CARL
LENOIR
S0-BNH-172

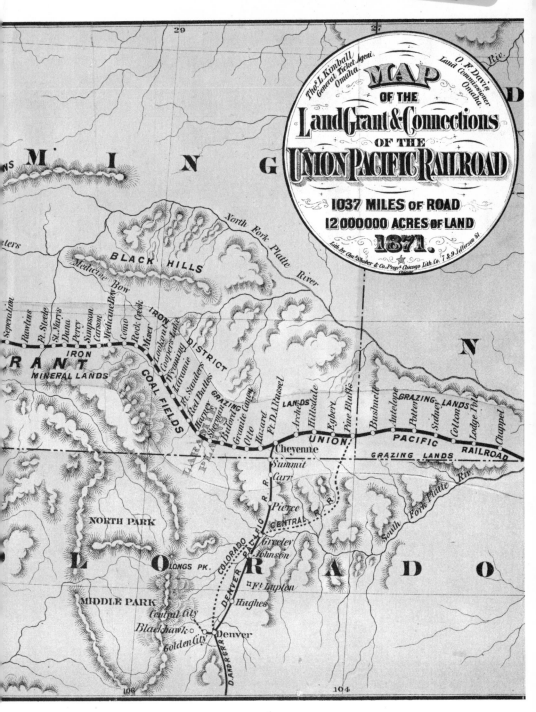

MAP
OF THE
Land Grant & Connections
OF THE
UNION PACIFIC RAILROAD
1037 MILES OF ROAD
12 000 000 ACRES OF LAND
1871.

The L. Kimball
General Ticket Agent
Omaha

O. F. Davis
Land Commissioner
Omaha

Lith. by Chas. Shober & Co. Props Chicago Lith Co. 7 & 9 Jefferson St.
Chicago

338.47
Am3p

99304

DATE DUE			

WITHDRAWN

PIONEERING

T H E   C

CARL A. RUDISILL LIBRARY
LENOIR RHYNE COLLEGE

PIONEERING THE UNION PACIFIC

A Reappraisal of the Builders of the Railroad

Charles Edgar Ames

APPLETON-CENTURY-CROFTS

EDUCATIONAL DIVISION

MEREDITH CORPORATION

New York

338.47

Am 3 P

99304

Nov. 1976

Copyright © 1969 by Meredith Corporation

All rights reserved.
This book, or parts thereof, must not be used or
reproduced in any manner without written permission.
For information address the publisher, Appleton-Century-Crofts,
Division of Meredith Corporation, 440 Park Avenue South,
New York, N.Y. 10016.

Library of Congress Catalog Card Number: 69-13448

Printed in the United States of America

R02970

ACKNOWLEDGMENTS

The Bobbs-Merrill Company: From *Trails, Rails and War,* by
J. R. Perkins, copyright, 1929, by The Bobbs-Merrill Company,
Inc., R. 1956, by J. R. Perkins, reprinted by permission of
the publishers.

The Johns Hopkins Press: Robert W. Fogel, *The Union
Pacific Railroad—A Case in Premature Enterprise,* 1960.

Paisano Press, Inc.: Edwin L. Sabin, *Building the Pacific
Railway.*

The Ronald Press Company: Nelson Trottman, *History of
the Union Pacific,* The Ronald Press Company, New York, 1923.

To the memory of
Winthrop Ames
without whose inspiration
this work never would have been attempted

FOREWORD

The centennial celebration of the completion of the first transcontinental railroad comes at a time when man is about to set foot on the moon for the first time. Although a century of dramatic technological progress separates the driving of the golden spike in 1869 and the prospective lunar landing in 1969, both events share a common basis in men's willingness to accept great risks.

Aside from differences of time and place, the two undertakings differ markedly in the blending of public and private resources and planning to minimize risk. One hundred years ago it was just as inconceivable that government itself would undertake to build a transcontinental railroad as it would be today to undertake space exploration under private auspices. Today NASA, a federal agency, directs the massive effort in which private industry is a vitally important but subordinate partner. The success of the moon shot hinges in the last analysis on the imaginative use of public funds by NASA. The success of the transcontinental railroad project a century ago hinged on the imaginative use of public credit and resources by private individuals. They achieved their goal by personal commitment and risk-taking, actual construction to qualify for government aid, and ingenuity in using this aid to attract private capital to their support.

The ways in which the promoters and builders of the Union Pacific Railway sought to minimize their financial risks and the resulting Credit Mobilier investigations are staples of American history. The role of the Ames brothers, Oakes and Oliver, of North Easton, Massachusetts, has been a familiar part of the story. Oakes Ames's censure by his Congressional colleagues, once accepted by some historians as probably deserved, has been viewed in a new light as the result of extensive research in primary sources during the past decade. The present volume adds significantly to this revisionist literature.

The author, a direct descendant of Oakes Ames, has devoted years of effort and applied the skills of a professional financial analyst to unravelling the extraordinarily complicated finances of the UP's construction company. The results give a new insight into the decision-making of the transcontinental's promoters and a fresh appreciation of the complex processes that move a nation forward whether in an age of steam or an age of space travel.

ARTHUR M. JOHNSON
Professor of Business History
Harvard University

Boston, Massachusetts
15 March 1969

PREFACE

Pioneering the Union Pacific is mainly a narrative of the ordeals and achievements of the builders of the Union Pacific Railroad—chiefly, Oakes and Oliver Ames, Grenville Dodge and Thomas Durant. The story is only one facet, to be sure, of a great accomplishment in American history, culminating in the first crossing of the continent by rail, and the opening, then development, of the Far West. Described for the first time in detail, however, this facet reveals some episodes which contribute significantly to the dramatic history of the railroad itself.

The Ameses did not start upon what, for them, seems an exceedingly bold venture until very late in life. No full biography of them has been written.[1] Hopefully, their experiences are here recounted as objectively as could be expected of one of their descendants who has access to some old writings and records which previously have not appeared in print. The author's primary task is to portray the past in its own setting by quoting as far as practicable the words of men then living. Another goal is to develop whatever facts may contribute importantly towards a fuller knowledge of the adolescent Union Pacific, particularly its financing and relations with a hostile Government.

The Ameses were the principal promoters and stockholders of the road, and leaders of the New England group of capitalists who joined them in 1865. Their history then became indivisible from that of the road. Oakes, as a Congressman in Washington, was not deeply involved in the particulars of management except in periods of crisis. For example, in 1867 he prevented stoppage of work on

[1] Winthrop Ames tells of their early lives at home, and of the construction of the road, not its financing, in his unfinished book, *The Ames Family of Easton, Massachusetts*, pp. 120–197.

the road by settling a bitter quarrel among the promoters. He alone underwrote an ingenious plan for financing the last two-thirds of the road in a way which could be approved by all. It became known as the Oakes Ames contract. On the other hand, Oliver was President during most of the building of the railway, occupied with monetary affairs and details of administration in New York or by remote control from Boston.

The Union Pacific already has been more heavily publicized than any other railway. Still, its history seems to suffer from strangely incomplete and sometimes inaccurate recording, particularly concerning the characters of the men involved. It was built during the period of reconstruction following the Civil War, when regional feelings remained bitter, and when transportation and finance were still dominated by the ideology of laissez-faire, or non-interference by the state with free enterprise. It is difficult to comprehend the extent to which changes have taken place in governmental regulation of railroads—in fact, in the ethics of all business—during a century of almost explosive expansion. Much that was then accepted as normal philosophy about profit-making is now outlawed. The censure of Oakes Ames by Congress in 1873 made him one of the earliest scapegoats of an awakening public conscience. Were it not for the governmental investigations of a mysterious tool of the Union Pacific called the Credit Mobilier of America, little would be known of the intricacies of the then common way of financing railroads. The subject perhaps appeared too complicated or word-consuming for more than meager coverage by past writers, with one exception.[2]

Much is told in this book about the Ameses' highly important personal relations with Chief Engineer Dodge and Vice President Durant. These four men were the key to the building of the Union Pacific from Council Bluffs on the eastern bank of the Missouri to Promontory high in the mountains north of Great Salt Lake. Because the influence of the Ames group carried on into the regime of Jay Gould, the story is continued very briefly up to the inevitable bankruptcy of the Union Pacific in 1893.

The book is arranged in chronological order, as far as practicable, for simplicity and minimum repetition.

CHARLES EDGAR AMES

Laurel Hollow, Syosset, New York
March 1969

2 Fogel, *The Union Pacific Railroad—A Case in Premature Enterprise.*

ACKNOWLEDGMENTS

I am indebted to a large number of friends who personally have been of real help, in one way or another, while my work was under way. Of these I am particularly grateful to *E. Roland Harriman,* former Chairman of the Board of Directors of the Union Pacific, for invaluable help in unearthing old company records and giving permission to make certain quotations. I must also warmly thank *Edwin C. Schafer,* General Director of Public Relations, for his courtesy and never-flagging aid in furnishing study material and many fine photographs of a century ago. Likewise, commendation goes to *Irene A. Keefe,* Director, Union Pacific Historical Museum, for short-cutting my research efforts. Other U.P. officers who helped were *A. O. Mercer, William R. Moore,* and *C. W. Rossworn.*

As to my research work, the late *Blanche A. Ames* was ever helpful and invigorating. She kindly allowed me to quote from the diaries and papers of Governor Oliver Ames. The late *John Stanley Ames* also assisted significantly by permitting me to quote freely from the newly found diaries of Oliver Ames Jr., written while President of the railroad. Others who contributed notably to my research endeavors were *Lilian Carlisle,* Executive Staff, Shelburne Museum, Vermont; *G. Hobart Chapman,* Civil Engineer, of Evanston, Wyoming; *Ronald L. Fingerson,* Special Collections Librarian, State University of Iowa, Iowa City, who allowed me to quote from the vast papers of Durant (Leonard Collection); *Robert W. Fogel,* Professor of Economics, University of Chicago, who switched me to the right track when I got lost in the subject of finances; *Katherine Halverson,* Chief, Historical Division, Wyoming State Archives and Historical Department, who among other helpful acts permitted me to quote from the "Annals of Wyoming"; and *Richard Harte,* who loaned me some rare books needed for repeated reference at home, and who encouragingly read my early manuscript. To *Jesse H. Jameson,* Director, Railroad Village Museum, Corinne, and Editorial Committee, "SUP News," go my thanks for interesting material. Particularly am I grateful to *Jack W. Musgrove,* Curator, Iowa State Department of History and Archives, Des Moines, for leading me through the maze of General Dodge's papers, for providing material for my use, and for allowing quotations from them and the "Annals of Iowa." *Elise Ames Parker* showed keen interest in the book and gave generous permission to reproduce several rare portraits and photos. *Edward O. Parry* granted consent to quote from published letters of his grandfather, Dr. Henry C. Parry. *William J. Peterson,* Superintendent, The State Historical Society of Iowa, Iowa City, was most helpful in Iowan subjects and gave permission to quote from "The Palimpsest." *Irene M. Poirier,* Librarian, Ames Free Library, was deft in finding Ames family material and assisted with several photos taken within the library. *Mildred K. Smock,* Librarian, Free Public Library, Council Bluffs, was most courteous and energetic—she not only led me to such Dodge papers as I had missed in Des Moines, but also provided a copy of a rare sketch by George Simons. At the National Archives *Philip R. Ward* of the Audio-Visual Branch dug up for me some unique photos in the Brady Collection.

For professional leadership in the complex transformation of typewritten matter into book form I was dependent on *Donald S. Benton,* Special Projects Editor, Appleton-Century-Crofts. He was ably assisted by *Dorothy DC. Thompson,* and other experts. To *Grace D. Burns,* my cheerful secretary for many years in Wall Street, goes credit for expertly typing, in off hours, the great bulk of my scribblings.

For reading my typewritten manuscript, with helpful comments, go my lasting thanks to *Cornelia Ames Abbot, David Ames, Oakes Ingalls Ames, Eleanor Ames Mattern,* and *Francis T. P. and Pauline Ames Plimpton.*

For inspiring encouragement I am very deeply indebted to *Amyas and Evelyn Perkins Ames,* who assisted me in no small way. On *George P. Baker,* Dean, Harvard University Graduate School of Business Administration, I would pin a medal for exceptionally courteous and able advice concerning the typescript. To *Helen Atkins Claflin* go my thanks for her keen interest. *Gene M. Gressley,* Director, Western History Research Center, University of Wyoming, by his gracious interest and advice became my good friend. To *Arthur M. Johnson,* Professor of Business History, Harvard University, go my deep thanks for reading both my manuscript and galley proof, for his welcome advice, and especially for his apt Foreword.

Finally, but far from least important, go never-ending thanks to my life partner, *Eleanor King Ames.* Always completely selfless, she gave up her own interests to proofreading, note-taking in libraries across the country, and patient discussions of the endless problems which arose from this composition. Yet, withal, she kept me healthy and happy.

C.E.A.

CONTENTS

ILLUSTRATIONS

GROUP 3 FOLLOWS PAGE 236

PIONEERING
THE UNION PACIFIC

1

The Union Pacific
Before Oakes and Oliver Ames

Historical Background—The Union Pacific's First Charter: The Act of 1862—First Attempts at Building End in Failure—John Adams Dix— Thomas Clark Durant—Ground Is Broken in Omaha—Lobbying for Better Bait—The Amended Charter: The Act of 1864—Problems of Financing Under the Charter—Durant Doesn't Have What It Takes

A. Historical Background

Truthfully, today we might not be one great nation from Atlantic to Pacific had it not so chanced that the first trunk line railroads were built during the very period when Pacific Coast pioneers were settling virgin land on the far side of our mighty mountain ranges and deserts. But for the Iron Horse, the Continental Divide, true to its name, might have parted two rival powers. The better to appreciate how opportune was this coincidence of history, this story starts with the early conception of a railroad to the Pacific and delves just briefly into some relevant bits of the history of the West during the first half of the 19th century.

Louisiana Purchase: It was in 1803, the same year that Oliver Ames Sr. settled in North Easton, that President Jefferson warily purchased from Napoleon the vast Province of Louisiana. This was the same territory that the Bourbon King of Spain had ceded back to France only three years earlier on a petty bribe by Napoleon. With New Orleans in the hands of a continental power, the whole Mississippi valley, already colonized to the eastward, had been cut off from the sea, much to the annoyance of the Americans, as some 40 per cent of the nation's produce was then passing through this busy Gulf port.

1

But, luckily for us, Napoleon had concluded that he might lose all his possessions in North America by an impending war with Great Britain, and he became a ready seller. Furthermore, he was adaptable enough at last to realize the futility of permanently holding Louisiana against a rising tide of American settlers using and crossing the Mississippi.

The deal nearly doubled the original 1783 area of the United States. Broadly speaking, it was bounded by the Mississippi River on the east, the watershed of the Rocky Mountains on the west, the present Canadian border on the north, and the Texas boundary as then set by the Red River and the Arkansas River on the south. A dozen new states were to rise in these 529 million acres. The price was $23,213,568 including interest—less than 5 cents an acre.[1] The exact nature of the purchase was to remain a mystery for many years, even with the boundaries in doubt, until explorations were made by Lewis and Clark, John Colter, Stephen Long, Kit Carson, Jedediah Smith, Benjamin Bonneville, and other bold and hardy pathfinders, especially John C. Fremont.

Jim Bridger: Of particular interest was the uncannily precise mapping talent of James Bridger (1804–1881), colorful "mountain man." As a hunter, trapper, fur trader, and guide, he became intimately acquainted with the mountains, streams, and contours to be crossed years later by the Union Pacific (hereafter referred to as the UP). Bridger was the first white man positively known to have seen Great Salt Lake and the hot geysers of the Yellowstone. In 1827 he discovered the South Pass in Wyoming, later to become the most widely followed emigrant trail over the Continental Divide. In 1843 he bought some land from the Mexican Government and there founded Fort Bridger, a trading post shrewdly located on the Black Fork of the Green River. At this point were to converge all the heavily used emigrant routes of the time: the Oregon Trail, the Mormon Trail, and the Pony Express route, all via the North Platte River and the South Pass; the Overland Stage route (which he opened) via the South Platte River; and Bridger's Pass over the Continental Divide. The UP was to run only nine miles north of Fort Bridger. General Grenville Dodge erected a monument to him in Mount Washington Cemetery, Kansas City, as a tribute to his friend and ofttimes guide.[2]

---

[1] U.S. Geological Survey Bulletin 1212, p. 36; U.S. Bureau of the Census, *Historical Statistics*, p. 236. (See list of Major References.)

[2] Dodge, *Biographical Sketch of James Bridger;* Charles Neider, *The Great West*, pp. 149–167; Dodge, *Autobiography*, p. 660.

The population of the United States at the time of the Louisiana Purchase was about 5,900,000, but it was destined to nearly double every 25 years during the period covered by this book. With the War of 1812, America was to turn her back on European politics and with ever-increasing enthusiasm face to the West, where any robust man with an axe and a gun could gain a frontier home, however crude. The expansive force of a strong, self-reliant breed was to cradle true democracy in the valley of the Mississippi. The labor shortage in the East was to be filled by immigrants from Europe.

Further Acquisitions: In 1818 the Canadian boundary was adjusted by agreement with the British to the 49th parallel all the way from Lake of the Woods (Minnesota) to the Rockies.[3]

The next year, by treaty with Spain, another 46 million acres were added by the accession of Florida and West Florida, including the seaboard areas of Mississippi and Alabama south of the 31st parallel.[4] The cost was nearly $6,500,000 with interest included.

Between 1845 and 1853, accessions far outstripped the Louisiana Purchase.[5] First, Texas was annexed as a State in 1845, receiving $10,000,000 for such of her area as became part of the public domain of the United States. However, a bit of a war with the Mexican Republic was necessary to push the boundary of Texas southwestward to the Rio Grande, where it remained, bringing the total gain from Texas to 250 million acres. Among the young army officers who saw Mexican action were Lieutenant Ulysses S. Grant, Colonel Jefferson Davis, and Captains Robert E. Lee and George B. McClellan.

Next, in 1846, title to the great Oregon Territory passed to us by peaceable diplomacy with the British at no cost. Its northern boundary was again fixed along the 49th parallel (the line east of the Rockies had been negotiated with the British in 1818), without the fight for "Fifty-Four Forty or Fight!" This was the entire area west of the Rockies and north of the 42nd parallel, amounting to 183 million acres, and comprising the present-day states of Oregon, Washington, and Idaho.

---

[3] U.S. Bureau of the Census, *Historical Statistics,* Series J2, p. 236, fn 1: "Continental U.S. territory in 1790 of 888,811 square miles [569 million acres] includes that part of drainage basin of Red River of the North, south of 49th parallel, sometimes considered part of Louisiana Purchase." Thus the Bureau of the Census assumes that the Red River area of nearly 30 million acres was acquired from Great Britain in the Treaty of 1783, and was not a part of the Louisiana Purchase. (The Red River of the North divides present Minnesota from North Dakota.) See also Bureau's Series A17, p. 8.

[4] U.S. Bureau of the Census, Series J3, p. 236.   [5] See map, Illus., Group 1.

Then, in 1848, just as gold was to be discovered along the American River in California, Mexico admitted defeat. She ceded the whole of California and what is now the southwest corner of Wyoming, all of Utah and Nevada, most of Arizona, and the western half of New Mexico. However, for these 338 million acres we paid our southern neighbor $18,250,000, not quite the bargain of the Louisiana Purchase—the price was over a nickel an acre.

Finally, the Gadsden Purchase of nearly 19 million acres was made in 1853 from Mexico for $10,000,000, extending the southern borders of present Arizona and New Mexico, in case a far-southern route for a railroad to the Coast was chosen.[6]

Thus, in the relatively short span of 50 years, mostly by purchase and negotiation, but partly by actual or threatened force, America was expanded by 1,365 million acres to nearly *3.4 times* its original size.[7] The purchase price totaled almost $59,750,000, or 4.3 cents an acre, to which was added the cost of the Mexican campaign. During the same period the population multiplied 4.4 times to nearly 26 million persons.[8]

"Westward Ho!"   The way was clear at last for the road of iron. The greatest railway yet conceived must stretch more than 2,000 miles across unknown lands from the Mississippi to the coast of isolated California or Oregon before it was too late. These new coastal possessions, with their treasures of salubrious climate, verdant valleys, fine timber, and precious minerals, were wide open to easy capture by a foreign power. Also, the inhabitants, while mostly American by birth and sympathy, were virtually independent of Washington authority and might readily secede from the Union. In 1857 came a severe business depression, blighting the economy up to the Civil War. Railroad building was dealt a hard blow.

By Sea: The difficulties of transportation of any kind were monstrous. The 5,250-mile, 35-day voyage by way of the malaria-infested trail across Panama was the usual route for California's Senators and Representatives to and from Washington. It was considered less dangerous than the Overland Stage route of 1859–69. The rough sail of some 13,300 miles around Cape Horn in cargo ships averaged about 130 days, but it often took up to 200 days. This route was longer by

---

[6] See p. 9.

[7] U.S. Bureau of the Census, *Historical Statistics*, Series A17, p. 8. See also map, Illus., Group 1.

[8] U.S. Bureau of the Census, Series A2, p. 7.

about 700 miles than the easier sea trip from New York to Calcutta around the Cape of Good Hope. Even the fastest of the American clipper ships, then in the heyday of their winged glory, could only reduce the Cape Horn passage to 100 days, sometimes a little less, from New York to San Francisco. The ocean-going steamship was about to displace canvas.

By Land: In the days of the Forty-Niners it took a whole summer, from early May to September, to painfully creep in an ox-drawn schooner to California. Sickness, accident, baking days, freezing nights, starvation, thirst, and vengeful Indians took their toll. To give overland travelers a degree of protection, the U.S. Army had to maintain a chain of forts and posts at heavy outlay for transportation of troops, munitions, and supplies. The best known of these were Forts Kearney and Bridger (the former on and the latter near the future route of the UP) and Forts Leavenworth, Riley, and Laramie. The Secretary of War stated that costs averaged over $2,000,000 annually between 1857 and 1861, but most likely it was much more, particularly if western postal service had been included.[9] Rowland Hazard put the average annual cost, including mail, at about $7,000,-000. The saving by rail proved to be nearly $5,000,000 yearly.[10] The rails carried freight and mail from Omaha to Salt Lake City in 1880 for one-tenth of the cost by wagon, which was over $27 per 100 pounds in 1865.

By Pony Express: Perhaps the most dramatic and colorful and certainly the shortest-lived effort at speeding up light transportation across the wastes was the Pony Express. Relays of lone horsemen hustled mail, news, and business documents back and forth between St. Joseph on the Mississippi and Sacramento, night and day, winter and summer, without a stop. By 3 April 1860, the Leavenworth freight-express firm of Russell, Majors and Waddell had established 190 lonely and dangerous stations along the fastest trail, tended by 300 or 400 older men, with nearly 500 horses valued at $200 apiece. Price was no consideration in this scheme. The 90 or so adventurous young riders were the lightest and hardiest—and soberest—that could be found in the West. One of them was "Buffalo Bill" Cody, then aged fifteen years. The Pony Express followed the old Oregon Trail of 1843 up the North Platte River past Fort Laramie and over

---

[9] Trottman, *History of the Union Pacific*, p. 124.
[10] Hazard, *The Credit Mobilier of America*, p. 25.

the South Pass as far as Fort Bridger. Thence it turned southwest away from the Oregon Trail for the old Mormon Trail of 1846–47 to Salt Lake City. Then, over an original route far from the Central Pacific (CP) tracks to come, it passed south of Great Salt Lake, crossed the seemingly endless Utah and Nevada salt deserts on nearly a straight line west to Carson City, and surmounted the Sierras south of Lake Tahoe at last to drop into Sacramento. This route, much of which was along mere Indian trails, coincided with that of the UP only on the Nebraska plains between Fort Kearney and Julesburg, and over that part of the Wasatch Range which lies between Fort Bridger and Henefer, via Echo Canyon. The entire 1,960 miles were ridden in an average of 10 days, at an overall gallop of 8 miles an hour. Lincoln's first inaugural message was carried to the West in less than 8 days, the fastest trip. Altogether, 650,000 miles were covered and 30,000 pieces of mail toted in 18 months. But the fee of $5 per half ounce (later reduced to $1), with no aid from the war-burdened Government, was not nearly enough to pay for the twice-a-week runs, costing $30,000 a month. By 24 October 1861, when Western Union's first telegraph line between East and West was hooked up, the Pony Express project was abandoned, with a loss of some $400,000 and one leather pouch.[11] Russell, Majors and Waddell, bankrupt, had to sell out their Overland Stage also.

By Stage: In the meantime, the Overland Stage, which continued to operate from 1858 through the Civil War until the Pacific Railway gradually displaced it, followed a more southerly route between Julesburg and Fort Bridger, winding up the South Platte River to Virginia Dale and Bridger's Pass—south of the Union Pacific. The total distance covered was 2,800 miles from St. Louis to San Francisco. The time—30 days. The fare—$200.

First Railroads: Credit for the first successful railroad company in the world goes to the engineering skill of the English. On 27 September 1825, the Stockton and Darlington Railway in northeastern England started the first train of 38 vehicles with "The Locomotion," which attained a startling speed of 15 miles an hour. The line proved a financial and mechanical success from its inception. Five years later

---

[11] Driggs, *The Pony Express Goes Through;* Driggs, *The Old West Speaks*, pp. 151–169; "There Goes the Pony Express," condensed from St. Louis *Post-Dispatch* of 2 Apr. 1944, by Donald Culross Peattie, appearing in *Reader's Digest*, May 1944, reprinted April 1960.

the 15-mile Baltimore and Ohio, with its experimental "Tom Thumb" engine, was the first to commence serious railroading in America. U.S. trackage in operation boomed to 2,818 miles by 1840.[12]

Asa Whitney Dreams: Already the construction of a transcontinental line from Lake Michigan or the Mississippi River to the Pacific Ocean, with shipping connections to the Orient, was being advocated by a prosperous and visionary New York merchant by the name of Asa Whitney, who was said to look like Napoleon Bonaparte. From 1840 to 1852 he worked fanatically to convince Congress and the public of the merits of his plan, which was prophetic as to the general route, the national grant of public lands, and the construction by private parties assisted by the Government. The concept of "mixed enterprise" had been born. His ideas were successful in that they aroused much public interest, but because of their impracticability and the sectional rivalry over the routes to be chosen, his pleas came to nought. Asa Whitney was remembered by history but left in poverty for his dreams.[13]

Rails to Chicago: By 1850 there were 9,021 miles of railroad in operation, all in the East, of course. With the rapid improvement in this new method of transportation, Chicago was to mushroom from a mere fort town of a few thousand frontiersmen into one of the great cities and railway centers of the country. Even before the Michigan and Southern, followed immediately by the Michigan Central, had triumphantly given Chicago its first rail connection with the East in the spring of 1852, far-seeing and more practical successors to Asa Whitney were painfully pushing spur railroads towards the Mississippi and the plains. The Chicago and Rock Island and the Chicago and North West Railways were already under way.

First U.S. Surveys: It was high time for the unknown mountains of the West to be mapped all the way to San Francisco, by now the obvious site for a terminus on the Pacific Coast. On 1 March 1853, Congress (the Thirty-Second) took its first faltering step toward promoting a transcontinental line by appropriating $150,000 (later increased to $340,000) for a survey "to ascertain the most practicable and economical route for a railroad from the Mississippi River to the

---

[12] U.S. Bureau of the Census, *Historical Statistics*, Series Q15, p. 427.
[13] Davis, *The Union Pacific Railway*, pp. 19–34; Asa Whitney, *Project for a Railroad to the Pacific*, 1849.

Pacific Ocean." [14] The Secretary of War, then Jefferson Davis, was authorized to employ the United States Corps of Topographical Engineers to explore the regions he deemed likely to be most practical. It took three and a half years and 11 volumes to present the picture, incompletely at that. In the process, however, the first professional maps of the entire West were drawn. The five routes that Jefferson Davis had chosen for survey may be broadly sketched as follows: [15]

1. The "North Route," between the 47th and 49th parallels, stretched 2,025 miles from St. Paul to Seattle. It was wisely located and is now generally followed by the Northern Pacific and Great Northern Railways. In the final report of December 1856, all routes were put on a cost scale under one formula. However, the costs were only guesses at best. Even over similar territory they varied from $35,000 to $50,000 per mile. The cost of the North Route was the highest, at $141,000,000.

2. The "Overland Route," "Mormon Trail," or "Central Route," near the 41st and 42nd parallels, extended 2,032 miles from Council Bluffs to Benicia (southwest of Sacramento) via the South Pass of Wyoming. The estimate was second highest, at $131,000,000, but nearly $65,000 a mile, and the line was to be followed by the UP and CP only for relatively short distances. The initial survey as far west as Fort Bridger was made in 1849 and 1850 by Captain Howard Stansbury of the U.S. Corps of Topographical Engineers. It is of interest to note that on the way out and back, guided by Jim Bridger in his prime at forty-six, Captain Stansbury claimed to have cut 61 miles from the emigrants' route over the Continental Divide at the South Pass by leaving the North Platte River in Nebraska and crossing the Black Hills (Laramie Mountains) near the Cheyenne Pass, proceeding directly over the Wyoming Basin. It was over this Laramie spur of the Rockies, the highest elevation reached, that the UP track was actually laid 17 years later, but over Evans (or Sherman) Pass 12 miles farther south. On the homeward journey, Stansbury was badly injured while descending from the Pass down Lodgepole Creek and had to turn back for Fort Laramie on the Oregon Trail. While his report argued for the Cheyenne Pass in preference to the South Pass, it was rejected in Washington, and for some obscure and unfortunate reason subsequent surveys of Jim Bridger's short cuts were never made by the Government. It finally fell to the lot of the

---

[14] 10 Statutes at Large 219.
[15] Senate Executive Document No. 78, 33rd Cong., 2nd Sess., Serial Nos. 758–768.

UP's own engineering enterprise under General Grenville Dodge to find the best route over the Rockies. A year or two after Stansbury's trip, Lieutenant E.G. Beckwith of the same Corps carried on west of Fort Bridger with the Government survey, down the Wasatch's Weber River (as built) but *south* of Salt Lake, and then, oddly enough, far out of the way into northern California and down the Upper Sacramento River. All in all, the Government's proposal was the least practical of the five routes, except the one described next.

3. The "Buffalo Trail," near the 38th and 39th parallels, was finally followed to some degree by the Denver and Rio Grande Western. The length was 2,080 miles from Westport (now Kansas City) to San Francisco, but an altitude of 10,032 feet over the rugged Colorado Rockies made it seem impracticable. The surveying party was massacred by Indians, and no estimate of the cost was ever made.

4. The route from Fort Smith, Arkansas, was well located near the 35th parallel around the southern end of the Rockies near Santa Fe, and was to form a large part of the present route of the Atchison, Topeka and Santa Fe. The distance to San Francisco was 2,096 miles, and the cost was guessed at $106,000,000.

5. Finally, the "Southern Route," near the 32nd parallel, from Fulton (near Texarkana) to San Francisco via El Paso, Fort Yuma, Los Angeles, and the Pacific Coast also looked good. The mileage was 2,024, and the estimated cost was the lowest of all, at $90,000,000. In general, it was to be the main line of the Southern Pacific Railroad. Little wonder that Jefferson Davis, the Southern leader, favored this route—just as the Northerners favored the "Overland Route." But the Southern line was not the most central one and could not serve the majority of the pioneers. The Gadsden Purchase, already mentioned, was to be the final addition to United States possessions on the continent, excluding Alaska. In the meantime, the construction of railways continued to boom in the North and East, and 22,016 miles were under operation in the nation by the time Secretary Jefferson Davis's final report was submitted in December 1856.

How to Finance? While the entire country was to benefit from a Pacific railway, Constitutional complications and questions of states' rights helped to block any legislation. Financing obviously would be most difficult, perhaps impossible. Even the route to be chosen produced such sectional rivalry that any decisive action was long delayed.[16] Some form of Federal aid was necessary: the venture was far

16 For a full account of sectionalism and localism see Davis, pp. 35–95.

too big and risky for private capital alone. Some argued well that the Government itself should build and operate the road, but such a radical step for a democracy had never before been attempted. For years, Government or state aid had been given to private lines in the form of valuable land grants along the right-of-way, yet in the case of the Pacific railway few persons believed that the land to be traversed was more than a barren waste, making land grants seem worth but little. Furthermore, it was generally thought that the cost of surmounting the Rockies would be almost prohibitive, necessitating not only land grants big in area, but large, direct Government subsidies in other forms.

Civil War: The black shape of slavery was already beginning to tear the country and Congress in two. The people were further divided between the farmers of the South and West on one side and the industrial and well-to-do classes of the North on the other. "Was it to be North and West against South, or South and West against North?" aptly queried Samuel E. Morison of Harvard. The menace of secession was slowly but surely leading to war. As stated, the South, led by Jefferson Davis, insisted on one of the southern routes. The North demanded the northern route, or at very least the central one, even if it did cost more. Both the Republican and Democratic platforms of 1856 and 1860 favored liberal Federal aid. The only trouble was that neither side would yield on the location.

Tragically enough, in the end it was secession from the Union of seven states in the Deep South, following Lincoln's election in November 1860, and the first frenzied guns of the Civil War on 12 April 1861 that cleared the way for action. The Southern representatives had quit Washington, and there was no faction left to hold out for their choice. The "Little Congress" was welded together with the common aim of winning the War. Also, the seizure by a Union cruiser of two Confederate agents, Mason and Slidell, who were on board the *Trent,* a British packet, and bound for London and Paris to represent the South, brought the Union to the brink of war with Great Britain. Had such a disaster occurred, the capture of our possessions on the Pacific by England could hardly have been prevented.[17] But Lincoln's wise decision was: "One war at a time." [18]

Thus it happened that military and political factors, including Indian control, finally outweighed commercial and economic con-

[17] *Cong. Globe,* 37th Cong., 2nd Sess., p. 1595.
[18] Sandburg, *Abraham Lincoln,* vol. 2, p. 128.

siderations when the Act of 1862 at long last gave painful birth to the Pacific Railroad.

B. The Union Pacific's First Charter: The Act of 1862 [19]

Such, in brief, was the background for the enabling Act of 1862, a creation of the Thirty-Seventh Congress of the United States at the Second Session, in which only 25 States were represented. Much of the credit for leadership must go to the persistent efforts of Congressman Samuel R. Curtis (1807–1866) of Iowa, who reported the bill before he entered the Union service in 1861. It was then taken up by Senator James Harlan of Iowa.[20] While the Seven Days Battle was raging on the outskirts of Richmond, the bill (H.R. No. 364), as finally amended on June 20 by the Senate 35 to 5, was passed by the House 104 to 21 on June 24.[21] It was signed with enthusiasm by President Lincoln on July 1. The motive of defense appears even in its title: "An Act to aid in the Construction of a Railroad and Telegraph Line from the Missouri River to the Pacific Ocean, and to secure to the Government the Use of the same for Postal, Military, and Other Purposes."

The appropriate choice of name for the new corporation created by this statute was "Union Pacific Railroad Company." It was probably inspired by the fact that a Union Congress was sponsoring the Pacific railway or, to be more generous, by the popularity of the idea that the Union would be strengthened by the Pacific railway.[22]

It could be assumed and operated by any group of individuals willing to risk buying its qualifying stock and building the line—a risk the Government itself would not take.

The corporation was, in brief, authorized and empowered to lay out, locate, construct, furnish, maintain, and enjoy a continuous single line of railroad and telegraph from a point on the 100th meridian of longitude west from Greenwich to the western boundary of Nevada Territory, by the most direct, central and practicable

---

[19] 12 Statutes at Large 489; Davis, pp. 96–110; Trottman, pp. 10–18; White, *History of the Union Pacific*, pp. 101–110 (the Act is quoted.)

[20] Dodge, *How We Built the Union Pacific*, p. 9.

[21] *Cong. Globe*, 37th Cong., 2nd Sess., pp. 2840, 2905.

[22] Dodge, *How We Built the Union Pacific*, p. 10; Trottman, p. 9. Congressman Curtis has been credited with the idea.

route, there to meet and connect with the already created Central Pacific Railroad Company of California.[23]

There was no difficulty in settling on Sacramento or San Francisco as the western terminus, but because of local jealousies it was not considered politically discreet to designate the exact eastern take-off point on the Missouri. Instead, a so-called "initial point" was set on the plains somewhere along the said 100th meridian, which passed through the center of Nebraska Territory about 247 miles west of Omaha. The "initial point" was between the south margin of the valley of the Republican River and the north margin of the valley of the Platte River, at a spot to be fixed by the President of the United States after actual surveys. From such an "initial point," four branch roads were to radiate *eastward* to the Missouri River at Omaha, Kansas City, Sioux City, and Atchison, where connections with railroads already pushing westward presumably could be made later.

The "Iowa Branch," which was to connect with a point, also to be fixed by the President, on the western boundary of the State of Iowa, was to be built by the UP and become its main line; the other branches went to other companies. It is not yet necessary to consider the Sioux City spur [24] nor the Atchison spur, which eventually were to be greatly changed in location.

The "Kansas City Branch" was to be built by the Leavenworth, Pawnee and Western Railway Company (later to be called the Union Pacific Railroad Company Eastern Division, and even later, the Kansas Pacific Railway Company) and was to run no further westward than the 100th meridian. When Congress subsequently canceled this clause and allowed it to run as a rival all the way to Denver, it created, in the words of Oakes Ames, a "well-nigh fatal" problem for the UP.

These "pestiferous and miserable" Missouri River branches, chartered to appease local prejudices, were to cause no end of trouble to all concerned.[25]

Central Pacific: Under the same Act of 1862, the Central Pacific Railroad Company of California, already privately incorporated under the laws of California on 28 June 1861, was

authorized to construct a railroad and telegraph line from the Pacific Coast, at or near San Francisco, or the navigable waters of the Sacra-

---

[23] *Act of 1862*, Sections 1, 8, 14.   [24] See p. 86.
[25] Davis, pp. 123, 134; White, pp. 13–14, 38–54.

mento River, to the eastern boundary of California, upon the same terms and conditions in all respects, as are contained in this act for the construction of said railroad and telegraph line first mentioned [the Union Pacific], and to meet and connect with . . . [the Union Pacific] on the eastern boundary of California.[26]

However, since the date of the possible formation of the UP could not be foretold, the Act also provided that the CP,

after completing its road across [California], is authorized to continue . . . construction . . . through the Territories of the United States to the Missouri river . . . on the terms and conditions provided in this act in relation to the said Union Pacific Railroad Company, until said roads shall meet and connect, and the whole line of said railroad and branches and telegraph is completed.[27]

Thus, if the UP should reach the Californian border before the CP did, it might continue on, with the consent of that State, to another meeting point; whereas, if the CP arrived there first, it might proceed to a meeting with the UP anywhere.

The practical effect of these involved sections of the Act was simply that either road could build as far as it wanted, under certain conditions, until a junction was made. In spite of two subsequent amending acts, *the meeting point was never clearly specified until too late.*

The CP had been created largely by the energy, salesmanship, and ample resources of a Connecticut Yankee by the name of Collis P. Huntington (1821–1900). He ultimately bore the responsibility for its financing,[28] much as did the Ames group for the UP. Helped by the prestige of Governor Leland Stanford (1824–1893), who became its President; by Mark Hopkins (1813–1878) and Charles Crocker (1822–1888); and especially by the initiative and engineering skill of Theodore D. Judah (1826–1863), another New Englander, the Central Pacific quietly broke ground at Sacramento on 8 January 1863 and proceeded initially in an insufficiently backed, discouraged sort of way. With the War on, its financing was dependent on the personal resources and credit of "The Big Four," on bank loans, and on the slow sale of hard-to-get city and county bonds, later supplemented by the proceeds of Government and company bonds. It was a smaller,

---

[26] *Act of 1862*, Section 9 (White, p. 105).   [27] *Ibid.*, Section 10 (White, p. 106).
[28] *Wilson Rep.*, pp. 696–722 (testimony of C.P. Huntington).

entirely private company, so the CP was freer from national politics and from Government Directors than was the UP.

It is of interest to discover this item in a leading newspaper:

A year or two after the first attempts to raise capital, meeting no encouragement from any source, Mr. Huntington, their energetic Vice President, was in Boston, and in the office of Glidden & Williams, California shippers, and seemed very much discouraged; there he was introduced to Oakes Ames, who loaned them $800,000 to start up the fearful and untried ascent of the lofty Sierra Nevadas. . . .[29]

Once the first and hardest part of the range was conquered, the CP won the confidence of rich Californian financiers and proceeded eastward somewhat faster than was originally expected. Indeed, as things turned out, it succeeded in building the entire way to Great Salt Lake before the UP could meet it. Practically all of the provisions of the Act of 1862 applied to the CP exactly as they did to the UP.

Act of 1862:   The raising of capital for the UP was to be splendidly simple and effective, Congress thought. A Board of 162 Commissioners of the Union Pacific Railroad and Telegraph Company was named to "open books of subscription to the capital stock in the principal cities of the country" and receive the orders that would flow in. No commissions were to be paid to salesmen or promoters for finding the venture capital. The national interest would be so keen it would sell itself, even though there were no surveys or assurance of earnings. The authorized capital was limited to $100,000,000 with shares of $1,000 par value. Subscribers were to pay no less than the *full par value in cash,* with 10 per cent down and the balance in semi-annual installments of 5 per cent each. As soon as $2,000,000 had been subscribed, and $200,000 thereon paid in, the subscribers would be authorized to organize the company and elect a board of directors and officers, who would, of course, gain control of the potential assets of the company, construct the line, and run its affairs. There were to be not less than 15 directors, of whom 2 were to be appointed by the United States President as "government directors to represent the interests of the government"; but they were not permitted to own any stock. By this unique provision, Government agents were to sit in on all meetings of the company and its commit-

---

[29] Dr. H. Latham in a letter to the editor of the New York *Herald*, 9 Jan. 1871.

tees and report on, or vote against, anything that they considered contrary to the best interests of the United States. The UP must build 100 miles of track within two years after agreeing to the provisions of the Act and 100 miles each year thereafter. Thus the entire line must be open to traffic before 1 July 1874.

The vitally important matters of "land grants" and "subsidies" as set forth in this Act have been misinterpreted by many politicians, article writers, and novelists from that day to this.

Land Grants: Having given the UP a right of way 200 feet wide through the new territories by extinguishing any Indian titles where conflicting,[30] the United States made an absolute *grant of land* to the company as follows: For each mile of track built, half the land for a distance of 10 miles on each side was to be given to the UP outright in the form of five alternate "sections" on each side. As a section consisted of one square mile, this meant a total grant of 10 square miles, or 6,400 acres per mile of track. The land had cost the Government less than a nickel an acre.[31] Actual land patents were not to be issued, however, until each 40-mile length of continuous track was certified by Government inspectors as being completed to the satisfaction of the United States. The Act avoided saying it, but naturally the other half of the land (the even numbered sections) was to be retained by the United States, and would become valuable only by reason of the railroad's being both built and operated. All mineral lands were to be retained by the Government, including coal and iron fields.

Bond Subsidies: A new feature in Federal aid to railroads was introduced. As a *subsidy,* when each 40-mile stretch of track was certified by the inspectors, the Secretary of the Treasury would be obligated to issue and deliver to the railroad certain bonds of the United States, payable in legal tender or U.S. currency notes (not gold), at varying amounts per mile, according to the estimated difficulties of building, namely, $16,000 par value per mile on the level plains, $32,000 per mile on the plateau between the Rockies and Sierras, and $48,000 per mile in these mountains. The $48,000 area covered the 150 miles west from the "eastern base" of the Rockies, and the 150 miles east from the "western base" of the Sierras, the points to be fixed by the President of the United States.[32] For the UP as built, *the average rate proved to be $26,222 per mile.*

[30] *Acts of 1862 and 1864,* Secs. 2, 3 respectively (White, pp. 102, 110 respectively).
[31] See pp. 2, 4.   [32] Section 11 (White, pp. 106–107).

The U.S. Subsidy bonds of $1,000 each were to be 6 per cent bonds maturing in 30 years from date of issue. But they were to be granted upon condition that the railroad company pay them at maturity. To secure such repayment to the United States of principal and interest, their delivery to the UP was to constitute, *ipso facto*, a *first mortgage* upon the railroad and all its appurtenances.[33] So the company's own bonds, payable in any lawful money, including gold and silver coin if so expressed, must be a second mortgage. The United States was not *giving* the company a penny. It was merely *lending* its good name and credit for a time, enabling the UP to either sell the Government bonds or use them as collateral for other loans to be raised in any way and amount possible under prevailing market conditions. Under this arrangement, the United States could lose only if the railroad was to fail and be unable to repay such principal and interest as might be due. Even then the Government could take title to the property and sell or operate it; thus it could recover at least a good part of its loss, if any.

Other Features: The UP (and CP), receiving these subsidies (limited to an aggregate of $50,000,000 for the entire Pacific Railway) as a temporary aid to financing construction, was bound, in return, to keep the road in repair and perform such railway services as the Government might require, such as transporting mail, troops, and supplies. (While special reduced rates for these services were not asked for, the UP voluntarily granted them from first to last, until "special rates" in general were repealed by Congress, effective 1 October 1946.) [34] Even such amounts as the United States might owe for these services were to be withheld and applied towards guaranty of the bonds and interest.

Of great importance, 5 per cent of "the net earnings" was also to be applied annually towards extinguishing the company's debt to the Government.[35] (The rate was increased to 25 per cent by the Thurman Act of 1878.) [36]

Finally, Uncle Sam was to withhold from 15 per cent to 25 per cent of the bonds due to be issued until the UP had "properly complied" with all the provisions of the Act. Otherwise, the railroad franchise was to be forfeited.

---

[33] Section 5. There was no specification as to whether the interest coupons paid by the United States were to be repaid by the railroad currently or upon maturity of the bonds. See p. 17.

[34] Union Pacific Railroad, *A Brief History*, pp. 15–18.

[35] Section 6 (White, p. 104).   [36] See p. 508.

Incidentally, all the iron used in construction had to be American, regardless of price. This high tariff policy, insisted upon by Thaddeus Stevens, was to be one of the reasons why building costs became so high. Again, grades and curves were not to exceed the maximum grade of 116 feet a mile and curve of 400 feet radius (14°) of the Baltimore and Ohio Railroad. On 3 March 1863, Congress decreed that the standard gauge of track be 4 feet 8½ inches.[37]

More important, Congress was to be empowered to reduce freight and passenger rates whenever "the net earnings of the entire road" for any one year should exceed 10 per cent of the road's "cost." Whether the entire road referred to the UP, or included the other lines named in the Act, was never specified. No suggestions were made for just how such basic matters as net earnings and cost were to be defined. Nor was there any provision regarding the dates when the company was to repay the interest paid by the U.S. on its bonds. Would it be semi-annually or at the 30-year maturity?

The Act Inadequate: All in all, the Act of 1862 was so loosely drawn as to cast doubt on the acumen of the Committee on the Pacific Railroad and the other members of the Thirty-Seventh Congress.[38] Even after amendments, its impracticalities, obscurities, and omissions were to burden all the Pacific railroads with unnecessary expenses, particularly the UP. Bitter litigation was to pour fuel on the political fires of the Reconstruction era. Finally, how could this proposition have offered such unattractive bait to private capital at the very moment when the Union was so desperately anxious for a road to be built, yet was unwilling to undertake it? As Lincoln allegedly remarked: "The government would do better to *give* its bonds to the company than to go without a road." [39]

However, in fairness to the "Little Congress," the Civil War was imposing tremendous pressures, many of them more important than mere railways; there was no legislative precedent to follow; and, to most politicians, the Rockies of the UP were little more than a figment. Most unfortunately of all, Congress boasted few legislators of proven business and financial abilities who could point out the practical way to the writers of the law. For all its defects, in the eyes of Congress it seemed to be about the best possible bill then capable of passage which offered some sort of compromise between Federal and private enterprise. So law it became—for a while.

[37] 12 Statutes 807.
[38] See p. 37.   [39] Ames Family, *Oakes Ames, A Memorial Volume,* p. 6.

C. First Attempts at Building End in Failure

With the Civil War raging on and the fortunes of the Union forces deteriorating, it is a wonder that any subscriptions at all were tendered for the UP stock. The Act of 1862 had come too late. Construction costs were spiraling with inflation; the purchasing power of the fixed government subsidies was shrinking; and labor for the required work was non-existent. In such a war economy there were plenty of opportunities for speculators to take other equity risks with far greater promise.

As prescribed by the Act, subscription books were opened on September 2 by the Board of 163 Commissioners, and "Notices of Sale" were printed in the newspapers of 24 cities.[40] But not a share was taken. Not until 25 September 1863, a year later, were 2,000 shares, the minimum required for lawful formation of the company, suddenly signed up.[41] The original subscription list contained 122 names underwriting 2,177 shares, for which $217,700 cash was paid on the 10 per cent deposit specified.[42] Most of the recorded subscriptions were for 20 shares, but there were eight for 50 shares, the largest amount. While a few well-known names appeared who took small amounts to "save the charter" or to lend their names to such a patriotic project, the nucleus of the subscribers turned out to be rather obscure persons or speculators of limited resources.[43] "On this subscription was the name of no recognized capitalist," said Oakes Ames.[44] Obviously, with little faith in the success of the company as a long-term investment, they had put up just enough capital to *acquire control* of the embryonic UP for the good thing that later might be made out of construction contracts, government land grants, and subsidies.

T. C. Durant, the first promoter, years later boasted to the Wilson investigating committee: "I procured a dozen or fifteen subscriptions by giving the parties the money to pay a 10 per cent installment, and agreeing to guarantee them against any loss. . . . I got my friends to make up subscriptions to the amount of $2,180,000 by furnishing

---

[40] *American Railroad Journal,* 13 Sept. 1862, pp. 705, 719–722.
[41] *Ibid.,* 3 Oct. 1863, p. 925.   [42] *Wilson Rep.,* pp. 740–742.
[43] Davis, pp. 116–117.
[44] Before Congress, 25 Feb. 1873; Ames Family, *Oakes Ames,* p. 110.

three-fourths of the money to make the subscriptions myself." [45] Even then, it developed, he was relying on further assistance from Congress by amendments to the Act of 1862, including elimination of the 200-share legal limit for one person. [46]

No one else wanted the UP at that time.

So, with such an uninspiring subscription, the Union Pacific Railroad Company was actually organized at a meeting of stockholders in New York on 29 October 1863. It was four months after the high water mark of the Confederacy at the Battle of Gettysburg. Thirty directors were elected for a year. The law provided for at least thirteen outside of the two Government Directors, who were Springer Harbaugh and T.J. Carter. Among them (about whom more will be written) were T.C. Durant, C.S. Bushnell, C.A. Lambard, H.S. McComb, J.I. Blair, and J.A. Dix. [47] Others were G.T.M. Davis, J. Edgar Thompson, and Brigham Young. The next day the directors appointed their officers: President, J.A. Dix (20 shares); Vice-President, T.C. Durant (50 shares); Secretary, H.V. Poor (10 shares); and Treasurer, J.J. Cisco (20 shares).

A "capital balance sheet" of the UP as of the end of 1863 appears in a report of the U.S. Pacific Railway Commission, pp. 4992–93.

D. *John Adams Dix*

Major-General Dix (1798–1879), a prominent statesman of New York, was then, at the age of sixty-five, in command of the Union Army's Department of the East. Although he was to remain the titular salaried head of the UP for a while, he was either unwilling to take active charge of the company's affairs or unable to do so because of his military duties. He had been prevailed upon by Durant to act as President because of his reputation and his experience with railroads as first President of the Chicago and Rock Island. [48] It was also a convenient arrangement for Durant, who could then rule. Later, Dix was appointed Minister to France and, in 1872, elected Governor of New York.

The following excerpts from a letter by Dix to Durant have more than one point of interest:

---

[45] *Wilson Rep.*, p. 515.   [46] *Act of 1862*, Section 1.

[47] *Wilson Rep.*, pp. 596–601; Union Pacific, *Official Register of Directors and Officers*, p. 3. Blair did not appear again as a director.

[48] See p. 192.

White House, Va., 6 July 1863

Dear Sir:

I received yours of the 3rd last evening. I have no objection that the Subscription of $20,000 for the Miss. & Mo. R.R. Co. to the Union Pacific R.R. Co. should be in my name if thought advisable and if it involves no personal liability. I am away from home, and, having no time to look after my own business, I ought not to have any liability of that nature thrown upon me.

In regard to the appointment of Director in the last named Company, I should like to know something about it first. . . . Is the road authorized by Congress and if so how are the Directors chosen. Send me the act if you can and let me know what has been done. . . . Remember me to the gentlemen at No. 13 Wm. St. and believe me

Yours truly,

T.C. Durant, Esq.   John A. Dix [49]

E.   Thomas Clark Durant

It was Dr. Durant who had projected the organization and taken the inside control of the UP from the very beginning. With varying success, he was to struggle desperately to retain power almost until the last stroke of the hammer at the Golden Spike in 1869.

Born in the Berkshires at Lee, Massachusetts, on 6 February 1820 into a family of colonial ancestry, T.C. Durant was sixteen years younger than Oakes Ames. Upsetting family hopes, he chose surgery as a profession, receiving a diploma *cum laude* from the Albany College of Medicine at the youthful age of twenty. For two years he was an assistant professor of surgery. But lectures and lessons seemed too humdrum and the profession too unprofitable. The Doctor moved to the big city for the more alluring possibilities of trading in commodity futures. At twenty-three he was made a partner in charge of the New York branch of his uncle's firm, Durant, Lathrop and Company of Albany, exporters of flour and grain, and active traders in foreign markets. There he soon found his aptitude—speculation. The granaries of the West were being opened up by the Erie Canal and new railroads, and opportunities for big profits in transportation were apparent. In 1847 he married Heloise Hannah Timbrel, by whom he had an only son, William West, and an only daughter, Heloise.[50] Nowhere is to be found any mention by him of his wife or children.

[49] Durant, *Papers*, 1–3–25–18.
[50] William Crapo Durant of Chevrolet motor fame was the son of William Clark Durant, a relative.

Getting to know some of the leading railroad promoters around Chicago, in 1853 he joined Henry Farnam (1803–1883), contractor for the building of the Chicago and Rock Island Railroad, of which Dix was President. This line reached the Mississippi River at Rock Island as early as February 1854. In the meantime, an extension of the Rock Island from the Mississippi had been organized with the intention of reaching the Missouri River. It was chartered in 1853 as the Mississippi and Missouri Railroad (M & M) with a stock issue of $6,000,000. The jobs of construction and raising capital were given to the new contracting firm of Farnam and Durant. Dix was elected President of this road, too. Peter A. Dey became chief engineer, with Grenville M. Dodge, then only twenty-two, his principal assistant. All but Farnam were to be with the UP years later. Having completed surveys from Davenport, Iowa, to Council Bluffs in November 1853, Farnam and Durant, at their own expense, ordered Dey and Dodge to "examine the country between the Missouri River and the Platte Valley to determine at what point on the Missouri River a railroad coming from the East should strike the river, with a view of connecting with a Pacific railroad that would run up the Platte Valley." [51]

The M & M laid its first rail (also Iowa's first) at Davenport on 29 June 1855, and within minutes of a time limit won a $50,000 bonus from Iowa City, then the capital, by hand-pushing a broken-down engine into that town before the bells began to ring in the New Year. This badly over-capitalized line never got further, as it went into receivership with the panic of 1857.[52] Durant had "pledged the paper of the firm of Farnam & Durant to meet his speculative ventures. This involved Mr. Farnam's collateral in litigation." [53] Farnam was badly hurt, and separated from his partner in a quarrel which was never reconciled.[54] Durant, with his usual acumen, fared much better than Farnam in the panic. From then on, until he encountered the Ames brothers, he was to be his own boss as best fitted his personality.

In 1863, the presidency of the Chicago, Rock Island and Pacific, upon Farnam's resignation, was passed on to the Doctor's brother, Charles W. Durant. The Doctor, his brother, and a third member of his family, William Clark Durant, had been on the board from the beginning. In December 1867 they got on the wrong side of a bull

51 Dodge, *How We Built the Union Pacific,* p. 47.
52 Hayes, *Iron Road to Empire,* pp. 39–53.
53 Dodge, *How We Built the Union Pacific,* p. 60.
54 Perkins, *Trails, Rails and War,* p. 139.

speculation in Rock Island stock. After losing a related lawsuit filed against the company by the Doctor, the Durant family all resigned.[55]

In the meantime, after having "externally dammed" [56] the M & M in 1857, the Doctor, back in New York, had turned his energies towards the allurement of a Pacific railway, even if the hope of dominating an eastern connection with it had been dimmed. Thus Durant can be seen as an old rival of Oakes Ames in railroading across Iowa, each man with an eye on the first track pointing to California.

Dr. Durant was rather tall and lean, somewhat stooped, with flashing, penetrating eyes and sharp features. His long brown hair, drooping dark mustache and somewhat straggly goatee were worn in the style of the day. He dressed expensively and ornately, preferring to wear his slouch hat, finely fitted velvet sackcoat and vest, corduroy breeches, and top-boots.[57] Restless and quick in action, his speech was rapid, quiet, and terse. In controversy, his manner was caustic and impatient; in salesmanship, suave and persuasive. When the time came for a decision, no one could be more adamant. Charles T. Sherman, a Government Director of the UP, said: "With his unexampled energy . . . Durant could drive work better than any man I ever saw." [58]

In his black walnut paneled office, with a marble fireplace and Oriental rugs, he kept palms, statues, and cages of singing canaries. His horses and carriages were the envy of Central Park. Early in 1865, while a resident of Brooklyn, he joined the New York Yacht Club and bought the well-known schooner *Idler*, 85 feet overall. On pleasant weekends he would entertain prospective investors, influential politicians, and judges with luxurious cruises up and down the placid Hudson. After leaving the UP, he also bought the 92-foot steam yacht *Minnehaha*, which could serve better on breezy days. He maintained both vessels until the panic of 1873, when he gave up yachting.[59]

Of all the persons connected with the UP during its construction, Durant was ever, for better or worse, the most conspicuous. With unceasing determination and unbridled ambition, he conceived the project, pressed Congress for the charter, took most of the first subscriptions, and made himself Vice-President, General Manager, and Chairman of both the Executive and Finance Committees of the UP and President of the Credit Mobilier of America. He took no salary.

---

[55] Hayes, p. 69.   [56] Perkins, p. 124 (Dey to Dodge).
[57] Leonard and Johnson, *A Railroad to the Sea*, p. 7.
[58] *Wilson Rep.*, p. 654.   [59] Records of the New York Yacht Club.

He was out on the line most of the time as construction neared the end. In fact, he took dictatorial charge of about everything, with little worry about such details as dual capacities and conflicts of interest. His own words portray his character: "I had rather have a man about me that did all his enemies claimed . . . [who] had pluck and energy and resources within himself to accomplish his work than to have a dolt, though he might be as honest as the sun." [60]

As a speculator, Durant was one of the boldest. He practically lived on a shoestring. To quote one of his closest associates, Silas Seymour:

He exhibited boldness, sagacity and tact in manipulating stocks, became one of the most successful operators of the stock exchange, and invested in railroad securities. . . . A sketch by one of the leading papers of New York says: . . . "His mainspring seems to be not love of money for itself, or of notoriety in any sense, but a love for large operations— a restless desire to be swinging great enterprises and doing everything on a magnificent scale." [61]

Taking no part in the Civil War, Durant devoted his powers during that period towards one goal. That was to make a fortune from contracts to build the UP, no matter how wastefully and regardless of where the chips might fall. "He was the most extravagant man I ever knew in my life," testified John M.S. Williams, a director of the Credit Mobilier.[62] His basic theory was that the operation of any railroad would never, as a legitimate business enterprise, yield a profit, and the UP would be no exception. One of the UP directors put it a bit more sharply:

Durant, McComb, and their supporters believed that everything that could be made must be made in the construction of the road, and that whoever depended like Mr. Ames for profitable returns upon his investment in the future earnings of the road, was, to use Durant's own expression, "a damned fool!" [63]

Few shrewder promoters ever operated in the early railroad history of America.

As an executive, Durant certainly was "not over-scrupulous," [64] yet he was smart enough to be seldom caught by the law, even though

---

[60] Leonard and Johnson, p. 11.
[61] James Parton, *Sketches of Men of Progress*, 1870–1871, p. 245.
[62] *Wilson Rep.*, p. 163.   [63] *Poland Rep.*, p. 87 (testimony of Alley).
[64] Hazard, p. 11.

many accusations were brought against him of misappropriation of company funds and other serious irregularities. Essentially secretive, he wrote few letters. When Durant became locked in battle with the Ames brothers for control, he hired Judge George G. Barnard, the notoriously corrupt judge of "Boss" Tweed's ring and tool of Jim Fisk and Daniel Drew, to impose crippling injunctions that impeded the financing of the UP. Durant's lawsuits seemingly were framed to be in the interests of the UP stockholders as a whole, whereas in fact they were attempts to fight those who were cramping his share of the gains. His long testimonies before the Wilson Committee [65] and the Poland Committee [66] in 1873 were masterpieces of clear memory, backed by voluminous documentary evidence designed to prove that he was always right. To some of those Congressmen, he must have made a smart impression as a witness, nothwithstanding his attitude of cool indifference, then being no longer with the UP.

In spite of such versatile talents, Durant had one fatal weakness: he did not know how to get along with people. One after the other, he first befriended and then fought his associates: Farnam, Blair, Dey, Hoxie, Lambard, J.M.S. Williams, J.L. Williams, Oakes Ames, Oliver Ames, Dodge, Reed, Evans, Henry, Blickensderfer, Train, McComb, and even the rascal Jim Fisk. He quarreled with his superintendents and construction crews. For example, the Superintendent of Construction, Samuel B. Reed, wrote home to his wife:

Dr. Durant is here [in Weber Canyon] and of all men to mix accounts and business, he is the chief. . . . Immense amounts of money were squandered uselessly [by his interference] and not as much work done [as could have been] . . . He costs hundreds of thousands of dollars extra every month he remains here and does not advance, but retards the work . . . No one can tell by Mr. Durant's talk what he thinks of a man, his best friends may not know what he means when talking to them.[67]

Sidney Dillon, once President of the Credit Mobilier and one of the Seven Trustees, waggishly declared to the Congressional Committee in 1873:

I can only say that Durant . . . is a fast man. He started fast, and I tried to hold him back awhile, but he got me going pretty fast before

---

[65] *Wilson Rep.*, pp. 62–137, 513–525.
[66] *Poland Rep.*, pp. 162–178, 239–243, 365–405.
[67] 12 and 16 Jan. 1869; Records of UP Historical Museum.

we got through. . . . What I meant by saying that he was a fast man was, that when he undertook to build a railroad he didn't stop at trifles in accomplishing his end.[68]

Oakes Ames, writing to McComb on 17 September 1867, said:

I do not think we should do right to put Durant in as a director, unless he withdraws his injunction suits and submits to the will of the majority. He cannot hurt us half as badly out of the direction as he can in, and there is no pleasure, peace, safety or comfort with him unless he agrees to abide by the decision of the majority, as the rest of us do.[69]

Dr. Durant was ejected from the management of the Credit Mobilier in May 1867, "after which it was in able and honest hands." [70] In March 1869, following President Grant's request to the Government Directors, he was finally ousted from office in the UP itself. Nevertheless, he walked away with a large fortune and retired to the Adirondacks. In the panic of 1873, he lost most of his gains in a local railroad venture and, still pursued by lawsuits, died broken in health and spirit on 5 October 1885.[71]

To this day, not a trace of the name of Durant can be found on the UP property. Perhaps he should have remained a doctor.

F. Ground Is Broken in Omaha

To return to events immediately following the tardy organization of the company, Vice-President Durant lost little time in having a few shovelfuls of ground broken at Omaha as a token of intention to start the road there and not somewhere else. The day was 2 December 1863, 11 months after the groundbreaking of the CP. The spot was in the Missouri River bottoms near the old ferry landing at Davenport and Seventh Street, between the present Ak-Sar-Ben highway bridge and the Abbott Drive viaduct.[72] The ceremony was also a promotion stunt at the expense of the meager first capital install-

---

[68] *Wilson Rep.*, pp. 510–511.   [69] *Ibid.*, p. 120.   [70] Hazard, p. 20, fn.
[71] Leonard and Johnson, pp. 270–272.
[72] Records of UP Historical Museum. This spot is not to be confused with the so-called "Initial Point" fixed by President Lincoln two miles farther north, since obliterated by the west arm of Carter Lake. (See map in Seymour, *Report of the Consulting Engineer*, 31 Dec. 1864; also p. 99).

ments paid in by the stockholders. Omaha declared a general holiday in honor of its selection as the place. Happy guns (unlike those at the siege of Knoxville that day) boomed on both sides of the river, horns blared and drums rolled to draw the crowd for the speeches. President Lincoln (two weeks after his Gettysburg address) and Brigham Young had been asked for messages of congratulations, which were read triumphantly by George Francis Train, the orator of the day. There were fireworks in the early dusk, followed by a large banquet at the nearby Herndon House—the center of social activities—with more flowery speeches by politicians and real estate promoters.

Lincoln's "Lost" Order: A strange complication arose. The President was required by the Act of 1862 to name "a point on the western boundary of the State of Iowa" with which the "Iowa Branch" of the UP would connect.[73] Pressed by Durant, Lincoln mailed him an executive order dated 17 November 1863, in which the "point" was not described too clearly.[74] Evidently he did not have the Pacific railroad uppermost in his mind when he hurriedly scribbled the order. In two days he would be making his immortal dedication address at Gettysburg. Durant shrewdly construed the point to mean Omaha, not a spot on the east side of the river, and proceeded with the ground-breaking. The Doctor also marked on the company map an "initial point" two miles further north. Then the order, of which there was no copy, mysteriously got "lost." Durant had kept it in his private possession throughout his lifetime. Some of the UP authorities became apprehensive and asked the President for confirmation. On 7 March 1864, Lincoln sent a second order, and at once explained it verbally before the Senate, definitely placing the point "on the western boundary of Iowa," *opposite* Omaha. Photos of both orders are now displayed in the UP Historical Museum. The President had acted on the general recommendations of two of the best engineers of the time, Dey and Dodge. John P. Usher, then Secretary of the Interior, years later related that the following conversation took place:

Dr. Durant said "Now the natural place for this terminal point is at the mouth of the Platte River, but Omaha is the principal town in Nebraska . . . the best thing is to start it from Omaha." I remember very well Mr. Lincoln looked at the map and said: "I have got a quarter section of land right across there, and if I fix it there they will say that

---

[73] See p. 12.   [74] Dodge, *How We Built the Union Pacific*, pp. 11–12.

I have done it to benefit my land. But," he added, "I will fix it there, anyhow." [75]

The fact that years before Dodge and Lincoln had each purchased residential sites in Council Bluffs near the spot where the Union depot of the UP was finally located need be given weight only in light of the fact that these men were the first to judge correctly that the best route for a Pacific railway was up the Platte Valley.

Durant's interpretation of Presidential orders started a tangle. After Lincoln's death a long, bitter lawsuit arose as to which company, the UP or one or more of the Iowan railroads to enter Council Bluffs, was finally to bear the entire cost of building the Missouri River bridge, "the most difficult engineering problem that the builders of the Union Pacific had to solve." [76]

G. Lobbying for Better Bait

The 1862 Act was unattractive, to be sure, but Durant and some of the individuals in his pool failed to inspire the confidence required to raise enough capital to build the first 40 miles and thereby receive Government assistance. "The enterprise was dragging along in the hands of men of little pecuniary responsibility," wrote Rowland Hazard. [77] One such man who was known to be involved was Durant's close friend Train. An erratic promoter and president of his Credit Foncier of America (a scheme for speculating in real estate, including good sites in Omaha), Train, with florid imagination and fluent tongue, was the stormy petrel of railroad politics and big-time speculation. To sum up, with responsible capitalists shunning the situation, it seemed most unlikely that the Act of 1862 would *ever* enable Durant to build the UP.

So, early in 1864, despite the preoccupation of the legislature with the War, Vice-President Durant commenced his lobbying in Washington for bigger and better bait. Just what he did and said, and how expenses were covered, will remain a closed book. However, there is no doubt that he was the leader in the fight for more aid. An investigation years later revealed that, in spite of the dangerously weakened condition of the UP's treasury, the astonishing sum of $435,754.21 was spent in Washington and charged upon the company's books as

---

[75] Senate Executive Document No. 51, 50th Cong., 1st Sess., pp. 1675–1676.
[76] Galloway, *The First Transcontinental Railroad*, p. 287.   [77] Hazard, p. 10.

"suspense-account," nearly all in Durant's name.[78] As an example, one item of $30,000 was found to have been paid on March 31 to a lobbyist lawyer by the name of Joseph B. Stewart for services in procuring the passage of the Act of 1864.[79] Stewart refused to divulge how a sum of over $250,000 which passed through his hands was disbursed, except that none of it was given to members of Congress.[80] For his contempt of Congress he spent a while in jail.

On this matter, Rowland Hazard wrote in 1881:

It transpires that they [the large amounts of bonds given by Durant to Stewart] were used largely, if not altogether, in promoting the interests of the Kansas Pacific Railroad, or, as it was then called, the Union Pacific Eastern Division. This was really a rival line to the Union Pacific proper, and the similarity of name has often caused confusion. It was to connect with the main line at the one hundredth meridian, and its actual terminus was the city of St. Louis.

Durant, Hallett, and a gentleman of St. Louis took the contract for building this line. At the time Durant took this one-third interest in this *rival* line, he was a Director and Vice-President of the Union Pacific. The operation illustrates his remarkable versatility.

But . . . there is no belief, on the part of those best informed, . . . that the passage of this amendment was procured either by bribery or by improper influences.[81]

Nevertheless, Durant's "suspense-account" of $435,754 caused much controversy. In September 1867 Oliver Ames and J.J. Cisco, having been appointed by the Directors as a committee to make a final allocation of the item on the books of the railroad, decided to charge it off to "construction." [82] They found that $163,020 had been paid by Durant on account of the Hoxie contract; $120,563 for construction; $102,127 for equipment; and $50,000 for the first installment on $500,000 stock.[83] All of these amounts, which were covered by signed vouchers, had been kept in "suspense" by Durant for the purpose of later spreading certain preliminary expenses over the whole road, instead of over the first 40 miles.[84]

The continual appearance of paid lobbyists seeking more aid for the Pacific railroads became noticeable in Congressional debates.

---

[78] *Wilson Rep.*, p. 137.   [79] *Ibid.*, p. 175 (testimony of Stewart).
[80] *Ibid.*, pp. 129, 177, 389.   [81] Hazard, pp. 11–12.
[82] *Wilson Rep.*, pp. 137, 103–113 (testimony of Durant), 297–299, 314; Durant, *Papers*, 3–17–17–18, 11 Sept. 1868.
[83] Durant, *Papers*, 1–2–32–33 (Credit Mobilier—Suspense account, n.d.).
[84] *Wilson Rep.*, pp. 103–113 (testimony of Durant).

C.P. Huntington of the CP had also hastened to the Capitol to feather his nest. Doubtless all this lobbying met with no little suspicion, and many Congressmen were to remain prejudiced against *anyone* who was building the Pacific railways.

In fact, one Congressman publicly raised a question at the time even about the good faith of the organization:

> Is it not notorious that one single individual owns or controls a majority of the stock, and has organized the company in such a way as completely to control it; and is it not alleged that there are directors in the board who are not *bona fide* owners of a single dollar of stock? . . . It must be understood that under the existing law, parties who have subscribed for $1,001,000 worth of stock (the whole amount subscribed being only $2,000,000) can control the whole concern. . . . The real management is in the hands of a set of Wall Street stockjobbers who are using this great engine for their own private ends, regardless of what should be the great objects of the company and of the interests of the country. Who are the men who are here to lobby this bill through? . . . The work . . . has gone into the hands of such men as Samuel Hallett and George Francis Train, *par nobile fratrum* . . . I believe the road will never be built under the present management even if the bill shall pass. . . . The whole business of the directors is done by an executive committee of the board . . . and one man is the executive committee.[85]

Oakes Ames to Washington: In the meantime, Oakes Ames answered his first Washington roll call when the Thirty-Eighth Congress, First Session, convened on 7 December 1863. As a member of the Pacific Railroad Committee of the House, he first learned the details of the dilemma of the UP under Durant. In fact, his Committee, headed by Cornelius Crole of California, endorsed the amended charter as set forth in the Act of 1864. There seems to be no record of Oakes's own stand on the matter. However, in his defense read before the House on 25 February 1873, Oakes had this to say:

> It is in testimony before a committee of the House that after the impracticability of building the road under the first act had been demonstrated, when it had become apparent that additional aid was necessary, to induce capitalists to embark in the enterprise, the late President Lincoln was urgent that Congress should not withhold the additional assistance asked, and that he personally advised the officers of the com-

[85] Congressman Elihu W. Washburne (Rep., Illinois), 21 June 1864, *Cong. Globe*, 38th Cong., 1st Sess., p. 3151; Davis, pp. 120–122.

pany to go to Congress for such legislation as would . . . place the construction of the road beyond a peradventure.[86]

Bushnell quoted Lincoln in his testimony:

I would like to make a statement to the committee as to the reason why we asked Congress for just what we did in 1864. We did it after a consultation—Mr. Dillon and myself—with Mr. Lincoln. Mr. Lincoln said to us that his experience in the West after many years was that every railroad that had been undertaken there had broken down before it was half completed, and the original projectors had lost all their money. He had but one advice to give us, and that was to ask sufficient aid of Congress, so that when we commenced the undertaking of building that road we should be able to carry it through to completion, and not break down and lose all we put into it. He said further that if they would hurry it up so that when he retired from the Presidency he could take a trip over it, it would be the proudest thing of his life that he had signed the bill in aid of its construction.[87]

H. The Amended Charter: The Act of 1864 [88]

By 1864 the Union Congress of 25 States had become convinced that the Act of 1862 must somehow, under the distressing circumstances, be liberalized and a start for the Pacific Coast undertaken at once. Members from the Western states quite naturally insisted on adequate aid regardless of cost. The burden of the War had now made it totally impossible for the Union to undertake the task alone, although there still remained some minority legislative sentiment in that direction.

So at last, even while the Confederates under General Early were within sight and sound of Washington, the "Act to Amend An Act" (H.R. No. 438) was passed on June 25 in the House by 70 to 38, with one member not voting.[89] Failing to answer the roll call were 73 Representatives, some of whom perhaps considered the rumble of guns a bit too loud. After much wrangling between the Senate and House over the proposed changes, interspersed by very conspicuous

---

[86] Ames Family, *Oakes Ames,* p. 111; *Cong. Globe,* 42nd Cong., 3rd Sess. See also p. 478. The speech was prepared by his lawyer.

[87] *Wilson Rep.,* p. 551 (Bushnell).

[88] 13 Statutes at Large 356; White, pp. 110–115 (in detail); Davis, pp. 110–135; Trottman, pp. 18–22.

[89] *Cong. Globe,* 38th Cong., 1st Sess., p. 3267; Davis, pp. 123–126.

lobbying, the report of a Joint Committee on Conference, headed by Senator James Harlan of Iowa and Congressman Thaddeus Stevens of Pennsylvania, was accepted by both branches on July 1, the next to the last day of the First Session, Thirty-Eighth Congress. The report was passed without being printed or read, and with only a meager verbal description by a member of the Committee in each house.[90] In this hasty and much criticized form, the Act of 1864 became law with the immediate signature of President Lincoln on 2 July 1864.

The principal changes from the original act are summarized as follows, more or less in order of importance:

1. The company could issue its *first* mortgage bonds, usual on completion of each section of *20* consecutive miles, instead of 40, *to an amount not exceeding the amount of the bonds of the United States*. The lien of the U.S. bonds was to be *subordinate* to that of the bonds of either Company (UP or CP) except as to the transmission of dispatches and the transportation of mails, troops, munitions of war, supplies, and public stores for the Government.[91] Thus it follows that the U.S. bonds should enable the first mortgage bonds to be sold in the market at substantially higher prices than under the Act of 1862. The only other difference between the two bonds was that the Government issue was payable in currency, the company issue in gold. The company's bonds rested on the property and the ability of the company to meet them. They were a lien on the company's capital, its expenditures on the road, its franchises, and its grants of land by Congress.

2. The land grants were *doubled,* with 10 alternate sections (one square mile each) on each side of every mile of track instead of five, making 12,800 acres per mile.[92] Previous restrictions on the sale of land were canceled. The land grants became *unconditional*. Furthermore, *ownership of coal and iron lands* found in the grants was no longer barred to the company.

3. Land patents and subsidy bonds were issuable as each *20-mile* stretch was completed and certified.[93] Thus the amount of working capital required for construction was cut in half.

4. Two-thirds of the subsidy bonds were to be issued *at once* for the value of approved *grading* work done in any section of 20 miles in the *mountain* regions, the remainder to wait until full completion of

---

[90] Davis, pp. 124–125; Hazard, p. 12; *Cong. Globe,* 38th Cong., 1st Sess., pp. 3154–3480.
[91] *Act of 1864,* Section 10 (White, p. 112).   [92] *Ibid.,* Section 4.
[93] *Ibid.,* Section 10.

said section, instead of a portion being withheld until the entire road was completed. Furthermore, "No such bonds shall be issued to the UP for work done west of Salt Lake City . . . more than 300 miles in advance of the completed continuous line . . . from 100° W." [94]

5. The CP could build *no further than 150 miles east of California,* instead of meeting the UP anywhere.[95] This vital item was to be changed again by the Act of 3 July 1866.[96]

6. The railroad was permitted to collect from time to time *one-half* of the sum due them on Government account, instead of the entire amount being withheld as security for repayment of the subsidy bonds.[97]

7. The capital stock, "the books for which were to be kept open to receive subscriptions," was changed to a par value of *$100* instead of $1,000 by what is now known as a split of ten shares for one.[98] Also, "the capital stock shall not be increased beyond the actual cost of said road," [99] which apparently indicated there were thoughts in Congress that the entire road might be built without any bonds at all!

8. The limit on the amount of stock one person could hold was canceled, but the subscription price was to remain fixed at the new par.[100] "The company shall make assessments upon its stockholders of not less than $5 per share and at intervals of not exceeding six months, until fully paid." [101] This meant at least 10 per cent per annum.

9. The directors were increased from not less than 15 to *20,* of whom 5 (not 2) were to be appointed by the President.[102] "At least one of said government directors is to be placed on each of the standing and special committees of the Company . . . and they must visit all parts of the line as often as necessary to gain a full knowledge of conditions and management of the line." Thus the interests of the Government were to be especially protected.[103]

10. Finally, "Congress may, at any time, alter, amend, or repeal this act." [104] And so it did make alterations, important ones.

11. Nowhere, however, were there any specifications as to just how the UP and CP were to connect.

Notwithstanding this much more favorable legislation, no capital was attracted, no additional stock was subscribed.

The obscurities and omissions of the clumsily drawn enabling

---

[94] *Ibid.,* Section 8.   [95] *Ibid.,* Section 16; see also p. 13.
[96] *Ibid.,* Section 16; see also p. 140.   [97] *Ibid.,* Section 5.   [98] *Ibid.,* Section 1.
[99] *Ibid.,* Section 2.   [100] *Ibid.,* Section 1.   [101] *Ibid.,* Section 2.
[102] *Ibid.,* Section 13.   [103] *Wilson Rep.,* p. ii.   [104] *Act of 1864,* Section 22.

Acts were not cleared up until too late. "They were among the Ifs of history." [105]

When Congress was in session, each day was started with a prayer. The Reverend Dr. Byron Sunderland, Chaplain of the Senate, in April 1864, made the following invocation: "O Lord, give us that Thou wilt, in Thine infinite wisdom, vouchsafe to our rulers and legislators in this Congress assembled more brains—more brains, Lord." [106]

I. Problems of Financing Under the Charter

The Pacific Railroad Acts of 1862 and 1864 taken together form the charter of the original Union Pacific Railroad and merit close attention.

Nelson Trottman, in his *History of the Union Pacific*, written in 1923, considered that:

They are among the most extraordinary, as well as important, acts ever passed by Congress. Congressional grants of land in aid of railroads were not unusual both before and after the Civil War; but this is the only instance where the national government aided a railroad by practically guaranteeing a portion of its bonded debt. Although the grants were generous, the obstacles which apparently stood in the way of the road's completion were large, and in the eyes of many, insuperable. . . .

To quote a Congressman: "This road could never be constructed on terms applicable to ordinary roads. . . . The government must come forward with a liberal hand, or the enterprise must be abandoned forever. The necessity is upon us. The question is whether we shall hold our Pacific possessions, and connect the nations on the Pacific with those on the Atlantic coast, or whether we shall abandon our Pacific possessions." [107]

The Acts contemplated a railroad which was to be built with money raised from three sources: cash subscriptions to the capital stock, a government subsidy, and first mortgage bonds. Congress unfortunately failed to take into consideration one important economic fact, which was that the method of financing railroad construction by means of cash subscriptions to the capital stock was then no longer employed in the con-

---

[105] Sabin, *Building the Pacific Railway,* p. 88.

[106] Noah Brooks, *Washington in Lincoln's Time,* edited by Herbert Mitgang (Rinehart), quoted in *Reader's Digest,* Jan. 1959, p. 186.

[107] *Cong. Globe,* 37th Cong., 1st Sess., p. 1912—speech of Rep. W.S. Holman of Indiana, "the watch-dog of the Treasury."

struction of new railroads. Formerly this had been done, with the result that the money invested in early railroads was usually lost. To invest in the stock of a projected railroad had been found to be extremely hazardous. At best, dividends could be expected only after a long period of waiting.[108]

Mervin H. Waterman, Professor of Finance, School of Business Administration at the University of Michigan, described in 1958 the general investment banking situation as follows:

So as we enter the post-Civil War period of industrial and geographical expansion and development of the United States we have the stage set for a new era of financing. The props are there: some individual capital available for investment and a growing amount of institutional capital in the background. The National Currency Act of 1864 had set the national banks up in the investment banking business by legalizing their right to discount and negotiate evidences of debt in general. . . . Participation in syndicates enabled the banks to procure issues which they might either redistribute or hold in their secondary reserves. Both as investors and underwriters these National Banks joined state banks and private bankers on the stage in what, by today's standards, might be considered a very confusing scene. . . .

Remember that this period after the war and into the 1900's was what history has recorded as a pioneering era. "Pioneers" in ever greater numbers took up land in the west; "pioneers" established businesses to foster and then to serve an increasing industrialization; there were "pioneers" [among] the bankers who moved readily between deposit banking and investment banking. . . . In the banking business as elsewhere there wasn't too sharp a line between "pioneering" and "buccaneering." . . . In their own field the bankers assumed the coloration of the times; the trouble was—or perhaps the virtue—that the bankers were human beings, and that is a broad classification including all kinds of people from the staid conservative to the speculator, from the highly ethical to the irresponsible.[109]

Historian John P. Davis, in writing his well-known *The Union Pacific Railway* in 1894, had the following to say on the financing of railroads in general and the UP in particular:

Such an exaggerated estimation was put on railway bonds in the period during and following the Rebellion that it was no difficult matter to

[108] Trottman, pp. 21–22.   [109] Waterman, pp. 25–26.

bond a railway for more than it was worth. . . . The investor in railway bonds seemed to be putting his faith not in a Vanderbilt or Gould (who ruled the markets), but in the manufacturers, farmers, producers and consumers of the tributary territory upon which the roads depended for their success. The autocratic influence of "railroad managers" had not been appreciably exerted. The disastrous results of competition and "rate wars" had not yet been felt. If a railway could not pay the interest on its bonds, rates could be increased; and if it could pay the interest on its bonds, it could by a little more pressure on the tributary territory be made to pay some interest even on stock or more bonds. Thus the value of railways came to be determined not by the expense of building them, but by the amount of bonds and stock that their tributary territory could carry; if bonds were at a high premium and stock should be paying a high rate of dividends, enough water was put into the capital of the company to make returns normal, by building branch lines and over-capitalizing them, by issuing stock dividends, or by some of the many other methods of stock-watering. The railway builder, urged on by the people whose towns, factories, and farms would be benefited by increased facilities of transportation, soon found, shrewdly enough, that he could usually build his road from the bonuses of the future patrons of the road, and the proceeds of the bonds that eastern investors . . . would invest in . . . .

The only safeguard the political economist and legislator of 1870 could find was in the principle of competition, by which, if one railway taxed its tributary community too heavily to pay interest and dividends on excessive issues of bonds and stock, another railway would compete with it for its traffic; hence, it was assumed, railway builders would, from prudential motives, refrain from excessive issues of bonds and stock . . . .

When Congress attempted to encourage the construction of the Pacific railway in 1862 and 1864, it blundered and groped about until it enacted laws that were fundamentally out of harmony with economic conditions. It expected a large body of patriotic citizens to buy shares in the Union Pacific, and to the money derived from the sale of stock the government would add a liberal bonus of land and bonds; then if such amount should not be sufficient to build the road, the company might issue enough first-mortgage bonds (not exceeding in amount the bonds of the government) to complete the project. A philanthropic scheme, indeed, by which patriotic capitalists and shareholders might provide their country with a Pacific railway and then wait for dividends on their stock as a reward for their patriotism! That may be the principle on which Congress makes laws, but it is not the principle on which, since 1860, capitalists have built railways, contractors have erected buildings, and clothing merchants have dealt in coats and socks in this *laissez faire,* competitive period of economic refinement . . . .

Indeed, Congress, state legislatures, and the people did not count the cost of a Pacific railway; the railway was what they wanted, no matter what the cost might be. Congress thought, until otherwise instructed by the Supreme Court, that the Union Pacific promoters were the agents and trustees of the government, inspired by the highest motives of patriotism to build the national highway,—they were only men of the nineteenth century, building a railway just as other men built railways, and making all the profit they could from the venture.[110]

Said Charles Francis Adams Jr. (1835–1915), a lawyer, prolific writer about railroads, and President of the UP from 1884 to 1890:

Ignorant legislation is at the root of the railway question. In this statute-ridden country two score of State legislatures each bungle their own work in their own way, while Congress sets an example of confusion to all. Knowledge cannot possibly creep into the legislature, because no one remains in the legislature long enough to learn. Committees shift with every year, and are constructed with an eye to current events; meanwhile the lobby is permanent, and the corporation is ever alert to defeat any scheme which may throw light on its operations. Knowledge, then, being the great desideratum in this matter, and the legislatures having wholly failed either to give evidence of possessing it themselves or of being able to impart it to others, it only remains for the community to provide other machinery through which the information so necessary may be procured. Bureaus, or boards of commissioners, having charge of questions in relation to railways, should be established, both State and national.[111]

More charitable towards human frailty is Robert William Fogel, Assistant Professor of Economics at the University of Rochester, in his scholarly, unique, and penetrating study, *The Union Pacific Railroad—A Case in Premature Enterprise.* He wrote in 1960:

Here then was the paradox with which the nation had to grapple: the paradox of a railroad that was both premature and late, both profitable and unprofitable, both essential and impractical. Nor was this an artificial paradox manufactured in the heat of political rhetoric. It reflected a real dichotomy between sound private investment principles and public or national economic necessity, a dichotomy that was inherent in premature enterprise. In mature enterprise the public and private interest are normally united. The first is contained in and is fulfilled as

---

[110] Davis, pp. 197–200. (Italics by C.E.A.)
[111] "Railroad Inflation," *North American Review,* Jan. 1869, pp. 162–163.

a result of the operation of the second, with private profit acting as the dynamic force which propels the work into being and insures its completion. The "invisible hand" works as it should. But in the case of the first Pacific railroad, as in all premature enterprise, the relentless compulsion of private profit was absent, and this absence created a formidable barrier to the project. The entire burden of the work rested on the public interest which alone had to provide the impelling force that would energize the enterprise. The existence of such a dichotomy gave opponents of premature construction a powerful argument. Few would contradict them when they asserted that by the principles of profitable private investment the road was sure to fail. Yet it was equally hard to deny that the road would create many new and highly lucrative business opportunities for merchants, manufacturers and farmers, thereby enriching both individuals and the nation as a whole.

The Pacific Railroad Acts of 1862 and 1864 did not resolve the paradox. They resolved the questions of whether or not the road should be built prematurely and whether or not the government should give its monies to the project, but not the seeming contradiction between the public and private interest in the line. Congress was well aware of the paradox, as even a cursory examination of the long debate (of seventeen years) will show, but its discussion never really probed the subtleties of this all too complicated problem. The tendency was rather to seize on one or another aspect of the paradox in order to use it as ammunition for or against premature construction. The Acts that climaxed the debate were measures of expediency by a Congressional majority which was anxious to get a Pacific railroad and was at last in a position to obtain it. Practical men who recognized that "the great railroad interests, and the great interests of the country had to be consulted," [112] these legislators had little time or inclination to dally with questions that bordered on the metaphysical.

To reproach Congress for not having been wiser would be inappropriate. For one thing it is much too late a date for disapprobation. For another, it asks for an understanding of issues that usually comes only with hindsight. Despite previous practical experiences, especially on state and local levels, the broader issues involved in premature and mixed enterprises were still basically unexplored in the mid-1860's. In a certain sense these issues and the problems they posed belonged more to the next century than to the one in which they appeared.[113]

Arthur M. Johnson, Professor of Business History at the Harvard Graduate School of Business Administration, and Barry E. Supple, Professor of Economic and Social History at the University of Sussex,

---

[112] Senator McDougall, *Cong. Globe*, 37th Cong., 2nd Sess., p. 2806.
[113] Fogel, *The Union Pacific Railroad*, pp. 23–24.

joint authors of *Boston Capitalists and Western Railroads, A Study in the Nineteenth-Century Railroad Investment Process,* published in 1967, concluded:

The plan that was actually adopted in financing the construction of the U.P. was as logical as any of the proposed alternatives involving private enterprise. Indeed, it was more logical than one that would have assigned primary responsibility to the government.[114]

Summary: It was, of course, impossible for a new enterprise to raise cash capital by *continuously* offering common stock at a fixed price, when $100,000,000 of it was for sale. The demand for UP stock was practically nil at $100 a share; the supply virtually open-ended. Earnings and dividends were conjectural at best. Anyway, most investors were not educated to buying common stocks of any kind in that era. The equity shares of most companies were held closely by a few people in the management or by the founding family. The shovel works of Oliver Ames and Sons is a good example. However, individual and institutional investors did understand and believe in *bonds,* where the rate of interest was fixed, where there was a definite maturity time, and where there was a priority claim on the assets and cumulative interest in case of trouble. Bonds, particularly national and state issues with active markets on the New York Stock Exchange, were far more popular investments than stocks. The Exchange had been organized as early as 1817, yet by 1869 there were only 73 companies whose shares were regularly quoted on the Exchange, and well over half of these were railroads.[115]

After the small amount of qualifying stock of the UP was subscribed at $100 a share for purposes of gaining control, no further issues were made except to the promoters in payment to themselves as contractors. If one of them then wished to dispose of his shares, he offered them for sale in the "over-the-counter" market, where the widely varying price was never above $50 a share until 1875, and sometimes as low as a few dollars a share before the stock was fully paid up. Of course, *the steadily increasing number of shares outstanding* had an important effect on the price. Earnings of a new road could not keep up with them, particularly on the UP.

Obviously, then, the bulk of the UP construction capital had to come from the public in the form of *bonds,* not stock. With the Civil

[114] Johnson and Supple, *Boston Capitalists and Western Railroads,* p. 263.
[115] *Commercial and Financial Register,* 1870, pp. 30–32.

War still on, and money exorbitantly tight, the U.S. 6 per cent Subsidy bonds, payable in an undermined currency rather than in gold (which had risen to a high of 285 or premium of 185 per cent in July 1864), yielded about 6 per cent. But the UP 6 per cent first mortgage bonds, even though payable in gold and senior to the U.S. bonds, sold at a discount and yielded nearly 9 per cent in gold.[116] The discount required a larger face amount to be issued and sold, which added to the danger of insolvency when the bonds came due. For instance, if the best price was only 84 per cent of par, $12,000 in bonds must be issued to raise $10,000 in cash, increasing the long term debt of the company by 20 per cent.

In the final analysis, however, it was the buyer who took all the bond risk, and obviously he paid only what he thought was a price commensurate with that risk. *Caveat emptor* was the dictum of those days. The financiers issued whatever first mortgage bonds they could sell at reasonable prices, but in the case of the UP, the amount was limited to the amount of the U.S. bonds issued.

If the buyer of a UP bond voluntarily took a risk at a yield he thought attractive, the financiers also took the great risk of not being able to find enough buyers of bonds in amounts and at prices that covered their expenses. The UP had no "tributary territory" except the Mormon settlements in Utah and a number of mining camps. It was dependent mostly on transcontinental traffic, yet there was no railroad connection until 1867 at its eastern terminus, and none until 1869 at its western terminus. It had the cutthroat competition of trying to meet the CP as far west as possible and, eventually, the rate competition from the Kansas Pacific Railway over one-half of its own length. Only the motive of making a handsome profit on the stock on the probability that all would go well could have enticed the promoters to push construction in the face of losing their fortunes if things were to go wrong.

Inefficient and well-nigh impossible as was the scheme of financing set up by the charter, the essential fact is that *Congress was unable to find any better, indeed any other, way of sponsoring the Union Pacific.* Yet Congress could hardly have anticipated that the initial control would fall into the hands of a very small group of men who were financially unable to carry out their own objectives and who, having seized the reins, would not yield control to others who could carry on.

[116] See p. 241.

All in all, this legislation was too impracticable as a political compromise to have any chance of success. It was a by-product of our system of representative government being soundly designed to prevent a small group of men, no matter how well intentioned or expertly informed, from negotiating on behalf of the Government and binding it to a bargain. Both houses of Congress and the President had to approve. To get such action, particularly in those Civil War years, required an amount of agitation the energy for which no one but an interested lobbyist was able to spare. To offset the lobbyist, the legislature applied brakes, sometimes most unwisely. Congress never seemed to understand, until corrected by the United States Supreme Court years later, that in the case of the UP they were surrendering to private capital something which the Government wanted but refused to undertake itself. Having gladly given the land grants and the Subsidy bonds, Congress failed to see that they had little to say about the profit or loss of the private venture, beyond some relatively minor restrictions set forth in the charter. Congress did not create, as they imagined they had, a great trust for the people. They released a "free" enterprise that wasn't really free.

To come to perhaps the deepest and most obscure difficulty, the Government, as creditor of the Pacific railways, was constantly liable to be drawn into disputes that involved it, the sovereign, in contests before its own courts with creatures of its own making, the railroads. As supreme lawmaker, the Government repeatedly altered its status as one of the parties to a contract by changing the laws that governed the railroads after construction had been committed.[117] Some regulation by legislation, even if piecemeal, clearly was necessary during the life of the Subsidy bonds. But the legislation often was injudicious, or simply amateurish, and defeating in its purpose. Regulation of these Pacific railroads in the 19th century was not by a permanent, trained public authority, like the Interstate Commerce Commission of today; rather, it was by imposition of one Congressional act after another, framed by lawyers who campaigned for their elections. Though experienced in adapting themselves to flitting demands of press and public, most of these statesmen were inexperienced in financing and managing new railroads. Too often they were motivated by an erroneous sense of trusteeship relations between themselves and the roads, and their laws put the Pacific railways at an unfair disadvantage in competing with other roads unhampered by regulation.

[117] White, p. 94.

Basically, it has been the *profit motive,* stemming from free competition (whence came ever-lower freight and passenger rates), that has spearheaded the nation's economic growth to heights unimagined in the 19th century. Perhaps it is reasonable to hope that, in the future, railroad regulation, in the hands of knowledgeable and understanding public agencies, will be able to balance competition and profit without destroying either.

To return to the UP, bitter conflicts were generated which were to continue for generations, to the frustration of all concerned. Quite naturally, UP affairs remained a source of discord. "No feature of it was ever brought before Congress without precipitating a conflict of opposing interests." [118] Ever startled by extreme statements of both politicians and press, the people came to distrust this whole experiment in quasi-Government railroading and to express increasingly resentful opinions of both management and Congressmen. So, as with the witches of Salem, there were some "sacrificial burnings," even one or two Congressmen of each party, for "good appearances."

Nevertheless, the military and political necessity for the Pacific railways at the time the charter was concocted cannot be overlooked when we pass judgment on events with hindsight.[119] As has been said, the UP was born under an evil star. But born it was, and somehow it lived and grew.

J. Durant Doesn't Have What It Takes

The Hoxie Contract: Strengthened by the much more liberal aid granted in the Act of July 1864, Durant now made a bolder try at financing that crucial first section of track, which had been cut to only 20 miles. Already, on 12 May 1864, the UP officers had appointed a Special Committee from among themselves, charged with letting a construction contract [120] to someone other than themselves. The Committee, inspired by Durant, consisted of General John A. Dix, C.S. Bushnell, and George T.M. Davis. On August 8, Durant arranged for the UP to receive a "contract" for building the first 100 miles out of Omaha.[121] It was signed "H.M. Hoxie, by H.C. Crane, Attorney" (Crane was Durant's "confidential man").[122] Herbert M. Hoxie of

---

[118] Davis, p. 113.   [119] *Ibid.,* pp. 133–134, on the Acts as military measures.
[120] *Wilson Rep.,* p. 63 (Durant's testimony).
[121] *Ibid.,* pp. 751–753; *Poland Rep.,* pp. 60–61, 389–391.
[122] *Wilson Rep.,* p. 101 (Durant's testimony).

Des Moines was a good friend of General Dodge; he was active in Iowan politics, was once a U.S. marshal; and at the time was operating a freight ferry across the Missouri. However, as Oliver Ames said: "Hoxie was a man of no means." [123] For his services as a convenient go-between, Durant promised to pay Hoxie "$5,000 in cash, plus $10,000 original UP stock." [124] (Five years later nothing had been paid, and Hoxie was ready to make trouble for Durant. On 13 March 1870, Oliver noted in his diary: "Settled with Hoxie." But he did not say for how much or who paid. Presumably, the Credit Mobilier put up the money.)

On September 23, the Special Committee formally accepted "the Hoxie Contract," exactly as originally submitted, to build the first 100 miles at a price of $50,000 a mile. The UP, not Hoxie, was to pay for any excess costs over $130 a ton for iron and was to assume any excess costs over specified limits for sidetracks, bridges, station-buildings, machine shops, machinery, tanks, equipment, and so forth.[125] The price to the UP of $5,000,000 under these conditions was considered by competent engineers to be an excessive charge for the terrain as a whole, notwithstanding the great rise in costs during the war. Then Hoxie was to "advance, or procure to be advanced, the necessary funds to the company . . . on 6% certificates of an amount to correspond with the first mortgage and Government bonds . . . at the rate of 80% of their par value, and on the land grant bonds 70%." In addition, he was to "subscribe, or cause to be subscribed, to the capital stock of your company $500,000."

Only 11 days later, on October 4, the contract was extended 147 miles further, under the same conditions, to the 100th meridian.[126] This made a total of 247 miles from Omaha at a price of $12,350,000 plus the extras. Hoxie's original "obligation to purchase" stock was doubled to $1,000,000. Such commitments, accepted by the same Special Committee of three, were of course out of all proportion to his financial ability. Only the Credit Mobilier itself could raise such sums. Years later, Durant swore that "the Hoxie contract was made (with no one interested in it) as a *bona fide* contract." [127]

Anyway, on October 7, Hoxie "consented" to assign his contract to such persons as Durant personally might designate. (Years later, Jay Gould's lawyers obtained from Hoxie a sworn statement that he

[123] *Ibid.*, pp. 256, 285.
[124] Hoxie to Dodge, 13 Aug. 1869, Dodge, *Autobiography*, p. 1107; *Wilson Rep.*, pp. 755–756 (agreement made 15 Mar. 1865 between the Credit Mobilier and Hoxie).
[125] *Wilson Rep.*, pp. 751–753; *Poland Rep.*, pp. 60–61, 389–391.
[126] *Wilson Rep.*, p. 753; *Poland Rep.*, pp. 61, 391.   [127] *Wilson Rep.*, p. 69.

had, prior to receiving the contract, agreed to assign it to the Vice-President of the UP and had acted merely as Durant's agent. The evidence was corroborated by Crane. On this showing of fraud, the UP, at the instance of Gould, filed suit against Durant.[128])

That same day a partnership pool consisting mostly of five principals, Durant, C.S. Bushnell, C.A. Lambard, H.S. McComb, and H.W. Gray (the persons so designated), agreed to subscribe the sum of $1,600,000—only 25 per cent in cash initially—for the purpose of carrying out the Hoxie contract. Each of them was to have an interest in whatever profit might accrue in proportion to the amount of his contribution to the pool. Durant's share was three-eighths; Bushnell's, one-quarter; Lambard's and McComb's, each, one-sixteenth; Gray's, one-eighth; and "etc., etc.'s" (combined), one-eighth.[129] Obviously, Hoxie himself had never been expected to carry out the contract, for as soon as he received it, he transferred it to the pool, which thereupon came back into full control of what was always to be known as "the Hoxie contract."

Peter A. Dey (1825–1911) of New York and in later years of Iowa City, who was a conservative and distinguished civil engineer of unquestioned integrity, had studied law two years but apparently was not well versed in the intricacies of construction financing. He was designated by Durant as "engineer in charge of surveys" of the UP on 1 January 1864, at the age of thirty-nine. Dey had served with Durant when the Mississippi and Missouri was under construction, and he was a close friend of Henry Farnam, who had fallen out with Durant. Many years later Dey served as Chairman of the Iowa Board of Railroad Commissioners. Dey gave Durant an estimate of the actual cost, including "equipments," of the new and longer Hoxie contract at only $30,000 a mile for the first 100 miles and $27,000 for the next 100—"large, full estimates," he believed.[130] Durant huffily returned it and hurried his agent, J.E. Henry, to Dey with verbal orders to make a second estimate at $50,000 a mile. He then let the contract to Hoxie at that figure, but with Dey's original and cheaper specifications for a $30,000 contract left in. When Dey learned of this on 7 December 1864, he resigned with the following often-quoted letter to President Dix:

I hereby tender you my resignation as chief engineer of the Union Pacific Railroad, to take effect 30 December 1864, one year from the

---

[128] Gould to Sidney Bartlett, 15 Sept. 1875; see p. 521.
[129] *Wilson Rep.*, pp. 753–754; *Poland Rep.*, pp. 391–392; Hazard, p. 14.
[130] *Wilson Rep.*, pp. 240–241.

date of my appointment. I am induced to delay until that time that I might combine the results of surveys of the present year and present them to the company and to myself in a satisfactory manner. My reasons for this step are simply that I do not approve of the contract made with Mr. Hoxie for building the first hundred miles from Omaha west, and I do not care to have my name so connected with the railroad that I shall appear to endorse this contract. Wishing the railroad success beyond the expectation of its members, I am, respectfully yours.[131]

He enclosed in the same envelope a second letter to Dix:

My views of the Pacific Railroad are perhaps peculiar. I look upon its managers as trustees of the bounty of Congress. I cannot willingly see them repeat the history of the M. and M by taking a step in the incipiency of the project that will, I believe, if followed out, swell the cost of construction so much that by the time the work reaches the mountains the representative capital will be accumulated so much that at the very time when the company will have need for all its resources, as well of capital as of credit, its securities will not be negotiable in the market. . . . You are doubtless uninformed how disproportionate the amount to be paid is to the work contracted for. I need not expatiate upon the sincerity of my course when you reflect upon the fact that I have resigned the best position in my profession this country has ever offered to any man.[132]

General Dix did not reply until February 27, when he rather coolly wrote:

We cannot get over 90% [for our U.S. bonds which are currency, not gold] and they are our only means of going on with the work. Under these circumstances we did the best we could. The arrangements for the first hundred miles had the approval of the Government directors. . . .[133]

But the Government Directors were reluctant in giving their approval. They thought the contract price was too high.[134]

Dey figured, correctly, that with the contractor guaranteeing funds on the first mortgage bonds at only 80 per cent and on the land grant bonds at only 70 per cent, the par amount of the bonds to be issued must be correspondingly increased. Hence the railroad had to borrow about $62,000, not $50,000, a mile for construction.[135]

[131] *Ibid.*, pp. v, 669.   [132] *Ibid.*, p. 670.   [133] *Ibid.*
[134] *Ibid.*, p. 652 (testimony of Charles T. Sherman, Government Director).
[135] *Ibid.*, p. 672 (testimony of Dey).

The partnership of the pool who signed the final agreement of 7 October 1864 to "take over" the Hoxie contract had so far paid down only $400,000 of the $1,600,000 subscribed. With that money all gone, and the second installment being demanded, they (or "many of them," said Durant) took fright at the unlimited liability they were assuming as partners, and defaulted.[136]

Rowland Hazard wrote:

It was perceived that the question of profit was wholly dependent on the success of the road as a commercial enterprise. Unless the road would pay a profit over running expenses, though the government bonds might be disposed of, the first mortgage bonds could not be sold. The public had little faith, and, so far as appeared to those early subscribers, they were in danger of losing what they had already put in. . . . The subscribers found that the enterprise was not only hazardous, but that they were liable to be regarded as partners with Hoxie, and so in danger of being involved to an unknown extent. They thought the risk too great for the expected profit, and they said we will stop just where we are, unless we can be protected from personal liability by an act of incorporation.[137]

As a result of the Vice-President and General Manager's decisions to date, the original $217,700 paid in on the UP stock had been exhausted, and, in addition, obligations for $200,000 or $300,000 for iron, cars, locomotives, grading, ties, and so forth, had been incurred.[138] Durant stopped all work and sold such material as was necessary to meet company debts. The 1864 UP "capital balance sheet" appears in a report of the U.S. Pacific Railway Commission, pp. 4994–95.

Thus the year 1864 came to an end with no track and less than 20 miles of grading completed. Most of it was in the Platte Valley, where the work was less costly than over the hills. The CP had already completed its first 31 miles of track to Newcastle.[139]

Quite obviously, the Doctor and his group did not have adequate personal resources or credit for the venture. But already he was taking steps towards a new scheme which should work: *the UP would have its own construction company.*

---

[136] *Ibid.,* p. 64 (testimony of Durant).   [137] Hazard, pp. 14–15.
[138] *Wilson Rep.,* p. 63 (testimony of Durant).   [139] See p. 92.

2

The Credit Mobilier
Before the Ameses' Connection

*The Union Pacific Gets a Construction Company—How a Construction
Company Functioned—The Civil War Ends with No Track Laid*

A. The Union Pacific Gets a Construction Company

In spite of its mysterious, foreign-sounding name, which most
Americans did not even know how to pronounce, the Credit Mobilier
of America was simply one more railroad "construction company."
Such *limited liability* corporations, designed for the purpose of creating a third party for legal and accounting convenience between the
UP and its financiers, had already come into widespread use in those
booming years of railroading. There were in 1864 about 34,000 miles
of railways operating in the U.S.; practically all the newer ones had
been built by construction companies, of which the stockholders
themselves were the promoters of the railroads. The CP had the
nearly unknown "Contract and Finance Company" for the purpose.[1]
Oakes Ames's Iowan railroads had been built that way.[2]

Durant finally had decided he must have his own construction
company, and it is difficult to understand why he had not arranged
for it from the beginning, nearly two years earlier. So, on 3 March
1864, he bought the charter of a totally obscure corporation, which
had never before done business, by the name of "Pennsylvania Fiscal
Agency." It had been created five years earlier for Duff Green by
authority of the legislature of the State of Pennsylvania, with such
broad and elastic powers in railroad financing and about any other

---

[1] *Wilson Rep.*, pp. 699–722 (testimony of Huntington).
[2] *Ibid.*, p. 164 (testimony of J.M.S. Williams). See also p. 88.

business, that it seemed as if the charter had been framed expressly for the purpose of profitable sale to the first high bidder. In fact, in the years 1850 to 1860, before general incorporation laws were common, "charter shops" were quite in vogue and served as a source of profit to certain persons of past political influence. One of the declared purposes of the incorporated Pennsylvania Fiscal Agency was "to become an agency for the purchase and sale of railroad bonds and other securities, and to make advances of money and credit to railroad and other improvement companies, and to aid in like manner contractors and manufacturers, and to authorize them as a company to make all requisite contracts. . . ."[3] The liability of the stockholders was limited to the payment in full for the stock to which they subscribed. Its authorized capital stock was 50,000 shares of $100 each. When 5,000 shares were subscribed and 5 per cent thereon paid in, the shareholders could elect five or more directors "to exercise its privileges." This was not accomplished until 1 June 1863, when 5,329 shares were subscribed for.

Durant paid for the charter of the Pennsylvania Fiscal Agency by charging to the UP the $26,645 the organizers had put up, plus their profit. He then subscribed for 5 shares ($25 down) in his own name, and had himself elected President. Three weeks later, on March 26, for a $500 legal fee, he changed its name to the "Credit Mobilier of America." This was the woeful suggestion of his strange friend, George Francis Train, whom many considered excitable and visionary to the verge of insanity. Train had just spent some time in France and was much impressed by a conspicuous company called *Crédit Mobilier de France*.[4] It had been set up in Paris in 1852 by the brothers Periere, and was, in 1864, at the height of its prosperity. However, after huge public works construction and railway operations in Europe from which the directors had made immense fortunes through malfeasance, the courts, in 1868, ordered its liquidation and awarded damages to the stockholders.[5] The term, *crédit mobilier,* means, simply, loans on stocks and bonds, but the words unfortunately came to savor of French corruption.

The Credit Mobilier of America at once transferred the full Pennsylvanian powers of the Board of Directors to a "New York Agency." There a "Railway Bureau" was established, at first consisting of five Managers, three to be Directors of the Company, ". . . who shall have

---

[3] *Ibid.,* pp. 7–9 (copy of charter and amendments); Hazard, pp. 15–17; Crawford, *The Credit Mobilier of America,* pp. 17–20; Davis, p. 164.
[4] Hazard, p. 17; Leonard and Johnson, pp. 103–105.　　　[5] Hazard, pp. 15–16.

the management of the railway contracts for which the Company may be the agent, which shall be subject to the approval of the President of the Company. . . . No business shall be done by said Company except that pertaining to the construction, as agent or attorney, or by lawful authority of the Union Pacific Railroad Company. . . ." [6] An office for the New York Agency of the Credit Mobilier was procured so as to adjoin and connect with that of the UP at 20 Nassau Street, New York. Then, on 7 October 1864, the original cash payments amounting to $400,000 (25 per cent of $1,600,000), which the partnership pool was required to make towards the Hoxie contract, were transferred as subscriptions to the *limited liability* stock of the Credit Mobilier (hereinafter usually referred to as CM for brevity). This payment made up 16,000 shares, 25 per cent paid.[7] At the same time, the remaining payments of 75 per cent were called for. Thus the capital of the CM started off at a figure of $1,600,000.

Stockholder Rowland Hazard years later described the next move as follows:

It was in the fall of 1864 that the proposition took this form. During that winter . . . the proposal [to subscribe] was made to capitalists whenever there was thought to be a chance of success. On 15 March 1865, after great effort, a subscription to the stock of the Credit Mobilier was obtained, amounting to something over $2,000,000.[8]

This effort brought the total subscriptions to 20,000 shares of $100 par value,[9] to be fully paid. Some $310,000 worth of Durant's friends had dropped out, but about $710,000 in new cash was found, largely among New England investors.[10]

It will be recalled that by the Act of 1864 each $1,000 share of the UP had been exchanged for ten $100 shares. *The Credit Mobilier now purchased all of the 21,770 new shares of the UP for the 10 per cent installment paid thereon, $217,700.*[11] For the amounts each had paid in, the UP stockholders were given the choice of either receiving an equivalent par value of CM stock free in exchange for their UP stock, or selling their UP shares at cost to the CM or the UP.[12] This was a fair proposition to the minority stockholders of the UP, as they could either get out entirely and have their money back, or, by

[6] *Wilson, Rep.,* pp. vii, 125–127 (testimony of Durant), 159–160.

[7] *Ibid.,* pp. 753–754; *Poland Rep.,* pp. 365–366 (testimony of Durant); Hazard, p. 18; see also p. 43.

[8] Hazard, p. 18.   [9] *Wilson Rep.,* p. 160.   [10] See p. 112.

[11] *Wilson Rep.,* p. vii.   [12] Davis, pp. 165–166; Hazard, pp. 23–24.

putting up all of the unpaid capital subscribed, take a pro rata interest in the construction company. *No one was frozen out.* This deal made the Credit Mobilier an exceptionally liberal construction company, for in most cases the small inside "ring" took all of the construction company profit by arbitrarily reserving to themselves the entire stock. The actual result was, at least for the time being, that practically all of the original UP stockholders in Durant's group became original CM stockholders, except for a few CM stockholders who did not pay for their UP shares until later.

Finally, on 15 March 1865, only 25 days before the end of the Civil War, Durant completed this intricate evolution, often challenged as collusive, fraudulent, and voidable, at least until ratified by the directors of the UP.[13] *He assigned the Hoxie contract to the Credit Mobilier,* exactly as he had planned five months earlier. So now it was the Credit Mobilier corporation, not individual persons, that guaranteed the performance of the Hoxie contract in return for the acquisition of all the contract rights and potential profits.[14]

When this assignment was made, an accounting was in order. Durant lost no time in recovering his outlays. Only five days later the CM, by H.C. Crane, Assistant Treasurer, issued a check for $302,700 to the order of T.C. Durant. Whether this was just a reimbursement of advances cannot be shown. However, R.G. Hazard later brought suit against him, claiming that it was an illegal payment made to Durant personally of the profits of the Hoxie contract previous to 1 December 1864. The check could not be found for years; the Doctor had removed it from the CM files.[15]

B. How a Construction Company Functioned

The use of construction, contracting, or finance corporations, like the Credit Mobilier, was the usual custom of building railroads during the period 1855–1880, as has been emphasized. Yet there has always been a widespread, persistent ignorance or misunderstanding of this practice, perhaps due to its complexity and the unfortunate atmosphere of secrecy in which it was shrouded.

---

[13] See p. 98.

[14] *Wilson Rep.,* pp. 755–756 (copy of agreement between the CM and Hoxie. The original is in Durant, *Papers,* 1–3–23–31).

[15] Records of UP Historical Museum: letter of S. Dillon to S. Bartlett, Aug. 1877. The check is on exhibit at the Museum.

The truth is, a construction corporation, which was merely a third party for legal and accounting convenience, was acquired, controlled, financed, and operated by the same, or nearly the same, capitalists who controlled the railroad company. The advantages of this ingenious arrangement follow.

Primarily, it was the only way of providing personal limited liability, to the extent of the par value of the stock, for the promoters who were undertaking the high risk of producing a new line.

Secondly, it was a lawful way of enabling the construction company, without cash cost beyond its paid-up capital, to take physical possession of all the railroad stock and bonds, when and as issued by the directors of the railroad. It could then hold or sell them as the promoters chose.

Thirdly, it was a practical way for the promoters to secure all of the building profits by hiring themselves, instead of outsiders, to construct their own line.

Finally, it was a convenient way of determining each promoter's profit or loss on the building contract and the railroad stocks and bonds allotted to him. Of course, most of the bonds had to be sold to outside investors to raise the huge amount of cash needed for building.

Thus the construction company, with the obvious consent of themselves as directors of the railroad, charged the railroad for such building costs as they might determine, *with the result that the road was usually built very largely by means of the sale of bonds, while all or most of the railroad stock was reserved for themselves as profit, if any.* Such relatively small amounts as were paid by outsiders on the early installments of qualifying stock were either voluntarily abandoned or refunded at cost, leaving the promoters as the only stockholders.[16] If the operation of the road became successful, the bond interest was paid and the principal redeemed when due. The railroad stock, which had been received free, would become valuable, it was hoped.

Each promoter's capital gain on his railroad stock could be determined by the market price at which he chose to sell out, less the cost at $100 a share of his construction company shares. The latter, of course, normally became worthless as soon as the road was completed, just as does the stock of a used-up mine. In addition, the capital gain or loss on his railroad bonds could be the difference between the cost

[16] *Wilson Rep.*, p. 247 (testimony of Oliver Ames: however, "some, like Fisk, were paid quite a large sum for their interest in the subscription").

prices specified in the construction contract (say, 80 per cent of par) [17] and the prices at which he elected to sell them.

As there was no recorded market for the stock and bonds during the period of building, the construction profit could be estimated only roughly. How much the securities became worth at any particular time *after* the day of receipt was obviously immaterial, as each promoter held or sold his portion according to his own judgment of the market and personal considerations. Furthermore, as the promoters and the contractors were the same persons, it made no difference to them what portion of their total profit came from construction, beyond the fact that construction profits were quick, and investment profits, if any, were slow. The hypothesis above is kept simple for the purpose of illustration. In actual fact, other figures would have to be brought into any estimate of real profit.

In answer to the question by the Chairman of the Wilson Committee, J.M. Wilson: "I want to know what explanation you have to give why the Union Pacific Railroad Company did not get dollar for dollar for its stock," John Alley replied:

Practically that could not be carried out. The road was built just as all other railroads are built, and I do not see how there was any wrong done to the stockholders of the Union Pacific, when all consented to it, and all participated in it to an equal degree [in pro rata proportion], and no director, trustee, or any other party had any advantage that was not shared in common by every stockholder of the Union Pacific. . . . If they did not choose to go in, we would buy their stock from them. They were all perfectly satisfied, and if there was any wrong done to anybody, I cannot see it. . . . Mr. Tilden [Samuel Jones Tilden, Oakes Ames's principal lawyer on his contract], I know, told me he regarded it as a compliance with the law.[18]

Further on, Alley said:

Of course it was the right of everybody to come in and subscribe for stock who chose to do so, but it would not have been profitable to do so. . . . The road was constructed by this construction company and stock taken in pay, and that stock could be bought for something less than par, and of course nobody was going to subscribe and pay par for the stock when they could buy it for anything less. . . . It was not until after the experiment was tried that this construction company scheme was resorted to.[19]

---

[17] See pp. 42, 44, 184.   [18] *Wilson Rep.*, pp. 324, 328.   [19] *Ibid.*, p. 568.

Horace F. Clark, then President of the UP, also was questioned by the same Chairman, J.M. Wilson:

Wilson: You said that the road cost about $114,000,000. Did you mean to say that it cost that amount in money, or that it cost that amount in the securities of the Company, estimating those securities at what they were considered to be worth at the time by the parties?

Clark: I have stated that that is the cost of the road appearing on the books. It seems to be the amount of the debts and the stock of the Company, but as to the real cost of the road, I do not know what it was. I have never been able to make the investigation.

Wilson: Do you not know as a fact that that $114,000,000 was swelled to that amount by letting the work at a higher price in consequence of the fact that it was to be paid for in the securities of the Company which were at a discount?

Clark: Of course. If you take at $100 a bond that is only worth $55 you have got to charge somebody the difference. The constructing company increases the price to that extent. That is human nature.

Wilson: The $114,000,000 is made up substantially by the capital stock, the two Mortgage loans, the Land Grant bonds, the Income bonds, and the floating debt?

Clark: Yes. The Company evidently gave that for the road.

Wilson: I understand you to say that contractors, when they agree to take the securities of a road in payment for their contract, increase the contract rate so as to make up the difference between the value of the securities and the par of the securities?

Clark: If they are sensible men they do.

Wilson: Do you know whether that was done in this case or not?

Clark: It may be supposed that the contractor estimated the value of the securities he was taking in lieu of money when he was fixing the price.

Wilson: Then, can you tell how the Union Pacific Railroad Company got par for its stock, as required by the law under which the Company is organized?

Clark: I did not say that it did. The Company got a road which it accepted at such a price which covered the par of the stock. Whether it got that road too cheap or not you do not want me to express an opinion.

Wilson: The practical effect of this was that the Union Pacific did not get par for its stock?

Clark: The practical effect of it was that these constructing companies got all the securities, stock and all, as full-paid stock, and gave the road. The practical effect of it is that the Union Pacific Railroad Company paid that for the road to the contracting parties; and somebody made a profit equal to the difference between the actual cost and the amount realized from those securities.[20]

It becomes clear that once the road was in operation, the only *sure* gainer would be the economy of the geographical areas affected. The mutual owners of the construction and railway companies' shares could, if lucky, gain only a puny portion of the wealth to follow the creation of this wondrous new invention, the road of iron—even if their two-way profit might be large.

To be sure, less secrecy on the part of the early promoters about the ways of construction companies might have led to some unwanted competition. Far more important, however, more elucidation would have soothed the suspicions of outsiders. As for the Credit Mobilier, this company came under prolonged examination by Government investigators and historians.

In the case of the UP, Congress *finally* had provided that each section of 20 miles of track be completed and paid for, and pass Government inspection, to obtain the Federal loans and land grants. Of course, tangible property on which to secure the company and Government bonds first had to be created. Then buyers for most of the bonds had to be found so as to replenish the promoters' cash for the next section, and so on. Like any other contractor, the promoters were of course entitled to be paid as they proceeded. Their original working capital would be employed time after time. Durant eventually learned, with the advice of Oakes Ames, that with the first contract at $50,000 a mile, a working capital of at least $3,750,000 cash in the construction company must be in hand for the first section before the bonds thereon could be sold. This *initial* working capital, which was the promoters' first big stumbling block, could come only from their own pockets, for the 10 per cent payments on the original subscriptions to the UP qualifying stock had produced only $217,700 cash, and that whole amount had been used up by Durant in preliminary expenses. Furthermore, outsiders would have to be repaid their investment.

But the real rub was that under the UP charter the promoters, like anyone else, always had to pay $100 a share for the stock, while the market price was much lower. Adjusting market prices to fully paid stock, "a holder would have been very glad to sell at 30 or 40," [21] and

---

[20] *Ibid.*, p. 448.
[21] *Ibid.*, pp. 250, 277, 293 (testimony of Oliver Ames); *Poland Rep.*, pp. 56–57.

the low was "not worth 10." [22] The average used by the Wilson Committee was 30,[23] but the actual average price was probably a bit
lower.[24] Large blocks such as those issued to the CM stockholders
were unsaleable at any price. During 1870, the year following completion, the price range was about 45 high in March and 9 low in
December.[25] But by that time the number of $100 shares outstanding
had gradually become huge, 367,623 to be exact, and amounted to
33 per cent of a total stated (book) capitalization of $110,966,812.[26]

*So, from time to time the promoters had the construction company
buy the shares, take the entire loss of $100 each, and distribute them
to themselves free. At the same time, the building contract price was
increased by an amount sufficient to cover the loss. The UP simply
handed the CM a check for the amount demanded on construction,
and the CM at once turned it back to the UP, who recorded it as
payment for the stock. "A check was considered cash."* [27]

There is another way of explaining this method of a construction
company. It is a significant way, for it is in the words of the principal
CM stockholders themselves, as filed in court. In H.S. McComb's
lawsuit against Oakes Ames and the CM, McComb's question Number 23 was worded:

Did the Credit Mobilier . . . give their check . . . to the Union Pacific
Railroad Company for the price or value of the shares, and receive the
check of the railroad for the same amount, and thus pretend to be paying for the stock, when in truth . . . no payment whatever was made?
If [this] question be answered in the affirmative, state what was the object
of the sham.[28]

The interesting answer of the defendant stockholders (Dillon,
J.M.S. Williams, Alley, Duff, Bushnell, R.G. Hazard and Oakes
Ames) to this question was:

The shares of stock in the Union Pacific Railroad, which were received
by the Credit Mobilier up to the date of the Ames contract, and those
received by the trustees of that contract afterward, were fully paid, and
by the parties receiving them, in this manner: That company and the
said trustees were successively contractors to build the road as already

---

[22] *Wilson Rep.*, p. 166 (testimony of J.M.S. Williams).   [23] *Ibid.*, p. xv.
[24] See Appendix A.   [25] See Appendix A.   [26] See p. 399.
[27] *Wilson Rep.*, pp. 375–376 (testimony of B.F. Ham, Auditor of the UP and Treasurer of CM, commencing early in 1867).
[28] *Poland Rep.*, p. 51: Supreme Court, Jan. term, 1868, No. 19, McComb *v.* CM.

stated, and by the contract they were obliged to receive the stock in payment of part of the sums due under their respective contracts.

Thus, the Union Pacific Railroad, instead of paying one hundred dollars to the contractors, delivered them a share of stock, the *face* of which was one hundred dollars, and extinguished a debt of that amount by receiving this in satisfaction as a payment to their capital.

It is believed the form generally observed was to exchange checks.

It is believed no one having any conception of what constitutes reality will suggest there is anything looking like a sham in this. Probably no corporation whose stock is not above par but would gladly receive subscription to capital on the same terms.[29]

Thus it can be understood why the contract price was set at an amount high enough to cover everything: the promotional expense of company organization, including lobbying and buying off competitors; the cost of surveys, rights of way, grading, tracks, engines, cars, bridges, tunnels, machine shops, buildings, water towers, snowplows, snowsheds, fencing, telegraph, tools, supplies, and equipment; payrolls, salaries, fees, and travel expenses of Government commissioners and Directors; legal fees and office rent; travel, advertising, revenue stamps, and other general overhead expenses; the cost of operating the land department; the discount, interest, and commissions on bonds issued, and interest on short-term construction loans;[30] and finally, of course, a profit to the capitalists commensurate with *their idea* of the risk being taken. Hindsight shows that the risk was in fact far greater than in any other railroad, before or after.

The remaining and extreme difficulty was that *the loss on the stock, combined with the heavy discounts on the bonds, caused far more bonds to be issued than otherwise.* Therefore, unless the earnings of the road were continuously favorable, there was the risk that the capital structure might indicate financial weakness before the time came around for the 30-year bonds to be paid off or refunded. The stock then would be adversely affected, too, perhaps even wiped out in a reorganization. This fear was what caused Durant to count only on quick profits for his remuneration.

It was obvious that the Government's price tag of $100 a share was to add enormously to the troubles, not only in money, but in public relations. Payment for the stock out of construction profits, instead of cash, was judged by the Wilson Committee as a circumvention of

[29] *Ibid.*, pp. 56–59: Supreme Court, Jan. term, 1868, No. 19, Equity.

[30] See *Wilson Rep.*, p. 637, for many of these items at their cost (testimony of B.F. Ham).

Section 1 of the charter, and the Committee recommended that the United States bring suit in equity against the UP and "all persons who received stock not paid for in full in money. . . ." [31] *Yet the Government Directors of the UP did nothing to prevent it. Indeed, it was the only possible way of effecting substantial subscriptions at the price fixed by law.*

If the charter was obsolete and impractical, Congress had only itself and previous Congresses to blame. Unfortunately, however, the purpose and the workings of the CM were too complicated to be understood by the Congressmen, the press, the public, and even many historians. The sinister name, "Credit Mobilier," when suddenly exposed to public view, seemed to signify some kind of corruption at the expense of the taxpayers. As a result, punitive legislation was fomented. The sweeping prejudice has been carried forth to this day, finally creating a national myth which may never die, no matter how many documented histories may prove that the prejudice is unjustified.

Davis is the authority for these considered words in 1894:

Of the Union Pacific and Central Pacific it must in justice be said, that of all the parts of the contemplated system, the Union Pacific Company, though most villified, has come nearest to the fulfillment of the purposes of its charter, with the least abuse of the mechanism of its construction company. . . . If the Credit Mobilier was a most iniquitous instrument of industrial development, it simply means that the system of railway building from 1860 to 1880 was iniquitous, and not that Oakes Ames was an arch villain among men . . . nor the shrewd swindler that he is often depicted. He was blunt, honest, and straight-forward, did not create conditions, but took them as he found them and made his actions fit them.[32]

Oakes Ames summed it up to Congress in 1873:

To give those who were willing to risk the capital required, to avail ourselves of the assistance or reward offered by Congress, it was necessary that we should be our own contractors, and thus receive for building the road what Congress offered to anyone who would do so.

To avoid the responsibility, as partners, this charter of the Credit Mobilier was purchased, it being intended that this corporation should be the contractor, and we, as its shareholders, should receive the profits

---

[31] *Ibid.*, p. xxvi.   [32] Davis, p. 196.

on the building. The profits were to be received in stock and bonds of the Union Pacific Railroad, which were paid on the building contract.

It must be observed our profits were merely nominal or contingent. If the road was completed, and when completed could earn interest on the debt, and profit besides, then our profits would be great. If our road was not completed, or, when completed, unprofitable, not only would our profits be lost, but our capital likewise.[33]

The greatest objection to the construction company method of financing, "one of the darkest phases of the railroad problem," [34] was that the promoters could, *if they wished,* let construction to themselves at *excessive* profits. As stated before, this could result in some railroads becoming over-capitalized with bonds. But that probably would have happened anyway, when only bonds, not stocks, were demanded by the investing public. Actually, it was the buyer's own fault if he put an excessive price on bonds and spurned equities. After all, the ultimate success of the earnings and finances of the enterprise was very largely a question of the integrity and ability of the financiers. As ever, the *personal* aspect was the trenchant one.

Even Trottman, who in 1923 had few kind words to say for the promoters, had to admit:

It is much easier to point out the evils of the Credit Mobilier scheme than it is to point out how the road could have been built in any other way. General Dodge has said that when he suggested to President Lincoln that the government build the Pacific railroad, the President refused to entertain any such project. In 1862 the United States was engaged in the Civil War and was too much occupied to enter the field of railroad construction. Lincoln was ready to offer ample governmental aid, but he insisted that private capitalists do the work. If the government had undertaken to build the Pacific railroad, it would have done so at a time when corruption permeated the national Civil Service, when fortunes were being made by corrupt army contractors, when "carpet-baggers" flourished, when frauds in the Indian and in the postal service were just beginning to reach enormous proportions, when the judiciary of the great city of New York, the financial center of the nation, was at the service of men like Fisk and Tweed, and when dishonesty affected many branches of the federal government. It is not improbable that a government-built road might have developed far greater abuses.[35]

---

[33] *Poland Rep.,* p. 16 (written testimony of Oakes Ames, prepared by his lawyer, before the Committee, 17 Dec. 1872).

[34] Davis, p. 163.   [35] Trottman, pp. 52–53.

Again, during the 1873 investigation by Congress, Horace A. Clark (Commodore Vanderbilt's son-in-law), who was then President of the UP but had had nothing to do with the CM, was asked whether the road could not have been built "at least $12,000,000 cheaper if the whole $36,000,000 of stock had been paid for in honest money at one time." He replied that he thought not, that the money never could have been raised; he added:

Taking into consideration the high prices of the times, the reckless extravagance of the construction, the fact that it was a road built in the first place without a route, no pass then discovered, . . . without timber, without fuel, without water, with gold, I think, at 160 [per cent of par] and with iron at $160 a ton, the work hurried up with night and day gangs, working with great rapidity, in order to get the advances from the Government; with half the force engaged in keeping the Indians off from the other half that was at work; if there had been thirty millions at that time in the treasury, I think the money would have been very soon squandered, and I do not believe that there would have been a road.[36]

Finally, John M.S. Williams of Cambridge, Massachusetts, and a partner of William T. Glidden in the well-known clipper shipping firm of Glidden and Williams, put it straight and frankly to the Wilson Committee in 1873. He was an original subscriber to the UP for $20,000.[37] At one time he held as much as $300,000 or $400,000 stock, but sold it all out early in 1872, when the price was between 30 and 40. Williams and Glidden each subscribed to 500 shares of the original CM stock in 1865 at the same time as did Oakes Ames, with whom they were associated in building the Iowan railways.[38] In the CM, J.M.S. Williams was the first secretary of the Railway Bureau of seven, a member of the first Executive Committee of three, and a Director until 1867. Later he was a Treasurer of the UP. Abstracts from his testimony follow:

The Credit Mobilier and the Union Pacific were the same identical parties. We were building it for ourselves, by ourselves and among ourselves. There was not $20,000 outside interest in it. . . . It was understood that we were dealing with ourselves, to get the control in the right hands. Mr. Durant had entire control, and we proposed to get it out of his hands. . . . Every stockholder in the Union Pacific had been invited

---

[36] *Wilson Rep.*, p. 403.   [37] *Ibid.*, p. 601.   [38] *Ibid.*, p. 160.

to come into the Credit Mobilier because it was understood that the road was to be built in that way, by contracting among ourselves for the common benefit of all. We had been building four railroads in Iowa that way, by contracting companies organized among the stockholders. We wanted no one to have an interest except in both alike. Therefore, every man who was a stockholder in the Union Pacific was invited to come into the Credit Mobilier. If he did not, then efforts were made to buy him out, so that there would be no outside interest, but the interest would be identical, and no man would suffer by these contracts.[39]

Question: Now, didn't you regard it as in any way a fraud upon the Pacific Railroad Company to make these dividends of stock?

Answer: They were the same parties; it could not be a fraud by any possibility; . . . They only took it from one pocket and put it in another.

Question: Was there any provision by which the actual cost of the road to the Credit Mobilier, exclusive of its profits, should be reported to Congress?

Answer: I do not think there was.

Question: Then, they were by no means the same thing so far as their relations to the Government were concerned?

Answer: They thought they were only dealing with their own property; they didn't think they had anything to do with the Government.

Question: Now you see they were not?

Answer: I do not. The Government could determine the cost of the road in any manner it thought proper.

Question: Do you understand that the provision of law which requires them to report the cost of the road would be complied with if they issued their own stock, worth ten cents on a dollar, at par, by calling the par value of that stock the cost of the road?

Answer: They supposed it was when they made their reports.

Question: Do you now suppose so?

Answer: I would require time to think of that question. . . . Allow me to say right here that Congress appears to be laboring under an entire misapprehension as to the nature and character of this Pacific Railroad act. It was not a special or private act, but an act to promote public interests and public welfare. The eighteenth section of the law of 1862 declares this to be its object, and I think it is due that it should be judged from the standpoint of the 37th and 38th Congress, and not of the 42nd, and that we ought to look at it contemporaneously with the event. There is a great misunderstanding about the whole thing. We understood that the Government was not to call upon us for the interest of 5 per cent of the net earnings; that both of those were done away with by that clause of the law which allows them only to retain

39 *Ibid.*, pp. 163–164.

one-half of the cost of Government transportation, and therefore in everything we did we thought nobody had any interest but ourselves. That is the view we acted upon. . . . The greatest sufferers were those who built the road, and not the Government.[40]

These forthright statements brought down on John Williams some further caustic questions by the Wilson Committee, who never did believe his reasoning. Yet, Congress had not declared or intended to suggest that only certain kinds of people could be stockholders in the UP, or that such persons could not own other stocks, or that only corporations of certain kinds could buy and hold UP stock.

C. The Civil War Ends with No Track Laid

In the meantime, Durant and his friends, with hands out for more construction company capital but with toes in the door of policy control, had *failed to lay even one mile of track* before the Civil War came to an utterly agonized end 9 April 1865.

Of about 4,200,000 Americans in uniform during the Civil War, some 619,000, or 14.7 per cent, had been killed in battle or had died of wounds or disease. This was a larger number of fatalities than occurred during World War I, World War II, and the Korean War combined, during which 589,991 of the 26,188,000 American servicemen had lost their lives.[41] However, the fatalities of the three wars represented only 2.2 per cent of the total in uniform, partly because of infinitely better medical and hygienic care. The Confederacy lost an estimated 19.9 per cent of its soldiers by death, the Union 12 per cent. Yet, because the Union army outnumbered the Confederate's by 2.2 to 1, its losses exceeded the South's by 1.4 to 1.

Historians Charles and Mary Beard wrote:

As of April 1, 1865, calculations reported the cost to the Union at about $3,250,000,000 and to the Confederacy at approximately $1,500,000,000, or $4,750,000,000 in all. After pensions, interest on the Federal debt, and the value of property destroyed were added, a conservative computation established the total cost of preserving the Union and abolishing slavery at above $10,000,000,000, (over $45 billions in today's money). For less than half this amount, freedom could have been bought for all the 3,953,857 slaves recorded in the census of 1860—

---

[40] *Ibid.*, pp. 165, 166, 167.   [41] U.S. War Dept.

the compensated emancipation which Congress and President Lincoln had proposed in 1862.[42]

The national defense motive for a transcontinental railroad, so vital when the charter had been written in 1862 and 1864, was now largely dissolved, and the project had assumed far more somber colors with the assassination of President Lincoln. Building costs had skyrocketed, and the purchasing power of the pre-war dollar had dropped to only 62 cents. In spite of the struggle between railroads pushing westward from Chicago to secure the first connection with the overland route to the Pacific, none had succeeded in reaching the Missouri. Omaha and its river neighbor, Council Bluffs, were still 150 miles from any railroad, despite their high expectations over the years. From the Pacific Coast, however, the CP was proceeding rapidly eastward with a unified and smoothly functioning construction company and with at least 5,000 Chinese coolies on the line. It even threatened to come all the way, leaving nothing at all for the UP to build. The only personal credit due Durant and his inactive President Dix during nearly three years of effort was that they had helped to obtain some favorable legislation and had formally organized the UP company with, at long last, its construction subsidiary.

Amazing progress under new capital and responsible management from virile New England was about to begin.[43] In spite of all misfortune, the Rockies and Sierras were destined to be conquered, and neither slavery nor the Continental Divide was to split the nation in two forever.

[42] From *The Beards' New Basic History of the United States* by Charles A. and Mary R. Beard. Copyright © 1944, 1960 by Doubleday & Company, Inc., 1960. Reprinted by permission of the publisher.
[43] Union Pacific Railroad, *A Brief History,* p. 18.

3

Oakes and Oliver Ames

Life at North Easton—Oakes Ames: Some Personal Notes—Oliver Ames Jr.: Some Personal Notes—Why Did the Ameses Undertake the Job?

A. Life at North Easton[1]

The parents of Oakes and Oliver were the Honorable Oliver Ames and Susanna Angier. Oliver, the senior of many Ameses of that name (without middle appellation), was born on 11 April 1779 at West Bridgewater, Massachusetts, the ancestral home for three generations. He was the youngest son of Captain John Ames (1738–1805) and Susannah Howard. A direct ancestor was the William Ames (1605–1654) who emigrated to Quincy, Massachusetts, probably in 1635, from the picturesque abbey town of Bruton, Somersetshire, England. The village is conspicuous for its fine perpendicular church and the ancient pack-horse bridge over the Brut. Oliver was also a descendant of Francis Cooke of the *Mayflower*.

Susanna was born on 8 March 1783, also at West Bridgewater, the daughter of Oakes Angier (1745–1786). He was an "eminent barrister" and direct descendant of the Reverend Dr. William Ames (1576–1633) of Ipswich, England. The latter, known as "Amesius," was the internationally known Puritan Calvinist, "master of theological controversy," and Professor of Divinity at Franeker University, the Netherlands. Urged to come to America by his relative, Governor John Winthrop of Massachusetts Bay, he expressed his intention to do so at first occasion. Samuel Eliot Morison, official historian of Harvard, wrote: "There can be little doubt that if William Ames had lived he would have been offered the first Harvard

---

[1] Principal sources: Chaffin, *History of the Town of Easton, Massachusetts;* Winthrop Ames, *The Ames Family;* Governor Oliver Ames, *Diaries;* and family records.

presidency. . . . He was the spiritual father of New England churches." [2]

Amesius's daughter, Ruth Ames, emigrated to Cambridge, Massachusetts, in 1637 at the age of eighteen, and in 1644 married Edmund Angier. They lived at Dunster and Mount Auburn Streets, so well known to Harvard students. He was the great-great-grandfather of Susanna Angier. Her marriage to Oliver on 7 April 1803 thus united two branches of the family, the Ameses of Bruton and the Ameses of Ipswich, just how closely related is unknown. Susanna was a descendant of two other passengers on the *Mayflower:* James Chilton and his daughter Mary, for whom the women's Chilton Club of Boston is named. A family portrait in oils shows Susanna in her fifties as a refined, kindly, and somewhat plump lady. Her eyes are blue and twinkling; her dark brown hair, parted to one side, is nearly concealed by a white bonnet; her very fair complexion is pink and white. She died at home at the age of sixty-four on 28 March 1847, many years before the death of her husband.

Oliver was the first Ames to settle in the small farming community of North Easton, to which he had been attracted by the abundance of water power on the Queset River, already turning the wheels of at least eight mills, forges, or factories. North Easton is a village 22 miles south of the State House, Boston, and 26 miles west of Plymouth. In September 1803, the year of the Louisiana Purchase, at the age of twenty-four, Oliver brought his young bride to a nearly new house he had just purchased on Pond Street (later numbered 46), close by the dam which formed what is now known as Shovel-Shop Pond. "Esteemed a fine house for those days . . . it was the first painted house in North Easton, exciting considerable notice on that account; it is the house in which Oakes Ames was born, and is still standing, unsuspected of ever having excited wonder and envy by a coat of paint." [3] A few months later he boldly relocated here, in a triphammer forge purchased for $1,600, the shovel and hoe shops started in West Bridgewater by his father before the Revolution, probably about 1773.[4] Thus began the "O. Ames" shovels of national fame.

Four years later, probably overextended financially, he removed to Plymouth with his wife and two young sons, Oakes and Horatio, to supervise the shovel-making plant of the then important Plymouth Iron Works. It was located on Town Brook behind Summer Street,

---

[2] Morison, *The Founding of Harvard College.*
[3] Chaffin, p. 280; Winthrop Ames, p. 233. The house is still there, although altered.
[4] Chaffin, pp. 593–595; Winthrop Ames, p. 233.

where the wide, lowest dam still spans the stream. Close by the dam, in a wooden dwelling known as the "Long House" (still standing and numbered 120–122 Summer Street), Oliver and family lived until March 1814, and here Oliver Jr. and William Leonard were born.[5] When the Plymouth business closed down after suffering heavily from the War of 1812–1814 (to which as an ardent Federalist he was bitterly opposed),[6] he returned to Pond Street, North Easton, where he still owned the plant at the lower end of Shovel-Shop Pond. Before 1814 was out, he had finished building a fine homestead on Main Street with a large tract of farmland in back. Here he settled down for his lifetime. In 1852, following a fire at the factory, the two-story "Long Shop" of granite, the largest of the Ames Shovel buildings, was erected between Pond and Oliver Streets, just across Main Street from his homestead. This changed the location of the main part of the business from Shovel-Shop Pond to Main Street.[7]

Starting with implements made *by hand,* which were carried to Boston in a one-horse wagon for the hardware dealers to sample, and successfully weathering the War of 1812 and the disastrous depression of 1837, Oliver Sr. lived to see up to 300 dozen shovels a day leave the mills by rail. The effective management and salesmanship of his two sons were telling. Later, the firm was to become the largest producer of earth-working implements in the world, occasionally turning out about 135,000 dozen shovels a year.[8] If the profit had been 20 cents on a one dollar shovel (as seems possible), a good year's net earnings would have been $324,000, mostly tax-free, when a dollar had a buying power about four and a half times the present amount.[9]

His early education was confined to simple instruction in the common school, along with the practical experience of hard work in his father's blacksmith shop.

"Broad-shouldered and erect, he stood over six feet even in old age; and, with his long broadcloth coat, white stock and ebony cane, his partially bald head protected by a wig, made so striking a figure that people turned to look after him in the street." [10] The wig was brown, his eyes deep set and brown. His weatherworn, heavily lined

---

[5] Winthrop Ames, pp. 92–93, 97, 234.

[6] Chaffin, pp. 373–375; Winthrop Ames, p. 235.

[7] Chaffin, pp. 595–596; Winthrop Ames, p. 237.

[8] Ames Family, *In Memory of Oliver Ames,* p. 7.

[9] During the years 1862 to 1872 a Federal tax, not exceeding a flat 10 per cent rate, was imposed on the income and profits of individuals in consequence of the Civil War. Massachusetts and 3 other states had a tax on personal income before the war.

[10] Winthrop Ames, p. 91.

face was handsome and strong, but stern of mien. Of very powerful physique, he excelled in sports of strength and skill, especially wrestling, in which he was long the town champion. A man of tireless energy, of adventurous yet stable character, he was far from being the benign type of village patriarch. Autocratic and obstinate in his opinions, he was much more inclined to order than to argue. Oakes and Oliver Jr. still stood somewhat in awe of him even when they were grown men, though *their* sons could hardly imagine either being awed by anybody.[11] Characteristically, when at the age of sixty-five, he turned over two-thirds of his interest in the business equally to his sons Oakes and Oliver, he stipulated that he was not to be "overruled" in the management. Oakes was then forty, Oliver thirty-seven. Starting that year, 1844, the "O. Ames" shovels were branded "Oliver Ames & Sons," the name of the new partnership.[12]

He was elected to the Massachusetts House of Representatives in 1828, 1833, and 1834, and, against his wishes, to the State Senate in 1844. He once wrote in his journal, "Went to Boston yesterday for the first time in 2½ years. Glad of it." The only public office he cared for was surveyor of the Easton highways, a post he held for life. Farming, raising prize oxen, and construction work occupied his limited leisure hours. In his day, the town was awakened at ten minutes before five by the shop bell. The factories started at seven, by lamplight in the winter, and, with an hour out at noon for dinner, continued until six, making a ten-hour work day. Usually, however, his sons and grandsons returned to the office in the evening to catch up with their correspondence (all letters were written and copied by hand), discuss business, and go over the accounts with the head bookkeeper. At nine, the shop bell sounded a curfew to advise bedtime.[13]

When Oliver came to Easton it was expected that a man of his standing would join one of the two existing congregations, Orthodox or Methodist. But he was an independent thinker. When the more liberal Unitarian doctrine, spread by the sermons of William Ellery Channing (1780–1842), began to be known in Massachusetts, it seemed a faith in which he might concur. So, he invited ministers of several different denominations to preach in succession, in a little, disused church building he had repaired. Finally, the parishioners were called together to vote for a permanent minister. Oliver settled the question promptly and without a vote. "Take the Unitarian," he said, "and I will pay half his salary." And so the family turned

[11] *Ibid.,* p. 114.   [12] *Ibid.,* pp. 109, 236.   [13] *Ibid.,* p. 129.

Unitarian.[14] In the Unity Church of North Easton is a tablet in marble to his memory. Again, on the corner of Main and Oliver Streets is a small plot, with a memorial seat of granite surmounted by a bronze bust of Oliver Sr. with these words below: "Would you behold his monument look about you." The bust (and several copies in marble or plaster) was modeled post-mortem from daguerreotypes taken at the age of seventy.

Oliver died at North Easton on 11 September 1863, having attained an age of eighty-five, not without realizing that his eldest son was soon to commence national service as a Congressman in Washington. His remains are marked by a large sarcophagus in the Village Cemetery, surrounded by the tombstones of his descendants. After providing by will for his other four children then living (Horatio, William Leonard, Mrs. Sarah Witherell, and Mrs. Harriet Mitchell), to Oakes and Oliver Jr. equally he bequeathed his share in the shovel works and the residue of his estate and named them his executors.[15]

B. Oakes Ames: Some Personal Notes [16]

1. PRIOR TO THE WAR

The Honorable Oakes Ames, the eldest of the eight children of Oliver and Susanna, was born 10 January 1804 at Pond Street in North Easton.[17] The senior of at least eight Oakes Ameses with no middle name, he was identified after his mother's great-great-grandfather, the Reverend Urian Oakes, the fourth President of Harvard College. That a strain of Puritan blood was his heritage becomes apparent. In fact, it is presumable that nearly all of his ancestors since 1620 were emigrants of southern English origin who had settled in the Plymouth Colony and environs.

Oakes, like his father, attended only the local district school, except for a few months at Dighton Academy, Massachusetts. At the age of sixteen he was put under a strict tutor to make sure he conned his book instead of going fishing or playing around the large homestead farm off Main Street. Oakes was no student, nor did he then desire to be one. After an apprenticeship in the Shovel Works, he

---

[14] *Ibid.*, p. 114. A somewhat different version appears in Chaffin, p. 409.

[15] Winthrop Ames, pp. 131–132.

[16] Principal sources: Chaffin; Winthrop Ames; Ames Family, *Oakes Ames, A Memorial Volume;* Evelina Gilmore Ames, *Diaries;* Ames Family, *Papers.*

[17] Winthrop Ames, pp. 233, 245; see also p. 63.

quickly and naturally rose to become its foreman and his father's chief reliance. The simple and undeviating rules of the plant were industry and integrity, qualities which were to stand him in good stead later on.

At the age of twenty-three, on 29 November 1827, Oakes married Evelina Orville Gilmore (1809–1882), daughter of Joshua and Hannah (Lothrop) Gilmore of the nearby town of Easton. She was not only a descendant of Francis Cooke, as was Oakes, but also an offspring of the widely known lovers from the *Mayflower*, John Alden and Priscilla Mullins.[18]

Oakes and Evelina lived a happy, frugal yet comfortable, and vastly busy village life. With them were their three sons, Oakes Angier, Oliver "2nd," and Frank Morton, and their only daughter, Susan. Home was in the northern half of the well-proportioned, four-square, wooden dwelling on Main Street (later numbered 25) near one end of Oliver Street and directly opposite the main factory. It had been built in 1814 by Oliver Sr., who moved into the southern half to make room for Oakes and his bride. The house was not torn down until 1951. Oakes was on intimate terms with his high-powered father, but he and Evelina rarely got out from under, living as they did at such close quarters on parental property. Thus Oakes, fifty-nine years old when his father died, missed the satisfaction and diversion of owning and developing his own home and farm. This close environment, as well as heredity, may partly account for his being such a workhorse for business, and may have accentuated his inborn thriftiness and simplicity. The house was plainly furnished, even for that period. He spent little on himself and nothing on the luxuries of life.

As Oakes and Oliver bent their energies to the task of building up their father's shovel business, it gained in sales and profits. A surge of highway and railroad building was getting under way. The demand for good shovels—strong yet light, competitive with British models—was quickening. Oakes was referred to as "the King of Spades for the whole land."[19] An article appearing in the *Atlantic Magazine* in 1836, titled "Ames Iron Works," is quoted as follows:

There is a great deal of Yankee enterprise in old Massachusetts. Perhaps no state goes before her in the extent and variety of manufacturing, compared with the amount of population. A striking instance of

[18] *Ibid.,* pp. 228–231.
[19] Quiett, *They Built the West*, p. 68, quoting "a contemporary writer."

this kind is found in the shovel works of Oliver Ames. . . . Now he has three extensive shovel factories, one at Easton, where he resides, one at Braintree, and one at West Bridgewater, and gives employment to three four-horse teams to carry his shovels to market. He has in his factories nine tilt hammers, which weigh about four tons apiece, and each cost from $1500 to $2000. His works turn about forty dozen shovels a day, and that is not sufficient to supply all the orders he receives. He employs about sixty workmen constantly. Each shovel goes through about twenty different hands. He pays his workman from $12 to $15 a month. His works cost upwards of $75,000. His profits are probably from $15,000 to $20,000 a year. So much for individual enterprise.[20]

In 1844, at forty, Oakes became a partner, as told, in Oliver Ames & Sons, with a one-third interest.

It is a pity that the records of the Ames wives and mothers are not nearly as full as those of the men—a neglect which Winthrop Ames also regretted when mustering the family genealogy. Fortunately, Evelina always kept a daily diary of her doings, and from one large book covering 1851 and 1852, much can be seen of her character and interests. A lovely, gentle lady, both in looks and personality, she must have been one of the most popular matrons in town. A portrait in middle age (by Blanche Ames Ames) shows her hair brown, eyes blue, and complexion fair with high color. Most democratic by nature, she had a tender, motherly interest not only in her own family, but also in her many nearby relatives and friends, whom she was always helping out, particularly in sickness, of which there was a startling amount in those days before hospitals and district nursing. Living at the hub of community activities, with "Father in the other part of the house," as she always put it, and with Oakes already the leader of the new Ames generation, people were constantly dropping in to pay their respects and exchange the latest news, not refusing impromptu invitations to dinner or tea. Possessing an energy second only to Oakes's, she was an extremely conscientious housekeeper. With but little domestic help, and rarely a holiday, the daily chores went on: cooking for large numbers, mending, cleaning, and "fixing." Her children were then all at home. Except on Sunday, family breakfast was at six; dinner at noon; and supper, always called "Tea" (the sociable occasion), at six-thirty or seven. Every week at least, the nearby Ames family, children, houseguests, and all, would assemble at one household, a custom which was carried on for generations. Fif-

[20] Ames Shovel Works, North Easton, framed copy.

teen or twenty was not an unusual gathering.[21] The duties that
Evelina enjoyed most were cutting and sewing the dresses, bonnets,
and so on, for herself and for ten-year-old Susan; she also made the
shirts for Oakes and the three grown boys, each of whom was working
in the factory. Her weekday relaxations were paying or receiving
afternoon calls, gardening, reading, and keeping her diary, which
she called her "book of nonsense." On 15 September 1851, she dryly
noted:

Have been sweeping and dusting the house and done little of everything & not much of anything. Have got the chambers in pretty good
order for once in my life. Have mended Mr. Ames coat & vest. Took
the time when he was from home because he has but one suit beside his
go to meeting, poor man!

Now and then she went to Boston by connecting stagecoach and
railroad to visit and shop, but was usually worn out by the effort.
"Mr. Ames," as she always wrote of Oakes (a custom of the time, with
the advantage of distinguishing him from son Oakes Angier), was at
the shop from Monday to Friday all day, except for noon dinner at
home; nearly every Saturday he went to Boston to "call on the trade."
Trips to New York were not infrequent then, either. Regularly,
every Sunday, with the few exceptions when he had to work, Oakes
and Evelina attended the little Unitarian church, sometimes twice
a day, taking their lunches with them.

In 1855, Oakes and Oliver built their first railway, the small Easton
Branch Railroad from the Shovel Works to Stoughton, where it con-
nected with the Boston and Providence Railroad.[22] That same year,
Oakes made his first investment in Iowa, as will be recounted.[23]

By astute management, the financial storm of 1857 was weathered
without serious dislocation. A new industrial era in the United States
was beginning, but the storm clouds of civil war had started to
gather. Perhaps the first forewarning of armed conflict was the bitter
political struggle to keep Kansas, a newly created Territory in 1854,
free from slavery, contrary to the interests of the pro-slavery faction in
the adjoining state of Missouri. "The Emigrant Aid Society" of
Boston was formed to help anti-slavery New Englanders settle in
Kansas, which they did in large numbers. Oakes and Oliver took an
active part in supporting this Society as "Free-Soilers," and Oakes
contributed $10,000.[24]

[21] Winthrop Ames, p. 128.   [22] *Ibid.,* p. 128.   [23] See p. 79.
[24] *Daily Republican,* Cedar Rapids, Iowa, 9 and 10 May 1873.

2. WAR AND CONGRESS

In 1860 the newly formed Republican Party unanimously named Oakes Ames in convention for Councilor from his county of Bristol. Thus, without solicitation on his part, he soon became a member of the Massachusetts Executive Council, a cabinet officer, chief adviser to, and finally, intimate friend of John Albion Andrew, the famous "War Governor" of Massachusetts. He served with him during the Civil War until moving to Washington. Early in the war he fitted out and fully equipped, from his own private means, two regiments of troops ready for service.[25]

At the age of fifty-eight, he was urged by Governor Andrew and many friends to run for the Thirty-Eighth Congress from the Second District of his state. On the informal ballot at the nominating convention, he received two-thirds of the votes cast, was nominated unanimously, and elected with a large popular vote. This was on 4 November 1862, only four days after the legal formation of the Union Pacific. The First Session of this Congress was not to convene until over a year later, on 7 December 1863.

Lincoln's preliminary Proclamation of Emancipation of 22 September 1862 had swollen the Republican losses even in the mid-term elections of 1862. In the Presidential election of 1864, with the very existence of the Union at stake, Oakes was aware of the wisdom of supporting Lincoln. He contributed $10,000 to the early campaign in Maine and about $20,000 more to the Republican national campaign.[26] The party won on a "National Union" ticket: Lincoln was elected for a second term, and Andrew Johnson, a Southern Democrat opposed to slavery and secession, became Vice-President. This odd ticket, as it turned out, was to become of high importance to the Ames brothers and the Union Pacific.

In Washington, Oakes served as a member of the Committee on Manufactures, the Committee on Revolutionary Claims, and the Committee on Roads and Canals. But it was as one of the nine members of the House Committee on the Pacific Railroad from December 1863 to March 1869 that he became familiar with the inside workings of legislation concerning the various Pacific railways. When Congress was in session, this Committee met weekly. His position in Congress, while influential, was not conspicuous except as to the Pacific roads. A taciturn, reserved man, he rarely, if ever, made a speech, yet his

25 *Ibid.*   26 *Ibid.*

practical knowledge of general business ways and his good judgment made him a valued working member of committees. On Capitol Hill, as well as on Wall Street and State Street, he was judged a successful, farsighted financier, and his business advice was highly rated.[27] Widely varied interests kept him busy traveling between Washington, New York, and Boston—a physical effort of no small proportions in those days. Freedom from slavery and the unity of the nation were his deeply rooted doctrines, from first to last. To his country's cause he freely devoted his time, his talents, and his means. Little wonder that he came to enjoy the friendship and confidence of President Lincoln, who counted on his opinion more than once.[28]

Only three days before Lincoln died, Oakes wrote him as follows:

N. Easton   April 11th 1865

His Excelency.   A. Lincoln
Pres of U. States

I see by the papers that a session of Congress is to be called to take measures to receive back the rebel states into full fellowship with the loyal states.

I hope you will not call Congress together for that purpose. I think we shall get along better and more harmoniously to let those states remain under Military law until they get time to conquer their prejudices and come to a realising sense of their position. I think more time is required to prepare for the change, excuse my boldness in making the suggestion.

I may be wrong. My only desire & object is for the public good.

Yours truly

Oakes Ames [29]

The S.S. Oakes Ames: The car-ferry *Oakes Ames* was built in Burlington, Vermont, in 1868 for the Rutland and Burlington Railroad, which ran the length of Vermont, with a branch from Plattsburg on the western shore of Lake Champlain to the Canadian border. The 24-mile water course between Burlington and Plattsburg cut off much rail distance. On board the powerful two-engined side-wheeler *Oakes Ames*, 258 feet long, six cars at a time could be shuttled across at the speed of a freight train, or even faster. Apparently it was built due to the enterprise and influence of John B. Page, Governor of Vermont, who was President of the road, and his good friends Peter Butler of Boston (also a Director) and Oakes Ames.

---

[27] Winthrop Ames, p. 132.   [28] Ames Family, *Oakes Ames*, p. 4.
[29] Abraham Lincoln, *Papers*, vol. 194, 11 Apr. 1865, Letter Folio nos. 41624, 41625.

However, a few years later the Delaware and Hudson Railroad sold the car-ferry to the venerable Champlain Transportation Company for $85,000. The latter converted it into a fine passenger vessel. In line with company tradition, but possibly also because Oakes, only that month, had fallen into Credit Mobilier disgrace, it was renamed the *Champlain II*, and scheduled opposite the S.S. *Adirondack*. On one bright, quiet July night in 1875 she was completely wrecked. The pilot, it seems, suffering from gout, was secretly under the influence of morphine. Running at full speed, he slammed her into the mountainside at Steam Mill Point. "I held her on the right course every minute," he swore.[30]

3. PERSONAL QUALITIES

In appearance, Oakes came by his father's powerful athletic frame. At middle age he was a full six feet in height and weighed over 200 pounds. Lincoln liked to call him "the broad shouldered Ames." Inheritance and a vigorous outdoor life had nurtured a robust constitution, which was to stand him well in late years. He never, it is said, took time out from work because of sickness. His very few photographs and the one bust seem to say: Here is no ordinary man, but a rugged, bold leader; an abrupt man of direct action, not of fine words. Here is a dynamic personality which exudes endurance and self-reliance. The long, thick hair, brown till graying; the deep-set, penetrating grayish-blue eyes; the long, straight nose, receding sharply above the shaven lip; the wide, straight mouth with thin, tightly set lips; the sturdy chin concealed by a short beard; the firm, ruddy face; the stocky neck set low in brawny shoulders of exceptional breadth; the barrel chest—all these seem to reveal determination and tenacity, possibly even to the point of impetuosity. Yet, along with a severe demeanor like his father's, here is a suggestion of a quiet, innate kindness which would lean to charity towards weaker men. Here is, perhaps, just a strong, simple man to wonder at.

Oakes's impulses of life appear to be founded on personal liberty and individual opportunity; on total honesty, truth, and fair play; on tolerance, loyalty, and spiritual piety; and on self-reliance, risk-taking, and hard work. Unpretentious and favoring social equality, he was

[30] Champlain Transportation Co., *The Steamboats of L. Champlain, 1809 to 1930*, 6 June 1930, pp. 123–125, Ralph N. Hill, Jr., editor of *Vermont Life Magazine*, Shelburne Museum, Shelburne, Vt. The original pencil drawing hangs in the Colchester Lighthouse at Shelburne.

proud to be a man of the people. Some of these precepts hardly differ from the natural impulses of the representative American of the 19th century, the pioneer.

Certainly Oakes had his shortcomings. He was reticent and self-contained, and his expressions by voice and letter were not fine-grained but plain-spoken, sometimes blunt, naive, and capable of being misinterpreted. Perhaps the scantiness of his schooling and the fast pace of big business had denied him the art of using meaningful words and precise phrases. He was not a reader. He had an inclination to rely on his excellent memory for important deals and details which sometimes might better have been recorded. Was he over-confident of his capacities, or was he overburdened by his pressures? How could he have underrated, so widely, the shrewdness of a Durant, the treachery of a McComb, and the political weakness of friends in Congress? He was not smart; rather, he was trusting.

Was he a victim of his own indomitable energy and endurance? No matter how unquestionable the probity of his character, were there not some conflicts of personal interests? For he was, all at one time, the senior partner of a great manufacturing concern; a private banker of a type rare today; a trustee or director of many important companies; a Representative of one of the leading states in the United States Congress, elected four times; and, in his late years, to cap it all, the financier and contractor of the greatest private industrial enterprise to date: the pioneering Union Pacific, deeply involved in national politics. Yet readers of American history know that after the Civil War, and until about the end of the 19th century, the economic philosophy of the nation was dominated by the doctrine of *laissez faire,* an attitude towards business which meant "hands off" as far as Government regulation was concerned. It was just a form of survival of the fittest, willy-nilly. Stemming from the teachings of Adam Smith, it encouraged private enterprise and increased the national wealth, at least during those decades of industrial expansion, virgin natural resources, and sparse population. To an American with his inwrought doctrine of freedom, to the frontiersman with his creed of individuality, *laissez faire* had a commanding appeal. To Oakes Ames, it was taken for granted and welcomed: it was just suited to his liking and capacity for challenging tasks.

Nevertheless, if Oakes Ames had not been the crusader that he was; had not done what he did, when he did; had not had a partner like Oliver; a railroad called the Union Pacific might never have been built. The Central Pacific might have gone all the way to Omaha;

or the Kansas Pacific to Denver, and then on to meet the Central Pacific, even in California.

General Dodge, who worked with him intimately during the last construction years, when the going was rough, said repeatedly, "Oakes Ames was the real pluck of the work." [31]

Without an Oakes Ames to contend with, what would Durant have done to the UP?

Without a Durant to contend with, would Oakes Ames have been able to build the UP without the troubles that developed with Congress?

C. *Oliver Ames Jr.: Some Personal Notes* [32]

The Honorable Oliver Ames, third son of Oliver and Susanna, was born 5 November 1807 in the "Long House" on Summer Street (now numbered 120–122), Plymouth, Massachusetts, during the only period when the family lived away from North Easton. He was nearly four years younger than his favorite brother, Oakes, and only a year older than Abraham Lincoln. His youth in North Easton was divided between school and the Shovel Works, where he became an expert in every phase of toolmaking. Unlike Oakes, he had aptitude for study, and at the age of twenty-one, having been temporarily disabled for active labor by a severe fall, he entered Franklin Academy at North Andover, Massachusetts, intending to prepare for college and ultimately to study law. However, after a year and a half at the Academy, and a period as a law student in an attorney's office in West Bridgewater, he regained his health to find that actually he disliked the confinement of an office. So, with the manufacturing business at home showing exceptional promise, he settled down with the Shovel Works. As stated, he was made a partner of Oliver Ames and Sons, with a one-third interest, at the age of thirty-seven. When only nineteen, he became interested in the temperance movement, and he was later a prominent officer and, till his death, a benefactor of the Massachusetts Total Abstinence Society from its first organization.

On 11 June 1833 he married Sarah Lothrop (1812–1877), a daughter of the Honorable Howard and Sally Williams Lothrop and a

---

[31] Dodge, *Romantic Realities*, p. 20; Winthrop Ames, p. 150.
[32] Principal sources: Chaffin; Winthrop Ames; Ames Family, *A Memorial of Oliver Ames*; Easton *Journal*, 17 Mar. 1877; Oliver Ames Jr., *Diaries*.

second cousin of Oakes's wife, Evelina Gilmore. Both girls had lived in the nearby town of Easton. Sarah was also a descendant of John and Priscilla Alden. An oil portrait depicts her as a middle-aged lady of refinement, with thick, braided, chestnut hair; hazel eyes; and fair complexion. As a wedding gift, Oliver Sr. built Sarah and Oliver Jr. a house on Main Street, opposite the end of Oliver Street, close by his own. In 1864, after his father's death, Oliver Jr. moved this attractive wooden house to Oliver Street (where it still stands in good condition), and in its place on the original site, a bit further back from the street, he built for himself a larger wooden house, in many ways similar to his father's. Named "Unity Close" and now numbered 23 Main Street, it is still occupied and finely maintained by his descendants.

Oliver's first political position was in the Senate of Massachusetts, to which he was appointed by the Legislature in 1852. Five years later he was elected to the same office by popular vote. While he could make effective speeches on the issues of the day, his fondness for active politics waned, as had his father's, and that was his last public office. Upon the dissolution of the Whig party, of which he had been a member, he took a lively interest in the Republican party, newly formed in 1860.

Oliver Jr. was distinguished by his friendliness and courtesy and by his quiet modesty and generosity. Energy, perseverance, and above all, unassailable integrity, were to carry him through to rare success in the business world. Like Oakes, he was chosen president or director of many banks and railroads, and was given positions of trust in numerous public and private enterprises.

In appearance, he was a tall, handsome gentleman of kindly mien. Although of slighter stature than his father or brother, he was robust enough also to be the town wrestling champion. From his bust and from an oil portrait hanging in the Ames Free Library, it can be seen that his face bore but small resemblance to Oakes's, despite the same brown hair (which became gray in his sixties), the short beard without mustache, and the ruddy complexion. The slate-blue eyes were larger, the nose was shorter and rather rounded at the tip, and the lips were a bit fuller and more relaxed.

Extremely wealthy for those times, particularly in his last few years, his public spirit led him to support various organizations of education, reform, and philanthropy. He shrank from publicity in these benefactions, many of which remained anonymous. He rarely missed a Sunday at church, even when away from home or worn out by problems with the railroad. He kept a daily diary from which many quotations appear in this book.

Early in 1865 Oliver Jr. first became interested in the UP by investment, inspired by the leadership of Oakes. The next year, in November, he became its unsalaried President, a Director, and a Member of the Executive Committee. His term in such key positions included the two-and-a-half-year period of construction from the 100th meridian in Nebraska to Promontory, Great Salt Lake, a distance of 839 miles. In the end, 1877, he held fully one-tenth of the UP common stock.[33] He was never a Director of the Credit Mobilier of America, nor was he engaged in its management in any way, except that he was a very large stockholder continuously from 1865. However, he was one of the Seven Trustees of the Oakes Ames Contract.

Perhaps his gentleness was a handicap in the rough-and-tumble world of the railroad builders. John Alley, co-director of the UP, said of Oliver: "Always honest and true, yet he often yielded reluctantly to these men [Durant, McComb, and Gould] because of his excessive amiability."[34] Surely he was the exact antithesis of Durant. His dislike of the Doctor was so intense as to preclude any chance of turning the tougher man's cunning and power to advantage. Not a domineering type, Oliver perhaps never quite had his whole heart in the vexatious job of being President of the UP. In his sixties, he was a conservative, pious, home-loving man, and probably would have preferred a calmer life in North Easton. Yet, without the convenience of telephones, he had to give up local affairs to make countless, tedious trips to the head office in New York, which was dominated by the Vice-President. But the Ames investment in the UP was so heavy as to demand his taking a leading part in its management.

Without Oliver's constant support, the UP probably would not have been built then, if ever. Oliver was the balance-wheel that steadied the Ameses over some of the rough spots.

D. Why Did the Ameses Undertake the Job?

In 1865, the year of their decision, Oakes and Oliver Ames were possessed of very large fortunes. They were the senior partners of an exceptionally profitable and reputable business. They had fine fami-

---

[33] Ames Family, *A Memorial of Oliver Ames*, p. 94. (From the *Shoe and Leather Reporter*, 15 Mar. 1877.)

[34] *Poland Rep.*, p. 89; see also p. 281.

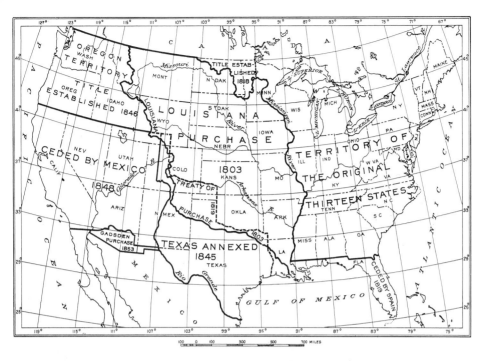

Accessions of territory, 1803 to 1853.
(U.S. Geological Survey Bulletin 1212.)

Pony express saluting the telegraph, 1861.
(Courtesy of Union Pacific.)

MAP 1. As Contemplated by Acts of 1862 and 1864.

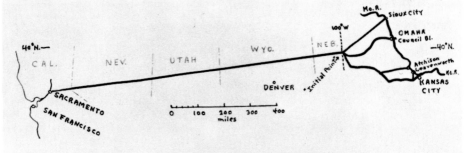

MAP 2. As Actually Built Under Acts of 1862, 1864, and 1866.

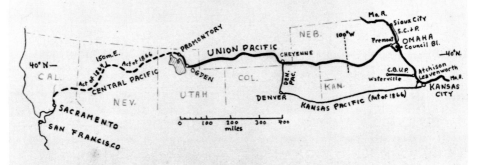

MAP 3. The Branch Lines As Contemplated By Acts and As Actually Built.

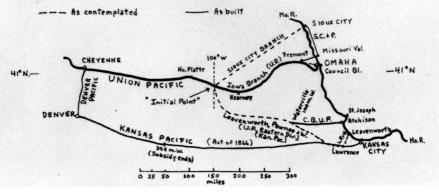

The Pacific Railway System to 1870.

Thomas C. Durant.
(Courtesy of Union Pacific.)

Susanna Angier Ames.
(Courtesy of Elise Ames Parker.)

The birthplace of Oakes Ames.

Oliver Ames Sr., *c.* 1849.
(Ames Family Records.)

Ames Shovel Works, North Easton, 1886.
(Chaffin.)

Label used on O. Ames shovels, spades, scoops.

Home of Oliver Sr. and Oakes Ames, from 1814 on.
Oliver Jr.'s house at far right; the Ames office at far left.
(Courtesy of Luella Ames Newcomb.)

Oakes Ames, *c.* 1862.
(Brady Collection, National Archives.)

Evelina Gilmore Ames.
(Painting by Blanche Ames Ames.)

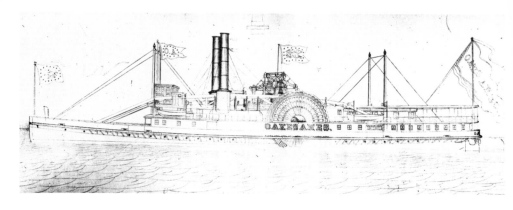

S.S. *Oakes Ames*, Lake Champlain, 1873.
(Courtesy of Shelburne Museum, Shelburne, Vermont.)

Sarah Lothrop Ames.
(Courtesy of Elise Ames Parker.)

Oliver Ames Jr.
(Ames Family, *A Memorial of Oliver Ames*.)

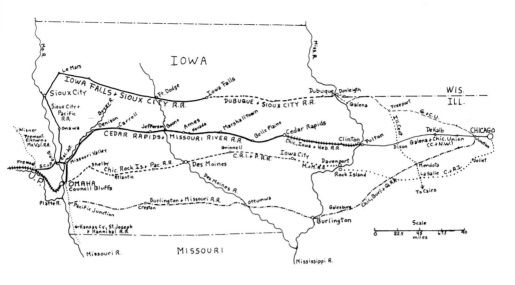

The Iowan railroads.

First temporary bridge between Council Bluffs and Omaha.
(Sketch by George Simons, February 1867.
Courtesy of Council Bluffs Free Public Library.)

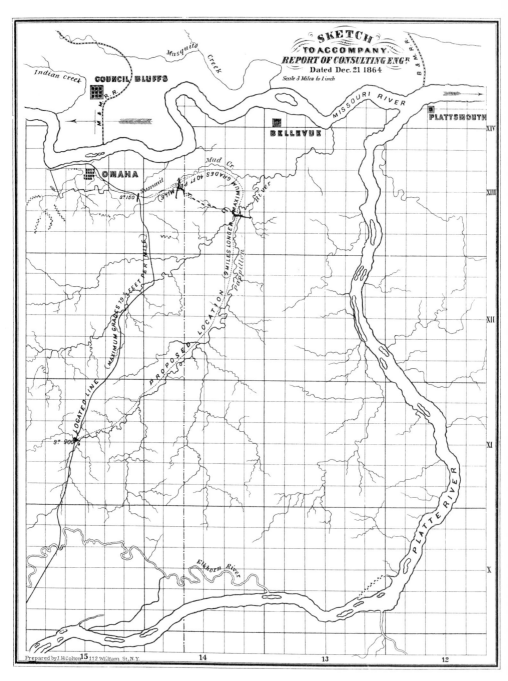

The "ox-bow" route out of Omaha.
(Sketch by Silas Seymour, 21 December 1864.)

lies with the closest of ties, social and political prestige, good health for their aging years, and a future seemingly without a cloud. *They risked all these—and why?*

A quick answer might be: for patriotism and for profit. In the aftermath of war, feelings of patriotism can be powerful, yet it is unrealistic to expect that businessmen would not weigh the chances between profit and loss. Here was the greatest creative task at the greatest risk yet faced by American private capital. Although firm believers in the rapid expansion of the country through railroads, the Ameses, particularly Oakes, were aware of many problems in the UP situation and were not men to act without reflection. For a full year their financial aid to the UP had been solicited from many quarters, particularly New York.[35] Many of their business associates had strongly advised against it.[36] In Oakes Ames's own words later: "There was universal distrust in financial circles of the ultimate completion of the road, and the general conviction that when completed it would fail to prove remunerative." [37] This much seems clear—if they were to go in, the inspiration must be supreme, the reasons strong and practical.

The question is pertinent, the answer unexpectedly involved. It is necessary to review, one by one, the dominant influences of the time:

1. The Iowan Railroad Investments
2. Abraham Lincoln—A Promise?
3. The Civil War Ended
4. The Central Pacific Coming On
5. The Construction Company Formed
6. The Pressure of Uninvested Capital
7. Superior Motives

1. THE IOWAN RAILROAD INVESTMENTS

Oakes Ames's vision of a Pacific Railway resolved into action as early as 1855, ten years before he undertook the Union Pacific. He became a leading financier-promoter and director of four pioneer Iowan railroads with an aggregate of 650 miles of line and a security capitalization of $28,591,000.[38] First and most important of these were the two roads comprising a trunk line which started at the Mis-

---

[35] Ames Family, *Oakes Ames*, p. 6.   [36] *Ibid.*, p. 133.
[37] *Ibid.*, p. 112, before the House of Representatives, 25 Feb. 1873.
[38] See table on p. 88.

sissippi, joined at Cedar Rapids, and ended at the Missouri—full across the gently rolling plains of the already prospering farming state of Iowa, with its deep, black, prairie soil; its corn and oats; its fatting hogs and cattle. Prophetically, this trunk line aimed straight along the 42nd parallel in the center of the state. It was the first road of iron to reach the pioneer Mecca of Council Bluffs on the Missouri and connect with the U.P. (See map of the Iowan railroads.) By then, January 1867, the UP had pushed its end-of-track more than 300 miles along the overland trail from Omaha into the setting sun.

Later, starting in 1867, Oakes Ames promoted the other two Iowan railroads, from Iowa Falls to Sioux City, and on to meet the UP. This Iowan story is recounted in some detail because of its close relationship to the UP, and because it has been overlooked in Oakes Ames's annals. Even Winthrop Ames barely mentioned it.

To revert to the background, by the year 1852 two rival roads, the Michigan Southern and the Michigan Central, each with connections to the Atlantic seaboard, were serving Chicago, the focus of the trek to the Golden West. Westbound from that booming town four new railroads shortly emerged, each a part of great independent systems to this day. They lie like a four-pronged fork with its short handle on Chicago and its points touching the sandy shores of the Mississippi along the Illinois border.[39]

First of these four to tap the then vital riverboat commerce of the Mississippi was the Chicago and Rock Island Railroad by way of Englewood, Joliet, and LaSalle, ceremoniously puffing into Rock Island opposite Davenport on 22 February 1854.[40] New York was only 42 hours away. Second came extensions of the present-day Chicago, Burlington and Quincy Railroad via Junction (now West Chicago), Mendota, and Galesburg, reaching the river opposite Burlington on 17 March 1855.[41] Third, and quickly following, was the largest system of the four, the Illinois Central Railroad. For its westbound traffic from Chicago, it used the northern branch of the Galena and Chicago Union Railroad as far as Freeport. There this traffic joined the Illinois Central's own main line, which traversed Illinois northward from Cairo, and ran onwards to Galena, and finally to Dunleith opposite Dubuque. The tracks met the Mississippi on 12 June 1855.[42]

Fourth, to Oakes Ames and his friends the most likely road to meet

---

[39] See map inside front and back covers.
[40] Hayes, pp. 27–30; *The Palimpsest*, Apr. 1960, pp. 177–192.
[41] *The Palimpsest*, Apr. 1960, pp. 226–240. [42] *Ibid.*, pp. 210–225.

a contemplated Pacific Railway was the highly profitable main and southernmost branch of the venerable "Galena," the Galena and Chicago Union Railroad of 1836, in 1864 consolidated with the Chicago and North-Western Railway Company (C & N-W).[43] Following part of the great circle track between Chicago and San Francisco, the Galena ran through Junction, DeKalb, and Dixon to Fulton nearly opposite Clinton on the Mississippi. Its first through train from Chicago proudly rolled into Fulton on 16 December 1855.[44] Oakes Ames must have agreed with the prophecy of its able chief engineer, John Van Nortwick, who had declared:

> There can be no doubt that this route must form the great trunk line west from Chicago to Council Bluffs and even west of that point, and that this is the one upon which Chicago must rely to secure the business of Central and Western Iowa rather than upon other western lines having eastern connections south of that city.[45]

In anticipation of the coming of the Galena, Oakes Ames's first move was to participate with friends in a little land speculation known as the Iowa Land Company, organized in May 1855.[46] (This company is not to be confused with the Iowa *Railroad* Land Company of 1869.)[47] The group bought 400 acres of fertile land across the river between Lyons and Clinton. To promote the sale of 150 acres of lots soon laid out, they organized a short railroad called the Mississippi and Iowa Central (not to be referred to again), and graded a half-mile northwesterly toward the plots. Among those interested in the Iowa Land Company with Oakes Ames were Charles A. Lambard of Maine, and William T. Glidden and J.M.S. Williams of Boston. Each was to become active with the UP. Incidentally, this was about the time that Durant's Mississippi and Missouri reached Iowa City and won the $50,000 bonus.[48]

Chicago, Iowa and Nebraska

From this little seed of bold speculation near Clinton grew the first elongation of the Galena prong of the fork, the profitable road known as the Chicago, Iowa and Nebraska Railroad (CI & N), in which Oakes Ames was a director and prominent figure, along with others of his New England group of capitalists. Besides the same

---

43 Stennett, *Yesterday and Today*, pp. 1–199.
44 *Ibid.*, pp. 27–28; *The Palimpsest*, Apr. 1960, pp. 193–209.
45 *The Palimpsest*, Apr. 1960, p. 206.
46 Stennett, pp. 37–38; *Daily Republican*, Cedar Rapids, 9 May 1873.
47 Stennett, pp. 40–41.   48 See p. 21; see also Hayes, pp. 39–43.

Glidden, Williams, and Lambard appeared some newcomers: Frederick Nickerson and the Honorable John B. Alley of Boston; R.G. Hazard of Peacedale, R.I.; Lucius B. Crocker of Oswego, N.Y.; and Captain John Bertram of Salem, Mass. More will be heard of these men, too. Horace Williams (not related to J.M.S.), the general representative of the New England interests in Iowa, came to Clinton in 1857 and was made president. Organized on 26 January 1856, the CI & N commenced tracklaying at Clinton that October, and carried on for 81 miles to Cedar Rapids, then having less than 2,000 inhabitants. The financial panic of 1857, with its sharp deflation of land values in the West, delayed its arrival there until June 1859.

Incidentally, it was at just this time, August 1859, that Abraham Lincoln held his well-known conversation with Grenville Dodge in Council Bluffs on the porch of the Pacific House, and became convinced more than ever that the Pacific Railway should start right there.[49]

Cedar Rapids and Missouri River [50]

Extending the Galena prong 272 miles still further from Cedar Rapids, Oakes Ames's second and principal Iowan road was the highly successful Cedar Rapids and Missouri River Railroad Company (CR & MR) organized on 14 June 1859 upon completion of the CI & N, largely by the same group. In March 1860 Iowa transferred one of its four railroad land grants from the defunct Iowa Central Air Line Railroad Company to the CR & MR, whereupon construction began in earnest. This was about the time that Lincoln was first nominated for President.

John I. Blair: The next year, despite the opening of the Civil War, John Insley Blair (1802–1899) of Blairstown, New Jersey, first joined Oakes Ames's CR & MR syndicate and before long, at the age of sixty, was given charge of the road's construction and management. In addition to becoming a Director and member of the Executive Committee, Blair was made President of the construction company, the Iowa Rail Road Contracting Company. *However, in none of the so-called "Blair Roads" of the West did he have more than one-sixth of the stock. The voting control was usually with the Ames group.*[51]

With but brief schooling, Blair had started in business at the age of only eleven. He was "a systematic and persevering sort of man," said

[49] See pp. 131–132.   [50] Stennett, pp. 39–40; *The Palimpsest,* Apr. 1960, pp. 193–209.
[51] Wick, *John I. Blair,* p. 490.

Dey.[52] A born financier and promoter, he rose sensationally through the grocery, iron, and railroad industries to build an empire in which he was President of 17 railroads (all at one time); the owner of over two million acres of Government land grants; the principal stockholder in several banks; and the founder of over 60 towns. Among the many companies organized by him was the Lackawanna Steel Company, with his son DeWitt Clinton Blair and Oakes Ames as partners, to make rails which theretofore had been largely imported from England.[53] Generous and kind when he felt like it, he was a very large donor to his Presbyterian church as well as a great benefactor to Blair Academy, Princeton University, and Lafayette, Grinnell, Coe, and Park Colleges. Yet, by nature he was close in his dealings, and stingy even with himself, foregoing many of the comforts of life. Perhaps for these reasons he was sometimes misunderstood. Always of tremendous vitality, he lived to be ninety-seven.

Dodge was reported to have said, "Blair, who was much more of a railroad man [than Oakes Ames], declined to take any part in the Union Pacific. He thought it was too far in advance of the times."[54] Actually, it is interesting that no record has been found as to just why Blair did not participate, although he was one of the original Directors in 1863.[55] Perhaps it was because Blair simply did not trust Durant.

In July 1862, the CR & MR, as then built and to be built, was leased to the Galena, which company and its successor, the C & N-W, controlled and operated it until 1884, when the latter purchased it outright.

When the CR & MR grading reached Nevada, 30 miles west of Marshalltown, in June 1863, Blair made a long trip west with Oakes Ames (then a Congressman, but not yet at Washington) to explore along the 42nd parallel for a junction with the newly organized UP, whose exact route was yet to be set. With keen inquisitiveness and perception, Blair jotted down in minute detail all that he saw and did. Space permits us to reprint only a few excerpts from his instructive Notebook of 1863:

History of J. I. Blair Traval to River Platt in 1863

J.I. Blair & Party exploring the Rout for the Cedar Rapids & M Riv Road to the Missouri & thence to the Platt River, for the Pacific line. 1863. June

---

[52] Dodge, *Autobiography*, p. 501.   [53] *The Palimpsest*, Dec. 1962, p. 550.
[54] Perkins, p. 269. Source not given by Perkins.   [55] See p. 19.

Boonsboro, Iowa,
Monday Morning June 15' 1863

J.I. Blair, Oakes Ames, James Blair, D.C. Blair, W.W. Walker, V.P. & Enginr L.C. Parder, Scty Mr. Octavis Cattle and Judge Whiting of Onawa, on the Missouri, with Our Cook, Team, Driver, with all our Camp Equipage, Provisions, Tents &co, with Three Waggons, all left Boonsborro for the Missouri River Endevouring to follow the 42 Parallel through the Center of Iowa & the Counties to the Missouri River.

. . . We arrived at Denison at 11 Oclk, 20 Miles Distance over a Hilly Country, or High Roles, the Most so of any I have Seen West of the Mississipi, too expensive to Construct a Rail Road. Not a House . . . .

. . . Left Denison at 3 Ock P.M. and drove down the Boyer River 15 Miles, and here we Camped. . . . The Flats down the Boyer is Handsom & quite wide, excellent for a Rail Road. . . . I Should Say from Denison to Councel Bluffs there is a Rout . . .

[Near Onawa 65 miles up river from Council Bluffs, June 20]: . . . the Feryman was & Indian Half Breed, by the Name of Kieugh, with Three other Half Breeds, took a Batteau Mr. Ames, James Clinton & Myself and they Rowed us across the River [Missouri], which is about 3/4 Mile wide. the River is Very deep on each Side in the Middle was a Sand Bar that we Rowed over not Covered over more than Two feet the Water is so Mudy You Cannot See & inch in it, and the Water is about a Light drab Collour, the Same as the Clay. This River is Generaly the Highest in June and is Now High . . . .

. . . The Mail Carrier lives at West point [on the Elkhorn] which has One House. . . . there is No deficulty in getting a Good line of Rail Road through to the Platt, So far [from the Missouri] . . . .

[At Columbus June 22] . . . Collumbus . . . is on a favourable Point to Strike the Platt for the Rail Road . . . [It] contains about 15 Houses, One Hotel and 3 Small Stores. . . . We found Ames Shovels here for sale in the Store. . . . We Passed Several Sod Houses—as Well as Stables. . . . We Saw the Loup River about 1200 feet across tho the Fery is Not over 200 Feet. the Current Swift . . . . Something is Passing here all the time . . . . in the Morning we will Turn our Eyes East . . . .

. . . We arrived at Fremont . . . has about a dosen Indiferent Houses. We Stoped at the Valley House, Kept by and old Widow Lady. . . . She left Massachusets 40 Years Since . . . . The Bluffs Runs out Thin, and the Rail Road Could be Turned West at that point which would be Near 40 Miles from Omaha. We Crossed the Elk Horn—which is about 120 feet across Banks not High. . . .

[Omaha, June 24] . . . the Bluffs & Land Lays High for Miles West of Omaha and I See No place that a Rail Road could be Made, except at Very High grads if at all—to the Platt. . . . This is a Flourishing town. they say it has 3500 Inhabitants. I doubt it. . . . I got Shaved here and paid 10 cents. All well . . . . We drove up to Council Bluffs . . . . Population estimated at 3000 to 3500. I Think & over estimate. We Stoped at the Pacific House, quite good. . . .

[60 miles West of Des Moines, June 26] . . . To Reach Des Moines . . . before the Land Office Closed on Satturday, to Morrow . . . we Charter a four Horse Stage of the Western Stage Compy and Ames, Walker, Clinton, Mr. Cattle & Myself Take this Stage. . . . paying Some Smart Money. . . . Our Stage Come on all Night . . . Ames & Myself took the Front Seat . . . we arrived at Desmoins 27 June . . . and Stoped at the Savary House which is used for First Story Stores, the Second Hotel Purposes. Ames and me had Room 33, Large Room with Two Beds. . . . Our Shirt Collars and Shirts Was Near the Colour of Black Kettles.

[Des Moines, June 28] . . . Mr. Ames & Myself with our Carriage & Horses left Desmoins City . . . and drove on to Peori City [Peoria], a village of 12 houses . . . 25 miles . . . . We crossed our Rail Road some 5 miles West of Marshaltown.

So the Reader Will See that We left Marshaltown at the end of the Rail Road on the 12th day of June 1863, and Returned on the 29th day of June 1863, Being Gone 18 Days. . . . The Distance . . . to Columbus or Loup Fork by the Way We Went was 300 Miles out & 300 Miles Back. . . . Our horses stood it well. . . . We left Marshaltown at 3 ½ Oclock and arrived at Ceder Rapids at 6 Oclk P.M. [by train]. Mr. Ames went direct to Chicago . . . .

Our Trip in a National Point of View was Likewise of Vast Importance. as it Was to See if there was a Feasible Rout for the extension of the Ceder Rapids & Missouri River Rail Road, from the Des moins River Near Boonsboro to the Missouri River, and Thence across to the North Bend of the Platt River, following through Iowa on the 42 Parallel to the Missouri River and Thence across to the Platt. there is & excellent Rout by Maple River as Well as the Boyer River, the Southing Can Be Made on the Missouri Flats; and the Platt Reached in 35 Miles, or Less if Necessary from the Missouri River. the Best Crossing Would appear Below Onowa.[56]

The main trouble with following the shorter route along the 42nd parallel beyond Denison, crossing the river near Onawa and then

[56] Blair, *Surveying the First Railroad Across Iowa,* in *The Journal of John I. Blair,* pp. 321–362.

turning southwestward to Fremont on the Platte, was that Council Bluffs and the flourishing town of Omaha would be by-passed. The CR & MR would have saved 40 miles by omitting Omaha and running straight to the UP at North Bend. Durant's proposal to unite the M & M with the CR & MR at Des Moines was rejected 18 February 1864 in a letter to him by L.B. Crocker, then President of the CR & MR.[57] The excuse was that they wanted to be free to save the 40 miles if they chose.

After the track of the CR & MR had reached Boone, 200 miles west of the Mississippi, mounting building costs due to the Civil War and the expense of crossing the deep, wide gorge of the Des Moines River delayed further financing. Only after additional land grants were made by Congress in July 1864 (the date of the UP's amended charter), and after authority was given to proceed 150 miles to Council Bluffs, was construction resumed. Oakes Ames's first subscription for the extension was $750,000 which he promptly paid.[58]

In the meantime, as lasting tribute to the pioneering spirit of his associate and good friend, Blair laid out a likely town on the line in May 1865, and named it Ames. Located exactly in the center of the state, Ames today is an attractive community of over 35,000 inhabitants, and well known as the seat of the finely equipped Iowa State University of Science and Technology. With a substantial land grant, this coeducational college was formally opened in 1869; it recently had about 14,000 students and 1,150 teachers.

General Dodge states that on 25 October 1865, he "received word from Mr. Durant that he had offered the Cedar Rapids Railroad $500,000 bonus if they would connect at Omaha in 18 months. They were now building a telegraph line from Boone along the projected line to Council Bluffs." [59] The CR & MR arrived within the time limit, but there is no record of such a big bonus having been paid. Durant probably had guessed that Oakes Ames, having just entered the CM, would never consent to the CM or UP paying big sums to his CR & MR. However, they did pay $75,000 and it is listed on the books as an actual cost of building the UP.[60]

From December 1865, construction proceeded steadily, straight along the high and gently rolling terrain from Boone through Jefferson and Carroll to Denison, which was reached the next spring. The

[57] Durant, *Papers*, 1–3–29–8.

[58] *Daily Republican*, Cedar Rapids, 9 May 1873; Poor, *Manual of the Railroads*, 1871, p. 414.

[59] Dodge, *Autobiography*, p. 434.

[60] *Wilson Rep.*, p. 637 (Rollin's list of UP's "actual cost").

great bridge (1,000 feet long, including its approaches) over the Des Moines River was crossed on April 26. At Denison, Blair and Ames wisely decided to turn southwestward down the extraordinarily level, broad flats of the Boyer River towards Omaha.

The Congressional Act of 3 July 1866 was "a sad blow" to the CR & MR, as Blair reported in November 1866:

The Union Pacific was now completed 325 miles west of Omaha . . . . When the Government passed the law allowing the Kansas City branch [U.P. Eastern Div.] to change its line, depriving the Atchison branch [Central Branch U.P.] from connecting with the U.P. main line, and making a line competing with the U.P., I had expended $2,000,000 on the C.R. & M.R. If the U.P. stopped, it would have been of little value. We might have discontinued further construction of the C.R. & M.R.[61]

Nevertheless, the Cedar Rapids and Missouri River entered Council Bluffs on Sunday, 17 January 1867, and on February 8 that goal of pioneers gaily welcomed its first passenger train from anywhere.[62] It came from Chicago, 491 miles away. From the brand new depot at Broadway and Sycamore (now 11th Street) a 2½-mile spur track was laid straight west to the bank of the river, whence Union Pacific steamers ferried cars across to the Omaha side near the foot of Davenport Street. In winter times, when river traffic was blocked, temporary pile bridges were thrown up, until the iron bridge was finished in 1872.[63]

The Union Pacific's official eastern terminus had been met at last.

Sioux City and Pacific [64]

The Sioux City and Pacific Railroad Company, organized on 1 August 1864, was the northernmost of the Pacific Railway branch lines that were considered by some historians as pesky to unravel. It was designed by the Acts of 1862 and 1864 to connect Sioux City with the main transcontinental road at, or somewhere east of, the "initial point" along the 100th meridian. U.S. Subsidy bonds and land grants were authorized for the same amount per mile ($16,000 and 12,800 acres) as for the UP, along with state grants, and no doubt the line was built partly for these compensations, as things worked out.

[61] Report of J.I. Blair, Pres. of "Sioux City Branch of UP" (Sioux City and Pacific R.R.), 20 Nov. 1866.
[62] Stennett, p. 40.   [63] See p. 412.
[64] Stennett, pp. 41–42, 70; *Wilson Rep.*, pp. 124–125 (testimony of Durant).

Actually, $1,628,000 U.S. bond subsidies were delivered for the 102 miles of main line between Sioux City and Fremont.[65] The cost of construction and equipment of $4,644,000 was financed jointly by John I. Blair, the first President; Oakes and Oliver Ames, Lambard, Glidden, Williams, Crocker, and others who were also Directors of the CR & MR. Oakes Ames's initial stock subscription in 1866 was for $210,000,[66] even though he was then moving into the UP in a big way. The construction company was the Sioux City Rail Road Contracting Co.

Grading was started in the spring of 1867 at the broad flats around Missouri Valley, a point 20 miles north of Council Bluffs on the CR & MR, and continued northward along the level Iowan bank of the Missouri for 75 miles to Sioux City, the tracks arriving there in February 1868. Next year the road was extended from Missouri Valley again, but this time westward to California Junction and over the river (by ferry in summer, by temporary bridges in winter—the current was very swift there) to the small town of Blair, Nebraska. Thence it connected in February 1869 at Fremont with both the UP and Blair's Fremont, Elkhorn and Missouri Valley Railroad. Its overall length, including 10 miles of branch lines, was 112 miles.

Congressional specifications were met, even if over a route hardly imagined by the authors of the charter. For the builders it was obviously better than crossing the river at Sioux City and then going southwestward. Traffic connections with the CR & MR and with Omaha were more lucrative, and land grant values were higher in Iowa than in Nebraska. But traffic was profitable only in its early non-competitive years, and later deficits had to be covered first by the sale of land grants and town lots, and then by both the CR & MR and CI & N through the C & N-W. In 1880, these companies purchased most of the Sioux City and Pacific stock from the individual stockholders.

Iowa Falls and Sioux City [67]

Finally, one more Iowan railroad of interest to the UP and the Ames family was the Iowa Falls and Sioux City Railroad Company. Another Blair undertaking, it was incorporated on 1 October 1867 (the UP had then reached Cheyenne) as an extension of the Dubuque

---

[65] Poor, *Manual*, 1871–1872, p. 494.

[66] *Daily Republican*, Cedar Rapids, 9 May 1873.

[67] *Poland Rep.* No. 82, "Credit Mobilier and Dubuque and Sioux City Railroad," pp. 1–53; Poor, *Manual*, 1871–1872, p. 497.

and Sioux City Railroad (Illinois Central) running parallel to and north of the C & N-W. It covered 184 miles from Iowa Falls via Fort Dodge to Sioux City, where in the summer of 1871 it connected with the Sioux City and Pacific just described, already tied to the UP in Fremont. Again, Blair was the first President, with Oakes Ames, Glidden, and Nickerson among the Directors.

In June 1868 Oakes Ames, joined by his three sons and a few other members of the family, subscribed for $950,000 of the stock of its construction company (Sioux City Contracting Company), the Blair family taking about $700,000.

Land grants of 688,563 acres were given by Congress as a subsidy.[68] Six or more members of Congress also were investors in the construction company stock, but in 1873 the Poland Committee of the Forty-Second Congress, in a separate report, cleared the financing without straining themselves.

The Race Ended: Thus it finally developed that the CR & MR (Chicago and North-Western, Iowa Division) won the four-pronged race across Iowa to connect the East with the UP, which was already operating to North Platte, 291 miles beyond Omaha. Not until 11 May 1869, the day after the far-away Golden Spike ceremony, did the closest rival, the Chicago, Rock Island and Pacific, reach the Council Bluffs goal. Third, in January 1870, came the Chicago, Burlington and Quincy. While the Sioux City and Pacific was second to reach the UP, its gap between Sioux City and the Iowa Falls and Sioux City Railroad was not closed until 1871, as we have seen, so it must be placed last. Of course, each of the new trunk lines brought ever-increasing transcontinental traffic to the completed UP.

The Fremont Elkhorn: Incidentally, although Blair's short Fremont, Elkhorn and Missouri Valley Railroad,[69] which had a land grant of about 100,000 acres from Nebraska, was not an Iowan Railroad, Oakes Ames was also a Director and one of its largest stockholders. It was organized in January 1869 to connect with the UP and the Sioux City and Pacific at Fremont. Thence it ran in a northwestwardly direction up the valley of the Elkhorn River 51 miles to Wisner, where its terminus remained until 1879. In the meantime, it was leased to the Sioux City and Pacific, and then purchased by the C & N-W.

[68] 15 Statutes at Large 39, 6 Mar. 1868.   [69] Stennett, p. 43.

STATISTICS OF OAKES AMES'S IOWAN RAILROADS, 1870 [a]

	Chicago, Iowa & Nebraska	Cedar Rapids & Mo. River	Sioux City & Pacific	Iowa Falls & Sioux City
Miles of Line [b]	82 [c]	272	112	184
Land grants (acres)		1,420,000	1,433,600 [d]	688,563
Common stock	$3,916,300	$ 6,850,400	$1,788,000	$4,625,000
Preferred stock	—	769,600	—	
Bonds	810,000	3,615,000	3,256,320 [e]	2,960,000
Total capital	$4,726,300	$11,235,000	$5,044,320	$7,585,000
Capital per mile	$ 58,350	$ 41,000	$ 45,028	$ 41,233
Cost per mile	$ 60,975		$ 43,250	$ 24,500 [f]
Gross earnings	$1,220,882	$ 1,865,167	$ 301,428	$ 140,672 [g]
Net earnings	$ 557,950		$ 111,528	
Leased to	C. & N.-W.	C. & N.-W.		Illinois Central
Rate of Lease (% of Gross Earnings)	47½ to 37½%	20% above $4,500 [h]		35%

a Poor, *Manual*, 1871–1872, pp. 414, 494–499.
b Main line, excluding branches and sidings.
c Including Clinton, Iowa, to east bank of Mississippi.
d 12,800 acres per mile; see p. 85.
e Of which one-half were U.S. subsidy bonds (Stennett, p. 42).
f *Poland Rep.*, p. 2.
g In operation to Fort Dodge, 49 miles, to 10 Oct. '70; thereafter the whole line.
h Originally $1,750 per mile, or $479,675.

Under the various leases outlined above, the stockholders received fixed dividends from the rentals paid by the lessors, but the stockholders thereupon relinquished actual control. Nevertheless, Oakes Ames's brother Oliver became a director of the C & N-W in 1877.

The Hastings and Dakota: The Hastings and Dakota Railroad also was not strictly an Iowan line. Starting at Hastings, Minnesota, on the Mississippi near St. Paul, it was designed to run 230 miles westward to Dakota Territory, with a land grant of 550,000 acres. In 1865, Oakes Ames invested $325,000 in the construction company. Among those on the Board with him five years later were Russell Sage, President, and L.P. Morton, both of New York. The road was operated by the Milwaukee and St. Paul Railway, of which Sage was Vice-President and Morton a Director.[70]

Conclusion: The important point of this Iowan sketch is to show that Oakes Ames was contemplating the coming of the Pacific Railway and sensing its route from Omaha up the great natural highway of the Platte River Valley years before he became a Congressman.

70 Poor, *Manual*, 1871–1872, p. 417; Johnson and Supple, p. 204, fn. 24.

Surely, at least one down-to-business reason for his final decision made early in 1865 to take on the faltering UP must have been the strong probability, at that time, that his Cedar Rapids and Missouri River road would win the race across Iowa, and via the best route, with all the ensuing business advantages of bringing exclusively to his Iowan railroads the early transcontinental traffic of the first railway to the Pacific. His foresightedness proved correct.

2. ABRAHAM LINCOLN—A PROMISE?

President Abraham Lincoln was, as has been emphasized, an ardent advocate of the Pacific railways. He was even willing that the Government *give* its bonds rather than go without the road. Yet the UP was in great danger of breaking down, the original promoters being unable to attract further capital. Chief Engineer Peter A. Dey had resigned in remonstrance to Durant's policies. Lincoln was about to commence his second term. The Civil War was obviously drawing to an end, and he had determined on a humane policy of reconciliation with the vanquished South.[71]

Now comes one of those good breaks to researchers of history where just a few recorded words may have important significance. On Friday, 20 January 1865, Mrs. Oakes Ames noted in her diary: *"Today Mr. Lincoln sent for Oakes to come to the White House. He went immediately after dinner and talked with the President until after midnight."* [72]

Even though the conversation that transpired will never be known, much can be guessed because of the date. At least Oakes Ames allegedly reported that in a conference about that time Lincoln had told him something like this: "Ames, you take hold of this. If the subsidies provided are not enough to build the road ask double and you shall have it. The road must be built, and you are the man to do it. Take hold of it yourself." And, he added pensively, in his typically humble way, "By building the Union Pacific, you will be the remembered man of your generation." [73]

It seems more than possible that on that night Oakes gave his word to Lincoln that he would try to rescue the Union Pacific from further misfortune by throwing in his own weight with Oliver's.[74] There is

[71] See p. 71.   [72] Winthrop Ames, p. 145. (The diary can no longer be found.)
[73] Ames Family, *Oakes Ames*, p. 6; Sabin, p. 130; Winthrop Ames, p. 145; see also p. 541.
[74] Ames Family, *Oakes Ames*, pp. 132–133 ("Oakes Ames and the Credit Mobilier," by his three sons, 9 Aug. 1880).

no recorded statement by Oakes which denies such a possibility. If indeed a fact, it could have been one of the most compelling reasons for his decision, especially in light of what was shortly to happen to the President. Oakes's word once given was good, come what may.

So, promise or just request, it must have been a fearful blow to the Ames brothers that on April 14, less than three months after this interview, President Abraham Lincoln was shot and died the next day. The UP lost its best friend in the high ranks of Government. Vice-President Andrew Johnson, who was to succeed Lincoln in the White House, was a highly controversial Southern Democrat, opposed to slavery and secession but jealous of Lincoln. Although it could not have been foreseen, Johnson, as President, showed little interest in the UP. Indeed, more than once, he deliberately retarded its progress. Lincoln's death alone might have stopped the Ameses, unless Oakes in fact had made a promise.

If the loss of Abraham Lincoln had been calamitous to the Ameses and to the UP, no adjective is left to describe the effect on the thinking American people of all the states, at last welded into one nation. This great unbroken Union, thrice by dint of blood and fire, was to become one of the leading world powers.

> ... *Great captains, with their guns and drums,*
> *Disturb our judgement for the hour;*
> *But at last silence comes;*
> *These are all gone, and, standing like a tower,*
> *Our children shall behold his fame,*
> *The kindly-earnest, brave, foreseeing man,*
> *Sagacious, patient, dreading praise, not blame,*
> *New birth of our new soil, the first American.*[75]

3. THE CIVIL WAR ENDED

Weeks, perhaps months, before Lee laid down his sword to Grant on 9 April 1865 at Appomattox Court House, it was judged that the War must soon end. Oakes and Oliver believed this, of course, before they determined to enter the UP. The cost of living had risen 69 per cent during the War to the highest level ever known till then. Oakes thought that economic conditions could hardly get any worse. Said he before Congress:

[75] James Russell Lowell, from *Ode Recited at the Commemoration of the Living and Dead Soldiers of Harvard University*, 21 July 1865.

The state of the country was exceedingly unfavorable to the prosecution of the work. Gold was one hundred and fifty; there was no market for the first mortgage bonds; and the government bonds, payable in currency, were of uncertain value and of difficult sale. . . . All materials were high, and all classes of labor scarce, and only to be obtained in limited quantities at extravagant prices.[76]

But with the War ended, the inflation could be expected to stop before long. There should be a long era of peace, reconstruction, and productive enterprise. Surely there would be a market for bonds, the backbone of railroad financing. There were even prospects of reward to venture capital. Actually, the cost of living started into a long, gradual deflation, declining 9 per cent by 1869 when the UP was finished, and 30 per cent to the depths of 1893, its receivership year.[77] At the beginning of the War there were 30,626 miles of railroad in operation in the nation. During hostilities only 3,282 miles were added, but during the eight years from the end of the War to 1873, while Oakes Ames was to be connected with the UP, he was to see railroads double to 66,171 miles.[78]

The Ameses' judgment proved correct. But great patience and effort would be needed.

4. THE CENTRAL PACIFIC COMING ON[79]

The Central Pacific was the first of the two railroads to be incorporated, and in spite of the far more difficult terrain to be encountered, wheels were set rolling on 10 November 1863, a year and a half ahead of the UP. The formality of groundbreaking took place on 8 January 1863 in Sacramento, at the end of the levee along Front Street where K Street meets the Sacramento River. Desperate for capital, staggered by rocketing costs, and hampered by scarcity of labor, all due largely to the War, "The Big Four" team of Huntington, Crocker, Hopkins, and Stanford, with Montague as Chief Engineer, though no more daring than the UP team, nevertheless had the advantages of being younger and much better coordinated.[80]

When they were hardest up for capital in 1864, Oakes Ames, interestingly enough, loaned them $800,000.

---

[76] Oakes Ames, 25 Feb. 1873; Ames Family, *Oakes Ames,* p. 112.

[77] U.S. Dept. of Labor, Bureau of Labor Statistics, Federal Reserve Bank of New York, 1938.

[78] U.S. Bureau of the Census, 1960, Series Q15, p. 427.

[79] See pp. 12–14.   [80] See p. 13.

The historic emigrant station of Clipper Gap at the 43rd milepost in the Sierras was reached in June 1865, a month before the first UP rail was laid. In September "end o'track" rested for the winter at Colfax (named for the Speaker of the House), while three regular trains a day huffed and puffed 55 miles to an elevation of 2,242 feet. Far different from the UP, the terminus was at the tidewater docks of a bustling town, while along the route traffic was waiting for service. Passenger rates were 10 cents a mile, freight rates 15 cents a ton per mile, all payable in gold. Gross revenues for 1865 were $405,592; construction expenses $3,200,000.[81]

Not even the Golden State, far less the East, had awakened yet to the reality that the snowbound Sierras were being scaled by an Iron Horse, which had been shipped around the Horn from the East Coast. The 1864 amendment had prohibited the CP from building further than 150 miles east of the state line.[82] To Oakes, early in 1865, there was no suspicion that still another change, the Act of July 1866,[83] would strike those "well-nigh fatal blows" to the UP, including permission for the CP to go as far east as it could before meeting the UP. To him, the feasibility of a Pacific Railway was merely being proven by Collis Huntington. His loan would be repaid. In any event, the incentive to meet the CP as far west as possible was quite apparent. A bigger railroad to operate, larger subsidies, and more lucrative construction profits were the prizes.

5. THE CONSTRUCTION COMPANY FORMED

It had taken a whole year for Durant to get his Credit Mobilier of America to function. The Ameses and other New England capitalists as well as the CP promoters knew enough about railroad financing to refuse to touch a road until it had a construction company.[84]

Until certain members of the Ames group became actual officers of the CM and the UP, and could get at the records, there was no way of their knowing that some of the philosophies of Durant were intolerable. Nor could they foresee that the UP would be led into a bitter internal quarrel which would nearly wreck it. Nor could they have sized up the treacherous character of a man like McComb. The Ameses already knew Bushnell and Lambard favorably, but they either never imagined the vastness of the difficulties to arise, or they believed the chief differences could be settled by reason or by the

[81] Sabin, p. 112.   [82] See p. 32.   [83] See p. 140.
[84] *Poland Rep.*, p. 77; *Wilson Rep.*, pp. 755–756; see also p. 50.

superior power of their own group. The fact stands that they were willing and ready to be sold by the salesmen. There could have been no other way of entering Durant's circles.

Be this as it may, it can be readily understood why the practical functioning of a corporation like the Credit Mobilier was a prerequisite to investment.

6. THE PRESSURE OF UNINVESTED CAPITAL

By 1865, the Shovel Works had accumulated earnings which hardly could have been imagined in 1844 when Oakes and Oliver Jr. first became partners. Now they possessed wealth far beyond the capital needs of the Shovel Works. Well could they ponder the words of Antonio of the *Merchant of Venice:*

> *I thank my fortune for it,*
> *My ventures are not in one bottom trusted,*
> *Nor to one place; nor is my whole estate*
> *Upon the fortune of the present year.*

The Boston *Traveller* Extra in a 14-page, finely printed booklet (price 30 cents) published the *Incomes of the Citizens of Boston and Other Cities and Towns in Massachusetts—1866* with this subheading: "As reported to Internal Revenue, published with concurrence of Revenue officers. Amounts for which actually assessed, and upon which required to pay tax, all deductions for exemptions, taxes, rent, losses, etc., having been made." Under the region "2nd District Easton," on page 14, appears this income information:

Ames, Oakes	$141,951
Ames, Oliver Jr.	147,118
Ames, Oliver 2d	24,497
Ames, Fred L.	25,450
Ames, Oakes A.	24,273

Oliver Ames Jr. paid an "excise tax" of $19,412.25 to the U.S. Internal Revenue in Mansfield, Massachusetts, for 1864. Of this sum, $19,396.80 was on "income." The rest was "$5.00 on 2 carriages, $2.00 on a gold watch, $4.00 on a pianoforte, and $4.45 on plate silver."

For that postwar year, 1866, the Federal Civil War tax on individuals' "annual gains, profits or income from any source whatsoever" was set at a 10 per cent flat rate.[85] Massachusetts long had had a tax on personal income in excess of $2,000 a year.

So Oakes and Oliver were now concerned with the quest not for treasure but for good investments. They were firm believers in the sound principle of a balanced portfolio—bonds for safety and income, and stocks for long term gain in principal and income—with action taken now and then to vary the proportion.

The common stocks and bonds of the new and growing railroad industry, especially in parts of the West, were just suited to the Ameses' resources, talents, and theories. To them, the large projects were the attractive ones. However, where each situation was to be managed, it was unwise to have too many companies to watch. On the other hand, it was not possible to buy a wide diversification of stocks which could be considered promising. In many ways, indeed, investment problems were different from what they are today.

So, not only did the Ames brothers have the capital in 1865 for a new risk like the Union Pacific—they were actually under pressure to find investments.

7. SUPERIOR MOTIVES

What did Oakes Ames himself say publicly about his altruistic motives? Following are about the only statements available. In November 1872, he sent a "card" to his constituents in which he said: "I have always regarded [my efforts to help the Union Pacific] as among the most creditable and patriotic acts of my life." [86] A month or so later, in a written communication to the Poland Committee, he reflected on his actions in a similar tone: "Those of us who were willing to aid this great enterprise were under the impression our acts were praiseworthy and patriotic. We certainly hoped we would make a profit, but we knew the risk was enormous." [87]

Later, however, in a spontaneous verbal reply to a loaded question by a member of the Wilson Committee, Oakes Ames seemed inclined to belittle his patriotism:

Question: Do you recollect having ever said that it was not the profits which you expected to derive from the construction of this road that

---

[85] Its maximum yield was $73 million in 1866, with 460,170 returns. Since 1862 the tax rate had been 10 per cent on income exceeding $5,000, and 5 per cent on income exceeding $600 but not exceeding $5,000. The income tax was abandoned in 1872.

[86] See p. 437.   [87] *Poland Rep.*, p. 16 (prepared by his lawyer).

influenced you, but that it was from a motive of patriotism that you threw yourself into the field to engineer and carry out this enterprise?

Ames: I never thought that, and I do not think *I* ever said it. Did you ever *hear me?*

Question: No, sir; I ask you the question.

Ames: I do not think I ever said it.[88]

But still later, in his speech of defense prepared by his lawyer and read on 25 February 1873 before the House of Representatives (his last and perhaps first speech in Congress), appear these statements:

It [the enabling Act] was universally esteemed not only a measure of sound policy, but a scheme appealing to the patriotism and loyalty of the capitalists of the United States, as the instrument whereby a future separation of the Pacific from the Atlantic States would be rendered forever impossible.[89]

To undertake the construction of a railroad, at any price, for a distance of nearly seven hundred miles in a desert and unexplored country, its line crossing three mountain ranges at the highest elevation yet attempted on this continent, extending through a country swarming with hostile Indians, by whom locating engineers and conductors of construction trains were repeatedly killed and scalped at their work; upon a route destitute of water, except as supplied by water-trains, hauled from one to one hundred and fifty miles, to thousands of men and animals engaged in construction; the immense mass of material, iron, ties, lumber, timber, provisions, and supplies necessary to be transported from five hundred to fifteen hundred miles,—I admit might well, in the light of subsequent history and the mutations of opinion, be regarded as the freak of a madman, if it did not challenge the recognition of a higher motive, namely, the desire to connect my name conspicuously with the greatest public work of the present century.[90]

As far as I am pecuniarily concerned, it would have been better that I had never heard of the Union Pacific Railroad.[91]

Horace Clark, then President of the UP and Director of the New York Central, said to a Congressional Committee in 1873:

I would not have put a dollar in the enterprise, because it occurred to me that it was a wild waste of money to think of doing such a thing. These men, however, determined to do it. There was a spirit of adven-

---

[88] *Wilson Rep.*, p. 29. (His lawyer had written it for him).
[89] Ames Family, *Oakes Ames*, p. 109.   [90] *Ibid.*, p. 113.   [91] *Ibid.*, p. 121.

ture about it, of loyalty and courage, such as I have never known in the history of railroad enterprises.[92]

America was in the midst of its great westward movement. Such an opportunity for a man to work out his own destiny and take his chances in his own way rarely has been equalled. "The Union Pacific project was thoroughly saturated and fairly dripping with the elements of adventure and romance." [93] Could it not have been that Oakes and Oliver, after nearly a lifetime spent at making hand tools in a provincial New England town, were also fired by the daring and stimulation of freely taking a leading part in this great new national development? Would not these words by Bishop Charles Brent (1862–1929) come close to fitting Oakes?

The one safe place for strength is in peril, swinging between risk and opportunity. . . . It is more reasonable to be in peril than in security, if the best things be at hair's-breadth beyond the peril. Everything worth having is found only at the yonder side of a risk. . . . We can live this life but once and it is only common sense to live it for all it is worth, and in a way that would count even if death were to close accounts forever. If it is a thing of value and of power, let us test its capacity to the breaking point and to the finish.[94]

[92] *Wilson Rep.*, p. 404.
[93] Davis, p. 137. Prof. Davis is the original author of this favorite sentence of UP historians.
[94] *A Bishop Brent Day-Book:* "A Day-Book Chosen from the Writings of Charles Henry Brent," Day 1; published by the Forward Movement of the Episcopal Church, Cincinnati, Ohio, 1943.

4

Building the Road: A Chronology

1865

Review of the Hoxie Contract—UP Directors Legalize Its Assignment to the Credit Mobilier—Muddles Around Omaha—Land Muddles, Too —Public Stock Subscription Fails Again—New York Bankers Make a Loan—New England to the Rescue—The Breach Begins—Surveys and Engineering—Construction and Equipment—Review of 1865

A. Review of the Hoxie Contract

It will be recalled that in October 1864 Durant caused Hoxie to assign his illegal construction contract to the partnership pool, in which the Doctor personally had a three-eighths interest, and that the pool thereupon agreed to subscribe $1,600,000 (only 25 per cent paid up) to take over the contract. When much of the unpaid balance was not forthcoming, Durant transferred the contract to the CM, whereby the partners were relieved of personal liability beyond the capital paid in. Thereupon they put up the remaining $1,200,000 as final payments on 16,000 shares of CM stock, par $100. The contract extending to 100° West continued to be known as "the Hoxie contract," even though the CM in reality had become the possessor. It was to develop that this would be the only contract the CM ever was to have.

B. UP Directors Legalize Its Assignment to the Credit Mobilier

On 6 April 1865, obviously at the request of Durant, the UP Directors unanimously voted to ratify the March 15th transfer of the

97

Hoxie contract to the CM. The principal UP Directors and members of the Executive Committee at the time were Dix, Durant, Bushnell, Davis, Lambard, and Opdyke. Other Directors were J.J. Cisco, H.S. McComb, J.E. Henry, Charles Tuttle, Brigham Young, Pickering Clark, Ebenezer Cook, E.H. Rosekrans, and J.F. Tracy. The Government Directors were Springer Harbaugh, J.L. Williams, T.J. Carter, C.T. Sherman, and George Ashmun—twenty directors in all.[1] "Their vote validated the contract as made between the CM and UP, and freed it from any taint or vice impairing its efficacy," according to a decision of the Massachusetts Supreme Court in a suit brought before it some years later.[2] In other words, if there had been fraud, the UP Directors had condoned it. However, Sidney Bartlett, UP General Counsel at the time of the suit, held the view that the vote was passed by the Directors in ignorance of the real facts.[3]

C. Muddles Around Omaha

Peter Dey had located the UP line out of Omaha in a consistently westward direction, up 264 feet over the plateau of rolling hills, and then down 147 feet to the level Platte Valley at the Elkhorn River, a distance of 21 miles. Durant had given his full approval. At first they agreed that the directness of the route adequately compensated for maximum grades of 66 feet per mile ascending westward and 80 feet ascending eastward, which could be reduced later. Dey's map was approved by President Lincoln on 4 November 1864.

Nevertheless, the very next month Durant, probably at the initiative of Silas Seymour, his right-hand man and consulting engineer, suddenly called off the original grading work and commenced building southward from Dey's summit (4 miles from the start in Omaha), down Mud Creek, and northwestward up the western Papillion River to rejoin Dey's line at a point about 16 miles from Omaha. *The change would add 9 miles of line to the original 13.*[4] From an engineer's point of view, this so-called "ox-bow" route probably was warranted. The over-all cost of the Doctor's eleventh hour decision would be $100,000 in abandoned grading work, plus a cash layout of at least $400,000 for extra construction. Nothing was then put in writing to the effect that the 9 additional miles would bring to the

---

[1] Union Pacific, *Official Register.*   [2] Records of UP Historical Museum.
[3] *Ibid.*
[4] Seymour's report to Durant, 21 Dec. 1864, and accompanying "Sketch"; see Profile, Illus., Group 3.

UP $144,000 additional subsidy bonds and 115,200 extra acres of land grants (not to mention the issue of $144,000 company bonds); the estimated profit under the Hoxie contract would rise by at least $180,000, as the work was easier.

The only step necessary would be to get the consent of the Government. Unlike Lincoln, President Andrew Johnson was wary of Pacific Railway affairs, particularly those of the Union Pacific.

On 12 May 1865, General Dix wrote the President for a prompt approval of the change, expecting no difficulty. He pointed out that $250,000 had been spent on the new ox-bow line already, and that costs were mounting at a rate of $2,500 a day. But the matter became involved "through the opposition of some parties interested in the terminus of the road." meaning Omaha, and Government action was delayed.[5]

Durant had been committed to build from the river by Lincoln's "lost" order of 17 November 1863 and second order of 7 March 1864.[6] He also had been obligated by his representations to the citizens of Omaha and Council Bluffs, by his acceptance of their donations of land for rights of way and other purposes, and by substantial investments that they had made in good faith.[7] He had broken ground in Omaha and had commenced grading there. The route had been approved by the UP Directors, and the inspectors had expressed their acceptance. Certainly Durant himself had recommended it.

Late in 1864 he threatened to radically change the route to Bellevue, which meant crossing the Missouri near this small town 9 miles south of the ferry, leaving Omaha only on a spur. On 4 February 1865, he tried to pacify the thoroughly alarmed citizens of Omaha by stating: "The line has been changed to avoid heavy grades, not with the intention of interfering with the terminus." [8] On 27 May 1865, he telegraphed D.H. Ainsworth, who had succeeded Dey as UP engineer in charge of surveys: "Make surveys immediately from river at Bellevue to nearest point on line and report probable cost of right of way. Also best location for shops at Bellevue or Fremont." [9]

Dodge noted that this dispatch was "simply to threaten and scare Omaha. I was overwhelmed with telegrams and protests from Council Bluffs and Omaha." [10] Perhaps Durant thought he thus could cause them to pressure the Government for quick acceptance of his ox-bow route, and wheedle them into larger contributions as well. For the

5 *Durant Rep.*, 10 Apr. 1866, p. 13.   6 See pp. 26–27.
7 Records of UP Historical Museum.   8 *Ibid.*   9 *Ibid.*
10 Dodge, *Autobiography*, p. 509.

UP was running out of cash in a desperate way. J.E. Henry wrote him from Omaha: "Our credit is so bad here that we cannot get Currency on sight drafts . . . to close up our pay Rolls for May and June." [11]

On June 6 General Dodge, worrying about his friends in Council Bluffs, wired the Doctor the following warning:

Your plan won't work. If you attempt it the government will stop you on the grounds of its decision. If you build on Mud Creek line, do so from Omaha. With iron down it will be more likely to be accepted if it goes to Congress, and if you build from Bellevue you will lose the ablest support the road has in the West. One thing certain, Government, Congress and the people will demand that over 40 miles west of Omaha be built before December first from the initial point as fixed by President Lincoln. Have written you.[12]

To this Durant flatly answered on June 9:

The plan will be carried out or the works abandoned . . . This is too important an enterprise to be controlled by local interest. The road can be built by the Kansas line if in no other way. No road through Iowa will terminate at Omaha.[13]

Durant had a one-third interest in the construction profits of this "Kansas line," and had loaned them between $300,000 and $400,-000.[14] Under Section 12 of the Act of 1864 the Kansas Pacific had the right to build, without subsidy, beyond 100° West and meet the CP, if it reached that point at a time when the UP "shall not be proceeding in good faith to build their railroad through the Territories."

At another time he threatened to cross the Missouri some 22 miles north of Omaha, perhaps by connecting with Oakes Ames's Cedar Rapids and Missouri River, if they decided to join the UP at Fremont instead of Omaha,[15] in spite of his close association with Dix and the latter's directorship in the rival Chicago and Rock Island.

In the meantime, Dey had written his friend Dodge as follows:

. . . Mr. Durant now has the whole thing in his hands, but is managing it as he has everything else. . . . A good deal spread and a good deal

---

[11] Durant, *Papers*, 1–1–49–14, 8 July 1865.   [12] Dodge, *Autobiography*, p. 511.

[13] *Ibid*. (The "Kansas line" is the Kansas Pacific group, aiming to build from Kansas City to the 100th meridian. Previously this railroad was the Union Pacific Eastern Division, and before that the Leavenworth, Pawnee & Western.)

[14] *Wilson Rep*., p. 516 (testimony of Durant).

[15] Dodge, *Autobiography*, p. 501; see also p. 84.

do nothing. . . . I am afraid that Blair, of the Northern road, who is a systematic and persevering sort of man will use him as he chooses. . . . Doctor needs common sense more than anything else and I have been so completely disgusted with his various wild ideas, that I have been disposed repeatedly to abandon the whole thing. I hate to do it as there is a great future in this thing, if judiciously and prudently managed. . . . We should have had all our ties and the grading under contract to Loup Fork before this. . . . Cannot advise as to investment, as the Doctor may want to connect tomorrow with the route through Texas.[16]

Even Seymour was puzzled by the Doctor's connivings. But he was not one to pass up a chance for a smart deal. In June he wrote him the following letter:

I feel somewhat in doubt as to your wishes respecting a change of termination—Am therefore to some extent embarrassed in my advice to Col. Simpson, who seems inclined to adopt my views—If you would really prefer that a change from Omaha to Bellevue should result from his report to the Secretary . . . I would like you to telegraph me to that effect immediately . . . substituting Chicago for Omaha and St. Louis for Bellevue (and Hoxie for Simpson), in any communication you may make . . . and no one shall know. . . . I feel anxious to serve you, but in order to do so intelligently and effectively you must keep me posted fully. . . . A great deal of money can be made at Bellevue if some things can be known in advance.[17]

Durant's reply, if any, is not to be found among his papers.

Upon the advice of the Honorable James Harlan (former Senator from Iowa and new Secretary of the Interior), Lieutenant Colonel James H. Simpson of the U.S. Engineer Corps was appointed to make a personal, independent examination and report of the situation.

The Doctor's real position can be described best by the following letter which he wrote to Harlan at Washington:

CONFIDENTIAL

New York   June 7, 1865

Dear Sir:

Thanks for the promptness displayed in procuring the appointment of a Government Engineer to examine the line in Nebraska.

There is no reason why they should not now be hurried to a definite settlement. The Company are however much Embarrassed by even the

---

[16] *Ibid.* The letter is dated Jan. 21, probably 1865. See also Perkins, p. 135.

[17] Durant, *Papers*, 1–3–24–17. No date shown.

CARL A. RUDISILL LIBRARY
LENOIR RHYNE COLLEGE

suspicion of delay, they are under obligation for a large amount that comes due within four months and relied upon completing 40 miles within that time. For them to go to protest would ruin the whole enterprise. . . . There is only about three months in the year that they can get Iron up the Missouri. . . . The Iron shipped for Omaha has been ordered to be landed at Belleview, this is absolutely necessary to save the Co, in case the old line is adopted for by no other means can they sure have road enough completed to save their Credit. An independent Company will take the Road from Belleview to the point of Junction off our hands. The only thing now to be decided is the Depot buildings, which must be built at once. . . . All we want is to act in concert with the Gov't and have the road built as rapidly as is possible. Tell us what you want us to do, and we will either do it or give you a good reason why it is not done.

Every day now is worth a week to us two months hence.[18]

Durant was being pressed further by Henry for payroll money and was desperate for an answer by the President. On September 19 he wrote another "private" letter to Harlan, in which he pleaded:

. . . The Company . . . cannot use their credit . . . and meet their payments with a controversy [going on] which is so little understood and which the company do not feel at liberty to explain and consequently are obliged to submit to all sorts of slander and the imputation of not prosecuting the work . . .[19]

Unfortunately, Colonel Simpson could not get to Omaha until July 4, and his reserved affirmative report to Secretary Harlan was not turned in until September 18. Harlan advised the President on September 23 that "the proposed line down the Missouri Valley and across the river bluff to Mud Creek . . . is 15% better than any other route that can be obtained . . . from the Company." The President endorsed Harlan's approval of such a route "on the express condition that the Company . . . make ruling grades [all the way between Omaha and the Elkhorn River], ascending westward and eastward, of 30 feet to the mile, as they propose." [20]

During the long delay Durant had taken the bold chance of going his own way. His road was retained and used much as built until 1908. That year Edward H. Harriman, then Chairman of the Executive Committee, opened the "Lane Cut-Off," a 12-mile, double-

---

[18] *Ibid.*, 1–1–42–47.   [19] *Ibid.*, 1–1–42–48.
[20] *Durant Rep.*, 10 Apr. 1866, Appendix D, pp. 63–64.

tracked, high-speed, main line—straight westward over the hills, almost identically along the route Dey had originally recommended —and saved the 9 miles.[21]

General Dodge, not yet with the UP, years later summed it up this way:

> The main argument for adding nine miles of distance in thirteen miles of road was that it eliminated the 80 and 66 foot grades of the direct line. If this had been done there would have been some argument for the change, but they only eliminated the grades from the Omaha summit west, while it took three miles of 60 and 66 foot grades from the Missouri River to reach this summit, and coming east the Elkhorn summit was an 80-foot grade, so by the change and addition of nine miles they made no reductions in the original maximum grades. . . . It was Mr. Dey's intention that when traffic demanded the original short line grades would be reduced to whatever maximum grade the road should finally adopt.
>
> After a long contest and many reports, the Government provided that the change should only be made if the Omaha and Elkhorn grades were eliminated, the first by a line running south from Omaha two miles down the Missouri Valley and cutting through the bluffs to Muddy Creek, giving a 35-foot maximum grade; and the Elkhorn by additional cutting and filling without changing the line; but this was never done. The company paid no attention to the decision but built on the changed line, letting the grades at Omaha and Elkhorn stand, and the Government commissioners accepted the road, ignoring the Government's conditions for the change, and bonds were issued upon it, although it was a direct violation of the Government order.[22]

The UP's first construction under Durant had been confused and controversial. The delay of many months was to have a critical effect on meeting the Central Pacific.

D. Land Muddles, Too

As stated, Durant had obtained city donations to the UP of extensive areas of blocks and lots within the limits of Omaha, and large acreages in adjoining counties. Included were 4,360 acres, mostly in Douglas County, valued at the time of conveyance at between

[21] Records of UP Historical Museum: *The Lane Cut-Off of the Union Pacific Railroad,* by Wm. W. Kratville, Univ. of Omaha, 1957. (When comparing present UP mileage with old, allowance must be made for the 9-mile difference.)

[22] Dodge, *How We Built the Union Pacific,* pp. 13–14, 63–64.

$200,000 and $300,000. They were taken in the name of "T.C. Durant, Trustee," without any language describing the beneficiary of the trust. This was for convenience when the property was to be re-conveyed to the UP, he claimed, and they were not subject to mortgages. Later, Durant denied the trust was for the benefit of the UP. A suit was brought against him which was carried to the U.S. Supreme Court, and the property was recovered by the UP.[23]

He also acquired in his name as trustee 951 acres in the vicinity of Council Bluffs. The UP law department had to sue Durant to secure title on 7 May 1874. These were valuable lands, but they had been frittered away by neglect and by tax sales until it became doubtful if they were worth recovering.[24]

The Doctor was not one to skip any interesting details. He gained some valuable Federal subsidies and land grants in the city when he telegraphed his younger brother, W.F. Durant, at Omaha on 8 December 1865: "You can make temporary grade to initial point. This must be included in first 40 miles." [25] While ground had been broken near the ferry landing at Davenport and 7th Street, the theoretical "initial point" was fixed two miles further north, a dead end later obliterated by Carter Lake.[26]

E. Public Stock Subscription Fails Again

With the capital all spent, Durant put on another campaign in the spring of 1865 to entice the public to subscribe to UP stock at $100 a share. Expensive advertisements announced the re-opening of the books in the principal cities of the Union. The results were more disheartening than ever. Said a Government Director: "I believe that not a dollar was subscribed. We considered, therefore, that the idea of building the road by means of subscription of stock was a failure." [27]

F. New York Bankers Make a Loan

The first large loan of money from the outside was obtained by Durant in May 1865. Secretary Harlan had introduced him to John Pondir of New York, "a man of voluble grievances and considerable

---

[23] Records of UP Historical Museum.   [24] *Ibid.*   [25] *Ibid.*   [26] See p. 26.
[27] *Wilson Rep.,* p. 664 (testimony of Charles T. Sherman, a cousin of the General).

aplomb," but a resourceful money broker.[28] The same day Pondir received a letter from Salmon P. Chase, then Chief Justice of the U.S. Supreme Court, who, Pondir claimed, "urged him to take hold of the road, to facilitate it with some money to build it." Pondir testified verbosely in 1887 that within several days he made the UP a short term loan of $1,000,000 (arranged by the Bank of Commerce) and secured by scrip on the still-unissued Government 6 per cent currency bonds, marked down to 90.[29] Oliver Ames said: "For a year or two . . . we paid 19% for money in New York . . . we were deeply in debt and very much embarrassed." [30] Presumably the discount on the Pondir note also came to about 19 per cent per annum.

G. *New England to the Rescue*

Certainly it was to have been expected that Durant and Cornelius Bushnell would be doing everything possible, in the face of this crisis, to get the financial backing of Congressman Oakes Ames. Durant later testified that he thought he had first met him in Washington in the fall of 1863.[31] They shrewdly guessed that Oliver would go along with his brother, and that the Ames prestige with other New England capitalists would attract enough working capital to set the wheels rolling before it was too late. As Bushnell himself put it later:

We had gone on one year and had done our best. . . . We came to Mr. Ames and got him to take a large amount of the stock . . . but we soon used up all the money that he put in. We then got Mr. Ames to intercede with his friends, and he got in Oliver Ames . . . and various other parties. . . . By the superhuman efforts almost of Mr. Ames with all his friends we got the capital stock that was finally paid in up to two and a half millions, and went through 1865 and 1866, and carried the road out to the one hundredth meridian.[32]

Durant must have been bitterly disappointed thus to be forced to give up any part of his three-eighths interest, particularly to New England financiers who, no doubt, would inject a bit of puritan conservatism into the management.

Oakes testified in writing that "My connection with the road began by a subscription to the CM in August 1865. My determination to do

---

[28] Sabin, pp. 91–94.
[29] U.S. Pacific Railway Commission, p. 437 (testimony of Pondir).
[30] *Wilson Rep.*, p. 252.   [31] *Ibid.*, p. 88.   [32] *Ibid.*, p. 40.

so, of course, preceded that some short time." [33] While he did not appear as a stockholder of record until 18 May 1866, with 900 shares,[34] in fact he had a joint interest in Oliver's 2,000 shares showing on the first subscription list of the CM as of 15 March 1865.[35] The actual shares, however, were not issued until some months later.

Whatever the details, it is likely that within a matter of months or even weeks after the end of the Civil War and Lincoln's death the two had decided to make the plunge.

Interesting details of just how and when Oakes made some of his first contributions to the Credit Mobilier are shown by the following correspondence:

Mr. Thos. C. Durant   *N. Easton   July 17, 1865*
Dear Sir

I have paid Mr. Lambard's two drafts on you amounting to 30,000$ Mr. John Bertram of Salem will take 25,000. in the Credit Mobilier for building the Pacific Rail Road. and I can get some more taken

When will you send the notes of the Pacific Rail Road signed by Gen Dix & Mr. Cisco to go with the bonds I took with me & when will you want the balance of the money. Mr. Lambard is away I expect him back tomorrow.

I spoke to Mr Dillon when in N.York about Mr Chapman & himself going out & over the road and seeing for themselves how matters were progressing and give such advice & instructions as they might think best in connection with Mr Henry

Mr. Chapman & Dillon will go if you approve & the company pay expenses I think it would be a good thing and strengthen the faith of our stockholders. What say to it

Yours truly

Oakes Ames

July 18th I have recd Note of the Co July 17th 4 mos for $40,000 Mr Lambard has not returned yet.[36]

In the following letter, Oakes first raised the question as to what degree of interest and control Durant was willing he should take at this time:

T. C. Durant Esq.   *N. Easton   July 22d 1865*
Dear Sir

I enclose you herewith the balance due on Note of Pacific R.R. Co. July 18 4 mos for 40.000—as per statement below. Say my check on Bank

[33] *Poland Rep.*, p. 19.   [34] *Wilson Rep.*, p. 155.
[35] *Ibid.*, pp. 160, 266 (testimony of Oliver Ames).
[36] Durant, *Papers*, 1–3–28–24 (original ms.).

of Commerce July 22 for Seventy Six Hundred and Fifty Six Dollars—
I have got Mr Bates the President of the Bank of Commerce to agree
to take either 50 or 100.000 of the C. Mobilier stock but he will not be
ready to pay for some two or three weeks. I am sorry you are so short
of money how is it—how many shares are there to be taken up. how
many may I dispose of if I can. I understand that we [have] the right
to take shares for the amount advanced on these bonds and to give the
bonds up—I expect Mr Blair will be in N.York on Monday & hope
you will get 85.000$ out of him as one share. Mr. Lambard is away
from here now keep your road all straight Shall I place some more of
these bonds for you at the same rate of these

Yours Truly
Oakes Ames [37]

Thos. C. Durant Esq.   *Boston   July 29th, 1865*
Dear Sir

I have yours of yesterdays date & have also seen Mr Williams I have
also recd the certificates for first Mortgage bonds. I am hard at work
to get stock taken in the Credit—Mr Nickerson thinks he will give us
25.000 $ Monday or Tuesday for his stock—I have got Mr Alley to agree
to take 50.m in our Company & will I think pay a part of it next week—
I am to meet Mr. Hooper on Monday & hope to get him to take 100.m
of the stock next week—I am in hopes to be able to write you Monday
or Tuesday that we have got some money for you on stock. I shall expect
that I have the privelege of selling off the stock—I want it in strong
hands & in the hands of men of character and standing and all the stock
not paid up to 85 per cent should be so placed shall I do it if I can.
Alley and Hooper are members of congress and will be a power on our
side if we do right ourselves Lambard is away—I am very short of money.
Mansfield is sending large amounts of Cotton & draws on Butler at sight
& it takes about 30 days to get the money for the cotton.

I have had to raise & pay nearly 600.000 this week and am all used
up. Will see what I can do for you the first of the week

Yours Truly
Oakes Ames [38]

Thos C Durant Esq.   *Boston   Sept 11th 1865*
Dear Sir

. . . How are you situated as to funds. Shall you raise what you can on
your bonds before calling in the other 15 per cent—how much more
stock is there to be issued and can I have $ 50.000 for my self—if I want
it soon.

---

[37] *Ibid.*, 1–3–28–27 (original ms.).   [38] *Ibid.*, 1–3–28–29 (original ms.).

How is the track laying progressing you must push it with all the force you can or you will not get the sixty miles done this year

Yours Truly

Oakes Ames [39]

Next, Oakes first recommended that the capital of the CM be increased, and that Blair be taken in. But Blair never came in:

T. C Durant Esq   *Boston   Sept 15th 1865*
Dear Sir
. . . I think you should increase the capital to 2½ or 3 millions and get the stock taken by Mr Blair and others. and not be so short of money. I will try to get some of those notes discounted if possible for you in course of a week. I am sorry to hear that you are coming short of ties. it is bad for us and will be against us in Congress next winter

Yours Truly

Oakes Ames [40]

Thos C. Durant Esq.   *Boston   Sept 18 1865*
Dear Sir
Yours of the 16th advising that you had made two drafts on me. one for 10.000 & one for 25.000—& also saying that you should draw on me to-day for 40.000—I don't see how I am to pay these drafts. I have accepted the two first & will try to provide for them. but don't see how I can manage the other. I have not recd the money for Gilberts stock and may not before next week—I am in advance to you on the notes in my hands 15.000. I have not been able to get them discounted. If I could get them discounted I could meet the drafts. but the notes are not known here and they are too large for our banks to discount beside all that we have so many other matters that absorb all our means that we are very poor

You better have the capital increased to 2½ millions or even three millions than to be so cramped for money

Mr. Blair has been on here and I expect to be in N.York next Thursday. in relation to our Iowa road extension and will then see you

Yours Truly

Oakes Ames [41]

Hon. Oakes Ames,
Boston   *Sept 18th, 1865*
Dear Sir:
I have drawn to-day for forty thousand at sight upon you which I will have credited you on stock or on the notes of the UPRR Co you

[39] *Ibid.,* 1–3–28–30 (original ms.).   [40] *Ibid.,* 1–3–28–22 (original ms.).
[41] *Ibid.,* 1–3–28–20 (original ms.).

have. If on stock you will want I suppose more than you have certificates for . . . I do not think it advisable to wait for a party now, as we need money and it is hardly fair to call on others. . . . If you gentlemen in Boston advise it we can increase the stock as you suggest to 2¼ or 2½ millions. . . . I think the sixty miles can be completed this year by prompt action. . . .

Thos. C. Durant [42]

Evidently, a corrected stockholders list as of March 15 was being made up belatedly:

Hon. Oakes Ames,
Boston   *Sept 27, 1865*
Dear Sir

I telegraph you today for a statement of your account as it is desirable to have the entries made on the *book* as soon as practicable. When I drew the last $ 10,000 I was under the impression that it just about used up the paper you had drawn leaving the 25m stock to be paid for . . . .

The work appears to be progressing rapidly but notwithstanding we have the assurances of Mr. Seymour that the prospect is fair for completing 60 miles this fall I am not over-sanguine about it.

Yours,
T.C. Durant [43]

Hon Oakes Ames
Boston   *Nov. 10, 1865*
Dear Sir

I have your favor of yesterday. . . . As to the $50,000 note it is the first I knew of its belonging to you. The arrangement was made with Mr Lambard who had the right to take 100m C.M. stock. When the first note became due he notified the Company that he would require stock in payment of the second one. . . . The track has been laid for several days past at the rate of ¾ of a mile per day. . . . I hope you will be able to place the stock as you propose.

Respectfully yours,
T.C. Durant [44]

Oliver S. Chapman (1811–1877) of Canton, Massachusetts, who was a close friend of the Ames family, and must have been also of John Duff's, now comes in:

Thos. C. Durant Esq.   *Boston   June 14 1865*
Enclosed you will find my Draft for Twenty one thousand two hundred & fifty Dolls., for which you will send me a scrip certificate of Credit

---

[42] Records of UP Historical Museum.   [43] *Ibid.*   [44] *Ibid.*

Mobilier of America Stock for Twenty five thousand Dolls, (being eighty five percent paid) in the name of Oliver S. Chapman. I hope to dispose of the ballance of the Fifty thousand in a few days. Please acknowledge receipt of this and also what progress the great Union Pacific R.R. is making, any thing relating to your operations will be interesting and acceptable and I shall be on hand whenever you require my services

Yours Truly
John Duff

P.S. Mr. Chapman is an old contractor and a first rate man, in all respects

JD [45]

J.E. Henry Esq.—Omaha   *Sept 21, 1865*
Dear Sir:

   Messrs. Ames & Chapman who are largely interested in the Credit Mobilier and in the Union Pacific Rail Road Company visit Omaha for the purpose of looking over the line and investigating affairs generally. You will please show them anything pertinent to the work . . . and advise with them . . .

Yours Respectfully
Thos. C. Durant [46]

Wm. F. Glidden	Glidden & Williams
J.M.S. Williams	California Packet Office
John A. Glidden	114 State Street
John M. Glidden	Boston

H C Crane Esq   *Oct 16 1865*
UPRR
New York
Dear Sir
. . . Am disappointed at you not giving figures showing why or how you are in so much need of money. The memo I took show Drafts to come in about $38,000

To pay Notes 16	$14862.15—17	$ 6,559.98	say	22,000
				60,000
You had on hand new $10,000—say	8,000			
Rec'd from Mr. Dillon	10,000			
" " " Hazard	15,000			
Sent you from Mr. Ames	20,000			
New from Mr. Duff	10,000			63,000

[45] Durant, *Papers*, 1–3–39–38 (original ms.).   [46] Records of UP Historical Museum.

Making $3,000 more than you got & I suppose to be needed & therefore wait yr explanation & enclose herewith

Yours very truly

Glidden & Williams

JMSW [47]

The Hazard Family: Among the important early newcomers to UP affairs from New England were the Hazard family of Peacedale, Rhode Island. Here, 28 miles south of Providence, and near the entrance to Narragansett Bay, Rowland Hazard Sr. set up a woolen mill in 1802, almost at the same time that Oliver Ames Sr. settled in North Easton with his Shovel Works. He named the community "Peacedale" after his wife, Mary Peace. About 1819 his sons Rowland Gibson and Isaac Peace, now in their early manhood, became associated with him and there helped to carry on the woolen industry for over 50 years.

The Honorable Rowland Gibson Hazard, the son (1801–1888), was a Free Soiler and later a Republican, and took part in the convention which nominated Abraham Lincoln in 1860. He was a member of the Rhode Island House of Representatives in 1851–1852, 1854–1855, and 1880–1881 and a member of the State Senate in 1866–1867. Urged to take part in the UP by his good friend, Oakes Ames, he was on the first CM stockholder list of 15 March 1865 with 500 shares, while his elder but inactive brother Isaac took 250 shares. In 1866 he loaned $404,000 to the UP, and smaller sums in later years, all of which were repaid with interest. Adding to their subscriptions as more capital was needed by the construction company, he and Isaac had bought a total of 1,990 shares by late 1868, almost exactly the same amount that Oakes held. They received their full share of the allotment of profits on the investment. Rowland G. Hazard at once became an intrepid opponent of Durant. When the latter was deposed in May 1867, he became a member of the CM Board and the Executive Committee and was so re-elected in 1868 and again in 1870. He served on the UP Board from 25 May 1869 until 8 March 1871, but was never one of the Seven Trustees. He was a courageous and vindictive litigant, at times suing Dillon and McComb, and did not hesitate to appeal to the U.S. Supreme Court. Later, Jay Gould also found him to be a formidable antagonist. These Gould-Hazard suits cost the UP $110,500. Largely retired after 1866, he left the Peacedale business to his two sons, and he spent much of his time at study, writing, travel,

[47] Durant, *Papers*, 1–1–22–14 (original ms.).

STOCKHOLDERS OF CREDIT MOBILIER AS OF 15 MARCH 1865 [a]

20,000 Shares of $100 par, Fully Paid

AMES GROUP (14) (All new except Lambard)		DURANT GROUP (8)		Change Since 7 Oct. '64 [d]
Oakes & Oliver Ames (joint)	2,000	Durant, T. C.	6,000	——
Lambard, C. A.	1,000 [b]	Bushnell, C. S.	2,000	− 2,000
Duff, John	1,000	Gray, H. W.	2,000	——
Glidden, W. T.	500	Gray, G. G.	1,100	+ 1,100
Williams, J. M. S.	500	Holladay, Benj.	500	+ 500
Hooper, Samuel & Co.	500	McComb, H. S.	250	− 750
Dillon, Sidney	500	Davis, G. T. M.	25	+ 25 [e]
Bates, B. E.	500	Train, G. P.	25	+ 25 [e]
Hazard, R. G.	500	Total	11,900	4,100 [f]
Hazard, I. P.	250			
Nickerson, Fred	250	GRAND TOTAL	20,000	+ 4,000
Nickerson, Joseph	250	(22 names)		
Chapman, O. S.	250			
Forbes, W. D.	100			
Total	8,100 [c]			

[a] *Wilson Rep.*, p. 160.

[b] Lambard was in the Durant Group before the Ames Group was formed. He had been with Oakes Ames in the Iowan railroads.

[c] Of which 7,100 shares ($710,000) were new subscriptions, excluding Lambard. Thus the Durant Group had made net sales of 3,100 shares. (See p. 48.)

[d] The changes in the Durant Group shown are those since 7 Oct. 1864, when the Hoxie contract was transferred from the partnership pool to the CM; this involved $1,600,000, or 16,000 shares.

[e] A total of 50 shares must have been divided between Davis and Train to make the total correct.

[f] The "Etc., etc." holding the equivalent of 2,000 shares were reduced to zero, in addition to the transfer of Lambard.

Thus, of a total of 20,000 shares ($2,000,000), the Ames Group started off with *40.5 per cent,* the Durant Group with 59.5 per cent. The Ameses together personally had 10 per cent of the total, and Durant personally 30 per cent.

and philanthropies. He was a Trustee of Brown University 1869–1875, and a Fellow thereof from 1875 until his death in 1888.

His son, the Honorable Rowland Hazard (no middle name, 1829–1898), held a maximum of 380 shares of CM in 1868, and received and held the allotments of profit thereon, but never became a Director or officer of either the CM or the UP. However, he made a valuable contribution to history by his study, *The Credit Mobilier of America, A Paper Read Before the Rhode Island Historical Society, February 22, 1881,* which is quoted in this book several times. He was a contributor to magazines on economic questions. Like his father, he became a State Representative and served two terms as State Senator, 1867 and 1868. Like his father again, he was a Trustee of Brown and a Fellow from 1889 to his death in 1898. He was survived by two sons and three daughters.[48]

H. The Breach Begins

On July 26 Durant had himself elected President of the CM,[49] thereby rounding out his one-man control. This was hardly glad tidings to the New England group, who were putting in their money but being left in the dark as to past and prospective maneuvers. John Williams was perhaps the first to take a stand in written words:

P R I V A T E
Thos. C. Durant Esq.
New York   *Boston   Novr. 6, 1865*
Dear Sir
 . . . We are associated with you in the management of the Credit Mobilier & thus become in fact (with you) the actual managing Builders of the U Pac R Road (*& will be held responsible as such*)—We have an Organization ahead of us—the *Rail Road Company*—in whose management *you* lead—but in which we are not recognized, thus you have power and authority which we do not.

 But, for the purposes of the Credit Mobilier, it is necessary that we should know *all* that is going on, & that I should have free access to all Books and papers; & from Mr. Bunker, his trial Balance, promptly at the first of the month—This I understand to be your wish. . . . I have not yet got the trial Balance—and so cannot tell how large the expenditures are to 1st Novr.—& we did not have the full opportunity to talk with you at the office that we expected. . . . The Directors meetings of course interfered.

 I do not propose to complain, but only to suggest, that when we are next in NYk, you place Mr. Bunker right, with me—so that he will cheerfully comply with my wishes—& also that you so arrange your own matters, as to give us at least two hours each day, of your time for two days in a week, so that we may keep thoroughly posted.

 The above has been shown to & approved by Mr. John Duff
                         Yours Very Truly
                                        John M.S. Williams [50]

---

[48] *New England Historical and Genealogical Register,* 1900, vol. 54; *National Cyclopedia of American Biography,* 1907, vol. 9; *Dictionary of American Biography,* 1932; Records of UP Historical Museum; Union Pacific, *Official Register of Directors and Officers.*
[49] *Wilson Rep.,* p. 13.   [50] Durant, *Papers,* 1–3–39–39 (original ms.).

Within a few weeks Sidney Dillon and John Duff were put on the Executive Committee of the Railway Bureau, of which Durant was the Chairman, of course. *No contract, payment of money, or appointment to any office could be made without the approval of this Committee.*[51]

I. Surveys and Engineering

General Dodge once said in a speech at Omaha:

There was no question, from an engineering point of view, where the line crossing Iowa and going west from this river, should cross the Missouri River. . . . The Lord had so constructed the country that any engineer who failed to take advantage of the great open road from here west to Salt Lake would not have been fit to belong to the profession; 600 miles of it up a single valley without a grade to exceed 15 feet; the natural pass over the Rocky Mountains, the lowest in the range, and the divide of the continent, instead of being a mountain summit, has a basin 500 feet below the general level.[52]

The Great Platte Valley had been the natural, easiest trail between the Missouri and the Rockies, first of the buffalo and Indians, then of the fur traders, Mormons, and overland emigrants to California and Oregon. The company's surveys of 1864 and earlier had enabled the road to be located under the first contract from Omaha to a point 100 miles west. Also, a final location had been set for 147 miles further to 100° West. Private engineering, not Government surveying, had proved the positive practicability of a continuous line from the head of the Great Platte Valley to the Black Hills either from (a) Camp Walbach (a deserted ruin 17 miles east of the Black Hills summit) along Lodge Pole Creek to Cheyenne Pass, or from (b) La Porte, Colorado, on the Cache la Poudre, to Antelope Pass; and from either of these passes across the Laramie Plain and the Wyoming Basin via Bridger's Pass to the Green River; and via Echo and Weber canyons to Salt Lake City. So now the most important questions remaining for Durant and the New Englanders to answer were:

(1) Could there be an even more favorable crossing of the Black Hills than the Cheyenne or Antelope Passes? Durant stated that "the profiles (of the Black Hills) show a country exceedingly rough, and

[51] *Wilson Rep.*, p. 162.   [52] Dodge, *How We Built the Union Pacific*, pp. 142–143.

broken by rocky can[y]ons and transverse gorges, which will render the graduation of the road exceedingly difficult and expensive." [53]

(2) Could there be a better route to the Green River via the *North Platte River*, either (a) along the Sweetwater to the South Pass, or (b) by a short cut from Fort Laramie through the Laramie River canyon?

(3) Could Salt Lake City be entered by passing south of the lake, or would it be better to omit the city and run north of the lake?

(4) Finally, could a favorable line be found from the lake to the California border? [54]

During 1865, Durant had some of these regions surveyed under his personal direction, with the help of Seymour. James A. Evans was named division engineer of the whole area east of the Continental Divide, while Samuel B. Reed was given everything west of the Divide.

Evans ran an entirely new line from Camp Walbach along the valley of Crow Creek to another pass which Durant thereupon named "Evans' Pass." It was only a few miles north of the pass over which the UP now runs. Evans assumed it to be "the *shortest* line that can be obtained over the Black Hills with grades less than 116 feet to the mile." While it was 20 miles longer than the Lodge Pole Creek-Cheyenne Pass line, the summit (8,424 feet) was 236 feet lower than Cheyenne Pass; and while 35 miles shorter than the Cache la Poudre-Antelope Pass line, it was 374 feet higher than Antelope Pass.[55] A choice among these three would be close. The Laramie River canyon was found to be far too difficult for any railroad.[56] A survey was made east of 100° West for a possible connection in the Republican Valley with the Kansas Pacific Branch. Evans reported that "the valley of the Republican, compared with that of the Platte, is narrow and crooked . . . making necessary a large amount of bridging. . . . The hostility of the Indians (everywhere) made explorations extremely difficult and dangerous. . . . Until they are exterminated, or so far reduced in numbers as to make their power contemptible, no safety will be found in that vast district extending from Fort Kearney to the mountains, and beyond." [57]

In the meantime, Reed failed to find a possible line from the Green River which would run south of the big snow-capped Uintah range of Utah to Salt Lake City. He, like Evans, had great difficulty with

---

[53] *Durant Rep.*, 10 Apr. 1866, p. 10.   [54] *Ibid.*, 10 Apr. 1866, pp. 1–3 (paraphrased).
[55] *Ibid.*, p. 4.   [56] See sketch in Dodge, *How We Built the Union Pacific*, p. 87.
[57] *Durant Rep.*, 10 Apr. 1866, Appendix B (Evans), pp. 20–21.

Indians. He found that a road over the South Pass of emigrant fame, while having an altitude of only 7,470 feet, was likely to meet excessive snow drifts, and was at least 70 miles longer. Taking the advice of Brigham Young, late in the year he made a preliminary survey from Salt Lake City, passing south of Salt Lake into the former Lake Bonneville, for 209 miles to the dead-ended Humboldt River in Nevada. Although grades did not exceed 60 feet, the general area was a saline-alkaline plain between mountain ranges, with little fresh water and none over one 60-mile stretch. Timber was very scarce, and there was no sign of coal. He recommended building the UP from the Californian border eastward to solve the lumber problem, using camels.[58]

Up to the close of this year 1,254 miles of continuous line from Omaha to the Humboldt had been surveyed. "The entire country between the rich agricultural region of the Platte Valley and the vicinity of Great Salt Lake City, is almost destitute of improvements and population, except miners, adventurers, and tribes of roving, hostile Indians; and the same may be said of the country between Salt Lake and Humboldt River Vallies." [59]

Dodge's Discovery: Before the winter closed in, the UP had a splendid break. General Dodge, returning home from his successful Indian campaign for the Army in the Powder River region of northeastern Wyoming [60] discovered, as luck would have it, what seemed like the ideal route for a railroad over the Black Hills. Later he would have it surveyed. It was to nullify Durant's pessimistic opinion of the Black Hills terrain. His account ran as follows:

On September 22nd (1865), after rounding up our stock, we continued our journey south (up Chugwater Creek). When we reached the Lodge Pole Creek, I took Leon Palladay (our hunter & guide, an Indian) and one of the other guides and about a dozen of the cavalry for the purpose of going up Cheyenne Pass to the summit of the Black Hills. I instructed the train to follow along the trail at the base of the hills as far as Crow Creek. We were now in sight of Long's Peak and the main Rocky Mountains. All the way (up) the Chug Water I had been watching the Black Hills with a view of seeing if there was any Pass that was superior to the Cheyenne Pass for a railroad crossing and I went up the Cheyenne Pass for the purpose of still following the divide south with

---

[58] *Ibid.,* 10 Apr. 1866, Appendix C (Reed), p. 17.   [59] *Ibid.,* 10 Apr. 1866, pp. 8–11.
[60] Dodge's own reports of this campaign appear in *War Records,* vol. 48, part 1, p. 335.

the same object in view. From letters I had been receiving and from the examinations that had been made on the Black Hills, I knew it was easy to get down into the Laramie Plains with a grade of 80 or 90 feet, but they could find no way on the East side of the Black Hills, unless with a grade of 116 feet or more.

We had proceeded along down the ridges keeping on the summit of the Black Hills for two or three hours, when one of the Indians with me discovered what he thought was a band of Crow Indians between us and the train. There was a large number of them, three or four hundred. I saw in a moment that we were likely to get into trouble (they were either after us or our stock). They had discovered us about the same time. I watched them very closely to see their motions and saw that they were hostile. I immediately dismounted my force and put the horses on the west side of the divide to protect them (where they were out of sight and gun shot). We moved down in a body, holding to the summit (of the ridge between Crow Creek and Lone Tree Creek). I knew with our rifles, which carried much further than any arms they had, we could keep them at bay. I immediately set a fire on the ridge to attract the cavalry. They had orders, when I was absent from the train, that if they saw smoke to come to us, but somehow, they did not see this smoke. We moved on down the range. I kept the guides towards the Indians. When the Indians undertook to come near us, they fired at them and I saw in several cases they hit some of them; if they did not hit an Indian they hit a horse and this forced the Indians to keep further away, but they did not show any disposition to leave us. I noticed that some of them were working ahead of us with a view of cutting us off but about 4 o'clock the Cavalry discovered our smoke signals. I held to this ridge, followed it right down and saw that I was going down a ridge into the plains and I said to the guides and others with me that if we saved our scalps, I believed I had found a route over the Black Hills for the Union Pacific road.

I discovered that as I was going down this ridge, I was on the divide between one of the branches of Crow Creek and another stream (Lone Tree Creek), and marked it very carefully by a lone tree (on Lone Tree Creek and a very steep cut Butte on Crow Creek). As soon as the Indians saw the cavalry they stopped following us and fled down one of the branches of Crow Creek. It was too late for me to follow them—the fact was we were all glad to see them go and joined the cavalry. I followed the ridge down to the valley to where we were camped, the train having made about 35 miles that day.

Over [along] this ridge which I came down, the Union Pacific railway was built. When the engineers, under my instructions came to examine it, they found a line with a grade not to exceed 90 feet, and where the sedimentary and granite formation came together instead of dropping off as it usually did, about 500 feet, there was only a depression here in the ridge which as soon as crossed took up its elevation again and kept it gradually falling to the plain (to near where Cheyenne now stands).[61]

It was not the discovery of the pass that counted—it was the long, gently sloping ridge descent from the pass to the plains. For this reason Dodge usually referred to it as the "Lone Tree and Crow Creek Divide Line," making the summit at Sherman Pass.[62]

J. Construction and Equipment

By July, due to the lack of both money and material as well as delays caused by the uncertainty of the route, no construction of importance had been accomplished, except the grading on the first 53 miles and the bridging and masonry on the first 32 miles. The road bed was 12½ to 14 feet wide, and in the Platte Valley generally 2 to 3 feet above the surface, with 2 foot ditches on each side for drainage. A number of patent excavators helped with the earth moving, and laborers had suddenly become abundant with the close of the War. Work was done largely with shovels and wheelbarrows, and with animals drawing scrapers and dump carts.

Good lumber for the crossties, bridges, and other purposes, including fuel, was very scarce and costly, and was to remain one of the UP's chief difficulties.[63] About 2,500 ties a mile were needed, of which only a third were of sound oak and walnut, and the balance of cheaper cottonwood. The latter, which skirted many of the streams, was in fair supply, but was very perishable, soft, and yielding. It would not hold the spikes well, and the rail would wear its way into the wood, making the track unsafe. The process of decay was slowed somewhat by the patented method of "Burnetizing," which under high pressure impregnated the tie with a solution of chloride of zinc, and which also made it less inflammable. But it cost $5 or $6 per 1,000 feet and did not make the wood either harder or more tenacious.[64]

[61] Dodge, *Autobiography*, pp. 408–410. (The words in parentheses are taken from a somewhat different version in Dodge, *How We Built the Union Pacific*, pp. 108–109.)

[62] Dodge, *Autobiography*, p. 592; see also map, Profile, map, Illus., Groups 2, 3, 4, respectively.

[63] S. Harbaugh's report to J. Harlan, Secretary of the Interior, 20 July 1865, pp. 1–9.

[64] Seymour to Durant, 19 Dec. 1864; Durant, *Papers*, 4-1-1-1.

On July 8 the first locomotive arrived at Omaha. It was No. 1, the "General Sherman," named after the war hero who was always a strong friend of the UP. It had been hauled on flatcars over the Hannibal and St. Joseph Railroad to St. Joseph, whence it had been shipped 175 miles up the Missouri River, while there was still enough water, to the Omaha ferry landing.

Two days later, July 10, the first rail was laid quietly on the river bottom lands near the ferry, with only a small force of men, as many had been discharged because of the company's inability to pay them.[65] The wheels of the UP began to roll at long last, even if the "General Sherman" for weeks was to have only a mile and half on which to bustle back and forth abjectly with materials. All of the original UP rails were of wrought iron, made in America as required by the charter. Steel rails did not appear until after the UP was finished. The first rails used on the main line mostly weighed only 50 pounds per yard, and were about 28 feet in length. They were shipped by river all the way from Pittsburgh.

On August 3 engine No. 2, the "General McPherson," from Paterson, New Jersey, was lowered to the tracks. Major-General James B. McPherson, a close friend of Sherman and one of General Dodge's commanders, had died for the cause at the Battle of Atlanta. Weighing only 28 tons, with four drivers of 50 inches, No. 2 was nicknamed "Grasshopper." After the eastern roads reached Council Bluffs, it did service switching cars between the terminal and the ferry boat at Omaha.

Track-laying proceeded painfully at only a quarter to half a mile a day, but as the New Englanders' cash began to flow in, some 1,000 laborers were rehired and this time paid. By September 25, eleven miles of track were joined, and on October 18 "eighteen miles were in running order, laying about half a mile a day," [66] with 100 miles of grading done.

The day had come for a little happy publicity. In November, Durant relaxed enough to direct his first passenger train on a "Grand Excursion" picnic to end-of-track at the Elkhorn, 29 miles out of Omaha. While the "General Sherman" hauled two dozen guests on a couple of flatcars, on a nail keg sat red-whiskered General William Tecumseh Sherman himself, highly amused but still skeptical that he would ever live to see the UP done at this rate.

The construction picture at the end of the year was at least more

[65] J. E. Henry to Durant, 11 July 1865; Durant, *Papers*, 1–1–49–15.
[66] Dodge, *Autobiography*, p. 420 (Hoxie to Dodge).

hopeful. Forty miles of continuous track with the necessary sidings, station houses, and water stations were completed. This took the tracks to within 7 miles of present Fremont. The first Government bonds were still to be delivered to the UP. At the terminus in Omaha,[67] large brick machine shops (with a stationary engine and ample tools for repairs), engine houses of brick, a large Burnetizing machine, and a big sawmill (plus 5 portable sawmills) were in operation. Four first-class locomotives, 2 first-class passenger cars, 25 second-class baggage and freight cars, 34 platform cars, and 9 hand cars were busily clanging on the tracks. Iron rails, connecting "chairs," spikes, and crossties for 22 additional miles, with several thousand cords of wood, were delivered and ready for use. Further west, the grading, masonry, and bridging required over the next 60 miles (except the bridge over the Loup Fork River) were done, and the grading over the second 100 miles was considerably advanced.

But Durant complained:

The track would have extended 60 miles out into the Platte Valley before the freezing of the ground, but for the delay of the Government, above referred to, in deciding upon the question of location. . . . If the parties who control the various railroad lines which are intended to connect with the eastern end of the Union Pacific, had been actuated by the same motives, and impelled by the same energy which have characterized the operations of this Company, this state of things would have been remedied long before the present time; but as it is I regret to say that we cannot reasonably hope for such a connection before the coming year.[68]

Naturally, he did not mention the erstwhile bankruptcy of his own Mississippi and Missouri Railway.[69] Nor was he so considerate of his new associate, Oakes Ames, whose Cedar Rapids and Missouri River tracks were just then crossing the Des Moines River gorge and obviously would reach Council Bluffs before the Chicago and Rock Island or any other Iowan road.[70]

As of the end of the year a "Trial Balance of Credit Mobilier of America" [71] shows the financial condition as follows:

[67] See p. 25. Near Davenport and 7th Street.

[68] *Durant Rep.*, 10 Apr. 1866, pp. 14–16; see also pp. 99–103.

[69] See p. 21.   [70] See p. 85.

[71] Durant, *Papers*, 1 Jan. 1866, 1-1-44-13 (original, amended by pencil). "DR" are expenses of the CM, "CR" receipts.

DR			CR	
Cash	$ 1,856		Capital Stock	$1,742,215
Construction Contract	2,621,763		Interest a/c	396
Expense a/c	49,953		UPRR Co.	1,176,992
UPRR Stock	279,750		D. Porter & Co.	923
Stock Cr. Mobr. Am.	18,000		UPRR Certif.	58,000
O M Barnes	2,500			
Glidden & Williams	500			
T.C. Durant	4,204			
	$2,978,526			$2,978,526

The 1865 Union Pacific "capital balance sheet" appears in a report of the U.S. Pacific Railway Commission, pp. 4998–99.

K. Review of 1865

The year opened ominously. Durant suddenly called off the grading work being done on his approved line across the hills west of Omaha and changed to the cheaper-per-mile route along the valley of the Papillion River. Nine miles were added to the length of the road. In direct violation of the Government's approval of the change, the Vice-President did not reduce the grade. At the same time, he stirred up between the various towns a muddle which never was to be cleared. Not only was at least $100,000 of work wasted, but the Doctor's vacillations caused a disastrous delay of many months in track-laying. He also became involved in long legal tangles about lands around Omaha donated by towns in trust for railroad account, but actually retained by him for his personal benefit.

With the Civil War ended, Durant made one last attempt to obtain public subscriptions for UP stock at $100 a share. Not a dollar was found. Thereupon he did obtain a million dollar short-term loan from New York bankers, but it cost 19 per cent per annum interest.

Come summer, the tide of the UP's fortune turned to flood at last. A group of financiers from New England, led by Oakes Ames and urged by Durant, decided to take a major position in the nearly defunct CM. But the eventual cost was unexpected. Even in 1865, a breach opened in the conduct of company policies, never to be closed until Durant was ejected.

In the autumn, General Dodge, still in service with the Army, almost accidentally discovered the Sherman Pass through the highest part of the Rockies to be traversed by the UP. If actual surveys were to confirm his belief, a great engineering problem would be solved.

The first rail was spiked down at Omaha in July. With real capital in hand, the bitter first 40 miles of track were completed by the year-end, bringing the road nearly to Fremont. From here on, the end-o-track would race westward with no stop until it met the Central Pacific.

5

Building the Road: A Chronology

1866

The Casements Take the Tracks—Finances—Major-General Grenville Mellen Dodge—The Act of 1866—Indians Get Aggressive—A Day in a Surveyor's Life—Samuel B. Reed—Sidney Dillon—John R. Duff Sr.— The Boomer Contract Bicker—Triumphant Excursion—Surveys and Engineering—Construction and Equipment—Review

A. The Casements Take the Tracks

Dodge had accepted appointment as Chief Engineer of the UP on January 1 but was unable to get mustered out of the Army until May. One of his first official moves was to look up his old Army friend, Brigadier General John Stephen Casement, and his younger brother, Daniel T. Casement, and to persuade them to take on the important job of laying the UP tracks. General Jack, now only thirty-seven and a stocky, muscular 5 feet 4 inches, had served with distinction throughout the War and had commanded a brigade under Sherman in the Atlanta campaign. Dan was even shorter, "five feet nothing," people said. Their parents had come to Geneva, New York, from the largely independent Isle of Man, halfway between England and Ireland. Both young men had already had some 13 years of experience laying track in the Midwest. Dan was the ingenious organizer and record keeper; Jack, the inspiring leader and disciplinarian with his pearl-handled Colt always slung on his hip. "I depended on him for policing the line," said Dodge, "and he was very prompt and active in such matters." [1]

[1] Dodge, *Autobiography*, p. 564.

On February 8 their first contract was made with Durant. The terms were to lay and fill the track according to instructions and acceptance of the Chief Engineer, starting at Fremont, for $900 a mile, soon reduced to $750, but much later raised to $1,100. They were to proceed "as fast as possible in a workmanlike manner," but not exceed 3 miles a day. The UP was to furnish all materials for the track, locomotives, cars, wood, and water; transfer free of charge all men and supplies needed; and pay for all delays of more than one day caused by want of motive power, track materials, or any UP neglect. The track was to be accepted upon completion of every 20 miles, and an approximate estimate was to be made by the Engineer in charge, with payments monthly. The Casements paid their 250 or so track laborers $2.50 a day, spikers $3.00, and ironmen $3.50 to $4.00, while foremen got $125 a month. The track men were charged uniformly $20 a month for their board.[2] The Casements stayed with the UP right through to the Golden Spike in 1869, laying a total of 1,046 miles of continuous main track plus the sidings.

Dodge described the Casement operation as follows:

Their force consisted of 100 teams and 1,000 men, living at the end of the track in boarding cars and tents, and moved forward with it every few days. It was the best organized, best equipped and best disciplined track force I have ever seen. I think every chief of the different units had been an officer of the army, and entered on the work the moment they were mustered out. They could lay from one to three miles a day [and one day laid eight and a half miles], a rate never excelled. I used it several times as a fighting force, and it took no longer to put it into fighting line than it did to form it for its daily work. They not only had to lay and surface the track, but had to bring forward to the front from each base all the material and supplies for the track and for all workmen in advance of the track. Bases were organized from 100 to 200 miles apart, as follows in order: Fremont, Fort Kearny, North Platte, Julesburg, Sidney, Cheyenne, Laramie, Benton, Green River, Evanston, Ogden, and finally Promotory.

At these bases large towns were established, which moved forward with the bases, and many miles of sidings were put in for switching purposes, unloading tracks, etc. At these prominent points I have seen as many as a 1,000 teams waiting for their loads to haul forward to the front. . . . After we crossed the first range of mountains we moved our bases so rapidly the towns could not afford to move with us.[3]

---

[2] Records of UP Historical Museum.
[3] Dodge, *How We Built the Union Pacific*, pp. 38–39.

The Casements had built an ingenious rolling headquarters capable of accommodating up to 250 of the track force. The other 750 were graders, teamsters, herdsmen, and cooks, all usually camping on the line. The boarding cars, as they were called, consisted of four 85-foot platform cars. On one of these was erected a house containing an office, a kitchen, and part of the mess hall. Another platform car held the mess hall only. The last two had tiers of bunks three deep. Some men slept under and over the cars for better air and relief from cooties. These cars were always kept forward at the end-of-track. Stacked in the ceilings was a veritable arsenal of a thousand rifles.

The actual work of placing the rails on the ties is described by a correspondent of the Chicago *Tribune:*

Each car [bringing material up] was laden with a certain number of rails, all of the same length, and the exact number of chairs and spikes required to lay them. . . . The material was thrown off behind the boarding cars, then the latter shoved back and the small cars used in laying the rails could come up to the piles of material. . . . A small car having been loaded in the same manner and with the same precision as the large ones had been, was run forward to the end of the track by a horse on the gallop. A couple of feet from the rails already down, checks were placed under the wheels, stopping the car at once. Before it was well stopped a dozen men grasped a rail and ran it forward of the car, laid it down in its chairs, gauged it, and ere its clang in falling had ceased to reverberate, the car was running over it and another pair of rails run out. The process was continuing as fast as a man could walk. Behind the car followed a man dropping spikes, another setting the ties well under the ends of the rails, and 30 or 40 others driving in the spikes and stamping the earth under the ties. The moment that one car was emptied of its iron, a number of men seized it and threw it off the track and into the ditch and the second followed on with its load. The work was all done with excessive rapidity.[4]

Of this speed, an anonymous journalist wrote:

Thirty seconds to a rail for each gang, and so 4 rails go down a minute. . . . Close behind the first gang come the gaugers, spikers and bolters, and a lively time they made of it. It is a grand Anvil Chorus that those sturdy sledges are playing across the plains. It is in triple time, three strokes to a spike. There are ten spikes to a rail, 400 rails to a mile.[5]

[4] Quoted by Galloway, pp. 280–281.

[5] Quoted by Davis, p. 143 (from W. A. Bell, "Pacific Railroads" in *Fortnightly Review,* May, 1869, pp. 572–573); Dodge, *How We Built the Union Pacific,* pp. 37–38.

The 1,000 or so men employed by the Casements were a motley, but largely Irish, force of Union and Confederate veterans, immigrants, disappointed miners and farmers, adventurers, gamblers, muleskinners, herdsmen, hunters, cooks, and, of course, plenty of ex-convicts. The high pay and exciting life in a new country were like honey to these bees, and there was always a chance to desert and go gold-mining. To the ex-soldiers, the prospect of a scuffle with Indians was more of a hope than a fear. No better stuff could have been found for the job ahead.

Altogether, it was a rough, dangerous, dirty, sweating, hard-working, hard-drinking, free-spending life that this army of track-layers lived as they pushed the steel rails across the plains. They worked long hours under a fiercely burning sun in summer and in bitter cold in winter, for the climate ranged the extremes. . . . In the late afternoon, "time" is called . . . . If the money from the last pay-day is not all spent, the men will probably wander into the town, that moving "hell-on-wheels," for a night of bad whiskey, gaudy dance-hall belles, crooked card games, and a morning-after headache. Of the raw night-life of these camp towns it was written, "They counted that day lost whose low descending sun, saw no man killed or other mischief done." [6]

By Christmas time, 265 miles of track had been well set by the Casement brothers in about nine months, an average of, say, a mile a day. From here on, as the men became used to their specialized tasks, the tempo was to step up.

B. Finances

On January 6 Dodge received a cheering telegram from the General Manager of the Overland Telegraph Company, Edward Creighton of Omaha: "The commissioners passed over the road today and telegraphed the Secretary that they find first section of 40 miles in superior order." [7] This took the UP nearly to Fremont and included the first two sections of 20 miles each built in 1865. On the 24th the work was accepted by the Secretary of the Interior, and on the 27th the first issue of U.S. Government 30-year 6 per cent currency bonds to the amount of $640,000 was promptly delivered to the UP as a subsidy loan. [8] It was, of course, at the rate of $16,000 a mile. The UP

[6] Quiett, pp. 36–38.   [7] Dodge, *Autobiography*, p. 450.
[8] Records of UP Historical Museum; *Wilson Rep.*, p. 738.

STOCKHOLDERS OF CREDIT MOBILIER AS OF 18 MAY 1866 [a]

25,000 Shares of $100 Par, Fully Paid

Ames Group (19)		Change Since 15 Mar. '65	Durant Group (6)		Change Since 15 Mar. '65
iver Ames (partly joint with Oakes)	3,125	+ 1,125	Durant, T. C.	6,041	+ 41
ıkes Ames	900	+ 900	Gray, G. G.	1,267	+ 167
ımbard, C. A.	1,250	+ 250	Bushnell, C. S.	750	+ 1,250
ıff, John	1,250	+ 250	Holladay, Benj.	500	——
ızard, R. G.	1,250	+ 750	McComb, H. S.	500	+ 250
azard, I. P.	250	——	Train, G. F.	125	+ 100
idden, W. T.	625	+ 125	Total	9,183	− 2,717 [c]
illiams, J. M. S.	625	+ 125			
llon, Sidney	625	+ 125	UNCERTAIN, ALL NEW (17)		
ıtes, B. E.	600	+ 100			
ooper, Samuel, & Co.	500	——	McCormick, C. H.	625	
ley, J. B. (new)	500	+ 500	Opdyke, Geo.	462	
rimes, J. W. (new) [b]	250	+ 250	Baker, E. H.	313	
ıckerson, Fred	250	——	Bardwell, J.	250	
ıckerson, Joseph	250	——	Jones, David	250	
ıckerson, Thomas (new)	100	+ 100	Macy, W. H.	250	
ıapman, O. S.	312	+ 62	Williams & Guion	250	
kins, Elisha (new)	312	+ 312	Gilbert, Horatio	125	
ırbes, W. D.	100	——	9 others, each less than 100	218	
Total	13,074	+ 4,974	Total	2,743	+ 2,743
			GRAND TOTAL (42 names)	25,000	+ 5,000

[a] *Wilson Rep.*, pp. 155, 377. See p. 112 for list as of 15 Mar. 1865.
[b] Owned jointly with Oakes Ames (*Poland Rep.*, p. 10.)
[c] H.W. Gray had sold his 2,000 shares, and G.T.M. Davis his 25 shares.

Thus, of a total of 25,000 shares ($2,500,000) the Ames Group now held *52.3 per cent,* the Durant Group 36.7 per cent, and "Uncertain" 11.0 per cent. For the first time, the Ames Group had a clear majority.

The holdings of the two Ameses together increased to *16 per cent,* while Durant's own holdings decreased to 24 per cent.

The Ameses personally now had $402,500 invested in the Credit Mobilier, having added $202,500 since 15 March 1865.

lost no time in issuing $640,000 of its own first mortgage 30-year 6 per cent gold bonds, as permitted by the charter. However, as they were unsalable, there being no buyers at any price, they were used only as collateral to replace the Certificates for first mortgage bonds in loans where exorbitant interest rates were being paid.

The money that came in from new subscriptions to the CM capital went out immediately to pay off Durant's previous obligations. Oakes

Ames testified on 17 December 1872 in writing: "I solicited [subscriptions from] my intimate friends and men in Congress possessed of means, and capitalists in large cities. Those whom I persuaded to do so I have no difficulty in naming, for they have continued to act with me. But it is not so easy to recall others I failed to persuade. Senator Grimes, and John B. Alley and Samuel Hooper of the House . . . subscribed very largely. . . . Our capital soon proved inadequate, and it was increased, and with difficulty." [9] He also got in Elisha Atkins and Thomas Nickerson, successful merchants and shipowners.[10]

On March 3 the CM stock was officially declared to be increased from $2,000,000 to $2,500,000, nearly all paid in. On May 1 the cash book of the CM stood as below: [11]

CM Receipts		CM Disbursements	
Capital stock	$2,365,915	Construction Contract	$3,433,574
UPRR Co.	2,633,162	Stock U.P.R.R. Co.	515,410
Sundry accts.	125,361	Scrip U.P.R.R. Co.	848,173
		Interest acct.	185,754
		Sundry accts.	141,528
TOTAL	$5,124,439	TOTAL	$5,124,439

During the year, the UP issued its stock at $100 a share as follows: during the first quarter, $229,800; the second, $150,000; the third, $1,744,040; and the fourth, $2,792,900—a total $4,916,830.[12] Of this amount $3,746,030 was issued against the receipt of scrip from CM stockholders who were paying installments on their partly paid up subscriptions to UP stock. "The stock was without market, and the expedient was resorted to of selling it to the CM stockholders, in proportion to their stock, at the rate of $4.50 a share—one dollar cash, balance scrip. This brought in many new stockholders in the Union Pacific." [13] The scrip was just a receipt for money paid for UP stock, into which it was convertible. For instance, "if a man had 10 shares of stock on which he had paid $100, which would be 10 per cent, leaving $900 to pay, then, if he had $900 worth of scrip and carried it to the railroad company, he got his certificate for 10 shares of stock." [14] Most of the remainder of the $4,916,830 stock was issued against "cash receipts from the CM for account of instalments."

[9] *Poland Rep.*, p. 19; also see p. 203 concerning stock sold to Congressmen.
[10] Johnson and Supple, pp. 204–205.
[11] *Wilson Rep.*, p. 154 (by H.C. Crane, Asst. Treas., CM).
[12] *Ibid.*, pp. 743–748   [13] Hazard, pp. 19, 27–28
[14] *Wilosn Rep.*, p. 381 (B.F. Ham).

(During 1867, $53,970 more scrip was sold at the same price.[15] Thus in all the CM sold to its stockholders $3,800,000 of scrip, convertible into an equal amount of UP stock, at 4.5 cents on the dollar, for a cash amount of $171,000. This was considered as additional capital invested by the promoters.[16]

Adding the $401,950 stock outstanding at the end of 1865, the total face amount of UP stock issued as of 31 December 1866 was $5,318,-780 or 53,187.8 shares.[17]

In the meantime, the UP was receiving more U.S. bonds every month or two as new sections of the road were accepted by the Government. By the end of the year the railroad had been subsidized with a total of $4,320,000 par value of U.S. bonds on 270 miles accepted at $16,000 a mile, including the 40 miles completed in 1865.[18] Of course, UP first mortgage bonds were also issued to the same value.

The 1866 UP "capital balance sheet" appears in a report of the U.S. Pacific Railway Commission, pp. 5004–5.

C. Major-General Grenville Mellen Dodge

Major-General Dodge arrived at Omaha to assume duties as Chief Engineer of the UP on 6 May 1866. The directors, officers, and employees of the company, delighted as they were, hardly could appreciate at the time how lucky they were to win the services of this renowned soldier-engineer. In retrospect, this was one of the brilliant events in the history of the UP.

Grenville Dodge was born 12 April 1831 in the small village of Danvers, near Salem, Massachusetts, the son of Sylvanus Dodge and Julia Theresa Phillips, a kinswoman of Wendell Phillips, the Abolitionist orator. His grandfather, Solomon Dodge, of nearby Rowley, ran one of the oldest and best sawmills in New England. Most of the Dodge ancestors were typical farmers, millwrights, tanners, weavers, small merchants, and town officeholders. But Sylvanus did not prosper in Danvers, and the family began a series of moves that added nothing to their fortunes. Having become an enthusiastic Democrat, Sylvanus was made postmaster of South Danvers, and opened a bookstore. His son "Gren," at the age of thirteen, by good fortune went to work on

---

[15] *Ibid.*, p. 748.   [16] Fogel, pp. 73–74, "Line 9" and fn.   [17] See Appendix E.
[18] *Wilson Rep.*, p. 738; see also Appendix D.

a large neighboring farm. The owner's son, Frederick W. Lander, was a graduate of Norwich University, Vermont, and became one of the ablest surveyors in the exploration of the West, serving with the U.S. Engineering Corps in 1854 under Captain Humphreys and Lieutenant Beckwith along the 41st parallel. He became greatly impressed with young Dodge and inspired him, too, to go to Norwich and become a civil engineer. So with visions of a great Pacific Railway in his head, at eighteen Gren enrolled at the military and scientific academy at Norwich, and there found that enthusiasm for railroad expansion was at a boiling pitch. He did various chores for pin-money, as help from home was rare.

He was a high-spirited lad and got into many scrapes, but in the end he wrote: "For three years I had drummed into me daily a respect for authority, obedience to orders, the disciplining of my mind and actions, loyalty to an employer, patriotism towards my government, and honor to the flag." [19] Can it be that such teaching is of a bygone style, now outmoded?

Soon after his graduation late in 1850, he left New England for good and joined some classmates at Peru, Illinois. Here he got a surveying job with the Illinois Central Railroad, and found the girl he later was to marry on 28 May 1854, deep-blue-eyed Ruth Anne Brown. She was a descendant of William Bradford of the *Mayflower*. In 1852 he met Peter A. Dey, who selected him as principal assistant in the first railroad survey ever made across Iowa, for the Mississippi and Missouri Railroad, of which Dey was the Chief Engineer. His salary was $1,500 a year. In Dodge's own words:

Henry Farnam and Durant, the then contractors of this road, instructed Dey to investigate the question of a proper point for it to strike the Missouri River to get a good connection with any road that might be built across the continent. I was assigned to the duty, and surveys were accordingly extended to and up the Platte Valley, to ascertain whether any road built on the central or then northern line would, from the formation of the country, follow the Platte and its tributaries over the plains, and thus overcome the Rockies.

Subsequently, under the patronage of Mr. Farnham, I extended the examination west to the eastern Rockies and beyond, examining practicable passes from the Sangre Christo to the South Pass; made maps of the country, and developed it as thoroughly as could be done without making purely instrumental surveys. The practicability of the route, the singular formation of the country between Long's Peak, the Medicine Bow Mountains, and Bridger's Pass on the South, and Laramie Peak, the Sweetwater and the Wind River ranges on the North demonstrated to me that through this region the road must eventually be built.[20]

In 1855 Gren took out a claim for his father and brother Nathan on the Elkhorn River 25 horse-miles west of the village of Omaha, then with only 500 settlers. Already he thought the Pacific Railway would cross just there. Trains of loaded covered wagons would pause at his claim. The Dodges began to farm in earnest, but soon found it was too lonely and dangerous. The Indians forced them to retreat back to civilization. At this time he decided to make his home in Council Bluffs, at 4th and Worth Streets. In 1856 he organized and equipped the Council Bluffs Guards, of which he was elected Captain. It played an important role in the opening days of the Civil War. Later it was known as the Dodge Light Guards. From the panic of 1857 to the outbreak of war he was active as a member of the mercantile firm of Baldwin, Pegram and Company, which engaged in freighting across the plains to Denver, and in real estate, merchandising, and contracting. He also established the banking house of Baldwin and Dodge, which later was merged into the Pacific National Bank, of which he became President. This bank is now the Council Bluffs Savings Bank.[21]

Abraham Lincoln, not yet hinting that he might run for the Presidency, but making political speeches over the western frontier, made a significant visit to Council Bluffs on 12 and 13 August 1859. He had a special interest in this old outfitters' town of 8,000 persons on the covered wagon trail, for he had bought a small plot of land there from his legal and political associate, Norman B. Judd, Attorney for the Mississippi and Missouri. The site was at the spot where the M & M had decided to make its terminus. On the broad porch of the Pacific House after dinner that hot evening, Lincoln was introduced to Grenville Dodge. In the two hours of conversation that followed, Lincoln, in his kindly way, soon drew out of Dodge all that he had discovered from his surveys for the M. & M. as to the best routes westward from the Missouri. As Dodge said: "He completely shelled my woods." [22] Lincoln became convinced more firmly than ever that the Pacific Railway, if ever chartered, should run up the Platte River

[20] Dodge, *Report to President Oliver Ames,* 1 Dec. 1869.

[21] Records of UP Historical Museum.

[22] Dodge, *How We Built the Union Pacific,* pp. 11, 141; Perkins, pp. 49, 50, 52; see also p. 80.

from Council Bluffs. "Not one, but many roads will center here," he prophesied.[23] Three railroad systems were already pointing to that town, where the great bulk of the emigration was concentrating for the best crossing of the Missouri River.

When the rebellion broke out, he was commissioned a Colonel of the 4th Iowa Volunteers, which he recruited and organized. In October 1861 his black-coated infantry regiment was assigned to the 1st Brigade, 4th Division, of the Army of the Southwest. Two months later, while in command of the military post at Rolla, Missouri, he got a leg wound in a skirmish. A lifelong friendship began with General Phil Sheridan. On 7 and 8 March 1862, his brigade took a heroic part in the bloody Battle of Pea Ridge in northwestern Arkansas. Colonel Dodge successfully blocked a surprise attack on the rear of his commander, General Sam Curtis. After three horses had been killed under him, he received a serious wound in the side from an exploding shell.[24] "It was a terrible three days to me," he wrote his father. "I got off a sick bed to go to the fight, and I never got a wink of sleep for three days and three nights. . . . We lacked sadly in numbers and artillery . . . but we won." [25] Unable to leave the battle-field for two weeks, he was hauled 250 miles over a rough road in an ambulance. However, on the way he received word of his promotion to Brigadier General, U.S. Volunteers, which, he said, "insured my getting well." [26] By the Battle of Pea Ridge, with 1,300 casualties on each side, Missouri was saved to the Union.[27]

After his recovery, General Grant put him in charge of repairing and building railroads, bridges, and telegraph lines in the South, such as the Mobile and Ohio Railroad in 1862, and the lines between Nashville, Chattanooga, and Decatur in 1863–1864. In this work with 8,000 troops, and in making pontoon bridges, he was in his element. Early in the War he also built up an effective secret service organization of 100 men for General Grant. About this difficult work behind the lines, very little was ever revealed.[28]

In April 1863, he was summoned to the White House by Lincoln, who wanted his advice on fixing the initial point of the Pacific Rail-road. They agreed that Council Bluffs was the place. Furthermore, Lincoln was more than willing to grant the UP more financial aid

[23] Perkins, p. 47 (quotes Carl Sandburg).
[24] J.T. Granger, *A Brief Biographical Sketch of Major General Dodge*, p. 99 (quotes Lt. Col. William H. Powell).
[25] *The Palimpsest,* Nov. 1966, p. 444.   [26] *Ibid.*
[27] Catton, Bruce, *Terrible Swift Sword,* Doubleday & Co., Inc., 1963, pp. 220–223.
[28] Perkins, pp. 105–120.

than was offered by the Act of 1862.[29] Dodge hurried to New York
to give the news to Durant, Dix, and Cisco. Congress was urged for
"bigger and better bait." In October the Union Pacific Railroad was
organized.

Next, Dodge served under Grant in the western campaigns, and had
command of the Central Division of the Army of the Tennessee. He
was in need of rest, his weight was down to 126, and Mrs. Dodge was
having a miserable time in Council Bluffs, where his business firm
had collapsed, and the "copperheads" were making life difficult for
the families of Union officers. On 9 March 1864, Lincoln placed
Grant in command of all armies of the Union as Lieutenant General.

At the age of thirty-three, Dodge was already in command of the
Sixteenth Corps under Sherman before being promoted to Major-
General on 7 June 1864. During the severe action around Atlanta,
in which Dodge's Corps suffered heavily, his brilliant commander and
close friend, General James B. McPherson, was killed by a rebel
volley.[30] At almost the same spot, on 19 August 1864, Dodge was
wounded a third time, being hit in the head by a ricocheting bullet
from a sniper. The injury was desperate, and he was unconscious for
two days. A rumor spread that he had expired.[31] His wife came on to
nurse him, and he recovered slowly. In September she brought him
back to their old home in Council Bluffs. For the Dodges, the fighting was over.

On December 2 Dodge was sent to St. Louis as Commander of the
Department of Missouri, an area in which irregular violence between
factions of the War was greatly distressing Lincoln. Dodge promptly
received an appeal from him about it on 15 January 1865. His response was a series of rough and unpopular repressive orders, which,
however, in the end brought quiet. The next month the Department
of Kansas was merged into his jurisdiction.

General Dodge was hurriedly awakened at midnight on 15 April
1865 by a messenger notifying him of the assassination of Lincoln.
Secretary of State Seward cautioned him to prepare against any up-
rising by the Union people against Southern sympathizers. So he
called into St. Louis at his nearby forces and posted them at police
stations, and issued in the morning papers a notice that all persons in
Missouri were to stay at home, and every place of business was to

[29] See pp. 29, 30.
[30] Dodge, *The Battle of Atlanta Fought July 22, 1864,* a 51-page paper read before
the New York Commandery, M.O.L.L.
[31] Perkins, pp. 151–152.

remain closed. Unexpectedly, the next day St. Louis was oppressively quiet. The Southerners seemed to be even more distressed than the others. Dodge said:

They knew what a friend Lincoln had been, and what a help he would have been in the reconstruction, and they were fearful of Andrew Johnson. I received word from the War Department to go to Springfield with my staff and part of my command to attend the burial services. I took my place at the head of the military procession and it was the saddest sight of my life. The streets were lined with thousands and thousands of people, evidently in great sorrow and distress and at every step, we could hear the sobs of the sorrowing crowd and every little while a negro would come out and drop down on his knees and offer a prayer. There was hardly a person who was not in tears, and when I looked around at my troops, I saw many of them in tears. As we paid the last rites to this great man, the sorrow was universal, for it was one of the greatest calamities of this or any other nation.

Lincoln was a man of keen vision, of almost prophetic ken . . . . He believed that in the main and on the average the plain people . . . are right. . . . In the discussion of great fundamental principles, he was a radical, and yet in the discharge of executive duties . . . he was a conservative . . . . Lincoln embodied in the mind of the people two great principles that were really only one—the preservation of the union and the abolition of slavery. . . . Back of him were the masses of the people, their eyes fixed with pathetic faith and loyalty upon that tall, gaunt, stooping, homely man, who to their minds meant everything that makes a cause worth dying for.[32]

On 26 July 1865 he was assigned to the command of all U.S. forces in Kansas, Nebraska, Colorado, and Utah, with headquarters in the field. The same day he moved to Leavenworth with his wife, their little daughters, Lettie and Ella, and his staff. His orders were to conduct a vigorous campaign against the hostile Indian tribes on the plains, re-open the stage and freight routes, and rebuild the telegraph lines the Indians had destroyed.[33] "It was my intention," wrote Dodge, "in the summer of 1865 to resign from the army and take up a position as Chief Engineer of the Union Pacific but neither General Grant or Sherman were willing for me to do this until the Indian campaigns were over. I therefore had to write Mr. Durant that it was impossible for me to carry out my agreement. . . . He answered on

---

[32] Dodge, *Autobiography*, pp. 343–345.
[33] It was in September 1865 that the Indians caused him to discover the Lone Tree–Crow Creek Divide. See also pp. 116–118.

April 27 that the place had been kept open, and when the proper time arrived, to let him know." [34]

On 7 March 1866 his third daughter, Annie, was born at Fort Leavenworth. It was the fourth anniversary of the Battle of Pea Ridge.

Dodge sent in his resignation as "Major General, U.S.V." on 10 March 1866. "Upon receipt of this General Grant wrote me saying he had approved it from May 30th. He was still anxious that I stay in the service until the conference with the Indians was held. I made no protest but I knew it would be impossible to get any agreement with the Indians which I thought the Government ought to accept at that time." [35] On May 1 he received a letter from General Sherman consenting to his going to Omaha "to begin what I trust will be the real beginning of the great road." [36] Dodge wrote this swan song:

Thus ended my active services in the Army of the United States . . . . I left it with a great deal of regret but my services had been very pleas-ant and I made many acquaintances which lasted all my life. It would be impossible for anyone to be more kindly or lenient with me than the officers I served under, commencing with Genl. Fremont, Genl. Hal-leck, then under Genl. Curtis, again under Genl. Halleck, then under Genl. Grant, next under Genl. Sherman, next under Genl. McPherson, then under Genl. Logan and then Genl. Howard . . . . Every one of these officers had recommended me for promotion or had asked for me to be assigned to their commands . . . . I was held by General Grant in an independent command most of the time . . . . There was no one to advise me . . . . I was in the habit of acting on my own judgement . . . . I was very fortunate in the selection of men . . . . They all knew that I was greatly opposed to any criticisms of orders simply because I knew it was impossible to criticize an officer's work unless you knew the cir-cumstances under which it was given.[37]

Edwin M. Stanton, Secretary of War, wrote to Senator Kirkwood on 25 July 1866: "My own high estimate of the services, ability, and distinguished merit of General Dodge has been repeatedly declared by many official acts; and I now add the assurances of my personal esteem for him as a gallant soldier and patriotic citizen." [38]

General Dodge gratefully praised General Grant on 16 July 1866:

I am now a citizen but shall take great interest in the army and shall always give it what aid there is in my power. I know that to your un-

---

[34] Dodge, *Autobiography*, pp. 356, 504. [35] *Ibid.*, p. 471. [36] *Ibid.*, p. 483.
[37] *Ibid.*, pp. 484–485. [38] *Ibid.*, p. 487.

failing support and your confidence in me I am greatly indebted for what little success I have achieved, and I desire now to thank you. . . . I grew up under yours, Sherman's and McPherson's orders and guidance, and I shall take into civil life my lesson that will be of lasting benefit to me. I trust if I can ever be of service to you in any way that you will not fail to command me, and that you will visit our section of the country in some of your travels. We are fast civilizing this Western country, and I believe our railroad will do more towards taming Indians than all else combined.[39]

Chief Engineer Dodge failed to appear as a witness at the Wilson Committee inquisition of 1873, "although diligent efforts were made to that end." The Committee concluded that he had "purposely avoided the service of the summons." [40] Subsequently he explained that he was then building the Texas Pacific Railroad between New Orleans and El Paso, had 40 days to make a connection to save the charter and the subsidy, and that President Thomas A. Scott told him it was not necessary to appear in Washington until the road was completed. "When it was completed," Dodge continued, "I came North and wired that I was prepared to appear before them, but they did not see proper to call me. . . . I did appear before the Judiciary Committee of the House in 1876." [41]

Meanwhile, the Wilson Committee found that Mrs. Dodge was the owner of 100 shares of CM stock, which had been issued in her name when the capital of that company was increased from $2,500,000 to $3,750,000 in 1868.[42] Her holding first appeared on the stockholders' list of 16 May 1868.[43] "This stock was paid for originally by John Duff, and General Dodge was written to by Mr. Ham, secretary of the Credit Mobilier, to forward $10,000 to re-imburse Duff," wrote the Wilson Committee. "Whether Dodge paid for this stock with money of his own . . . or of his wife, is of little consequence. One way or the other, it placed him in a position where his pecuniary interests were adverse to the interests of the railroad company he was representing in this most vital capacity." [44] On its face, the last sentence was a serious reflection on his character, made in the light of suspicion of his motives for failing to appear. That he ever did permit the small holding to influence him in any way is not indicated by the records, nor by the testimony produced in subsequent Congressional investi-

[39] *Ibid.*, p. 488.   [40] *Wilson Rep.*, p. xxii.
[41] U.S. Pacific Railway Commission, p. 3791.   [42] See pp. 166–167.
[43] *Wilson Rep.*, p. 158.   [44] *Wilson Rep.*, p. xii.

gations, nor by the engineers who revised and improved the original line after 1898.[45] Indeed, his character was most admirable.

In the year of the Golden Spike he built a fine brick mansion of 14 rooms at 605 Third Street and Story Street, on one of the bluffs overlooking his hometown, the three railroads, and in the distance the winding river. This was his residence for the rest of his long life. It was restored and registered as a National Historic Landmark in 1964, and will become a museum, owned by the Council Bluffs Park Board.

Contemporaries who knew General Dodge well stated that he was a very rapid thinker, talker, and writer, quickly reaching sound conclusions. With a remarkable faculty of observing, he listened more than he talked. He was very ambitious and inclined to continually overwork himself. Perhaps this was why he was never really strong in health, particularly after his wounds. His habits as to record-keeping were very loose, and he always relied on his staff and employees to keep the necessary records. His attitude was genial but not witty. Earnest in his convictions, he was never afraid to express them, if he thought doing so would produce results. Only rarely did his temper fire. Essentially, he was a man of action, prompt and energetic. In no sense was he a politician. He was elected to the U.S. Congress only once, in 1866, and then without electioneering. His service as a Republican in the 40th Congress extended from 4 March 1867 to 3 March 1869. He refused renomination.[46]

The editor of the Omaha *Herald,* Dr. George L. Miller, commented to a memoir writer:

He appeared to me a very ordinary man, small in stature, narrow in figure, with a small head on narrow shoulders. He struck me as being the average civil engineer, subordinate to a chief. He was self asserting and, in some measure, egotistical. It was his modest demeanor that gave him these impressions. I never knew him to spend much time in quarreling with enemies. One of the most beautiful things in his life was his devotion to General Grant. Men who knew him best liked him most. A man of great resolution, he carved his own name by his intuitiveness, intelligence and judgement. I bear testimony to his personal worth and strength of character.[47]

Of special merit are excerpts from an authoritative sketch of his character:

---

[45] Records of UP Historical Museum.   [46] Dodge, *Autobiography,* pp. 343–345.
[47] *Ibid.,* pp. 376–381.

It may be concluded that Dodge, as an engineer, was a man of much more than ordinary good judgement, clear-headed and possessed of an unusual degree of acumen in the selection, direction and supervision of capable and trustworthy subordinates. He adhered unswervingly to a high professional standard. He had confidence in the soundness of his own conclusions as to the correct, true, and economic location of the road. His estimates of quantities and costs, having been reached only after exhaustive explorations, surveys, and careful study of the terrain to be crossed, could not be shaken by extraneous influences or by the opinions of men of ulterior purposes. He had the good sense to avoid involvement in the internal dissensions which disrupted the relations of the financiers who dominated the affairs of the Union Pacific during the construction period. . . . He had a type of mentality which can adapt itself to the views and actions of others which he might deem unsound, but for which he bore no personal responsibility.

Dodge was more, however, than a professional engineer. As a successful merchant, soldier, banker and executive, he displayed exceptional qualities. Further, he had the gift of foresight and an ability to judge the trend of values, which, combined with a faculty of inquisitiveness, enabled him in time to amass a considerable fortune . . . .

The choice of Dodge for the Union Pacific was wise and logical, not only because of his proven abilities and experience under difficult conditions in the Civil War, and his knowledge of Indians, but especially because of years of exploration in the mountainous regions through which the Union Pacific must be run. He was aware of and took advantage of the experience of previous explorers, notably Captain Stansbury, who traversed the approximate route used by the Union Pacific; and of many plainsmen, trappers, and mountain men, notably Bridger, whose friendship and admiration Dodge acquired.[48]

After the completion of the UP, Dodge continued with civil engineering in the location and construction of numerous lines amounting to over 9,000 miles, chiefly in the Southwest under Jay Gould. First was the Texas and Pacific Railroad, from Shreveport to Dallas and from Marshall to Sherman. Between 1874 and 1879 he spent much time abroad on German, Italian, and Russian railroads. Later he became President of the American, the Pacific, and the International Railway Improvement Companies, and of the Missouri, Kansas and Texas Railroad, as well as of others, and built a line to Mexico City.[49]

---

[48] Records of UP Historical Museum. For a life sketch of Dodge, with numerous illustrations, some in color, see *The Palimpsest,* Nov. 1966, pp. 433–480.
[49] Records of UP Historical Museum.

He was a Director of the UP during most of the years between 1869 and 1897.

He outlived nearly all of his engineering, railroading, political, and military acquaintances of the Union Pacific and earlier days, dying of cancer at his 1869 Council Bluffs home on 3 January 1916, aged eighty-five. His remains lie nearby in Walnut Hill Cemetery in a fine mausoleum which faces the setting sun, the wide flood-plain of the Missouri, and a shining network of great railroads.

For posterity, he left in several secure public places a massive collection of original source material, which has contributed much to the history of one of the most interesting eras of America. It should be added, however, that his memory occasionally betrayed him in late years, so that as far as the UP is concerned, only his reminiscences and correspondence written prior to 1870, when he stopped his memoirs, can be completely depended on. Sadly enough, his voluminous autobiography was never sifted, edited, and published. It was not through any fault of Dodge's. His biographer, J.R. Perkins, in 1928 completed *Trails, Rails and War, The Life of General G. M. Dodge,* under the auspices of the Iowa State Department of History and Archives at Des Moines, where there is a special room for the Dodge Papers.

He was survived by his wife and three daughters: Lettie (Mrs. Robert E. Montgomery), Ella (Mrs. Frank S. Pusey), and Anne (unmarried). Mrs. Dodge died only nine months after her husband. In Fairview Cemetery, Council Bluffs, is a beautiful and famous memorial fountain and statue known as "The Black Angel," dedicated to Mrs. Dodge by her daughters, Ella and Anne. It is symbolic of a recurring dream she had described just before her death.

In 1934 his estate was valued at $3,385,735.[50]

With the UP: In January 1866, Dodge received a "peculiar" dispatch from Durant. It seemed to indicate that he was to go into the field instead of being head of the Engineering parties. After rejecting the offer, he went to see Durant in St. Joseph and told him he "would not accept and be responsible for the road unless given absolute control, that he had seen in the army the disastrous effect of a divided command. There was a lack of discipline, and we were going into a country without law, where right was might." [51] Durant agreed fully. The General's influence with the Army, if the Indians attacked could be an asset.

[50] Council Bluffs *Nonpareil,* 31 Jan. 1934.   [51] Dodge, *Autobiography,* pp. 554–555.

When Dodge arrived at Omaha on 6 May 1866 to take over his duties as Chief Engineer, at a salary of $10,000 plus some stock in the CM, he found a blundering, frustrated organization, some of the men unpaid for months, and liaison with various groups of officials in New York non-existent. "I soon got the whole organization upon a sound basis . . . so everyone west of the Missouri River would obey my requests and orders. It was necessary to arm all the forces on the line." [52] He assigned S.B. Reed to construction; W.B. Snyder to railway operations; H.M. Hoxie to transfer of materials; J.E. House to the Omaha office; and G.W. Frost to purchases; and made J.A. Evans assistant of surveys.

From this time on, the building of the UP progressed as rapidly as the Ames group could get it financed. There was no time to waste. The Central Pacific trains were chugging 67 miles to Dutch Flat in the Sierras and about to get a ticket from Uncle Sam good to Nebraska—if.

D. *The Act of 1866* [53]

The act of 3 July 1866 dealt the UP what Oakes Ames called "two well-nigh fatal blows, from the effect of which complete recovery is impossible."

Section 1 provided that "the Union Pacific Railway Company, Eastern Division [the Kansas Pacific: originally the Leavenworth, Pawnee and Western] . . . shall connect their line of railroad and telegraph with the Union Pacific railroad, but not at a point more than 50 miles westwardly from the meridian of Denver in Colorado." Originally it had been limited to joining the UP no further west than the 100th meridian. "The result is a rival parallel road connecting with the Union Pacific at a point 516 miles west of the Missouri River [now Cheyenne]—being one half the length of the Union Pacific—and claiming equal advantages and facilities in all running connections and interchange of business." [54]

But it was the second blow (Section 2) that brought on the gladiator scene. It authorized the Central Pacific "to continue their road eastward, in a continuous completed line, until they shall meet and connect with the Union Pacific." Again in the words of Oakes Ames:

---

[52] *Ibid.*, pp. 563–564. [53] 14 Statutes at Large 79, 39th Cong., 1st Sess.
[54] Oakes Ames's speech before Congress, 25 Feb. 1873 (Ames Family, *Oakes Ames,* pp. 110–111).

Union Pacific Engine No. 2, "General McPherson" (or "Grasshopper"),
3 August 1865.
(Courtesy of Union Pacific.)

Building the Union Pacific Railroad in Nebraska, 1866.
(Courtesy of Union Pacific.)

John S. Casement.
(Courtesy of Union Pacific.)

Lincoln and Dodge in Council Bluffs,
13 August 1859.
(Reproduction of painting by C. Everett Johnson.
U.P. Annual Report, 1962.)

Samuel B. Reed,
Superintendent of Operations.
(Courtesy of Union Pacific.)

Grenville M. Dodge,
Chief Engineer, 1866–1869.
(Engraving by A. H. Ritchie.
Courtesy of Iowa State Dept. of History and Archives.)

Sidney Dillon.
(Courtesy of Union Pacific.)

John Robertson Duff Sr., 1882.
(Courtesy of Union Pacific.)

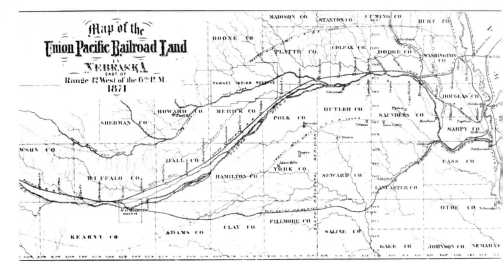

The Union Pacific Railroad land in Nebraska. 1871.
(Union Pacific, *Guide to Railroad Lands, 12,000,000 Acres*.)

SATURDAY, MAY 4, 1867.

The rain of last Evening made roads very muddy this Morning — Pleasant day. Any our appointed ... officers to-day and they are approved as far as appointed. Had a plain talk with Durant to day about his lawless way of doing work taking the whole thing into his own hands — & forbid his doing it without Consultation

SUNDAY 5

Oliver Ames's diary, 4 May 1867.

Cornelius S. Bushnell, 1862.
(Courtesy of Yale University Library.)

Oakes Ames, *c.* 1867.
(Engraving by George E. Perine.)

John B. Alley prior to 1872.
(Brady Collection, National Archives.)

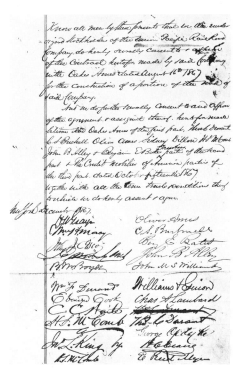

UP stockholders' consent to
Oakes Ames's contract, December 1867.
(Leonard Collection.
Courtesy of State University of Iowa.)

Wagon box fight near Fort Phil Kearney, Wyoming, 2 August 1867.
(U.S. War Office.)

Cheyenne Indians attacking a working party on the Union Pacific,
4 August 1867.
(*Harper's Weekly,* 7 September 1867.)

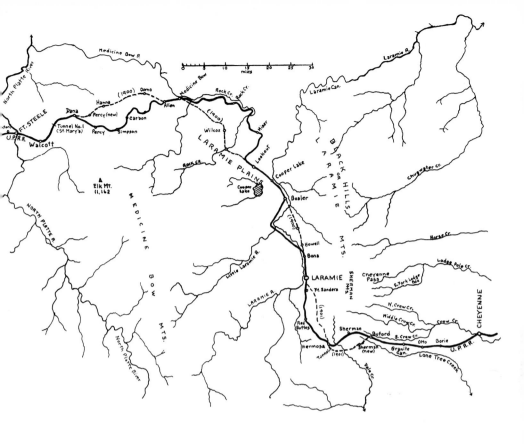

Cheyenne to Fort Steele, showing changes in line.

16th Street, Cheyenne, 1868.
(Courtesy of Union Pacific.)

Supply trains, last siding, near Archer, Wyoming, October 1867.
(Courtesy of Union Pacific.)

Great embankment, Granite Canyon, 1867.
Dug-outs of graders, and, in distance, water tower.
(Courtesy of Union Pacific.)

"Thus, by Act of Congress, these two corporations were sent forth upon a race across the continent, which finally culminated in the construction of 500 miles of road by each company in a single season . . . at a necessary cost largely in excess of the most extravagant estimates."

It will be recalled that the Act of 1864, Section 16, had restricted the CP from building into Nevada further than 150 miles to meet the UP.[55] Huntington had never worried much about this 1864 amendment to the Act of 1862. "One hundred and fifty miles ought not to have gone into the bill," he said. ". . . I would take that out as soon as I wanted it out. In 1866 I went to Washington. I got a large majority of them without the use of a dollar." [56] Senator Conness of California charged that the printing of this section of the Act of 1864 had been tampered with so as to favor the UP.[57]

While the UP was permitted to build to the eastern boundary of California, there was no legal authority for the CP to construct further east than the point where it should meet and connect with the UP.[58]

E. Indians Get Aggressive

The American Indian was, after all, the true discoverer of this continent, not Leif Ericson or Columbus. His descendants were making their last hopeless stand in the 19th century against the irresistible surge of the white man's civilization.

The tribes making the most trouble in the lands about to be opened by the UP were the Sioux, the Cheyennes, and the Arapahoes, all mounted. The Sioux ("Cut-Throats") generally roamed the big area north of the Platte and North Platte Rivers and fought both whites and other tribes.[59] South and west of the North Platte lay the country of the Cheyennes and Arapahoes, generally at peace with the Sioux. The Cheyennes were usually very hostile to the white man, while the Arapahoes were occasionally friendly. Dodge often claimed, "There were really no friendly Indians." [60] Their bands were largely broken

[55] See p. 32.

[56] Bancroft, *History of California*, vol. 7, p. 551, n.; Davis, p. 149; *Wilson Rep.*, p. 563 (Alley).

[57] *Cong. Globe*, 19 June 1866, p. 3261.   [58] Records of UP Historical Museum.

[59] U.S. Dept. of the Interior, Bureau of Indian Affairs, *Indians of the Central Plains,* 1966; *Indians of Montana & Wyoming*, 1966.

[60] Dodge, *Autobiography*, p. 376. But the Pawnees of Nebraska never fought the whites.

up, with many head men, and there was no chief with supreme authority—a tremendous disadvantage. All were nomadic, wandering hither and thither with the seasons to better hunting and pasturage grounds, more favorable climate, and sources of good water.

The U.S. Indian Agents, generally a poor lot licensed by the Department of the Interior, had repeatedly come into policy conflict with the U.S. military commanders, and were providing the "friendly" Indians with arms so that they could "hunt game better," although before the white invasion the bow and arrow had been quite adequate. Also, much graft was practiced by unscrupulous agents and settlers in the sale to redskins of rifles, ammunition, animals, provisions, and hay. As much as $20 to $50 a ton was being paid for hay to feed the live stock.

The Quartermaster and Commissary depots at Leavenworth and elsewhere were under the orders of the Chiefs of those Departments in Washington, and so were not in any way under control of the military commanders. Dodge reported that the citizens of Denver, at least, expressed themselves in favor of the policy of the Army officers as against that of the Interior Department and the Indian Agency.[61] To General Sherman he wrote:

They did not seem to know in Washington how easy it was for Indians to slip into a small station and capture the stock, drive off the soldiers, cut the telegraph line, attack a wagon train, and get away with it without being hurt . . . . Unless we could set apart some large scope of country for these Indians, where they would be free from the immigrants, it would be impossible to make any peace until they were thoroughly whipped. . . .

President Johnson was very determined that the war on the Indians should be stopped and peace made on any terms. . . . However, there could be no end of hostilities until these Indians were put upon reservations and cared for directly by the Government. It was impossible to keep civilization from encroaching upon their country.[62]

Major-General John Pope, Commander of the Department of the Missouri, had answered the latest of many complaints coming from Washington about the mounting redskin problem. He had written the Assistant Adjutant General, Military Division of the Mississippi, explaining his problems as follows:

[61] *Ibid.*, p. 413.   [62] *Ibid.*, pp. 420, 431.

All the tribes of Indians east of the mountains are in open hostility. They attack the mail coaches, emigrant trains, and small posts continually. The United States is required to protect the great overland routes passing in several directions through this great Indian region. Protection is thus required along 3,500 miles of road, nearly all of which lies in an uninhabited country . . . . This demands a considerable military force if the Government means to assure security of life and property . . . . I do not see how the Indian question is to be solved without an entire change of policy under the laws. The rich mining regions have attracted great throngs of emigrants and their number has been tenfold increased by the results of the civil war. Thousands of families who sympathized with the South have left to make their permanent homes in the new Territories. Many thousands of men who have been discharged from the Army are also seeking the mining regions. Not alone are the great overland routes pursued. Every route supposed to be practicable is explored by them. They drive off or destroy the game . . . . Neither the movements nor the conduct of these parties can be controlled. No man can say what wrongs they do to the Indians by robbing, by violence, or by dispossessing them of country which they have occupied unmolested for centuries. It is only what the Indian does to the white man which reaches the public.

The Indian, in truth, has no longer a country. He is reduced to starvation or to warring to the death . . . . The U.S. Troops, small in number and utterly incapable of affording security to the whites or protection to the Indians, have been strictly on the defensive. Expeditions are now moving in the hope of restoring peace, but in my judgement with little prospect of doing so, except by violent extermination of the Indians . . . . The Indians' first demand is that the white man shall not drive off his game and dispossess him of his lands. How can we promise this unless we prohibit emigration and settlement? The Government every day is stimulating emigration, and building roads guarded by soldiers.

I do not know of any district west of the Mississippi where the Indians can be located and protected, and support themselves. I explained all these difficulties very fully in the conference which was had between the Secretaries of War and the Interior, General Grant and myself.

It is idle to talk of treaties of peace when no promise can be fulfilled. It is useless to think of the Government subsisting large bodies of Indians in remote districts. Whatever may be the abstract right or wrong, the result must inevitably be the dispossession of all his lands and their occupation by civilized men. The only practical question is how this can be done with the least inhumanity.

My duties as a military commander require me to protect the emigration, the mails, and the settlements against hostile acts of the Indians. This necessity demands a large military force on the plains, which will have to be increased as the Indians are driven to desperation. The end is sure and dreadful to contemplate. Military force and heavy expenditures must either be accepted, or the plains given back to the Indians. . . . Treaties such as we have made with them in times past will no longer answer the purpose.

I reiterate my views only because the General-in-chief seems to indicate dissatisfaction that so many troops are employed in the Indian country. Either a large force must for a time be kept there, or we must furnish insufficient protection to our citizens in that region.

In case treaties are made by the proper officers of the Indian Department, and troops withdrawn, is the army commander to be held responsible if the Indians violate the treaty and renew the war? [63]

In July, Secretary of the Interior James Harlan resigned in a disagreement with President Johnson. Two months later he was succeeded by Orville H. Browning, a lawyer-politician and ex-U.S. Senator from Illinois. Unlike Harlan in every way, Browning took a dismal view of General Grant, General Dodge, the U.S. Army in general, and the UP in particular. President Lincoln, who knew him well, came to the conclusion that he was a strangely befuddled character. The "humanitarian" Secretary was strong for both the Indians and the Indian Agency policies. Not only by his astounding subversiveness in facilitating the sale of Government rifles to tribesmen known to be warring, but in many other ways, as will be seen, he was to be a constantly festering sore in the progress of the UP.

In the intervening August, as the tracks began to penetrate far into the Nebraska plains, the UP suffered its first damage from redskins on the warpath. At Plum Creek (now Lexington), 230 miles from Omaha, a powerful band captured the crew of a freight train and set it on fire. Notified by an observant telegraph operator, Dodge raced back ten miles in his heavily armed car hooked up to an engine, opened fire with twenty men, and sent the marauders scrambling for their ponies. That there were no white casualties was due to his lightning action.

Far worse, on December 21, at Fort Phil Kearney in north central Wyoming, Lieutenant Colonel William J. Fetterman and 81 of his cavalrymen were trickily ambushed by some 2,000 Sioux, Cheyennes, and Arapahoes, massacred to the last man, and their bodies horribly mutilated. General Sherman was forced to retract his repeatedly expressed hopes for peace. The war was rekindled in earnest, and the UP was to be led into its worst year of Indian aggressions.

[63] *Ibid.*, pp. 380–383.

F. A Day in a Surveyor's Life

In the late autumn, Arthur N. Ferguson took part in one of Evan's engineering parties locating, for Durant's purposes, a possible line for the UP across the divide between the valleys of the Platte and Republican Rivers, south of Fort Kearney. He was a young man and had not yet earned his law degree at the University of Iowa. Later, he married the sister of A.J. Poppleton (an attorney for the UP), practiced at Omaha, served in the Nebraska Senate, and became a state's attorney as Judge.[64] Ferguson's journal for 14 October 1866 relates the typical life of a railroad surveyor on the Nebraska plains.

This evening I endeavored to have a light in my tent, but the wind was so heavy that it was next to impossible to keep a candle burning, so I had to go to bed in the dark. Early on the morrow we made preparations for passing the divide between the Platte & Republican Rivers. As we intended to run a preliminary line across, we divided our party into two bodies, a portion of the troops remaining with the transit and level parties, & the remainder going with the main body who were to cross the divide as fast as possible and make a camp in some favorable place in the valley. The party going into the field with Mr. Evans would have to camp several nights on the divide where no water could be had, & therefore they had several barrels filled & placed in the army wagons that went with them. They also took about 20 cavalrymen.

I took the balance of the party & the rest of the soldiers & started for the Republican. We are now in the midst of the worst Indian country in the entire West; in fact it is the very stamping ground of the war parties of various tribes now at war with the whites. Large bodies of troops have been killed in this region after hard battles with the Indians, & months afterwards their bones have been found bleeching on the prairies.

This is the great Buffalo country of the west, & sometimes a dense black, surging mass can be seen extending in every direction as far as the eye can reach, the herd running up into thousands & thousands.

Large herds of Antelope roam the plain in every direction, & the cavalry were riding all over the country & wasting their ammunition by shooting them in sport—having no use for the meat—but killing the animals & leaving them on the ground for the wolf and the vulture, which always follow these vast herds.

This is a terrible country, the stillness, wildness & desolation of which

64 Records of UP Historical Museum.

is awful. Not a tree to be seen . . . . We have game in great abundance. The boys brought in a large buffalo today, but it was almighty tough for it was an old bull with nearly all its teeth gone. When a buffalo bull becomes very old, the young bulls drive it from the herd, & it strays off by itself & feeds alone, until it dies of old age, or is killed by the hunter or Indians. This buffalo was shot about a mile from camp & we had to send a wagon to bring it in.

We have any amount of Elk, Antelope & wild turkeys, nearly all the soldiers coming into camp having several of the latter tied to their saddles. They are so tame that you can walk within a few feet of them, & there is no trouble in shooting all a person can carry.

The weather is very cold & stormy—& we have occasional snow. The troops have no covering, & they suffer very much, being without suitable tents . . . . They are very vigilant, as we are in bad Indian country. The other detachment joined us today, having run the line to this point. We feel safer now as we are all together. We have been running line down Turkey Creek to the bank of the Republican River . . . .

We have plenty of wood, however, & keep large fires burning day & night under the lee of a bluff . . . . We feel thankful enough. It has become too late in the year to apprehend much trouble from Indians, except we should run into a war party, which is not likely.[65]

G. Samuel B. Reed

Samuel Benedict Reed was born at Arlington, Vermont, on 18 November 1818. Educated at Middleport Academy, his first job was working on the Erie Canal. He went to Illinois in 1842 and became locating engineer on the Michigan Southern (where he became a friend of Farnham and Peter Dey), and on the Chicago and Rock Island Railroad. Later, under Dey, he was construction boss of Durant's ill-fated Mississippi and Missouri. In the meantime, in April 1855, he married Jane Eliza Earl, and they made their home at Joliet, Illinois.

In March 1864, Durant hired him as locating engineer of the UP, and that year he spent six months surveying between Green River and Salt Lake Valley, recommending the route over which the railroad was finally built. In 1865 he was put in charge of all surveys west of the Continental Divide.[66] During this period he became a cordial friend of Brigham Young, which act proved to be fortuitous for the UP.

[65] Diary of Judge A.N. Ferguson, UP Historical Museum.   [66] See p. 115.

In January 1866 Durant switched him from surveying to Engineer of Construction and Superintendent of Operations of the line as it advanced. Thus, he had the supervision of all grading, bridging, tunneling, and track-laying. He maintained records of the quantities of material handled, miles of track laid, and bridging built as well as estimates of payments due currently to contractors. Fortunately, these records and personal correspondence, appearing to be substantially complete, were secured from the Reed estate and donated to the Union Pacific Historical Museum by Levi O. Leonard, the historian.[67]

Sam Reed is best known today by his voluminous collection of devoted letters to his wife, "Dearest Jennie." In these, he recounts in profuse and unrestricted detail his experiences and reflections while working for the UP. The letters are invariably engaging, but for lack of space only a few colorful samples are quoted in this book.

Reed was a friendly man, stanch and conscientious; a vigorous, competent, and methodical engineer. But, in the end, he also could not tolerate Durant. He considered Durant's policies ill-advised and extravagant: "immense amounts of money were squandered." [68] General Dodge, who knew him as thoroughly as anyone, had this to say:

No one can read the letters of Mr. Reed . . . without seeing what an able, well-poised man he was. He disliked a controversy or fight very much. He was too apt to acquiesce, while he disapproved, and Mr. Snyder was just the reverse. He was aggressive, fighting everything laggard on the road; he could not put up with Mr. Reed's desire to compromise and avoid friction and I had to quiet them often and several times went to New York to keep them from being dismissed by Durant or the company.[69]

Reed remained faithful to the UP to the end. At Promontory, with Strobridge, he placed in position the polished laurel tie that held the Golden Spike. After working with the Illinois Central in the early 70's and then with the Santa Fe, he became Chief Engineer of the Canadian Pacific Railroad. He died on 25 December 1891. His grave in Joliet is marked by a bronze tablet set in a huge granite boulder taken from the place he knew so thoroughly, Echo Canyon. It is the joint gift of the Rock Island and the Union Pacific, in commemoration of his loyal services.

[67] Records of UP Historical Museum.   [68] *Ibid.*
[69] Dodge, *Autobiography*, p. 1109.

H. Sidney Dillon

Sidney Dillon already had had more experience in railroad contracting and building than anyone else in the UP when he made his debut with the purchase of 500 shares of CM stock in April 1865. He had probably been approached by Oakes Ames and John Duff, for his experience as well as his capital was needed.[70] He stayed with the UP in one official way or the other longer than anyone else also. He was born on 7 May 1812 at Northampton, Long Island, where the family had resided since his grandfather had served in the Revolution. The Dillons had two daughters, Cora A., wife of Peter B. Wyckoff, and Julia, wife of J. Dwight Ripley. The family home was at Litchfield, Connecticut.

Virtually his whole life was spent in railroading, starting as an errand boy on the Mohawk and Hudson. At the age of twenty-eight, he took part of a large contract for the Western Railroad from Boston to Albany. He then entered the contracting business on his own account, building various important lines in New England and New Jersey, and later the Canada Southern and the Northern Central. He also had an interest with J.I. Blair in some of his Iowan contracts. Altogether, he helped to create some 30 different railroads. "I would not take a contract unless I thought I could make 20% on it," he testified in 1873—and he meant 20 per cent on the total dollar amount of the contract.[71] His firm was Dillon, Clyde & Co., 50 Wall Street, New York. He did not move to Boston with the UP.

In the CM, he was elected to the Executive Committee almost immediately upon subscribing, and then President when Durant was deposed in 1867. His maximum holding in the CM was 1,005 shares, only a fraction of the amounts held by Durant or the Ameses. He was one of the Seven Trustees under the Ames and Davis contracts.

In the UP, he was first elected a Director in October 1866 and continued as such until his death on 9 June 1892, the year before the UP went into receivership. He had been made President in March 1874 when Jay Gould took control, and held that position until succeeded by Charles Francis Adams ten years later. In 1890, when Gould re-entered the UP, he again became President, to serve until his death. His maximum holding of UP stock was 27,800 shares in 1879.

As long as Jay Gould headed the UP (and the Kansas Pacific, start-

---

[70] Records of UP Historical Museum.   [71] *Wilson Rep.*, p. 511; see also p. 444.

ing in 1878), Gould's control was personal and absolute. Officially, Dillon was President of both companies, but in their administration he was wholly subservient to Gould's influence and policies. Therefore, the history of Dillon's presidencies was the history of the regime of Gould.[72]

A self-made, busy man, he was considered the most impressive looking of all the Union Pacific personages. Tall and well-proportioned, with finely chiseled features and luxuriant sideburns already turned white at fifty-four, he was brisk, yet courteous. "Courtly" was a word once used. Between his single-minded concentration on railroads, his tireless efficiency as an executive of big business, and his unfailing loyalty to the notorious speculator, Jay Gould, he succeeded in accumulating no small fortune.

I. John R. Duff Sr.

John Robertson Duff Sr., of the same age as Governor Oliver Ames and Dodge, was an energetic Boston stockbroker, railroad capitalist, and speculator. His first connection with the UP was a subscription to 1,000 shares of the CM early in 1865. In this move he was largely influenced by his friends, Oliver S. Chapman and Sidney Dillon.[73] He was at once made one of the five managers of the Railway Bureau of the CM in 1865.[74] In October 1866 he was elected a Director and Member of the Executive Committee of the UP.[75] At about this time, he loaned the UP $433,000 and increased his CM stock to 1,880 shares.[76] In April 1867 he was made one of the two Trustees of the Land Grant Mortgage,[77] and in the spring of 1869, Vice-President of the UP. At that time he was described as "portly and white-haired."

He retained all of these UP positions until March 1874, when Jay Gould took over complete control and dropped him from the Executive Committee and Directorate. Having put in a claim against the UP for services as Vice-President and Trustee at $10,000 a year each, with interest, Gould ordered him sued for $10,000,000 at least, "for his failure to relinquish, upon order, his share of the controversial $2,000,000 note of the UP to the CM."

In 1867 Duff originally voted as a Director against the Oakes Ames contract. He explained his opposition as follows:

[72] Records of UP Historical Museum.   [73] *Ibid.;* Durant, *Papers,* 1–3–39–38.
[74] *Wilson Rep.,* p. 162.   [75] Union Pacific, *Official Register.*
[76] Records of UP Historical Museum; *Poland Rep.,* p. 59.
[77] Records of UP Historical Museum.

I thought there might be a simpler and better method of doing it, and I thought that he was not the proper person to build a railroad, being a member of Congress. I opposed it to that extent that the majority would not have me in the management [as one of the Seven Trustees] . . . . There were some parties connected with it who I did not think were efficient railroad men or understood the construction of railroads. . . . At the time the contract was made with Mr. Oakes Ames, I did not know the disposition that was going to be made of it. I understood afterwards that it was to be assigned to trustees. Mr. Oakes Ames had no experience in building railroads. Mr. Oliver Ames had no experience, neither had Mr. John B. Alley nor Mr. B.E. Bates. . . . I was not on very intimate terms with the people who were discussing the matter. They all favored it, I believe, but myself . . . . It would not have been made with Oakes Ames without the understanding [that it was to be assigned to trustees].[78]

He did not go on to explain that Durant had vowed that the CM would never have another contract and had brought court injunctions against the UP for that purpose. So Duff was not elected one of the original Seven Trustees. However, in March 1868 he replaced Alley, who had resigned as such a Trustee at Durant's insistence.

He also testified that he had repeatedly tried to get competent outside contractors for the UP, but could not find one willing to touch it. Among the reasons given, he said (besides the obvious difficulties of the country), was the presence of the Government Directors "who had not any interest in the road except to get their traveling expenses and per diem salary. . . . The work was subject to the approval of these commissioners, who were likely to be appointed for political considerations. And, of course, my own opinion was that they would be men not likely to know anything about the construction of railroads, and that they would harass and embarrass us a good deal." [79]

Duff was an experienced railroad builder, operator, and financier, being, among other things, one of the promoters and Directors of the Hannibal and St. Joseph Railroad. "I got $600,000 of that stock, which I offered to sell at 10 per cent, so that the value of railroad stock before the road is built is not much." He added: "The UP stock [at the time of the Ames contract] had no market-value at all. You could not borrow on it or sell it, except to people who would take a risk as they would at a faro-bank." [80] He accepted every opportunity

---

[78] *Wilson Rep.*, pp. 488–489 (testimony of Duff).
[79] *Ibid.*, pp. 493–495.
[80] *Ibid.*, p. 492 (testimony of Duff).

to make trips over the UP during its construction, but frequently was in controversy over policies. In 1873 the bills payable account of the UP showed that John Duff was due the sum of $298,000.[81]

John Robertson Duff, his son, often batted for him in visits over the road and in other ways. On 25 May 1869, he was elected a Director of the UP until Dodge could succeed him in August.[82] Their names often have been confused.

John R. Duff died in Boston on 27 February 1891, aged sixty.[83]

J. The Boomer Contract Bicker

The wrangle which developed over the Boomer (Gessner) contract was a repercussion of the growing breach between the Ames and Durant factions. Through new purchases the Ames group, as of May 18, had gained a majority of over 52 per cent of the CM stock,[84] and their relative proportion of the UP stock was growing as shares were issued to the CM stockholders. So in the annual election of 3 October 1866 Oliver Ames, Dillon, and Duff were added to the UP Board of 15 (excluding Government Directors), at the expense of three of Durant's figureheads. At the same time, Oliver and Duff were substituted on the Executive Committee of seven. Furthermore, on November 24 Oliver was elected "President *pro tem*" [85] when Dix took leave of the Board to go to Paris as U.S. Minister. But Durant still commanded a majority on both the Board and the Executive Committee of the UP. He was not going to give up his rule until smarter brains than his would prevail.

The Hoxie contract, assumed by the CM, had been completed at the 100th meridian, and the Act of 1866 was hurtling both roads towards a head-on collision somewhere, sometime. The UP had passed a resolution which Durant claimed "authorized the officers to go on as fast as possible, making all their contracts subject to any future general contract that should be given." [86] The Ames group, as well as the others, upon putting up their cash had had a distinct understanding, even if only verbal, that all contracts would be for the benefit of the CM.[87] Little did they suspect that the CM, as such, would never have another true contract.

On 10 November 1866, Durant, as "agent," quietly signed up a contract for the UP on his own terms with L.B. Boomer of Chicago,

---

[81] Records of UP Historical Museum.   [82] Union Pacific, *Official Register.*
[83] Boston *Evening Transcript,* 28 Feb. 1891, p. 9.   [84] See p. 127.   [85] See p. 155.
[86] *Wilson Rep.,* p. 115.   [87] *Ibid.,* p. 41 (testimony of Bushnell).

a bridge-builder he had used on his Mississippi and Missouri, to construct 153 miles beyond 100° West.[88] Actually, only 58 miles were thus built, accepted by the Government, and subsidized, bringing the track just beyond the site of North Platte early in December. Boomer employed one N.A. Gessner as his agent, and then sold the contract to him. Thus, on the books of the UP, the deal was known as the Gessner contract. Contrary to his own Hoxie contract at $50,000 a mile,[89] Durant stipulated a surprisingly low and non-profit price of about $27,500 a mile, including equipment, but excluding the bridge over the North Platte. Durant (and H.C. Crane) testified that $1,700,-000 ($29,310 per mile), including bridges, had been spent on it.[90] Durant now reversed himself and claimed that it was illegal for the CM to let UP contracts to themselves, unless *every* UP stockholder had approved. This ingenious idea, which at face value sounded so virtuous, would give Durant a veto power over every move. It also would be a protection against lawsuits. Of course, he did not mention either reason.

But the UP Directors, led by the Ames group, refused to ratify his Boomer contract, and on 5 January 1867, while Durant was away, passed a resolution (over the objection of most of the Government Directors) extending the Hoxie–CM contract terms to the point already completed at $50,000 a mile.[91] Upon his return, Durant forced them to rescind the action on January 27 by getting out an injunction in Judge Barnard's corrupt court. Notwithstanding, the CM subsequently received a payment of $1,104,000 representing the profits, of which Durant received his normal share.[92]

Furthermore, he vowed that the CM would never have another contract while the Ames party was in control,[93] even though he owned over 6,000 shares personally. He was able to make this declaration good by repeated injunctions. From North Platte on, until the Oakes Ames contract was signed, construction was carried on without any contract, under Durant's direction.

K. Triumphant Excursion

As no other railroad had reached the 100th meridian before the UP did on October 6, the right had been won to go on and build to a

[88] *Ibid.*, pp. 756–757 (copy of contract).   [89] See pp. 42–45.
[90] *Wilson Rep.*, pp. 66–69.
[91] *Ibid.*, pp. 66–69; see also p. 163; *Poland Rep.*, p. 54 (12th answer).
[92] Records of UP Historical Museum.   [93] *Wilson Rep.*, p. 4 (testimony of Alley).

connection with the Central Pacific. Also, the charter had been "saved" by opening the first 100 miles of regular service on June 2, just before the deadline of June 27.[94] The tempo of construction was being stepped up steadily, thanks to the New England working capital. Durant was elated. He thought that his accomplishments would attract public capital, if only they could be properly advertised. So he began planning a second excursion, this one to be the most lavish publicity event ever concocted by a railroad to that date. Stocks had been going up nicely on the New York Stock Exchange since the end of the war, and gold was off nearly 50 per cent from its high of 285 in 1864. Crane telegraphed Durant from New York on October 17: "Erie 83⅜, New York Central 119¾, Northwestern 51¼, Rock Island Chicago 109⅝, Gold 147⅛." [95]

He issued invitations to several hundred persons in the public eye to a "Great Pacific Railway Excursion to the One Hundredth Meridian," with the UP acting as host. Wide notice was given to the press, naturally. Those favored by bids were President Johnson and his Cabinet, all members of the Senate and House, all foreign diplomats in Washington, all Army and Navy "high brass," Government Directors and Commissioners of the UP, and leading railroad financiers throughout the country—including their families. There would be the choice of two trains, one to start from New York, pick up guests at Chicago, and proceed over the Chicago, Burlington and Quincy and the Hannibal and St. Joseph, whence two fine steamers would make a 48-hour sail upriver to Omaha. The other train was to leave Chicago via the Chicago and Northwestern to its end-o-track, where coaches (also provided by the UP) would drive the remaining 60 miles to Omaha.

Oakes and Oliver did not go, perhaps because they could not exactly cherish such extravagance, which would be partly at their own expense as stockholders; or perhaps because they could not relish two solid weeks in such close company with Durant. But 140 persons accepted, including Directors Dillon, Duff, Lambard, Cook, and three Government Commissioners. Among the notables were five Senators; a number of Congressmen, Governors, and Judges; Robert Todd Lincoln, just out of Harvard; two picturesque noblemen, one from Scotland and the other from France; and, of course, numerous newspapermen; and . . . oh, yes, the merry George Francis Train, with wife and maid. Details were entrusted to Dodge, Snyder, and

[94] *History of the Union Pacific Railroad,* p. 25.
[95] Records of UP Historical Museum.

Hoxie, and no item was left unplanned. Sam Reed said he had been dreading the conclave, and was quite satisfied to be laid up with typhoid fever.[96]

Everybody arrived happy and well wined and dined for the opening ball at Omaha's finest hotel, the Herndon House, on October 22. For the next three days, two shiny, powerful locomotives, bedecked with bunting, antler horns, and appropriate mottoes, hauled nine new cars, including four of George Pullman's latest "Palace Sleeping Cars," out to the track-end and back, at comfortable speeds of 20 miles an hour, "the better to enjoy the scenery." Another train went ahead with 100 employees, tents, buffalo robes, wood for bonfires, and provisions. Events included encampments on the prairie; a war dance by five dozen friendly Pawnees; a "Sioux" raid on the guests at dawn (which was almost too realistic); and a screaming battle, including scalping, between Pawnees and "Sioux"—all sham. There was the choice between watching a sample of the Casements' track-laying arts, and a buffalo or antelope hunt. At the end of the day, game dinners were served with champagne and rosy speeches, band concerts, vaudeville acts, and fireworks. There were no "dog feasts," however. On the way back, after a visit to a vast prairie dog colony, the grand finale was an evening prairie fire 20 miles wide, set at a safe distance. Then some went on to a speechy banquet at the Chicago Opera House.

Dodge wrote his appraisal of the affair:

The representatives of the press took full notes of the road. I had had prepared in my office, ready to turn over to them, such information as I knew would be attractive and of benefit to the road and they used it, adding a great deal of romance to it so that the Eastern papers were full of the excursion and books were written on it. The result of the trip was the negotiation of some of our bonds. There is no doubt but what the excursion had a very beneficial effect upon the East and while it must have cost a great deal in money, from a sight-seeing point of view, it may be considered as very successful.[97]

At this time, the UP was paying up to 19 per cent per annum for large amounts of borrowed money: "We were deeply in debt and very much embarrassed," said Oliver Ames.[98] By the end of the year, the capital of the CM was exhausted, and the UP was three or four million dollars in debt.[99] Not a bond had yet been sold for cash. On

[96] *Ibid.*   [97] Dodge, *Autobiography*, p. 587.   [98] *Wilson Rep.*, p. 252.
[99] *Ibid.*, p. 40; *Poland Rep.*, p. 179 (testimony of Bushnell).

December 31, the CM paid $1,714,580 for UP stock, being 70 per cent in scrip on 24,494 UP shares.[100]

Dodge Elected Congressman: In the fall, Dodge was elected to the Fortieth Congress from the 1st District of Iowa. His comment on this event, which was to have effects both good and bad on the UP, was:

The 10th of October was election day. We were in the mountains and I had forgotten all about it. . . . I got a large package of telegrams . . . notifying me that I had been elected to Congress by the largest majority ever given in that District. I think I am the only man who has ever been elected to Congress who forgot the day of election . . . . I had not been in the district to take any part in the election during the campaign . . . . I was greatly astonished.[101]

His first session convened 4 March 1867, and his last expired 3 March 1869.

Oliver Ames President: Oliver Ames, who had been elected a Director of the UP for the first time on 3 October 1866, was elected "President *Pro Tem*" on 24 November 1866, as has been stated.[102] He was "regularly elected" President on 12 March 1868. Former President Dix "took leave of the Board of Directors" on 24 November 1866 [103] and was never again on the official roster in any capacity, so Oliver Ames was actually President from November 1866.[104]

"Until the Ames brothers came in," wrote Winthrop Ames, "Durant had a free hand, and he resented their check on his activities. He also expected to succeed General Dix as president of the road, and when Oliver Ames was elected instead his animus became acute." [105]

L. Surveys and Engineering

On August 23, Evans sent Dodge his preliminary line over the Black Hills, via the Lone Tree-Crow Creek divide discovered by Dodge a year previous. Dodge at once forwarded it to Durant, saying it was far superior to any of the others.[106] The next month he went

---

[100] *Wilson Rep.,* pp. 747–748.   [101] Dodge, *Autobiography,* p. 584.
[102] See pp. 151, 178.   [103] Union Pacific, *Official Register,* list of presidents.
[104] *Wilson Rep.,* p. 241 (testimony of Oliver Ames).   [105] Winthrop Ames, p. 141.
[106] Dodge, *Autobiography,* p. 574; see also maps, Illus., Group 2.

out to the Black Hills, and with Evans went over the preliminary line himself, finding it even "much more favorable" than he had expected.[107] In the meantime, Jesse L. Williams and Seymour, who had not been over that line, were wedded to the Cache la Poudre line, and were prepared to use their influence to get it adopted.[108]

Dodge decided he had better go to New York, explain his report dated November 15 personally, and make plans for next year. It was on November 22 that he submitted the following information, in substance:

To date, the lines through the Black Hills are confined to a choice between Cheyenne Pass and Antelope Pass, and both are impracticable because the rises from the stream heads are so rapid, an abrupt 500 to 1,000 feet, that the summits cannot be reached without tunneling. Furthermore, the canyons are tortuous, with bad curvatures and direction. Even on the slopes of the mountains, or on the divides between the different streams, there is the same sharp rise in the end—except for one divide, the Lone Tree and Crow Creek divide.

Here, the pass is reached with easy grades and light work. The divide crosses the junction of the sedimentary and granite rocks at a point where they come together at nearly the same level—the only such point so far discovered. The mountains here run out into the plains in a succession of ridges some 20 miles in length. The line follows the ridge between Lone Tree and Crow [South Fork] Creeks, making the summit at Evans Pass with an elevation of 8,242 feet, thence to the crossing of Dale Creek near its head, thereby avoiding the heavy crossing of Dale Creek made by the Cache la Poudre line. It crosses the divide between Dale Creek and Laramie Plains just north of Antelope Pass and descends immediately with uniform slope not exceeding the maximum grade ascending west. Total ascent and descent on the Lone Tree line is 2,865 feet; on the Cache la Poudre 4,589 feet. Maximum grade on the Lone Tree line can be reduced to 90 feet, but the Cache la Poudre only to 100 feet, and with a tunnel at that. Curves on the former will not exceed 6 degrees; on the latter at least 12 degrees. The cost per mile will be about one-third to one-half less than on the latter. From snow there will be no trouble, as it will not drift so easily as in valleys and on slopes. Finally, it is the shortest and easiest approach from the mouth of Lodge Pole Creek (Julesburg), and is as good as the Cache la Poudre in approach from Denver, except for distance.

We should without doubt choose the Crow Creek and Lone Tree divide line.[109]

[107] *Ibid.*, p. 579.   [108] *Ibid.*, p. 580.   [109] *Ibid.*, p. 593.

This decision was no snap judgment. It was the result of thorough explorations over all of the Black Hills during the past three years.

After full consideration by the Board, the following action was taken on 23 November 1866: "The Committee on Location and Construction . . . unanimously recommend the adoption of the Lodge Pole Creek line, crossing the mountains via the Lone Tree and Crow Creek divide line. . . ." [110]

Dodge continued to write in his autobiography:

The company was being pressed to raise money for work, but the unexpected favorability of the crossing of the Black Hills, at so small a cost, gave them great encouragement, and also the fact that as soon as we reached the Black Hills we would receive $48,000 per mile in U.S. bonds for 150 miles. . . . Up to that time we had been receiving only $16,000 per mile from the Government, but the great cost of the road required more funds than they were receiving . . . . Iron was costing us about $130 a ton laid down, and our ties ran from $1.50 to $3.00 and bridge lumber in the same proportion . . . . I was in hopes of reducing the cost of Material early in 1867, by having the Northwestern road connect with us.[111]

On 10 December 1866, from North Easton, Oliver Ames wrote O.H. Browning, Secretary of the Interior:

The Directors of the Union Pacific Railroad Company are about making contracts for the vigorous prosecution of the Road next year . . . . They have decided to build on the line known as the Lodge Pole Creek, Lone Tree and Crow Creek divide line. It becomes important from the great expensiveness of the work that the President of the United States should, under Section eleven of the act of Congress approved July 1st 1862, fix the point where the loan to the Company of $48,000 dollar of Govt Bonds per mile should commence.

The maps prepared by Gen Dodge Chief Engineer of the UPRR Co show that the ascent of the Mountains commence when the new line adopted by the Company crosses Crow Creek. I would therefore respectfully suggest that the Forty Eight Thousand dollars of Bonds of the United States . . . shall commence on the crossing of Crow Creek . . . as shown on the (enclosed) Map.[112]

This was Oliver's first of many letters to the Secretary of the Interior. It was received 2 January 1867. The facts are clear that this

---

[110] *Ibid.*, p. 593. [111] *Ibid.*, p. 596.

[112] U.S. Secretary of the Interior, Record Group 48 (letters received from the Ames brothers, 1866–1870).

favorable route along the Divide and over Evans (Sherman) Pass was known, even though not finally staked out for grading, to all the Directors and the Government at least eight months before the signing of the Oakes Ames contract in August 1867. Furthermore, the final location was completed early in the summer of 1867.[113] Six years later, Hoar of the Wilson Committee, examining Oliver Ames, asked: "Was not the road located at the time you made the contract with your brother, by the way it [the railroad] now goes?" Oliver answered: "No sir; I think not." [114] Obviously, Oliver's wavering memory was in error. This was not the only time that memories failed at the Wilson and Poland inquisitions. Oakes made the same slip when he said, "After this contract was made, and after we found the easy grade over the Rocky Mountains, I thought we would make a good deal of money." [115] Too many years had passed by. Nothing further need be construed, notwithstanding the Wilson Committee and questions raised by some historians as the result of incomplete research.

When field work became impossible as cold weather approached, Dodge sent a small group of his engineers to winter down at Dale Creek, 8,000 feet up in the Black Hills near Evans Pass. They built a comfortable log cabin and took some livestock along for food. Their primary duty was to observe the weather and the drifting of the snows over the pass.

Dodge was unable to turn in his formal annual report for 1866 to President Ames until 19 June 1867.[116] As to the engineers, he said that during the season Evans had marched 956 miles and run 624 miles of instrumental lines east of Evans Pass, including the preliminary line over the Lone Tree-Crow Creek divide already described. Evans demonstrated that a low-grade, shorter route through the Laramie River canyon was impossible for the UP then. It took him three weeks to push through 25 miles of that "narrow, wild, precipitous gorge, never before passed by man; everything had to be packed by the men, as pack mules could not find a footing." [117]

Percy T. Browne, First Assistant Engineer, ran 500 miles of line altogether, moving up the Republican Valley and west for a route to Denver, then into the main Rocky Mountain range. In September his party was driven off by snowstorms in the 10,000 foot passes. Tunneling would have been necessary, so Denver had to be by-passed.

---

[113] Records of UP Historical Museum.   [114] *Wilson Rep.*, pp. 253–255.
[115] *Ibid.*, p. 28; Fogel, pp. 85–86, 117. (See Durant's testimony, *Wilson Rep.*, p. 85.)
[116] Dodge, *Autobiography*, pp. 601–609.
[117] *Ibid.*, pp. 601–602; Dodge, *Report of the Chief Engineer*, 1866, pp. 4–6.

Browne then located 105 miles of line up Lodge Pole Creek in severe weather to connect with Evans's line.[118]

L.L. Hills, also a First Assistant Engineer, who made the final location of the third 100 miles under Ainsworth, ran a total of 823 miles on the plains, including the feasibility of a branch from several points on the adopted line to Denver.[119]

Thomas H. Bates, Division Engineer, was the first to find a practicable line from Reed's Pass in the Humboldt Mountains to the California boundary via the Humboldt and Truckee river valleys (which the Central Pacific was to follow). He reported the mountainous areas rich in coal, iron, copper, silver, and gold. Thus the UP found no obstacle all the way to California, whether going north or south of Salt Lake. Surveys already indicated that the northern side was better. Bates ran 371 miles of line and had to march about 1,000 miles to do it.[120]

Dodge had some good words for his surveyors who had thus located over 2,300 miles of lines in one season:

All working parties have shown energy and perseverance. Often threatened by Indian attacks, sometimes without escort, and obliged to examine the country alone, a portion of the time during winter, they have all had narrow escapes, have had stock stolen, camps attacked, and been caught in heavy snowstorms, in extreme cold without fires, but, as yet, we have not lost any lives or any stock of great value . . . . The young men composing the parties are, as a general thing, far above the average, many of them of fine education, and who not only performed their duty well, but intelligently.[121]

The General came to be known to the superstitious Indians as "Long Eye." Awed by the telescope on his ever-present surveying instrument, they thought he must have "Big Medicine" power.

M. Construction and Equipment

Early in the year, Durant had bought the Lincoln Car, made especially for the President in 1864, from the War Department for himself and important guests. Its interior was of black walnut, upholstered in dark green plush. Between the inner and outer walls

118 Dodge, *Report of the Chief Engineer, 1866*, pp. 6–8.
119 *Ibid.*, pp. 8–11. 120 *Ibid.*, pp. 11–12.
121 Dodge, *Autobiography*, p. 608; Dodge, *Report of the Chief Engineer, 1866*, p. 20.

were sheets of boiler iron. Lincoln was said to have considered it inappropriately ornate and probably used it little. When the more convenient Pullman cars became available late in the year, Durant ordered one of the finest for himself and the Directors and turned the Lincoln Car over to the Government Commissioners for their inspection trips.

On 24 February, Lieutenant Colonel J.H. Simpson, Chairman, submitted to Secretary Harlan a 50-page report of "The Board Convened to Determine on a Standard for Construction of the Pacific Railroad," signed by five Government Commissioners and five Government Directors. The report was to be used as a "guide for their action in directing or accepting the work, without retarding the progress." Sections of the road could be accepted even though not finished to perfection, where the work was proceeding vigorously in good faith. Where the road had already been completed, some exceptions to the specifications were tolerated.

All in all, it was a liberal document, which in the end would produce, the Board said, "a good track . . . with due consideration to questions of economy, of first cost, and of ultimate working, as well as to rapid progress and final adaption to the traffic to be expected from this great work." [122]

Springer Harbaugh, Government Director, reported to Secretary Harlan on May 17 that "the public spirited gentlemen who are contributing so largely of their means in the prosecution of this work, which is destined to conduct a traffic of extraordinary magnitude, merit substantial returns on their investment." Work had been suspended for two weeks by a flood early in May which submerged the tracks and some of the company buildings at Omaha by one to three feet. He found that track-laying (which had been resumed in April) was now progressing at about 7,000 feet a day, and that the Casements were planning to use artificial lights at night so as to complete one and a half to two miles in a twenty-four hour day. A 1,700-foot temporary bridge over the Loup Fork 84 miles from Omaha was completed on May 2 and replaced before the end of the year with Howe truss spans resting on masonry piers. This was one of the largest rivers crossed and was subject to destructive ice floods.

Surveys and soundings for the big problem bridge over the Missouri were under way.

On the Fourth of July, in the sixth section of 20 miles, there were

[122] Chairman J.H. Simpson to Harlan, 24 Feb. 1866 (Report of Board Convened to Determine a Standard, p. 5).

11 engines, 81 flat cars, 40 box cars, 3 passenger cars, 3 baggage and caboose cars, and 20 hand cars in operation. On the same day, the located line for the third 100 miles was sent to Washington.[123] Next month Dodge laid out the town of Kearney 191 miles from Omaha, and fixed the price of corner lots at $150 and inside lots at $100. Further from the station, prices were reduced to $75 and $50, respectively.[124] One-third of the price was payable cash down, the balance over one or two years. Purchasers agreed to plant shade trees within 12 months. Jacob E. House, Division Engineer, was in charge of right of way and depot towns, already some 12 in number.[125]

On September 4 Durant wrote Reed from the office of the CM that Reed would be discharged if he, or any engineer or head of department, corresponded with any Director or Government officer upon affairs of his department. "You can show this letter wherever necessary." This was another reflection of his growing antagonism to the Ames group.[126]

On October 6 the track crossed the figmental 100th meridian close to old Willow Island and present Cozad, 247 miles from Omaha. The fertile valley there was flat as a pancake for 8 miles on each side of the track.

Just after Durant's excursion celebrating this event, Dodge went to the projected site of North Platte to select the station grounds. It was to be a railroad division point 291 miles from Omaha, at the junction of the North and South Platte rivers. He described his policy as follows:

I selected a large acreage for the station, division station, and sidings for the future. I went on the principle that it was best to take all the property needed or that ever would be needed while the land was vacant, and that policy has been of the greatest benefit to the Union Pacific Railroad Company, for the large number of acres, at some of its points 160 to 640 acres of lands, which were selected at that time is still held today and is of great value to the property.[127]

On December 3, UP service reached North Platte, crossing the river by a cedar pile trestle bridge 2,300 feet long. Track-laying continued 14 miles beyond to near O'Fallons Bluffs, a pioneer landmark, before stopping for the winter 305 miles from Omaha. Thus North Platte became the first of the notorious "Hell-on-Wheels" towns.[128]

---

[123] Dodge, *Autobiography*, pp. 569–570. [124] *Ibid.*, p. 575. [125] *Ibid.*, p. 604.
[126] Records of UP Historical Museum. [127] Dodge, *Autobiography*, pp. 587–588.
[128] Samuel Bowles, editor of the Springfield (Mass.) *Republican,* is credited with the expression.

Between April and December, 265 miles of track had been completed, more road than had ever been built anywhere in nine months. The Casements had averaged 1¾ miles per day for the days worked, sometimes reaching 3 miles in one day. Two days after being laid down, the track took cars smoothly at 30 to 40 miles per hour. Wrote Dodge:

> The road in its grades, alignments, superstructure, stations, tanks, turnouts, and equipment is a first-class American road . . . not one mile has been rejected as not coming fully up to the requirements of the law.
> The road . . . enters the heart of the best mining country yet developed, with superior advantages for building lines north to Montana, or northwest to Idaho or Oregon, south to Denver, and southwest to Pahranagat.[129] To all of these places are natural outlets from the main line, and valleys through which they can be reached without meeting any of the great mountain barriers or deserts that the general topography of the country indicates, and which must be encountered in reaching these places on any other of the proposed routes across the continent.[130]

N. Review

On balance, 1866 was a good year for the adolescent UP; in retrospect, the happiest and most hopeful one it was to see. General Dodge was an invaluable addition to the team. Splendid reconnaissance and engineering, before the Indians quite realized what was happening to them, had revealed at last a practicable route, including Evans (Sherman) Pass, all the way to California. The construction of 265 miles was much better than could have been expected with no rail connection to the East. Adequate working capital for the construction company was in sight. U.S. bonds in the amount of $4,320,000 had been received so far.

However, the company bonds had no market, for the public had no faith yet in such a venture. Vicious rates were being paid for the money which had to be borrowed as the track pushed rapidly westward. The Act of 1866 boded ill for the UP. Apprehension about the Indians rose as the year ended. Worst of all, thunderheads of grave dissension within the management were gathering.

---

[129] Apparently this refers to the Pahranagat Range north of Las Vegas, Nevada, on a proposed route from Salt Lake City to southern California.
[130] Dodge, *Autobiography*, pp. 607–608.

6

Building the Road: A Chronology

1867

Battle for Control of Policy—The Compromise—Financing Steps Up—
Congressman Ames Sells Some Stock to Congressmen—Indians Open
War on the Union Pacific—Surveys and Engineering—Construction and
Equipment—Highlights of 1867

A. Battle for Control of Policy

The Doctor's contract with Boomer [1] brought to a head the now
bitter battle for control of policies. On January 5, while Durant was
away on business, the UP Directors, by a vote of 8 to 4 (four of the
five Government Directors dissenting), assigned this work to the
Credit Mobilier and at $50,000 a mile instead of $27,500 in the following words:

Resolved: That the Union Pacific Railroad Company will and do
hereby consider the Hoxie contract extended to the point already completed, namely, 305 miles from Omaha, and that the officers of this company are hereby authorized to settle with the Credit Mobilier at $50,000
per mile for the additional 58 miles. [2]

Upon his return, Durant was furious and filed a protest which was
promptly "expunged" from the records by the Board. He correctly
claimed that the 58 miles had been built at much less than $50,000 a
mile, had been accepted by the Government as complete, was not
done under the Hoxie contract, and had been largely paid for before
the resolution was passed. But he closed with the contention that

[1] See pp. 151–152. [2] *Wilson Rep.,* p. 67; see also p. 152.

"the resolution did not provide any compensation or advantage to the company by requiring stock subscription or stipulations for the construction of additional portions of the company's road, or by any other means or stipulations whatsoever, which leaves the company to sustain a very great and unrequited loss." [3]

He stated before the Wilson Committee: "The Hoxie contract was made (with no one interested in it) as a *bona fide* contract." At the same time, he bluffed: "The parties who became subsequently interested in the Hoxie contract and in the Credit Mobilier, became directors of the Union Pacific Railroad Company; and then, to extend that contract over a piece of road that was already completed, was simply letting the contract to themselves." [4]

More effectively, Durant got out an injunction in Judge Barnard's infamous New York court. As that meant disastrous delay in the distribution of the company's securities, on January 24, upon motion of Bushnell, the Hoxie extension of January 5 was rescinded by the Directors.[5]

On January 10, while in New York, President Oliver Ames noted in his diary: "$560,000 Govt. Bonds rec'd today but all pledged before we got them," and the next day went on: "Meeting of Finance Committee who favor an increase of our Capital by increasing Cr. Mobilier. The first mortgage bonds if gold bearing should be sold for 90." Gold was then at 140, so currency certificates would have been at 64, and lower if used as collateral for loans. Back home he noted: "Think our exhibit of Cr. Mob. is very flattering and should induce subscriptions." [6] Such optimism was not shared by Durant, even though the Cedar Rapids and Missouri River Railroad track was then only a few miles short of a connection.

General Dodge wrote: "The meetings of the Board in New York were very stormy. There was a desire among a large number of directors to take the management of the road away from Mr. Durant . . . Mr. Reed thought that 'Durant, full of suggestions, would set some trap into which they will all fall and allow the work to go on as heretofore.' " [7] Reed made a prophecy which came true: "If the Doctor and his friends are thrown out he can, if disposed, throw such obstacles in the way as to prevent the rapid prosecution of the work,

---

[3] *Ibid.,* p. 68 (alleged protest as quoted to the Wilson Committee by Durant in 1873).
[4] *Ibid.,* pp. 69–70 (testimony of Durant).   [5] *Ibid.,* p. 68 (testimony of Durant).
[6] Jan. 15. Unfortunately, Oliver Ames' diaries for 1865 and 1866 and after 1871 are missing from his family records. The diaries quoted hereafter are bound in black leather, about 7 by 3 inches, with 3 days on each page.
[7] Dodge, *Autobiography,* p. 599 (quotes Reed's letter of 17 Jan.).

and I would not be disappointed if he does so, even to the ruining of himself and friends financially." [8]

Oliver Ames noted on January 26: "We agreed to increase the Capital Stock of Cr. Mob. 1,000,000$. I subscribed for 100,000$ of it." But two days later he wrote an artless letter, to which, as can be imagined, there was no reply.

Dr. T.C. Durant V P   *N. Easton   Jany 28th 1867*
Dear Sir:
Having once settled up to the 305 mile, and accepted the report of the Committee to settle with Cr. Mobr, by which Report there appears to be a Balance due the Cr. Mobr of $2,500,000—and an amt. of Stock and other assets still in hands of Cr Mobr of about 1,000,000$ and this report having been made to Stockholders in Cr Mobr, as an inducement to subscribe to more Stock would it be right to put all this finished Road into this new contract? It will be giving an advantage to the New Stockholders at the expense of the Old—I shall see Duff today and will talk it over with him.

Yours truly
Oliver Ames [9]

On February 13, Durant wrote an interesting suggestion to the Executive Committee of the UP:

I hand you herewith the statement of John J. Cisco Treas of this Co showing its indebtedness for borrowed money at the present time to be $3,459,677.55. In addition to this the Company owe the Contractors a large sum of money for work due prior to Jany 1st 1867. The Company is greatly embarrassed in its operations and cannot sustain its credit much longer unless some means are adopted at once to raise money for its present necessities, and the prosecution of the work for the ensuing year will have to be abandoned.

I would suggest that the Company at once put their available securities in the best shape to realize money and offer a portion of their Land Grant and 1st Mortgage Bonds for sale at a fair price. The Stockholders of the Credit Mobilier propose to increase their Capital and will become purchasers of the Bonds to a considerable extent if terms can be made satisfactory.[10]

Following this up the same day, the Executive Committee of the CM made a proposition to the Executive Committee of the UP, part of which is quoted below:

[8] Records of UP Historical Museum.   [9] Durant, *Papers,* 1–3–26–58 (original ms.).
[10] *Ibid.,* 3–3–4–11.

Gentlemen: The Credit Mobilier of America propose to purchase of your company $3,000,000 of land-grant bonds at 80% of their par value; $2,060,000 of first-mortgage bonds at 85%; $750,000 of the certificates of the company convertible into first-mortgage bonds at 80%, the said certificates to bear 6% interest until the bonds are issued and exchanged.

They will loan . . . to the company $1,250,000 on four months' time, at the rate of 7% interest per annum, and 2½% commission, with first-mortgage bonds as collateral security at 66⅔% of their par value, . . . payments to be made in installments before April 26, 1867.

This proposition is made on the express condition that . . . the present contract for which this company is the agent shall be extended to include 100 miles westward from the 100th meridian . . . for the sum of *$42,000* per mile . . . etc.[11]

Although the UP Executive Committee accepted the proposition, which would have raised about $6,000,000 in cash, said Durant,[12] the CM Board was unwilling to compromise, and nothing was done.

1. FINAL INCREASE IN CAPITAL OF CREDIT MOBILIER

Shortly after, sometime in February, at a meeting in the Fifth Avenue Hotel in New York, an agreement was finally reached. The CM made its third and last increase in capital by voting to raise $1,250,000 in cash through the sale of stock at par. If successful, it would bring the capital to $3,750,000. To entice new subscriptions, a most liberal bonus of a certificate for a $1,000 UP first mortgage bond was offered free with every new 10 shares of CM stock bought. "At that time," later testified the Honorable John B. Alley, "the Union Pacific was in a very precarious condition . . . pledging its bonds, which were then entirely unsaleable, at 40 and 50 cents on the dollar, and in some instances at 25 cents on the dollar, and requiring that the personal credit of the directors and stockholders and parties in interest should be used to a very great extent in putting the road through." [13] Professor Fogel states: "The actual prices could well have been and very likely were, as Alley claimed, below 40 or even below 25." [14]

When asked what he regarded as the "actual, intrinsic value" of the two classes of bonds, John Duff replied: "At that time I would not have considered the first-mortgage bonds worth more than 50 cents on the dollar, and the Government bonds 80 cents. I think that

[11] *Poland Rep.*, pp. 171–172.   [12] *Ibid.*, p. 172.
[13] *Wilson Rep.*, p. 557; Hazard, p. 20.   [14] Fogel, p. 78.

the Government bonds were sold at 85. I know that I bought a good many for 90, and held them a long time." [15]

Thus it can be seen that, if the temporary *certificate* for one bond was loanable only at 25 per cent, the stock was being offered at 75. If the bond was at 40 per cent, the stock was at 60. It all depended on how the buyer chose to apportion his $1,000 cash, and on the vagaries of loans and gold premiums.

In spite of such a bargain, none of the original Durant group was tempted. Durant even sold $100,000 of his CM stock and gave Bushnell 5 per cent commission to get prices between 95 and 100 in New York.[16] Durant realized he already had lost control of the CM, and he angrily declared that "the CM should never have another contract while it was under the control of the men who were called the 'Ames party.'" [17] His compromise offer had been rejected. Or had the Durant group already put up as much as their credit would stand? Be that as it may, actually all of the new stock with bonus was taken up by the "Ames party" and by some four dozen new and smaller persons, and others whose allegiance cannot surely be traced to either side.[18]

These subscriptions, like all the others, had been made with the distinct, although unwritten, understanding that the CM stockholders were to receive the benefit of the profits on any and all contracts for the building of the UP.[19]

The fresh $1,250,000 cash now raised was paid over piecemeal to the UP for the bond certificates it issued, enabling a reduction of its $3,500,000 bank loans.[20]

2. DARKEST DAYS IN THE EAST

As to further construction, on March 1 John Williams submitted his first proposition to the UP Directors to build 268 miles westward from the 100th meridian, reaching to the "base of the Rocky Mountains" (at about the future site of Cheyenne), at the rate of $42,000 a mile for the first 100 miles and $45,000 a mile for the remainder. He agreed to procure $1,500,000 subscriptions to the UP stock.[21]

---

[15] *Wilson Rep.*, p. 492.   [16] *Ibid.*, p. 41 (testimony of Bushnell).
[17] *Ibid.*, p. 4 (testimony of Alley).
[18] For a list of CM stockholders of 18 May 1866 and 12 Dec. 1867, see p. 127 and p. 194, respectively.
[19] *Poland Rep.*, p. 183 (testimony of Bushnell).
[20] *Wilson Rep.*, p. 40 (testimony of Bushnell), pp. 619–621.
[21] *Ibid.*, p. 70 (gives full text); *Poland Rep.*, p. 54 (13th answer).

STOCKHOLDERS OF CREDIT MOBILIER AS OF 17 MAY 1867 [a]

34,482 Shares of $100 Par, Fully Paid

AMES GROUP (25)	Change Since 18 May '66		DURANT GROUP (6)		Change Since 18 May '66
Oliver Ames (partly joint with Oakes) [b]	4,685	+ 1,560	Durant, T. C.	5,558	− 483
Oakes Ames	1,330	+ 430	Gray, G. C.	1,287	+ 20
Lambard, C. A.	1,400	+ 150	Bushnell, C. S.	910	+ 160
Duff, John	1,180	− 70	Holladay, Benj.	500	——
Hazard, R. G.	1,618	+ 368	McComb, H. S.	750	+ 250
Hazard, I. P.	380	+ 130	Train, G. F.	115	− 10
Hazard, Rowland (new)	372	+ 372	Total	9,120	− 63
4 other Hazards (new)	77	+ 77			
Glidden, W. T.	625		UNCERTAIN (44)		
Williams, J. M. S.	620	− 5	McCormick, C. H.	945	+ 20
Dillon, Sidney	945	+ 320	Opdycke, George	712	+ 250
Bates, B. E.	600	− 100	Baker, E. H.	473	+ 160
Hooper, Samuel, & Co.	750	+ 250	Bardwell, Joseph	480	+ 230
Alley, J. B.	500	——	Macy, W. H.	375	+ 125
Grimes, J. W.	380	+ 130	Jones, David	250	——
Nickerson, Fred	250	——	Gilbert, Horatio	185	+ 60
Nickerson, Joseph	380	+ 130	Williams & Guion	380	+ 130
Nickerson, Thomas	150	+ 50	Jenks, B. H. (new)	500	+ 500
Chapman, O. S.	312	——	Lockwood, LeGrand (new)	500	+ 500
Atkins, Elisha	622	+ 310	Pigot, J. B. (new)	200	+ 200
Gilmore, E. W. (new)	150	+ 150	Robbins, R. E. (new)	200	+ 200
French, C. H. (new)	160	+ 160	Sanford, Harvey (new)	125	+ 125
Total	17,386	+ 4,312 [c]	Bowman, A. H. (new)	150	+ 150
			Gilbert, H., Jr. (new)	137	+ 137
			Hotchkiss, Henry (new)	150	+ 150
			28 others, each 100 or less	1,514	+ 1,596
			Error in itemization by Wilson Report	700	+ 700
			Total	7,976	+ 5,233
			GRAND TOTAL (75 names)	34,482	+ 9,482

[a] *Wilson Rep.*, pp. 156–157. See p. 127 for list of 18 May 1866.
[b] Partly on the books of Oakes Ames & Sons. (*Poland Rep.*, p. 223, testimony of G.W. Kennedy.)
[c] W. D. Forbes had sold his 100 shares.

Thus, of a total of 34,482 shares ($3,448,200) the Ames Group now held *50.4 per cent,* the Durant Group 26.4 per cent, and "Uncertain" 23.2 per cent. The Ames Group retained their clear majority.

The two Ameses together were reduced to *17.4 per cent* of the total, while Durant's own holdings were reduced to 16.6 per cent, both reductions largely by reason of the increase in "Uncertain" from 11.0 to 23.2 per cent during the past 12 months.

The Ameses personally now had $601,500 invested in the CM, having added $199,000 in the past 12 months.

Separately, it was agreed that he would assign his contract, if accepted, to the CM. The UP Board ordered his proposition drawn up and entered in the minutes, whereupon they accepted it. But on March 27, Durant again filed a protest (also expunged), on the grounds that a section already accepted by the Government had been included, and that "the company did not derive any benefit adequate to the price paid over the cost of construction." [22] Before the Wilson Committee in 1873, he pointed out that: "As Mr. Williams at that time had made an assignment of his contract, in case he obtained it, to the Credit Mobilier, it was simply contracting with themselves again." [23] The Doctor followed up with another restraining order, this time from Judge Wells of New York, and that was the end of that.

Sam Reed wrote to his wife from Omaha on April 5: "Mr. Ham, the tool of Ames & Co. is trying to overhaul our books & vouchers. He will not find out much until I get word from the Dr. to give him access to the books & papers." [24] It is doubtful that all of them were made available.

On April 6, Oliver noted in his diary: "Met R.G. Hazard on the Glidden & Williams [private car]. Says some radical change must be made in Financial Management of UP Rr & Cr Mob."

On May 4, while on a one-week inspection trip over the road with Durant, Duff, Harbaugh, and Dodge, President Oliver Ames wrote a classic note in his diary: "Had a plain talk with Durant today about his lawless way of doing work taking the whole thing into his hands— & forbid his doing it without consultation."

3. THE AMES GROUP TAKES LEADERSHIP OF THE CREDIT MOBILIER

The Ameses and their friends had finally come to the end of the rope with the Doctor and decided to strike hard. On May 18, at a meeting of CM Directors in Philadelphia, Thomas C. Durant was forced out as President, Director, and Member of the Executive Committee of the CM. Sidney Dillon was elected to these offices in his place. Rowland G. Hazard and John B. Alley were elected to the Executive Committee, replacing G. Griswold Gray and John M.S. Williams. Gray was ousted as Director also, along with Director Williams. The latter presumably was not a candidate in view of the contract he was proposing. Oliver W. Barnes retained his position as Director, Secretary, and Treasurer.[25]

---

[22] *Wilson Rep.*, pp. 70–71 (gives full text).   [23] *Ibid.*, p. 71.
[24] Records of UP Historical Museum.   [25] *Wilson Rep.*, pp. 13–14; *Poland Rep.*, 87.

Thus, the direction of Credit Mobilier affairs fell firmly and permanently into the hands of the New England group. From here on Durant was to be only the Vice-President, Director, and Member of the Executive Committee of the *UP*.[26]

Oliver wrote Dodge on May 20: "I think that the new Board will have all the efficiency of the old & will carry every needful economy into construction." [27]

Oliver's diary notes on these events were:

May 18: At Cr Mob. meeting in Philadelphia Durant Williams & Gray put out and Alley, Dillon & Hazard put in their places—no opposition to new board.

May 22 (New York): Had a meeting of Directors of UPRR. Durant is feeling very Beligerent for being left off of Board of Directors of Cr. Mobr. and has put an injunction on us forbidding the execution of the Wms contract.

May 23: Meeting of Board of Directors (of the UP) at 12 o'clock a good deal of excitement against Durant for his course against Pacific RR. Chose a committee to prosecute the work without regard to Wm Contract.

Oliver ordinarily was a mild-mannered man, so he must have been in a fever of wrath on May 25 while penning the following letter from Boston to General Dodge:

The ejectment of Durant from Pres't of Cr. Mobr. has raised the very devil in that amiable Gent, & he has come down upon us with injunctions and proposes to visit us with every form of Legal Document to keep us honest. Such a lover of honesty and fair open dealing can't bear to see the money of the U.P.R.R. wasted on such scoundrels as make up the balance of the Board of Directors. I cannot understand such a change as has come over the Dr. The man . . . who is today we think holding Stock and a large portion of his Stock on fictitious claims and trumped-up-a/cs. He is now in open hostility to the Road and any orders he may give you or any parties under you should be entirely disregarded. Dr. Durant has been and is now seeking to favor other roads and other interests and at our meeting [of the UP the day before] yesterday it was voted that the power to direct action on the Road [for completion to the base of the Rockies] should be placed in the hands of a Committee and that Committee is Duff Dillon [Chairman] Carter Bushnell & Ames.[28]

---

[26] Union Pacific, *Official Register.*   [27] Dodge, *Autobiography*, p. 621.
[28] This and the letter below are from Dodge, *Papers*, vol. 152 (original ms.).

The UP Directors on May 23 also approved Harbaugh (Chairman), Cisco, and J.L. Williams, as a Committee of Three to settle with the CM for construction of the railroad. Williams declined, and George Ashmun, Government Director, was appointed by Oliver in Williams's place.[29]

Oliver then continued with his diary:

May 24: Signed yesterday 320 RR certificates on 19th Section and have signed today 640 first Mortgage Bonds in anticipation of having 40 more miles of the Road finished tomorrow. Appointed Alley Hazard & Bushnell to look after the finances.

May 27: Mr. Hazard proposed to make a new Co. to build the UPRR instead of Cr. Mob. which was not favored.

May 28: Bushnell is talking about buying him [Durant] out.

May 30: Telegraphed to Omaha that Durant had no authority to act for the Co.

June 3: Agreed with Mr. Alley to pay him 1/10 of profit on my Cr. Mob. stock above 6% if he will give ½ of his time to the finances and use his best efforts to protect the interests of the UPR and our own.

June 25: Shop doing about 250 to 300 doz. [shovels] per day.[30]

Oliver wrote Dodge again on June 6, from the UP's office in New York:

. . . I and all in connection with the road here have never been so sanguine of the success and great merit of this Road as we are since Durant has been put out of its management We are now selling from 15 to 20,000 $ of our Bonds Daily and are getting our money at much better rates than formerly. The Moneyed Interests here have now much more confidence in us and will I have no doubt soon be applicants for our paper . . .

John Williams made a second bid for a contract on June 24, but it met with the same fate—an injunction in the same court. This proposal (accepted by the UP) was the same as his first of March 1, including assignment to the CM, except that the rate was $50,000 a mile, a stock subscription was omitted, and the work was to be completed before the end of the year.[31] In the meanwhile, the railroad had been completed to Julesburg,[32] 130 miles west of the 100th meridian, leaving only 138 miles of his proposition to be built.

29 Records of UP Historical Museum.
30 This was about 60 per cent of their best production rate. See p. 64.
31 *Wilson Rep.,* pp. 162–163 (testimony of J.M.S. Williams).
32 Records of UP Historical Museum.

4. A MARKET IS FOUND FOR THE BONDS

On April 12 President Ames had written the following letter to Clark Dodge and Company, a New York firm of private bankers:

Referring to our proposal to your House this day in reference to a loan of One Million Dollars & the sale of Ten Millions of Bonds. We have to say that we have no objection to your receiving any portion of said money which you loan or procure to be loaned to this company from C.S. Bushnell . . . on such terms as you are pleased to arrange with them. We will receive such portion of the One Million Dollars to be advanced under our proposition to you as you may agree to from C.S. Bushnell Geo Opdyke or other parties designated by them & credit the same as part of the One Million Dollars referred to in another letter of this date.[33]

On June 21 Oliver commented in his diary: "Bushnell decided to accept the Clark Dodge & Co. loan. Had conference with Durant, wants to get back into management of Co."

"The Union Pacific Railroad Company had not sold a bond up to the spring of 1867," testified Bushnell later.[34] Bids had been so low that they had preferred short-term bank loans at 19 per cent interest to a public sales campaign.[35] "Mr. Duff," said Bushnell, "thought it would be impossible to sell the Union Pacific Railroad bonds until they extended the line to some place where the [revenue] cars would be running, and I contended that the affair would be an utter failure if we had to wait till that time, and that we could sell the bonds." [36]

After his talks with Clark Dodge and Company, salesman Bushnell believed the time for action had come. What he then did he related to the Wilson Committee some five years later in the following words:

They left me with authority to sell ten millions of bonds . . . . I went to work, employed an advertising agent, and started advertisements in every leading paper in the Northwest and New England, and I sent travelling agents to every leading city. My most sanguine expectations were realized, and in less than six months I sold ten millions of bonds,[37]

---

[33] *Ibid.*   [34] *Wilson Rep.,* p. 40.   [35] See p. 154.   [36] *Wilson Rep.,* p. 41.

[37] The actual amount of sales to the public entered on the company's "Abstract Ledger A" appears to have been only about $7,000,000 by the end of the year; but in Jan. 1868 an additional net amount of $1,944,000 was sold (after allowing for conversions from certificates for bonds), and in February alone $3,240,000 more was entered, making a total of about $12,000,000 in nine months. See *Wilson Rep.,* pp. 619–621.

and put the price up from 90, at which we had started, to 95. That furnished us with money, so that we were out of the woods so far as financial difficulties were concerned . . . . Not a cent was paid to the Credit Mobilier. . . . I acted as agent for their sale. . . . They were sold exclusively for the benefit of the Union Pacific Railroad Company.[38]

This was indeed a remarkable turning point in the financial history of the Union Pacific. *Commencing in July 1867, the promoters were able to get from the public all the money they seemed to need for constructing the rest of the UP, and at a tolerable cost, considering the market conditions of the time.* The best reason for the reversal in the attitude of the public was the world's-record rapidity and the high quality of the construction work, which were being excitedly lauded by the nation's press. "The eager newspaper correspondent was out there, his pencil poised, his eyes roving, his ears thirsty. . . . No such railroading had ever been dreamed of . . . 260 miles of track laid in exactly eight months. . . . Truly, the dusty, rusty cowhide brogans of the sweating, swearing toilers with tools and arms had betaken to themselves the proclivities of the seven-league boots." [39] Furthermore, this was the first opportunity, widely advertised in glowing terms by the Union Pacific Railroad Company, that had been given to investors to buy the bonds of a new and grandiose railroad which at last seemed likely to close the gap between the oceans and create the shortest route to the Orient. Durant's power in the CM had been broken by the Ames group. Connections with the East had just been made, the crest of the Sierras had just been conquered by the CP, and the rumor began to spread that the Rocky Mountains were to be overcome by newly found easy routes. Before long, the Government Subsidy would rise to $48,000 a mile. No doubt the UP promoters, buried in a black cloud of internal wrangling, had lost sight of the intrinsic worth of their project until Bushnell had the vision and diligence to put on his public drive.

An example of how sales of first mortgage bonds were solicited from the public for the first time is shown by a circular letter issued under the letterhead of the UP dated August 31. It stated that over the 325 miles in operation during the three months which had ended July 31 the earnings from *commercial business* alone were $723,755; the expenses $237,966; and the net operating profit $485,789. This was a highly favorable operating ratio of only about 33 per cent. Receipts for hauling contractors' material and men were usually

[38] *Ibid.,* p. 42.   [39] Sabin, pp. 147, 156.

treated by railroads under construction as legitimate earnings, the letter said. But the UP, "to give the clearest understanding of their affairs," in this statement had thrown out such earnings of $479,283 and had deducted about 33 per cent of them ($157,564) from actual total expenses of $395,531, thus making the commercial expenses $237,966, as stated above. The rest of the circular follows:

The amount of Bonds the Company can issue on 325 miles, at $16,000 a mile, is $5,200,000. Interest in gold, three months, at 6 per cent. on this sum, is $78,000; add 40 per cent. premium, to correspond with currency earnings, is $109,200,—showing that the net earnings for this quarter were *more than four times the interest* on the First Mortgage Bonds on this length of road. These Bonds are:

First. A first mortgage on what will be for a long time to come the only railroad to the Pacific. As the road will have no competition, it can always charge remunerative rates.

Second. As the United States Government invests Fifty Million Dollars by its advances, for which it takes a *Second Mortgage,* it practically guarantees the completion of the work. As further aid, it makes a donation of more than twenty million acres of land.

Third. Exclusive of the land grant, the bonds represent but about one third of the property on which they are secured. The Company is restrained by its Charter from issuing its bonds except as the work progresses, *and to the same amount on the various sections as are issued by the Government.* The mortgage which secures the bondholders is made to Hon. E.D. Morgan, U.S. Senator from New York, and Hon. Oakes Ames, Member of the U.S. House of Representatives from Massachusetts, as Trustees, who alone can deliver the bonds to the Company, and who are responsible for their issue in strict accordance with the terms of the law.

The bonds have thirty years to run, with interest at the rate of Six per cent. in Gold, payable semi-annually; and as they are offered for the present at ninety cents on the dollar, they pay over Nine per cent. on the investment. Government securities can be converted into these bonds at an average profit of over fifteen per cent.

Subscriptions are received by the advertised agents of the Company, and by banks and bankers generally, from whom full particulars may be obtained.

First Mortgage Bonds whose interest is so amply provided for and so thoroughly secured must be classed among the SAFEST investments.

                                                                John J. Cisco, Treasurer.[40]

[40] Records of UP Historical Museum.

5. CORNELIUS SCRANTON BUSHNELL

Bushnell was born 19 July 1829 in Madison, Connecticut, a descendant of English emigrants to the New Haven Colony in 1638. He was about the same age as Oakes Ames's eldest son. He gave up schooling at fifteen for the coastal shipping business. Largely through his efforts in 1858, the main line of the New Haven was completed between New London and Stonington. As a shipbuilder and financier, he became impressed by Captain John Ericsson's plan for an ironclad warship, "that floating cheesebox on a raft." He determined to sell the idea directly to the President, who was always enthusiastic for ironclads and other new weapons of war. Lincoln, who had signed his discharge from the service, with thanks, shortly after the Fort Sumter bombardment, was convinced by this "massive, vigorous, fine-looking man" and at once promised his support.[41] But the Navy would make a contract only after Bushnell, together with Congressman D.N. Sperry and Daniel Drew, gave a surety bond to guarantee satisfactory performance.[42] Sure enough, on 9 March 1862 his *Monitor* worsted the rebel, slant-armored *Merrimac*, which had been devastating the Federal wooden frigates. Naval warfare was revolutionized. During the war, in his shipyard at Fair Haven, he built more ships for the Government than had any other man.[43]

Bushnell's most conspicuous part in the UP and CM was played during the years before the Ameses came in, but he was always active, even after the road was finished. "I was originally a corporator in the bill of 1862," he explained. "I went to Chicago with the other corporators and helped to organize the company. In 1863 I was appointed on a committee to procure the first two millions subscription, necessary to organize the stockholders' company. . . . I was elected a member of the first board of [UP] directors and have been elected a member every year since [until 1874], and on the executive committee every year until 1872." [44] Also, he was one of the Seven Trustees of the Oakes Ames contract, as well as a member of the Missouri Bridge Committee and many working committees. He had a 25 per cent interest in Durant's original partnership pool which underwrote the Hoxie contract, and thus received 4,000 of the original 16,000

[41] Bruce, *Lincoln and the Tools of War*, p. 172; W.S. Sells, *The Original U.S. Warship Monitor*, 1899.
[42] Records of UP Historical Museum; Sells.
[43] Herringshaw, *Encyclopedia of American Biography*, 1898, p. 179.
[44] *Wilson Rep.*, p. 38.

CM shares. At that time he was a Director and Member of the Executive Committee of the CM, but was not re-elected after serving one year. As the New England group came into the picture, he sold his CM holdings down to 510 shares, or only 1.4 per cent of the 37,500 shares finally issued. Thereby, although reducing his risk, he failed to participate in a lion's share of the profits. In the UP he had started with 50 shares, reached a maximum of 4,926 shares in 1870, and sold down to only 711 shares by 1872.[45] It is a tribute to his ability, versatility, broad vision, and conscientious faith in the UP objective that, even after Durant had been ejected, he was the only member of the Durant group chosen to remain a Director and Member of the Executive Committee of the UP. Certainly, Cornelius Bushnell was a super-salesman in everything he undertook. He even claimed part of the credit of signing up Oakes and Oliver,[46] and testified:

I did not think there was any delicacy in asking Mr. Ames in 1865 to advance a million or two dollars, and when he got other friends in Congress to aid in the enterprise, I thought he had induced them to do an act that every man in Congress or out of Congress ought to be proud of. There is no act in my life which I look upon with so much satisfaction, and I think my children will be proud of it to the last generation.[47]

In addition to finding the first real market for the bonds in 1867, as just described, during the financial crisis of December 1870 Bushnell put over a huge, heroic sale of UP securities to save the company's credit, taking a substantial part of them with his own money. His reward was a bonus of $82,500 from the company—and an attempted smear by the Wilson Committee for accepting it.[48] To Bushnell, Dillon, and Duff fell the desperate task of straightening out the wild tangle of finances left behind by Durant.[49] Oliver seemed rather puzzled by Bushnell at times, perhaps because the latter and Seymour were the closest associates of Durant. He once sarcastically noted in his diary: "Bushnell full of notions. Can fix everything up right." [50] Later, Oliver said, "I feel like doing what I can for him." [51] The town of Bushnell in extreme western Nebraska was named for him. It is now only a station on the UP, with a population of less than

---

[45] *Ibid.*, pp. 599, 601, 605.   [46] *Ibid.*, p. 40.   [47] *Poland Rep.*, p. 180.
[48] Records of UP Historical Museum; see also pp. 407–409.
[49] Ibid.; see also p. 356.   [50] 6 Aug. 1868.   [51] See p. 399.

300. He died on 6 May 1896 in New Haven, survived by seven sons and a daughter.

6. BUT THE BATTLE RAGES ON

As the second half of 1867 opened, the acrimonius wrangle was far from over. As Bushnell put it: "The Boston and New York interests, as we termed them, were at loggerheads; they did not agree upon some line of policy." [52]

On July 3 Oliver wrote: "Meeting of Directors of UP. Was presented general feeling of indignation against Durant for his conduct." On the eleventh he noted: "Brother Oakes came on last night to see if the Committee to settle up with Durant of which he is one could make any satisfactory settlement for him to disgorge ill got gains withdraw his injunctions and go on again smoothly."

Oakes also had a plan to discuss with Samuel J. Tilden, one of his lawyers. He wrote one of his few letters. It was to General Dodge, from Washington, dated July 8, part of which follows:

. . . Bunker has been here a long time trying to get those accounts brought here by Durant last March, settled, and has not as yet succeeded. I don't exactly know where the block is, but intend to find out about it this week. . . . I want to see the road go ahead to the mountains, and a piece up, this year, and if you have no Indian troubles, I suppose you will do so . . . .[53]

Oakes also received heartening news from Ham, his "tool," writing from New York on July 20. "Money is plenty now and we have more offered than we can take. Our wants for this month are all supplied with what we shall realize from sales of Bonds of which we are selling 15 or 20 per day. . . ." [54]

Oliver wrote with a suspicious tone on July 17, "Committee unable to report yesterday and finally unable to agree on the mode of and parties to carry out contract for building 600 additional miles of R.R. Govt. directors evidently bought to support Durant's schemes." On the twenty-second, "Bushnell sent on by Durant to see if something might not be done to have us harmonize with Durant. Nothing effective." And the next day, "Durant wants his old position in the Road." Finally, on August 12, he penned Dodge, "We have one of

[52] *Wilson Rep.*, p. 54.   [53] Dodge, *Autobiography,* p. 640.
[54] Records of UP Historical Museum.

4 OCTOBER 1865 TO 3 OCTOBER 1866

Ames Group	Durant Group	Government	Uncertain
DIRECTORS AND MEMBERS EXECUTIVE COMMITTEE (7)			
C. A. Lambard	C. S. Bushnell	S. Harbaugh	G. Opdyke
	J. A. Dix (Pres.)		
	T. C. Durant (V.P.)		
	C. Tuttle (Secy.)		
DIRECTORS (13)			
	J. J. Cisco (Treas.)	G. Ashmun	E. Cook
	P. Clark	T. J. Carter	C. H. McCormick
	J. E. Henry	C. T. Sherman	B. Young
	H. S. McComb	J. L. Williams	
	E. H. Rosekranz		
	J. F. Tracy		
TOT. DIRS.: 1	10	5	4

3 OCTOBER 1866 TO 4 OCTOBER 1867

DIRECTORS AND MEMBERS EXECUTIVE COMMITTEE (7)

Ames Group	Durant Group	Government	Uncertain
Oliver Ames	C. S. Bushnell	S. Harbaugh	
(Pres., Nov. 24)	J. A. Dix (Pres.		
J. Duff	to Nov. 24) [b]		
C. A. Lambard	T. C. Durant (V.P.)		
DIRECTORS (13)			
S. Dillon	J. J. Cisco (Treas.)	G. Ashmun	J. Bardwell
	H. S. McComb	T. J. Carter	E. Cook
	J. F. Tracy	C. T. Sherman	W. H. Macy
	C. Tuttle (Secy.)	J. L. Williams	C. H. McCormick
TOT. DIRS.: 4	7	5	4

4 OCTOBER 1867 TO 11 MARCH 1868

DIRECTORS AND MEMBERS EXECUTIVE COMMITTEE (7)

Ames Group	Durant Group	Government	Uncertain
Oliver Ames (Pres.)	C. S. Bushnell	J. Brooks	
J. Duff	T. C. Durant (V.P.)		
W. T. Glidden	H. S. McComb		
(to 10 May '68)			
C. A. Lambard			
(10 May '68)			
DIRECTORS (13)			
J. B. Alley	J. J. Cisco	G. Ashmun	J. Bardwell
B. E. Bates	J. F. Tracy	S. McKee	E. Cook
F. G. Dexter		J. S. Rollins	W. H. Macy
S. Dillon		J. L. Williams	
TOT. DIRS.: 7	5	5	3

[a] Adapted from Union Pacific, *Official Register; Wilson Rep.*, pp. 596–599.
[b] Dix "took leave" of the Board and resigned as President on 24 Nov. 1866.

Durant's special meeting this week to see if he can't get some contract that will enable him to again take direction of the Road. I think he will be disappointed. His injunction does not work to suit him. He will soon find that he is not General Manager." [55]

7. JOHN B. ALLEY

On 18 May 1867, when Durant was ejected from office in the CM, the Honorable John Bassett Alley, ex-Congressman from Massachusetts, first was elected a Director and Member of the Executive Committee of the CM.[56] His initial investment of $50,000 in the venture had been made the year before, with Oakes guaranteeing him against loss.[57] On October 4 he joined the Board of Directors of the UP, to remain until March 1871, with the exception of six months shortly after the Golden Spike.[58] On 15 October 1867, he reached the top of his influence in the road's affairs by being chosen one of the Seven Trustees and one of the three members of their Executive Committee.[59] During these critical days, however, he reduced his holding of CM stock from 500 to 290 shares, stating that he was opposed, on a business basis, to the policy of early large distributions of construction profits which was about to begin.[60] In March 1868 he resigned as Trustee in favor of Duff, at the insistence of Durant.

John Alley was born 17 January 1817 at Lynn, Massachusetts. He was 13 years younger than Oakes Ames. Attending the common schools, he apprenticed as a shoemaker, at the age of fourteen, for five years. Disliking the confinement, he moved to Cincinnati, bought a flatboat, and freighted merchandise up and down the Mississippi. In 1838, however, he returned to Lynn and began the manufacture of shoes on his own account, establishing, successively, the firms of Alley, Choate and Cummings; John B. Alley and Company; and Alley Brothers and Place.

In politics, where he found an aptitude, his career was quite remarkable. Joining the Free-Soil Party in 1848, he served on the Board of Aldermen of Lynn and, later on, Governor Boutwell's Executive Council. Then he became a State Senator and a member of both the Constitutional Convention of 1853 and the State Central Committee of the Republican party in 1857. As an ardent member of that party,

[55] Dodge, *Papers*, vol. 152 (original ms.).   [56] See p. 169.
[57] *Poland Rep.*, pp. 77–78 (testimony of Alley).   [58] Union Pacific, *Official Register*.
[59] See p. 188; also Davis, p. 169.
[60] See pp. 168, 194, 208; *Wilson Rep.*, pp. 308, 335 (Alley); *Poland Rep.*, p. 93 (Alley).

he was four times elected U.S. Congressman from Lynn, serving from 4 March 1859, through the War, to 3 March 1867. In Washington, he was at one time Chairman of the Standing Committee on the Pacific Railroad and held various other important posts.[61] Not a candidate for renomination in 1866, he turned his energy towards his business and the building of the Union Pacific. Oliver agreed to give him 10 per cent of the profits on his own CM stock above 6 per cent, if Alley would devote one-half of his time to the finances of the road.[62] After selling all his allotments on construction, he made $93,456. "I have got no money that I earned harder or took more risk for," he said.[63]

In 1841, he married Hannah, daughter of William Rhodes, and they had two sons and two daughters. He died in West Newton, Massachusetts, on 19 January 1896, at the age of seventy-nine.

Alley was a dynamic, emotional character and a great talker. He had strong opinions about everything and frank likes and dislikes of people. As a result he made some enemies, foremost of whom was the Doctor himself. McComb was a close second. While he always remained friendly with the Ameses, he sometimes disagreed with their policies, and on occasion had tiffs with them over personal money matters, for his leather dealings had made him a sharp trader. While under examination by the Wilson and Poland Committees, he annoyed them, perhaps, by insisting on his right to lengthy replies. But he seemed to have the best memory of all the witnesses, as lawyer McMurtrie said.[64] His colorful remarks revealed to history many interesting details of the problems in financing the road, which otherwise never would have come to light. All in all, he was a "clear-headed and far-seeing son of Massachusetts." [65]

8. THE CONFLICTING PERSONALITIES

Dr. Thomas Clark Durant had reason to feel angry about his ejection from every office in his Credit Mobilier. The vision of how to actually build the Pacific Railway to California had been his, he thought. Was it not he who had finally coerced Congress into the enabling acts, organized the first surveys, contributed the first large capital, secured the Pondir loan, and set up the construction company? Was it not he who had built the first 247 miles virtually single-

---

[61] *Biographical Directory of the American Congress;* New York *Times,* 20 Jan. 1896, p. 5.
[62] See p. 171 (Oliver Ames's diary of 3 June 1867). [63] *Poland Rep.,* p. 86.
[64] *Ibid.,* pp. 85, 103. [65] Boston *Commonwealth,* 11 Mar. 1875.

handed? Had he not found General Dodge as Chief Engineer, Sam Reed and Jim Evans as surveyors and construction managers, and Silas Seymour as his own Consulting Engineer? Surely he had earned leadership by all these accomplishments. Anyway, he thought, he was certainly the shrewdest brain in the venture and could make more money, quicker, for *all* the promoters than anyone else could. He had procured the rich shovelmakers and other manufacturers down east with all their reputation and following and expected to dominate them. The surprise was that the conservative Ameses, who couldn't even write English as the king would have it, and their friends were such obstinate "damn fools" [66] as to be scrupulous about the surveying and construction, and to count on profits through the continuous operation of a sound railroad. Far better, thought the Doctor, to construct the road just as cheaply as the Government inspectors would permit, and with all the mileage they would let him lay on, and so make the most from the bond and land subsidies he had won. With the market price of his stock up, he would sell out and leave the operating losses to others.

But the Ameses and their friends also had reasons to be bitter. Oakes had cherished a vision of the way to build the Union Pacific as early as Durant, but had been preoccupied with the War, with Congress, with making shovels, and with beating Durant and the others across Iowa to Council Bluffs. Having put up the most working capital, with Durant's consent,[67] the Bostonians had won control of the CM more than a year earlier,[68] with the understanding that all contracts were to go to the CM.[69] They assumed that control of the CM would bring working control of UP policies. But at the UP stockholders' annual election as late as 3 October 1866, Durant had allowed the Ames group only four of the 15 directorships (excluding the five Government Directors), and only three of the seven key positions on the Executive Committee;[70] even though by December 1867, as new stock was issued, the New Englanders were to own over 55 per cent of the *UP* stock.[71] A reason well may be that Oakes, as a Congressman, always declined to be a Director or officer of either the CM or UP. The Boston crowd were not averse to a generous profit in exchange for an unprecedented risk on a contract for a good, honest road. Oakes Ames repeatedly said, "I supposed I was going to

[66] *Poland Rep.*, p. 87 (testimony of Alley).   [67] See p. 107.
[68] The Ames group had 52.3 per cent of the 25,000 shares of CM outstanding on 18 May 1866; *Wilson Rep.*, p. 155; see also p. 127.
[69] See p. 167.   [70] Union Pacific, *Official Register;* see also p. 178.
[71] *Wilson Rep.*, pp. 725–727; *Poland Rep.*, p. 59; see also p. 195.

make 20 per cent on it." [72] They had learned much from their Iowan pioneering. That the Ameses had intended to keep their investment for lifetime to the fullest extent possible is proven by the fact that: (a) Oakes held 20,319 shares prior to his insolvency; [73] (b) Oliver died with over 36,000 shares; [74] and (c) there never was a time in the history of the UP down to 1929 that the Ames family was not represented on the directorate.[75] On the other hand, Durant fulfilled his prophecy by selling out completely after the road was finished, but for quite a different reason than he had expected.

The frugal Ameses were also distrustful of Durant's wastefulness with the road and of his personal extravagance. They had discovered serious "irregularities." [76] His obstruction to examination of official records and accounts aroused deep suspicions, even though many of them later were proved unfounded. His suave intolerance of their soft-spoken, plodding, but sometimes artless ways irritated them. Especially, his employment of fraudulent courts to block progress of the road was insufferable. Indeed, no two personalities could have been more antithetical than Durant and Oliver. Their only interest in common was the projection of the road before both failed. If it was to be failure, the New Englanders would lose more than the New Yorkers.

B. The Compromise

1. THE OAKES AMES CONTRACT

Firmly convinced that Durant would never under any conditions submit to the rule of the majority, the New England group determined that there must be a major shake-up at the coming stockholders' meeting on October 2. To build on with no contract was unthinkable. So Oakes submitted a startling plan dated August 16, New York:

To the president and board of directors of the Union Pacific Railroad Company:
Gentlemen: I propose to construct for your company 667 miles of your road, commencing at the 100th meridian westward, for the following

---

[72] *Wilson Rep.*, pp. 28–30.   [73] *Ibid.*, p. 605 (26 Feb. 1870).   [74] See p. 76.
[75] Oliver Ames (1864–1929), grandson of Oliver Ames, Jr., the president, was the last to serve.
[76] See p. 170.

prices, viz: First 100 miles, at $42,000 per mile; second 167 miles, at $45,000 per mile; third 100 miles, at $96,000 per mile; fourth 100 miles, at $80,000 per mile; fifth 100 miles at $90,000 per mile; sixth 100 miles, at $96,000 per mile; provided the details of a contract can be arranged by a committee of your board and myself satisfactory.

Respectfully,

Oakes Ames [77]

There was not a word about the Credit Mobilier.

"On the same day," stated Durant, "this proposition was accepted, and referred to the Executive Committee by the following resolution:

"*Resolved:* That the contracts adopted this day be referred to the executive committee, with authority to settle the details; and when the same is approved by said executive committee, that the president *pro tem.* and secretary are hereby authorized to execute the same in the name of the company." [78]

A form of contract was carefully drawn up and signed by the available members of the committee on August 18, with Harbaugh appending a letter "reserving an opinion," and Durant adding a note which read: "I recommend the above with the understanding that the assent of all the stockholders is to be obtained." [79]

The detailed contract as drawn up by the Executive Committee and predated August 16 [80] would, if effected, bind Oakes, his heirs, executors, administrators, and assigns, to build and equip 667 miles of railroad and telegraph line, commencing at the 100th meridian (and reaching to near the present site of Bridger, in western Wyoming), at a total price of $47,915,000, or $71,837 per mile. It may be added that by the Act of 1864 the total of U.S. Government Subsidy bonds and UP first mortgage bonds (equally divided in amounts) that could be issued over the same 667 miles was $38,592,000, or $57,858 per mile, as shown in the accompanying table.

To paraphrase the main features of the contract, if the Government bonds received could not be sold at par net, or if the same amount of first mortgage bonds could not be sold at 90 cents on the dollar net, then Oakes Ames would be charged with the difference between the

[77] *Poland Rep.*, p. 375.

[78] Records of UP Historical Museum; *Poland Rep.*, p. 375 (prepared statement by Durant).

[79] *Poland Rep.*, pp. 375–376.　　[80] *Wilson Rep.*, pp. 759–761; *Poland Rep.*, pp. 62–64.

	OAKES AMES'S CONTRACT			TOTAL U.S. AND UP 1ST MORTGAGE BONDS TO BE ISSUED [a]		
Mile Posts from Omaha	*Near Site of Later Stations*	*Rate per Mile*	*Amount*	*Mile Posts from Omaha*	*Rate per Mile*	*Par Value Amount*
247–347	Ogallala	$42,000	$ 4,200,000⎫	247–525 [b]	$32,000	$ 8,896,000
347–514	Cheyenne	45,000	7,515,000⎭			
514–614	Rock Creek	96,000	9,600,000	525–675	96,000	14,400,000
614–714	Rawlins	80,000	8,000,000			
714–814	Salt Wells	90,000	9,000,000⎫	675–914	64,000	15,296,000
814–914	Bridger	96,000	9,600,000⎭			
Total: 667 miles [c]		$71,837	$47,915,000	Total: 667 miles	$57,858	$38,592,000

[a] *Wilson Rep.*, pp. 738–739 (Secretary of the Treasury G. S. Boutwell to J. M. Wilson, 21 Jan. 1873).
[b] East base of Rocky Mts. was fixed by President Johnson at 525 miles west of Omaha and 7 miles west of Cheyenne. (Secretary Browning to Oliver Ames, 25 Nov. 1867; Records of the Secretary of the Interior, vol. 2, p. 182). The west base of the Rockies was 150 miles farther along.
[c] See pp. 182–183.

amount actually realized and the amount specified in the table by the contract rates—provided the first mortgage bonds were not sold below 80. *If the amount realized from all bonds was not enough to cover the cost of the work as stipulated in the contract, he was to make up the deficiency, from time to time, with subscriptions to UP stock at par; and the proceeds of such subscriptions were to be repaid to him.*[81] This meant, of course, that such deficiency, if any, was to be recovered by the sale of issues to him of UP stock.

The whole work was to be constructed in a good and workmanlike manner, upon the same general plan and specifications as adopted east of the 100th meridian. Oakes was to provide, at a cost of not less than $7,500 per mile, all necessary depots, machine shops, rolling stock and sidetracks, and so forth.[82] The cost of bridges and tunnels, however, was excluded.[83]

He was to have the right to increase the grade and curvatures within the limits of the Act of Congress "for the temporary purpose of hastening the completion of the road," but the estimated cost of reducing the same to the Chief Engineer's specifications, or as approved by the company, was to be deducted and retained by the company until such grades and curvatures were so reduced.[84]

He was to receive from the UP the benefit of all existing contracts

[81] *Ibid.*, 11th section, pp. 760–761; *ibid.*, p. 277; Fogel, p. 62; see also p. 54.
[82] *Wilson Rep.*, 2nd section, p. 759.   [83] *Ibid.*, 9th section, p. 760.
[84] *Ibid.*, 4th section, p. 759.

and *all work already done* or to be done and to assume all liabilities thereon west of the 100th meridian, *but he must "credit the UP on this contract for all moneys already expended thereon."* [85] (Thus, as the bonds of course were issued only once for each section, it will be seen there was *no duplication* of receipts or payments by the UP by reason of previous contracts—the conclusions of other historians notwithstanding.)

He was to agree that "the speed of construction and time of completion was the essence of this contract," [86] *yet the road and equipment were to be first-class. If, in the opinion of the Chief Engineer, the entire work was not so prosecuted, both as to quality and dispatch, the UP could, through an officer designated for the purpose, take charge of the work and carry it on at the proper cost and expense of Oakes Ames.*[87]

All the expenses of engineering were to be paid by Oakes, except the salaries of the Chief Engineer and Consulting Engineer and their immediate assistants and the expenses of the general survey of the route.[88]

The document closed with these words: "This contract having been submitted to the Executive Committee by resolution of the Board of Directors, August 16, 1867, and we having examined the details of the same, recommend its execution by the proper officers of the company with the Hon. Oakes Ames. (Signed) Oliver Ames, C.S. Bushnell, Springer Harbaugh, Thomas C. Durant, Executive Committee, Union Pacific Railroad Company." [89] The contract was approved on October 1, subject to written approval of all UP stockholders.

The other three members of the committee were Duff, Lambard, and Dix. Duff would not sign, and the last two were in Europe.

On August 16 Oliver noted in his diary: "Meeting of Board of Directors at 11 o'clock at which the Board accepted bid of Oakes Ames to build 667 miles of Road west of 100 Meridian (naming the different rates). Left completion of contract to Ex Committee and Adjourned to 4th Wednesday of Sep." On August 21 he went on: "Meeting of Executive Committee could not be had for want of quorum. Bushnell & Duff sick. Durant & self present. [I] signed contract to Mr. O. Ames."

Oliver wrote Dodge an explanation from North Easton on August 18:

[85] *Ibid.*, 5th section, p. 760; *Poland Rep.*, pp. 54–55 (14th and 15th answers).
[86] *Wilson Rep.*, 6th section, p. 760.   [87] *Ibid.*, 6th and 7th sections, p. 760.
[88] *Ibid.*, 8th section, p. 760.   [89] *Ibid.*, p. 761.

Your letter from Fort Sanders said the Indians held the country West of you and we naturally felt anxious for your safety. We have been a little stirred up here about our matters and from the course of Durant who can never be relied upon. We have felt a little anxious that things should run smoothly untill the Annual Election the 2d of Oct when we calculated to put enough reliable men in the Board of Directors to have things in the future run on correctly . . . . This contract of my Brother Mr Oakes Ames has no provision to favor Durant or any other individual & will be managed very much as the Road Construction is now being managed. Only we hope to every year have additional economies . . . and by better line and better management make the road a paying institution . . . .[90]

Oakes Ames wrote an often quoted letter to McComb:

H.S. McCombs Esq   *N. Easton   Sept 17th 1867*
Dear Sir
    I have called on Gov. John A. Andrew and got his consent to act as one of the Govt Directors if he should be appointed, and it is our wish to have him
    I wish you to put the matter in the hands of Judge Black if that is the best channel to do it [91]
    I don't suppose the change will be made until October
    Hope you will get every thing ready to run smooth on the contract
    I don't feel that we should do right to put Durant in as director unless he withdraws his injunction suits and submits to the will of the majority. he cannot hurt us half as badly out of the direction as he can in. and there is no pleasure peace safety or comfort with him unless he agrees to abide the decisions of the majority as the rest of us do.
                                                          Yours Truly
                                                          Oakes Ames [92]

2. DURANT HATCHES A PLOT WITH JIM FISK

Oliver penned in his diary on September 19 at New York: "Made no progress in settling up with Durant and hope we shall not until he comes to our terms." Two days later he wrote: "Telegram from New York that Durant had subscribed for 20,000 shares of UPR stock. subscribed for same amount through Thomas." On the 25th: "Was made today a stock subscription on books of UPRR by Mr. Alley and

[90] Dodge, *Papers,* vol. 152 (original ms.).
[91] According to Oliver Ames's diary, 12 Sept., Judges Black and Allen were to look over the contract.
[92] Durant, *Papers,* 1–3–28–21 (original ms.).

others of 50,000,000$ which places our stock where it cannot be over-slaughed. Durant and party greatly surprised at the extent of sub-scription and amt of money used."

The cause of this farcical scene was that Durant and McComb, Alley alleged, in their desperation had connived with the notorious rascal James Fisk Jr. to wrest control of the UP by subscribing for stock before the coming election.[93] Oliver checkmated them by in-voking the charter provision that all subscriptions be paid in full in cash. Fisk's subscriptions of September 21 for 10,000 UP shares were never paid for, and he never got the stock.[94] Durant claimed that the subscriptions of Alley and his friends of about $60,000,000 were fictitious, because they obviously were not and could not be properly paid for in cash, and anyway had been made only about five days before the election of directors, whereas the bylaws specified at least ten days of record for voting privileges.[95]

Oliver must have been deeply disturbed by the whole affair, for on September 26 he made this surprising entry: "Agreed to resign my place as Prest and give it to McCombs he to join us in electing new board of directors & such things as an honest administration of Pac RR interests required. Signed the contract of the 7."

At a meeting of the Executive Committee held on October 1, a resolution to approve the contract without reservation failed to carry. Thereupon resolutions were adopted: (a) to approve the contract and execute it *"subject, however, to the written approval of the stock-holders of the company, as understood by the board of directors when the same was voted upon";* and (b) "that the option to extend this contract to Salt Lake be referred to the board, with recommendation that said option be accepted." [96]

3. THE AMES GROUP TAKES LEADERSHIP IN THE UNION PACIFIC

Oliver noted on October 1: "Large meeting of Stockholders of UPRR on hand to take part in election tomorrow. Ashmun got the start of Bushnell and nominated a Board of Inspectors averse to us & it was carried." On October 2: "Alley chosen Chairman. By Law

---

[93] Records of UP Historical Museum; *Poland Rep.,* p. 421 (testimony of Alley).

[94] *Wilson Rep.,* pp. 244, 297 (testimony of Oliver Ames; nevertheless, he later filed a suit).

[95] *Poland Rep.,* p. 372 (prepared statement by Durant).

[96] *Wilson Rep.,* p. 761. (Italics by C.E.A.)

amended." And on October 3: "The Board of Directors chosen yesterday met at 5th Avenue Hotel and chose their officers last evening."

At the meeting of October 2, each of the two parties put up their own slate of Directors. The Ames slate excluded Durant,[97] and each side got out injunctions to prevent the other from voting; each alleging that the stock held by the other was illegal.[98] The meeting was finally deemed null and void. Two days later, after agreeing among themselves: that *no one* would be barred from participating in the profits; that Oakes would assign his contract to a board of trustees; that he would be relieved from liability for its execution; and that the trustees would administer it for the benefit of the stockholders in common of the UP and CM, a "compromise" board was elected.[99]

Oliver noted the results of the second meeting, this time valid, in his diary of October 4: "Agreed to a compromise Board of Dirs. Voted out Dix, McCormick & Lambard & Tuttle resigned & put in their places Bates Glidden Dexter & J.B. Alley." [100]

Thus, until the next annual stockholders' meeting, the Ames group were to have seven of the 13 Directors (excluding the five Government Directors). But on the Executive Committee of seven, soon to be replaced in effect by the Seven Trustees, the rival groups still would have three members each (at first Oliver Ames, Duff, and Glidden versus Durant, Bushnell, and McComb), with Government Director Harbaugh replaced by James Brooks.[101]

Thus Oakes Ames won his efforts to break the deadlock. He was the only large stockholder who had the confidence of nearly all. Durant won his two main conditions, that the CM would have no more contracts, and that no action could be taken without the written consent of all UP stockholders. More important, his position on the Board was ensured. But the wrangling went on—in fact, it never ended.

4. THE SEVEN TRUSTEES TAKE HOLD: THE TRIPARTITE AGREEMENT[102]

On October 15, Oakes Ames assigned to Durant, Oliver Ames, Alley, Dillon, Bushnell, McComb, and Bates, as the Seven Trustees, all of his right, title, and interest in the contract he had made with

[97] See p. 186 (Oakes Ames's letter to McComb).
[98] *Wilson Rep.*, p. 683 (testimony of Benjamin F. Butler).
[99] Records of UP Historical Museum.   [100] See pp. 178, 182.
[101] Records of UP Historical Museum.
[102] *Wilson Rep.*, pp. 762–765, and *Poland Rep.*, pp. 62–66 (full text in each); *ibid.*, p. 55 (16th answer).

the Union Pacific bearing the date of August 16. The transfer became known as the Tripartite Agreement, being made between Oakes Ames, the Seven Trustees, and the Credit Mobilier. The more important of the conditions to which it was subject are paraphrased as follows:

The Seven Trustees were to pay over all of the estimated net proceeds of Oakes's contract to the stockholders of the CM in proportion to their shareholdings on 15 October 1867 (after service compensation to themselves of not over $3,000 per annum per Trustee). The payments, to be made on the first Wednesday of each June and December, were limited to such CM stockholders who, *being also UP stockholders, had executed their irrevocable proxies to the Trustees* empowering the latter to vote upon at least six-tenths of their UP stock.[103] In turn, on October 16, the Trustees mutually agreed to vote for the persons nominated as Directors at each election by a majority of the then existing Board of Directors, not appointed by the President of the United States, and no others.[104]

The Seven Trustees were to act only by the concurrent assent of four of their number in a meeting recorded by their secretary. Meetings could be called by any two Trustees. The secretary was to keep a faithful record of all their acts, proceedings, and contracts in books always available to any of the Trustees. The Trustees were to prepare a monthly statement showing the amount due from the UP for work done, or equipment or material furnished under the contract, with a copy to the CM.

If any Trustee were to neglect his duties, or willfully attempt to interfere with the execution or performance of the contract, or appropriate for his own use anything belonging to the trust, he could no longer act as Trustee. Any vacancies were to be filled by vote of the remaining Trustees. (No changes in Trustees were made, except that in March 1868, Alley resigned in favor of John Duff, at the insistence of Durant.) [105]

The CM was to advance, as upon a loan, to the Trustees, all such sums of money and at such times as necessary as would enable the Trustees promptly to perform the conditions of the contract. Such sums were to be paid to the CM by the UP, including interest at 7 per cent per annum and a commission of 2½ per cent. The CM was to hold Oakes and the Trustees free of liability.

---

[103] *Wilson Rep.*, pp. 272 (testimony of Oliver Ames), 723 (testimony of Oakes Ames, and the agreement in full), 72 (testimony of Durant).
[104] *Ibid.*, p. xi; see also p. 446.   [105] see p. 179.

Finally, the Trustees were to pay over to the CM such portion of the net profits of the work performed and material furnished on the first 100 miles west of the 100th meridian as was done *prior to 1 January 1867.* As on that date work had stopped for the winter at O'Fallons Bluff only 58 miles beyond 100° West,[106] the reference was to the Boomer contract. Under Oakes's contract this portion was covered, but at $42,000 per mile, whereas the CM under Durant had charged a non-profit rate of $27,500 per mile.[107] If Oakes had not included it, presumably his rates on the rest of the road would have been higher. Actually, the difference, plus bridges, and so forth, was finally adjusted by the UP paying the CM $1,104,000.[108] There was no duplication of Subsidy bonds, of course—the cost to the UP was merely legitimately higher than Durant had arranged.

The Tripartite Agreement was signed as of October 15 by Oakes Ames and the Seven Trustees named above and by Dillon as President of the CM. Durant explained:

Previous to such assignment of [the Oakes Ames] contract the board, by resolution, agreed to recognize said assignment, and accepted the guarantee of the Credit Mobilier Company, and to release the said Oakes Ames from all liabilities under the same, referring the details of such assignment to the executive committee. A full release from all liabilities under the contract was duly executed by the proper officers of the company. The enormous responsibility which Mr. Ames had assumed . . . was thus completely wiped out.[109]

The Tripartite Agreement thus cleverly divided the profits among the CM stockholders in proportion to the stock which each one held, without giving the CM itself a contract. Yet it kept the control of policies nearly evenly divided between the New England and New York interests. Trustee Benjamin E. Bates of Boston, President of the Bank of Commerce, held the balance of control between Trustees Oliver Ames, Dillon, and Alley on one side, and Trustees Durant, Bushnell, and McComb on the other. But any one of them, including Durant, and for that matter any other UP stockholder, held a veto power. With consent unanimous, there would be no lawsuits among themselves. At least, that was the theory. As the CM guaranteed the contract, there was no personal liability to any CM stockholder.

The provisions of both the Contract and the Agreement were formulated by attorneys representing the divergent interests within

---

[106] See p. 161.   [107] See pp. 151–152.
[108] Records of UP Historical Museum; *Wilson Rep.,* pp. 373–375, 641.
[109] *Poland Rep.,* p. 376 (prepared statement F).

the UP Board. They were primarily Samuel J. Tilden, but also Judge W.F. Allen and Benjamin F. Butler for Oakes Ames; [110] Charles Tracy and Clark Bell for Durant; and J.S. Black for McComb.[111] "The instruments were drawn with great care by eminent counsel." [112]

Questions arose in lawsuits later during the Gould regime whether the Oakes Ames contract indicated collusion or connivance. Neither Oakes nor Oliver was ever a Director or officer of the CM. It was never proved beyond a reasonable doubt that, prior to presenting his proposal to the UP Board, Oakes had conspired with Directors of the CM and UP to permit them to participate in the profits.[113] In the Wilson investigation, Oakes testified: "I took that contract without any regard to anyone else." [114] In answer to the question, "Was there any understanding between the UP and Mr. Ames that any profits that might be made out of his contract should be participated in by any other persons than himself?" Durant replied, "None to my knowledge." [115] Oakes himself denied having had any understanding, even with Oliver, that the latter would be permitted to acquire an interest. Oliver confirmed this.[116]

Alley swore: "Mr. Ames took it upon himself with only this condition being attached to it: that it should receive the assent of all the stockholders of the Union Pacific Railroad Company; other than that there were no conditions and he would make no pledges. . . . After the contract was given to him he then said: 'I knew that this contract in honor and honesty belongs to the stockholders of the Credit Mobilier. I will assign it to seven trustees upon certain condition, and every individual member of that corporation shall be offered the opportunity of taking an interest in that contract in pro rata proportion to his ownership in the stock!' " [117]

Sidney Bartlett wrote to Jay Gould on 1 December 1877: ". . . I believe all Credit Mobilier parties and directors, except Mr Hazard, have testified on more than one occasion that the contract was made with Mr. Ames alone, with no agreement he should give its benefits to Credit Mobilier stockholders, although it is confessed that he would naturally include them, if he saw fit, in the enterprise." [118]

---

[110] However, Butler did not see the contract until after it was prepared. *Wilson Rep.*, p. 684 (testimony of Butler).
[111] Records of UP Historical Museum.　　[112] Hazard, p. 22.
[113] Records of UP Historical Museum; *Poland Rep.*, pp. 54–55.
[114] *Wilson Rep.*, p. 27.　　[115] *Ibid.*, p. 88.　　[116] *Ibid.*, p. 251 (Oliver Ames).
[117] *Poland Rep.*, pp. 87–88; see also *Wilson Rep.*, pp. 4–5 (Alley).
[118] Records of UP Historical Museum.

The consent of all the UP stockholders was completed during the month of December.[119] Durant and McComb did not sign until December 20, according to Oliver's diary of that date. So it was not a contract until then.[120]

Dix Holds Out: When it came to getting consents, the only real rebel was General John Dix. He was unhappy about losing a job paying $8,000 a year as inactive President and not being re-elected a Director. He owned 500 UP shares, at least part of which had been paid for by Durant.[121] According to Bushnell, Dix's lawyer (Dix was in Europe) apparently threatened that "the Union Pacific bonds would meet with unfavorable reception in Europe," unless Dix was given $100 a share for his stock.[122] Its worth at that time was not over $20.[123] There was no market. Wrote Oliver on 5 March 1868: "Agreed to carry out Bushnell's agreement to pay him [Dix] 50,000$ which is a complete swindle of the Co." And the next day: "Dr. Durant got home from Europe. Does not like settlement with Gen'l Dix." Said Oakes: "They paid him $50,000 to get rid of him, and to get rid of the claim, or the threat, or whatever you call it. . . . It was a hard thing on the company." [124]

All the rest of the Union Pacific was destined to be built under such an instrument as the Oakes Ames contract with its complements, the Tripartite Agreement and the Seven Trustees.[125] At least the way was cleared to meet the rival Central Pacific as far west as was humanly possible.

C. Financing Steps Up

The promoters renewed their efforts to sell first mortgage bonds. Some of them even thought that at 89 a good turn might be made. In three months the price would be at par for the first time.

On October 22, Ham wrote Oliver:

Mr. Bushnell wishes to know if you have any objection to a special meeting to accept a proposition for the sale of Five Million Bonds at the present rate. . . . The parties are Mr. Cisco, Mr. Opdyke, Mr. Mur-

119 Durant, *Papers*, 1–2–48–18. See Illus., Group 2.
120 *Wilson Rep.*, p. 88 (testimony of Durant).
121 *Ibid.*, p. 542 (testimony of Bushnell).   122 *Ibid.*, p. 544 (testimony of Bushnell).
123 *Ibid.*, p. 680 (testimony of Oakes Ames); Hazard, p. 21.
124 *Wilson Rep.*, pp. 679–680.   125 *Poland Rep.*, p. 55.

dock and Mr. Bardwell are to take $1,000,000 per month, *the Co to sell to no one else.* Mr. Dillon will explain to you fully. . . .[126]

Bushnell wrote Durant the same day:

The parties of whom we were talking have made up Four parties out of Five to take Five Millions of our Bonds and I have pledged you for one fifth of the purchase and would like to go you halves as I think the Road will make $250,000 in three months. The terms proposed are 89 same as we now get, and take them in $500,000 sums—semi monthly— the Company giving them the market for 6 months—and to expend if necessary $100,000 more of the Clark Dodge & Co commission fund in advertising and popularising them.

But some of the parties calculate in making a strike of the entire lot abroad.

Please write Tuttle if you consent to a special meeting of the Board to act on this proposal and nothing else in your absence and the absence of Ames and Dillon—the call of course would specify the object and nothing else would be in order. The parties are quite anxious to have immediate action as they think the time is now very favorable for the consumation of the negotiation abroad. Mr. Cisco sold $100,000 to go to France today. . . .[127]

In October, $672,000 bonds were sold; in November, $700,000; and in December, $2,450,000, a total of $3,822,000.[128] During the year $3,840,000 of them had been issued, matching the U.S. Bonds. For the Government had accepted 240 miles of track, all at $16,000 a mile (the last mileage at this rate). The cumulative total to date was $8,160,000 of each type.[129]

The UP stock was increased during 1867 from $5,318,780 to $5,467,980.[130] Of this moderate gain of $149,200 the additional scrip previously described accounted for $53,970.[131]

Stock of the CM was and would remain at 37,500 shares outstanding; no more was ever authorized.

Profits of the UP for the year 1867, according to the general ledger of the operating department, were: total earnings, $3,465,000; total operating expenses (including taxes), $1,404,000; and net earnings, $2,061,000.[132]

The 1867 UP "capital balance sheet" appears in a report of the U.S. Pacific Railway Commission, pp. 5012–13.

[126] Records of UP Historical Museum. (Italics by C.E.A.) Murdock was never a Director and Opdyke was not one at the time.
[127] Durant, *Papers*, 1–3–30–15. [128] *Wilson Rep.*, pp. 619–621.
[129] *Ibid.*, p. 738. See also Appendix D. [130] *Ibid.*, pp. 748–749. See also Appendix E.
[131] See p. 129. [132] U.S. Pacific Railway Commission, p. 5266.

STOCKHOLDERS OF CREDIT MOBILIER AS OF 12 DECEMBER 1867 [a]

37,400 Shares of $100 Par, Fully Paid [b]

AMES GROUP (27)		Change Since 17 May '67		DURANT GROUP (9)		Change Si 17 May '	
Oliver Ames (partly				Durant, T. C.	4,915 }	+	107
joint with Oakes)	4,680	−	5	do. (Fourth Nat. Bk.)	750 }		
Oakes Ames	1,955	+	625	Gray, G. G.	1,620	+	333
Oakes, Ames, Trustee (new)	93	+	93	Bushnell, C. S.	410	−	500
Lambard, C. A.	775	−	625	Holladay, Benj.	750	+	250
Duff, John	1,880	+	700	McComb, H. S.	750		——
Hazard, R. G.	1,690	+	72	Train, W. D. (or G. F.)	175	+	60
Hazard, I. P.	380		——	Boyer, B. M. (new)	75	+	75
Hazard, Rowland	300	−	72	Crane, H. C. (new)	128	+	128
4 other Hazards	77		——	Crane, H. C., Trustee (new)	60	+	60
Glidden, W. T.	625		——	Total	9,633	+	515
Williams, J. M. S.	620		——				
Dillon, Sidney, Pres.	400	+	400	UNCERTAIN (49)			
Dillon, Sidney	1,005	+	60				
Bates, B. E.	500		——	McCormick, C. H.	945		——
Hooper, Samuel, & Co.	750		——	Opdyke, George	712		——
Alley, J. B.	290	−	210	Baker, E. H.	623	+	150
Grimes. J. W.	380		——	Bardwell, Josiah	710	+	230
Nickerson, Frederick	250		——	Bardwell, Josiah,			
Nickerson, Joseph	380		——	Trustee (new)	300	+	300
Nickerson, Thomas	150		——	Macy, W. H.	300	−	75
Chapman, O. S.	412	+	100	Jones, David	380	+	130
Atkins, Elisha	622		——	Gilbert, Horatio	185		——
Gilmore, E. W.	150		——	Gilbert, H., Jr. (new)	137	+	137
Total	18,364	+	978 [c]	Jenks, B. H.	500		——
				Lockwood, Le Grand	500		——
				Pigot, J. B.	200		——
				Robbins, R. E.	200		——
				Sanford, Harvey	125		——
				Hotchkiss, Henry	150		——
				Davies, J. M. (new)	500	+	500
				Johnston, J. B. (new)	200	+	200
				Neilson, C. H. (new)	150	+	150
				Skinner, F., & Co. (new)	500	+	500
				Smith, John (new)	405	+	405
				29 others, each 100 or less	1,731	+	217
				Total	9,403	+	1,427
				GRAND TOTAL (85 names)	37,400	+	2,918

[a] *Wilson Rep.,* pp. 725–727; *Poland Rep.,* pp. 59–60. See p. 168 for list of 17 May 1867.

[b] 100 shares short of the maximum of 37,500 finally issued.

[c] 160 shares had been sold by C.H. French.

[d] 380 shares had been sold by Williams & Guion, 150 shares had been sold by A.H. Bowman, 700 share e in Wilson Report of 17 May 1867 is eliminated, and 197 shares had been sold by various persons.

Thus, of a total of 37,400 shares ($3,740,000) the Ames Group now held *49.0 per cent,* the Durant Group 25.8 per cent, and "Uncertain" 25.2 per cent.

The two Ameses together were increased to *18 per cent,* while Durant's own holdings were decreased to *15 per cent.*

The Ameses personally now had $672,800 invested in the CM, having added $71,300 since 17 May 1867.

The control of the CM was no longer of importance since the Oakes Ames contract. The list merely shows at what pro rata rates the allotments of profits were made by the Seven Trustees to such CM stockholders as were also UP stockholders and had signed proxies.

STOCKHOLDERS OF UNION PACIFIC ALSO AS OF 12 DECEMBER 1867 [a]
44,164 Shares of $100 Par, Fully Paid

Ames Group (20)		Durant Group (7)	
Oliver Ames	6,251	Durant, T. C.	7,564
Oakes Ames	2,849	Gray, G. G.	2,534
Oakes Ames, Trustee	——	Bushnell, C. S.	1,450
Lambard, C. A.	1,250	Holladay, Benj.	1,000
Duff, John	500	McComb, H. S.	1,075
Hazard, R. G.	2,000	Train, W. D. (or G. F.)	230
Hazard, I. P.	500	Boyer, B. M.	100
Hazard, Rowland	500	Crane, H. C.	——
4 other Hazards	——	Crane, H. C., Trustee	——
Glidden, W. T.	1,250	Total	13,953 (31.7%)
Williams, J. M. S.	1,245		
Dillon, Sidney	1,848	Uncertain (20)	
Bates, B. E.	1,000		
Hooper, Samuel, & Co.	1,000	McCormick, C. H.	1,251
Alley, J. B.	1,000	Opdyke, George	931
Grimes, J. W.	500	Baker, E. H.	625
Nickerson, Frederick	500	Bardwell, Josiah	500
Nickerson, Joseph	500	Bardwell, Josiah, Trustee	200
Nickerson, Thomas	200	Macy, W. H.	650
Chapman, O. S.	624	Jones, David	500
Atkins, Elisha	674	Gilbert, Horatio	251
E. W. Gilmore	200	Gilbert, H., Jr.	175
Total	24,391 (55.2%)	Jenks, B. H.	80
		Lockwood, Le Grand	——
		Pigot, J. B.	——
		Robbins, R. E.	——
		Sanford, Harvey	——
		Hotchkiss, Henry	——
		Davies, J. M.	——
		Johnston, J. B.	——
		Neilson, C. H.	200
		Skinner, F., & Co.	——
		Smith, John	——
		9 others	457
		Total	5,820 (13.1%)
		GRAND TOTAL (47 names)	44,164

[a] *Wilson Rep.*, pp. 725–727.

Thus, at this date, of 44,164 shares of UP stock outstanding, the Ames Group (20 names) held *55.2 per cent,* the Durant Group (7 names) held 31.7 per cent, and "Uncertain" (20 names) held 13.1 per cent. It is interesting to compare this list with that of the CM stockholders on the same day.

On 12 December 1867, the Seven Trustees declared the first allotment of accumulated construction profits to the CM stockholders, payable on January 3. Oliver noted: "Meeting of Contractors or Trustees & to talk over matters. Decided to pay off the earnings of the past season in part to Stockholders of Cr. Mob, 60% in Bonds & 60% in Stock." [133] To each holder of 10 shares ($1,000 par value) of CM stock, then, was given $600 par value of first mortgage bonds and six shares of UP stock, with odd-lot holders pro rata.[134] At the then current market prices of 97 and 30, respectively,[135] the bonds had a value of $582 and the stock $180, a total of $762. On this basis, each holder received the *equivalent of a cash payment of 76 per cent* on his working-capital investment in the construction company, not "120%." What the subsequent value might be is irrelevant. It would vary according to the market at any given date. Total securities thus paid out on the 37,400 shares of CM were $2,244,000 par in bonds and 22,440 shares in stock. The principal recipients of the allotments are listed in "Stockholders of Credit Mobilier as of the List of 12 December 1867—37,400 Shares." [136]

On December 28, no interest or other payment ever having been allowed to the CM stockholders, the CM Executive Committee declared the only true dividend, at 6 per cent for each of the two years 1866 and 1867, payable also on January 3.[137] "Money was . . . very low in the treasury, and Union Pacific stock was plenty." [138] So it was decided to pay this 12 per cent interest in UP stock at *30 per cent of its par value.*[139] Thus each holder of 10 CM shares was credited with four UP shares, which, at a market price of 30, were worth $120 in cash at the time. On the records this was called a "40% dividend," but its value was only 12 per cent of par. To effect it, a total of 14,960 shares of UP stock were credited to the holders of 37,400 shares of CM outstanding.[140] The stock was sold, and the proceeds divided pro rata.[141]

Oakes, co-trustee of the first mortgages, must have spent much of his Christmas shopping period in Washington endorsing those bonds at 65 cents a signature.[142] On December 19, Alley wrote him: "Out of bonds, send without fail tonight." [143] Oliver's Christmas probably was not too merry, either. On December 27, he noted: "Whole day

---

133 Diary, 12 Dec.   134 *Wilson Rep.,* pp. 725–727 (gives names and amounts in full).
135 See pp. 238, 259.   136 See p. 194.
137 Hazard, p. 21; *Wilson Rep.,* p. 19; *Poland Rep.,* p. 56.   138 Hazard, pp. 21–22, 28.
139 *Wilson Rep.,* p. 154 (the resolution), also pp. 15, 19.   140 *Ibid.,* pp. 385 (Ham), 749.
141 *Poland Rep.,* p. 56.   142 *Wilson Rep.,* p. 549 (Bushnell).
143 Records of UP Historical Museum.

wasted. Durant willing to do but never willing to come to any definite practical mode of effecting a settlement." Perhaps the Doctor secretly enjoyed letting Oliver stew about details which would have been easy enough for a New Yorker to master. But the Doctor was having a poor Christmas, too. He and his brothers were being squeezed in an attempted corner on the Chicago and Rock Island stock and would be forced to resign as Directors of that railroad, an Iowan rival of Oakes's Cedar Rapids & Missouri River.[144]

Rowland Hazard summed up the position of the CM stockholders as follows:

Technically, the connection of the Credit Mobilier Company with the Union Pacific Railroad ends here. It constructed 247 miles of road, upon which very little profit was realized; it invested all its capital in the operation; and it made two dividends only, of 6% each. Besides this, it sold its stockholders 200% of Union Pacific stock at $4.50 a share,[145] and sold them $1,250,000 in bonds as before explained. Each stockholder, after an investment of two years, had in hand, for each $100 invested (one share CM) $200 (par) in Union Pacific stock, worth at that time not over $20 (per share), and thirty-three and one-third ($33⅓) in Union Pacific bond *certificates* worth say $30 (30%) and the Credit Mobilier stock, considered to be worthless.[146] So, on this showing, each stockholder would lose half the money he put in. This, though technically true, was practically avoided by the perfected arrangement (the Oakes Ames contract).[147]

D. *Congressman Ames Sells Some Stock to Congressmen*

1. WHERE IT CAME FROM

Sidney Dillon had been elected President of the CM in May to replace Durant. Upon examining the records a month later, he found that a block of 650 shares stood in the name of Thomas C. Durant

---

[144] Hayes, pp. 55, 69; see also p. 21.

[145] *Wilson Rep.*, pp. 745–748; see also p. 129.

[146] However, this is hardly fair, as the CM stock then had a "market" value of at least $50 a share. On this basis, each CM stockholder would have stood about even some time prior to the Oakes Ames contract of 1 Oct. 1867. Only *eventually* would the investment in the CM stock become worthless, either in a failure or upon completion of the road.

[147] Hazard, p. 21 and fn. Parenthetical items have been added by C.E.A. to simplify the calculation. For $100 invested, an investor had a market value of $40 in stock, less the small amount paid for it, and $10 in bond certificates—a total less than $50, if the CM stock had no value as claimed.

which had never been paid for. Durant alleged he held this stock for persons who had agreed to take it, but who had not paid in their subscriptions.[148] The persons were not named. Oakes claimed that at least a portion of it should be assigned to him to fulfill his own engagements.[149] The CM ordered the block transferred to Dillon in trust about October. Upon full payment at par and interest from July 1, it was divided and transferred, 280 shares to Oakes in trust, and 370 to Durant who still was claiming prior commitments. The authorization for the division was signed by nine principal CM stockholders, *including McComb.* At a later date about the same nine stockholders, but excluding McComb, agreed to issue 93 additional shares at par to Oakes Ames, Trustee. Thus, as of 12 December 1867, the CM stock outstanding was raised to 37,400 shares, within 100 shares of the final limit.[150]

The Poland Committee stated:

Mr. McComb, who was present at the time, claimed he had also made engagements for stock which he should have stock given him to carry out. This claim of McComb was refused, but after the stock was assigned to Mr. Ames, McComb insisted that Ames should distribute some of his stock to his (McComb's) friends, and named Senators Bayard and Fowler, and Representatives Allison and Wilson, of Iowa.[151]

McComb had demanded 250 of the original shares, together with the 50 per cent increase, making 375 shares in all.[152] He already had 750 shares.[153] Oakes then accommodated McComb by transferring and lending to him 500 shares on 28 December 1867, so that McComb could receive the allotments of profits on 1,250 shares paid on 3 January 1868.[154] McComb returned the shares, or equivalent ones, with the allotments in full, sometime after February 1, as agreed. Presumably by then McComb had completed a purchase of 500 shares from B.H. Jenks.[155] Oakes's original letter is on exhibit at the UP Historical Museum, on Panel 22. His kindly loan is not mentioned in the Poland or Wilson Reports.

2. OAKES'S PURPOSE

After his contract for the remainder of the road had been assigned to the Seven Trustees on October 15, Oakes was more willing than

---

[148] *Poland Rep.*, pp. 57 (evidence taken in Chancery Court, 1869, McComb v. Credit Mobilier), 18, 335 (Oakes Ames), 174, 241–242, 386 (Durant), 406 (Alley).
[149] *Ibid.*, pp. iii, 57.   [150] See p. 194.   [151] *Poland Rep.*, p. iii.
[152] Ibid., p. 3 (McComb).   [153] See p. 168.   [154] See p. 259.   [155] See p. 194.

ever to sell to his good friends as much Credit Mobilier stock as they could properly afford. The company bonds were selling well for the first time. The details of an expeditious route over the first range of the Rockies, known in a general way for over a year,[156] had been ironed out. Probably no overwhelming difficulties would be met in obtaining enough capital to meet the Central Pacific well out, even beyond Salt Lake. Oakes talked with his intimate friends in Boston, particularly those to whom he wished to return a favor. He approached capitalists in large cities wherever he went.

Also, between November 21, when Congress convened, and December 12, when the first allotment "dividend" was declared, he talked with a number of his influential friends in the Capitol. But time was running out; the CM stock was beginning to be in general demand as the favorable news spread via the market grapevine. Perhaps it took hours, in those days of no telephone, automobiles, or planes, to reach and explain the essential investment facts to each prospect. "There were so many who talked to me," said Oakes, "about getting an interest in it, when they began to think it was a good thing, I cannot recollect all the names; I do not know whether they had all spoken to me before; I know that several of them did." [157] To some he offered a guarantee against loss. "He asked no one to take a risk that he was not willing to take more largely himself." [158]

Testified Oakes in writing to the Poland Committee in 1873, in his consistently frank manner:

We wanted capital and influence. Influence not in legislation alone, but on credit, good, wide, and a general favorable feeling. If the community had confidence in our ultimate success, that success was insured. . . . For unless we could get off our bonds and land-grants, to raise money to pay our way, we must certainly fail. When, then, I tell you in the light of these circumstances that I wished to enlist our public men as well as capitalists, to obtain their influence, have I not the right to ask you to infer that I meant a *proper* influence? [159]

To the Committee again:

During 1865–66, and until late in 1867, there were neither dividends nor profits. During all this time I was constantly at work endeavoring to enlist others. Confident of ultimate success, and of the profit that

---

[156] See p. 156.   [157] *Poland Rep.*, p. 32.   [158] Ames Family, *Oakes Ames*, p. 8.
[159] *Poland Rep.*, p. 16.

would come, I held out every inducement, and made every representation that I believed to be justifiable for this purpose. Precisely who I spoke to or who formally agreed to take shares, but desired to postpone the time of payment, it is quite impossible for me to recall. When the stock was *obtained in 1868* there was a difficulty about this, and time has not aided me in this respect. . . . The number of shares that remained, and with which I could fulfill many engagements I had made, or supposed I had made, was very small . . . . From first to last I was influenced by the same motive—*to aid the credit of the road*.[160]

Congressman Alley swore to the Poland Committee:

Mr. Ames was trying to sell the stock to everybody, especially to those who had influence, power and money. He had a very heavy load on his shoulders. He felt that he had a big enterprise, and he was soliciting men from every quarter to come in.[161]

Cornelius Bushnell voluntarily made a prepared statement under oath before the Poland Committee:

He [Mr. Ames] said that he had promised, during the spring [of 1867], in our dark days, some two or three hundred shares of stock, and that the parties were fairly entitled to it. I knew that he had done it. During the spring he had placed a great deal of it, and I had done the same. He asked us to sign a paper or an agreement that he might have this stock and fulfill his promises made in the spring. I had no hesitation in signing that agreement. The view I took of it was, that if parties in Congress or out of Congress had taken that stock they ought to be proud of it. . . . I believed his word when he said he had promised it, and it was nothing to me whom he had promised it to.[162]

Nothing ever happens in this world until somebody sells something to somebody.

3. WHEN IT WAS SOLD

It seems certain that every one of the CM shares which Oakes sold to Congressmen after the Tripartite Agreement was *negotiated* in Washington while Congress was in session. *That year the First Session of the 40th Congress, which had adjourned on July 20, convened again for a Special Session at noon on November 21 and met every*

[160] *Ibid.*, pp. 19–20 (Oakes Ames). (Italics by C.E.A.)
[161] *Ibid.*, p. 78.   [162] *Ibid.*, p. 180.

day until Monday, December 2, when the regular Second Session opened.[163] Strangely, this fact was not understood by the Poland Committee at any time. "The session commenced about the beginning of December," they claimed.[164] Unfortunately, the fact was overlooked also by Oakes, his lawyers, and everyone else, except Alley. Alley mentioned it so briefly in one or two of his many profusive statements that apparently it escaped attention.[165] *Also, it is very probable that all of Oakes's negotiations were carried on before the declaration of the first CM "dividend" of December 12.* At least, no one testified to the contrary.[166]

4. THE LITTLE BLACK MEMORANDUM BOOK

All of Oakes's actual transactions were entered concisely and accurately in the little black memorandum book which he habitually carried in his pocket.[167] All entries were made systematically from a sample form that he devised, and can be summed up as follows: [168]

First, all sales were made in even lots of 10, 20, or 30 shares. *Second,* the price of the CM stock was invariably par, $100 a share, regardless of the so-called "market" price. Par was the price which Oakes had paid for it, in cash to the CM.[169] *Third,* to the price was added interest at 7 per cent from 1 July 1867 to the settlement date, a period of 7 months and 10 days.[170] The settlement date was that upon which the stock had been, or was supposed to have been, delivered to Oakes. *Fourth,* each account was credited with the proceeds of sale at 97 per cent (the estimated market value) of an "80% dividend" payable in UP first mortgage bonds at par. The 80 per cent was the sum of the 60 per cent dividend declared by the CM on 12 December 1867 [171] and a 20 per cent dividend declared on 3 January 1868, both payable on January 3. The money so credited was sufficient to recover 73 per cent of the CM investment, principal, and interest. *Finally,* at the bottom Oakes noted the par value amount of both the CM stock purchased and the 100 per cent UP stock dividend received free. The latter was the sum of a 60 per cent stock dividend declared on 12

---

[163] *Cong. Globe,* 21 Nov.; *Biographical Directory of the American Congress,* p. 1950; Crawford, pp. 179–180; Hazard, p. 32.

[164] *Poland Rep.,* p. ii; Ames Family, *Oakes Ames,* p. 112.

[165] *Poland Rep.,* p. 407 (Alley); *Wilson Rep.,* pp. 281 (Alley), 283 (Oliver Ames).

[166] Ames Family, *Oakes Ames,* p. 25; Crawford, pp. 179–180; Hazard, p. 32.

[167] The booklet cannot be found today. It is not filed in the National Archives or in the Library of Congress.

[168] *Poland Rep.,* p. 452 (Oakes Ames).   [169] *Ibid.,* p. 58 (Chancery Court testimony).

[170] *Ibid.,* p. 139 (B.F. Ham to Oakes Ames).   [171] See p. 196.

December (along with the 60 per cent bond dividend above), and a 40 per cent stock dividend declared on 17 June 1868.[172] So Oakes must have entered these accounts at about this date.[173]

The CM stock sold was not transferred to the name of the buyer until years later. It remained in the name of Oakes Ames, Trustee, and was kept in his possession. The reasons for this were good. There was a chance that the legal title might be involved in a lawsuit which McComb was threatening to bring against Oakes and the CM.[174] The Poland Committee believed the true reason was that any transfer would cut off the right to "dividends" from the Seven Trustees, unless the new owners (including the Congressmen) also became parties to the Tripartite Agreement.[175] In some cases, however, Oakes delivered a "certificate" for stock in lieu of the actual stock.[176]

Oakes sent out but few statements of the status of the accounts, probably for the same reasons. Judging from the testimony of the owners, this was an error of judgment on the part of Oakes or his counsel. It led to irritations and misunderstandings. Later, it opened up a temptation for some of the Congressmen, during the Poland inquisition, to publicly disclaim ownership of the stock which they had bought. The sequel appears in Chapter 11.

5. WHO BOUGHT IT, AND WHO DID NOT

In all, nine U.S. Representatives and two U.S. Senators, from seven states, made purchases of CM stock from Oakes, amounting in all to 160 shares for $16,000 and interest.[177] These shares were less than one-half of one per cent of the total CM stock outstanding. They added only 5 per cent to all stock previously held by U.S. Congressmen. They were less than 8 per cent of the 2,048 shares then standing in the name of Oakes, personally and in Trust.

The circumstances of the original negotiation and agreement preliminary to settlement with each of the 11 fellow Congressmen to whom Oakes sold late in 1867 are given in alphabetical order below:

William Boyd Allison, Representative from Dubuque, Iowa—
10 Shares

Some time late in 1867 (no one was able to remember exact dates after the passage of over five years), Congressman (and Lieutenant

---

[172] *Wilson Rep.*, p. 630.   [173] *Poland Rep.*, p. 451 (Oakes Ames).
[174] *Ibid.*, pp. 129, 292.   [175] *Ibid.*, pp. viii, 339 (Oakes Ames).
[176] *Ibid.*, p. 104 (Alley).   [177] See p. 203.

23 U.S. CONGRESSMEN INTERROGATED BY POLAND COMMITTEE REGARDING THEIR HOLDINGS OF CREDIT MOBILIZER STOCK, IF ANY

Congressman	S: Sen. R: Repr.	State	Shs. Sold Late 1867 by		Shares Held 17 May 1867	Remarks
			Oakes Ames	Durant		
Alley	R	Mass.	——	——	500	Bought in 1866 through Oakes Ames. Dir. of CM and UP.
Allison	R	Iowa	10 *a*	——	——	
Oakes Ames	R	Mass.	——	——	1,330	Dir. of UP after 1869. Never Dir. of CM.
Bayard	S	Del.	——	——	——	Never held any.*b, e*
Bingham	R	Ohio	20	——	——	
Blaine	R	Me.	——	——	——	Never held any.*e, d*
Boutwell	R	Mass.	——	——	——	Never held any.*e, d*
Boyer	R	Pa.	——		100	Bought in 1866 through Durant.
Brooks	R	N.Y.	——	150 *e*	——	
Colfax	R	Ind.	20	——	——	
Conkling	S	N.Y.	——	——	——	Never held any.*e*
Dawes	R	Mass.	10	——	——	
Eliot	R	Mass.	——	——	——	Never held any.*e, d*
Fowler	S	Tenn.	——	——	——	Never held any.*b, e, f*
Garfield	R	Ohio	10	——	——	
Grimes	S	Iowa	——	——	380	Bought in 1866 through Oakes Ames.
Hooper	R	Mass.	——	——	750	Bought in 1865 through Oakes Ames.
Kelley	R	Pa.	10	——	——	
Logan	R	Ill.	10	——	——	
Patterson	S	N.H.	30	——	——	
Scofield	R	Pa.	10	——	——	
Henry Wilson	S	Mass.	20	——	——	
Jas. F. Wilson	R	Iowa	10 *a*	——	——	
Total shares held			160	150	3,060	
Total Congressmen			11	1	5	
Shares Per Congressman			15	150 *e*	612	

a Oakes Ames complied with McComb's request.
b Urged by McComb to take some of Oakes Ames's shares, but turned down the offer.
e Notwithstanding McComb's claim to the contrary (*Poland Rep.*, p. 6).
d Oakes Ames offered him stock, but was turned down.
e Durant sold 100 shares, the Credit Mobilier sold 50.
f Oakes never offered any.

Colonel) Allison, a lawyer, because of his interest in Oakes's Sioux City and Pacific Railroad, of which he was for a time a Director and stockholder, asked Oakes if he could have some CM stock.[178] Oakes,

[178] *Poland Rep.*, pp. 304–308 (Allison).

at the request of McComb, finally agreed on only 10 shares, and on 24 April 1868 debited them at $1,000 plus interest of $47. The same date Allison was credited with an 80 per cent dividend of $800 of UP bonds, which Oakes had sold for him at 97, or $776. The net debit balance of *$271* was paid by Allison that day.[179] Whereupon Oakes delivered the shares to him against receipt, but bought them back at cost in 1868.[180] The sequel appears in Chapter 11.

John Armor Bingham, Representative from Cadiz, Ohio— 20 Shares

Desiring to recoup for Congressman and Major Bingham, a lawyer, a total loss of $2,000 in another stock he had once recommended, Oakes advised him in the spring of 1867 and again in November or December to buy 20 shares of CM. Bingham did so. Shortly afterwards Oakes exchanged them for $2,000 UP bonds at 95, keeping in his possession both the stock and the bonds, but treating Bingham as the real owner of the stock. He made proper adjustments to Bingham's satisfaction.[181] The sequel appears in Chapter 11.

Schuyler Colfax, Representative from South Bend, Indiana— 20 Shares *(Speaker of the House)*

"I cannot remember which of us first mentioned the subject," said Oakes, "but I know he wanted to get some stock." [182] They agreed on 20 shares in November or December 1867. The price was $2,000 plus $86.72 interest. After being credited with the 80 per cent bond dividend sold at 97, or $1,552.00, on March 5 Colfax paid Oakes the net debit balance of *$534.72* with a check on the House Sergeant-at-Arms. He thereby became the owner of 20 CM shares and 20 UP shares.[183] The unfortunate sequel appears in Chapter 11.

Henry Laurens Dawes, Representative from Pittsfield, Massachusetts —10 Shares *(Committee on Indian Affairs)*

Prior to 1867, Congressman Dawes, a lawyer and graduate of Yale in 1839, had made some small investments in railroad bonds through

---

[179] *Ibid.*, p. 293 (Oakes Ames's memorandum book).   [180] *Ibid.*, p. 292 (Oakes Ames).
[181] *Ibid.*, pp. vi, 21, 336, 458 (Oakes Ames), 191–197 (Bingham).   [182] *Ibid.*, p. 20.
[183] *Ibid.*, pp. 279, 451 (Oakes Ames).

Oakes. Sometime in November or December 1867, Dawes asked him to buy a bond of the Cedar Rapids and Missouri River. Oakes said 10 shares of CM would be a better investment and guaranteed to take it off his hands any time with 10 per cent interest on his money. After making inquiries, Dawes took the stock for $1,000 plus $35 interest, *paying Oakes in full* in cash, $800 on 11 January 1868 and $235 three days later.[184] The sequel appears in Chapter 11.

James Abram Garfield, Representative from Hiram, Ohio—
10 Shares
(Chairman of the Committee on Military Affairs)

Congressman and Major-General Garfield, a lawyer and graduate of Williams in 1858, first heard of the CM in 1866 or 1867 through George Francis Train, and Oakes had told him the investment would be safe and profitable.[185] Oakes said, "I agreed to get ten shares of stock for him and hold it until he could pay for it." [186] This was some time in 1867. Garfield never paid any cash down for it. Oakes put up the purchase money of $1,047, including interest. The first 80 per cent bond dividend sold at 97 raised $776. Part of the 60 per cent cash dividend of $600 of June 17 was needed to fully cover the cost. On 19 June 1868, Oakes sent him a check or currency for the net credit balance of *$329*. Oakes received all the subsequent dividends,[187] and the account had not been finally settled by the time of the Poland investigation.[188] The sequel appears in Chapter 11.

William Darrah Kelley, Representative from Philadelphia,
Pennsylvania—10 Shares

Early in December 1867, during a session of Congress, Oakes recommended that Congressman Kelley, a lawyer, purchase 10 shares of CM. Not being prepared to pay for the stock then, Oakes volunteered to carry it for him at 7 per cent interest until he had the money. From there on the case resembled Garfield's. Kelley put up no money and on June 23 received from Oakes *$329* in a check on the Sergeant-at-Arms of the House. That was the net credit balance after the original purchase debit of $1,047, the 80 per cent bond dividend at 97 of $776, and the 60 per cent cash dividend credit of $600 of June

[184] *Ibid.,* pp. v, 20, 449–450 (Oakes Ames), 112–115 (Dawes).
[185] *Ibid.,* pp. 128–131 (Garfield).   [186] *Ibid.,* pp. 21, 297, 459 (Oakes Ames).
[187] *Ibid.,* p. vii.   [188] *Ibid.,* p. 460 (Oakes Ames).

17.[189] The account remained open until McComb's suit, if any, could be settled. The sequel appears in Chapter 11.

John Alexander Logan, Representative from Carbondale, Illinois— 10 Shares

In November or December 1867, Congressman and Major-General Logan, a lawyer and graduate of the University of Louisville, upon Oakes's recommendation made an arrangement with Oakes whereby he purchased 10 shares. As in the case of Garfield and Kelley, the cost of $1,047 was not fully paid until after the 60 per cent cash dividend of June 17 was credited. Thereupon, on June 20, Oakes sent him a check for *$329*, the net credit balance.[190] All the securities were held by Oakes. The sequel appears in Chapter 11.

James Wills Patterson, Senator from Hanover, New Hampshire— 30 Shares

At the suggestion of Oakes, Senator Patterson, a graduate of Dartmouth in 1848 and later a professor there, purchased 30 shares on 31 August 1867 [191] for $3,000 plus $105 interest. He paid only $3,000. Oakes credited him with $2,328 for the 80 per cent bond dividend at 97, deducted the $105, and on 14 February 1868 paid Patterson in cash the net credit balance of *$2,223*. The securities were not transferred to Patterson's name, but Oakes handed him certificates for 30 CM and 30 UP shares.[192] The sequel appears in Chapter 11.

Glenni William Scofield, Representative from Warren, Pennsylvania —10 Shares

Late in 1866, Congressman Scofield, a lawyer and graduate of Hamilton in 1840, bought some Cedar Rapids and Missouri River bonds from Oakes. A year later, in November or December, Scofield wanted more, and Oakes suggested some CM stock instead. Scofield bought 10 shares. Preferring to be a cash customer, he paid Oakes $1,041 principal and interest on January 29 and took a certificate, but

---

[189] *Ibid.*, pp. vii, 21, 298, 330, 451 (Oakes Ames), 197–204 (Kelley).

[190] *Ibid.*, pp. 335, 460 (Oakes Ames), 346–347 (Logan).

[191] Crawford, pp. 147–148 (Select Committee from the Senate, 27 Feb. 1873); *Poland Rep.*, p. 185.

[192] *Poland Rep.*, pp. 266–273, 457–458 (Oakes Ames), 184–186, 261–266, 270–272 (Patterson).

not the stock itself. Scofield stated he had no idea of the market price at the time of sale; Oakes had said nothing about it.[193] Oakes delivered a $1,000 UP bond to him in Washington on Sunday, February 9, taking in payment *$195.33* in cash from Scofield for "the balance due on his bond over his dividend." [194] When the 60 per cent cash dividend was received, Oakes paid him the $600 for it by a Sergeant-at-Arms check on June 22. Oakes then held for him the 10 UP shares and the 10 shares of CM stock.[195] The sequel appears in Chapter 11.

Henry Wilson, Senator from Natick, Massachusetts— 20 Shares

Senator Wilson (1812–1875) and Oakes boarded at the same house in Washington and often sat at the same table. The Senator, a schoolteacher and shoemaker, who became Vice-President of the United States in 1873, seemed rather proud that he had to live in the strictest economy. He had paid $150 for his home lot, he said. The salary of a Congressman was hardly $5,000 a year.[196] On their silver wedding anniversary in 1865, his wife had received a gift package of $3,800 in bills from many friends, in amounts from $50 to $200 each. Oakes's contribution had been $200, Alley's $100. William H. Claflin, soon to become Governor of the Commonwealth, had presented the package.[197] Wilson consulted Oakes about its investment, and the bonds of some of Oakes's Iowan railroads were purchased for Mrs. Wilson. In December 1867, or earlier, Wilson spoke to Oakes about her buying some more. Oakes recommended 20 shares of CM instead and offered a guarantee against loss, with 10 per cent interest, if the Wilsons would give up half the profit, if any, above that. After checking with Alley,[198] Wilson agreed, and gave Oakes *$2,000*.[199] Some months later, however, he changed his mind, "believing that much of the money put into the Pacific Railroad would be lost." [200] He also pointed out that there was a lawsuit pending, and that "he would purchase no property that could be affected by legislation." Oakes felt bound to take the stock off their hands, and he returned to the Wilsons all the money he had received for their account, plus 10 per cent interest.[201] The sequel appears in Chapter 11.

---

193 *Ibid.*, p. 205 (Scofield).   194 *Ibid.*, pp. 455–456 (Oakes Ames).
195 *Ibid.*, pp. vi, 299–300, 336, 352 (Oakes Ames), 204–207 (Scofield).
196 *Ibid.*, p. 481 (Moses Dillon).   197 *Ibid.*, p. 187 (Henry Wilson).
198 *Ibid.*, pp. 78–79 (Alley).   199 *Ibid.*, pp. 20, 187, 288–289 (Oakes Ames).
200 *Ibid.*, pp. 187–188 (Henry Wilson).
201 *Ibid.*, pp. 26, 336, 448–449, 461, 481 (Oakes Ames), 186–190 (Henry Wilson).

James Falconer Wilson, Representative from Fairfield, Iowa—
10 Shares

Urged by his friend McComb, Congressman Wilson, who in 1882 became a U.S. Senator, applied to Oakes for 50 CM shares but was turned down because it was too much. Upon further consultation in November or December 1867, Oakes let him have 10 shares on the basis of not putting up any money, but paying Wilson $329 after the 60 per cent cash dividend. Soon becoming aware of serious differences between Oakes and McComb,[202] Wilson decided to sell his CM and UP stocks in 1869, before he became a Government Director of the UP.[203] Oliver Ames bought them from him.[204] The sequel appears in Chapter 11.

In addition to the 160 shares summarized above, Oakes had influenced *Samuel Hooper* and *John Bassett Alley*, Representatives from Boston and Lynn, respectively, to join him in 1865 and 1866, respectively, in the Union Pacific venture. Hooper and his partners bought and kept throughout the construction period 750 shares of CM, Alley at least 290 shares.[205] Also, in May 1866 Oakes got *James Wilson Grimes*, Representative from Burlington, Iowa, to go joint account with him on 380 shares of CM.[206] Oakes offered to guarantee all three Congressmen against loss.[207]

Oakes tried, but failed, to get *George S. Boutwell* and *Thomas D. Eliot*, both Representatives from Massachusetts, and *James G. Blaine*, Representative from Maine, to purchase CM stock in November or December 1867.[208] None of them ever held title to any CM or UP shares, notwithstanding McComb's claim to the contrary.[209] Blaine said in 1873: "It never once occurred to me that Mr. Ames was attempting to bribe me." [210]

McComb failed in his efforts to sell some of Oakes's CM shares to *James A. Bayard*, Representative from Delaware.[211] Oakes declined McComb's request to offer any to Senator *Joseph S. Fowler* from Tennessee.[212] Neither ever held title to any CM or UP shares, despite

---

[202] *Ibid.*, p. 212 (J.F. Wilson).
[203] *Ibid.*, pp. 21, 29, 40, 333, 336, 457 (Oakes Ames), 211–220 (J.F. Wilson).
[204] *Ibid.*, p. 38 (Oakes Ames).   [205] *Ibid.*, pp. 59–60, 77–78.
[206] *Ibid.*, pp. 19, 21 (Oakes Ames), 220 (J.F. Wilson).   [207] *Ibid.*, p. 19.
[208] *Ibid.*, pp. 20–21, 28, 32, 80, 303–304 (Oakes Ames), 1 (Blaine).
[209] *Ibid.*, p. 6 (McComb).   [210] *Ibid.*, p. 1.
[211] *Ibid.*, pp. 4 (Oakes Ames to McComb, 25 Jan. 1868), 9 (McComb), 30, 33, 293, 336 (Oakes Ames), 74 (Bayard to McComb, 14 Jan. 1868).
[212] *Ibid.*, pp. 516–519 (Fowler).

the claims of McComb.[213] Nor did Senator *Roscoe Conkling* from New York.[214]

Durant obtained subscriptions in 1866 for 75 shares CM from *Benjamin M. Boyer,* Representative from Norristown, Pennsylvania, and 25 shares from his wife. The Boyers kept them and all the allotments throughout and were entirely happy about their investment. They were model clients, indeed. Boyer said in 1873, "My only regret was that it was no larger in amount. There was no legislation whatever concerning the Credit Mobilier. I can . . . find nothing in my conduct to regret." [215]

Late in December 1867, *after* the 80 per cent bond dividend was declared, *James Brooks,* Representative from New York City, and a Democrat for a change, purchased from Durant 100 shares of CM for $10,000 and received from him $5,000 UP bonds and 200 shares of UP, not the full amounts the others got, as he was late. Later, in January or February 1868, Brooks claimed an additional 50 shares of CM by reason of his purchase of 100 shares, and the principal stockholders approved it upon President Dillon's recommendation. As Brooks was then a Government Director of the UP, and therefore was not allowed to hold any stock, he bought the shares in the name of his son-in-law, Charles H. Neilsen.[216] Oakes had nothing to do with Brooks's deals.

Thus concludes an outline of the original negotiations with 17 of the 23 U.S. Congressmen examined by the Poland Committee.[217] The Committee was appointed in December 1872 "to investigate whether any member of this House was bribed by Oakes Ames, or any other person or corporation, in any matter touching his legislative duty." [218] The perplexing sequel to the story appears in Chapter 11.

6. OAKES'S UNGUARDED LETTERS

During January and February, the Honorable Oakes Ames wrote McComb three careless letters. Carefully locked up, they became key evidence in a lawsuit marred by blackmail, which in turn led directly to two simultaneous Congressional inquisitions into the affairs of the Credit Mobilier and the Union Pacific. The letters were surprisingly open and over-confident, particularly so when it is considered that Oakes well knew the chances he was running. This he confirmed when he said, "Before that time I had ascertained facts connected

---

[213] *Ibid.,* p. 6 (McComb).   [214] *Ibid.,* p. 21 (Oakes Ames).   [215] *Ibid.,* p. 208 (Boyer).
[216] *Ibid.,* pp. x-xiii.   [217] See p. 203.   [218] *Poland Rep.,* p. i.

with McComb that would prevent me placing any confidence in him." [219] Oakes not only knew McComb well, but had been put on his guard further when Congressman Alley repeated what Jackson Shultz, a prominent citizen of New York and a leader in the leather trade (as were McComb and Alley), had told him about McComb. Shultz regarded him "as the most infamous scoundrel he knew, and that he ought to be in the penitentiary; that he had robbed and cheated the soldiers and the Government [during the war] . . . and the archives of the Government would show it." [220] Alley had been a U.S. Congressman at the time.

But Oakes went right ahead in his trusting, ingenuous manner. Perhaps Oakes had some slight feeling of obligation towards Mc-Comb.[221] Perhaps his sense of fair play [222] led him to a rather sympathetic and generous attitude towards this UP Director, one of the Seven Trustees, who had been given a shorter end of a deal by the Board than he had. Unable to express himself warily, he was just simple and forthright about it. Certainly, Oakes was *positive* that at no time did he ever, or would he ever, exert what he believed was an *improper* influence upon any of his co-Congressmen.[223]

Quotations from his three impatient, hasty letters follow.

H. S. McComb, Esq.   *Washington   Jan. 25, 1868*
Dear Sir: Yours of the 23rd is at hand, in which you say Senators Bayard & Fowler have written you in regard to the stock. I have spoken to Fowler, but not to Bayard. I have never been introduced to Bayard, but will see him soon. You say I must not put too much in one locality. I have assigned as far as I have gone to 4 [Congressmen] from Mass., 1 from N.H., 1 Delaware, 1 Tenn., 1 Ohio, 2 Penn., 1 Ind., 1 Maine & I have 3 to place, which I shall put where they will do the most good to us. I am here on the spot, and can better judge where they should go . . . .

Yours, truly,

Oakes Ames [224]

The remainder of the letter is about a proposed further increase in the CM stock which never took place, and about the 80 per cent dividend in bonds which had already been paid, and is omitted for the sake of brevity.

[219] *Ibid.*, p. 22.   [220] *Ibid.*, p. 93 (Alley).
[221] See p. 187 (Oliver Ames's offer to let McComb take his place as president of the Union Pacific).
[222] *Poland Rep.*, p. 22 (Oakes Ames).   [223] See p. 199; *Poland Rep.* p. 16.
[224] *Poland Rep.*, pp. 4–5 (Oakes Ames's letter quoted by McComb).

H.S. McComb, Esq. *Washington, Jan. 30, 1868*

Dear Sir: Yours of the 28th is at hand, inclosing copy of letter from, or rather to, Mr. King. I don't fear any investigation here. What some of Durant's friends may do in N.Y. courts can't be counted upon with any certainty. You do not understand by your letter what I have done, & am to do with my sales of stock. You say none to N.Y. I have placed some with N.Y., or have agreed to. You must remember that it was nearly all placed as you saw on the list in N.Y., & there was but 6 or 8 m. [60 or 80 shares] for me to place. I could not give all the world all they might want out of that. You would not want me to offer less than 1,000 m. [10 shares] to any one. We allow Durant to place 58,000 [580 shares] [225] to some 3 or 4 of his friends, or keep it himself.

I have used this where it will produce most good to us, I think. In view of King's letter and Washburn's move here,[226] I go in for making our bond dividend in full.[227] We can do it with perfect safety. I understand the opposition to it comes from Alley; he is on the finance com'ee, and can raise money easy if we come short, which I don't believe we shall, & if we do we can loan our bonds to the company, or loan them the money we get from the bonds. The contract calls for the division, & I say have it. When shall I see you in Washington?

Yours, truly,

Oakes Ames

[P.S.] We stand about like this:

Bonds, 1st mortgage, rec'd. on	525	miles	at	16m	8,400,000
" " " " "	15	"	"	48m	720,000
" " " " "	100	"	"	48m	4,800,000
					13,920,000
10,000,000 sold & to sell to pay our debts					10,000,000
					3,920,000
80 p'r cent. dividend on 3,700,000 C.M. of A.					3,000
					920,000
Govt. bonds received this day					960,000
Due for transportation 400 m, one-half cash					200,000
					2,080,000

In addition to this we can draw Gov't bonds for $2/3$ of the work done in advance of the track, if we desire it.

[225] Actually it was 370 shares (see p. 198). Shares in brackets are corrections by C.E.A.

[226] See p. 213.

[227] The issue of UP bonds was limited to the amount of U.S. bonds issued, of which only $9,117,000 had been issued to date. (*Wilson Rep.,* p. 738; see also Appendix D.) "Mr. King" is John L. King of Springfield, who held 80 shares of CM (*Poland Rep.,* pp. 6, 60).

Then McComb added below that, on the same sheet, in his own handwriting, a list of names which led to the commotion in Congress during the Presidential elections of 1872:

Oakes Ames's list of names as showed today to me for C.M.:

Blaine, of Maine, 3,000.	Elliott, Mass., 3
Patterson, N.Hamp., 3,000.	Dawes, " 2.
Wilson, Mass., 2	Boutwell, " 2.
Painter, Rep. for Inq., 3	Bingham & Garfield, Ohio
(Reporter for Inquirer)	Schofield & Kelley, Penn.
S. Colfax, Speaker, 2.	Fowler, Tenn.
Feb'y 1, '68 [228]	

McComb later swore, "I wrote those names as Mr. Ames read them to me from his memorandum book. He sat one side of the table and I sat the other." [229]

Oakes replied, "Mr. McComb says I dictated a list of names for him to write down. It is not true. . . . I have no doubt I mentioned the names of some that I *expected* would take it." [230]

Oakes's third letter follows:

H.S. McComb, Esq.   *Washington, Feb. 22, 1868*
Dear Sir: Yours of the 21st is at hand. . . . You ask me if I will sell some of my U.P.R.R. stock. I will sell some of it at par C.M. of A.[231] I don't care to sell. I hear that Mr. Bates offered his [CM stock] at $300, but I don't want Bates to sell out. I think Grimes may sell a part of his at $350. I want that $14,000 increase of the Credit Mobilier to sell here.[232] We want more friends in this Congress, & if a man will look into the law, (& it is difficult to get them to do it unless they have an interest to do so,) he cannot help being convinced that we should not be interfered with. Hope to see you here or at N.Y. the 11th.

Yours, truly,

Oakes Ames [233]

Oakes admitted rather ruefully in 1873: "My friends say that I never ought to be trusted to write a letter; that I never conceal anything. . . . It seems that I make statements that are not wholly understood, and write letters that are not understood." [234]

In his second letter to McComb (January 30) Oakes had said, "In

---

[228] *Poland Rep.,* pp. 5–6 (Oakes Ames' letter quoted by McComb).   [229] *Ibid.,* p. 6.
[230] *Ibid.,* p. 19.   [231] Did he mean $100 a share, or at a price equal to that of the CM?
[232] See p. 194.   [233] *Poland Rep.,* p. 7 (Oakes Ames's letter quoted by McComb).
[234] *Ibid.,* pp. 269–270.

view of King's letter and Washburn's move here, I go in for making our bond dividend in full."[235] McComb and the Poland Committee picked up these words as evidence that Oakes, "in his distributions of stock, had specially in mind the hostile efforts of the Messrs. Washburn, and desired to gain strength to secure their defeat."[236] On December 9, Cadwalader C. Washburn, U.S. Representative from Wisconsin and notoriously a turbulent demagogue, had introduced a bill to regulate and reduce freight and passenger rates on the Pacific Railway so as not to exceed double the rates charged on the eastern roads.[237] Without debate, the House had sent the bill to the Standing Committee on the Pacific Railroad, of which Oakes had been a member for years. There is no record of any action being taken.[238] When questioned by the Poland Committee about the bill, Oakes replied:

Mr. Washburn was complaining . . . and wanted to fix a rate by Congressional legislation. . . . I know that it was *for* our interest while the road was being built, and before it was completed. We required all the transportation we had to carry our railroad-iron and other material. All the freight we carried for private parties was a damage and nuisance to us. . . . We were building the road rapidly. . . . The rates he proposed to fix, let me say, were a great deal higher than we are now charging. That was the substance of this "move"; there was nothing else.[239]

In his written statement before the House, Oakes maintained:

To say that the Washburn bill, which professed to deal exclusively with the operation of the road . . . *after* it had been built . . . was a measure feared, and to protect the railroad company against which the stock in question was sold to members of Congress, seems to me to invoke the last extreme of credulity.[240]

Nevertheless, the coincidental timing of the "Washburn move" seems to have led many historians to assume it must have influenced Oakes to make the sales. Perhaps they did not find all the evidence.

An account of McComb's lawsuit and its disastrous results follows in Chapters 9 and 11.

7. ITS PRICES

All *subscriptions* to the CM stock had been at par, fully paid in cash.[241] In some cases, payments were long delayed, as with Durant's

---

[235] See p. 211.   [236] *Poland Rep.*, p. iv.   [237] *Cong. Globe*, 40th Cong., 2nd Sess.
[238] Minutes of the Committee.   [239] *Poland Rep.*, p. 273.
[240] 25 Feb. 1873; Ames Family, *Oakes Ames*, pp. 115–116. (Italics by C.E.A.)
[241] See Appendix F.

650 shares.[242] The *prices* at which it sold in the "market," if that is the word for it, was quite another thing. Such market was extremely inactive and thin, as with other very closely held companies. There were only 85 names on the stockholders' list of 12 December 1867.[243] There were no published "over the counter" bid and asked prices, such as we find today in the papers. If a holder wished to sell, he could either visit a stockbroker who would hunt around for a buyer, or he could let his wants be known to his friends. Because no records were kept, and because the Government inquisitions took place more than five years after the events, no confidence can be placed in the wildly contradictory testimony about the "market price" of the CM stock on a particular date.

It is true, however, that for the first three years the stock went begging. It never sold above 100 until two or three months after the Seven Trustees' agreement was reached on 15 October 1867. Durant and McComb did not sign up until December 20.[244] By that time, all of the company treasury shares had been taken at 100, except for Durant's 650. If a buyer could not get some of those, he would have to bid above 100 until some one was tempted to sell. Oliver testified, "My recollections are that at the time we increased the stock it was not thought to be worth par." [245]

There was no substantial change in the intrinsic value until December 12, when the first allotment of profits was declared.[246] The 60 per cent allotment of bonds, assuming a market price now of 97,[247] added $58.20 to the value of each share of CM; the 60 per cent allotment of stock, assuming a market price of 30,[248] added another $18.00. Combined, one share of CM was worth $76.20 more than previously —that is, until the year-end. Then, on January 3, a further 20 per cent allotment of bonds was declared,[249] which at 97 added $19.40, making $95.60 per share of CM. If consideration is given to the 12 per cent interest declared in stock at 30 per cent on December 28, $12.00 more can be added. All four of the above declarations were payable on 3 January 1868.

Alley testified, "It was hard work to get people to take it at first. I do not know that it actually could have been sold at par before early in January, 1868, and then it was sold at 160 . . . it went to 200 before the end of January. After that some of it was sold at 225. I do not remember of any being sold higher than that—it may have been." [250]

[242] See p. 198.   [243] See p. 194.   [244] See p. 192.   [245] *Wilson Rep.*, p. 283.
[246] *Ibid.*, p. 283 (Oliver Ames); Hazard, p. 32; Crawford, pp. 179–180.   [247] See p. 196.
[248] *Wilson Rep.*, p. 154; see also p. 196.   [249] See p. 196.   [250] *Poland Rep.*, p. 104.

Oakes said, in a written statement to the Poland Committee, "You were told that the stock was, in January, 1868, worth more than par. That is true, though the value stated by McComb[251] is very much exaggerated. The best test is actual sales. These were made at 160 or thereabout."[252] But "worth" is different from "price." On February 22, he wrote McComb: "I hear that Mr. Bates offered his at $300."[253] Actually, Bates did not sell any part of his 500 shares.[254]

No more distributions were made until 17 June 1868.[255] Theoretically, at least, each one added still more to the worth of the stock, so that eventually it could have sold higher than Alley's top figure of 225. But each allotment was non-recurring. They were very different from the regular quarterly cash dividends now paid, upon which a stock is capitalized in the market. Indeed, each one brought the stock nearer to the date when it would be worth nothing at all, as the contract would be fulfilled. So at some point the price would have to start coming down in anticipation of the end.

E. *Indians Open War on the Union Pacific*

While the financial men in the East brought their personal war to a crisis without shedding a drop of blood, the Sioux and Cheyenne wars on the railroad in the West opened in full crescendo with the coming of the spring days. Many men in the surveying parties, workmen, and train crews, not to speak of the Redskins, laid down their lives in violence and cruelty, without ever a medal or even honorable mention. Horses, mules, and livestock were run off by the hundreds, perhaps by the thousands. Major-General and now Congressman Dodge took the brunt of the responsibility the whole length of the UP and was lucky to come out unwounded. Without his unfaltering example and the loyal aid of the tough cavalrymen and infantrymen of the United States Army, the railroad would have been long delayed, if not permanently stopped. "The bulk of the defense fell upon the Second Cavalry and the Twenty-first, Thirtieth and Thirty-sixth Regiments of Infantry, stationed at Forts Kearney, McPherson and Sedgwick along the Platte; Fort D.A. Russell at Cheyenne; Fort Laramie Headquarters to the north; Fort Sanders at Laramie; Fort Bridger in western Wyoming; and Camp Douglas at Salt Lake City;

[251] "600 or 700" (*ibid.*, p. 10).   [252] *Ibid.*, p. 17.   [253] See p. 212.
[254] *Wilson Rep.*, p. 158.   [255] See p. 247.

assisted upon the plains by the free-roving Pawnees of Major Frank J. North, the white chief." [256]

Dodge put it this way:

Our Indian troubles commenced in 1864 and lasted until the tracks joined at Promotory. We lost most of our men and stock while building from Fort Kearney to Bitter Creek. At that time every mile of road had to be surveyed, graded, tied and bridged under military protection. The order to the workers . . . was never to run when attacked. All were required to be armed . . . Our success depended in a great measure on the cordial and active support of the army, especially its commander-in-chief, General Grant, and the commander of the Military Division of the West, General Sherman. He took a personal interest in the project. He visited the work several times each year, and I communicated with him each month, detailing my progress and laying before him my plans. In return I received letters from him almost every month. We also had the cordial support of the district commanders of the country through which we operated—General C. C. Augur, General P. S. Cooke, General J. C. Gibbons and General J. H. Stevenson, and their subordinates. General Grant had given full and positive instructions that every support should be given to me, and General Sherman in the detailed instructions practically left it to my judgement as to what support should be given by the troops on the plains. They were also instructed to furnish my surveying parties with provisions from the posts whenever our provisions should give out, and the subordinate officers . . . responded to every demand made, no matter at what time of day or night, what time of year or in what weather, and took as much interest in the matter as we did.[257]

In spite of such military aid, the Indians, particularly the horse-riding, buffalo-eating, and rifle-swinging Sioux, with their stealthy hit-and-run raids, scalping, and horse-stealing, were almost a match for the UP. Today it would be known as guerrilla warfare.

Rock Creek: The trouble began about May 12 near Rock Creek, Wyoming. Percy T. Browne's surveying party was hit in camp by a swirl of Sioux, who killed Sergeant Clair of the escort and Stephen Clark of Albany and captured the mules, harness, and firearms.[258]

Ogallala: On May 18, 800 Indians crossed the Platte near Ogallala, Wyoming, and pulled up one mile of stakes just laid out, in sight of the surveyors.[259]

---

[256] Sabin, p. 234 (abridged by C.E.A.).
[257] Dodge, *How We Built the Union Pacific*, pp. 18–19.
[258] Dodge, *Reports of the Chief Engineer*, 1867, p. 33.
[259] Records of UP Historical Museum (Ferguson).

Dodge wrote Sherman on May 20:

The Indians are getting to be very troublesome. . . . The great difficulty is that General Augur has only two companies of cavalry to scout
the whole line and seven or eight companies of infantry to protect 300
miles of opened work. . . . It seems to me that we are at the mercy of
the Red Man. . . . We are now at Alkali, 40 miles west of North Platte,
and I tremble every day for fear of a stampede by the workmen.[260]

Greatly troubled, Dodge reported on the same day to Durant:

. . . It is hard to get more protection from Military. I have made a
strong appeal to Sherman to abandon the Powder River expedition and
then run troops along our line, as they have done some damage East of
Sedgwick and the depredations extend west to Bridger Pass showing a
concerted movement all along the line, at same time they struck us they
burnt Stage Stations beyond Sedgwick, also at Rock and Cooper Creeks,
on Laramie Plains. I have pushed Brown out again taking part of Black
Hills party escort and adding to his thus giving him about 70 men.
    I think if they are vigilant active and will fight, they can whip what
ever comes against them, we must however expect loss of stock, perhaps
some men this summer and think ourselves lucky if we get through a
lot for the Indians mean work and the Military are crippled having no
adequate force to cope with them. If my health permits . . . I am out
of the house for first time since you left . . . and can get out on the work
I think I can hold most of our men, they stick to us yet.[261]

Durant followed this up on May 23 with a dire warning to General
U. S. Grant in Washington:

. . . The Indians are interfering very seriously with our operations . . . .
Unless some relief can be afforded by your Department immediately, I
beg leave to assure you that the entire work will be suspended . . . .[262]

Overton and Brule: On May 25, five out of six men in a section gang
improving the track near Overton, Nebraska, 220 miles west of
Omaha, were killed and scalped. The same day Sioux Indians attacked the train at the end of the track near Brule, Nebraska, killed
three men, wounded one, and took 31 animals; while at McArthur's
camp, opposite Bowen's, they herded off another 30 head of stock
and killed one of McArthur's men.[263]

[260] Dodge, *Autobiography*, p. 621.   [261] Durant, *Papers*, 1–1–32–65 (original ms.).
[262] Records of UP Historical Museum.   [263] Dodge, *Autobiography*, p. 626.

Ogallala Again: Only two days later, on May 27, Dodge was with
three Government commissioners, General J.H. Simpson, General
F.B. Blair, and Congressman W.M. White, inspecting the newly laid
track near Ogallala (milepost 342) for approval of U.S. bonds. About
100 Indians sprang from a ravine upon the grading camp at noon,
within sound of end-o-track and only five miles from the post of the
military guard. "In plain view of us," said Dodge, "they cut out several mules and horses and got away with them before the graders
could get to their muskets, which were stacked along the work while
eating their dinner. The Commissioners showed their grit by running
to my car for arms to aid in the fight . . . and on returning to the East
dwelt earnestly on the necessity of our being protected." [264] Following a strong appeal to General Augur, Dodge succeeded in getting
three additional companies of cavalry stationed along the line for
scouting purposes.[265]

Lodge Pole Valley: UP surveyor Arthur N. Ferguson left a vivid
account in his "Journals" of a typical attack, this time on his camp in
the Lodge Pole Creek valley on Sunday, June 2:

This morning, shortly after sunrise, the camp was aroused by the cry
of "here they come, here they come, boys!," and for the next few minutes
the interior of our tent presented a lively picture—the soldiers, Mr. Boyd
and myself grasping our arms, and regardless of our clothing and everything else we rushed out of our tent, and there we saw the Indians
charging down upon us from the northern bluffs. Mr. Boyd commenced
the action . . . and our men started firing with great rapidity. It was an
exciting time—some of our men were almost naked; I had nothing on
but shirt, drawers and stockings. . . . Report followed report in rapid
succession; men cheering, Indians yelling, and the entire camp a scene
of intense action and extreme excitement. I saw the blue smoke wreath
up from Mr. Clark's gun as he fired over the earthwork in front of our
tent. He shot at a mounted Indian who was sitting on his horse motion-
less and alone to our left, and seemed from his appearance to be the
chief. As a musket ball passed nearer to him than he liked, he started his
horse to a full run and came around to our front where all the heavy
firing was going on. Here I saw one of the most daring Indians that I
ever saw or ever heard of. He had dismounted from his own horse, and
was endeavoring to pull up a "picket pin" to which was tied one of our
horses, and while trying to do this he was subjected to the fire from the

[264] *Ibid.,* p. 628; Dodge, *How We Built the Union Pacific,* p. 18.
[265] Dodge, *Autobiography,* p. 629.

muzzles of at least ten guns, and that within only two or three hundred feet of him. He, however, succeeded in his purpose, and in the meanwhile escaped as by a miracle from our shots. Now he springs to the back of his horse and endeavors to ride up the steep bluff immediately in front of us, when all at once a bullet strikes him, he sways to and fro in his saddle, as if the force of the bullet came very near to dismounting him; another shot strikes him, he reels and falls to the ground. "Joe" [the hunter] ran up to dispatch him when one of the boys shouted to him to run under the bluff as another Indian who was in close vicinity to us was preparing to shoot him as he came up; and by this short delay we lost the chance of getting a fine scalp; and the other Indians got this wounded man away from us . . . The Indians finally succeeded in driving off all our stock but four head . . . The entire Lodge Pole valley for a distance of 20 miles has been attacked this morning . . . One of the engineers captured from the Indians a white woman's scalp, which was quite green, having been killed but a few days, to judge from the appearance of it . . . *June 12, 1867:* I kept a sharp lookout for Indians, and while I stood at the instrument I had a gun lying at my feet.[266]

Julesburg: Even while Sherman was issuing orders for all ranchers to gather at the nearest stage station, and all stages to bunch up and travel at irregular times, an attack was being made on Julesburg, Colorado, only two weeks before the railroad came through. Dr. Henry C. Parry, a Major in the Army Medical Corps who was stationed at Fort Sedgwick close by, wrote in his diary on June 10:

A report has just come in that 50 Cheyennes are attacking Julesburg. It is true, for we can hear their yelling. "To Horse!" is sounded in the cavalry barracks at the fort, and soon a company will be dashing down the road to the rescue . . . .

I have just got back from Julesburg. The Cheyennes came down on the place last night about 7 o'clock and were handsomely repulsed. They killed two men, scalped them, and mutilated their bodies in the most brutal manner. Several Indians were wounded and only one killed. I visited five men who were wounded by arrows. I never saw an arrow wound before and regard them as worse than a bullet wound. One of the men killed was lying on the ground, pinned to the earth by an arrow through his neck. He must have been shot after he had been scalped.[267]

Cheyenne Twice: On June 14, L.L. Hills, a civil engineer for the UP in charge of a party making location over the divide between the

266 Records of UP Historical Museum; see also pp. 145–146.
267 "Letters from the Frontier," *Annals of Wyoming,* Oct. 1958, p. 132.

valleys of Lodge Pole Creek and Crow Creek, was ambushed and murdered in a mounted raid some 6 miles east of present Cheyenne, near Archer to be. Had it not been for the prompt leadership of Axeman J. M. Eddy, a lad scarcely of age, who organized the defense and made a running fight of it, the whole crew of 10 surveyors and six troopers might have been wiped out. It developed that Eddy had fought in Dodge's Sixteenth Army Corps at the age of sixteen or seventeen. Dodge at once promoted him, and kept him in his service until long after the UP was completed.[268]

Dodge and General Rawlins had celebrated the Fourth of July by formally christening the community as "Cheyenne." The next day, at the same spot, a band of Sioux rushed off the hills, attacked the train, killed two or three men, and got away with part of the stock before our cavalry got saddled and got after them. The men killed were buried in Cheyenne and became the first inhabitants of that city." [269]

Bitter Creek: The hardest blow to the UP, particularly to the Chief Engineer, was the killing of Percy T. Browne, a veteran of the Civil War. "He was one of the brightest of our young engineers," said Dodge, then ill. "He was a great loss to me, and I see no way to replace him. This put another party out of commission. I am beginning to think that engineering is no sinecure with the load I am carrying, but if I should stop now a lick would not be struck west of here this year." [270] On July 23, Browne and his surveying party of eight, including escorts, were attacked by 300 Sioux on the warpath in the flat, waterless, sagebrushed Red Desert near Bitter Creek, 785 miles from Omaha. After fighting from noon to dark, Browne was shot through the abdomen. His men had to give up their stampeding horses, whereupon the Indians fled. Browne begged his party to leave him and make their way to safety. They refused and carried him on a litter of carbines for 15 miles during the night to the Laclede stage station, where he soon died.[271]

Fort Phil Kearney: On August 2, near Fort Phil Kearney, not far from present Sheridan, Wyoming, 30 escort soldiers of the Ninth Infantry, led by Brevet Major James Powell, were rushed in the early

[268] Dodge, *How We Built the Union Pacific*, p. 24; Dodge, *Reports of the Chief Engineer*, 1867, pp. 3–4, 30; Sabin, pp. 235–236; see also p. 158.

[269] Dodge, *Autobiography*, pp. 637–638.   [270] *Ibid.*, pp. 643–644.

[271] Dodge, *Reports of the Chief Engineer*, 1867, pp. 3, 34; Dodge, *How We Built the Union Pacific*, pp. 25, 112; see also p. 158.

morning hours by some 2,000 Sioux under Chief Red Cloud. Hastily erecting a barricade of wooden boxes from the wagons, the small force stood off charge after charge during the entire morning. Luckily, they had been equipped with the new single shot but *breech-loading* "Allin Alteration" Springfield rifles, a conversion of the now obsolete Civil War muzzleloaders. After several hundred of his best mounted fighters had been killed or wounded so unexpectedly, while only three palefaces had been wounded, Red Cloud called it quits and fled away. "The Wagon Box Fight," as it was called, became one of the great traditions of the Infantry in the West. As the news spread, it had considerable demoralizing effect on all the Redskins warring on the Union Pacific. Probably the year of 1867 had seen the worst of it, as far as slowing down of work on the road was concerned.

Plum Creek: On August 4 the Indians, this time Cheyennes under Chief Turkey Leg, tried their hand at disrupting established traffic. Four miles west of Plum Creek (now Lexington) and only 234 miles out of Omaha, they fastened a "big stick" (tie) to the rails with cut telegraph wire and sat down by a bonfire to see what would happen. It was diabolic. At 9 o'clock William Thompson, head lineman, and five of his repair crew were sent out from Plum Creek on a handcar to investigate the break. They saw the fire, then Indians on all sides, and, although rolling at full speed, leaped off just before the car, guns and all, turned a somersault on the tie. A mounted Cheyenne chased the dazed Thompson, shot him through the arm, clubbed him, stabbed him in the neck, and then scalped him alive. The brave galloped off, but his trophy slipped away. Thompson retrieved it, and finally staggered 15 miles through the night to safety. His long, blond scalp was put in a pail of water in a vain hope of saving it. But the doctors were unable to graft it back on. It now reposes in the Omaha Public Library, in the Boys' and Girls' Department.

The Cheyennes, emboldened with success, tried their Satanism again. By firelight they pried up a pair of rails and banked them with ties. Soon a westbound freight with five cars crashed in at full steam and burst into flames on top of the derailed engine (No. 53). The fireman was roasted alive; the engineer, thrown through the cab window, soon died. "The bursting box cars were plundered of bales of calico, cottons, boxes of tobacco, sacks of flour, sugar, coffee, boots, bonnets, hats, ribbons, and velvet—and a barrel of whiskey. . . . Having gorged themselves, the Indians bore firebrands from car to car. Speedily the whole train was a mass of roaring flames, with drunken savages encircling in a furious dance." [272] The hardy Thompson had been an eyewitness to all this, hidden in the tall grass. A second freight train close behind very nearly smashed into the inferno. Warned just in time by a shouting survivor, it picked him up and backed full speed to Plum Creek.

Dodge, called in, drove the Indians away the next day.[273] Oliver noted in his diary on August 8: "Bad news that the Indians had piled ties on the track ditched a train & kill seven men and burned up the cars.—Govt. is not giving sufficient protection."

F. Surveys and Engineering

As 1867 began, Chief Engineer and Congressman Dodge had no time to lose in locating the best line to a Central Pacific rendezvous. At the rate the Casements were advancing, he prophesied to General Sherman that the track would be at Fort Sanders (near Laramie to be) by the end of good weather. Sherman wrote back on January 16: "That would be almost a miracle. . . . I regard this road as the solution of the Indian affairs and the Mormon question, and therefore give you all the aid I possibly can." [274] During January, Dodge carefully drew up some plans: (1) To L.L. Hills he assigned a revision of all of Lodge Pole Creek to Crow Creek as far as the "eastern base of the Rockies." This meant some 140 miles from Julesburg to the coming site of Cheyenne. (2) To J.A. Evans went the tricky job of polishing off the final exact location of 55 miles over the Black Hills between Cheyenne and Fort Sanders. (3) To P.T. Browne was given the arduous and dangerous task of developing some 275 miles from Fort Sanders to Green River. This included Laramie Plains "park" and the comparatively unknown, arid, but highly colorful Red Desert plain. The latter is in the center of the Great Divide Basin, where the UP could cross the Continental Divide at a surprisingly low elevation of 7,100 feet. Finally, (4) Dodge set T.H. Bates and F.S. Hodges, in separate parties, to finding the best way from Green River through the rugged Wasatch Mountains to Ogden, a distance of perhaps another 190 miles, if all went well. They also were to reconnoiter from Salt Lake up the Bear River, and around the northernmost spur of the Wasatches to Black's Fork, to connect with a revision of S.B. Reed's surveys of 1864 and 1865; if the latter proved practicable.[275]

---

[272] Sabin, pp. 249–251.   [273] Dodge, *How We Built the Union Pacific*, p. 36.
[274] *Ibid.*, pp. 17, 53.   [275] See p. 116.

"The parties got into the field early [in March], with pretty strong escorts," reported Dodge, "and were progressing remarkably well . . . when the combined attacks of the Indians, apparently along our whole line, not only on the parties far west, but on our graders, etc., the killing of our chiefs, the depletion of our escorts, etc., virtually broke up our work, forced me to change my orders, and to use the parties wherever we could do so to advantage." [276] So, late in June, he took direct charge of the field for the remainder of the year. Congressman Dodge had answered his first roll call on March 4, but stayed in Washington only until March 30. He did not return until December 2, when the Second Session convened.

The exploration of each of the four areas is briefly reviewed below.

Julesburg to Cheyenne—139 miles: This was the most pressing work, as the track was coming on fast from O'Fallons Bluffs. L.L. Hills was perfecting Evans's preliminary line up the Lodge Pole from Julesburg and was nearly at Cheyenne site when he was killed and his party driven out, as told.[277] Evans took over from the Wyoming border, with difficulty keeping the grade down to the 35 feet per mile maximum which had prevailed from Omaha, and located a good line across the divide between Lodge Pole and Crow Creeks to a point 7 miles east of Cheyenne.

There he connected with his excellent, finally located line of 1866 over the Black Hills.[278] At the point where the line crossed Crow Creek, on July 2 Dodge staked out land for the town of Cheyenne and reserved 320 acres for a railroad terminal. "It was about 6100 feet above the Sea," wrote Dodge, "and even then it was uncomfortably cold. In the middle of the day the sun burns but at night I wore an overcoat and slept under two blankets. Before we left Cheyenne the people commenced flocking there. They had heard of the location and they came up from Denver in large numbers." [279]

He then moved on to Fort Sanders for explorations further west, regardless of the opening of a session of his Congress on July 3. "My constituents thought I should be there, but I felt it was my duty to be out upon the work, thinking I could do more good than I could in Washington," he mused. He left behind two parties under J. R. Maxwell and O'Neill, although they were much needed westward, for some new surveys desired by Seymour, who was determined to "im-

[276] Dodge, *Reports of the Chief Engineer*, 1867, p. 4.   [277] See pp. 219–220.
[278] See p. 156.   [279] Dodge, *Autobiography*, pp. 637–639.

prove" on Evans's line up the Black Hills. For Evans had gone East upon the sudden death of his wife.

Cheyenne to Fort Sanders (Laramie)—54 miles:[280] If Seymour, probably under secret orders from Durant, had not interfered, and actually changed a radical amount of finished grading, which had to be done over at heavy expense and delay, Dodge would have accomplished his prophecy of reaching Fort Sanders by the end of the year,[281] and the UP might have met the CP well beyond Promontory. Unless it was to cheapen the construction and increase the subsidies, Seymour's actions were most mysterious. His curvatures were increased to such an extent that more locomotive power was needed than on the 90 foot grade. However, he was jealous of Dodge, and was always sure to back up his boss, who just had been demoted.

Sam Reed, writing to his wife from Julesburg on July 15, made the following comment on Seymour:

Col. Seymour was outfitted after the following style: First, the horse which he selected and paid a good round price for was, or ought to have been, the twin brother of old "Knockumstiff." On the horse he would have placed the saddle, attached to which was his carbine in its case securely strapped and buckled to be convenient in case of a sudden Indian attack; also his poncho, bed, etc., in bulk about a barrel, leaving very little room for the colonel. When mounted he would hoist his umbrella and leisurely follow in the wake of the [military] escort or perhaps leading them a few paces. The Pawnees made fun of him from beginning to end.[282]

On 23 January 1867, the UP Board had resolved that "Hereafter no material changes of grade shall be made from that established in the final location of each section of the road without the examination and approval of the chief engineer of the company, and that such shall be the provision in future contracts." [283] But it was overlooked. Dodge, as Chief Engineer, was employed by, paid by, and responsible to the UP. *He had no responsibility to the contractors.* His direct authority was limited to the location of the route and to the land and lots departments. Yet the Ames group relied on him to counterbalance Durant's questionable moves. When the sections of the location were completed, they were subject to the approval of the Chief Engineer.

---

[280] See Profile, Illus., Group 3; see also sketch of Sherman Pass, Group 4.
[281] Dodge, *Reports of the Chief Engineer*, 1867, pp. 18 (Dodge), 30–32 (Evans).
[282] Records of UP Historical Museum (Reed letters).   [283] *Ibid.*

When so approved, they were turned over to the Construction Engineer (S.B. Reed), who was employed by the contractors, the CM.[284]

Nevertheless, there was much New York interference, done or attempted, with Dodge's official authority which had a seriously adverse effect on the "economic accuracy" of the location, as well as upon the cost of construction.[285]

On June 13 President Oliver gave a hint of what was up when he wrote Dodge:

Your favor of June 7th in reference to Road over Black Hills is received and we are greatly pleased with the very favorable aspect that it bears. I am only fearful if the thing looks so very fine that it may influence the Judgement of our Mr. Blickenderfer in fixing the Base of the Rocky Mts. I do not see however how he can materially change it.[286]

Both cheered and puzzled by this, Dodge sent the following telegram to Oliver from Carmichael's supply camp on July 20:

I have obtained an eighty-foot grade from Summit of Black Hills to Laramie Plains (Ft. Sanders). I can obtain the same maximum from Crow Creek to Summit on *East* side at not to exceed $200,000 additional cash. *I recommend it be done.* Answer to Fort Saunders.[287]

Something was done about it in New York. It was not only rejected, but there emerged some further policy ideas which proved to be confusing, to say the least, to the Chief Engineer. For on July 26, Oliver answered Dodge as follows:

. . . We did not have sufficient data to be able to decide the question. The great desire of the Country is a rapid completion of this Road and we do not wish to delay the work by any very heavy cuts when we can do this work after the road gets in operation. When we are running the Road we can reduce grades. But to get it running we will make the grades in all places, if it will more rapidly complete the work, at the Maximum grades allowed by the Charter. Durant and his Friends are endeavoring to injure your and our standing before the Country by calling us Slow. I don't wish to be liable to that charge by attempting to reduce grades to delay the work. Let everything be pushed ahead as fast as possible.[288]

[284] *Ibid.*   [285] *Ibid.*   [286] Dodge, *Papers,* vol. 152.
[287] *Ibid.* (Italics by C.E.A.)   [288] *Ibid,*

Dodge was hurrying as best he could, and he protested earnestly.[289] On July 30 Oliver answered, still ambiguously: "Your letters are received. . . . The Doctor is infusing the minds of Govt Directors that we are not pressing forward. . . . The feeling of our Committee is to push the road along . . . even if we have to put the largest grades and curves that our charter allows. You know very well what our feelings are about the Road—to make it as perfect as possible consistent with the rapidity of construction demanded by the Country. . . ." [290]

He followed this up with six other similar letters to Dodge, dated August 1 to 12, from which a few extracts are quoted:

I do not of course mean by this that you should put in a heavy grade or short curve merely to save a little money but to save time so that the grading may at all times if possible be ahead of track laying by 150 or 200 miles, and we shall not merely for a good Allignment run into heavy cuts that will stop the progress of the track for months . . . .

We hoped that . . . yourself Carter & Seymour after looking carefully over Evans Line would have been able to suggest such alterations as would hasten the construction and save Hundreds of Thousands of Dollars . . . .

If we make the Road cost too much it will never pay dividends—all these things must be taken into consideration—and to get this best line the Best Engineering talent will be required that can be procured. . . .

Your favor of July 26th is received. I entirely concur with you in opinion of Seymour as an indolent man with a strong desire to criticize others work and do nothing himself . . . He has been kept more for the purpose of writing the Dr Reports and doing his correspondence than meets the public eye and whitewashing his rascalities than for any real engr service he has done or will do the Co . . . I have told Seymour to make a survey of his proposed changes and report the comparative gain. *If he has found a better line* it is our duty to adopt it. If a 2 or 3° curve will throw us out of heavy work and hasten completion of the Road I should do it. You understand our views and for the present act up to them. After Oct. we shall stand better.

. . . We must acknowledge Seymour is an extremely plausible man with excellent ability as a writer and if he has anything of a show for a decent line he will be able to make the most if it . . . If he can make a point against us and in the interest of Durant will do it . . . One or two years

---

[289] Dodge, *Reports of the Chief Engineer*, 1867, p. 18.

[290] Dodge, *Papers*, vol. 152. See p. 185 for provision of the Oakes Ames contract. (The charter called for curves not to exceed those of the Baltimore & Ohio, which reached a maximum radius of 400 feet—about 14 degrees. See p. 17.)

use of the Road will pay all the amendments that may be necessary to make it a perfect line . . . .[291]

Oliver had been forced by the Committee into a decision. Moving the "eastern base" of the Rockies 3 miles east would increase the Subsidy bonds by $48,000. On August 28 he wrote to Seymour to go ahead with the change, provided all he said was accurate.[292]

On August 30 Dodge received this conclusive letter (with one catch) from Oliver:

Seymour states he and Blickensderfer had run the eastern slope of the Black Hills and had found line that could be built on 80-ft grade with $120,000 less money to the summit and bringing E. base of Rockies 3 miles further East. This will be certainly the most desirable route, and *if so,* should be adopted.[293]

Dodge, much discouraged, made the following remarks in his autobiography:

It was very evident to me now that for some reason the Board of Directors were not disposed to follow the advice of their engineers, but were influenced by Seymour and his continuous telegrams and misrepresentations. On September 1 from dispatches to and from Reed, it was clear what a fearful mix-up there was about changes in the Black Hills line, but I saw it was impossible for me to remedy where I was.[294]

Evans wrote Dodge on September 22:

The folks are still sweating in the Black Hills. As I came along three separate lines of grading could be distinctly traced in places showing that some of the changes had been changed . . . . A considerable ingenuity is being used to avoid Dale Creek crossing, and as a consequence Evans' Pass. Alas, for my immortality.[295]

On October 2, Dodge telegraphed Seymour to suspend all further surveys in the Black Hills, whereupon Seymour challenged Dodge's authority, without success.

The crowning touch of this affair, which wasted so much time, money, and correspondence all around, came when Seymour's "80

[291] Dodge, *Papers*, vol. 152 (original ms.). (Italics by C.E.A.)
[292] Records of UP Historical Museum.
[293] Dodge, *Autobiography*, p. 683; Oliver Ames's diary, Aug. 28. (Italics by C.E.A.)
[294] Dodge, *Autobiography*, p. 682. (He was in the Great Basin.)   [295] *Ibid.*, p. 684.

foot" grade reached downward to the eastern foot of the mountains. There he found he was obliged to put in a 90-foot grade for 1,500 feet as he dropped off the foothills to the plains. A portion of this abandoned grading remains today. The company had finally concluded that all of Seymour's changes amounted to nothing.[296] The railroad was built over Evans's original line, and is still there, a splendid tribute to the engineering skill of Dodge and Evans.

These two already had found a fine 80-foot grade down the 21-mile west slope of the Black Hills to Fort Sanders. But they could not bypass the deeply gorged Dale Creek at the highest elevation of the whole Pacific Railway, over 8,000 feet. The tallest trestle of the UP would have to surmount it.[297]

Fort Sanders to Green River—275 miles: Alhough the final location had risen 2,201 feet from Cheyenne to Sherman, it fell only 1,079 feet to the Laramie Plains at Fort Sanders. From there on to the Green River a generally descending but somewhat tortuous route would be located before winter. Its elevation would vary only between 7,163 feet at Fort Sanders and 6,140 at Green River, even though, curiously enough, the road would cross the Continental Divide at only 7,100 feet. Many explorations would be needed to prove there was no better line before the work was finished. Everywhere were steep ravines and washouts, dry except in the spring, which must be avoided, while grades and curvatures still must be held to the minimum.

Percy Browne followed the lowlands of the Big and Little Laramie Rivers and of Rock Creek in a generally northern direction as far as Medicine Bow, the scene of Owen Wister's immortal *The Virginian.* From there, turning westwardly to get out of the Laramie Plains "park," he finally decided to surmount the 7,125-foot rim formed by the Rattlesnake Hills (now known as the Saddleback Hills) at a new point which Dodge later named "Browne's Pass," 664 miles from Omaha. It is 13 miles north by east of the lone Elk Mountain, 11,162 feet high, and conspicuous to UP passengers throughout a hundred miles of riding. The key to the choice of passes was the 27-mile, westerly-flowing St. Mary's Creek, which cut between lone St. Mary's Hill and the 7,900-foot Pass Creek Ridge on its zigzag way down to Fort Fred Steele on the North Platte River, where the elevation dropped to 6,540 feet at milepost 696.

---

[296] Dodge, *How We Built the Union Pacific,* p. 32; Dodge, *Autobiography,* p. 686.
[297] See p. 273.

But just before Percy Browne completed these surveys, he was killed by Indians on July 23.[298] "His death before I could reach his party," reported Dodge, "with the loss of notes and all the information he had obtained in a thorough reconnaissance of that entire country, added greatly to our labors, and in many cases forced us to cover the same ground twice." [299] In memory of Browne, Dodge also gave the name of Percy to a station at milepost 667 on the ridge at the head of St. Mary's Creek.[300] (When, at the turn of the century, some 30 miles of this road was moved a bit northward to serve the coal mines at Hanna, and to straighten curves and reduce grades, Percy station also was moved to *new* milepost 645, 15 miles north by west of Elk Mountain. But the road over Browne's Pass was forsaken.)

From here on the adopted line followed the southern portion of the generally level but frequently ravined plain across the Great Divide Basin, Wyoming Basin, or Red Desert Basin, as it was variously known. "This entire plain, 200 miles east and west, and from 40 to 100 miles north and south, has no living streams traversing it, and but few living springs throughout its entire extent . . . . It is singularly marked by a succession of independent basins, each having its own drainage, . . . in some cases as much as 300 feet below the surrounding country." [301] Fifteen miles westward from the North Platte River, Dodge found a cold, fresh spring gushing from a rock. It was such a welcome rarity in the basins that he later named it Rawlins for the ailing General, who was one of the party.[302] He then almost imperceptibly crossed the Continental Divide at the present site of Creston station, 737 miles from Omaha, and 20 miles northwest of mountain-man Jim Bridger's famous pass, where the Overland Stage was still running. Four miles west of the prominent landmark called Table Rock he dropped into Bitter Creek, at milepost 775, and followed Evans's line of 1864 along its winding valley for 70 miles down to Green River. He reached this long tributary to the great Colorado River on August 12. Here he was met by Hodges of the Salt Lake party working eastward.

Green River to Ogden—187 miles: [303] From Green River to Salt Lake there were no Indian troubles, but two serious obstacles slowed the work: the high western rim of the Great Divide Basin and the

---

[298] See p. 220.   [299] Dodge, *Report of the Chief Engineer,* 1867, p. 7.
[300] See Profile, Illus., Group 3; map, Cheyenne to Ft. Steele (Illus., Group 2), shows changes in the line.
[301] Dodge, *Report of the Chief Engineer,* 1867, p. 7.
[302] Dodge, *Autobiography,* p. 649.   [303] See Profile, Illus., Group 3.

very rugged Wasatch Mountains. In addition, Dodge had to be absolutely sure that the South Pass-Sweetwater River route along the northern rim of the Basin really was inferior, as he had always suspected. Furthermore, he wanted to explore some short pass from Ham's Fork to the Snake River, whence a whole new railroad could readily be built all the way to Portland, Oregon and Puget Sound (the "Oregon Short Line" route).[304] He spent the rest of the good weather in all these efforts.

From Green River there was no difficulty in reaching the depression worn by Blacks Fork and following it upstream to the present site of Granger, at milepost 876, where Ham's Fork was crossed. But thence, working up Muddy Creek for 50 miles, the tracks would have to rise 1,276 feet to top the western rim of the Great Divide Basin. A big rock cut would be needed at Aspen, the second highest point on the UP: elevation 7,546, milepost 937. From the rim the grade then eased downward 807 feet in 18 miles to the oddly coursing Bear River and the future site of Evanston, elevation 6,739, milepost 955.[305] Like all streams west of Aspen, Bear River ended futilely in the Great Basin in which Salt Lake is located. (Thirty-four years later the line over the rim between LeRoy and Millis was abandoned. The elevation was reduced 363 feet, but at the expense of two tunnels at Altamount, several miles north of the original Aspen.)

Once the long Muddy Creek route had been settled upon, the remainder of the line to the Great Salt Lake was obvious, and already had been run by Reed, Bates, and Hodges. There would be a fall of 2,316 feet down the narrow, high-walled Echo and Weber Canyons for 56 miles of the most picturesque and odd scenery on the UP. Ogden, only 4,340 feet above the sea, would be 1,028 miles west of Omaha. Some very difficult engineering would be involved, particularly in getting over the 6,876-foot-high winding ravines at the head of Echo, where the longest tunnel of the railroad would be needed.

Arriving at Salt Lake City on August 30, Dodge refitted his transportation and replenished his supplies at Camp Douglas. In the interval, he and Rawlins conferred with Brigham Young about grading through the Wasatch Mountains. He also took another look westward, and became convinced that his true line west was *north* of Salt Lake, and perhaps even across the Bear River arm of that evaporating sea. Starting homeward on September 4, with one company of infantry added to his escort, he explored northward up the Bear River

[304] Dodge, *Report to the Board of Directors*, 1 Dec. 1867.   [305] See p. 294.

and over to Snake River, confirming his feasible route to Oregon and Puget Sound. "It would be by far the best line from the Atlantic to the Pacific, would avoid the high elevation of the Wasatch and Sierra Nevadas, with their heavy grades and troublesome snows, and no doubt ere long it will become the great through route from the northwest, and control the trade and traffic of the Indies," he prophesied.[306] At the northern spur of the Wasatch Mountains he turned eastward and traversed again part of the South Pass–Sweetwater River trail of the emigrants. "But it was impracticable for a railroad, the routes south having lighter work and easier grades . . . its winds and deep snows . . . its high foot-hills and numerous canons . . . Browne's line is the shortest, with the least curvature, lightest grades and cheapest work, the least length of road without running water, the most accessible to building material, and the least liable to obstruction from snow." [307]

During the season the UP engineers staked out 1,675 miles of instrumental lines, reconnoitered 3,310 miles, and traveled 5,193 miles in parties.[308] In spite of the trials suffered, 655 miles of continuous line from Julesburg to Ogden were tentatively fixed. "I shall strain every nerve," said Dodge in closing his 85-page report, "to get the location so advanced in the spring of 1868 as to be far out of reach of the construction corps, but success will depend upon the severity of the weather . . . . The responsibility for detention of the work in the Black Hills will rest solely on the company."

In the meantime, during 1867, the CP engineers had made some purely preliminary surveys, without any locations, all the way east to the head of Echo Canyon, and on that basis the next year had filed in the Interior Department a "map" in order to obtain a call on the subsidy bonds. Dodge claimed it was fraudulent.[309] They also explored the Wasatch and Uintah Mountains, Fort Bridger Basin and the valleys of the Muddy, Blacks Fork, and Hams Fork. All this ground had been explored previously by Dey, Reed, Hodges, and Dodge. The CP developed nothing that the UP had not discovered before.[310] But in 1866, Bates of the UP had found a practicable line from Reed's Pass in the Humboldt Mountains of Nevada to the California border, which the CP was now following.[311] So here was the beginning of the "gladiator scene" which was to rock the Capitol halls and the press in 1869, as will be told.

[306] Dodge, *Report of the Chief Engineer*, 1867, p. 12.   [307] *Ibid.*, pp. 13–17.
[308] *Ibid.*, p. 18.   [309] See pp. 312–313.   [310] Records of UP Historical Museum.
[311] See p. 159.

All in all, 1867 proved to be both the most important and the most disastrous year for the UP in surveying.

G. Construction and Equipment

It will be recalled that track-laying had stopped for the winter at O'Fallons Bluffs, 17 miles beyond North Platte.[312] Not until January 1867 did the UP attain a railroad connection with the East, when Oakes's Cedar Rapids & Missouri River Railroad entered Council Bluffs.[313] The price of rail at Omaha dropped from $135 a ton to $97.50.

North Platte: Now the town of North Platte sprang up like the first weeds of spring with construction workers, teamsters, traders, stagecoach travelers, miners, adventurers, and soldiers until the population reached more than 5,000; all in half a year.

Wrote Major Henry C. Parry, age twenty-eight, Dodge's medical officer, on May 16:

I found as I passed through North Platte that the Indians had driven all the traders and miners in from the mountains, and at North Platte they [the miners and traders] were having a good time, gambling, drinking, and shooting each other. There are fifteen houses in North Platte: One hotel, nine eating or drinking saloons, one billiard room, three groceries, and one engine house, belonging to the Pacific Railroad Company. The last named building is the finest structure in the station. I observed that in every establishment the persons behind the counters attended to their customers with loaded and half-cocked revolvers in their hands. Law is unknown here, and the people are about to get up a vigilance committee.[314]

Fortunately, the Casements had stored up an enormous amount of material during the winter. They signed a contract at $850 per mile for laying track during the coming season, including transportation of required material from the last terminal base. Just as Nebraska changed from a Territory to a State (over President Johnson's veto), Dodge wired Reed on March 7 to open work on the fourth hundred miles and to have it graded by May 1.

Flooding Rivers: The past winter had been exceptionally severe. North Platte had been shut in repeatedly, once for a week. "During

---

[312] See p. 161.   [313] See p. 55.   [314] Parry, *Observations on the Prairies*, p. 24.

April," wrote Dodge, "we had great floods. . . . It cost $50,000 to repair the damage to the Loup Fork Bridge. . . . East of Grand Island the river became one-half mile wide, cutting the road in two and sweeping over the country for 20 miles. At Elkhorn one mile of track was gone. . . . The height of the water was beyond all precedent." [315] Even in Omaha some of the track was under water. Reed was under heavy pressure, but by April 27 his swarms of repairmen had all trains back on schedule.

Official Visit from New York: Just at this inopportune moment, an official inspection party from the New York office arrived, to remain until May 6. In it were Directors Oliver Ames, Durant, Duff Sr., Government Director Harbaugh (all members of the UP Executive Committee), and Director Dillon. On behalf of the UP they had come to take formal acceptance of the completed road from the CM. During the ride out to O'Fallons and back with Dodge, Oliver expressed his deep disappointment in the nature of the countryside, and Durant countered again with his opinion that the only profit in the venture would be in its construction and not in its operation.

"They broke up in a row," wrote Sam Reed to his wife on May 6, "and no one knows what will be the end. No work has been let west of the fourth hundred and will not be until they come to some agreement among themselves in N.Y. . . . This fight places me in a very unpleasant position and I have a mind to resign my position but shall remain a few days until I hear from New York. The Dr. is jealous of every one and I think dare not let any more work until he goes East." [316] These were the darkest days of the wrangle among the promoters, and the demoralization was reflected throughout the working forces in the West.[317] Webster Snyder was appointed General Superintendent at Omaha, with Hoxie as his assistant. Dodge's salary from the UP was again set by the Directors at $10,000 a year.

Julesburg: On June 24 the railroad and telegraph line were completed to Julesburg and in readiness to deliver U.S. mail.[318] That community was in its third location and was destined to be changed by a few miles once more. Almost immediately, many of the shacks were moved in from North Platte, and the population mushroomed to several thousand persons. Sam Reed wrote "Dearest Jennie" about the Bacchanalia he witnessed on July 30:

[315] Dodge, *Autobiography*, p. 618; Records of UP Historical Museum.
[316] Durant, *Papers*, 1–2–45–27 (Reed).   [317] See pp. 167, 169.
[318] Records of UP Historical Museum.

Julesburg continues to grow with magic rapidity, vice and crime stalk unblushingly in the midday sun . . . I sent for Dan Casement to pilot us (I knew he could show us the sights) . . . By gas light . . . the first place we visited was a dance house, where a fresh importation of strumpets had been received. The hall was crowded with bad men and lewd women. Such profanity, vulgarity and indecency . . . would disgust a more hardened person than I. The next place visited was a gambling hell where all the games of chance were being played. Men excited with drink and dally were recklessly staking their last dollar on the turn of a card or the throw of a dice. Women were cajoling and coaxing the tipsy men to stake their money on various games; the pockets were shrewdly picked by the fallen women of the more sober of the crowd. We soon tired of this place and started forth for new dens of vice and crime . . . At last, about 10 p.m., we visited the theater and were asked behind the curtains to see the girls. From here I left the party and retired to my tent fully satisfied with my first visit to such places.[319]

Dodge told this story about General Jack Casement:

I wired him, "Go and clean the town out. Hold it until the citizens are willing to obey orders of the officers I placed in charge, and pay for their lots." This was fun for Casement . . . . When I saw him later, he said, "I will show you what I did". . . . He took me to a hill where there was quite a burial ground and he said, "General, they all died in their boots and Julesburg has been quiet since." [320]

Cheyenne: On November 13 the track reached Cheyenne, which Dodge had staked out on July 2 and named for "one of the most important tribes of Indians on the plains." [321] The Julesburg "shebangs" —the stores, saloons, and haunts of vice—were now moved on, leaving a litter of cans to mark the site of a five-months' town. So Cheyenne became the third burgeoning "Hell-on-Wheels." In a few months it had 5,000 inhabitants, under the police control of General J. H. Stevenson at Fort Russell. But Cheyenne, instead of withering when the trains rolled westward, was soon to have a branch railroad to Denver. It survived to become the capital of Wyoming, with a population today of some 45,000. Dr. Henry C. Parry, arriving at new Fort D. A. Russell "after a long, tedious, windy, dusty, cold, and perilous journey from Salt Lake City," noted on October 7:

---

[319] Dodge, *Autobiography*, p. 646; Records of UP Historical Museum (Reed's letters).
[320] *Ibid.*, p. 647.   [321] *Ibid.*, p. 641; see also p. 223.

PROGRESS OF THE TRACK [a]

Date	End of Track at or Near	End of Track Miles from Omaha	Miles per Day Excl. Suns.	Elevation [b]	Grade in Feet per Mile
22 Apr. '67 [c]	O'Fallons Bluff	305		2,976	
			1.32		7
May 24	Ogallala	342		3,190	
			0.90		8
June 5	Brule	351		3,266	
			1.73		12
June 24	Julesburg	377		3,500	
			1.33		14
July 12	Lodge Pole	397		3,800	
			1.32		18
Aug. 29	Antelope (Kimball)	451		4,712	
			0.90		18
Oct. 26	Hillsdale	496		5,591	
			1.33		27
Nov. 13	Cheyenne	516		6,041	
			0.71		46
Dec. 7	Otto	531		6,724	
			0.25		96
31 Dec. '67	Granite Canyon	536		7,298	
			0.11		80
14 Mar. '68	Buford	542		7,780	
			0.33		66
5 Apr. '68	Sherman	549		8,242	

Total miles laid in 1867: 231.
Average miles laid per day, excluding Sundays: 1.06.

[a] Compiled by author from Records of UP Historical Museum.
[b] Dodge, *Annual Report*, 1869, pp. 24–27; UP, "Time Table No. 24, June 20th, 1870," with several adjustments to correspond with UP, *Freight Tariff to Take Effect June 1st, 1870.* See Profile, Illus., Group 3.
[c] The date of commencing spring track-laying is estimated by the author.

The Fort is three miles from the town of Cheyenne which is building up rapidly. When I left here last July [trekking westward] all the land was bare and the only habitations were tents. Cheyenne now has a population of 1,500, two papers, stores, warehouses, hotels, restaurants, gambling halls, etc., etc. Three months ago it was nothing but bare prairie land.[322]

Thanks to Seymour the machinator, the track got no further than Granite Canyon, halfway up the heavy grade beyond Cheyenne. All construction material possible was accumulated and stored in Cheyenne, including timber for the Dale Creek Bridge. Urgent calls for hundreds more workmen were sent out. The company now had on hand for the 517 miles in regular operation 53 locomotives, 17 pas-

322 Parry, *Observations on the Prairies*, p. 31.

senger cars, 6 baggage cars, 838 freight cars, and 99 handcars. These were exclusive of the large amount of rolling stock owned and run by the contractors for building the road. Snyder was having snowplows built for immediate use.

From April 1 to the end of the year, the company carried 15,022 passengers for 3,381,088 passenger miles and moved nearly 26 million tons of freight. Total government service performed in the transportation of troops, freight, mail, and the use of telegraph lines brought in $813,000.[323]

Progress of the Track: During the year 1867, the Casements advanced the track 231 miles from near O'Fallons Bluff to Granite Canyon, where they practically laid off for the winter. By 5 April 1868, they reached the summit at Sherman, 13 miles further on. How their rate slowed down to only ¼ mile per day during December while the grade steadily increased from only 7 feet per mile to 96 (later reduced to the maximum of 90) is shown in the accompanying table.

H. Highlights of 1867

This was the year of crisis in the discord among the promoters. The Ames group had purchased their way to control of the CM and had ejected Durant from that office, but Durant had blocked the construction company from another contract and any possible profit. After reaching $3,750,000 no further CM capital was ever needed. By springtime the UP, east and west, was at its lowest ebb of demoralization, with no money and its securities unsalable. But for the energy, perseverance, and financial ability of the New Englanders, the company would have failed. A truce was not called until after Oakes Ames came forward in August with an offer to himself contract for the rest of the road. Through the Tripartite Agreement which ensued, the contract was vested in the Seven Trustees, of whom Durant was one. The consent of every UP stockholder was now required on every policy decision, and the profits were to be prorated among such CM stockholders as executed proxies to the Trustees.

The Redskins raised Cain with the surveyors, along the tracks, and with ranchers and travelers throughout the West. Army protec-

[323] Dodge, *Report of the Chief Engineer*, 1867, p. 20.

UP Treasurer John J. Cisco's
bond circular of 2 April 1868.

THE

Union Pacific Railroad Co.

OFFER A LIMITED AMOUNT OF THEIR

FIRST MORTGAGE BONDS,

AT PAR, PRINCIPAL AND INTEREST

PAYABLE IN GOLD.

These Bonds are for $1,000 each, and have Coupons attached. They have thirty
years to run, and bear annual interest, payable on the first days of January and
July at the Company's Office in the City of New York, at the rate of six per cent.
in gold.

At the present rate of premium on gold, these Bonds pay an annual income on their
cost of

NEARLY NINE PER CENT.,

And it is believed that they will soon be at a premium.

The Company have but a very limited supply of their Bonds remaining on hand—
but it is expected that the first installment of the New Bonds, to be issued on that
portion of the road to be completed this year, will be ready in May.

Any subscriptions accepted to a greater amount than can be filled from Bonds
now in the Company's possession, will be supplied from the New Bonds in the order
in which they are received.

The Company reserve the right to advance the price of their bonds to a rate above
par at any time, and will not fill any orders or receive any subscriptions on which
the money has not been actually paid at the Company's office before the time of
such advance.

Parties subscribing will remit the par value of the bonds and the accrued interest
in currency at the rate of six per cent. per annum, from the date on which the last
coupon was paid. Subscriptions will be received in New York

AT

THE COMPANY'S OFFICE, No. 20 Nassau Street,

AND BY

JOHN J. CISCO & SON, BANKERS, No. 59 Wall Street,

AND BY THE

Company's Advertised Agents throughout the United States.

*Remittances should be made in drafts or other funds par in New York, and the Bonds
will be sent free of charge by return express. Parties subscribing through local agents,
will look to them for their safe delivery.*

JOHN J. CISCO, *Treasurer.*

NEW YORK, APRIL 2, 1868.

The Union Pacific and its connections, early 1868.
(Courtesy of Union Pacific.)

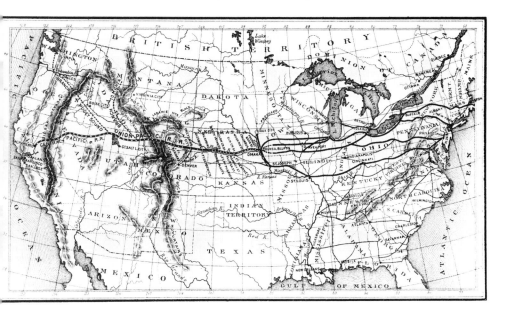

Dale Creek Bridge, 1868.
(Courtesy of Union Pacific.)

Grant settles the argument at Fort Sanders, 26 July 1868.
Front, left to right: Dillon (straw hat), Gen. Sheridan (hand in pocket),
Gen. Grant (hands on fence), Gen. Sherman (coat on arm),
Gen. Harney (top hat), and Durant (straw hat).
(Courtesy of Union Pacific.)

Union Pacific construction train, 1868.
(Courtesy of Union Pacific.)

Iron men laying rails, 1868.
(Courtesy of Union Pacific.)

Supply train, Echo Canyon, 1868.
(Courtesy of Union Pacific.)

Wilhemina Pass, Echo Canyon, 1868.
(Courtesy of Union Pacific.)

Z-track switchback, Echo, Summit, 1868–1869.
(Courtesy of Union Pacific.)

Union Pacific Railroad, Weber Canyon and River.
(*Frank Leslie's Illustrated Newspaper,* November 1877.)

Tunnel No. 3, Weber Canyon, May 1868.

Bear River City, the forsaken, November 1868.
R.R. Restaurant and telegraph pole from near the track. Main Street at right.
(Courtesy of Union Pacific.)

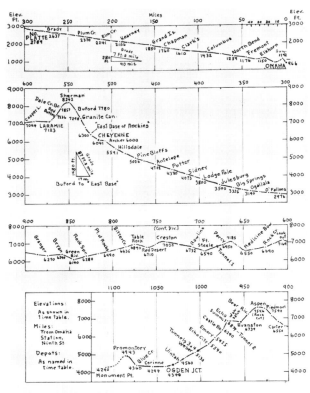

Source: U.P. Time Table No. 24, June 20th, 1870, and other original records.

Profile of Union Pacific as first built.

Across the Continent—Through line, New York to San Francisco.
(Currier & Ives print, 1868. Courtesy of Mr. Kenneth M. Newman,
The Old Print Shop, Inc., New York City.)

Conference in Directors' car, early 1869.
Left to right at table: Seymour, Dillon, Durant, and Duff Sr.
Reed standing, right rear.
(Courtesy of Union Pacific.)

Union Pacific certificate for 6 shares in name of Fisk,
23 June 1868.
(Courtesy of Union Pacific.)

Oakes to Durant, 16 January 1869.
(Durant, *Papers.*
Courtesy of State University of Iowa.)

ONE THOUSAND MILES
OF THE
UNION PACIFIC RAILROAD
ARE NOW COMPLETED.

As 500 miles of the western portion of the line, beginning at Sacramento, are also done, but

267 MILES REMAIN

To be Finished. To Open the Grand Through Line to the Pacific. This Opening will certainly take place Early this Season.

Besides a donation from the Government of 12,800 acres of land per mile, the Company is entitled to a subsidy in United States Bonds on its line as completed and accepted at the average rate of about $26,500 per mile, according to the difficulties encountered, for which the Government takes a second lien as security. Whether subsidies are given to any other companies or not, the Government will comply with all its contracts with the Union Pacific Railroad Company. Nearly the whole amount of bonds to which the Company will be entitled have already been delivered.

FIRST MORTGAGE BONDS
AT PAR.

By its charter the Company is permitted to issue its own FIRST MORTGAGE BONDS to the same amount as the Government Bonds; AND NO MORE. These Bonds are a First Mortgage upon the entire road and all its equipments.

THEY HAVE THIRTY YEARS TO RUN, AT SIX PER CENT, and both

PRINCIPAL AND INTEREST ARE PAYABLE IN GOLD.

Such securities are generally valuable in proportion to the length of time they have to run. The longest six per cent gold interest bonds of the U. S. (the '81's) will be due in 12 years, and they are worth 112. If they had 30 years to run, they would stand at not less than 125. A perfectly safe First Mortgage Bond like the Union Pacific should approach this rate. The demand for European investment is already considerable, and on the completion of the work will doubtless carry the price to a large premium.

SECURITY OF THE BONDS.

It needs no argument to show that a First Mortgage of $26,500 per mile upon what for a long time must be the only railroad connecting the Atlantic and Pacific States is PERFECTLY SECURE. The entire amount of the mortgage will be about $30,000,000, and the interest $1,800,000 per annum in gold. The present currency cost of this interest is less than $2,500,000 per annum, while the gross earnings for the year 1868, FROM WAY BUSINESS only, on AN AVERAGE OF LESS THAN 700 MILES OF ROAD IN OPERATION, WERE MORE THAN

FIVE MILLION DOLLARS.

The details of which are as follows:

From Passengers	$1,094,005 97
" Freight	2,040,233 19
" Express	51,423 08
" Mails	136,235 59
" Miscellaneous	91,626 27
" Government troops	104,077 77
" " freight	649,440 33
" Contractors' men	201,179 49
" " material	968,630 52
Total	$5,066,651 61

This large amount is only an indication of the immense traffic that must go over the through line in a few months, when the great tide of Pacific coast travel and trade will begin. It is estimated that this business must make the earnings of the road from FIFTEEN TO TWENTY MILLIONS A YEAR.

As the supply of these Bonds will soon cease, parties who desire to invest in them will find it for their interest to do so at once. The price for the present is par and accrued interest from January 1, in currency.

Subscriptions will be received in New York

At the Company's Office, No. 20 Nassau Street
AND BY
John J. Cisco & Son, Bankers, No. 59 Wall Street.

And by the Company's advertised agents throughout the United States.

Bonds sent free, but parties subscribing through local agents, will look to them for their safe delivery.

A NEW PAMPHLET AND MAP was issued October 1st, containing a report of the progress of the work to that date, and a more complete statement in relation to the value of the bonds than can be given in an advertisement, which will be sent free on application at the Company's offices or to any of the advertised agents.

JOHN J. CISCO, Treasurer New York.

January 20th, 1869.

Financial.

EXTENSION TABLES
(EXCLUSIVELY),
of Every Style and Quality, at Greatly Reduced Prices.
WM. HERBDT, Manufacturer,
150 WOOSTER STREET,
BETWEEN PRINCE AND HOUSTON STREET
NEW YORK.

THE ONLY
Genuine Oroide Watches

JAS. GERARD & CO., Sole Agents,
85 NASSAU STREET, NEW YORK CITY.

Safes For Sale
AT A VERY LOW PRICE.

"SAFE," P.O. Box 5.650.

LARGE FIRE!
Brooklyn, May 15, 1866

SHERMAN BROS.

PERFECT

SAFES

MARVIN'S
Chrome Iron Spherical

Burglar Safe
Will resist 11 Burglar Implements for any length of time.
Please send for Catalogue.

MARVIN & Co.,
PRINCIPAL WAREHOUSES
No. 265 Broadway, New York.
No. 721 Chestnut st, Philadelphia.
No. 108 Bank st, Cleveland, Ohio.
Sale by our agents in the principal cities through the United States.

HEBBARD, STRONG & CO.,
SILVERSMITHS,
NO. 17 JOHN STREET.

Union Pacific advertisement of bonds for sale.
(The *Chronicle*, 13 February 1869.)

Temporary trestle near Promontory, April 1869.
UP Engine No. 119 westbound.
(Courtesy of Union Pacific.)

tion proved to be inadequate. Seymour slowed down construction on the key Black Hills section of the road just when speed was paramount. The first rumblings of new trouble came as the UP and CP surveys began to overlap.

Oakes naively sold $16,000 worth of Durant's belatedly paid CM stock to 11 Congressmen in November or early December, an average of 15 shares each. Soon after that, on December 12, the first allotments of profits were declared, and later the stock kited. But his unwary letters to McComb induced a blackmail lawsuit, the threat of which forced Oakes to keep in his name all of the shares he had sold.

There were happy events, also, in 1867. Rail connection with the East was finally secured in January. Starting about June, large buyers of UP bonds were uncovered for the first time, and for a while the financiers would have no serious difficulty in raising all the capital seemingly needed just through sales of these and the Subsidy bonds. Furthermore, the allowable issue of bonds was to triple to $96,000 per mile after the "east base of the Rockies" was fixed. Dodge's far-flung surveys led to a good line all the way into Nevada, plus an economical route for a possible UP branch to Portland, Oregon. The promising town of Cheyenne was staked out. Some 231 more miles of track were bedded, to Granite Canyon near Sherman Summit. Uncle Sam had handed over $3,840,000 of his subsidies on 240 miles, bringing the cumulative total to $8,160,000 by the year end.

But the CP was already at the western Nevada border, except for a gap of 7 miles near the summit of the Sierras. Their hardest work was over. By amended law, they could now build eastward until they connected with the UP.

7

Building the Road: A Chronology

1868

Finances—The Last of the Indian Troubles—Surveys and Engineering
—Construction and Equipment—Summary

A. Finances

1. DIVISION OF PROFITS TO CM STOCKHOLDERS BEGINS

Now that all the cash necessary for building probably could be raised through bond sales, the Seven Trustees decided the time had come to start settling with the contractors, who were the CM stockholders. The first allotment of estimated profits on construction of the past season was paid out on 3 January 1868. As previously described, this allotment (or "dividend," as it was incorrectly called at first) had been declared by the Trustees on 12 December 1867.[1] To repeat, it was in the form of: (a) 60 per cent in UP bonds on the 37,400 CM shares, amounting to $2,244,000 at par, and $2,176,680 at the estimated market price of 97; and (b) 60 per cent in UP stock, amounting to $2,244,000 at par, and $673,200 at the estimated market price of 30.[2] From now on, all UP stock was to be fully paid up.

On January 3 the Trustees declared a second allotment, payable on the same day, consisting of 20 per cent in bonds, which amounted to $748,000 at par, and $725,560 at the market price of 97.

On January 8 Durant left for Europe, to return on March 5.[3]

---

[1] See p. 196.
[2] See table, p. 259; Oliver Ames's diary of Jan. 3; see also Appendix G.
[3] *Poland Rep.*, p. 110 (McComb).

2. BOND PRICES AND SALES RISE FURTHER

Oliver noted in his diary on January 21: "Full of work at the office and very large sale of Bonds—800 or more ordered today. The 10,000,000 $ of old Bonds sold and have commenced on the new lot today. Increased the price to 95 to save us from being entirely run out." These were UP bonds.[4]

On January 27 the Government increased the rate of issue of subsidy bonds from $16,000 to $48,000 a mile, as the "eastern base of the Rockies," officially fixed at 525.078 miles from Omaha, had been reached and the road approved. The issue of first mortgage bonds also could now be raised to $48,000 a mile—a total of $96,000. This highest rate was to continue until 150 miles would be completed (near Percy on 24 July 1868); then the rate would drop to $32,000 a mile.[5]

Benjamin Ham was having his troubles making up the inevitable free passes. "Enclosed I send passes for remainder of M.C.s," he wrote the Honorable Oakes Ames on January 25, "and also for President Johnson and his Cabinet. Shall I make them out for the Judges of the Supreme Court and also Gen'l. Grant and staff and Gen'l. Sherman & staff. If for the latter please have them furnished list of Staff officers . . . ."[6]

And on February 3, Ham to Oakes again, better news: "The increase of price of Pacific Bonds . . . made quite a stir amongst moneyed men who designed investing. We had orders for $1,000,000 at old rates but did not deliver. We received Cash for $258,000 and 398,000 most of which were delivered and for only 7 did we receive 96 less 1. We now have on hand Cash $700,000 besides a special deposit with Mr. Cisco of $900,000." Again, February 12: "Shall have about one million left after filling all orders at 95%."[7]

Oliver entered a note in his diary on February 6: "Meeting of Board of Directors at which we decided to pay 97 for certificates issued for Bonds—Bonds raised to Par yesterday. Had a very harmonious meeting." And nine days later: "Received check from UPR for 170,802.30."

On April 16 Oliver noted that money was going higher: "McCombs had to pay for 200,000 $ from Park Bank for 60 days at rate of 18% per annum . . . The UPR is paying 13% for money."

[4] *Wilson Rep.*, p. 621; Fogel, p. 60. [5] *Wilson Rep.*, pp. 738–739.
[6] Records of UP Historical Museum. [7] *Ibid.*

COMPOSITION OF UP BOARD BY GROUPS [a]

11 MARCH 1868 TO 25 MAY 1869

Ames Group	Durant Group	Government	Uncertain
DIRECTORS AND MEMBERS EXECUTIVE COMMITTEE (7)			
Oliver Ames (Pres.)	C. S. Bushnell	J. Brooks	
J. Duff	T. C. Durant (V.P.)		
C. A. Lambard	H. S. McComb		
DIRECTORS (13)			
J. B. Alley	J. J. Cisco	G. Ashmun	J. Bardwell
B. E. Bates	H. C. Crane	S. McKee	W. H. Macy
F. G. Dexter	J. F. Tracy	J. S. Rollins	
S. Dillon		J. L. Williams	
TOT. DIRS.: 7	6	5	2

25 MAY 1869 TO 9 MARCH 1870

Ames Group	Durant Group	Government	Uncertain
DIRECTORS AND MEMBERS EXECUTIVE COMMITTEE (7)			
Oliver Ames (Pres.)	C. S. Bushnell	J. Brooks (to 7/14)	
E. Atkins		Jas. F. Wilson (7/14)	
S. Dillon			
J. Duff (V.P.)			
W. T. Glidden			
DIRECTORS (13)			
J. B. Alley (11/19)		J. W. Burson (11/8)	E. H. Baker
O. S. Chapman		D. L. Harris (3/6)	(to 8/18)
F. G. Dexter		H. Price (3/6)	C. H. McCormick
J. R. Duff (to 8/18)		B. F. Wade (5/31)	
G. M. Dodge (8/18)		J. D. Webster (3/16	
R. G. Hazard		to 5/31)	
C. A. Lambard		J. L. Williams (to 11/8)	
F. Nickerson			
TOT. DIRS.: 13	1	5	1

9 MARCH 1870 TO 8 MARCH 1871

Ames Group	Durant Group	Government	Uncertain
DIRECTORS AND MEMBERS EXECUTIVE COMMITTEE (7)			
Oliver Ames (Pres.)	C. S. Bushnell	Jas. F. Wilson	
E. Atkins			
S. Dillon			
J. Duff (V.P.)			
W. T. Glidden			
DIRECTORS (13)			
Oakes Ames		J. W. Burson	C. H. McCormick
J. B. Alley		(to 1/23)	
J. Brooks		D. L. Harris	
O. S. Chapman		J. C. S. Harrison	
G. M. Dodge		(from 1/23)	
R. G. Hazard		H. Price	
C. A. Lambard		B. F. Wade	
F. Nickerson			
TOT. DIRS.: 13	1	5	1

[a] Adapted from Union Pacific, *Official Register; Wilson Rep.*, pp. 596–599. (For period 4 Oct. 1865 to 11 Mar. 1868 see p. 178).

The date of the annual meeting of UP stockholders was changed from October to March, and this would be the last such meeting until after the Golden Spike. The only change in Directors made at the meeting on March 11 put H.C. Crane in place of Ebenezer Cook, who, after serving since 1863, had sold his small holding and was never re-elected. This brought the Durant group up to six Directors, but the Ames group still had seven, as shown in the accompanying table. The margin of control was too small, as will be seen.

The UP Plays Up Its Bonds: Treasurer John J. Cisco put out a new and attractive 32-page printed pamphlet to help sell first mortgage bonds. Its inside title was, briefly: "THE UNION PACIFIC RAILROAD COMPANY, Chartered By The United States—*Progress Of Their Road West From Omaha, Nebraska, Across The Continent.* Making, With Its Connections, An Unbroken Line From The Atlantic To The Pacific Ocean. *Five Hundred and Forty Miles Completed December, 1867*—Offices, No. 20 Nassau Street, New York. Published By The Company. Pamphlet Edition, April 2, 1868."

After commenting fully on such subjects as the progress of the work; agricultural, timber, and mineral resources; how the railroad was being built; the branch and connecting roads; financial resources for construction; and the anticipated business and profits, he reported on actual earnings for the 8 months from 1 May 1867 to 31 December 1867. This period was taken because "the road was run by the contractors until April." His figures were as follows:

Earnings		*Expenses*	
Passengers	$ 526,779	Conducting Transportation	$ 282,022
Freight	1,912,028	Motive Power, Engines, etc.	567,355
Express	17,886	Maintenance of Way	430,641
Mails	32,274	Maintenance of Cars	91,208
Miscellaneous	7,223	General	55,827
	$2,496,190		$1,427,054

Net Earnings $1,069,136 [8]

The *average* length of road in operation during this period was 386 miles, he said. The amount of first mortgage bonds issuable on such mileage at $16,000 per mile was $6,176,000. Interest for 8 months at 6 per cent per annum was $247,040, to which was added the 40 per cent premium for gold of $98,816—a total of $345,856. Therefore, he

[8] See p. 193.

figured, interest on the first mortgage bonds was earned about 3.1 times.

"Transportation for the government and for the mining regions is at present the principal source of already large revenue . . . . Mails and passengers have already been brought through (to New York) from San Francisco, by the Union Pacific Railroad and Wells, Fargo & Co.'s stages, in 15 days (the steamer requires 21 to 24 days), and, as the eastern and western ends of the track are brought nearer together, there can be no doubt that by next season, at least one-half of the California passenger travel will take this route," Cisco concluded.

On 3 October 1868, the first weekly quotations on the first mortgage bonds appeared in the *Commercial & Financial Chronicle*. But weekly quotations on the stock and all three bonds were not published until 26 March 1870.

3. "WASHBURN'S BILL" AGAIN

Dodge's Speech: Washburn had introduced a second bill to reduce Pacific Railroad rates.[9] General Dodge made his first and only speech in Congress on March 25, refuting many important statements made by Washburn as misrepresentations and mere hearsay. Dodge gave some detailed facts and figures, a few of which follow. The UP was charging about 7 mills (7/10ths of one cent) per 100 pounds of freight per mile. The great eastern roads, competing for freight between large cities, were getting $2\frac{1}{2}$ to 4 mills, with all the advantages of civilization, concentration, and cheapness of material, fuel, and repairs. The western roads east of the Missouri were charging 4 to 5 mills, and many local southern roads 4 to 7 mills.

As to passenger fares, the UP was charging 10 cents per mile, the Chicago and Northwestern 4, the Rock Island $3\frac{1}{2}$, and some others 6—all in heavily settled country—while the UP was running 500 miles into a wilderness, with nearly all freight and travel going only westward.

During 1867, coal for fuel cost the UP from $28 to $42 per ton, delivered at places for use. Wood averaged $18 to $20 per cord. Labor and living costs exceeded those of eastern roads by 33 per cent. As soon as the road reached the rich coal fields 100 miles west, the UP proposed to reduce rates and fares.

The average cost to the Government during 1864–1867 for freight

9 See p. 213.

hauled by wagon trains had been about 2 cents per 100 pounds per mile, nearly three times the cost over the railroad. In 1867 alone the Government thus saved about $1,040,000 on 20 million pounds of freight hauled for an average of 400 miles on just the UP.

The rest of the speech was largely on a broad basis, describing the difficult conditions, defending the aims, and praising the accomplishments of the UP.[10]

Oliver Ames congratulated him promptly:

We are very greatly delighted with your success in the controversy with Washburn. It shows the necessity of having some one there that thoroughly understands the whole subject . . . . The law allows us 10% on our stock and I think the most of us will be satisfied with that, and the Committee would not be allowed to cut us down below that.[11]

Oliver wrote Dodge in an over-optimistic mood on March 30:

. . . I think I have never seen the Doctor more pliable & anxious to please everybody than now. It may, however, be for the purpose of getting power in construction of road. I hope, however, he will be as he now pretends only anxious to push forward the road.[12]

Durant had just been voted extensive powers.

Oakes's Proposal: The same day Oakes wrote Durant about a possible amendment he was proposing to Section 18 of the Act of July 1862, pertaining to the "reduction of fares if the net earnings exceeded 10% upon its cost": [13]

> *Fortieth Congress, House of Representatives*
> *Washington, D.C.   March 30, 1868*

Thos C Durant, Esq.

Dear Sir: You have seen by the papers that our Road has been the subject of attack from some of our enemies & we have succeeded in getting the resolution refered to our committee [Committee on the Pacific Railroad]. We promised to give it attention and have concluded to report to the house when our committee is called, something like the following, thinking it will be as well or better for us than to have Congress do it as the law now has it. ((Be it enacted, that for the purpose of carrying into effect the intent & meaning of Section 18 of the Act of July 1862,

---

[10] Dodge, *How We Built the Union Pacific Railway*, pp. 87–95.
[11] Dodge, *Autobiography*, pp. 745–746.
[12] Dodge, *Papers*, vol. 154 (original ms.).   [13] See p. 16.

the Sec of War, Interior & Atty General of the U.S., and two other persons of experience in constructing and operating R Rds. to be appointed by the Pres of the U.S. are hereby appointed a board of Commissioners, whose duty it shall be on the 1st of July in each year, to establish a tariff of prices for freight and passengers on said Pacific R Roads & branches at which prices so established the sd RR. Cos shall be compelled to transport the same, and the said Companies shall keep posted in all their stations along the line of sd road the bill of prices so established. Provided However that this shall not take effect until there shall be a continuous line of Rail Road completed and in running order from Omaha to Sacramento.))

I dont think the com will be called for some days and if you think of anything better that will probably pass send it down & I will try to get it substituted if I think it better.

I think our bill we have agreed on will put the thing of until after the road is done. & I think we can get along with 5 men better than we can with congress as a body. & they cannot act under this report unless we make over 10 per cent. It is a great thing to us to keep them off until the road is done. Will you please give me the views and wishes of your people in regard to matters here. will Oliver be in N.Y. this week please post me on road matters and finance & Oblige Yours

Oakes Ames [14]

Apparently Durant never sent in any proposals.

Although Washburn's amended bill finally passed the House on May 12, the Senate merely referred it back to Oakes's Committee on the Pacific Railroad, where it died. After the line was completed, the companies voluntarily reduced their rates, and further trouble was avoided.

4. STOCKHOLDERS OF CREDIT MOBILIER AS OF 16 MAY 1868

A new CM list was made up to aid the Seven Trustees in settling further allotments of profits on the Oakes Ames contract with such UP stockholders as also owned CM stock and had executed proxies. It was found that there were only a few changes in individual holdings from the list of 12 December 1867.[15] The 26 names in the Ames Group now held 47.1 per cent of the final 37,500 shares of CM outstanding; the 9 names in the Durant Group had 26.9 per cent; and

[14] Durant, *Papers*, 1–3–28–16 (original ms.).
[15] *Wilson Rep.*, pp. 157–159; Durant, *Papers*, 3–3–8–11; see also pp. 194, 189.

the remaining 56 names, who are classified in this book as uncertain in their preference, owned 26.0 per cent.

The Ames brothers alone now had $697,800, or 18.6 per cent of the total, invested in the CM, Oakes as Trustee having bought $25,-000 additional since 12 December 1867. The Doctor himself had nearly the same as before, $565,800, or 15.1 per cent. At times he still could influence enough UP Directors, regular and governmental, to block the New Englanders, even though the latter held some 55 per cent of the UP stock.[16]

5. PRESIDENT JOHNSON IS NEARLY IMPEACHED

The attempted impeachment of President Johnson by the Senate failed by only one vote on May 16. As Vice-President he had succeeded Lincoln, and, to the great detriment of the Union Pacific, served until 4 March 1869, when General Grant took office. The impeachment trial was one of the most notorious on record and is covered thoroughly in most histories. For that reason, only a bare outline of events will be given here.

Congress was still in firm control of the Republicans, but Johnson vetoed many of their resolutions in such a way as to favor the Southern states in the problems of reconstruction, only to have his vetoes overridden. Johnson thereupon characterized the course of Congress as a rebellion, and great excitement arose throughout the nation. Twice he removed Stanton as his Secretary of War. The second time, Stanton refused to move out, protesting that his removal was in violation of the Tenure of Office Law which Congress had passed over Johnson's veto in March 1867. Congress had taken from the President practically all control, and the Senate had resolved that "the President has no power to remove the Secretary of War and designate any other person to perform the duties of that office."

The next day, February 24, the House of Representatives determined upon the President's impeachment by a unanimous Republican vote. The House recited many offenses, the principal of which were the removal of Stanton; the public expression of disregard of and contempt for the legislative branch of the Government; the Congress in session was not a constitutional one; and, particularly, his obstruction to the execution of Congressional acts. The main points of defense were that Johnson's course in the work of reconstruction

[16] See pp. 240, 168, 195.

was merely a continuation of the plans of President Lincoln and his cabinet, and that the Tenure of Office Act was unconstitutional.

The vote of the Senators from all 27 states (excluding the unrecognized Southern states) was guilty 35, not guilty 19. The necessary two-thirds majority for impeachment called for a vote of 36 to 18, so Johnson was barely saved. Obviously, the voting was highly partisan. All 12 Democrats voted for acquittal, while 35 of the 42 Republicans decided "guilty." The seven courageous Republican Senators put what they believed were the best interests of the country and its form of government ahead of all the merciless abuse they knew would be heaped on them. They were Edmund G. Ross of Kansas (the only one who refused to reveal how he would vote until his ballot was cast); William Pitt Fessenden of Maine, who died shortly after; John B. Henderson of Missouri; Peter Van Winkle of West Virginia; Lyman Trumbull of Illinois; Joseph Smith Fowler of Tennessee; and finally, James Wilson Grimes of Iowa, Oakes Ames's close friend and a bitter enemy of Johnson. Under stress, Grimes had suffered a stroke of paralysis only two days before his vote and was carried to his seat. He never recovered. Before dying, he said:

I shall ever thank God that . . . I had the courage to be true to my oath and my conscience . . . and no power could force me to decide on such a case contrary to my convictions, whether that party was composed of my friends or my enemies.

All seven were ruined for life, politically and socially. But history is belatedly vindicating them.

6. ALLOTMENTS OF PROFITS SOAR

On May 21 Oliver noted: "Govt bonds received for 40 miles of Road 1,920,000 Sold to Cisco for 99½. Money getting easy. Road going along well. Had meeting of Contractors and purchased 10,000 tons of Rails at 82$ per ton." These bonds, for mileposts 540 to 580, had been issued and received, one-half on May 16 and one-half on May 18.[17]

A contract was made with the Post Office Department at this time to carry the mails twice daily from Omaha to stations as far as Cheyenne and back at the rate of $150 per mile per annum, and to points in the mountain area at $300 per mile per annum. One-half of the

[17] *Wilson Rep.*, pp. 738, 615.

mail pay was to apply to payment of the Government Subsidy bonds.[18]

On June 2 the offering price of the first mortgage bonds was advanced to 102.[19] This was to be the highest price until 1874.[20] Oakes "paid $25,000 for 500 shares" of UP on May 27.[21] The price of 50 was the highest of which there is a record until 1875.

Within a period of three weeks, the Seven Trustees made their third, fourth, and fifth profit allotments under the Oakes Ames contract to such CM stockholders as also owned UP shares and had executed proxies.[22] On June 17 they declared and paid: (a) 40 per cent in Stock amounting to $1,500,000 face value, or $450,000 at market value, estimating the price at 30; and (b) 60 per cent in cash, or $2,250,000. On July 3 they declared and paid 75 per cent in Bonds amounting to $2,812,500 face value and market value, estimating the price at 100. And on July 8, they made another cash allotment of 30 per cent, or $1,125,000.[23] (The sixth and final action would come at the end of the year.)

On June 18 Oliver noted in his diary from New York: "Let Mr. Oakes Ames have my dividend of 280,800." This was the entire 40 per cent cash "dividend" on the 4,680 shares of CM with which he was "partly joint account" with Oakes.[24] On the same day, he wrote: "Made a sale of 1,920,000 Govts to Dillon—which is the best sale we have ever made." Oliver was out West on the road from June 21 to about July 4, according to his diary.

In June, Oakes and his sons subscribed $950,000 to the stock of the construction company of the Iowa Falls and Sioux City Railroad.[25] His Sioux City and Pacific had completed its connection with the UP in February.[26] Sioux City then had a population of nearly 3,000.

7. THE WARDELL COAL CONTRACT AND THE WYOMING COAL AND MINING COMPANY

The Act of 1864 allowed the UP to possess any coal lands found in the land grants. Valuable coal deposits fortunately were discovered along the road, especially at Rock Springs; Almy (near Evanston); and Grass Creek, Utah. On 16 July 1868, a contract with certain Directors acting for the UP (Oliver signed it as President of the UP) was negotiated with a man named Thomas Wardell and his associate,

---

[18] Durant, *Papers,* 1–3–39–42.   [19] Records of UP Historical Museum.
[20] See Appendix A.   [21] Oakes Ames's cash book, p. 3.   [22] See p. 189.
[23] See table on p. 259;; *Wilson Rep.,* p. 245.   [24] *Wilson Rep.,* p. 157.
[25] See p. 87.   [26] See p. 86,

C.O. Godfrey. These two were to operate the mines and supply coal to the UP for 15 years at fixed prices, starting at $6 a ton and declining gradually to $3 the last year. Some of the coal also could be sold commercially, with a 25 per cent rebate to the contractors. The actual cost of the mining started at a bit over $2 a ton, to fall gradually to about $1.10.[27]

The story becomes complex. In January 1869 a corporation, the Wyoming Coal and Mining Company, was formed under Nebraska law. *By pre-arrangement* (as found later by the courts), Wardell and Godfrey assigned their contract to this company on April Fool's Day, 1869. The new company supposedly had capital stock of $500,000, although it is not clear whether all was issued. Wardell claimed that John Duff (President), Durant, Oliver Ames, Dillon, Lambard, and he each took 10 per cent, Bushnell 5 per cent, and J.W. Davis 2 per cent. Godfrey had retired. Duff, Ames, Dillon, and Bushnell often stated in court that they held their interest in it "in trust for the use and benefit of the Union Pacific." [28] Durant swore: "The Union Pacific only paid the actual cost of the coal, $1.82 per ton, and any dividend would go to the Union Pacific. I hold $20,000 of stock, which I paid for in instalments out of the trust-funds. The only reason that it stands in my name now [1873] is because the Union Pacific will not release the parties that subscribed from any liability in case of debt. I believe that all the stock except 15% is held in trust for the Union Pacific road." [29] On the other hand, the Government Directors, in several reports, continued to denounce the contract as a "bad one." But it carried on until Gould took over in 1874, when he broke the contract and forcibly took over the coal lands as the sole property of the UP. Wardell, however, attempted to force the railroad to continue under the contract. Finally, in 1880, the U.S. Supreme Court ruled that the original contract had been fraudulent and was void. Wardell received $100,000 plus interest of $28,286 in settlement.[30]

8.　SECRETARY BROWNING INJURES THE FINANCING

Williams Wants a Deficiency Reserve:　Government Director Jesse L. Williams was an able, energetic, and honest civil engineer from

[27] *Wilson Rep.,* pp. 591–593 (contains copy of contract); Trottman, pp. 42–44.
[28] Records of UP Historical Museum; *Wilson Rep.,* pp. 232–235 (testimony of J. F. Wilson).
[29] *Wilson Rep.,* p. 122.
[30] *U.S. Reports,* 13 Otto 651, Law Department Library No. 103.

Fort Wayne, Indiana. He had been appointed by President Lincoln in October 1864, and had served continuously since. He felt that the road was being built too fast to meet Government standards. On June 16 he wrote to Johnson's Secretary of the Interior, Orville H. Browning, in one of those periodic reports which the Government Directors were supposed to make, introducing a new idea, which probably would call for an amendment to the law:

> While expressing gratification with these preparations for a full and prompt completion of the road by permanent structure, I further suggested [to the Directors] an adequate *reserve fund* for this purpose . . . . The existence of a contract for construction of the road, the provision of which this suggestion might seem to interfere with, should not prevent a prudential measure like this, so beneficial for the road, since the contractors and the company are mainly the same parties, . . . the contract system having been resorted to for greater convenience . . . . If binding agreements could be made under the law by the commissioners, on the acceptance of each 20-miles section hereafter received, which would authorize the proper department of the government to withhold a part of the bonds due to such section, or to any section in advance and not yet constructed, equal to the cost of substituting permanent work . . . such action would be far more effectual than any measure which the Government directors can enforce or suggest.[31]

On August 15, in conscientious pursuit of duty, Williams next reported to Browning that he could see actual and estimated deficiencies of about $3,000,000. They were largely due, he said again, to work that had been too hasty for "the substantial character" of the UP. "The gentlemen now owning the road might be relied upon to add fresh money to the extent needed," he pointed out, "but the control might pass speedily to others . . . . The additional expense now needed should be paid out of *government subsidies* rather than upon a surplus income later." [32]

Oliver complained about the letter to Browning on August 21, saying, "The withholding of bonds is damaging to the Company's credit and destructive to the progress of the road." [33] Nevertheless, on September 2 the UP Directors decided to set up a reserve fund of $3,000,000 in trust for the proper completion of the road. It was done

[31] Government Directors of the Union Pacific Railroad, *Reports to the Secretary of the Interior*, 1864–1885, pp. 37–39.

[32] *Ibid.*, pp. 44–49.

[33] Secretary of the Interior, *Correspondence with Oliver and Oakes Ames*, 1866–1870, Record Group 48.

late in December.[34] It was in first mortgage bonds issued on the most recent 100 miles. "The Company is endeavoring to meet government demand," conceded Williams to Browning.

Browning Withholds Bonds: Browning, along with others in Washington, was becoming increasingly concerned by the continual wrangles between factions within the New York office, and between them and the officers out on the line.[35] Grant just had been nominated by the G.O.P. for President, and the odds were high that he would be in the White House the following March, while Browning would be out of a job. Anyway, Browning openly favored the CP over the UP, largely because of his animosity to Durant. He decided to impose penalties where it would hurt.

Early in October *he withheld delivery of $2,560,000 Subsidy bonds* on 80 miles that had been approved by the Commissioners. Apparently they were between mileposts 780 near Table Rock and 860 near Bryan. This was contrary to the law, imposed serious strains on the financial program, and was a factor in a market decline of UP bonds and stock. Some of the certificates for bonds already had been sold and could not be retrieved.

When Oliver heard of it, he telegraphed Williams, who was at Fort Wayne: "Your letter to Browning has caused him to withhold Bonds. Telegraph the Secretary immediately that you did not intend to have this confirmation put upon your Report. Send me a copy of your telegram." [36] Oliver probably meant "interpretation" rather than "confirmation." No reply can be found.

Browning Demands Information: Next, on October 7, the Secretary wrote the Government Directors, demanding that they report full details of the whole financial and physical status of the UP—cost of construction and equipment, the amount of debt, expenses of operation, dividends paid, etc.[37] Government Directors Williams, Brooks, and McKee in turn requested the information from President Oliver, and on October 20 Oliver delivered his answers, with the comment, "Have always held our books open to Directors and Government Directors."

Among the many facts submitted by Oliver were the following:

---

[34] Oliver Ames's diary, Dec. 23.   [35] Dodge, *Autobiography*, p. 824.
[36] Records of UP Historical Museum.
[37] Government Directors, *Reports*, pp. 50–52.

a) Amount paid for construction (unadjusted balance due contractors not included):

Prior to 1 Jan. '67	$14,215,835.90
1867	15,782,976.54
1 Jan. '68 to 30 Sep. '68	26,204,094.11
	$56,202,906.55

"These amounts," he said, "were paid to chief engineer for preliminary surveys and location of line; to contractors on estimates of chief engineer, and according to the terms of the contracts, to officers for services, to banks and capitalists for discount on loans, 1st mortgage bonds, and U.S. 6% 30-Yr. currency bonds, to the U.S. for revenue stamps, to advertising agent for advertising bonds, and to stationers and others for incidental and general expenses."

b) Indebtedness:

1st Mortgage bonds	$21,408,000 [38]
U.S. loan	18,958,000
Pay-rolls & unpaid bills	1,790,214
Bills payable and loans in excess of cash on hand and other assets	1,836,170
	$43,992,384

c) Expenses incurred for year ended 30 Sept. '68: $3,213,566.

d) Dividends: None declared or paid to UP stockholders.[39]

Williams wrote Browning in further explanation:

Assuming the junction with the Central Pacific will be a little west of Monument Point, the Union Pacific will be 1,110 miles long. The cost as shown on the Union Pacific books is, of course, equivalent to the contract price per mile. I am uncertain about the last 200 miles. But the *actual* cost to the contracting company is shown only by their private book, of which the Government Directors have no knowledge. In the present state of the work even a full statement of expenses to date would throw little light on the cost of the entire line . . . The gentlemen composing the contracting company, whose enterprise and experience so rapidly builds the road, merit large compensation.[40]

Browning Forms Special Commission: Also on October 7, Browning appointed a Special Commission to examine the entire road, consist-

---

[38] Probably included the $3,000,000 set aside in trust for deficiencies.

[39] Government Directors, *Reports*, pp. 52–53.

[40] *Ibid.*, pp. 52–53. (The date was Nov. 14.)

ing of G.K. Warren, Brevet Major-General, U.S. Army; J. Blickensderfer Jr., civil engineer employed by the UP; and James Barnes,
civil engineer. They started west on October 25, Dodge accompanying them.

Oliver wrote Dodge on October 24 from North Easton:

We are really now needing our bonds and as we have now 80 miles
of road done on which we have rec'd no bonds nor can we issue our
1st Mtg. Bonds until we receive the Govts, it virtually keeps 5,000,000$
out of us which we have to raise in the market to keep the Road moving
along.[41]

Stockholders Are Asked to Help Out: Bushnell wrote a long letter
to Durant on October 28, in which he said:

Our salvation is the adoption of a plan that I suggested some weeks
since to get from all our own people in three or four months some 4
millions which has made us comparatively easy . . . We will borrow or
steal all the money you need.[42]

The same day Oliver wrote Durant from New York about a very
important matter:

We have been raising money from our Stockholders pro rata at 14½
per cent to carry our work along and I hope will be able to meet all
our payments promptly, and defeat the purpose of Huntington and his
clique to embarrass our operations. Money has been very close here for
the past 10 days and Dillon's bonds have been in the way of our sales . . .
The Commissioners to Re Examine the Road I think are first class men
and will do what is right.[43]

Not all of the CM stockholders were jumping forward to put up
their share. The following letter by B. F. Ham to R. G. Hazard on
October 12 illustrates the scheme adopted to encourage them:

The Co. not getting funds fast enough from its sales of securities has
decided to make a loan of $2½ millions from its stockholders on the
following terms—4 months time at 7% and 2½% commission. You will
be entitled to take for yourselves and friends of this loan $200,000—
Security 1st Mtg Bonds—110 for each $100,000 . . . Please reply.[44]

[41] Dodge, *Papers*, vol. 155 (original ms.).
[42] Durant, *Papers*, 1–3–25–7 (original ms.).
[43] *Ibid.*, 1–3–26–65.   [44] Records of UP Historical Museum.

The Commission's Report: Browning's Special Committee came back with a long report on November 23. Most of it was about defects in construction to the end of track amounting to $6,489,550. That part will be summarized further on.[45] Their concluding remarks, however, were most gratifying to the promoters:

Taken as a whole, the Union Pacific Railroad has been well constructed. The general route of the line is exceedingly well selected . . . . The energy and perseverance with which the work has been urged forward, and the rapidity with which it has been executed, are without parallel in history. In the grandeur and magnitude of the undertaking, it has never been equalled, and no other line compares with this in the arid and barren character of the country it traverses . . . . Deficiencies exist, but they are almost without exception incident to all new roads, or of a character growing out of the peculiar difficulties encountered, or inseparably connected with the unexampled progress of the work, a matter of the greatest importance and highly creditable to the able managers of the company; and they can all be supplied at an outlay but little exceeding that which would have obviated them in the first instance, but at the cost of materially retarding the progress of the work. Under the circumstances it is much more a matter of surprise that so few mistakes were made . . . . The country has reason to congratulate itself that this great work of national importance is so rapidly approaching completion under such favorable auspices.

G.K. Warren, J. Blickensderfer, Jr., James Barnes.[46]

In his Annual Report to the President dated November 30, Browning said in part:

J. L. Williams estimated [on November 14] that the cost of the full 1,100 miles, based on the cost of the first 710 miles, just for locating, construction and completely equipping it and the telegraph line, is $38,824,821, an average per mile of $34,977.[47] The Government subsidy in bonds for that distance at par amounts to $29,504,000, an average of $26,580 per mile. The company's first mortgage bonds are estimated at 92%, and yield $27,143,680. The fund realized from these two sources amounts to $56,647,680, an average per mile of $51,034, exceeding by $16,057 per mile the actual cost of constructing and fully equipping the road, and yielding a profit of more than $17,750,000.

I have the honor to recommend that the issue of patents for land and of bonds be suspended until such deficiencies shall have been supplied.

[45] See p. 347.   [46] Dodge, *Autobiography*, pp. 841–843.

[47] Obviously much too low. Many items of cost were omitted. The last 390 miles were the costliest. See p. 289; Dodge, *Autobiography*, pp. 848–851.

Oliver Informs the President: Some time about the middle of December, Oliver wrote a 32-page letter to the President of the United States, from Washington. It was received by the Interior Department on December 19. A paraphrased extract follows:

The Special Commission had examined 90 miles which had not yet been submitted to the Govt. for acceptance, and upon which nothing had been done except the grading, the tracks laid, and bridging partially completed. The Government was proposing to withhold the bonds for the completion of this 90 miles. Since the examination by the Special Commission, most of the deficiencies had been made good, and the regular Commissioners had approved the mileage. Therefore there was no ground for withholding the $2,880,000 bonds.

All in all, the Special Commissioners had found deficiencies on 890 miles of $6,489,550 from which the Company claimed a reduction of $3,973,056, leaving an admitted deficiency of $2,516,494.

No road is ever finally "completed." The road *once* well built for business is all the Government can ask. That we have these qualities now, or will soon attain them, we here assert. The progress and character of the road should be sufficient guarantee of our intention to meet the requirements of the law.

The Company now respectfully demands that the Central Pacific be examined on the same basis as the UP, under the same rules, under the same restrictions, and by the same men with the same instructions.

We ask nothing but what is just and right.[48]

But no bonds were forthcoming from Browning until December 31. At the eleventh hour, he delivered $2,560,000 bonds withheld since early October.[49] Apparently he had given in under pressure from the President when the reserve fund of $3,000,000 was set up by the UP late in December.[50]

9. THE LAST CONTRACT—THE "DAVIS" CONTRACT

When the track reached milepost 914, one mile beyond Bridger, Wyoming, in the middle of November, the Oakes Ames contract was completed. Two months earlier Oakes had gone to New York for the purpose of extending his contract to Salt Lake.[51] For reasons that cannot be found, he decided not to exercise his option to carry on fur-

---

[48] Secretary of the Interior, *Correspondence with Oliver and Oakes Ames*, pp. 1–32.
[49] *Wilson Rep.*, p. 615.   [50] See p. 249.   [51] Oliver Ames's diary, Sept. 10.

ther. He was nearly 65. The pace was tightening, and the problems arising on the next and last 200 miles or so looked like the worst yet.

Durant, not yet forty-nine, with energy and nerve unlimited, lost no time in stepping into the breach. On November 1, as Vice-President and General Agent of the UP, he quietly arranged a contract with James W. Davis of Omaha for all mileage west of Bridger, using the Oakes Ames contract as a base.[52] He was a son of G.T.M. Davis, who was the father-in-law of George Francis Train and a Director and Member of the Executive Committee under Durant in 1863 and 1864. Young Davis had studied law and had been working a sub-contract from Durant under the name of "Davis & Associates" to cut and deliver ties and timber for the UP.[53] *Five days later, on November 6, Davis assigned the new contract, as previously agreed, to the Seven Trustees for the stockholders of the UP, subject to their approval.*[54] However, Durant did not report the new contract to the UP Directors until 26 February 1869, when he handed the Executive Committee a letter dated three months earlier, November 27, which read:

I hand you herewith copy of contract and an assignment of the same in trust to the same parties who are trustees for the assignees of the Ames contract, the whole subject to the approval of the stockholders of the Union Pacific. I found it absolutely necessary, in order to carry out the wishes of the board, to commence work on this portion of the road at once. The present organization, with its large outfit of teams, tools, and men, presented the most available means of doing the same. To have created an entirely new organization would cause much delay . . . If approved, the work can go on . . . as heretofore. Referring the whole subject for your action, I remain, etc.

P.S.—There having been no meeting of your board since the date hereof, I hand the report to your executive committee. You will perceive I have taken the terms of the Oakes Ames contract as a base, believing that to be the wishes of the stockholders who approved said contract.[55]

Davis declared afterwards that he was promised $5,000 for his services in the matter. The contract was not approved by the stockholders until a meeting in Boston on 28 May 1869. The road as finally built extended from near Bridger to Promontory—about 172 miles.[56] Needless to say, Durant took personal charge of about every-

[52] *Wilson Rep.*, pp. 765–766, 285; *Poland Rep.*, p. 55.
[53] Records of UP Historical Museum.
[54] *Wilson Rep.*, p. 117 (testimony of Durant).
[55] *Ibid.*, pp. 765–766, 272. [56] Records of UP Historical Museum.

thing that went on under the Davis contract. The cost of this mileage to the UP, as it apparently appeared on the company books, was put by the Wilson Committee, with all securities at *par* value, at over $23,400,000, or $136,900 a mile.[57] But their estimate was grossly excessive, as will be shown later.

Grant Becomes President: On November 3, General of the Army Ulysses S. Grant of Galena, Illinois, was elected President, as was widely expected. The UP would get much fairer and more friendly treatment from the Executive Branch of the Government than from Johnson. He won by 214 electoral votes to only 80 for Horatio Seymour, a lawyer, ex-Governor of New York—and, *mirabile dictu,* a brother of Colonel Silas Seymour. Riding into the Vice-Presidency on the coattails of the war hero was Schuyler Colfax of Indiana. Oliver noted on Election Day: "North Easton voted 362 Republican and 67 Democratic, with a very strong vote for Grant throughout the State."

A Way of Financing: A sample of the various methods of borrowing money for the UP is shown by the following letter of John J. Cisco, Treasurer, to Messrs. Brown Brothers and Company,[58] private bankers of New York, on November 7:

Gentlemen—We hereby acknowledge the receipt from you of £100,000 say 100,000 pounds Sterling of your 60 day Sight Bills which we agree to return in a like amt. of 1st Class Bankers 60 day Sight Bills endorsed by us & approved by you & to be delivered at our option within 60 days from this date. We agree to pay you a Commission of ½ of 1% on the £100,000, and also interest at the rate of 7%. We deposit with you as security.[59]

McComb Files Suit: On November 11 McComb served notice of suit against Oakes and the Directors of the CM for possession of the 375 shares (250 plus 125) which had been assigned to and bought by Oakes.[60] This blackmail suit was still pending when the Congressional investigation began four years later.

Financial Notes by Oliver: Oliver made a series of interesting notes in his diary. On November 24: "Sold off all Govt Bonds we have at 99

---

[57] *Wilson Rep.,* pp. xiv, 373–375, 641.
[58] Became Brown Brothers, Harriman & Co. in 1931.
[59] Records of UP Historical Museum.
[60] *Poland Rep.,* pp. 4, 14 (testimony of McComb).

A decided ease in money market." On December 1: "Dr Durant & Brooks do not feel well on Report as it requires 6,489,000$ to complete Road." On December 2 (the fifth anniversary of "groundbreaking"): "Durant & Brooks in Wash urging Govt to give us our bonds . . . Dixon [Dix] goes on tonight and will see the Prest and thinks he can get him to issue the Bonds." On December 3: "The papers this morning favorable to Road which enables us to raise necessary money easily for our wants." And, on December 5: "President has ordered the issue of 40 miles of Bonds."

On December 3 Oliver wrote Durant from New York:

By Section 8 of the Act of 1864 we have a right to call upon the Govt to advance us ⅔ of the cost of work done in advance of the track. We have now expended three millions in advance of the track and we have nearly 4,000,000 of iron ties and superstructures on hand and most of it paid for . . . . Your telegraph to Associated Press and quotation from the close of the Comm'rs' Report is having a good effect . . . . Your idea of letting them have the lands or Land Bonds as security is a good one and I think will be a good get off for them from the infamous position they have taken.[61]

Oakes and Dodge returned to Washington for the convening of the Third Session, 40th Congress on December 7.

On December 23 Oliver wrote Durant a long letter from Washington, in which he mentioned: "I understand from Ewing [Thomas Ewing, former Secretary of the Treasury and Interior] that their proposition is to give us our Govt Bonds as fast as the Road is accepted, and withhold ½ of the 1st Mortgage Bonds till they amount to 3,000,000, for the completion of the Road." [62]

10. THE FINAL PROFITS PAYMENT

On December 29 Oliver wrote in his diary: "Gen'l Dodge still in NY Had meeting of Contractors and made dividend of 200% of Stock to Contractors. Money very short and had great difficulty in getting what we want for our payments [on the road]." The next day he added: "Had an exhibit of Finances which look as though we were to have a hard winter to meet our payments. Returns from Road of expenses look very hard."

---

61 Durant, *Papers*, 1–3–26–66 (original ms.).   62 *Ibid.*, 1–3–26–67 (original ms.).

As the amount realized from all sales of Government and company bonds was not enough to cover the estimated cost of the stipulated work, the Trustees were *obliged* by the eleventh section of the Oakes Ames Contract to make up the expected deficiency with subscriptions to UP stock at par.[63] So this sixth and last allotment, payable on 1 January 1869, was 200 per cent in stock, or $7,500,000 at par value. But with the market price calculated at 35, its value then was only $2,625,000.[64]

Thus *all* the allotments of estimated profit on construction were paid or declared during this one year, 1868. The total of the cash and par value of the securities involved was $20,423,500, while its value *at the estimated market prices on the dates of payment was $13,137,940*. There had been almost no profits prior to the Oakes Ames Contract (Durant's Hoxie Contract was a washout),[65] and now Durant's Davis Contract was beginning to look dubious as a money-maker. *So the promoters probably were commencing to realize at the end of 1868 that their construction profit for sweating over the UP might be only $9,000,000 or so*. For from the $13,137,940 must be deducted the $3,750,000 capital they had paid in to the CM, which, theoretically at least, would be worth nothing after the Golden Spike. Furthermore, there was no assurance, of course, that the values of the UP securities not sold at the time received would not go lower—as indeed they did for a dismal period to come soon. However, other major factors enter into any guess of the final real profit on the whole road.[66] These will be examined later.[67]

There has been much criticism by historians of the release of construction profits in 1868. "They should have been kept in the company's reserves" it is claimed. But the reproaches seem to be based partly on hindsight. Several disasters occurred later which could not have been imagined. In defense of the men taking all the risks, it should be recalled now that their capital had been tied up for three or four years, during which period over 900 miles of railroad had been built, competently and speedily. Contractors generally are paid for their services as they go, not all at the end. Unforeseeable contingencies might wipe out the company's surplus, even cause bankruptcy; and a possible severe bear market is always a consideration of investment. Indeed, already Fisk was under suspicion of sizing up the

---

[63] *Wilson Rep.*, pp. 760–761; see also p. 184. The terms of the Davis contract were based on the Oakes Ames contract.

[64] See table, p. 259.　　　[65] See p. 197; Hazard, p. 21.

[66] Fogel, pp. 66–74.　　　[67] See pp. 454–457.

ALLOTMENTS OF PROFITS MADE TO CM STOCKHOLDERS UNDER THE OAKES AMES CONTRACT [a]
(Excluding 6% interest allotments for 1866 and 1867)

Date Decl'd.	Date Paid	CM Shares Outst'g.	Title of Allotment	Paid in Cash	Paid in UP Bonds at Par	Paid in UP Stock at Par	Market Price	Market Value
12/12/67	1/3/68	37,400	60% Bonds		$2,244,000 [b]		97 [c]	$ 2,176,680
12/12/67	1/3/68	37,400	60% Stock			$ 2,244,000 [b]	30 [d]	673,200
1/3/68	1/3/68	37,400	20% Bonds		748,000 [e]		97 [c]	725,560
6/17/68	6/17/68	37,500	40% Stock			1,500,000 [f,g]	50 [h]	750,000
6/17/68	6/17/68	37,500	60% Cash	$2,250,000 [f,g]				2,250,000
7/3/68	7/8/68	37,500	75% Bonds		2,812,500 [g,i]		100 [j]	2,812,500
7/8/68	7/8/68	37,500	30% Cash	1,125,000 [h,k]				1,125,000
12/29/68	1/1/69	37,500	200% Stock			7,500,000 [g,l]	35 [m]	2,625,000
		Total		$3,375,000	$5,804,500	$11,244,000		$13,137,940

Summary at *PAR*

Cash	$ 3,375,000
Bonds	5,804,500
	9,179,500
Stock	11,244,000
Total	$20,423,500 [n]

Summary at *MARKET*

Cash, Bonds and Stock	$13,137,940
Less: Cost of CM Stock	− 3,750,000
Profit	$ 9,387,940 [o]

[a] *Wilson Rep.*, p. 630 (see note n below). Allotments were were voted by the seven trustees. *PolandRep.*, pp. 55–56; see also Appendix G.
[b] *Wilson Rep.*, pp. 725–728.
[c] *Poland Rep.*, p. 452 (Oakes Ames).
[d] *Wilson Rep.*, p. 154.
[e] *Ibid.*, pp. 728–730.
[f] *Ibid.*, pp. 731–732.
[g] *Ibid.*, pp. 630, 245–246.
[h] See p. 247 (Oakes Ames).
[i] *Wilson Rep.*, pp. 733–734, 245–246.
[j] Oliver Ames's diary, 6/18, 8/28.
[k] *Wilson Rep.*, p. 784.
[l] *Ibid.*, p. 736.
[m] *Ibid.*, p. 35 (Crane).
[n] Add $14,000 to check with *Wilson Rep.*, p. 630. Add $48,168 to check with *ibid.*, p. xvi.
[o] Oakes Ames stated that the total profit on his contract was about 8 to 9 mils. See p. 456.

UP for his next raid. Furthermore, the Government and the press were now viewing the quarrels within the UP through jaundiced eyes. The CP under the leadership of Collis Huntington was proving itself smarter and faster than had been reckoned. Finally, the promoters were expecting to make at least some money on the Davis contract by building from Bridger to Monument Point, particularly so if Humboldt Wells could be reached. The majority of the Directors did not yet believe, in spite of Dodge's warning, that Durant, in his welcomed haste to earn $32,000 a mile subsidies which otherwise would fall to the CP, and to save heavy interest charges during construction, would soon roll up such appalling expenditures during the winter that the final profit on the whole road would be reduced, rather than increased. Nor could they guess that the CP would be met as far east as Promontory.

On the other hand, not all the Directors were in favor of all the allotments being made in 1868. Alley, one of the Seven Trustees, was vehement about it, and proved it by resigning as a Director in March 1869.[68] He testified in 1873 that the last allotment, the obligatory one, was issued partly in *anticipation* of profits on the Davis contract—but there were none.[69] However, he added: "[The profits were] distributed with the understanding, and, I believe, written condition, that if the money was required to complete the road, that they would pay back the amount . . . I do not mean return; they *loaned* several millions . . .[70] I think the money was mostly raised by the purchase of securities—land-grant bonds and income-bonds, . . . to finish the road and pay their debts. . . . Impolitic they were; there was no impropriety in it, because nobody was wronged, unless it was themselves." [71]

Bushnell admitted, "Unwisely, as we see now, we had divided the profit of 1867, instead of keeping it on hand, as we now see we ought to have done; but we supposed we were going to make some money on the rest of the road." [72]

Perhaps there was no great difference, in this case, whether the profits were kept in the coffers of the company for a number of months more, or transferred to the personal accounts of the company's contractors. The same people possessed them, wherever they were held. Either way, the profits could be, and it was supposed would

[68] See p. 127; *Poland Rep.,* p. 93 (testimony of Alley).
[69] *Wilson Rep.,* p. 335.   [70] See p. 178.
[71] *Wilson Rep.,* p. 335; see also pp. 302–305, *passim.*
[72] *Ibid.,* p. 553.

be, used for the benefit of the company in the end. Nevertheless, if fewer allotments had been made, the balance sheet of the UP would have been somewhat stronger, probably enabling some company junior bonds to be sold at higher prices. Also, interest charges on heavy new funded debt would not have been paid out of capital.

In summary, it does seem, looking at affairs as they existed in June and July, 1868, that it would have been better business judgment to have put off at least the two *cash* payments totalling $3,375,000 (which almost covered the cost of the CM stock) until the actual junction with the CP had been made, wherever that might be. But the more conservative Directors had the Doctor to contend with. His avowed intention was to hit and run. "There will be no profit in operating the completed road," he had warned repeatedly.[73] He was ejected less than a year later, along with his friends (except Bushnell),[74] and, naturally, none of that large amount of profit was made available. *This increased the burden on the Ames group.*

11.   EARNINGS AND INTEREST CHARGES

The Act of 1 June 1868 had required the subsidized railroads to issue a report of earnings as of June 30 in order to synchronize with the Government's fiscal year. The UP report was given to the *Commercial & Financial Chronicle,* which printed it as follows:

UNION PACIFIC RAILROAD [a]

The following are the earnings & expenses of the UP Rd. for yr. end Jun 30, '68.

Earnings		*Expenses*	
From passengers	$ 888,335.05	For conducting transportation	$ 517,802.86
From freight	3,233,971.61	For motive power	977,010.62
From express	30,954.79	For maint. of cars	209,150.57
From Mails	66,800.00	For maint. of way	831,537.66
From miscellaneous	26,579.28	For general expenses	149,255.43
	$4,246,040.73	TOTAL	$2,684,757.14
		Net earnings to balance	1,561,283.59
		TOTAL (on Average of 472 miles)	4,246,040.73

[73] See p. 23.   [74] See p. 345.

The amount of First Mortgage Bonds the Company can issue on this 472 miles is $7,520,000.

Gold interest for one year, at the rate of 6 per cent, is	$ 451,260
Add 40% premium for gold	180,480
TOTAL	$ 631,680
Surplus for the year, after paying interest on first mortgage bonds	$ 929,603.59

We will now add to the account the interest on the United States second mortgage bonds, and it will stand as follows:

Net earning for one year		$1,561,283.50
Interest on first mortgage bonds reduced to currency	$631,680	
Interest on second mortgage bonds reduced to currency	451,200	1,082,880.00
Surplus, after paying all interest		$ 478,403.59

It is stated by the officers of the Board that the earnings for the first half of the financial year were so large that the Company reduce their charges twenty-five per cent.

ᵃ *Commercial & Financial Chronicle,* Sept. 19, 1868, p. 364.

Only meager information is available on earnings and expenses of railroad operations at this period, prior to the issuance of regular annual reports to stockholders. Records revealed much later indicate that the full year 1868 showed an all time record low in net income, before or after, of only $894,000. According to the general ledger of the operating department, the figures were as follows: [75]

	1868	1867 [76]
Total Earnings	$5,063,000	$3,465,000
Total Operating Expenses (including taxes)	4,169,000	1,404,000
Net Income	$ 894,000	$2,061,000

While earnings gained 46 per cent over 1867, operating expenses jumped 197 per cent, presumably because of the servicing of the very long mileage suddenly added. After this year net operating income would slowly but steadily increase. The 1868 UP "capital balance sheet" appears in a report of the U.S. Pacific Railway Commission, pp. 5022–23.

However, such income was woefully far from even covering the annual interest charges arising on all the new bonds just issued. By the year-end, the $24,000,000 or so first mortgage 6 per cent bonds (with their gold premium currently at 35 per cent) alone would call for annual interest payments of about $1,944,000.[77] But another annual $1,444,680 of interest was pledged for payment sometime under the $24,078,000 second mortgage, the U.S. Subsidy 6 per cent

[75] U.S. Pacific Railway Commission, p. 5266.   [76] *Ibid.;* see also p. 241.
[77] These bonds could not exceed the subsidy bonds.

currency bonds.[78] Furthermore, still more debt, relatively small, would be created next year. Perhaps the Doctor would be right about net profits—after interest.

B. *The Last of the Indian Troubles*

The Second Session of the Fortieth Congress adjourned on March 3, virtually for the rest of the year; and on April 1, Dodge went West, to remain for the working season. "I found the Indians very aggressive and our escorts and military not yet fully furnished us," he noted.[79] By late spring, however, and for the rest of the year the Army had some 5,000 troops spread out along the road as far as Salt Lake, with a thousand or so headquartered at Fort Russell near Cheyenne.

When the season for maraudings opened in April, way back at Elm Creek, 212 miles from Omaha, five section men working at repairs were surprised and killed. At the same time, two off-duty conductors were badly mauled while fishing in Lodge Pole Creek near the Sidney station. One of them, Tom Cahoon, was scalped, but lived to tell the tale. On April 23 about 200 young bucks attacked the construction party working three miles east of Dale Creek bridge, killing two men, wounding four, and carrying off a dozen head of stock.[80] Oliver complained to Dodge the next day: "I see nothing but extermination to the Indians as the result of their thieving disposition, and we shall probably have to come to this before we can run the road safely." [81]

A fortnight later the Doctor issued his tough "General Order No. 3," worded as follows:

The military authorities have done, and are doing everything in their power to protect the Road and its Employees from depredations by the few roving bands of Indians which occasionally make their appearance upon the Plains, and it only remains for those connected with the Road, to use due diligence in order to avoid any further annoyance from that source.

It is therefore ordered:

1. The Engineer in charge of Construction will direct each Contractor or Foreman in charge of work to see that their men are well armed when they go upon the work, and that their arms are in good condition, properly stacked and within easy reach, in case of an alarm. Also that proper precautions are taken to guard against surprise.

[78] *Wilson Rep.,* pp. 738–739; see also Appendix D.
[79] Dodge, *Autobiography,* p. 747.   [80] *Ibid.,* p. 748.   [81] *Ibid.*

2. Inasmuch as the only casualties that have happened along the line from this source have been occasioned by the most gross and almost criminal neglect on the part of those in charge of the work—It is further ordered, that, at the direction of the Engineer in charge, in case the Contractors fail to obey instructions in this matter and neglect to make the proper use of the means placed at their disposal by the Military Authorities and the Company for the protection of their men, *these means will be taken from them.*

Thos. C. Durant, Vice President [82]

Early in June, Dodge was notified that, in addition to the casualties noted above, "Four men were killed on Boyle's work and 6 teams captured; at least 4 men killed on Hall's work; and Mr. G.M. Davis, Jr. was killed at one of the saw mills." [83]

UP surveyor Arthur N. Ferguson, while at Fort Steele on July 21, made the following entry in his journal:

The first passenger train ever west of the North Fork of the Platte crossed the bridge about noon today. . . . While sitting in one of our tents a few days ago a bullet entered the canvas, making quite a hole in it. . . . The Indians made an attack on Sunday, and killed and scalped 4 men besides severely wounding another. On Saturday a band of 500 Indians made their appearance before Fort Sanders and killed 2 men. . . . The time is coming, and fast too, when in the sense it is now understood, THERE WILL BE NO WEST.[84]

The Redskins wrecked their last UP train in September at their favorite point of attack near Ogallala in the same manner as in August 1867 at Plum Creek.[85] A freight train, this time with only one passenger car, was derailed by ties lashed with telegraph wire to the track. The fireman, hopelessly pinned against the firebox, was roasted to death. The passengers effectively held off the murderers with rifle fire, thereby saving their own scalps. The next and last attack on the UP was in November, when a small bridge near the Wyoming border at Pine Bluffs was burned. Fortunately, no casualties occurred. West of the Continental Divide there never were any serious troubles with the Indians. The CP never suffered from them.

Thus ended a nasty three-year guerrilla warfare which, without the aid of the United States Army, might well have prevented the UP

[82] Durant, *Papers*, 3–3–18–5, dated May 8 from Ft. Saunders. (Italics by C.E.A.)
[83] Dodge, *Autobiography*, p. 760.
[84] Records of UP Historical Museum. See also pp. 145–146, 218–219.
[85] See pp. 221–222.

from building even to the eastern Utah border ahead of the Central Pacific. The Chairman of the House Committee on Indian Affairs estimated that the recent cost of the Government's war on the Indians had been running at $1,000,000 a week.[86]

C. Surveys and Engineering

1. DODGE'S REPORT

As 1868 opened, Congressman Dodge was in Washington giving full instructions to his men weekly from a special office in the Department of Interior. "It was a fortunate thing," he wrote, "that I happened to be there . . . as there was a great deal of friction on account of the attitude of the Central Pacific and the friendliness of the Government, and as I was right on the ground, I could generally meet and solve them." [87]

Road to Oregon: Oliver wrote Dodge on January 8 about the latter's proposed branch railroad to Oregon:

[It] has great merit. . . . The Union Pacific Railroad Company will use their best efforts to secure the construction of this Road whenever the people on its line shall awake to its importance. It cannot be built without good aid, but our Co should not appear as applicants for this Charter, but it should come through the exertions of Representatives of Oregon. . . . I trust you will be able to enlist active workers . . . without cloging it with too many other interests.[88]

On October 1 Dodge gave instructions to J.O. Hudnutt to survey a line to Portland from Monument Point (near the projected road about 24 miles west of Promontory) via Raft River and Snake River.[89] Obviously, it was then expected that the UP would get at least as far west as Monument Point.

Evans: In March, although the snow was still deep in a late spring, the Chief Engineer sent James Evans with four parties, without escort, to make the final location from Laramie to Green River. Durant had ordered this work to be finished by June 1. It was done

---

[86] Senator W.M. Stewart (Nev.) in debate on 19 Feb. 1869.
[87] Dodge, *Autobiography*, p. 705.   [88] Dodge, *Papers*, vol. 153 (original ms.).
[89] Dodge, *Autobiography*, p. 823; see also p. 231.

by May 2. Evans was then transferred by Dodge to Superintendent of Construction under Reed, and his duties with the Engineering Corps were ended for good. Evans had spent most of his time on the UP developing the country east of Green River. Dodge praised him highly as "a man devoted to the interests of the company—a great aid, able, efficient, energetic." [90]

Blickensderfer: In the meantime, on February 26, Blickensderfer with three parties had started work on the final location from Green River to Salt Lake. The snow was above the telegraph poles in the Wasatch Mountains. He had orders to locate up the Muddy, *to allow no grade over 90 feet at the head of Echo,* to build no tunnels except two short ones in the lower Weber River, and to hug the north slope of Echo Canyon where the snow was always lightest. But, late in April, Durant had ordered Dodge to "cover the road with men from Green River to Salt Lake within one month, and to Humboldt Wells in three months." Once again, as in 1867, Dodge's plans had to be reorganized, causing costly delays. "The forcing of the parties forward so fast gave us no time to review our lines," complained Dodge. "We had to use 116 foot grades. The men worked day and night, even to the full seven days of the week. The company will understand that if [there are] any complaints on account of want of time, the blame will rest with it." [91]

Blickensderfer finished his final location in July. "His choice at the head of Echo was better than any other," said Dodge.[92]

Rock Creek Muddle: On May 20 Dodge, as a delegate-at-large from Iowa, went to Chicago for the convention which nominated Grant for President. On June 30 he met Oliver, Evans, and Reed at Laramie and with them went to end-o-track near Rock Creek, where questions long had been brewing as to the best route to follow between Cooper Lake (on the Laramie River) and Medicine Bow. Dodge explained:

There had been submitted to the company from the Laramie River west, two locations. One by way of Cooper Lake through the Rattlesnake Pass to Medicine Bow. This direct line was with 60-foot grades and considerable heavy work, but it saved 20 miles in distance. . . . The line by way of Rock Creek was in the valley, was of light work, but had heavy curvature and about the same grade. . . . But the contractors claimed

[90] Dodge, *Report of the Chief Engineer,* 1868–1869, p. 5.
[91] *Ibid.,* p. 2.   [92] *Ibid.,* p. 7.

that they could build this [longer] line in one-half the time. . . . It was adopted against my recommendation.[93]

In 1901 the UP shortened the main line 12 miles by relocating to Dodge's preferred route over Rattlesnake Pass.[94]

Salt Lake City By-Passed: On August 14, Dodge met Lewis M. Clement, one of the principal engineers of the CP, and was informed for the first time that they would not build any line south of Great Salt Lake. Dodge had already made the same decision. So, regardless of whose main line it was, Salt Lake City would be by-passed. Brigham Young's inevitable storming would have to be tolerated.

Dodge reported:

The northern route was shorter by 76 miles, had less ascent and descent, less elevation to overcome, less curvature, and the total cost was $2,500,000 less. There was more running water, more lumber, and better land for agriculture and grazing . . .[95] When I made the decision to build north I immediately notified Brigham Young. He was greatly disappointed and much dissatisfied, and appealed to our directors . . . The UP's decision was that when they built to the north end of the Lake, they would build a branch to Salt Lake City . . . When Brigham Young learned the Central Pacific [also was going north] he immediately changed his policy, and came to us turning all his forces to help us out, as now the great conflict had begun between the two companies.[96]

Promontory Problems: On August 19, Dodge started his trip over the line to Humboldt Wells. At Ogden he dined at Bishop John Sharp's home with Brigham Young and his 16 wives, "quite an interesting dinner." [97] By September 26, the final location to Humboldt was completed. The principal difficulty to be encountered was the surmounting of the rugged, barren Promontory Range, which Dodge described as follows:

Promotory Point, the most difficult summit to make, and where the most intricate line, the heaviest work, the highest grades, and the sharpest curves occur, is a bold backbone running north and south . . . and for a distance of 30 miles dividing the waters of Great Salt Lake . . .

---

[93] Dodge, *Autobiography*, p. 776.   [94] See map, Illus., Group 2.

[95] Dodge, *Report of the Chief Engineer*, 1868–1869, p. 14.

[96] Dodge, *Autobiography*, pp. 802–802A; James McCague, *Moguls and Iron Men*, New York, Harper & Row, 1964, pp. 211–216.

[97] Dodge, *Autobiography*, p. 804.

The ridge is 600 feet high, with scarcely 4 miles of direct ascent from the east, and 12 of descent on the west, devoid of natural ravine or watercourse. To approach the summit the line has to overcome the elevation by clinging to the rough sides of the ridge, and gaining distance by running up Blue Spring Creek Valley, and winding back again on its opposite side . . . The 80-foot line was adopted, reviewed, and, on final location, considerably improved. The 6 miles of line on the east slope of the mountains has heavy work and a few 6 degree [955-foot radius] curves as a maximum, and is by far the most difficult portion of the line west of Weber Canon. Foreseeing that this would probably be in the vicinity of the terminus of our work, I caused the passage over this range to be carefully surveyed in August; and in September, after surveying a number of lines, we made a location over it. Subsequently, after a still more minute examination . . . we adopted the 85-foot grade line . . . and turned it over to the construction department in October.[98]

Dodge had written Durant on August 27: "Six miles of a 90-foot grade up Promontory will cost a Liberal estimate of $70,000 a mile. . . . The entire 18 miles of crossing the Range . . . will cost about $30,000 a mile, including the light work on the western slope . . . . The C.P.R.R. told me tonight that they should adopt virtually my line." [99]

Far beyond Promontory the final location of the main line was made to within 6 miles of Humboldt Wells (now Wells, Nevada), at latitude 41° 09′ and longitude 115° 03′, elevation 5,565 feet above the sea.[100] The CP finally followed that easy route almost exactly.

The remainder of Dodge's last report appears in Chapter 9, page 373.

2. SECRETARY BROWNING FAVORS THE CENTRAL PACIFIC AGAIN

Early in May, Dodge heard the first unexpected rumblings of parallel grading troubles, and wrote: "The Central Pacific was trying to take advantage of a clause in the charter which authorized each party to file a line 100 miles in advance of their work, *and they were endeavoring to file a good deal more than that, reaching nearly to Echo Canon,* almost a 100 miles east of Ogden . . . I had consulted Mr. Oakes Ames on it." [101]

[98] Dodge, *Report of the Chief Engineer,* 1868–1869, pp. 9–10.

[99] Durant, *Papers,* 1–3–35–34.

[100] Dodge, *Report of the Chief Engineer,* 1868–1869, p. 14. Humboldt Wells was 222 miles west of Ogden by rail.

[101] Dodge, *Autobiography,* p. 755; see also p. 231. (Italics by C.E.A.)

On May 15, Oliver wrote back to Dodge from New York:

I had a letter from my Brother yesterday saying that the Central Pacific RR Co were pressing their map & location upon the Secy of Interior to allow them to lap over to the East side of Salt Lake. This should not be granted and I think my Brother feels that you will be able to check its adoption. I think it is our duty to put on parties of Surveyors West of Salt Lake, and thoroughly survey and locate a line West of Salt Lake as far as we are able to complete it.[102]

On May 23, Ham wrote Oakes: "I enclose copies of letters rec'd from Secty. Browning . . . He states that the Central had filed a map which he had not accepted." [103] This was evasive. On May 15 he had accepted their map of 24 July 1867 as far as Monument Point, but not to Weber Canyon, as applied for.[104]

On June 11, Hammond wrote Browning, "With this note we forward a map of the located line of the U.P.R.R. from Weber Canon to N. point of Great Salt Lake—80 miles." [105]

On September 20, Oliver, happily expectant, wrote Dodge, "I have no doubt but we shall be able to lay the track from one to 200 miles west of the Lake. It is clearly our right to lay the Rails till the two Roads meet and their giving out Contracts to grade beyond their ability to lay their Rails should not stop us nor the Road from completion." [106]

On September 4, Oliver sent Browning a map of the ninth 100 miles, to beyond Echo station. It was amended on October 16.

Oliver sent Browning his "Report of the Progress and Condition of the Union Pacific Railroad," dated October 15, in which he said: "The Road is completed for 847 miles (near Green River) and grading and masonry will be completed (except for tunneling at head of Echo Canon) to Salt Lake in November. The location of the line has been definitely made to Humboldt Wells." [107]

Notwithstanding these vital facts, on October 20 the Secretary of the Interior quietly approved and accepted the Central's map and profile from Monument Point to Echo Summit which had been filed on October 14.[108] *He did this even though the UP had already finished grading and bridging nearly all of that mileage.* However, it was not

---

[102] Dodge, *Papers,* vol. 154.   [103] Records of UP Historical Museum.

[104] Dodge, *Papers,* vol. 157 (Secretary of the Interior J. D. Cox to Dodge, 1 Apr. 1869).

[105] Records of UP Historical Museum.   [106] Dodge, *Papers,* vol. 155 (original ms.).

[107] Secretary of the Interior, *Correspondence,* RG 48.

[108] Secretary of the Interior, *Annual Report,* 1868, p. 15; Dodge, *Papers,* vol. 157.

until about the middle of December that the UP officials learned of this action of Browning's by reading his Annual Report. Abraham Lincoln had finally come to look at Browning as "one of the most peculiarly befuddled individuals that had come out of the war." [109]

On December 15 Browning, following his determination to favor the CP, wrote Oliver:

On 20th October last ... I gave "my consent and approval" to the location of the C.P.R.R. from "Monument Point" to "Echo Summit." It is necessary under the law that your road and the Central Pacific shall be so located as to unite and form one continuous road. You are therefore requested to cause the Union Pacific Railroad to be located to Echo Summit so as to unite and form a continuous line with the Central Pacific Railroad as already located to that point and forward the necessary map and profile for file in this Department.[110]

Following this foul blow, on December 19 Oakes, Oliver, and Dodge went to Browning in person and hotly protested the whole inexplicable situation. Dodge described the inconclusive interview this way:

Secretary Browning stated that the acceptance gave no rights to one company over the other; that the map was only accepted as a general route which both companies must conform to; that each company should keep on building and that it should receive its bonds as fast as the road should be completed and accepted by the commissioners. He made these statements over and over again, and in answer to my suggestion that the Central Pacific road claimed to have acquired rights by this acceptance, he scouted the idea; said that such a construction was impossible, and that we should have our bonds as fast as our road should be completed. I asked if we must conform to the grades and alignments of this map, which were far inferior to our own located line. He replied that we need not conform to them; that such was not his intention; that he wanted the best possible line, so that the two roads would meet and connect and not pass each other.[111]

On December 22, Dodge telegraphed from New York to Oakes, "Get date of filing and acceptance of CP maps also ascertain where end of CP track was at those dates also how many miles Government had notice of as built at those dates." [112]

[109] Sandburg, *The War Years*, p. 600.
[110] Secretary of the Interior, *Correspondence*, RG 48, vol. 2, p. 406.
[111] Dodge, *Autobiography*, p. 916.   [112] Dodge, *Papers*, vol. 155; see also p. 295.

Their suspicions of mischief were confirmed. Was this one of the primary reasons why the gradings of the two roads finally ran parallel to each other? Congress also must have been at fault, as well as the President.

On December 30, Oliver prepared a very long letter of protest to Browning. Dodge admitted that he had written most of it himself for Oliver. But Oliver did not deliver it until 10 February 1869.[113] Some key extracts follow:

> Today the Central Pacific is . . . 188 miles from Monument Point and 328 miles from the head of Echo. . . . The track of the Union Pacific is now 10 miles west of Echo, covering 10 miles of the ground that the alleged location [of the CP] assumes to cover, and is within 130 miles of Monument Point, and nearly three-quarters of the grading and bridging over the entire distance is complete. . . . From this data it will be seen that the Union Pacific railroad is 58 miles nearer to Monument Point than that of the Central Pacific.
>
> Again: our final location was made, the contract let, and our work opened between head of Echo and Monument Point, long before the Central Pacific railroad were within 300 miles of that point, while the end of our track from July [the date of the certificates of the map] has been all the time about 50 miles nearer to Monument Point than theirs. . . . Our curvatures are less, our grades less, our distances shorter . . . .
>
> Finally, the great injustice of the matter appears when the fact is presented . . . that they file over a country that they had done no work upon at the time the map was accepted. . . . *You will see the physical impossibility of our complying with your request.*[114]

D. Construction and Equipment

1. DURANT TAKES OVER ONCE MORE

When the year 1868 opened, the track was halfway up the eastern slope of the Black Hills at Granite Canyon.[115] Sam Reed was working desperately to speed what was then the most important and expensive bridge on the Pacific Railway, over Dale Creek just beyond Sherman. On January 13 there was a fearful snowstorm along the entire line. More than two feet of snow blocked work all around for some time. Reed wrote to his wife:

[113] See p. 309.
[114] Dodge, *Autobiography*, pp. 852–854. (Italics by C.E.A.) See also p. 295.
[115] See p. 235.

I was delayed two days on a trip to Fort Saunders . . . The wind blew a gale & a large amount of snow fell and was blown furiously over the country, being deposited in high piles behind rocks, in ravines canyons & railroad cuts. After the storm it was intensely cold, thermometer sank to 30° below zero.[116]

At this time, Dodge reported 1800 men working on the heavy grading in the Black Hills and 500 more sawing ties at the heads of the two Laramie Rivers. But the snow in the woods was three feet deep on the level, which prevented any timber-hauling to the streams.

Reed had his worries about the flourishing whiskey traffic, among other things. On March 29 he wrote Dodge:

A few nights since two men in Carmichaels Camp were shot . . . Welch contractor robed of $1100 dollars and nearly killed . . . one man shot through a window at Creighton's camp. Horses & mules frequently stolen. . . . Let us have martial law if necessary to keep off the whiskey. Every pay day the men loose several days the work is materially retarded . . . Dale Creek bridge is not completed we are doing well on it. Boomer is raising the truss work. The trestles will be nearly completed this week. . . . Just have worst storm of season loose two weeks in clearing cuts of snow.[117]

Durant went West about April 4 to push the work along. The construction army of some 10,000 men were sallying from winter quarters at Cheyenne.[118] He remained until November 28 (Aspen), with the exception of a month, between June 15 and July 13, and another month, between August 6 and September 4. For this work, after being ejected from the UP, he put in a service bill of $4,400 for 1868 alone.[119]

Sherman Summit: The highest railroad summit on the continent was belatedly surmounted on April 5 at Sherman (first site), 549 miles from Omaha, elevation 8,242 feet.[120] Durant arrived just in time to ceremoniously spike down the last rails.

Dale Creek Bridge: On April 23, Reed wrote his wife, "Dale Creek bridge finished [about April 16] & all excavations through the first range of mountains done, track over bridge & through most of rock cuts. Great load off my mind." [121] Strangely, very little information

---

[116] Records of UP Historical Museum (Reed letters).
[117] Dodge, *Papers*, vol. 154 (original ms.).
[118] Sabin, p. 170.   [119] Durant, *Papers*, 3–1–13–19.
[120] See p. 235.   [121] Records of UP Historical Museum (Reed letters).

can be found as to the detailed plans of the bridge and the actual work of building it. The Engineering Department of the UP advised in October, 1946, that the only description in its records was:

Dale Creek on the western slope of the Black Hills range, running in a granite gorge 120 feet deep and near 600 feet wide at grade line, is crossed by a pine timber trestle bridge of 40-foot spans, with double bents resting on piers of granite masonry raised only to a small height. The roadway is suspended by a low truss frame resting on these bents. The structure is in part of mountain pine, but chiefly of the better pine from Chicago . . . The timber trestle was replaced in 1876 with an iron bridge known as the "spider web," it appeared so slender, 707 feet long, 127 feet high at the deepest point.[122]

The cost of the original bridge was $200,000.[123] A furious squall almost destroyed the structure when it was half way up, and only prompt and heroic action by Hezekiah Bissell and his gang with guy ropes saved it. Otherwise, there would have been a critical delay in track-laying.

Costs of Construction Secret: Dodge was having his troubles getting the facts on the true cost of building the UP. He wrote:

On March 9th Mr. J.E. House, under my instructions, had made up an estimate of the actual cost from the 100th meridian to the 600th mile post. When Mr. House applied to the superintendent of construction for the cost of their work, they failed to give it to him, giving him to understand that we were not supposed to know what the railroad cost the contractors, I immediately asked for information . . . and how they expected me to make an estimate. . . . They did not make a direct answer to me but indicated that I should make them from my own estimates . . . and then they would compare them later with the actual estimates. . . . Notwithstanding, . . . I was able at all times, through Mr. Reed and the Division engineers, to obtain this information myself; while they did not like to give it to subordinates, they were always ready to give it to me, confidentially.[124]

Durant Given Broad Powers to Hasten the Road: The Chief Engineer suffered a blow to his prestige when Oliver informed him on

---

[122] Records of UP Historical Museum.
[123] Dodge, *Autobiography*, p. 975 (affidavit of W. Snyder, 29 May 1869).
[124] *Ibid.*, p. 738.

March 13 that the following resolution had been passed by the Board of Directors at the annual meeting on March 11: *"Resolved*—That the Vice President be appointed the General Agent of this road with power to assent to a change of the grades and location of the road, as provided in the contract with Ames, and do all other things necessary to expedite the construction of the road and telegraph in connection with the contractors." [125] This pungent little bylaw, inspired by Durant, was the first link in a new chain of agitation.

Oliver's letter to Dodge, enclosing a copy, attempted an explanation:

In passing [this] it was understood that the power conferred applied only to the road under construction and was not to give power over the Chief Engineer or his parties in their location of the road. I understand this to be as heretofore . . . . We have a committee on location & construction who last year took charge of the location & construction. That Committee this year have undoubtedly the power of location, but the construction has been put out to contractors. The location is in the Board of Directors and by them conferred upon the Committee.

I hope you will not consider this assumption of authority by Durant as a final settlement of this question. If he could by these annoying exhibitions of his peculiar character drive us all out of the road, he would do it, but I don't intend to be driven out or coaxed out, but will adhere to the strict interpretation of the Resolution, and if he abuses the power we must repeal the resolution conferring it.[126]

Dodge, naturally, was much upset. He noted in his autobiography:

Upon receipt of this resolution I could see Durant was again obtaining the power which he had been deprived of during his absence in Europe and since his being relieved of control of construction matters had moved along very smoothly, but I saw that this meant trouble and that it also meant that I would also have to fight to maintain my lines and perhaps another demoralization of the forces. I immediately answered Mr. Ames' letter and told him that a great mistake had been made; that it would not be a month before Mr. Durant would be changing things all along the lines and it would bring on a conflict with the Government as I would not stand for any changes which were made for the purpose of saving work and hurt the commercial value of the road; that the Government depended on me . . . and that [neither] Mr. Durant, nor the Company, had any right to change these lines after we had sub-

[125] *Ibid.,* p. 739.   [126] *Ibid.,* p. 739.

mitted our maps and profiles . . . . I saw the hand of Seymour was also in this work.[127]

Fort Sanders Reached: On April 3 the track reached Fort Sanders in the Laramie valley, and the new town was opened for business a month later.[128] At this latter time, the CP track was at Lake's Crossing (now Reno), and the race was on. Casement was laying over three miles a day in Laramie valley, but Strobridge, Reed's counterpart in the CP, was over the Sierras, with mostly flat country ahead, and going at the same rate or better.

Missouri River Bridge: Work began on the high 2,750-foot bridge over the Missouri between Omaha and Council Bluffs. This vital structure would increase the speed of deliveries enormously when ready, but because the UP charter prevented the issue of securities to finance it, work was soon suspended until 26 July 1869, as will be related later.[129] "The bridge letting, I knew, was a blind." [130]

Dodge Warns Durant: On April 23, Dodge met Dillon, Durant, and Seymour at Cheyenne and had "a very plain talk." The Doctor smoothly assured him that "he had no desire to interfere with the work or delay it, but only wanted to help." Dodge vowed that "nobody could go over his work superficially and change it. Mr. Dillon agreed with me." [131]

General Orders No. 1: Durant's elation with his new power led him into an error of judgment. On May 6, while at Fort Sanders, he issued his brazen "General Order No. 1." Its last paragraph was worded as follows: "In order to prevent unnecessary delay in the work during the absence of the Chief Engineer from the line of the road, the consulting engineer is hereby invested with full power to perform all the duties pertaining to the office of acting Chief engineer and his orders will be obeyed accordingly by everyone connected with the engineer department. Any orders heretofore given by the chief engineer conflicting with orders that may be given by the consulting engineer during his absence, are hereby rescinded." [132] The order, printed on circulars for posting, was unsigned.

Dodge knew this meant real trouble, but as he did not intend to be

---

[127] *Ibid.*, pp. 739–740.   [128] *Ibid.*, p. 751.
[129] Dodge, *How We Built the Union Pacific*, pp. 64–66; see also p. 419.
[130] Dodge, *Autobiography*, p. 821; see also p. 421.   [131] *Ibid.*, pp. 747–748.
[132] *Ibid.*, pp. 752–753; *Poland Rep.*, p. 377 (testimony of Durant).

absent from the line during the summer, he saw that Seymour could not accomplish much. He sent the order to Oliver, saying that he would resign if his lines were changed. It was a direct contradiction of the assurance Durant had given him.[133]

Evans sent in his resignation to Dodge on May 11. "Nothing can ever induce me to do business with the man Seymour," he declared. Dodge tactfully wrote him to accept charge of construction from Fort Sanders west to Green River, as an assistant to Reed.[134]

Oliver rationalized to Dodge on May 14:

The whole circular shows the impolicy of giving him power which he is sure to abuse always. I think at our next meeting, we should definitely fix up the powers we intended to give him or repeal altogether the resolution making him agent for this work . . . I understand that Blickensderfer wants to resign . . . Durant has no power over the location . . . When you return from Chicago come this way. We would like to fix the powers that Durant shall have, if any such thing can be done.[135]

Oliver penned Durant on May 18 rather mildly, all things considered:

The resolution . . . did not intend to confer on you the power to direct the Chief Engineer where he should locate the Road . . . the changes to be made were only such as might expedite the construction by such slight modifications as might be made on the ground to avoid hard points. The responsibility of the Chief Engineer is to the Board of Directors—and they must say whether the location is properly made.[136]

Upon returning from Grant's nomination at Chicago on May 20, Dodge told Durant he would pay no attention to his or Seymour's orders and so instructed all of his employees.[137]

Durant Cramps Cheyenne: When Durant arrived at Cheyenne and Fort Sanders early in May, he attempted to move the extensive roundhouses, machine shops, and so forth, already well under way, to Laramie. His reasons are not made clear. Dodge had staked out a large town at Cheyenne the last July, on the sound basis that any road connecting the UP with Denver, 105 miles south, or with points north, would thereby avoid the range of the Rockies. One-tenth of the lots already had been sold. The UP had advertised that eventually

---

[133] Dodge, *Autobiography*, pp. 753–754.　　[134] *Ibid.*, p. 754.　　[135] *Ibid.*, p. 755.
[136] Durant, *Papers*, 1–3–26–61 (original ms.).　　[137] Dodge, *Autobiography*, p. 757.

it would build a branch to Denver. But Durant's threat was causing a great loss to the company by stopping sales, those who had bought were up in arms, and the UP's good faith was at stake.[138] Dodge appealed to Oliver, and Durant's plan was thrown out by the Executive Committee,[139] fortunately, because only a month later the Senate passed a bill organizing the Territory of Wyoming with Cheyenne as its capital. It became law within a year. Also, a U.S. Arsenal was planned for the same town. But Durant had irretrievably slowed the growth of Cheyenne for a long time to come and stimulated Laramie. "If the company had devoted their time and energy to Cheyenne," wrote Dodge some years later, "in my opinion it would have been a much larger place than it is." [140]

Durant's Powers Canceled—Another Injunction: "When the company took its recently bestowed authority over me and the contractors away from Durant, the Doctor served still another injunction against the Company, virtually preventing the carrying out of orders," wrote Dodge.[141] On May 29 Oliver had flashed the following Western Union telegram from New York: "To Sidney Dillon Or G.M. Dodge, Chief Engineer: Injunction dissolved Durant gone supposedly to Omaha advertise Dillon's election and that [the] committee naming them alone have power to contract for Union Pacific R R notify personally banks and all officers of both companies that Durant has no authority." [142] Dillon had been made "Chairman of the Board of Construction." [143]

On the same day, President Oliver wrote Silas Seymour, Consulting Engineer, a "rather indecisive" letter:

The authority given to Dr. Durant was simply an authority to change the line in construction & under the Ames contract. All matters pertaining to location are in the hands of Genl Dodge Chief Engr. of U.P.R.R. Co. & parties on location subject to his order & his reports are to be made to Board of Directors. Our Co. have always been jealous of giving power to contractors to change the grades or location of road & the authority should not be exercised unless in cases of very urgent necessity & when the construction would be greatly expedited by the change.

You will therefore in any action you may take in regard to the original

[138] *Ibid.,* pp. 750–751, 765 (Dodge to Oliver Ames, 9 June).
[139] No record of the voting is available. [140] Dodge, *Autobiography,* p. 751.
[141] *Ibid.,* p. 757; Records of UP Historical Museum. [142] Dodge, *Papers,* vol. 154.
[143] Dodge, *Autobiography,* p. 765.

location consider it subject to change only when placed in hands of constructing engineer. Trusting you will use your best discretion to have everything harmonized in the Engr. Dept. I am

Very Truly Yours

Oliver Ames Prest.[144]

The Row Continues: For the next two months this new ruckus over Durant's authority vortexed like a prairie twister, and upset letters poured out in such volume that lack of space prevents quoting but one or two. In the eye of the disturbance lay the control of the "Committee on Location and Construction."

It is most unfortunate that the minute books of this and all other UP committees prior to 1912 seem to be lost forever. They were in the office of the Union Pacific at 120 Broadway, New York, when that building, the Equitable, was destroyed by fire in 1912.[145] So it is impossible to say just who were present at meetings, except for some random notations made outside of the official minutes. However, a complete list of the UP Executive Committee, and the make-up of the Trustees under the Ames contract are shown elsewhere here.[146] It is certain that the potential control was nearly evenly balanced now, with only a slight edge favoring the Ames group. With Oliver away, Durant held sway—or the opposite way. Just why Oliver did not get back to New York until a day or so after the critical meetings of July 3 is not apparent.[147] Perhaps Vice-President Durant called the meeting then deliberately, to take advantage of his absence.

On June 4 Durant arrogantly telegraphed Dodge: "All Division Engineers not complying with General Order No. 1 will be discharged. I do not know as the Board will sustain me but I shall not stay in the Company if they see fit to keep you in their service to run politics to the neglect of your duties as Chief Engineer." [148] Dodge was on the road practically all of the normal grading season.

Oliver, in New York, noted in his diary of June 5, "Gen. Dodge came on from Washington is not satisfied with Durant's orders— Durant very sanguine of building the road to Salt Lake & don't want any trouble." Yet a week later he wrote Dodge from New York an inexplicable note: "I have never seen the Dr. so entirely courteous and confiding as he has been since I have been here these two days

---

[144] Records of UP Historical Museum.

[145] Information supplied by C.W. Rossworn, Secretary of the Union Pacific, New York, Sept. 1964.

[146] See pp. 240 and 188–189, respectively.   [147] See pp. 280–281.

[148] Durant, *Papers*, 1–3–36–16.

. . . I will meet you in Omaha the last of next week Rollins and Williams will go out with us over the Road." [149]

Contract with the Mormons: Oliver, in New York on June 10, made an important notation in his diary: "B. Young takes contract on our Rd of 100 miles from Salt Lake east at regular rates pd to our Contractors." This deal was to develop some ramifications over the coming months, even years. It seems that Sam Reed, popular in the Mormon colony since his 1864 surveys, on May 21 had signed a $2,000,000 subcontract with Brigham Young.[150] The Mormon leader, then sixty-seven, had subcontracted with Sharp and Young, a firm owned by Bishop John Sharp (the "Railroad Bishop") and Joseph A. Young, Brigham's oldest son. The agreement covered all grading, tunneling, and bridge masonry from the head of Echo Canyon to Ogden. Later it was extended to Promontory. The unit prices specified were no greater, and in some instances materially less, than those allowed other contractors. Durant promptly sent an order to Snyder: "In consideration of the large contract made with Brigham Young, this company will transport passengers on his orders or those of his agents, at the same rate charged contractors." The concession was of considerable value to Young, materially reducing the cost of transportation to Utah of the large number of converts to the Mormon faith in the East and in European countries.

The followers of the Church of Jesus Christ of Latter Day Saints were, in general, good workers on the road: well disciplined and honest; thrifty and temperate. Without their loyal efforts under the severe winter conditions, the UP might have been beaten by the Central into Ogden. Brigham Young's relations with Oliver and Dodge so far had been cordial, until he learned Salt Lake City was to be by-passed. He was an original purchaser of $5,000 par of the UP stock, on which he failed to execute proxies for the profit allotments. Also, he was a UP Director during 1864, 1865, and 1866. Unfortunately, the UP, due to financial difficulties, for a long time was unable to pay some $750,000 remaining due to Young after the contract was satisfactorily completed in May 1869.[151]

Reed Resigns: Sam Reed, as might be expected, sent in his resignation on June 12 because of Seymour's interference and Durant's

149 Dodge, *Papers,* vol. 154.

150 Records of UP Historical Museum; U.S. Pacific Railway Commission, pp. 2154, 2173.

151 See pp. 356, 360.

orders.[152] But it was not accepted, as he was too valuable. Dodge defended him with these words: "The interest Durant had with Davis & Co. and with others was very detrimental to Reed as he could not force the discipline or push them as he could other contractors . . . Reed had been accused of having interest in various contracts (as Durant, Seymour and others actually had), but that was absolutely false . . . . He looked upon Seymour as a spy and on the work for the purpose of finding fault with others." [153]

On June 21, Oliver departed from New York for the West, and on the 30th left Laramie to go over the line with Dodge, Alley, Jesse Williams, Reed, and Evans.[154] "Mr. Reed talked very plainly with Mr. Ames," said Dodge, "in regard to the way matters were being handled. Every change and every order received by Durant and Seymour interfered with operations on the ground, was costly to the company and detrimental to the surveys and only kept the engineers undecided as to what they should do. . . . I have never known Mr. Reed to be so positive . . . . He said the only object of Seymour was to get rid of the Chief Engineer, if he could." [155]

Seymour addressed a "Private" letter to Durant on June 23, in which he said:

I have given you my views frankly and you have discarded them & gone it blind on Dodge whose opinion upon such matters you know as well as I, is not worth the snap of your fingers. He is trying to recover from the blunder about grades that he made on the Black Hills . . . . Reed & I have agreed so far about everything and would have saved you a good deal of time & money if our plans had been carried out & Dodge had not interfered with General Order No. 1.[156]

Oakes wrote Dodge rather plaintively on June 27: "I saw Hooper today of Utah and he says they had a great meeting at Salt Lake for Mr. Seymour and Reed and had speeches, etc., etc. Great men Seymour & Reed. They must have astonished the Saints. . . . The weather is very hot and we have had night sessions. . . . Wish I were out on the Road with you. Write me when you have a chance." [157]

Durant's Powers Renewed by Executive Committee: Durant now closed in, slugging. On July 3, just before Oliver and Alley got back

[152] Dodge, *Autobiography*, p. 763.   [153] *Ibid.*, p. 766.
[154] Oliver Ames's diary. See pp. 266–267.   [155] Dodge, *Autobiography*, p. 775.
[156] Durant, *Papers*, 4–1–1–11 (original ms.).
[157] Dodge, *Papers*, vol. 154 (original ms.).

from the West,[158] the Executive Committee of the UP held a meeting. This group then consisted of Durant, Bushnell, and McComb on one side; Oliver Ames, Duff, and Lambard on the other; and James Brooks, Government Director.[159] Obviously, Durant dominated it. *Result: a resolution again officially granting Vice-President Durant plenary authority over construction.*[160] This meant supervision of the affairs of the company on the line, including such surveys, preliminary or final, as were being made. Hurrying construction was the real objective. All officers and employees were subject to his instructions. It was intended to give him full powers under Bylaws No. 3 and 4. He was accountable only to this Committee and the Directors. Dodge openly threatened to resign.[161]

Alley Pleads with Oliver: John B. Alley, Director and ex-Trustee, furious, put it this way, rather too eloquently, as usual:

On our return home we found that the executive committee had . . . conferred full authority to act upon the line of the road upon Mr. Durant, the vice president, amenable only to the executive committee, chiefly composed of his friends, practically ignoring the president and chief engineer; Mr. Oliver Ames, always honest and true, yet often yielding reluctantly to these men, as I thought, because of the excessive amiability of his nature. I denounced the action to Mr. Oakes Ames . . . and predicted the ruin of the enterprise if the management was to be given to such men as Durant and McComb; that the Government would be wronged and cheated . . . Mr. Ames concurred with me. I need only add that the passage of that resolution did nearly bankrupt the company. In my disgust I wrote to Mr. Oliver Ames . . . as follows on July 25:

". . . Dissatisfied and uneasy as you and others know I have been ever since I have been engaged with the road, I have never known anything in the action of these men that has alarmed me more. . . . If our associates had been all of them like you and your brother, disposed and desirous to do right and doing justice to the stockholders and the Government, we should not now have been troubled with the injunctions and rascalities which, I fear, may injure us seriously.

"You have acquiesced in and submitted to wrong; and to the view of outsiders even appeared to countenance and encourage it, until there is great danger, I think, of compromising your character. . . . Now what do we find upon our return? The executive committee practically ignor-

---

158 *Ibid.,* Oliver Ames to Dodge (telegram), July 25.   159 See pp. 240, 278.
160 Records of UP Historical Museum. The voting is shown on p. 329.
161 Dodge, *Papers,* vol. 155, Oliver Ames to Dodge, July 27; Records of UP Historical Museum.

ing the board of directors, and no meeting of the board for four months; the chief engineer subordinated and insulted because he is fearless and honest; your authority . . . almost destroyed. . . .

"Now, Mr. Ames, I advise you as a friend . . . to resist, by all the power which you possess, these encroachments upon your rights and ours. For one, I will stand by you and defend you with all the ability which God has given me. If you will, however, allow yourself to be subordinated by such men and the board of directors ignored, the rights of the stockholders trifled with, and our pledges to a beneficent Government trampled upon, then I must enter my solemn protest; and if such a state of things must continue, then let me retire from the contest." [162]

Oliver, in North Easton, his teeth bothering him a great deal, struggled with a lengthy letter to Dodge on July 27, in which he brought out a new swirl of forebodings:

As our great object is to complete the Road we must as far as possible set aside all these annoyances and let no ordinary thing turn us from this object . . .

Duff Green got out an injunction on Cr Mobr and we supposed it was of no a/c and was put off until the 8th of August Dillon and Durant went out on the Road with that understanding . . . By some Hocus Pocus they got it on the 21st of July . . . and it was represented in the Herald that they had run away to avoid testifying . . . quite a damaging article . . .

Jas Fisk now claims that Durant and Bardwell agreed to pay him expenses [for help in last fall's elections] and don't come up, and he will now get what he can. He has served an injunction on Cisco and will serve one on me if he gets a chance to tye up the Road . . . and make us pay him a liberal sum to withdraw his suits. Bushnell thinks he can buy him off with 50,000$.[163]

Grant Settles All Questions About Dodge: General of the Army Grant had been in the Indian country in July for a Treaty Council at Fort Laramie and on the side was doing some campaigning against Horatio Seymour for the November elections. Now, in company with Lieutenant General Sherman and Major-General Philip Sheridan, Commander of the Department of the Missouri, he wanted to inspect the latest work on the UP. At the same time, he would get the whole truth about the fuss the Chief Engineer was getting into with Vice-President Durant. The rumors that were stirring in Washington had

---

[162] *Poland Rep.*, pp. 89–90 (testimony of Alley).
[163] Dodge, *Papers*, vol. 155 (original ms.).

become unsavory and were appearing in the press. Overconfident, Durant took this occasion to wire Sherman, who in turn wired Grant for an interview. A date was set for July 26 at Fort Sanders. Dillon telegraphed Dodge on the 23rd to hotfoot it to the meeting, that he feared Durant was going to bring charges against Dodge and get him put down.

But Major-General Dodge, when in command of the Sixteenth Army Corps under Sherman, had learned something about the art of counterattack. Because of possible adverse political effects on Grant's campaign, he very quietly arranged to show his three warm Army friends the end of the track at Benton, 124 miles beyond Fort Sanders. It was there, on July 25, that he must have "taken great pains on this trip to post them thoroughly about everything connected with the Union Pacific," declaring that he was ready to quit if his final locations were altered.[164] Playing it safe, Grant exacted a personal promise from him that he would not resign until the railroad was done.[165]

On that baking Sunday afternoon, July 26, the showdown took place in the big log bungalow which served as the Officers' Club at Fort Sanders. Among those known to attend were Durant and Seymour; Dodge, Dillon, and Jesse Williams; and Grant, Sherman, and Sheridan. Seven other famous generals waited outside.[166]

The Doctor, assuming that with his new powers came unquestioned authority, took the floor. He boldly accused Dodge of having selected extravagant routes, wasted precious time and money on useless surveys, ignored the sound judgment of his associates (meaning Silas Seymour), by-passed Salt Lake City, neglected his engineering duties while a Congressman, and so on.[167] Dodge refuted every charge, one by one.

"What will you do about it, Dodge?" queried Grant, an almost imperceptible twinkle in his eye.

"Just this," he answered stoutly, "if Durant, or anybody connected with the Union Pacific, or anybody connected with the Government, changes my lines, I'll quit the road."

Grant paused for a moment in the tense hush.

"The Government expects this railroad to be finished," he ordered, as if already the Chief Executive. "The Government expects you to remain with the road as its Chief Engineer until it is completed."

Durant stared at the tough, dark little man in front of him, glanced at the paling face of henchman Seymour, and did some quick think-

[164] Dodge, *Autobiography*, pp. 787, 792.   [165] *Ibid.*, p. 788.
[166] *Ibid.*, pp. 787–788.   [167] *Ibid.*

ing. Pulling at his straggly goatee, he mumbled: "I withdraw my objections. Of course we all want Dodge to stay with the road." [168]

Durant was never to forgive Dodge for the humiliation.[169] From then on, Dodge insisted on written orders from Durant and Dillon, which he obtained.[170]

Three days later, Dodge entertained Grant, Sherman, and Sheridan at his modest house in Council Bluffs, and went over more details about Durant's interference. He also opened up with them "the question that was then being started about the overlapping of the lines." Then they relaxed, choosing descriptive names for the new stations over the Continental Divide between Rawlins and Green River.[171]

Dodge Flails Oliver: But the same troubles continued, Durant insisting on raising the permanent grade over Echo Summit to between 90 and 116 feet.[172] This drove Dodge to his first really bitter letter to Oliver on August 8:

Under my orders I am obliged to make all my official communications to the Vice President. I suppose, however, that I am allowed the privilege of writing you privately. You can put such construction on the action of Durant and the Executive Committee as you deem best. I know what it means and where it will end. He has accomplished his end. Seymour has supreme control here and he in New York. If the country knew it today more than one injunction would be served on you. Nothing is being done on repairs and the orders of the Vice President is to skin and skip everything for the purpose of getting track down. Your temporary bridges will now hardly stand to get trains over them and winter will close in on you with nothing done. Your immense subsidy will be spent in dividends and what few men you have among you who had name or reputation will be, in the eyes of the country, disgraced.

I am sent out here under orders to look after 200 miles of line. Seymour is sent here with orders to break up the finest location that was ever made by putting in 116 foot grades and 8° curvature and I am not even under the order, allowed to say a word or give an opinion; however, the company may go on and do all this, but I doubt whether a mile of the road will be accepted ⋅ . . .

I expect to remain here until my lines are located, and I trust for that short time, I will not be interfered with. . . . After that I shall be at liberty and the men I brought here and whom I consider I was bound in a

[168] Adapted from Perkins' very free version of the story (Perkins, pp. 221–222).
[169] Records of UP Historical Museum.
[170] Dodge, *Autobiography*, p. 792.   [171] *Ibid.*, pp. 792–793.
[172] Durant, *Papers*, 1–3–26–63 (Oliver Ames to Durant, Aug. 7); Government Directors, *Reports*, p. 46 (Williams to Oliver Ames, Aug. 6); Dodge, *Annual Report*, 1868, pp. 6–7.

certain degree to protect, will be through and I shall feel them at liberty to take such course as circumstances dictate.[173]

"This letter created a great many comments in Boston," Dodge noted later. "The Government Directors entered a strong protest against the Executive Committee and caused Mr. Durant . . . and Mr. Dillon . . . to desist from further attempts to change my lines."[174]

Fine Track-Laying: In the meantime, the Casements were making record progress, once on the relatively level ground and light curves of the desert between Fort Steele and Granger from July 21 to October 20. During these 78 working days (excluding Sundays) they laid 181 miles of track, an average of 2.3 miles a day. Apparently, the hardy Irish thrived on the scorching sun, cold nights, and skimpy, bad-tasting water. Always moving in one direction (which took longer than closing a gap between rails), there were a number of 3- to 7-mile days. Their record was $8\frac{1}{2}$ miles from rise to set of sun, the day and mileposts unrecorded.[175] At one time they caught up with the graders, and General Jack collected $3,000 a day for waiting, as specified in the contract. All the preliminary work of preparing roadbed, bedding ties, and bending rails for curvature was done with simple tools by hand labor. The rails were handled with tongs, picked up and set into place on the ties by squads of "iron men," eight men to the squad, four on each side of the track. These were expert rail layers, selected for their physical strength, endurance, coordination, and experience. On both the UP and Central the "iron men" were white, predominantly Irish. No Chinese were employed on the UP. The rails were of iron, chiefly in 30-foot lengths, weighing 560 pounds each at 56 pounds a yard.[176]

On July 21, at end-o-track beyond Rawlins, a large party of leading newspaper men ("editorial gentlemen," they were then called), from New York, Boston, Philadelphia, Baltimore, Pittsburgh, and Chicago, quartered in a special four-car train from New York, witnessed some of this "Union Pacific tracklaying science." They gave it "full measure of commendation," and wrote with enthusiasm of the accomplishments of the company and the condition of the road and rolling stock. All in all, it was a good piece of publicity, gotten up by the UP's advertising agency, Peaslee and Company.[177]

[173] Dodge, *Autobiography,* pp. 794–795.   [174] *Ibid.,* p. 795.
[175] According to Dodge (Records of UP Historical Museum).
[176] Records of UP Historical Museum.
[177] Leonard and Johnson, pp. 175–179; Sabin, pp. 171–175. (The articles are in a scrapbook in the Leonard Collection of the State Historical Society of Iowa at Iowa City.)

Echo Canyon Problems: Oliver wrote Durant in a firmer tone on August 12:

The telegrams from Reed, Seymour & Gen. Dodge this morning on Echo Cannon Line which Mr Crane forwards to you shows very clearly that the 90 feet grade will not delay the Track and is a line which in the end will not cost us any more than the 115 f line. We have put the Road through on such favorable grades I think it will be now our true policy to keep them down to 90 feet . . . . [This is] the best possible thing for the Road & the Govt . . . and ourselves.[178]

On August 23, Oliver sent Dodge a long letter about Durant, in which he added:

Durant and Dillon are away on a/c of this Fisk Suit. It is now fixed so they can return. I have called a meeting of the Board of Directors for the 2nd of Sept and we will have the final acceptance of Located Lines fixed with the Committee on Location which is Ames Dillon Durant Duff & Williams. . . . Though the line of the Road will be fixed all along the Route where *your* Engineers have laid it It is exceedingly annoying to have to fight for it all the way. . . . My opinion is the Dr wants the best line just as much as any of us and when talking about taking the long line it was with the idea of its being cheaper to get this line through at once and work out the long Tunnel after Road was running . . . by Machinery at about 10 $ per yd. . . . We are now within 300 miles of Salt Lake and as we have the right to work 300 miles ahead of our track we can now put our men on the heavy work west of Salt Lake at once.[179]

Parallel Lines Developing: On September 4, Dodge wrote Oliver from Wilton Springs, Utah, recounting the whole situation and movements of the CP. He concluded:

The Central Pacific has just let grading work for 100 miles *west from* Monument Point, which is 345 miles from the track of both the roads. It seems very poor policy for two companies to go on and build or grade over the same 100 miles beyond this point. They can reach it by the time we do, with less work and snow. . . . At least limit our grading to the summit of Toans Pass, 200 miles west of Weber Canon, where the work gets rough. . . . By this plan you would have heavy work only over 6 miles on the east slope of Promotory . . . . You do not want to be

178 Durant, *Papers,* 1–3–26–64 (original ms.).
179 Dodge, *Papers,* vol. 155 (original ms.).

grading 100 miles on an uncertainty. The CPRR are not grasping, commencing only at a point now halfway between the two roads. I know I can save $50,000 perhaps more if I am not driven to death.[180]

But the General was far too optimistic this time. Anyway, the day before, Durant had telegraphed Reed to "cover the line from Humboldt Wells east with men." [181] This was 222 miles west of Ogden.

Reed, at Echo City, informed Dodge on September 21 as to his progress:

The track is at Point of Rocks [805 miles from Omaha]. Bent has gone west with large outfit to commence [grading] operations at Humboldt Wells and work east. Casement's outfit are on road to commence 100 miles east of Wells and work east. Shall have 500 or more teams there very soon . . . . All work at head of Echo is proceeding satisfactorily. Deep cut at rim of basin will be completed by October 10th. Tunnel [there] drove 60 feet at each end. Rock soft, make 6 feet per day at heading, obliged to timber it.[182]

In October, Dodge tried to "impress upon Durant the folly of spending any money west of Promotory, but he storms a good deal about it." [183]

Durant Gets Reckless: By September 14, Durant was back on the road, pumping up pressure for more speed, more speed. To Reed went a telegram on September 25, "Work day and night with Malloy's force. Increase track-laying to 4 miles a day." [184] To Evans, now Construction Superintendent, the same day, "Notify Casement that 16,000 feet of track per day won't do." In October, to Casement, "What prevents your doing 5 miles per day." [185] On one day, October 26 (near Granger), Casement responded with 7¾ miles of new rail and rewarded his men with triple pay. But a few days later, at Granger, he complained, "Durant here and only creates delays." Evans wrote to Durant at Bear River on November 19, "The work is too fast . . . I prefer to be out." [186] And on December 18, Durant to Snyder, "How fast are you sending men to head of Echo? We want 2,000 as soon as can be had." [187]

Sam Reed wrote "Dearest Jennie" on December 6, from Carmichael's Camp at the head of Echo Canyon:

[180] Dodge, *Autobiography,* pp. 802, 802A.   [181] *Ibid.,* p. 811; see also p. 266.
[182] *Ibid.,* p. 818.   [183] *Ibid.,* p. 826.   [184] Leonard and Johnson, p. 207.
[185] *Ibid.,* p. 160.   [186] Durant, *Papers,* 1–3–40–19.
[187] Leonard and Johnson, p. 208.

Another week has passed & I am still working hard to get the grading done. It goes very slowly on account of the hard frozen ground which it is impossible to move without powder. We are working nt & dy without cessation. The Dr. made a great mistake when he put our grading forces on ties and timber. Had he left them as they were all the grading to Weber Canyon would have been done long ago, . . . & the ties & timber would have been as well advanced as now, it will take twice as long now to do the light grading with double the force . . . . I shall remain here until the grading is completed to the head of Echo Canyon. No rest for the weary until the road is finished. I fear my dinner at home must be postponed a few days. My horse is at the door of my tent & I must go over the work. A ride of 20 mis. on this cold day would be dreary in the states but here I think but little of it.[188]

Again, on December 16, from the head of Echo, Reed wrote:

. . . At my [field] office I have a good cook & 2 black boys, 1 to take care of the horses & outdoor work . . . . The ground is frozen about 2 ft. deep. Very expensive work. I am writing in a tent that has just been put up for me. All the forces have to be sent west & placed on new work before I can possibly leave for the East.[189]

He never got home for Christmas. On the 28th, from Weber, he wrote:

The track is laid to the stage station in Echo Canyon where we stayed 1 nt on our trip out. Grading forces are being distributed on new work. Dr Durant arrived at the head of Echo on the 25th. . . . You do not know how I want to be home. If anything goes wrong the H-1 is to pay, the same if all goes swimmingly. I do not care whether I remain another day or not. Evans has gone east. I do not know the reasons. Dr. is just driving up & I must close.[190]

Blackmail on the Tracks: A disgraceful blackmailing incident occurred in October when Cornelius Wendell, one of the UP Commissioners appointed by President Johnson, demanded $25,000 in cash for his approval of the first 25 miles of track west of Green River. Webster Snyder saw fit to have it paid by the UP as "construction— particular exigency." [191] "It was kept a secret for some time but it finally came out," said Dodge.[192] In 1873, the Wilson Committee

---

[188] Records of UP Historical Museum (Reed letters).   [189] *Ibid.*
[190] *Ibid.* (Reed letters).
[191] *Wilson Rep.,* pp. 467–475 (testimony of Snyder), pp. 287–290 (testimony of Oliver Ames).
[192] Dodge, *Autobiography,* p. 860.

demanded its repayment to the UP by those responsible for an illegal disbursement.[193]

Promoters Shocked by Costs: While the majority of the Directors had cheered Durant onward in his rush to beat the CP to the Salt Lake valley, now, as the bills began to pile up, they became appalled. Another Christmas would bear no cheer. Reed had sent news that his estimate of the cost of just grading, masonry, ties, and bridge timber from the head of Echo to Salt Lake, 55 miles, was $54,000 per mile. Adding $11,000 per mile for iron would bring the estimate to $3,575,000 or *$65,000 per mile.* Furthermore, there was much yet to be done. Up to December 31, an additional $500,000 was spent.[194]

Oliver wrote an anguished letter to Durant, again on the road, from Washington, on December 23:

. . . The demands for money are perfectly frightfull . . . . Some how the Road must be costing us very much more than we are getting for it, or every one out there is stealing. Awful stories come down here from outsiders of the competition of the Contractors Engineers and everyone in connection with the Road. If something is not done to stop it at once and discharge all supernumaries on the work we shall be largely in debt when the tracks meet. I believed up to within two months that at the end of our work we should have a handsome surplus. It now looks as though we should have a large floating Debt. Do something to stop the thieves from stealing our last cent and making the Road suffer. We have Snyder asking for 700,000$ Kennedy for 1,500,000. This will take a large portion of our Govt and with the 900,000 wanted for interest on our Bonds will take 100 miles of our Road. We owe outside of this 1,500,000 more on which we have no securities, the 5000000 we owe on a pledge of our 1st Mtg Bonds leaves us with almost nothing to finish up the Road. It looks to me as if Kennedy was drawing or asking to draw for double the amt needed. . . . The Tunnels should be pressed. The Central say they are going to meet us at the Big Tunnel. . . . You know how to get through the Tunnel as well as any one and meet them at Head of Salt Lake. The work at Promotory Point is costing or will cost for 5 miles there 100000$ per mile if there is danger of their getting up to that point leave it for them to do. Cut off all useless expense and economize everywhere, where it will not delay work. We dont want any surplus material on hand when the work is done.[195]

[193] *Wilson Rep.,* p. xvii.   [194] Dodge, *Autobiography,* p. 864.
[195] Durant, *Papers,* 1–3–26–67 (original ms.).

Oliver wrote Durant more calmly the next day from New York:

... It cant be that it has cost over 40,000$ per mile for 54 miles from Echo West for grading as reported by Reed and not done. That wood business should be looked up—But should not make contract giving such exorbitant prices for wood. I hear that Bent [196] has an interest in it that will give him a handsome sum. We have got to get the work through and we must weed out the thieves or we shall come out minus. The President Evarts & Browning seemed yesterday very pleasant—and will give us our Bonds as fast as we earn them. Was you to give Ewing ten. I suppose he wants it and if so write me.[197]

2. THE FOUR TUNNELS

There were only four tunnels on the original UP (compared with 15 on the CP), all started in 1868. They were about 19 feet wide and 20 feet high, very small compared with modern railroad tunnels. Tunnel 1, the shortest, was in sharply winding St. Mary's Creek, 680 miles from Omaha. Only 215 feet long, it was dug through brown sandstone that had to be timbered. During its construction in June and July, a sharply curving temporary track was built around it.[198]

Tunnel 2, at Echo Summit, was by far the longest and most difficult. It was approached by deep rock cuts with the aid of some new power drills,[199] driven 772 feet straight through the ridge, 7,000 feet above the sea. Started in July, it also had to be timbered, as stone and cement were not available then. As it was not opened until shortly after the Golden Spike, for nearly six months all traffic had to be diverted 8 miles around on flimsy, temporary tracks. The climb over the ridge was so steep that a switchback shuttle, or "Z-track," had to be used. The engine would first pull the train forward to the track-end, then push it up and backwards a way to the next track-end, and so on. In the winter rush, the rails sometimes were just laid upon the thick ice and glaring snow. During a thaw, Dodge watched a whole train, from engine to caboose, slide sideways into the deep ditch below, carrying with it all the track and ties.[200]

Tunnels 3 and 4 were only three-quarters of a mile apart in the narrowest part of the steep, rock-cliffed gorge of Weber Canyon, 3

[196] Union Pacific grading contractor and transport teams.
[197] Durant, *Papers*, 1–3–26–68 (original ms.).
[198] Records of UP Historical Museum.
[199] Dodge, *Autobiography*, p. 738 (Oliver Ames to Dodge, 9 Mar. 1868).
[200] Records of UP Historical Museum; Dodge, *How We Built the Union Pacific*, p. 117.

miles west of Devil's Slide. Work was begun in September. Tunnel 3 was 508 feet long on a $3\frac{1}{2}°$ curve, while Tunnel 4 was 297 feet long on a 4° curve. Both were cut through sharp spurs of black limestone and dark blue quartzite. The use of newly invented nitroglycerine greatly expedited the work. Number 4 was finished in January, but longer Number 3 not until April. So, for a few months, trains had to creep dangerously around sharp curves at the edge of the turbulent river.[201]

3. BENTON, THE GHOST TOWN

Benton had been planned as a terminal division by Dodge before the tracks reached it about July 22. In central Wyoming, but no longer shown on maps, it was only 3 miles west of the North Fork of the Platte, at the 696th milepost from Omaha, and within the military reservation, and about 2 miles west of Fort Fred Steele, which was built in 1866 to protect the UP workers and emigrants from the Indians. For a short while, it was a stage terminus and a distribution station for freighting lines operating by wagon haul to Utah, Montana, and Idaho. It was named after Senator Thomas Hart Benton of Missouri, one of the earliest champions of a Pacific Railway from St. Louis to Oregon. Abundant good timber for ties was floated down the river from the Medicine Bow Mountains. The spacing between terminals was good. In fact, the location had many advantages, so Dodge laid out a townsite in blocks. The company sold $10,000 worth of lots at rather fancy prices, indicating a permanent settlement.[202] Within a few weeks, Benton became the new "Hell-on-Wheels," with a population of some 3,000. For 10 hours a day, the streets were thronged with motley crowds of railroad men and soldiers; merchants and miners; saloon-keepers and mule-whackers. Among them, of course, was the usual large quota of parasitic adventurers, men and women. Saloons numbered 23, dance houses 5. The center of activity was the same old "Big Tent," moved on from the previous end-o-track town. It was 100 feet long and 40 wide, floored for dancing and tables. Here the mob played poker, dice, and every species of gambling known, including monte, keno, faro, and rondo coolo. One side was lined with a splendid bar, supplied with every variety of liquor and cigars, with cut glass goblets, ice pitchers, and splendid mirrors and pictures brought on from eastern cities. At another side a raised platform supported a full band ready to play day and night.

[201] Records of UP Historical Museum.   [202] Dodge, *Autobiography*, p. 777.

Prefabricated houses, 20 by 40 feet, with wooden imitation red brick or stuccoed fronts and canvas sides, were hurried on from Chicago. It was said that a dozen men could thus fill up a whole block in a day, and that two boys with screwdrivers could put up a $300 habitable store in three hours. When the town moved on, the structure could be taken to pieces, shipped on a platform car, and set up again.

It will be recalled that it was at Benton on July 25 that Dodge had his hushed-up meeting with Grant, Sherman, and Sheridan before meeting Durant at Fort Sanders.[203]

But Benton was at the worst, eastern edge of the Red Desert. Drinking water from the river had to be carried 3 miles by wagon in barrels—at one dollar each, ten cents a pail. Wells 25 feet deep had brought up only brackish water.[204] Fine alkali dust covered the ground inches deep and sifted into every crevice. "A man in black clothes looked like a cockroach struggling through a flour barrel." Not a green tree, shrub, or spear of grass could be seen from town.[205]

But excellent spring water, adequate for humans and engines, had been discovered by Dodge a year previously near Rawlins, 11 miles west of Benton.[206] So, rather reluctantly, the Chief Engineer decided to move Division headquarters over there. Benton was abandoned in October.[207] Shortly after, not a trace of the site could be found, except a few iron barrel hoops and tin cans, some half-destroyed mud chimneys, and a hundred or so nameless graves.

The UP was not free of troubles following its move, however. For instance, the owner of Lot No.C in Block 33 brought suit for recovery of the $500 paid, when a deed was refused by the railroad. The matter went to President Oliver for settlement on September 24. Benton lot holders were offered equivalent lots in Rawlins.[208]

The ghost of Benton will carry on, however. Its drama is too tempting for the writer of western novels. The best of these is Zane Grey's *The U.P. Trail,* an exciting story woven around the building of this part of the road and the raw life of Benton.

4. BEAR RIVER CITY, THE FORSAKEN

Old Bear City, or Bear Town as it was locally known, lay in the extreme southwestern corner of present Wyoming, on small Sulphur

[203] See p. 283. [204] Dodge, *Autobiography,* pp. 776–777.
[205] Records of UP Historical Museum; J. H. Beadle, *The Undeveloped West, or Five Years in the Territories,* pp. 87–99, quoted in Davis, pp. 144–148, and Sabin, pp. 263–265.
[206] See p. 229. [207] Dodge, *Autobiography,* p. 828. Dodge visited it on Oct. 17.
[208] Records of UP Historical Museum; Dodge, *Autobiography,* p. 777.

Creek 2 miles east of Bear River and at original milepost 944. Today, by motoring from the Evanston station 10½ miles southeastward on State Highway 150, the site can be found, tucked away between hills, near an historic marker on the roadside. It is a mile west of the dam for the very new Sulphur Creek Reservoir. Only gray sagebrush covers the habitat. The reservoir inundates over half a mile of the original UP roadbed, which further on serves as the foundation for a county motor road from the lake to old Hilliard, 2 miles to the east, through the rock cut at the original Aspen pass, and on to abandoned Piedmont and the present station at Leroy.[209]

Bear Town's history is unique and has a moral. Originally, it was probably a resting place, after the climb over the pass,[210] on the early emigrant routes between venerable Fort Bridger and Salt Lake City, including the Mormon Trail, the Pony Express, and the Overland Stage. It was also once a logging and coal mining camp known as Gilmer. When the UP graders bore down on Bear Town in the autumn of 1868, the nefarious crowd from Green River also moved in, creating still another Hell-on-Wheels of nearly 2,000 persons, with well over a hundred shacks, log cabins, tents, and saloons. A character by the name of Leigh Freeman, editor of a local newspaper called *The Frontier Index,* assumed leadership of an aggressive group of merchant vigilantes, it seems, and started to clean up the town, not distinguishing much between the Green River riffraff and some hard drinking UP graders. A misfit, irresponsible Southerner, Freeman next printed outrageous personal attacks on newly elected President Grant, respected by all workers on the railroad.

Soon the inevitable riot came off. About November 19, a large group of Union veterans and Irishmen apparently broke open the jail, released their pals, and advanced on *The Frontier Index* hovel. They were said to be armed only with picks and shovels, and were easily mowed down on the street by vigilante rifle fire from cabins. At least 14 UP men were killed and dozens more wounded.[211] Embroiling white men could hurt the UP more than the Indians could.

The track reached Bear Town only days later, but the trains passed by without a stop. Not so much as a siding was put in. Thus ruined, the vigilantes began to move away, and soon Bear River City became just a bad memory. Unlike Benton, it was nearly forgotten, as even

[209] Visited in 1965 by the author with G. Hobart Chapman of Evanston, a civil engineer and grandson of Oliver S. Chapman, a CM stockholder.
[210] See Profile, Illus., Group 3.
[211] McCague, *Moguls and Iron Men,* pp. 258–260; Stone, pp. 83–84.

the track was abandoned in 1901. The railroad grade between Millis and Leroy was greatly reduced by moving several miles northward and boring two tunnels, each well over a mile long, between the new Altamont and the new Aspen.

5. EVANSTON

After this, Dodge determined to make a Division point of Evanston, lower down on the Bear River at milepost 955, naming it after his engineer, John A. Evans. "It was only 10 miles from the stage line and there was no road nearer," he wrote,[212] apparently glad to blot out any reference to the fracas. Not a word of Bear Town is to be found in all his writings,[213] and the records of the UP Historical Museum give it only a few words.

The track reached Evanston on December 4,[214] but, delayed by severe snowstorms for two weeks, the first train did not pull in until December 16.[215] The mail contract was thereupon extended 97 miles from Bryan.[216] Nearby, at present Almy, were found some excellent coal beds.

General J.A. Williamson, one of the UP land agents, wrote Dodge on December 28 that "he could not sell any lots at Evanston as everyone wanted to go to the town in the valley." He then added:

Echo City . . . which killed Evanston . . . is owned mostly by the [Mormon] railroad men and they do all they can against the town laid out by the company [in Evanston]. I was over in the valley a few days ago and saw McCabe [217] who you know is trying to find the original government surveys. He told me he could not find any of the corners. I saw Gen. Clark the Surveyor General of Utah, and he says the Government will have to cause a re-survey to be made.[218]

Today Evanston, the county seat, has a population of over 5,000; Echo, only 85.

6. STATIONS AND ROLLING STOCK

Snyder reported to Dodge on December 13 that there had been built 64 stations, 73 water tanks, and 15 coal houses. The total rolling

---

[212] Dodge, *Autobiography*, p. 835.

[213] *Ibid.* Perhaps Dodge just erred when he here noted that Evanston, not Bear Town, was the place into which "the crowd that was at Green River City had moved, bringing the same influence to bear at Evanston."

[214] *Ibid.*, p. 837.   [215] *Ibid.*, p. 860.   [216] *Ibid.*, p. 859.

[217] J.F. McCabe, a Union Pacific engineer.   [218] Dodge, *Autobiography*, p. 865.

stock on the road consisted of 124 engines; 21 first class coaches, 10 second class coaches, and 8 sleeping coaches; 81 cabooses, 16 baggage and mail cars, 520 box cars, 1,734 flat cars, and 100 coal cars.[219]

PROGRESS OF THE TRACK, 1868

		UP	UP	UP	CP	
		Approximate Miles from				
			Ogden Junc-	*Monu- ment*		*Eleva-*
Date	*End of UP Track at or Near*	*Omaha* [a]	*tion* [a]	*Point* [b]		*tion* [a]
Jan. 1	Granite Canyon [c]	536	496	572		7,298
Apr. 5	Sherman (Ames Monument) [c]	549	483	559		8,242
June 7	Laramie [d]	573	459	535		7,123
July 1	Carbon [e]	656	376	452		6,750
July 19	St. Mary's (Tunnel No. 1) [e]	679	353	429	470 [f]	6,751
July 21	Fort Steele (Benton) [g]	696	336	- 414		6,540
Aug.	Creston (Continental Divide)	737	295	371		7,030
Sept. 18	Point of Rocks [h]	805	227	303		6,490
Oct. 1	Green River [e]	845	187	263		6,140
Oct. 20	Granger [e]	876 [i]	156	232 [i]	295 [f]	6,270
Nov. 28	Aspen (heavy rock cut at summit)	937	95	171		7,546
Dec. 4	Evanston [j]	955	77	153		6,739
Dec. 10	Wasatch	966	66	142		6,824
Dec. 28	"Echo Summit" (Head of Echo Canyon) [e]	969	63	139		6,879
Dec. 29	Castle Rock	975	58 [g]	133		6,290
Dec. 30	"Ten miles west of Echo Summit" [f]	979	53	129		6,050
Dec. 31	"Stage station at foot of Echo grade." [k] (Probably Emory, later a UP Station.)	982	50	126	188 [f]	5,925

Total miles laid in 1868: 446
Average miles laid per day, excluding Sundays: 1.42

[a] Dodge, *Annual Report*, 1869, pp. 24–27; UP, "Time Table No. 24, June 20th, 1870," with several adjustments in mileage to correspond with UP, *Freight Tariff to Take Effect June 1st, 1870.* Ogden Junction was 1,032 miles from Omaha. See Profile, Illus., Group 3.
[b] Monument Point was 1,108 miles from Omaha.
[c] Progress of Track, 1867, see p. 235.
[d] Dodge, *Autobiography,* p. 760, J.E. House.
[e] *Ibid.,* p. 915, Dodge.
[f] *Ibid.,* p. 853, Oliver Ames.
[g] Records of UP Historical Museum.
[h] Dodge, *Autobiography,* p. 818, Reed.
[i] *Ibid.,* p. 909, Oliver to Sen. J.M. Howard of Senate Railroad Commission, 2 Apr. 1869.
[j] *Ibid.,* p. 837, Evans.
[k] *Ibid.,* p. 866, Blickensderfer.

E. Summary

All in all, 1868 was a mixed-up year of tremendous accomplishments marred by distressing setbacks and mistakes, and the never-ending quarrels at headquarters.

[219] *Ibid.,* p. 859.

The finest feat was the unprecedented rapidity of construction. Nearly the whole length of present Wyoming was crossed, and Utah was penetrated. There was no grade over 90 feet to the mile, although three mountain ranges were surmounted. From Granite Canyon up the east slope of the Black Hills, the line topped the highest point of the entire Pacific Railway at Sherman, then dropped sharply to Laramie. Thence it raced 330 miles across the bunch and buffalo grass, sagebrush and greasewood, and alkali deserts, over the Continental Divide to Carter—all this distance at elevations between only 7,169 and 6,140 feet. Next, it conquered the very difficult crests at Aspen and Echo Summit and ended the year with a steep drop well into the picturesque Echo Canyon, as far as the present station of Emory. Thus the progress during 12 months of work burgeoned into 446 miles of track and telegraph, complete with sidetracks, bridges, tunnels, station houses, machine shops, and town plots. The company's engineering and construction performance was superb. Congressman Dodge was active in the field most of the year, yet managed to maintain contacts with valuable friends in Washington and the Army. These 446 miles compared with 536 miles built during the three previous years combined. The length of single track main line from Omaha was now 982 miles.[220]

Before Bridger station was reached in mid-November at milepost 914, which was the end of the 667-mile Ames contract, Oakes decided to drop out. It was quietly extended on the same terms by Durant with the so-called Davis contract, which was supplemented by Reed's contract with the Mormons. Much to Brigham Young's distress, both the Central Pacific and the UP decided it was well worthwhile to by-pass Salt Lake City by skirting the Lake to the north. As the year ended, the only remaining problem was how best to mount the bold ridge of the Promontory range.

The crowning reward of the year, besides the satisfaction of accomplishment, was the receipt of $15,918,000 United States bonds for the 430 miles accepted, of which $7,200,000 was earned on the 150 miles subsidized at the maximum rate of $48,000 a mile. The total was nearly double all the bonds previously received and brought the cumulative total to date up to $24,078,000 for the 940 miles accepted. Sales of corresponding amounts of the company's first mortgage

[220] See p. 295. According to the Union Pacific's widely distributed free brochure, *A Brief History* (pp. 15, 18), only 955 miles were laid. Year by year the mileage was: 1868—425; 1867–240; 1866–260; 1865–30. In 1869 the mileage was 125, it is claimed, making the correct 1,080 miles to Promontory.

bonds were successful, with assists by Treasurer Cisco's advertising circulars and some good orders from British and Continental investors.

The time was approaching for the issuance of some long awaited "dividends," and the Seven Trustees selected 1868 in which to make the first (and the last) allotments of construction profits to the contractors, who were also the CM stockholders. They delivered $5,804,-500 par value of first mortgage bonds, $11,244,000 par value of common stock, and $3,375,000 in cash—a total of $20,423,500. At estimated market prices at the times of payment, however, this total was reduced to $12,837,400. At least part of these allotments should have been delayed.

The best run of luck for the UP was the election of General Grant as President of the United States, to take office the following March; another was the end of interference by the Indians as the road advanced beyond their hunting grounds.

The worst error in judgment was a majority vote in March of the UP Directors (the Ames group generally dissenting), appointing Durant the General Agent of the road with power to change grades and locations and generally speed up the work. His prompt General Order No.1 brought about widespread demoralization in the field. His plan to move Division headquarters, already established at Cheyenne, to Laramie was not approved. His change of route through narrowly winding Rock Creek was a cheapening mistake which could not be corrected without excessive cost and loss of 20 miles of subsidies. After a short period of repeal by the majority, which produced another tiresome injunction, the Executive Committee, dominated by Durant in Oliver's absence out West, restored his powers in July. But now his attempts to lengthen and cheapen the route without tunnel, causing grades of over 90 feet at Echo Summit, only brought about costly delays. Dodge threatened to resign because of the interference. Government standards would never be met, he claimed. Only after the Doctor was challenged face to face by Generals Grant, Sherman, Sheridan, and Dodge at Fort Sanders late in July was Dodge's authority on all engineering matters restored. Durant then became absolutely reckless in his impatience, and by carrying on the work in mid-winter, at high altitudes, with inefficient use of laborers and money, he ran up awful bills. Normal costs were often doubled, even quadrupled, said Dodge. The Directors were appalled when they finally realized what Durant had done, and that there would be losses, not profits. But it was too late. The Doctor had frittered away his time and had been far too extravagant to attain even his one objective—profits on construction.

The meanest break was the trouble stirred up by the "strangely befuddled" Secretary of the Interior, H.O. Browning. Hating and fearing Durant, and roused by Government Director Williams's idea of creating a reserve fund of several millions to ensure the remedy of some deficiencies in construction caused by undue haste, he unlawfully held up until the last day of the year the delivery of Subsidy bonds worth $2,560,000. As a result, the CM stockholders were entreated to dig up or loan some of the profits already received. In addition, net operating income was not sufficient to cover interest charges on the heavy new funded debt, causing further drain on capital. Worst of all, Browning stipulated that the Central Pacific was to build into the area already partly constructed by the UP, which would allocate to the CP all the Subsidy bonds as far east as Echo Summit. Oliver wrote Browning that this was "impossible to accept."

The final clash between the railroads was under way.

8

Building the Road: A Chronology

1869 Through May 10

Finances—Fisk Raids the Union Pacific—Construction Under Durant Until March 11—Construction After Durant—The Golden Spike

A. Finances

1. PUBLICITY BECOMES HOSTILE TO THE UP

As the final months of building came around, rumors were spreading that by corrupt devices the promoters of the UP were channeling to themselves a large part of the Government subsidies intended to strengthen the railroad. An ominous subsidiary known as the Credit Mobilier somehow had seized possession of the road's assets. The talk was born of ignorance and suspicion, nurtured by rivalry and personal ambition. But it hurt.

A Series of Detractions: Charles Francis Adams Jr., a descendant of two U.S. Presidents, a member of the Massachusetts Board of Railroad Commissioners, and, oddly enough, a later President of the UP, opened fire on the CM with a tirade, "The Pacific Railroad Ring," in the reputable *North American Review* of January 1869, part of which is quoted:

Who, then constitute the Credit Mobilier? It is but another name for the Pacific Railroad Ring. The members of it are in Congress [but only Congressman Oakes Ames, Hooper, Alley, Grimes, Brooks, Dodge and Boyer had over 30 shares];[1] they are trustees for the bondholders, they

[1] See pp. 203, 208–209.

are directors, they are stockholders, they are contractors; in Congress they vote the subsidies, in New York they receive them, on the plains they expend them, and in the Credit Mobilier they divide them; as stockholders they own the road, as mortgagees they have a lien upon it, as directors they contract for its construction, and as members of the Credit Mobilier they build it . . .

Ever-shifting characters, they are ever ubiquitous; they receive money into one hand as a corporation and pay it into the other as a contractor . . . Under one name or another, a ring of a few persons [there were 91 in May 1868] [2] is struck at whatever point the Union Pacific is approached . . . .

Shortly after, Congressman Philadelph Van Trump of Ohio aired some hearsays in the House. The Credit Mobilier people, he said, are working "gigantic schemes of public plunder . . . the amount of which is unknown because . . . the actual cost of the road is shown only by their private books. . . . It is a situation so delicate and so full of temptation that no honest man . . . would desire to be in their position." [3]

The Doctor arbitrarily discharged Blickensderfer with the following letter on January 2, "You will please consider your services for this company at an end from and after the time you left your work to accept an appointment under the Government." [4] Dodge, who was then in Washington, commented:

Of course this letter was a very injudicious one and made the Interior Department [who had appointed him to the Special Commission to examine the roads] very angry. I immediately sent an order to Mr. Blickensderfer countermanding Durant's orders, and took it up with Company, but the mischief had been done . . . Our great difficulty in contending with the Central Pacific was that the administration and the Departments had lost all confidence in Mr. Durant, and many of the decisions against us came on account of his interference and statements . . . The Central Pacific could use his statements with great effect. [5]

A crackpot by the name of C. H. Snow, who stated that he had been appointed a Government Director by the President on January 9, [6] wired Andrew Johnson on February 1, "I do not think any more money should be given to the Union Pacific until it is better constructed and managed better." [7] It seems that Snow had brought two

---

[2] See pp. 244–245. [3] *Cong. Globe*, 40th Cong., 3rd Sess., pp. 528–530.
[4] Dodge, *Autobiography*, pp. 867–868. [5] *Ibid.*
[6] Government Directors, *Reports*, pp. 56–64. [7] Dodge, *Autobiography*, p. 885.

long reports on the general character of the road to Dodge, one highly derogatory and the other favorable. He offered the latter for sale at $1,000. Dodge refused to pay the blackmail, and wrote a frank letter of protest about the incident to Secretary Browning.[8] Nevertheless, on March 5, Snow delivered his defaming report, addressed to "The President of the United States," who, by then, was Grant. To this day it lies shamelessly in the records of the Secretary of the Interior. Significantly, Snow's name does not appear in the "UP Official Register of Directors and Officers, 1863–1897."

The $25,000 blackmail paid to Wendell, another Johnson appointee, already has been recounted.[9]

James Fisk's outrageous manipulations of railroad stocks had not reflected yet directly upon the UP, but the well-founded whispers that Durant and McComb had connived with him in the stockholders' election of Directors in October 1867[10] did the UP no good, especially so now that Fisk was preparing for a raid, charging that the UP was facing bankruptcy.[11]

On April 5, Senator W. M. Stewart of Nevada, seconded by Senator J. W. Nye of the same state, both naturally firm supporters of the Central and against the UP, made a violent attack on the Credit Mobilier as corrupt and incompetent,[12] but then relapsed into silence when he was reminded that the Central had its counterpart construction company which also might bear investigation.

After the Golden Spike, all these and many more charges of corruption were gradually forgotten, until suddenly resurrected in the Presidential election of 1872.

2. THE UP SHORT OF WORKING CAPITAL

No Money to Pay Bills: Oliver wrote "Doctor Durant" on the first day of the new year:

To raise what money was necessary to meet our Payments we have used up all our Securities and have had to raise on Certificates Gold to pay our interest on Bonds. There are now 2,000,000$ of money required to meet the drafts now asked for from Line of Road and really nothing to raise the money with. Our Chicago Creditors are clamorous for money and say they have loaded themselves down with bills of ours to their

---

[8] *Ibid.,* p. 861; *Wilson Rep.,* p. 290 (testimony of Oliver Ames). [9] See p. 288.
[10] See p. 187; Dodge, *Autobiography,* p. 934. [11] See p. 324.
[12] *Cong. Globe,* 5 Apr. 1869.

utmost capacity and must have money to keep along. Blair [Government Commissioner] was in N.Y. yesterday and is ordered out to examine Road. We shall get sometime hence the 640000 on this Section and if another can be got ready they might examine this but this would be but little help for the pressing claims upon us. The next remedy for us is estimation of work done in advance of track. This would help us and if the estimate could be promptly ordered it would give us temporary relief. You ought to discharge all unnecessary men at once and get no more ties and timber than is absolutely necessary for the work.

It would be an eternal disgrace to us, and to you in particular as the manager of the construction to be forced to suspend for want of funds to continue the work. Cut down expenditures remeasure the work as proposed and have a heavy stock of ties and timber on hand. When the Road is completed we can buy them at better rates than now. And the exorbitant rates of interest we are now paying will eat us out—Was Ewing [Thomas, former Secretary of the Treasury and Interior] to have 10,000$ write me he wants the money.[13]

On January 4, Oliver sent Durant another very similar letter.[14]

At this time, according to Ham, the short term indebtedness of the UP was $12,960,000 consisting of: loans, $5,225,000; bills payable, $4,455,000; and Certificates for first mortgage bonds, $3,280,000. Assets, however, were only $11,063,000, made up of $6,762,000 of first mortgage bonds and $4,301,000 of U.S. 6 per cent 30-year bonds. The company was entitled to receive $2,278,000 first mortgage bonds.[15]

Oliver wrote from New York in his diary of January 6: "Had a meeting of Executive Committee agreed to raise money among ourselves Pro Rata 5% Com 7% interest for 1st 10 [days] deducting 1% for every 10 days delay after today till it gets as low as we can afford to take it."

And again, on January 9, this time from Boston, "Had meeting of Stockholders in Cr Mobr and Pacific RR at G&W [Glidden and Williams] office to get them to advance money to UPRR to help them along. All seemed willing to do what they could, if all would come in meeting of Society at office."

Oliver Asks Oakes to Retrench: The next day Oliver, much troubled by the road's affairs, wrote a long letter to Oakes, now nearly sixty-six, imploring Oakes to join him in making no new speculations

---

[13] Durant, *Papers,* 1–3–26–59 (original ms.).
[14] *Ibid.,* 1–3–26–69.   [15] Records of UP Historical Museum.

and reducing indebtedness.[16] Oakes had just become a Director and one of the largest stockholders of John Blair's newly organized Fremont, Elkhorn and Missouri Valley Railroad, starting from the UP at Fremont.[17] The Sioux City and Pacific Railroad was about to complete its UP connection at the same place.[18] His large investments in the Cedar Rapids and Missouri River Railroad were still committed.[19] The important subject will be pursued further in Chapter 10, pages 385–386.

Diary Notes: A series of diary notations by Oliver follows:

January 21, in Boston: Pleasant meeting of Executive Committee . . . Chose Duff & Self a committee to purchase cars like those on Express train from Boston to NY—Price of them, 4800$ . . . Ordered 18 new Sleeping Cars.

January 22, in New York: Executive Committee closed the Stock Books so that no New Stock can be subscribed to influence Election. Money easy. pd Boomer on Bridge 100,000$.[20]

January 28: Got to NY about 8 o'clock last night. Everything going very well. Money is coming in rapidly and we have 500,000$ ahead . . . Signed passes for members of Congress.

February 19: A very large amount has been expended in transportation of construction material which has increased cost of operating Road.

February 25, 5th Avenue Hotel: Great rise in Govt Bonds which has carried up all other securities based on Gov.

February 27: Oakes is feeling quite anxious about the cost of work and management on Line of Road—as we all are, and feel that our interests are being sacrificed.

March 2, New York: Left on the 3 p m train for NY had a slow passage not getting in to NY till about 12 o'clock. McCombs went on with me—feels sore on our view of his conduct.

March 27: Duff wants all things fixed to suit him before he does anything to help us in finances.[21]

Dodge sent a wire from Washington on April 6 to cheer up Snyder out West: "I have been at work on finances, they are getting better. Keep good courage. Tell your banks and merchants we are going to see them through all right. We are just now trammeled by injudicious fights, etc., but are, nevertheless, able to take care of ourselves." [22]

---

[16] See pp. 385–386.   [17] See p. 87.   [18] See pp. 85–86.   [19] See pp. 80–85.
[20] See p. 275.   [21] See pp. 149–151.   [22] Dodge, *Autobiography,* p. 926.

UP Taps Its Stockholders: On April 10, the Union Pacific offered
to sell first mortgage bonds and land grant bonds at bargain rates
exclusively to its stockholders, through the medium of what is now
known as "rights." The printed offering "Circular" stated the proposition this way:

To the Stockholders of the Union Pacific Railroad Company

The Union Pacific Railroad Company, for the purposes of paying the
advances which it has procured, and to obtain further means to complete and equip its road, has resolved to offer to its Stockholders, *pro
rata,* bonds of the Company, upon the following terms:

1. To each Stockholder First Mortgage Bonds to an amount equal at
par to 50% of the par amount of the stock held by him; the price to be
85% and accrued interest. Payments will be made in cash to Wm. T.
Glidden, Chairman, at his Office, No. 114 State Street, Boston, at various
specified dates on or before May 20th, with delivery at time of payment.
Certificates, not bearing interest, will be given for fractional amounts
of less than one bond.

2. To each Stockholder Land Grant Bonds to an amount equal at par
to 50% of the par amount of the Stock held by him; the price to be 55%
and accrued interest. The Committee reserves the right to buy back these
Land Grant Bonds, within four months, at 60% and accrued interest.
Payment, delivery, and fractions as under the 1st Mortgage Bonds.

Any portion of the Bonds so offered which may not be accepted by
the Stockholders, will be alloted, *pro rata,* to such of the Stockholders
as shall sign, with their acceptance, the accompanying printed notice
that they agree to take their shares of the remaining bonds.

Committee—William T. Glidden   William T. Glidden, *Chairman.*[23]
           C. S. Bushnell
           Oakes Ames
           James Brooks
           Benjamin E. Bates

On April 16, Oakes Ames agreed to buy the amount of both classes
of bonds to which he was entitled. In addition, in case any stockholders failed to take up their proportions, Oakes agreed to accept
further amounts of $250,000 par of each class or such less amounts as
might be allotted by the Committee.[24]

The subscriptions thus accepted on behalf of the UP by Chairman
Glidden apparently were first mortgage bonds $4,796,000 and land

grant bonds $6,509,000 at par.[25] However, at prices of 85 per cent and 55 per cent the market values were only $4,076,600 and $3,579,950 respectively. So, by this honorable appeal, the UP seems to have netted in all $7,656,550 and interest, which was used to pay off the short term advances already made by important stockholders, and to build up desperately needed working capital. Presumably the money came from such UP stockholders as were also CM stockholders and had received $12,837,940 market value of profit allotments in 1868. This reversal cast quite a different light on such allotments, which had been the subject of some criticism.[26]

On April 24, Glidden wrote Bushnell:

Hope you will get the N. Haven people to pay up all *at once,* & those who have notes send them in & get the advantage of interest. . . . Fear we may come short of 1st Mtg Bonds to deliver—& those who come first, will be first served.[27]

Oakes wrote Glidden and Williams from New York on April 27:

I wish you to make up for Messrs. Morton Bliss & Co 150,000 of each kind of Bonds which they will take on account with me and will be a part of my options. Bushnell and Hazard are both here they are hard up for money yet and Mr. Hazard has not yet done anything of any account.[28]

Oakes wrote to "Bro Oliver" on the same day that Morton Bliss and Company were taking the bonds on joint account with him, the bankers to carry them and divide the profits.[29]

Congress Finally Acts: Finally, after much thrashing about, the Forty-First Congress pulled itself together, and, on the last day of the First Session, April 10, passed a very important law which will be mentioned further. It was designated a "Joint Resolution for the Protection of the Interests of the United States in the Union Pacific Railroad Company, the Central Pacific Railroad Company, and for Other Purposes." *Section 3* thereof, pertaining to issues of Subsidy bonds, specified that the President "must withold from each company an amount of U.S. Bonds . . . sufficient to secure its full completion as a first-class road . . . or in lieu of such bonds, the President may re-

---

[25] *Wilson Rep.,* pp. 622–625 (Abstract Ledger B, Rollins).   [26] See pp. 258–261.
[27] Records of UP Historical Museum.   [28] *Ibid.*   [29] *Ibid.*

ceive an equal amount of the first mortgage bonds of each company";
or, if that were insufficient, he could requisition any bonds already
issued.[30]

Under *Section 2* of the same law, pertaining to deficiencies, the
President was to appoint "a board of eminent citizens, not exceeding
five in number, and who shall not be interested in either road, to
examine and report upon the condition of, and what sum or sums, if
any, will be required to complete each, for the entire length thereof,
as a first-class road." The expenses of the board, including an allowance of $10 a day for each member, were to be paid equally by the
railroads. The five eminent citizens appointed by Grant in August
turned in a generally favorable report on October 30.[31]

Drafts Pour In: On May 1, Dillon wired Glidden from Echo, "We
must have $500,000 to pay contractors men immediately or road
cannot run. When will Oliver Ames be here." [32]

On the same day, Oliver wired Duff and Dillon to "End of track
UPRR Utah": "Draw no more drafts on New York. Telegraphed you
authority to draw on Glidden for $200,000 on the 28th April. You
may draw for one or two hundred thousand more at sight if very
necessary." [33]

On May 4, Oakes, in New York, wrote Glidden and Williams: "I
do not understand Mr. Dillon's telegrams he wants to draw on N.York
and Boston both, and for all kinds of sums and think he must be
confused in his operations and the large amounts he wants to draw
rather surprises me." [34] Oakes was to get the sad answer a few weeks
later, after the Golden Spike.

3. MORE TROUBLES WITH BROWNING

Browning Repeats Demand: Secretary Browning again made his
demand on Oliver January 6:

On the 15th ultimo you were requested to cause the Union Pacific RR
to be located to Echo summit so as to unite and form a continuous line
with the Central Pacific RR as already located to that point, and forward
the necessary map and profile for file in this department.

The law requires the Union and the Central roads to be so located

---

[30] 16 Statutes at Large 56; *Poland Rep.*, pp. 196–197 (gives the Resolution in full).
[31] See p. 337.   [32] Dodge, *Papers*, vol. 158; Dodge, *Autobiography*, p. 943.
[33] Dodge, *Papers*, vol. 157.   [34] Records of UP Historical Museum.

as to unite and form one continuous line of roads, and I have to repeat my request . . . . In the meantime action will be witheld upon your present application.[35]

Oliver sent a copy to Dodge the same day, remarking:

Is there no way for us to avoid this and are we to lose our subsidy on a/c of the line of Central being located in advance of ours. If this is so we better give up our Road where it is and stop our work. I have no idea of doing this as Browning desires. He evidently wants to force us to give up our grading and take that of the Central and build our Road on their line or lose our subsidy—The old Hipocrite I thought when he was saying to us that the location of their line in advance of ours gave them no rights he meant what he said and would simply ask that the Roads should be joined where they met. You must get some immediate action of Congress to have this matter put Right and not let our line be sacrificed in this way . . . . We can't go on without the subsidy and if it is to be applied to their line we must pull up our track and put it on their line or quit.[36]

Continuing from North Easton, he added in a separate letter:

It would be infamous for such action as Browning is talking to be sustained and your documents cant be used too quick—to show him up in Congress. Our hope is in Congress. The Cabinet will be too differential to the Head of the Interior Department and will avoid action. I think Congress would like to ventilate the Interior Department just now that its corruption is being exposed and this action of Browning shows that the Head is corrupt.[37]

Dodge commented, much later, "The action of the Secretary was creating a great deal of discussion in Congress, and the Senate and I were utilizing it very effectively. It was very evident to everyone that there was a nigger in the wood-pile somewhere; that this effort of Browning's . . . was beyond all reason. We were fast nearing Ogden. The Central was still 150 miles West of there . . . . We were keeping close watch on the Central's movements. I had organized an investigating force both in Washington and in the West so that every move they made was known to us." [38] Certainly, Dodge had had valuable experience during the war with his secret service.[39]

---

[35] Dodge, *Papers*, vol. 156 (original ms.).   [36] *Ibid.*   [37] *Ibid.*
[38] Dodge, *Autobiography*, pp. 876–877.   [39] See p. 132.

Oliver Worried About a UP Failure: In the middle of Oliver's long
letter to Oakes of 9 January 1869 (about cutting down on speculations) appear these words:

I am troubled about the Pacific R R affairs and we must have a failure to meet our call or prompt relief from our Stockholders. If this can
be done cordially and promptly we may meet our Liabilities and save
the failure of our Creditors West who are now suffering for want of
funds from us. It will take 2,500,000$ to save us if we get our dues from
Govt promptly. If there is holding back as Browning is now doing a
larger amt will be required. Govt ought to be willing to pay us in to
bring the Roads to-gether and if the point is fixed where we shall meet
and the line on which we shall build I see no reason why Govt might
not give us all the bonds for the Road where we have graded and wait
for us to put down the iron when we have it all on Road.[40]

Browning to Fix Junction: Browning, having appointed a commission of three to examine just the Central, was finally informed by
them that there were only $310,000 deficiencies. "This was a white-
washing report," said Dodge, who then appealed to Browning "to
have only one commission examine *both* roads again, in simple
justice to both." [41] Apparently in response to this, on January 14
Browning made up a new commission to "examine both roads and
determine on a point of meeting, *even if it takes a completely new
location.*" [42] For this important work he again chose General Warren,
Blickensderfer, and Lieutenant Colonel R.S. Williamson of the Army,
but at the urgent request of the Central added Lewis M. Clement,
their principal locating engineer.

   Oliver wrote in his diary January 14: "Mr. Oakes Ames thinks he
has got Browning overruled and we will be able to get along well
hereafter. Signed a lot of Land Bonds." Just why Oakes was led to
believe this is not clear, unless he had seen the President.[43]

Huntington Goes After Bonds: On January 18, Collis Huntington
traveled East, observing on the way that UP graders were burning ties
at $6 each to keep from freezing in the mountains.[44] His first move
was to write a long, bitter letter to President Johnson dated the 19th,
complaining that the UP were trying to get the bonds unfairly, as
they had advanced their track into Weber Canyon only by hasty and

---

[40] See pp. 385–386.
[41] Dodge, *Autobiography*, p. 844 (letter dated Jan. 11); see also pp. 329–330.
[42] *Ibid.*, pp. 845–848.   [43] See p. 309.   [44] Sabin, p. 192.

incomplete construction during the winter.[45] He then concentrated all his dynamic efforts in getting the subsidies for the Central. His reputation, and that of his company, still stood high in Washington, quite contrary to those of Durant and the Credit Mobilier. He took advantage of this to interview the President and members of his Cabinet, including, of course, Browning and Secretary of the Treasury Hugh McCulloch; Attorney General James Speed; Senators Stewart, Nye and Howard; and many other influential and friendly persons in Government circles. His approach was unvarying—logical, clear, and forceful. "The bonds had been lawfully authorized," he insisted.

Oliver Protests: On February 10, Oliver, after learning that Huntington was applying for bonds 100 miles in advance of what he claimed to be the end of their track, forwarded the protest which he and Dodge had prepared for Browning on December 30,[46] but had not mailed then, along with the following letter:

I have been informed that the Central Pacific RR have applied for an advance of U.S. bonds under the 8th section of the act of July 2, 1864, on that part of the route lying between Monument Point and Ogden. The Union Pacific RR is constructing the road on this part . . . and will very soon apply for the bonds . . . The Union Pacific began . . . this work under the authority of the act of July 3, 1866, the same being at the time within 300 miles from the end of their completed track, and being at that time more than 300 miles beyond the end of the Central Pacific's completed track.

Nor are the rights of these companies affected by the fact that the Secretary of the Interior . . . approved a map filed by the Central Pacific.[47]

Huntington Captures $2,400,000: Time was running out on Johnson and his retinue, still baffled since the attempt at impeachment.[48] After several meetings with his Cabinet, the last one as late as March 1, Huntington's application was approved unanimously, and the reluctant McCulloch was ordered adamantly to hand over the contested bonds. According to Dodge's affidavit: "Towards the end of February Mr. Oakes Ames called on Secretary McCulloch, who said we might rest assured that no bonds would be issued in advance of the completed track . . . that the commissioners were out examining

---

[45] *Andrew Johnson Papers,* Manuscript Division, Library of Congress; Dodge, *Autobiography,* pp. 854–855.
[46] See p. 271.   [47] Dodge, *Autobiography,* p. 855.   [48] See pp. 245–246.

the very question involved . . . *and we also obtained assurances from President Johnson that no such bonds should be issued.*" [49] McCulloch seemed to be greatly relieved to have the decision taken off his hands, as the craftily patient Huntington had been calling on him over and over, camping outside his office by the hour, and when let in, demanding explanations as to why he would not come up.

So, at the eleventh hour, Hugh McCulloch finally issued the following order:

Treasury Department, March 2, 1869

In pursuance of the acts of Congress in such case made and provided, and in consideration of the completion of certain work upon four sections of 20 miles each of their road by the Central Pacific Railroad Company of California, commencing at the 660th and terminating at the 740th mile-post east from the initial point at Sacremento, California, please issue $1,066,666.67 in bonds of the United States to bear interest from the 17th day of February, 1869, and deliver to said company bonds to the amount of $566,666.67 retaining $500,000 until security is given by the company for the completion of the road according to the requirements of the law.[50]

"This order," wrote Dodge later, "covered line from a point 8 miles East of Monument Point to a point 6 miles East of Ogden. This was on the line which we built over and which was at that time mostly graded. This alone shows the injustice of the order. The Central Pacific had done some grading on this line but not much." [51]

Some explanation is needed to understand McCulloch's figures. The odd fraction of bonds delivered perhaps was to even out previous or subsequent issues. The Act of 1864, Section 8, specified that "The Secretary is . . . authorized and required, upon the delivery of such certificate [of the commissioners] to issue . . . a proportion of said bonds, not exceeding two-thirds of the amount of bonds authorized to be issued under the provisions of the act, to aid in the construction of such section of 20 miles, nor in any case exceeding two-thirds of the value of work done, the remaining one-third to remain until the said section is fully completed and certified by the commissioners. . . ." [52]

The commissioners had certified that, based on the Central's statements, the value of the grading work already done on these 80 miles

---

[49] Dodge, *Autobiography* (affidavit of Mar. 30). (Italics by C.E.A.)
[50] *Ibid.*, p. 856 (order quoted in full).   [51] *Ibid.*
[52] See pp. 31–32, 257; White, p. 111 (quotes Section 8 in full).

was $1,600,000.[53] Two-thirds of 1,600,000 is 1,066,666.67, and 566,-666.67 plus 500,000 makes 1,066,666.67.

Dodge Protests: However, Dodge submitted a protesting affidavit on March 30, too late, part of which said:

It is not possible that on the 19th of January, 1869 [the date of the certificate] there had been work performed by the Central . . . on the 80 miles above described, necessary to prepare the road for the super-structure of the value of not less than $1,600,000 . . . . The well-known character of the country . . . and of prices for work in the vicinity of Salt Lake, as well as our actual estimates for the UP . . . of excavation and embankment of $1,149,110 . . . all prove the falsity of the certificate of the commissioners . . . I make the foregoing statements in aid of the application of the Union Pacific to have the acceptance of the map on October 20, 1868, revoked, and the order to issue bonds to said Central Pacific cancelled . . . I assert . . . that this action . . . was an unworthy device, secretly perpetrated during the closing moments of the adminis-tration of Andrew Johnson, for the purpose of obtaining an unfair advantage of the Union Pacific . . . and obtaining bonds to which the Central Pacific had no legal or equitable right.[54]

The eventual bond subsidy seemingly lost by the UP at $32,000 a mile was $2,560,000, plus the right to issue the same amount of first mortgages, and plus the grants of land. But the die had been cast, irretrievably, by Browning.

Another $1,333,333.33 of bonds, this time with interest from March 2, were assigned to the Central by McCulloch in a second order, this one dated March 3. Of these, $833,333.33 were handed to Huntington along with the first lot on that last day; and an-other $500,000 were withheld for security.[55] This issue was based on the commissioner's certificate that $2,000,000 of grading had been "done" on January 19 [56] between their 560th and 660th mileposts, which was 100 miles from the vicinity of Ives Pass (50 miles east of Humboldt Wells) to the vicinity of Monument Point.[57] "This did not cover the line which we built over but it covered the line that we had graded over," noted Dodge. However, despite Dodge's claims, there

---

[53] Dodge, *Autobiography*, pp. 917–918 (last page of his sworn statement to the House Committee on Pacific Railroads).
[54] *Ibid.*, pp. 917–918.   [55] *Ibid.*, p. 856 (quotes McCulloch's order in full).
[56] *Ibid.*, pp. 917–918.   [57] *Ibid.*, pp. 856, 917.

can be little doubt that the Central had some logical rights to this stretch.

To sum up, Huntington walked off that evening with exactly $1,400,000 U.S. bonds in his suitcase, together with a promise of exactly $1,000,000 more as soon as the grading was done. This would ensure the CP a total of $5,760,000 U.S. Bonds by the time the 180 miles of finished track were accepted at $32,000 a mile. Durant's scheme of building east from Humboldt Wells had failed, and about $200,000 had been wasted on grading there.[58] "Our great loss," wrote Bushnell, "grew out of our crazy attempt in sending men last summer to Humboldt Wells who should have been kept at work through the line this side and beyond Wahsatch, instead of doing it in midwinter at a fabulous cost to the contractors." [59]

Grant, President: On March 4, General Grant was inaugurated as President, and Johnson went out, a good break for the UP at last. In the new Cabinet as Secretary of the Interior was Jacob Dolson Cox, a Major-General under Sherman, an ex-Governor of Ohio, and now a lawyer and distinguished writer, aged forty-one. He was "a great friend of the Union Pacific," said Dodge.[60] For Secretary of the Treasury, Grant chose George Sewall Boutwell. He was an organizer of the Republican party and the new Department of Internal Revenue; a U.S. Congressman from Massachusetts since 1863, when Oakes Ames was elected; and already a renowned author at the age of fifty-one. With the opening of the Forty-First Congress, Dodge was out, and Oakes was no longer on the House Committee on the Pacific Railroad.

Grant's very first order, released on the evening of March 4, instructed both Secretaries to suspend action on the issue of further Subsidy bonds to *both* roads.[61] Needless to say, the CP was more disappointed than the UP.

On March 29 a resolution was introduced in the House which challenged the propriety of the issue of $2,400,000 bonds to the CP only a few hours before the dissolution of the old administration, and directed the Committee on the Pacific Railroads to investigate immediately and recommend action to protect the interests of the Government. As a result, Dodge prepared an affidavit to the said committee

---

[58] Records of UP Historical Museum.

[59] Bushnell (at Echo) to J. M. S. Williams, 5 July 1869, Records of UP Historical Museum. See also pp. 372, 376.

[60] Dodge, *Autobiography,* p. 900.   [61] *Ibid.*

dated March 30. An important part which has not yet been quoted follows:

The map filed in the Interior Department, which pretends to be a location [made during 1867] of the Central Pacific railroad from Echo Summit to . . . Humboldt Wells, I know to be false and fraudulent, as I have been over the entire ground since the maps were sworn to May 15 and July 18, and no located line existed on the ground. I met the Central Pacific engineers during August, September and October [1867], locating their lines on the ground, conversed with them, and obtained from them copies of profiles and maps, and they never pretended that the line that had been filed was anything but a trial line; and every foot of line that the Central Pacific railroad has graded or worked on between Humboldt Wells and Ogden has been located since their maps were filed, and very little of the entire location is upon the same line represented on the map accepted October 20, 1868. The line is only a trial line, without curves, with stakes 500 feet apart, and run in 1867, and the map, in my opinion, was intentionally so made that it is perfectly useless in an engineering point of view. . . . *It has no topography, no stations, no courses, no angles, no scale, nothing by which any line could be identified by it on the ground.*

It was received in direct violation of the instructions of the Interior Department, and does not comply with the requirements of the Department made upon the Union Pacific upon their filing maps.[62]

Oliver filed an overly long protest on April 2 with Senator John M. Howard of Michigan, Chairman of the influential Senate Committee on the Pacific Railway, which is not quoted for lack of space. He recounted the feud for control of the Salt Lake traffic and lashed Browning and Huntington for unlawful acts.[63]

The result of all this was the pertinent Joint Resolution of Congress on April 10, Section 3, which directed the President to withhold bonds (which he already was doing) under certain conditions, as previously recounted.[64]

Total U.S. Bonds issued by the Treasury during the year 1869 ended up at $2,997,000 for 93.68 miles at $32,000 a mile, as far as Ogden. But only $2,674,000 were actually received by the road during the same year. This brought the cumulative total for the entire road to $27,075,000, close to the $27,236,512 ever to be issued.[65]

---

[62] *Ibid.*, pp. 915–916. (Italics by C.E.A.) See also p. 231.   [63] *Ibid.*, pp. 909–912.
[64] See pp. 305–306.   [65] See table, p. 314.

RECORD OF U.S. BONDS ISSUED ON MILEAGE ACCEPTED
BY YEARS, TO FIVE MILES WEST OF OGDEN

Year Issued	Miles Accepted	Cumulative Miles	Rate per Mile	Bonds Issued (Par Value) [a]	Cumulative Total [a]	Received by UP [b]
1866	270	270	$16,000	$ 4,320,000	$ 4,320,000	$ 4,320,000
1867	240	510	$16,000	3,840,000	8,160,000	3,840,000
1868	15.078		$16,000	241,000		
	150.000		$48,000	7,200,000		
	264.922		$32,000	8,477,000		
	430.000	940		$15,918,000	24,078,000	15,918,000
1869	93.680	1,033.68 (Ogden)	$32,000	2,997,000	27,075,000	2,674,000
1870	5	1,038.68	$32,000	160,000		163,000
	Bonds withheld on 52nd section.					320,000
	Bond previously withheld a/c fractions.			1,000		1,000
	Cash in lieu of fractional bond.			512		512
				$161,512		484,512
Total	1,038.68 miles (5 miles west of Ogden)				$27,236,512	$27,236,512

Recapitulation

	Miles	Rate per Mile	Bonds
	525.078	$16,000	$ 8,401,248
	150.000	$48,000	7,200,000
	363.602	$32,000	11,634,264
	1,038.680	$26,222	$27,236,512

[a] *Wilson Rep.*, pp. 738–739 (Secretary of the Treasury Boutwell to J.M. Wilson, 21 Jan. 1873). See Appendix D.
[b] *Ibid.*, pp. 615–616 (Rollins, Abstract Ledger A of UP).

4. DURANT SHORN OF AUTHORITY ON CONSTRUCTION

On March 1, General Grant sent for Dodge and told him there was evidence of a "great swindle" in estimates for UP work done in Weber Canyon. "I saw from our conversation," wrote Dodge, "that as soon as he got in power he was determined to have a complete re-organization of the road East as far as the Government was concerned." [66] As President, he then gave orders to Hiram Price, a Government Director, that at the next UP meeting for election of Directors Durant must be put out, and named his choice of Government Directors—Price, Jesse Williams, and Congressman James Brooks.[67]

But the annual meeting of stockholders to elect Directors, scheduled for March 10, was forcibly prevented. In spite of that, some

[66] Dodge, *Autobiography*, p. 898.   [67] See table, p. 240.

actions were taken, for Oliver noted that day, "Agreed on Board of Directors and Bates cast the vote. Sheriffs with injunctions of Fisk present which were finally served upon us." The postponed meeting was not held until May 25, and in Boston. On March 11 Oliver penned, "Board of Directors gave all powers into hands of a Committee to go out on line of Road, and rescinded all authority given to Durant."

That same day, March 11, the Doctor addressed the Directors with a letter: "The object of the resolution of the executive committee adopted on July 3, 1868, having been fully accomplished, I therefore resign all authority conferred by said resolution, or by any resolution of the board." [68] That was all, so far.

Dillon wrote Dodge three days later from the West: "We have had a lively time of it since you left, but . . . have barricaded the old lion in his den, and if we all stand firm he will have to remain there. He seems very tame at this time yet he may be preparing for another leap . . . don't fail to have our election [of March 10] made valid." [69]

By an odd quirk in the UP's habitual mishaps, Durant would have been fired by this time if Fisk's injunction had not stopped the election of Directors that March 10. So Vice-President Durant appeared as the company's top brass at the Golden Spike ceremony two months later.

5. KANSAS PACIFIC CONNECTS WITH THE UP AT CHEYENNE

Off in another direction, the Congressional Act of 3 March 1869,[70] having allowed the stalled Union Pacific Railway Eastern Division to change to the less plagiaristic name of Kansas Pacific Railway, authorized it to contract with or lease the Denver Pacific Railroad. This independent company, led by John Evans, Governor of Colorado, was building from Cheyenne south to Denver, a distance of 106 miles, unsubsidized except for land grants. It will be recalled that the Act of 3 July 1866, amending the Act of 1864, already had authorized the Kansas Pacific, which was building west from Kansas City, to connect with the UP no more than 50 miles west of the meridian of Denver.[71] Congress thereby had created a rival road (subsidized with bonds and land grants to the 100th meridian) for over half of the length of the

---

[68] Records of UP Historical Museum; see also p. 281.
[69] Dodge, *Autobiography*, p. 903.
[70] 15 Statutes at Large 324, 348.   [71] See p. 140.

UP. Under the leadership of young General William J. Palmer, the KP finally reached Denver on 3 October 1870, and there connected with its leased Denver Pacific, which arrived shortly after. This completed a continuous line of 745 miles from Kansas City to Cheyenne.

Rivalry between the KP and UP remained keen, even bitter, for the next nine years. The issue of proper freight rates was fought in Congress and in the courts. Both the KP and DP became failures from an investment point of view, and in 1880 Jay Gould finally consolidated them and the Union Pacific *Railroad* Company into the new Union Pacific *Railway* Company.[72] To this day, the original line from Kansas City to Denver and thence to Cheyenne is a part of the UP.

6. RAILROADS TO MEET AT PROMONTORY

In the second week of March, about the time the UP entered Ogden, Grant called Dodge to the White House and told him he wanted the railroads to fix a meeting point at once, or Congress would do it for them. The President was now treating his trusted friend as an emissary to the Union Pacific. Soon after, Dodge met Montague on the road, and apparently they agreed on Promontory.[73] Other matters must have been settled, too, for on March 12 Oliver addressed a letter from North Easton to Dodge in angry terms:

I wrote you yesterday on matters of U.P.R.R. but today I have your letter of 10th and also agreement made with Central Pacific RR. That part of the agreement giving the Central Road the Bonds on the Road we build beyond Ogden is an outrage upon us and ought never to have been consented to. We have burdens enough to bear to have some little help in bearing them. But for us to give to the Central these bonds and let them pay us for the Road when they get ready will I fear break us down. I cant conceive how you should ever have consented to it. If you had known the condition of the Co you would not have done it. Certificates for these Bonds have already been sold and it calls upon us to raise money at once to redeem them & when if you had stood for Bonds of Govt on all the road we build we should have got them and had part of our pay While as it now stands we shall have a quarrel with CP to get any pay out of them. The rock and earth work is put down very much below what it is costing us. The feeling of our people is very strong against surrender of the bonds and limiting us to actual cost of the road . . . .[74]

---

[72] Records of UP Historical Museum; see also p. 509.   [73] *Ibid.*
[74] Dodge, *Papers*, vol. 157 (original ms.); Dodge, *Autobiography*, p. 920.

On April 9, from Boston, Oliver noted in his diary, "Instructed General Dodge to fix with Central point of junction at 1100 mile post." The next day, however, he disgustedly wrote: "Learned from papers that point of Junction is fixed (at Promontory) and am not satisfied at all with it."

UP and CP Agree: On April 9, in Washington, Vice-President Huntington and Chief Engineer Dodge, accompanied by stockholders Samuel Hooper and Rowland G. Hazard, met and the four signed an agreement. Huntington is said to have made the first move. He would buy the UP track between Ogden and Promontory; if the UP declined, the CP would build into Ogden anyway. The exact agreement reached that day follows:

For the purpose of settling all existing controversies between the Central Pacific and the Union Pacific railroad companies, of fixing the place of meeting between the two roads, and of securing harmonious and united action between them in future, the following agreement has been entered into between them, to-wit:

First: The place where the two roads shall meet and connect shall be at some point within eight miles west of Ogden to be hereafter mutually agreed on by said companies. Both companies to have an equal interest and share in the town site at such junction which shall include not less than eight sections of land.

Second: The Union Pacific company shall complete the track to the summit of Promontory Point to which place the Central shall build from the west, and the Central Pacific company shall pay to the Union the cost of the road without rolling stock from the terminus near Ogden as aforesaid to said Promontory Point, and shall pay to the Union one half the cost of the grading by the Union between the summit of Promontory and Monument Point done at this date.

Third: The Union shall draw U.S. bonds to the full amount per mile to the terminus near Ogden as aforesaid and the Central shall draw the balance of bonds and have the subsidy allowed by law on all that part of the track from the terminus westward.

Provided, the Central shall pay to the Union one half the net proceeds of all lands up to Bear River and if the City of Bear River [75] is located west of Bear River the sale of lots up to this date shall belong to the Union, the balance shall belong to the Central, and the sale of lots in said city of Bear River by the Union shall be valid; and upon making payment as provided in the second article, the Central shall own and

[75] A city of this name was never established. The site, 8 miles north of Ogden, became the UP station called Bonneville, now Hot Springs on the Oregon Short Line.

control the track from said terminus westward subject to the rights of said companies hereinafter, provided, the deficiency of Government bonds, if any, shall fall on the road west of the terminus, near Ogden, as aforesaid.

Fourth: In building any branches north or south between Humboldt Wells and Green River, both companies shall have equal privileges and both companies shall have the right to reach the traffic of or from said branches upon equal terms without any discrimination against either, and in their own cars.

If there is any disagreement or misunderstanding as to the terms of this agreement, it shall be referred to three referees, to be chosen as follows: One by the Union, one by the Central, and the third by those two; and it is further agreed that in estimating the cost earth work shall not exceed 50 cents per cubic yard, and solid rock $4.50 per cubic yard.

It is understood that the line agreed upon will be recognized by the Government as the established line of the Pacific Railroad.[76]

That same day the Senate happened to be debating the House resolution of March 29.[77] Senator Howard suddenly rose to make an important announcement. The railroads had just reached an agreement. Its intent should be adopted, he advised.

Congress Makes Up Its Mind: The next day, Saturday, April 10, the Joint Resolution was carried by the Forty-First Congress and became law. Under Section I appeared the pungent words: "The common terminus . . . shall be at or near Ogden; and the Union Pacific . . . shall build, and the Central Pacific . . . shall pay for and own, the railroad from the terminus aforesaid to Promontory Summit, at which point the rails shall meet and connect and form one continuous line." [78]

Now parallel grading over a distance of 200 miles became only a matter of history, and the UP/CP furor waned. Both companies relaxed, discharged all the men they could, and took their time in finishing up. The Central would roll along with about 60 easy, desert miles to go, while the UP had some 16 miles of slow, expensive work ahead.[79] At least, rationalized the Easterners, "We bagged Ogden and the Salt Lake trade, even if we failed to keep the Central out in the desert."

Oliver wrote Dodge again on the 12th from home:

---

[76] Records of UP Historical Museum.   [77] See p. 312.
[78] *Poland Rep.*, p. 197; see 16 Statutes at Large 56 for the complete Joint Resolution.
[79] See p. 336.

We have not yet learned the arrangement definitely, as we have only the Rumors of the papers. Any settlement is better than a constant fight, but the information is not as favorable as we hoped. The Central probably is not paying near as much as it has cost us. . . . Our money matters are in a sad state and I fear . . . we shall have some more difficulty with our men on line of Road Though I hope just as soon as we get our office removed to Boston to run things very much smoother. I want you to take full charge of the Engineering . . . and we must use the utmost economy.[80]

Poor Oliver! Next Sunday, he conscientiously noted, "Chaffin preached. So sleepy could not keep awake."

Dodge Justifies the Deal: General Dodge, too, was dead weary at home in Council Bluffs, but somehow he managed to stir himself enough on the 19th to answer Oliver's discontented letter of March 12.[81] The reply was both lucid and acerbic:

I am in receipt of your letter complaining of the agreement. I will state the case as plainly as I can and you must be the judge.

1st. Central Pacific bonds at the rate of $13,500 per mile were issued and delivered to and receipted for by the Central as far east as Ogden.

2nd. Our Attorneys concluded that we would be unable to break up that issue, or if it was broken, it must be in court, as a last resort in the U.S. Supreme Court.

3rd. The cabinet (Grant's) concluded it would be impossible to revoke it without legislation, which you are aware it was impossible to get, and advised a compromise, especially when we ascertained that we could not reach Monument Point.

4th. They were also of the opinion that it would be impossible to issue bonds to us over the same country until the other issue was legally nullified.

5th. On the decision and record as made by the Secretaries of the Interior and Treasury the Central had clear right to stop our crossing their grading (as we did and will). See Poppleton's letter that Hazard has, and Poppleton to Mr. Snyder on April 1st, 1869.[82]

6th. We could get no order for examination of our road beyond Ogden, while the law places examination of the Central entirely in the hands of the Surveyor General of California, and General Cox informed me he could not interfere . . . that the only remedy was to refuse to issue bonds . . . on grounds of uncompleted road.

[80] Dodge, *Papers*, vol. 157.   [81] See p. 316.   [82] Dodge, *Autobiography*, p. 921.

7th. Now, if under this state of affairs you can see where you were to get any pay for work west of Ogden, I cannot. You could have fought them as long as you pleased, but instead of compromising now you would finally have been forced to make your junction where the Central intersected you at Ogden. It is even impossible for us to reach Promotory Summit by the time the CP does . . . .

8th. The agreement enabled us to get the law [of April 10th] and the CP have now no right east of Promotory, until they pay us the cost of our work up to the common terminus; they cannot draw [any more] bonds on it. We have to have road accepted to Promotory and draw [the remaining] bonds therefor. The agreement, as far as it conflicts with the law in this case, is subordinate to it.

9th. Under the law you have the right to issue 1st mortgage bonds 190 miles in advance; your 1st mortgage bonds hold as far as your completed road; nothing in law or agreement takes off that lien; therefore all you could possibly get is the [balance of the] $32,000 per mile of government bonds, and whether you would rather have them at some future time, when your road is completed, as required in the report of the Commissioners, or whether you prefer cash for your work done as soon as you turn it over to the Central, is a matter for you to decide. If the CP do not choose to pay you for the road, then you can hold it until they do . . . .

On all these points . . . I have the written opinions of Cushing and Chandler [83] and am confident what the decisions of the Secretary of the Interior and Cabinet will be.

I made the best arrangement I could—it was that or nothing. I submitted it to Oakes Ames and informed him that it could be disagreed to before 12 o'clock the next day, but I do not believe there is a man in the board who, had he been present and known all the circumstances, but would have agreed to it, and would consider it a good bargain. I expect all who knew nothing of the circumstances would find fault with it. The great mistake you all labor under is the supposition that you were to override all the acts of the past administration, revoke what they had done and get a double issue of Bonds over the same ground—none of which would have done, as our lawyers told us the legal question was a prima facie case against us and we had to show fraud on it to break it up. The bonds were issued and receipted for by the Central Pacific Company [and] gave them the legal title to them, and how were you to get around it?

The cost of grading at 50 cents and rock at $4.50 I am told by the men in charge out there, is ample to cover it all, our contract price is much less.[84]

---

[83] Caleb Cushing and W.E. Chandler, lawyers for the UP.
[84] Dodge, *Autobiography*, pp. 933–934.

On the 28th, Oliver wired Duff, Dillon, and Price from Boston: "Must remain here on money matters—You have full powers of Board—Exercise your authority—Sidney Bartlett says while I am on hand at the Company headquarters here the Vice President has no power to act as President." [85] The next day Oliver also telegraphed to the same three at End of Track U.P.R.R. Utah: "You will make no permanent arrangement for connection—Change car only at end of the track laid by us—till they pay us—otherwise shall find it difficult making settlement with them—get matters into best shape you can— come home soon and let new Board authorize future arrangement." [86] At the same time he wired Dodge at end-o-track, "Duff, Dillon and Price have full power—and no one else."

These messages inspired J.M.S. Williams, the Treasurer of the UP, to write Dodge from Boston the same day: "Oliver Ames has sent out some good telegrams. They have the right ring of authority. He is disposed to take more responsibility than in N.Y. Sidney Bartlett, our ablest lawyer, says it is a mistaken idea that our by-law gives any power to the V.P." [87] But Oliver must have been having a bit of a jolt of some kind. His troubles as President had been mounting cruelly. In his diary of May 4, he said, "Had a very bad headache all day," and the next day, "Head ache this morning and most of the day very bad towards night. Took some whiskey which relieved it." He had always been a leader in the temperance movement.[88]

On May 6, Dodge wired Oliver that the track would be joined on the 10th.[89]

7. DURANT IS "KIDNAPPED" BY DAVIS'S TIE-CUTTERS

Durant and Duff were on their way west for the ceremonies when a strange incident occurred on May 6. It could have such serious effect on the unpaid labor situation over the entire road that the UP did their best to hush it up. As a result, many incorrect versions of the event have appeared in print. Their train was pulling into Piedmont, near the Aspen summit, when like a bolt from the blue rifles blazed, and the engine was stopped by ties piled on the track. A mob of some 300 armed men, all tie-cutters and graders on the UP, was waiting outside. Uncoupling the official car and waving the train

[85] Dodge, *Papers*, vol. 157 (original ms.).
[86] Records of UP Historical Museum; Dodge, *Autobiography*, p. 941.
[87] Dodge, *Autobiography*, p. 942.   [88] See p. 74.
[89] Dodge, *Autobiography*, p. 943.

onward, they swarmed around Durant. The spokesmen angrily demanded their back pay, overdue for months. They would hold Durant and Duff there until it was paid. The sum was said to be something like $200,000 or even more. Durant had no such amount, of course, but quietly assuring his captors that he was in full sympathy with their plight, he telegraphed Oliver Ames in Boston to send the money. Oliver flashed a wire to Dodge in Salt Lake City to send the troops instead.[90] Dodge ordered up a company of infantry from the nearest Army post at Fort Bridger. But Dillon, who had been appealed to by Dodge, for some unknown reason ordered the troop train not to stop at Piedmont. The kidnappers then wired Dodge to put up the money within 24 hours, or else.

Certain facts are verified. On May 7, Dodge wired Oliver from Echo City, "Tie outfit at Piedmont hold Duff & Durant under guard as hostage for payment of amount due them. You must furnish funds on Dillon's call." [91] That was done. The next day Dodge sent a second wire to Oliver from "End Track Utah": "Trouble at Piedmont will cause trouble in running department unless Snyder gets immediate help—if you wait until trains are stopped [everywhere] it will be too late to release them until we are forced to pay in fact everything due on line—half million at once will relieve necessities and enable us to keep moving—actions at Piedmont known everywhere & all know company was obliged to pay before officers were released—answer care Snyder." [92]

Durant Arranged It: Some years later, Dodge wrote a startling explanation of the damaging affair:

On May 6th, when Durant and Duff were coming west to attend the joining of the tracks, at the tie siding at Piedmont the Davis outfit captured their car and held them, refusing to let them go until they were paid for the estimates they had made on their contracts. There is no doubt this was an arrangement made by Durant for the purpose of forcing the Company to pay. It was a dispute between James W. Davis and Co. and Reed, the Superintendent of Construction, upon the amount due and he had refused to accept a great deal of the timber and ties they had brought in.[93] I was in Salt Lake at the time and immediately wired the commanding officer at Ft. Bridger to put a company on the train . . . to go to Piedmont and take possession of the car and the

---

[90] This message cannot be found in the records.

[91] Dodge, *Papers*, vol. 158 (original ms.); Dodge, *Autobiography*, p. 945.

[92] Dodge, *Papers*.   [93] See pp. 302 (Oliver Ames to Durant, 1 Jan. 1869), 255.

crowd that was there . . . But Dillon ordered the train, with the company aboard, to go through without stopping, which was a great mistake, but I did not hear of it until it was too late to stop it. There was nothing to do now but furnish the money to . . . release Duff. I knew Durant would be released any time he wanted to.[94]

Oliver expressed his suspicion of Durant in a letter to Dodge of May 12:

. . . Their seems to be no relief and we feel that the vortex out there will swallow all that can be raised out of our securities—and then perhaps the mobs on line of Road will stop the trains and the next thing we shall hear is that the trains have been stoped and Passengers Robed to pay starving men. It would have been better to have called out the Military and stoped this 1st mob and then we should have had no more trouble.

I am informed that Davis & Associate men were the parties stoping the train. Could it be one of Durants plans to have these men get their pay out of the Road and we suffer for his benefit   Durant is so strange a man that I am prepared to believe any sort of rascality that may be charged agnst him.[95]

B. Fisk Raids the Union Pacific

The Background: Youthful James Fisk Jr., the most improbable human parasite in the era of the Tweed Ring, and often called the "Barnum of Wall Street," had cast avaricious eyes on the budding Union Pacific as early as September 1867. Undoubtedly with the connivance of Durant, and probably with the counsel of their mutual good friend George G. Barnard, Justice of the New York State Supreme Court in Manhattan, he had attempted to seize control of the UP Board of Directors jointly with Durant by pretending to enter orders for 20,000 shares just prior to election day.[96] But his subscriptions had been checkmated on technical grounds by President Oliver Ames, and the meeting had been declared null and void, as has been told.[97] Fisk had warned he would "break" the UP anyway and had demanded delivery of the 20,000 shares. His next step had been the proper purchase of 6 UP shares. A pre-signed certificate (then customary for very small lots), dated 23 June 1868, had been delivered

[94] Dodge, *Autobiography*, pp. 944–945.   [95] Dodge, *Papers*, vol. 158 (original ms.).
[96] Records of UP Historical Museum.   [97] See pp. 186–187.

to him, registered in his name by the Register of Transfers.[98] It did not bear Fisk's "consent" to the Oakes Ames Contract, as thereby it might have more legal weight. No dividend was ever paid on it, nor was it ever endorsed or assigned on the back. Thus Fisk had become a legal stockholder and was to use that fact for all its $240 worth. A month later, Oliver had made this diary notation, "Our Fisk law suit not yet removed to U.S. Court . . . . Thought case dangerous and should not expose myself to injunction." Finally, on 27 July 1868, he had written Dodge:

> Jas. Fisk the fellow who figured in the Rock Island & Erie R.R. controversy and made a good deal of money out of them and is also one of the parties Durant got in to subscribe to 2,000,000$ of our Stock last fall and got out injunctions then for Durant in his fight against the Road. He now claims that Durant and [CM stockholder Josiah] Bardwell agreed to pay him expenses and don't come up, and he will now get what he can. He will . . . do every possible thing . . . to annoy us and make us pay him a liberal sum to withdraw his suits. Bushnell thinks he can buy him off with 50,000$.[99]

Blackmail Demanded: By March, 1869, Jim Fisk was in earnest tooth and nail. He warned that he would proceed with tactics like those where, in company with Jay Gould, and assisted by Boss William M. Tweed and Judge Barnard, he craftily had just wrested the control of the Erie Railroad away from financiers no less renowned than Cornelius Vanderbilt and Daniel Drew. "I will break you up," he bragged, "so that you cannot pay your obligations, and the first one you default on I will buy it up, and so on, until I get control of the road."[100] He demanded $75,000 blackmail, and if refused he would bring suit.[101] The UP refused, but by some kind of misunderstanding did pay $50,000 to some attorneys, who may have used it for the purpose of settling.[102] Next, on March 10, he broke up the annual election of Directors with sheriffs[103] and issued warrants for the arrest of all the Directors in New York. The day after, Oliver noted, "Went this morning to Court to have our case fixed up and to

---

[98] A photo of the certificate now hanging in the UP Museum, the gift of UP Director Oliver Ames (1864–1929; grandson of Oliver Ames Jr.), appears in Illus., Group 3.

[99] Dodge, *Papers,* vol. 155 (original ms.); Dodge, *Autobiography,* p. 791. See p. 282.

[100] *Wilson Rep.,* p. 48 (testimony of Bushnell).

[101] Testimony taken by the Judiciary Committee of the N.Y. Assembly in regard to Judges Cardoza and Barnard, p. 953.

[102] *Wilson Rep.,* pp. 295–296 (Oliver Ames), 317 (Alley). Both objected to the payment.

[103] See pp. 314–315.

answer for contempt. Case was put off. Gave bail in 20,000$ . . . Durant full of ways to come it over Fisk, which is to cover himself . . . *I would sooner lose the whole than compromise with Fisk.*" [104]

Receiver Appointed: Then, on March 17, Fisk caused Barnard to order the appointment of William M. Tweed Jr., son of the Boss of Tammany Hall, as receiver of the CM. Durant wrote Oliver at the Willard Hotel, Washington, two days later: "Receiver appointed of Credit Mobilier. Indirectly he has authority to take securities or money of Pacific Company, but will get nothing—He has nothing to do with books or papers of Pacific Company—and has found none of those of other Company (the CM)." [105]

The Safe Broken Into: But Fisk figured he had a lot to do with all the records, securities, and cash of both companies. By April 2, young Tweed, the "receiver," and eight deputies armed with sledge hammers and chisels were breaking open the office safe with great difficulty. Charles F. Tracy, Durant's lawyer for this case of the UP, strutted in and loudly exclaimed, "I order you burglars to cease this work and leave the building within five minutes, or I'll proceed against you both civilly and criminally." [106] But no one scattered, except the spectators who had been attracted by the general commotion. The UP entered a suit against Fisk for trespass, with $1,000,000 damages. Durant soon appeared and caustically remarked that while he hoped Tweed would be satisfied when he reached the contents, the lock was already injured so much that his key would never work. Tweed was said to reply, "I'm just going to make sure all those papers and bonds will not be stolen by someone." When the door at last was broken open, there was a skirmish between clerks and deputies to grab the contents. Nothing important was there.

Only just in time, it seems, Durant, through a CM clerk to whom he had given the key, had removed the documents for his (Durant's) own purposes, knowing he was about to be fired, and had them copied so as to be prepared for another legal fight if he felt so disposed. Many, if not all, of these copies now repose among Durant's *Papers,* the gift of one of the Doctor's descendants.[107]

As to the money and securities in the safe, Bushnell testified much later:

[104] Italics by C.E.A.   [105] Records of UP Historical Museum.
[106] New York *Post,* 2 Apr. 1869.   [107] Records of UP Historical Museum.

When the trouble arose in the spring of 1869, we had on hand in New York ten millions of the first-mortgage bonds; we had on hand seven millions and odd of land-grant bonds, on all of which we had borrowed every dollar we could get on them. We had made the fatal mistake of putting the price of our bonds so high that the sales had stopped completely . . . We had an immense debt on hand, not less than thirteen or fourteen millions, and just then Fisk came down upon us with his blackmailing suit, just as we were going to hold an election. You know the history of Judge Barnard's taking possession of our office. Our bonds were scattered, and every single director of the road was driven out of New York, with some apprehension of Ludlow Street Jail—every single one of them except myself. The book-keepers were driven out, and the bonds, in the great hurry to get them away from the reach of the sheriff, were scattered, and many of them lost [over $400,000]. I gathered them up, all I could, and disposed of them at 85 for the first-mortgages bonds, and 55 for the land-grants, to raise money to meet the obligations . . . and I suppose the company had to sacrifice six or seven millions on account of that attack on us.[108]

But Bushnell was often prone to exaggerate. James Brooks said, "the cost was a million, some think as much as $3,000,000." [109] Probably several millions was near enough by way of the temporary depreciation of market prices.[110] The first Mortgages suddenly broke from 102 to 65 when the "receivership" became known.[111] However, by May 11 they were "back to 93 bid, very few offering." [112]

In the meantime, Oliver noted in his diary on March 25, "Judge Blatchford [Samuel, of the U.S. Circuit Court in New York] issued Mandamus to have the Fisk case brought before him. Came home in noon train to dinner. Had a large party and it went off very slow." And, on April 1, "Duff went with Bushnell to NY to see if he could do anything with Durant to find out his true views on the matter & see whether he is interested in Fisk's suit."

On April 6, Glidden and Williams sent a message to Dodge: "The statement of Oakes Ames and others published today must help the Senate, it is a good statement." [113] It was an affidavit before a referee, taking three long columns in the New York *Times*. It declared, among many other things, that the six shares of UP which Fisk had

---

[108] *Wilson Rep.*, pp. 47–48.   [109] *Poland Rep.*, p. 260.
[110] Records of UP Historical Museum.
[111] Judiciary Committee of the New York Assembly in regard to Judges Cardoza and Barnard, p. 955 (testimony of Bushnell); Trottman, p. 50.
[112] Dodge, *Papers*, vol. 158 (J. M. S. Williams' telegram to Duff and Dillon).
[113] Dodge, *Autobiography*, p. 928.

bought in his name were purely for the purpose of bringing an annoying suit against the company; that Fisk had never paid any money on his subscriptions prior to the election of Directors; that he had raised his price for settlement to $75,000—later to $100,000; and if no settlement then was made, he would have the UP put into receivership.[114] Considering the special hazards of the work, the affidavit went on, no contract could have been made with anyone other than stockholders for less than 15 per cent of the actual cost. Finally, all the allegations of McComb in his threatened suit against Oakes and the Directors of the CM were erroneous and untrue in fact. The affidavit, dated April 5, was signed by Oakes Ames, Durant, Bushnell, Dillon, and Alley.[115]

Even in the Federal Court the intricate affair dragged on for years, at a very considerable legal expense to the UP. Jim Fisk, as might have been expected, was murdered in cold blood at the age of thirty-seven in January 1872, the target of his former partner and suitor of his favorite mistress. That same year, Judge Barnard was impeached for outrageous corruption. Not until June 1877, after Oliver's death, was this grotesque episode in the affairs of the UP finally ended by the payment to Fisk's widow of $20,000—plus the then market price of 65 for the contentious little six shares.[116]

The UP Moves to Boston: Thus, Congress had a fourth good reason, and an urgent one, to enact the Joint Resolution of April 10. The opening words are quoted: "Resolved, That the stockholders of the Union Pacific Railroad Company, at a meeting to be held on 22 April 1869 at the city of Boston (with power to adjourn from day to day), shall elect a board of directors for the ensuing year; and said stockholders are hereby authorized to establish their general office at such place in the United States as they may select at said meeting . . . ." [117]

Following this more cheering news, the stockholders voted to move the office to Boston, and on May 2 Oliver wrote Dodge, "We have taken down our sign in New York and given up the offices . . . . When we can get our books away from New York and cleaned out from that sink of corruption, we shall feel safe and not till then." [118] The change was a great relief to Oliver and the other Boston Directors, who were being worn down by the incessant trips to and from New York. Also

[114] See p. 323.   [115] New York *Times*, 6 Apr. 1869, p. 8.
[116] Records of UP Historical Museum.
[117] *Poland Rep.*, pp. 196–197 (Resolution in full, 16 Statutes at Large 56).
[118] Dodge, *Autobiography*, p. 943.

the Ameses, particularly Oliver, could devote much more time to the Shovel Works. The full postponed meeting for election of Directors was held on May 25, with the organization meeting following the next day.[119]

C. Construction Under Durant Until March 11

1. BUILDING IN THE WINTER

Now surrounded in the Wasatch, there upon the high divide between the waters of the Bear and the Weber, almost at the Promised Land but not quite, the Union Pacific was experiencing all the rigors of the Central's Sierra. Winter enfolded deeper and deeper, burying shack and tent and grade; behind, 200 miles of track at a time were put out of commission when the blizzards swept the Laramie Plains; for weeks at a time neither supplies nor material moved forward; during three months the construction force fought doggedly, cut off, and tortured by the delays and by the thought that the Central was forging on. The work continued. Those were the orders: work all winter, as all summer and fall. Thaws succeeded freezes, but the snow had gathered twenty feet, and the grade, shovelled partially bare, was a white-walled galley . . . . The tracks sought the canyon bottom; and here the mushy ground yielded until crowbars were used to steady the superstructure while the construction train crept over. The track-men stuck, but they demanded $3.50 a day; so did the company graders; they got it. Sunday was forgotten, except in doubled price. The Mormon workers at $5 a day to man and team required their $10 on Sunday. It was given, and earned. Where sub-contractors dodged the spring-sinks and the heavy cuts, Casement flung his tireless Irish into the breach.[120]

In his last annual report to President Ames, dated 1 December 1869, Chief Engineer Dodge gave official praise to his men:

Too much credit cannot be given for the successful battle with the elements, thus demonstrating the possibility of building railroads under such difficulties, in altitudes so high and at any season of the year. No one can obtain at this time an intelligent idea of the difficulties met and overcome; to appreciate them one had to be present and witness the work. . . . Men who went out in the morning with overcoats on, and would have to work with overcoats on all day, were not able to do very large days' works.

[119] See pp. 345–346.   [120] Sabin, pp. 190–191.

There was a mighty blizzard late in February, blockading the tracks west of Cheyenne for 10 days. It stopped all movement of material needed at the front. Casement wired that his men were "all worked out and frozen," and that it was "impossible to get work done." All passenger trains were being sent out fully provisioned, with cooking arrangements aboard.[121] Casement wired Snyder, "You can't get trains over this division by sending a snow outfit ahead with provisions, and as soon as you get through a cut have train follow. Have seen a cut fill up in two hours which took 100 men 10 hours to shovel out . . . . Cant more than keep engines alive when it blows."[122]

2. DURANT'S WILD EXTRAVAGANCE CONTINUES

General Superintendent Webster Snyder, out on the line January 4, reported to Dodge:

. . . In construction the waste of money is awful . . . . The track west of Aspen is not fit to run over and we are ditching trains daily. Grading is done at an enormous expense . . . . Track tonight is at Castle Rock . . . . The ties cost $4.50 each on the ground . . . . The company can't stand such drafts as I know the Construction Department must be making . . . . Would like to know what I am to be paid. Reed and Seymour have salaries of $8,000.[123]

On January 11, from Boston, J.M.S. Williams wrote Dodge a long, caustic letter about the Doctor, and happened to reveal the names of the Executive Committee who voted in favor of that key resolution of 3 July 1868:

Since the Executive Committee on the 2nd of July last (Duff, Lambard, McComb and Brooks) passed that order . . . putting the locating engineers under Durant's control,[124] I have no faith or hope in their operations. The Executive Committee deserve to be swindled out of two millions as they will by Durant.[125]

Oliver warned Durant on January 14:

. . . It is very important that you should have the line built without change from Location as fixed by Blickensderfer if possible . . . essential

---

[121] Dodge, *Autobiography*, p. 895.   [122] *Ibid.*, p. 897 (Feb. 27).   [123] *Ibid.*, p. 869.
[124] See p. 281. The date of the meeting was July 3; these four made a majority.
[125] Dodge, *Autobiography*, p. 880.

changes might affect the opinion of Com'rs . . . . We should do everything possible to secure their favor. Warren, Blickensderfer and Williamson are the Commission . . . to examine Central and fix the Point of
Junction.[126]

Echo City: On January 15 the track reached the mouth of Echo
Canyon and entered the little settlement of Echo City, which "held
high carnival and general jubilee on the occasion." [127] Here the first
Mormons had turned south, not north like the railroad, and trekked
up the Weber River and over very steep grades in the Wahsatches to
drop into the Promised Land. That day Oliver reassured Dodge,
". . . I hope you will feel that though the Dr may want power and
exercises it without judgement frequently yet the Board of Directors
are strongly your friends and I hope you will not let your feelings against Durant lead you into any demonstrations against the
Road." [128]

Blickensderfer, now serving on Browning's commission of four,[129]
wrote Dodge the next day from Salt Lake City:

> I regret to hear that the work west of Green River has cost so largely.
> . . . There is no doubt that the thing has been mismanaged and that the
> same results could often have been obtained at a greatly reduced cost.
> . . . It cannot be that rottenness has never visited Echo City and its
> vicinity . . . . What excites my wonder is that such men as Ames and
> some others could not foresee this last summer.[130]

Oakes's Last Letter to the Doctor: Oakes, in Washington, on the
16th had just handed in his large bond subscriptions [131] and felt
stirred to brush up Durant a bit:

> We have had a hard time here to get our bonds for our completed
> road and find that the Secy of the Interior claims that we should build
> on the Central P line to the head of Echo. that he had accepted their
> map to that place I find that the Central claim that they will meet us
> at the mouth of the Tunnel. and that we cannot go beyond a completed
> continuous line by the Law of 66.
> We have now got commissioner appointed by the Govt to go out and
> decide the line between the end of completed track of the two roads. I

---

[126] Durant, *Papers,* 1–3–26–70; see also p. 308. The point of junction was fixed before
they could do anything about it.
[127] Sacramento *Union,* 19 Jan. 1869.   [128] Dodge, *Papers,* vol. 156 (original ms.).
[129] See p. 308.   [130] Dodge, *Autobiography,* p. 886.   [131] See p. 304.

would suggest that you conform to our line run by Blinckensdofer as closely as possible or we may have our line rejected, and the bonds withheld if they should do that we shall have hard work financially and may be broken down entirely we cannot afford to fight the Government now if we can in the future and as the Govt have selected their Commissioners we must treat them properly. and conform to the line so closely that our line and road shall be accepted. I hope you will have the road in shape to get 60 miles at least accepted. while the commissioners are out there now.

I was at N.Y. yesterday Mr. Crane was not in during the day Money is very hard with them and the stockholders are raising their pro Rata of 80 per cent on their Stock in the Contracting Co   Mr. Crane I suppose will attend to yours Some of the Co say they will do their share if *all* the rest will. You better write them that you will do your share. Hope the road is progressing fast and that we shall win our line 1200 miles of road.[132]

Oliver, in New York, penned Durant the same day that Oakes did:

. . . Everything depends on the economy and vigor with which you press the work on construction. We hear here awful stories of the cost of the work and the thieving of our employees—I hope you will pay no estimates until the work has been remeasured by disinterested engineers. Ties are said to cost $4 each laid on the track when contract price is but one dollar. I hope you will be able to protect the Road. Let us also have your approval of our arrangements to raise money on the Land Grants.[133]

The mystic 1,000th milepost, where stood a large lone fir between the track and the Weber, was passed on January 20.[134] Back in New York, salesman Cisco took the occasion to run another ad in the *Chronicle,* dated February 13, 1869 (see Illus., Group 3).

Snyder again complained to Dodge on February 3:

. . . From Bryan to Wahsatch [108 miles] it will cost an average of $4,000 per mile to put the road in good shape. From Aspen to Wahsatch our trains make but 6 miles per hour on account of condition of road bed . . . Track laying has not been advanced one foot because we caught [up to] the graders twice west of Aspen . . . I will get out unless there is certainty of a change in March [stockholders' meeting].[135]

---

[132] Durant, *Papers,* 1–3–28–15 (original ms.).

[133] *Ibid.,* 1–3–26–71 (original ms.). See also p. 304.

[134] See p. 336; Sabin, 198 (photo).   [135] Dodge, *Autobiography,* p. 885.

On February 4, J.W. Davis, tie contractor, telegraphed Durant, "Private conference. Snow wants coal contract 200 tons per day at $6 This will make all right if I am authorized to pledge it. Regard this very important to you." [136] This might indicate that Durant did have "an interest" in the Davis contract.[137] No one east knew until February 26 that Durant had assigned the extension of the Oakes Ames Contract to Davis the previous November.[138]

"Vice President" Durant telegraphed "G.M. Dodge, M.C." via Western Union from New York on February 3: "I telegraphed you some time since not to send instructions west without first submitting the same to me. You are away from the work attending to other business and are not sufficiently posted if you cannot find time to report here I shall of necessity be obliged to supercede you." [139]

Durant wired Snyder on February 25 to send 800 flat cars at once, adding, "If you can't send the cars, send your resignation on and let some one operate the road who can." [140]

On February 29 the track reached Devil's Gate bridge, six miles from the mouth of Weber Canyon, and 66 miles from Promontory. The Central was 40 miles east of Humboldt Wells [141] and more than 144 miles from Promontory.

Ogden: The UP track arrived at 25th Street and Wall Avenue in the key city of Ogden at 2:30 p.m. on Sunday, March 7. This was 1,028 miles from Omaha.[142] Crocker's rails were then 184 miles away.[143] But the celebrations were delayed until the next day. Most of the Mormon population of 1,500 turned out when the brass band, artillery salutes, and locomotive whistles all opened up at once. Then came the long, official speeches under the banners hung between arching trees: "Hail to the Highway of Nations! Utah Bids you Welcome!" Indeed, Utah had been sorely isolated through many years. Ogden had been laid out by Brigham Young 19 years earlier. Today its population is over 70,000 and it is an important junction for several railroads. That same day, 8 March 1869, Brigham Young organized the Utah Central Railroad Company to cover the 37 miles from Ogden to Salt Lake City. He sold its control to the UP three years later.

[136] *Ibid.* [137] See p. 332.
[138] Dodge, *Autobiography*, p. 890; see also p. 255; Oliver Ames's diary, 26 Feb. 1869.
[139] Dodge, *Papers*, vol. 156; see also pp. 275–278. [140] Dodge, *Autobiography*, p. 896.
[141] *Ibid.*, p. 898; see also p. 336. [142] Dodge, *Annual Report*, 1869, p. 27.
[143] Dodge, *Autobiography*, p. 915.

Union Pacific poster for 10 May 1869.
(Courtesy of Union Pacific.)

Oliver Jr.'s diary, 22 May 1869.

The rails are joined at Promontory,
10 May 1869. Dodge (*right*) and
Montague, rival Chief Engineers, clasp hands.
"No. 119" (*right*) and "Jupiter" (*left*).
(Photo by Col. Savage. Courtesy of Union Pacific.)

Omaha in 1871. Ferry *H.C. Nutt* unloading cars.
Left: Missouri River Bridge under construction.
(Painting by Vic Donahue. Courtesy of Northwestern Bell Telephone Co., Omaha.)

First bridge over the Missouri under construction, 1872;
looking towards Council Bluffs.
(Courtesy of Union Pacific.)

Oakes to "Dear Katie,"
his daughter-in-law,
22 February 1873.
(Courtesy of Richard Harte.)

Last photo of Oakes Ames, *c.* 1872.
(Ames Family, *Oakes Ames, A Memorial Volume.*)

Jay Gould.
(Courtesy of Union Pacific.)

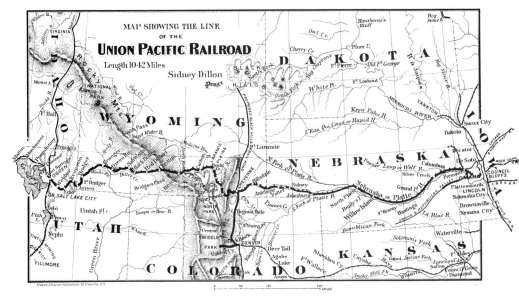

Map of Union Pacific, 1042 miles, 1878.
(Courtesy of Union Pacific.)

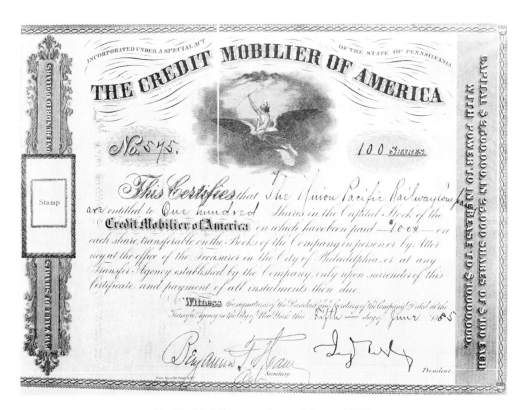

Credit Mobilier stock certificate, 1885.
(Courtesy of Union Pacific.)

Governor Oliver Ames, 1880.
(Gov. Oliver Ames, *Papers.*)

7 Friday

In N.Y. At 11 o'clock met Gould and in about 30 minutes made a trade with him selling 6250 shares of C B & P stock at $250 per share payable ½ in New UP 6% bonds & ½ in Kansas Consolidated bonds, 6%. Gould wrote agreement which we both signed. Gould & Sage were delighted with their trade & so was I, and all our party. Gould told me he would allow me 200 for 1000 shares more. Left for home on the boat. Sale amt to $1562500. Gould & Dillon say they want me to be a director in the Union Pacific RR.

Governor Oliver's diary,
7 November 1879.

Unity Church and parsonage, North Easton, 1877.
(Chaffin.)

Ames Free Library, North Easton, 1883.
(Chaffin.)

Oliver Ames Jr., *c.* 1875.
(Portrait by Lazaro.
Courtesy of Ames Free Library.)

Oliver Ames Jr.
(Bronze medallion by Augustus Saint-Gaudens.
Courtesy of Ames Free Library.)

Monument to Oakes and Oliver Ames, 1881, at site of
original station in Sherman. Plaque of Oakes, east side.
Inset: Quarrying rock for the Monument, 1880–1881.
(Courtesy of Union Pacific.)

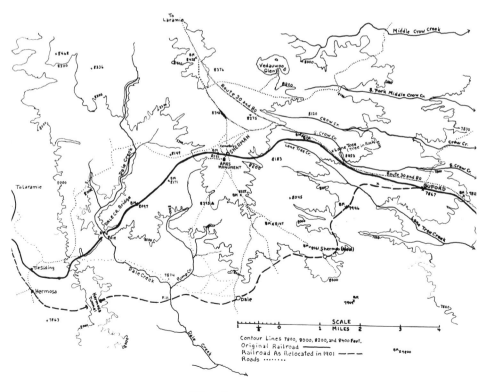

The Sherman Pass.

View of North Easton *c.* 1881.
Oakes Ames Memorial Hall at left center.
(Courtesy of Elise Ames Parker.)

Oakes Ames Memorial Hall, 1881.
(Chaffin.)

Durant's Davis Contract Backfires: Durant now opened up the Davis contract fight[144] by wiring Dodge, who was in Washington, on March 8:

You have so largely over estimated the amounts due Contractors, that it becomes my duty to suspend your acting as Chief Engineer until you give a satisfactory explanation of the same . . . before the report becomes public . . . . When it gives Contractors hundreds of thousands of dollars it creates suspicion that all is not right.[145]

Dodge, knowing the Doctor was now leading from weakness, simply wired back, "The last estimate was made up from data furnished by Mr. Reed and Mr. Crane. If there is any mistake in it I could not detect it."[146] Years later, Durant testified: "I am aware that I expended more money in building the road than some thought advisable. This I did in order to secure good work. The railroad company was not the loser, for it was to pay a fixed sum per mile, and by my action the contractors only were deprived of a portion of their profits by the increased expenditure."[147]

Reed's records indicate that the actual cost of the road west of Piedmont was more than $80,000 a mile.[148]

Furthermore, Dodge testified years later that on the 46 miles east of Promontory the actual contract cost of track, grading, masonry, bridging, and rock work—without equipment—was over $4,000,000, or $87,189 a mile. If equipment had been added, the contract cost would have been $94,700 a mile.[149]

Thus ended the bewildering winter fiasco of the lonely Doctor, for on March 11 the Directors revoked all of his authority on the line.[150]

D. Construction After Durant

Durant was off the line, to be sure, but his trails of the past 12 months kept turning up. For instance, some bridges and foundations for permanent masonry on Black's Fork and near Green River were found placed as far as 200 feet away from the completed track.[151] Oliver issued notice to the sub-contractors that unless the work was "first class," as agreed, he would have it done over at their expense.

---

[144] *Ibid.,* p. 902; see also pp. 254–255.
[145] Durant, *Papers,* 1–3–36–16; see also p. 289.   [146] *Poland Rep.,* p. 378.
[147] *Ibid.*   [148] Records of UP Historical Museum.
[149] U.S. Pacific Railway Commission, pp. 3799–3801.   [150] See pp. 314–315.
[151] Dodge, *Autobiography,* p. 906 (Blickensderfer to Dodge, Mar. 27).

Thieving, as Oliver put it, continued mysteriously in the construction department. Indians stole four teams from Boyle's camp and shot four men on April 4.[152] There were many other serious mistakes and troubles, far too many to mention.

Corinne and Parallel Roads: On April 7, the first train pulled into Corinne at the then navigable mouth of Bear River, 27 miles beyond Ogden City. The townsite had been laid out on March 25 for a terminal base.[153] It was a pretty name, and it was to flourish in a fevered sort of way as a large freighting center with more than 100 saloons and gambling houses. But the scandalized Mormons, hearing of the early pistol feuds, religiously kept distance from this new and last gentile Hell-on-Wheels. Nevertheless, for some years it was Utah's second largest city, with a population of 5,000.[154]

The Central's bare grading could be seen right in Corinne, eroding dismally a foot or two above the table-flat, glaring-white, salt-encrusted bed of ancient Lake Bonneville, closely parallel to the tracks the UP had laid. To this day, one can cautiously motor down from Promontory on the surface of curving sections of the original but abandoned UP roadbed, over the high fills and through long, deep rock cuts; and there can be traced the Central's never-used grading alongside, criss-crossing now and then—stark mementos both of human failure and achievement—both of Government and builders.[155]

All work slowed down after April 10, when Congress fixed the junction point at long last. The UP stopped grading west of Promontory at once, and by the 15th the Central withdrew their entire construction force from all points east of the Summit.[156]

Dodge wired Oliver on the 21st to stop any more drafts being drawn on subcontractors' accounts unless authorized by Dodge's own letters. This was to thwart any drafts by Durant, or anyone else, in attempts to pay off contractors.[157] These were not the only persons who would wait long months for money properly due them.

Ten Miles of Track in a Day: April 28 the Central came within 3½ miles of Promontory, largely by dint of joining just over 10 miles of

---

[152] *Ibid.,* pp. 927–928.

[153] Harold E. Jensen and Jesse H. Jameson, "A Railroad to the Pacific," *SUP News* (Salt Lake City), Apr.–May 1959. Records of UP Historical Museum.

[154] Village Railroad Museum, Corinne, Utah; tablet erected by Utah Road Commission, 1959.

[155] A photo of the parallel tracks appears in Galloway near p. 183.

[156] Records of UP Historical Museum.   [157] Dodge, *Autobiography,* p. 941.

winding, uphill track in 11 hours of extreme exertion. Crocker's "pets," as the gang of coolies were known, and their Irish foremen under Jim Strobridge, had relentlessly spiked down into ties (all bedded previously) 3,520 rails, each 30 feet long and weighing 560 pounds. That amounted to the eight Irish rail-lifters handling 11.2 short tons per man per hour, without mechanical aid and with no relief. The long-hardened lifters earned and got four days' wages for one day's sweating. The all-time record feat was witnessed by Dodge, Durant, and the Casements—probably a bigger crowd, including the laborers, than appeared at the Golden Spike ceremony. Apparently the show was the outcome of an old $10,000 bet between Durant and Crocker, which the latter won hands down.[158]

Promontory Reached: On April 30, eight days ahead of the original appointed time, the Central's track reached the meeting point at Promontory, while the UP still had a bit more than 6 miles to go over some very difficult ground.[159] A temporary wooden trestle 450 feet long and 60 feet high, only a mile east of Promontory, was not passable until May 5, and a very long rock cut was not opened up until May 8. Dodge wisely decided to save time by hauling rails and material by wagon around these obstacles. On April 29, according to the diary of Colonel Leonard H. Eicholtz, the top bridge engineer since 1867, track-laying was started *eastward from Promontory.* As an afterthought, by laying down a complete siding and Y-track at Promontory during the night of May 9–10, Dodge established claim to the use of the terminal.[160]

UP Delayed by Washouts: By mutual consent the date of meeting had been fixed for Saturday, May 8. It had been done "far enough ahead so that the trains coming from New York and San Francisco would have ample time to reach Promontory in time to take part in the ceremonies." [161] But outrageous weather held up the ill-fated UP contingent, much to the chagrin and discomfort of Governor Leland Stanford and his parties, who had arrived on May 7. They now could twiddle their thumbs in the cars or make sightseeing tours to Salt Lake City, Weber Canyon, or nearer points. When Durant and Duff had been released from the suspicious episode at Piedmont, they had

[158] Records of UP Historical Museum.

[159] *Ibid.;* Dodge, *Autobiography,* p. 943; Perkins, p. 238 (Dodge's letter to his wife, 2 May).

[160] Records of UP Historical Museum.

[161] Dodge, *How We Built the Union Pacific,* p. 68.

PROGRESS OF THE TRACK, 1869

Date	End of UP Track at or Near	UP Miles from Omaha [a]	UP Miles from Ogden Junction [a]	UP Miles from Monument Point [b]	CP Miles from Monument Point [b]	UP Elev.[a]
Jan. 1 [b]	"Stage station at foot of Echo Grade" (probably Emory, later a UP station) [b]	982	50	126	188 [b]	5,925 [c]
Jan. 15 [d]	Echo (City), entrance to Weber Valley	991	41	117		5,540
Jan. 20 [e]	"1,000 Mile-Post" [e]	1,000	32	108	145 [e]	5,200 [c]
Jan. 21 [c]	Tunnels 3 and 4 (not then finished) 3 miles W. of Devil's Slide	1,003	29	105		5,150 [c]
Feb. 29 [c]	Devil's Gate	1,018	14	90		4,870
Mar. 2 [f]	Uintah ("Mouth of Weber River")	1,023	9	85	120 [f]	4,560
Mar. 7 [g]	Ogden (City)	1,028	4	80		4,340 [c]
Mar. 9 [c]	Ogden (at point of ultimate junction with CP)	1,032	0	76	108 [g]	4,340 [c]
Mar. 12 [c]	Hot Springs (Bonneville)	1,041	9 W.	67	100 [c]	4,310
Mar. 27 [e]	Corinne ("22 miles W. of Ogden")	1,055	23 W.	53	70 [e]	4,294
Apr. 10	Date of Junction at Promontory set by Congress	1,068 [c]	36 W.	40	35 [e]	4,300 [c]
Apr. 21 [h]	Blue Creek	1,074	42 W.	34	6 E.[h]	4,360
Apr. 30 [i]	3 miles E. of Promontory	1,081	49 W.	27	24 E.[i]	4,750 [c]
May 9	Promontory [j]	1,084 [k]	52 W.	24	24 E.[i]	4,934
	Monument Point	1,108	76 W.	0	0	4,290

Total miles laid in 1869: 102
Average miles laid per day, excluding Sundays: 0.93

[a] Dodge, *Annual Report*, 1869, pp 24–27; UP, "Time Table No. 24, June 20th, 1870," with several adjustments in mileage to correspond with UP, *Freight Tariff to Take Effect June 1st, 1870*. See Profile, Illus., Group 3.
[b] Progress of Track, 1868, see p. 295.
[c] Author's estimate.
[d] Sacramento *Union*, 19 Jan. 1869.
[e] Dodge, *Autobiography*, p. 915.
[f] *Ibid.*, p. 914.
[g] *Ibid.*, p. 915. Celebration at Ogden the next day.
[h] Dodge, *Autobiography*, p. 937. Snyder wired Dodge on Apr. 21 that the UP was within 12 miles of Promontory Point and the CP within 18 miles. The CP laid 10 miles on Apr. 28.
[i] Perkins, p. 238, quotes Dodge's letter of May 2 to his wife that the CP arrived at Promontory on Apr. 30. See p. 338.
[j] The Golden Spike celebration took place on May 10. See pp. 337–343.
[k] All the above mileages *exclude* the 2 miles north of Omaha to the "initial point."

E.—East of Monument Point.   W.—West of Ogden.

rejoined the official party bound west; but on reaching lower Weber Canyon, the melting snows funneling off the mountains and a prolonged downpour combined with too hasty construction work, slowed the train to a dog-trot. The Strawberry Ford bridge was unsafe. Worse, at Devil's Gate the new bridge was declared impassable, and Eicholtz had to rush in a new 50-foot truss. Passengers were transferred around it in the rain. Not till late Sunday afternoon was the party able to get out of the gorge. Thus, their special train never arrived at Promontory until 10 o'clock Monday morning, May 10, only barely in time for the postponed rituals.[162] However, as far as the weather at Promontory was concerned, the delay proved most fortunate.

In the meantime, it was just too late for Stanford to put off the celebrations already set at San Francisco and Sacramento. So these joyous Californians held their elaborate affairs on the 8th anyway, and continued on with them for the next two days. Thus, some West Coast journals published inaccurate details of the Promontory story before the event.

Back in Promontory, on May 9, Dodge finally telegraphed Oliver in Boston: *"The end of the Union Pacific is 1,085 miles and 4,680 feet from the initial point.*[163] *You can make affidavit of completion of road to Promontory Summit."* [164]

E. The Golden Spike

May 10 at Promontory: Monday, May 10, dawned with a skim of ice on water left standing. The storm had rolled by, and a fresh northwesterly was snapping the Star-Spangled Banner above the telegraph pole which marked the gap between the track-ends topping the pass between the North and South Promontory Mountains. A brilliant morning sun in a deep blue, cloudless sky flooded this brownish, red and yellow little saucer of a valley dotted with pungent, blue-gray clumps of unchanging sagebrush and greenish, stunted cedars high on the slopes amidst an occasional snow patch. The thermometer warmed steadily into the 60's as noon approached. "Promontory town, of a single miserable street lined with canvas and rough board shacks, was arrayed, the drab, in all her festal clothes. It was her hour. For one brief heyday she occupied the centre of the National stage and acted as hostess to giants of finance and industry . . . . She stood upon her present, not upon her rather dubious past, short and turbulent." [165] The visitors, grateful for the change to fine weather, rolled slowly up the sharply winding grade, and reveled in the lovely spectacle of the rugged, snow-capped Wasatch Range towering behind white Corinne and the great lake hundreds of feet below, shimmering with foam-flecked waves that gradually vanished in a blue haze.

---

[162] Records of UP Historical Museum.
[163] To be exact, it had just been measured by chain all the way from Omaha.
[164] Dodge, *Autobiography*, p. 945; Records of UP Historical Museum.
[165] Sabin, p. 212.

Surely, this was a moment to forget toils and tussles and just enjoy a simple spot of history in the making.

Many of the great libraries of the nation have innumerable pages on the day of the Golden Spike, but "there is no single and accurate account of all the details." [166] The words that follow draw a little composite picture based on the more authentic records.

The two UP trains and one CP train were waiting when Governor Stanford's special pulled up near the flag at about eleven o'clock. Officials and their guests, reporters of the press, infantrymen, and bandsmen were surrounded by hundreds of curious, jostling, cheering Chinese and Irish workers of the track. Altogether, it was a crowd of just about 1,000 persons, using the average of a dozen widely varying guesses.

Who Were There: Arriving from the East that morning were only three UP Directors: Vice-President Durant, "in a smart black velvet coat and a modish New York tie that in brilliancy rivalled, according to a chronicler, the other 'last tie' "; [167] courtly Sidney Dillon, also one of the Seven Trustees; and portly, white-haired John Duff, another of the Seven Trustees and a member of the UP Executive Committee. Of course, there was Chief Engineer Dodge, looking like business, and co-master with Edgar Mills of arrangements, perforce made on short notice. Other UP associates already noticed in this book were Sam Reed, James Evans, Silas Seymour, and the two Casement brothers; also, H.M. Hoxie, L.H. Eicholtz, M.F. Hurd, J.W. Davis, J.A. Williamson, H. Bissell, and Edward Creighton.

Coming from the West, Leland Stanford, the forty-five-year-old Governor of California and President of the CP, had with him in his special car only one Director, Charles Marsh; three Federal Commissioners of Inspection for the CP, the Honorable F.A. Tritle, W.G. Sherman (a brother of the General), and J.W. Haines; also, Governor Safford of Arizona, Judge Sanderson of the Supreme Court of California, Collector Gates of Nevada, Dr. Harkness of the Sacramento *Press,* and Edgar Mills, son of a leading banker of Sacramento. In the second train, the only other important CP officials who appear in this volume were Chief Engineer Samuel S. Montague and Superintendent of Construction James H. Strobridge.

Important guests joined in from both directions: Governors of Wyoming and Utah, a member or two of Congress, and a couple of

---

[166] Records of UP Historical Museum.   [167] Sabin, p. 215; see also p. 315.

Mayors. Under orders were 250 men of the U.S. 21st Regiment of Infantry, including a large band, and Ogden's 10th Ward band "resplendent in the gayest of uniforms and $1200 worth of the brightest of new instruments." Earning their way were some twenty "Knights of the Quill" from the presses of New York, Boston, Springfield, Chicago, Omaha, Salt Lake City, Sacramento, and San Francisco; plus, of course, the Associated Press. Three official photographers with their bulky, slow, wet-plate cameras were welcomed to make some vivid, lasting records—Major A. J. Russell and Colonel Charles R. Savage for the UP, and Alfred A. Hart for the CP.

Who Were Not There: Conspicuously absent from the UP delegation were Oakes and Oliver Ames. They were tied down by their financial burdens in the East and the Fisk fiasco. Oakes, not yet a Director, may have felt it necessary to remain in Washington and New York (as did Huntington), even though Congress was adjourned. Anyway, Oliver was advised by counsel to remain at the brand new Boston office, opened on May 2, to forestall any schemeful moves by the Vice-President, who might have commanding power if the President were absent.[168] The other Directors who did not show up were Alley, Bardwell, Bates, Bushnell, Cisco, Crane, Dexter, Lambard, Macy, McComb, Tracy, and the five Government Directors.[169]

Absent, equally noticeably, from the Central's group were their other officials: Directors Collis P. Huntington (also Vice-President); E. B. Crocker; Mark Hopkins (also Treasurer); E. H. Miller (also Secretary); and A. P. Stanford (brother of the Governor). Nor did Superintendent Charles Crocker turn up. Presumably they, too, were struggling with finances and urgent affairs at the home office.

Neither did President Grant come, although he had expressed intention to do so; an important meeting of the State Department had been called. Nor did Brigham Young, who was on business in southern Utah and preparing for his new railway; he was represented, however, by Bishop John Sharp, sub-contractor for the UP.

The Last Tie: While the last two rails were being spiked down, one by the UP and one by the CP, "The Last Tie" was solemnly carried by Strobridge and Reed from Stanford's special and gently bedded in. It was one of several fine gifts from the sentimental and generous states of California, Nevada, Arizona, Idaho, and Montana. Eight feet

[168] See p. 321.   [169] See p. 240.

long, eight inches wide, and six inches thick, it was of Californian laurel, beautifully polished, bound with silver, and ornamented with a silver plate bearing the names of the Central's Directors and officers. Holes had been drilled so that the soft metal spikes would not be injured by the hammering and extracting. It was presented to Stanford by West Evans, a CP tie contractor. (Sad to say, the laurel tie was destroyed, along with all the Central's records, in the earthquake and fire which devastated San Francisco in April 1906.)

The Golden Spike Is Placed:　Finally, after some long delays in the program, Stanford stepped up to the rail over the last tie and stood ready with a large, silver-headed maul presented for the occasion. A wire led from the hammer to the instruments of W.N. Shilling, a Western Union telegrapher from Ogden, sitting at a table near by. The idea was that the impact of the hammer on metal would create a "dot" on the transmitter which would be instantly relayed to the entire Western Union circuit, from Atlantic to Pacific, from the Great Lakes to the Gulf of Mexico. In effect it worked, at most places. Shilling now tapped out a message to his nationwide hook-up of operators:

"Everyone keep quiet. Just before the last spike is driven we will say 'done.' Then listen for the strokes of the hammer." Minutes later: "Almost ready. Hats off. We are praying." Stanford, Durant, and Dodge made very brief speeches, then led cheers; the bands played, the engines tooted, and "we all," said one spectator, "yelled fit to bust."

Shilling fingered his key: "All ready now. The spike will soon be driven. The signal will be three dots for the commencement of the blows."

Dot, Dot, Dot, *DONE!*

At nearly 12:30, Governor Stanford had made his only stroke at "The Last Spike." It was a moderately lusty blow, and he missed the spike and hit the rail instead, sparking the first electric impulse. Durant, who had a bad headache, followed but also missed, hitting the rail resoundingly again. The two "misses" well may have been intentional.[170] The expert sledgers of the crews could hardly restrain

---

[170] There seems to be no written corroboration of this idea of the author. Apparently one story is as good as another. But a blow on a rail could be "heard" electronically better than one on a spike; the head of the soft, solid gold spike was engraved, and apparently came through unmarred; the spike could move easily in and out of the hole made to fit it; and hitting the rail was surer.

their groans at these bungling swings, but Shilling "obligingly" signaled them as though the spikes had been struck—sounds compared by an enthusiastic press to the shot at Lexington heard around the world. The Golden Spike was then gently tapped home by the two Chief Engineers, Dodge and Montague, followed by General Jack Casement and Jim Strobridge.

Echoes: The tick recording the Governor's blow reached Washington at exactly 2:47 p.m. (allowing about 2 hours for difference in time, which was not yet standard time) and sounded the bell of the Capitol. In San Francisco the fire-bell in the City Hall tower pealed, and 220 cannons at Fort Point roared in answer. In New York, 100 guns were fired, and the chimes of Trinity Church chanted a *Te Deum.* The Liberty Bell in Philadelphia sounded its cracked note. Chicago celebrated with a four-mile-long procession. There was a long parade in Omaha, while 100 guns boomed from Capitol Hill. At Ogden, all business places were closed, and 7,000 Mormons gathered at its new Tabernacle, while in Salt Lake City the great Tabernacle overflowed. Back in Boston's Faneuil Hall, cradle of American liberty, there were patriotic speeches.

The first message, telegraphed to President Grant and the Associated Press, read:

Promontory Summit, May 10, 1869.
The last rail is laid! The last spike is driven! The Pacific Railroad is completed! The point of junction is 1086 miles west of the Missouri River and 690 miles east of Sacramento City. *(Signed)* Leland Stanford, Central Pacific Railroad; T. C. Durant, Sidney Dillon, John Duff, Union Pacific Railroad.[171]

The second wire was to President Oliver Ames from Duff, Dillon, Durant, and Dodge:

The last rail was laid today connecting the Union Pacific with the Central Pacific at Promontory Summit. This act quietly performed 2500 miles west of Boston, 690 east of Sacramento will have an influence upon the future and upon the commerce and travel of the world that no one can today estimate. We congratulate you upon the success of the enterprise.[172]

[171] Union Pacific Railroad, *A Brief History,* p. 10; *History of the Union Pacific Railroad,* pp. 39–42.
[172] Dodge, *Autobiography,* p. 946.

It sounded like Dodge's words. Unfortunately, Oliver did not get it until the next afternoon, too late for the evening papers of even May 11. So the Boston office heard nothing from Promontory on May 10.[173]

The Last Spike: The world-famous Golden Spike was a gift to Governor Stanford from David Hewes, a sand contractor of San Francisco. Of solid gold, it was only about 5½ inches long and ½-inch square, nearly of the regulation size of the time. Upon its head was inscribed the legend, "The Last Spike"; on one side, "The Pacific Railroad. Ground broken Jany. 8th, 1863, and completed May 8th, 1869"; on another side, "May God continue the unity of our Country as this Railroad unites the two great Oceans of the world"; on the third side, "Presented by David Hewes, San Francisco"; and on the fourth, the names of the company Directors and officers. The original can be seen at the Leland Stanford Museum at Palo Alto. A gold-plated replica is at the UP Historical Museum. Originally the spike was extended by a large nugget of solid gold designed to be broken off at the ceremony and melted into souvenirs. Four tiny golden watchfobs and rings were fashioned from it and presented to President Grant, Secretary of State Seward, Governor Stanford, and Oliver Ames. At least one was inscribed "The Mountain Wedding, May 10, 1869." Oliver's are on view at the UP Historical Museum, the gifts of his grandson, UP Director Oliver Ames.[174]

The Engines Talk It Over: To complete the ceremony, the locomotives were uncoupled, and, loaded with everyone who could find a place to cling, crept forward until their pilots touched, and the engineers clashed together bottles of champagne which foamed on the laurel tie. There proudly purred Union Pacific's brawny, unnamed, Rogers-made "No. 119," with a tall pipe of a stack, a coal-burner born last year, and Central Pacific's lighter "Jupiter" (No. 60) with a flaring funnel stack, a survivor of the storms of Cape Horn and the Sierras. Both were gracefully 4–4–0 wheeled, highly polished, and ornate with brazen bands and filigree—lions of the day. A classic photo by Savage shows Dodge and Montague clasping hands, the last tie visible between them, and the dark steeds of iron behind.[175]

> *What was it the engines said,*
> *Pilots touching, head to head,*

---

[173] *Ibid.*, p. 955 (Oliver Ames to Dodge, May 11).
[174] Union Pacific Railroad, *A Brief History*, p. 6.   [175] See Illus., Group 4.

Facing on a single track,
Half a world behind each back? [176]

Whatever they said, surely they were the best, the truest of all the immortal words uttered that day.

After a lavish luncheon for the combined party in Governor Stanford's car, the steamers backed to work again, picking up their cars. No. 119 gently drew the first train full across the joined tracks and then pushed it back over; Jupiter repeated the ritual. All precious spikes and mauls, and the laurel tie, were put under guard. The jackknives of souvenir-seekers whittled to splinters the "last last tie" —at least six of them before count was lost and the sun had sunk behind the valley ridge in its own cloudless blaze of yellow and red gold.

The Golden Spike Monument: Today waterless Promontory consists only of a white, pyramidal monument, about twice the height of an adult, and a few dilapidated buildings. On a summer day, little whirlwinds of dust go chasing around through the sagebrush seeking a place to rest. Probably the only persons to be seen will be other curious motorists, for the Southern Pacific Railroad abandoned and dismantled this section in 1942. The monument is surrounded by a neat, black iron fence, outside of which are two short, undersized and undergauged rails anchored in concrete. On the west side of the pyramid is fixed a bronze tablet. Under a little bronze eagle (whose head is gone) appear the following words:

National Historic Site

GOLDEN SPIKE

"The last rail is laid, the spike is driven. The Pacific Railway is completed." Here at Promontory, Utah, at 12:47 p.m., on May 10, 1869, the driving of a golden spike completed the first Transcontinental Railroad. Climax of a dramatic railroad-building race between the Union Pacific building from the East and the Central Pacific building from the West, this event symbolized attainment of a long-sought goal—a direct transportation route to the Pacific Ocean and the China Trade. And it achieved the great political objective of binding together by iron bonds the extremities of continental United States, a rail link from ocean to ocean.

National Park Service
United States
Department of the Interior

[176] Bret Harte; Sabin, p. 227.

Oliver: Back in Boston, Oliver faithfully filled in his diary for
May 10:

Pleasant. The joining of the Rails and completion of Road to Pacific.
The greatest event of the age. Celebration throughout the country by
Speeches Bell-Ringing and firing of Guns. Boston did nothing. I invited
a few and had a pleasant dinner at Young's [hotel] in celebration of the
joining of Rails.

And the next day, rather grumpily:

No special news from Pacific Road today. The Telegram that we
should have received yesterday from Duff & Dillon [and Dodge and
Durant] got along this PM.[177] Bushnell here from NY full of confidence
as usual, but does not present any way to raise money except at high
Rates.

The first mortgage bonds were at 93.
Oliver also took the occasion to write Dodge from North Easton
on May 10:

Let us rejoice that Last Rail is laid and we have a Road complete
as far as Engineering and Grading and all the Exciting contest for Length
of Line is concerned. It is the great Event of the age in Railroad Construction.
The question now with us is how shall we put the road in the best
running order and our Finances in satisfactory shape. We have used up
all our securities. . . . I have loaned the Co every 1st Mtg Bond I have
after buying them of the Co and putting up my money on them. . . .[178]

---

[177] See pp. 341–342.   [178] Dodge, *Papers,* vol. 158 (original ms.).

9

Cleaning Up—May 11 to End of 1869

Durant Removed as Director and Vice-President—Unpaid Bills and Critical Finances—Freight Rates, Passenger Fares, Wages, and Services—The Five Eminent Citizens' Report—McComb's Injunction—The UP Sells Its Ogden-Promontory Track to the Central—Dodge's Last Annual Report—Summary of 1869

A. Durant Removed as Director and Vice-President

Review of Durant's Authority: It will be recalled that the annual meeting of UP stockholders set for 10 March 1869 in New York had been broken up by Fisk's sheriffs and warrants for arrest,[1] so that Durant could not be fired then from the Board of Directors,[2] as requested by President Grant.[3] But the next day, the Directors at least had rescinded all of Durant's plenary authority as General Agent to hurry construction at will, a power so unwisely given first by the Directors[4] and then by the UP Executive Committee.[5] Congress had authorized the company to move headquarters to Boston and the stockholders to elect a new Board of Directors on 22 April 1869, or later.[6]

Durant Out At Last: The Boston annual meeting had to be postponed until 25 May, awaiting the return of Dillon and Duff from Echo. The day before, Durant, knowing he was beaten, made the best of it for the record, turned in a resignation as Vice-President, and declined re-election as Director.[7] So the axe did not fall until May 25, over 5½ years after the legal organization of the Union Pacific Rail-

---

[1] See p. 325.   [2] See p. 240.   [3] See p. 315.   [4] See p. 275.
[5] See pp. 281, 329 (J.M.S. Williams to Dodge, 11 Jan. 1869).   [6] See p. 327.
[7] Records of UP Historical Museum.

road Company. But the Doctor still had his CM and UP stocks, and his probable interests in some sub-contracts; there still were judges who could be bought. In 1869, he was sued in Rhode Island courts by Rowland G. Hazard for recovery of huge sums allegedly expropriated from the assets of the CM. Hazard brought criminal charges of embezzlement and caused Durant's arrest and confinement in jail.[8]

The New Management: Oliver's diary notes on May 25 follow: "Went into Boston on the 7 a.m. train to attend Stockholders meeting of UPRR. Elected a new Board of Directors leaving off Durant, McCombs, Bardwell, Cisco & Macy putting in their place Hazard, Gen Dodge, Chapman, Baker & Atkins. Bates will decline because Bardwell is left off & Dillon reports a larger amt. of debt than we expected." However, Dodge was not elected until August 18. Oakes had written him on May 22 that someone would be chosen to serve in his place temporarily, until he could finish up on the road.[9] It proved to be J. R. Duff Jr. Oliver forgot to mention, however, that William T. Glidden and Fred Nickerson were also newcomers on the Board, as well as Rowland G. Hazard, Elisha Atkins, and Oliver S. Chapman. Thus, *but too late,* now that connection with the CP was made, the Ames-New England group (including Alley, to be elected on November 19) gained overwhelming control of the 15 non-Government members of the Board, only Bushnell being honored as one of the former Durant group.[10]

On the next day, the organization meeting of the new Board was held. Oliver noted, "Pleasant meeting of the Directors of UPRR to organize. Chose Oliver Ames Pres., John Duff V.P., J.M.S. Williams Treas., E.M. Rollins Secty & Asst. Treas. Bates took no part in the meeting and will probably resign." New members of the Executive Committee were Glidden and Atkins, displacing Durant and McComb; re-elected were Oliver, Duff Sr., Dillon, Bushnell, and Government Director Brooks.

Other changes among officers included the obvious resignation of Colonel Silas Seymour on June 1; the removal of Webster Snyder as General Superintendent (General Manager) by Bushnell and Duff; and the appointment in his place on July 29 of Colonel C.G. Hammond of Chicago, an experienced railroad operator, and a Commissioner under the Act of 1862 to organize the UP.[11]

[8] See p. 24.   [9] Dodge, *Papers,* vol. 158.   [10] See p. 240.
[11] Records of UP Historical Museum.

B. Unpaid Bills and Critical Finances

Report of Browning's Commission of Four: The Special Commission appointed by Secretary of the Interior Browning on January 14 (consisting of General Warren, Blickensderfer, Lieutenant Colonel R.S. Williamson, and L.M. Clement) was to examine both roads and determine on a point of meeting, even if it involved completely new locations of the lines.[12] They finally turned in their report to Secretary Cox on May 14. They decided that the UP's location was superior to the CP's west of Ogden, but that the UP had deficiencies in construction of $6,771,770 from Omaha (on 1,035 miles), while the CP was incomplete by a value of $4,493,800 (on 551 miles). In reconsidering the UP, they found the UP track varied considerably in half a dozen cases from locations made by Dodge, "the only apparent reason being a desire to effect savings in construction, a result not always attained, and in no instance commensurate with the damage inflicted on the commercial value of the road." [13] In the case of the CP, the biggest item was $1,600,000 "for correcting errors of location, reducing curvatures, lengthening radii of curves, reducing grades, and obviating loss of elevations"; the next largest, $628,000 for various defects in the track-laying. "The report settled all questions of location and construction of the two roads in favor of the Union Pacific," wrote Dodge, "but the question of the acceptance of the line was still undecided." [14] The roads had already met, so part of the Commission's task had disappeared.

On May 15, Dodge wrote an encouraging word of advice to Treasurer J.M.S. Williams, prior to the postponed annual meeting:

... All see the difficulties that we are in ... I have great faith in the future if you only have nerve, letting nothing turn you from putting at the head of your concern men whom you know the country has faith in, and who will deal, one with the other, honorably and straightforwardly and we can command a great trade .... We have got to let the Central Pacific understand that we are ready all the time for business .... These Californians begin to see that their interests lie where ours do .... Had I not made that agreement, we never would have gotten a cent west of Ogden. They see that now.[15]

[12] See p. 308.   [13] Dodge, *Autobiography*, pp. 846–847.   [14] *Ibid.*, p. 848.
[15] *Ibid.*, p. 957.

Subsidy Bond Status: The Chief Engineer made a rough calculation of the condition of the U.S. Subsidy bond accounts of both roads and the total on May 17 as follows: [16]

U.P.R.R. Bonds delivered to 1,000th mile	$25,998,000
86 miles *undelivered* (at $32,000 a mile)	2,752,000 [a]
	$28,750,000
C.P.R.R. Bonds delivered to 510th mile	$18,604,000
About 46 miles in addition, delivered	1,400,000
About 134 miles in addition, *undelivered*	4,360,000 [17]
	$24,364,000
UP and CP Bonds delivered about 1,556 miles	46,002,000
UP and CP Bonds *undelivered* about 220 miles	7,112,000
Total issue would be on 1,776 miles	$53,114,000

If there is a fifty million limitation [18] C.P.R.R. will lose $ 3,114,000

[a] Of which the Bonds on about 46 miles are $1,472,000, which will in the end go to the C.P.R.R., leaving to remain with the Union Pacific R.R. $1,280,000.

In the end, the UP received $27,236,512 U.S. bonds on 1,038.68 miles of mainline track, which started 2 miles north of Omaha and ended 5 miles west of Ogden.[19] The Central apparently got $25,885,120 U.S. Bonds par value, turned into gold at a discount of about $7,000,000.[20]

Ames-Dodge Letters Get Sharp: Oakes wrote a long letter to Dodge from North Easton on May 22, in which he again unfairly laid on him matters which were really contracting items:

Mr. Duff got back this morning. Have had a long talk with him and am sorry to hear so bad an account . . . of the reckless and extravagant manner in which our affairs have been and still are managed out there and his inability to find out the amount of our indebtedness on the road, and our liabilities to contractors. . . . You should not pay for rock when it was earth . . . and hold back something for our stone work that has been so poor. Duff tells large stories about the amount of Stone hammers, Drills and Scrapers we have on hand that never was used. . . . Those rotten ties must be replaced at once. . . . I don't see where the money is coming from to meet all these claims . . . and pay the interest on our bonds, unless we earn a great deal.[21]

[16] *Ibid.,* p. 957.
[17] This figure (4,360,000) was omitted in Dodge's calculation, apparently by typographical error, but is supplied by the author in order to complete and prove Dodge's figures.
[18] *Act of 1862,* Section 11; see also p. 16.   [19] See p. 314.   [20] Sabin, p. 306.
[21] Dodge, *Papers,* vol. 158 (original manuscript).

Oliver wrote a long and most unhappy letter to Dodge from Boston on May 24:

The terrible state of our affairs on the line, and the cost of Road and our indebtedness is so much larger than I anticipated that I have felt too blue to write. Duff and Dillon have not written a letter since they left Omaha and really all the information we got was from you, except Dillon's Drafts which came down upon us quite as fast as we could raise the money . . . . The purpose for which this committee went out has not been at all accomplished . . . . We must have an entire reorganization of the road . . . . We want daily returns and weekly returns promptly made but we have never been able to get them . . . . If we had a good purchasing Agt we should not have 1,500,000$ of *stuff* in our shops at Omaha. I think Snyder is quite as much at fault as is Frost (purchasing agent). . . . What is being now done about Shops at Cheyenne. We have spent 200,000$ or more there and I understand we have nothing . . . . *I am so thoroughly sick of my connection with the Road that I propose to get out of it just as soon as I possibly can.*[22]

Dodge, also down-mouthed, answered Oliver on May 26, also from his home, Council Bluffs:

I have no access to any data by which I can determine Reed's expenditures. Everything relating to contractors' are kept from me, I suppose under instructions. We have no knowledge of what is under contract East . . . . The C.P. folks will be in New York next week, and you want to settle with them immediately and sell them the road built to Hot Springs or to the 1040th mile post . . . . At any rate, we must run West of Ogden from there. We do not want the road, we want to get rid of it. It has 116 feet grades, 10° curves, in fact its grades are equal to 132 feet, with high, rough trestles and good deal to be done. If you have not got the cost, Reed should furnish it to you . . . . You will have the entire construction outfit out there on your hands all summer . . . . It is not very easy to run a road with a class of discharged men around, growling and looking for the coming of Durant, or some one to give them a new lease on life. The C.P. are doing all they can to discourage travel. Stop passengers 22 hours at Promontory going west—hold up freights going to your road and charge 10 cts. per mile. I am in favor of bringing through freights down immediately to 3 cents per mile per ton. If you do you will get all your cars can carry.

One thing certain your hesitating about the establishing of lines, has

---

[22] *Ibid.*, vol. 158 (original manuscript; italics by C.E.A.); Dodge, *Autobiography*, pp. 962–963.

been, with your business methods, etc., losing you in all quarters what little confidence people might have had in you, and we cannot long even expect to hold the good-will of the powers that be.[23]

Dodge fired again from Council Bluffs, on May 29, in an extremely long and critical, yet constructive, letter to Oliver:

I have your letter and Oakes. After seeing Mr. Duff, you take a gloomy view of matters just as I begin to feel better. You were aware of this state of things for nearly a year. Now we are just emerging from it; all I have to say is, meet as it should be met, not by charging it to subordinates but bring it right home to New York where the root of the mischief is, where the foundation for all your trouble has been laid and where corruption, dishonesty, extravagance, has been held at a premium. Men out here have only followed the open example set them and none of you can plead ignorance of the state of affairs for you have been told and plead with to change it.

I am not disappointed, matters are not as bad as I expected, and the running department of the road is in far better condition than any one could expect. Employees unpaid for four months, over two millions of dollars and hardly one cent yet received to pay it off. What men do you suppose could get efficiency out of any work with that state of affairs in existence?

We see now great improvement, having paid our labor up to March 1st and gotten rid of construction forces and our men on west end are doing better. We lose now very little by thieving, our depots are not robbed daily, our cars broken into and our trains ditched; we run on time smoothly and the two new division superintendents west are doing well. As soon as we can get Chinese labor instead of Irish we can reduce cost of labor 50% . . . .

As to reports . . . it seems to me, daily reports of earnings and monthly report of expenditures, purchases, condition of road, etc., is all that you require. The system of accounts out here are the same as on C.R.I. & P. and other roads, only they are much fuller in detail on U.P.

Material on hand. I have written of this before; of material needed for the road you have no great surplus. $1,500,000 worth of material of all kinds so far west as we are for 1,086 miles of road is no great amount . . . Frost, Reed, Evans and Snyder all tell me that if they had observed the orders they would have twice as much as they have . . . . *But then we were going to build to Humboldt Wells;* if we had, our material would be short. The material that you have which is not needed is that used in construction . . . . You want to come out here and look

---

[23] Dodge, *Autobiography*, pp. 964–965. Presumably by "you" Dodge meant the company, not Oliver personally.

for yourself . . . . Out of 147 engines we now have only 12 out of repair, and this after a terrific winter and springs work . . . . At Cheyenne we have spent $90,000, have the 20-stall roundhouse completed, etc. It will take $125,000 to complete the Blacksmith and machine shops . . . . Three 10-stall roundhouses should go up, at Bryan, Wahsatch or Piedmont, and at end of the road wherever it may be.

Now, I have been over all these subjects before. You are as much at sea out here as ever. Men are unpaid; I have raised $100,000 on my own personal security. Snyder has raised as much more, and we live along from hand to mouth. If I could get $350,000 I would agree to carry the running department. We can float a million easy but we cannot float four millions with our labor unpaid. The contractors out west talk of raising mobs on us, stopping trains, and you see the condition of matters by dispatch I enclose. My way of settlement is to order the construction outfit to Omaha to make its settlements, get it away from line of road, draw the subcontractors down to this end, where we can handle them; now at Echo they are just where we don't want them.

Make arrangements for fare and freight with Central Pacific and we can run in, but as we are now we are losing one-half of our business, and the good season is passing away.[24]

On June 2, Oakes commented to Dodge from North Easton:

We are working every way we can to raise money to meet the coupons maturing July 1st and the debts out on the road. it seems as though there was no end to the debts due out there and at Omaha Chicago and at other places & N York the Lawyers will eat us all up at the rate they charge in Washington and New York . . . We here in Boston are econo- mising in every way we can and if we can ever get out of the hands of thieves swindlers and Lawyers in New York, and a prudent economical honest administration of affairs on the line of the road our stock may be of value . . .

We must make some different plan about free passes or we shall get no room in the cars for anything but dead heads. Has Casement been charged with the ballasting up his track that he left for us to do . . .

N.B. You must take care of the 5 Eminent men as Commissioners when they go over the road. I intend to go out to Iowa and over to Omaha as soon as we can see our way clear for funds to pay coupons.[25]

Cox Releases $2,000,000 Bonds: Dodge sent a sworn affidavit to Secretary Cox on May 29 as to the amount spent on the completed road *east* of the 1035 milepost since its examination by the Special

24 *Ibid.,* pp. 967–968. (Italics by C.E.A.)
25 Dodge, *Papers,* vol. 158 (original manuscript).

Commission of Four appointed by Browning on January 14.[26] Such
expenditures totalled $2,221,803 to which were added $1,373,475 for
locomotives, cars, bridges, and buildings on hand, and $677,000 on
rolling stock contracted for: a total of $4,272,277.[27] "On this state-
ment the Secretary of the Interior released some $2,000,000 of bonds
which was a great relief to the company," said Dodge.

Oliver Fires Back: Oliver, usually an equable man, showed a rare
bit of acrimony in his reply to Dodge's severe letter of May 29. Both
friends seemed to be letting off steam back home.

Genl G M Dodge Chf Engr   *N Easton   June 5th 69*
   . . . I have never had any interest in any contract never any sallary or
derived anything but labor and anxiety from my connection with the
Road. There has been great fraud on line of Road the past year, and
if today the work was measured up and pd for strictly according to contracts Millions of dollars would be saved to the Co. I have always thought
that the contract price on line of Road was low enough, and if it had
been measured up honestly and paid for as contracted Gravel for Gravel,
Earth for Earth & Rock for Rock we should have got through within
our Estimates. *But Engineers who have measured up the work have been
tampered with* and the quantities have been enlarged Rock has been
given for Gravel and a general system of swindling has been had by
Engineers in cohesion with Contractors
                                    Yours truly
                                        Oliver Ames [28]

   Dodge, now cooled off at Wahsatch, wrote Oliver at length again
on June 14, after making some investigations of the losses suffered,
and submitted some plans for action.

   I am in receipt of two letters from you, in one of which you intimated
that in some letter I had charged you with fraud. I cannot think what
letter you refer to, as I do not remember any such language and I know
it never entered my mind. It must have been in a letter in which I said
New York was to blame for our trouble out here; if you have any doubt
of that, you had better come out here and see the orders and instructions
that have been given from New York, and *I do not hesitate to say that
all our troubles and all our losses are due to Mr. Durant.*
   As I have heretofore said, *engineers and subordinates cannot be
charged with these matters;* they were powerless in most things and the

26 See p. 308.   27 Dodge, *Autobiography,* pp. 974–977, gives details of all items.
28 Dodge, *Papers,* vol. 158 (original manuscript; italics by C.E.A.).

worse reputation a man had, the quicker he was employed or given a contract, and you are aware that engineers were kept on construction after I had discharged them and notified the company officially that they were not trustworthy. Mr. Evans I believe to be honest; he had no interest in masonry; it was put in against his protest by direct order of Mr. Durant, and he says, in just the shape ordered for the purpose of avoiding cost and making it pass muster. He, unfortunately, I think, after taking a contract, remained as an engineer at the urgent and repeated requests of Durant, he, the Dr., stating it would save him trouble, and Evans was merely to see that the work was pushed . . . . What astonishes me is that how, today, you are paying $27½ per yard to put in the masonry at Devil's Gate, Ogden, Bear River and other points, when I can get better masonry done for $12½ per yard, right here on the ground. *Are you tied up by a contract? If not, then stop the leak. I could stop a hundred here today had I the power . . . . Had Evans been placed in charge last fall of work west of Aspen, and Durant had kept away, your track would be 50 miles further west, and it would have saved us millions.*

I can better give you an idea of how men are changed here by stating what I know. You remember the coal contracts made last year.[29] Well, Durant came out here after it was made, denounced it to me, to Snyder and gave Snyder to understand that he was to pay no attention to it. Durant then made contracts, or ordered others to, with Hall, Morrow, Vandyke, Gessner and others for coal. Now, when Duff and Dillon were out here, I heard Durant denounce Snyder to them in the bitterest terms because he, S. has not carried out that contract and I was led to believe that Duff and Dillon believe it. I said nothing about this as Duff informed me that Snyder would be brought up on it and I wanted him and Durant brought face to face on it . . . .

Before you come out here make a note, as I do, of every complaint you hear on road and probe it when you get here without saying a word to any one, and you can get at the facts, that is the only way . . . I would like to have you see Reed's orders, and others', and you would open your eyes. We have picked up on side of road whole car loads of construction supplies reported lost on books, when the fact is they have been neglected until some thief, through some rascally conductor or agent would rebill them, forge marks and have them delivered to some other person and away they go. I got track today of a large amount that went to Salt Lake.

Bent [of transport teams] has a charge against the Company of $100,000 of overcharges on his supplies. I looked at his bills today and at our books and find him charged with nearly doubled prices on them. Now, who got the profits? . . . We have lost most of our money by Co. work, by Co. agents, in our supply Dept. in false rolls, in double prices for teams that laid still in movement of material when it was not neces-

[29] See pp. 247–248.

sary . . . . Grading between Monument Point and Ogden, even at the prices you paid, will not cost much over $15,000 per mile. The C.P.'s grading, when they made their affidavit, was not one-third done . . . . *My opinion is that C.P. will endeavor to get our road for their price, failing in this, will build themselves to Ogden* . . . . If you do fail to agree, that moment issue an order to me to take our line over Promontory to 80 foot grade. See now that our line is accepted to Summit and make in writing to C.P. proposition to sell at cost, stating what is is and say you are ready to turn it over the moment they pay for it.[30]

Oakes wrote Oliver on June 13, "I think it important to get the stock and bonds [listed] on the board [New York Stock Exchange] . . . so that we can sell them or borrow money on them it would give us facilities for using them that may be useful. I will do my part towards it." [31]

Reed, at Echo, wrote Oliver on June 14, "It is very important that payments be made immediately for all team work & other labor. The men are very much excited and cannot be controlled much longer." [32]

Oliver wrote Dodge from Boston, on June 17, far too hopefully:

. . . Also [received] your telegram that the 53½ miles of road West of Ogden has cost 4,387,000$ [$82,000 a mile]. If we can get this valuation accepted by the Central Pacific and the Govt will issue their Bonds to us now due we shall be in position to pay up promptly all our Bills and have something handsome left for the Omaha Bridge.

We are getting in much better shape here . . . . Carmichael and Hall [transport teams] are Durant's pets could they have been in, in some way to divide the spoil . . . . Something ought to be done to hold these swindlers up to the Public gaze.[33]

Oliver noted in his diary of June 18, "Letter from Dodge in explanation of cost of work where done by Co costing 6 times as much as when done by contract." This letter was not found.

Dodge wrote some interesting comments to Treasurer J.M.S. Williams from Promontory on June 14:

. . . Do you appreciate that you have 1086 miles of road out here, with all kinds of questions arising *with no person here to say yes or no to a man or even give him satisfaction enough to keep him quiet?* . . . You

---

[30] Dodge, *Autobiography*, pp. 977–979. (Italics by C.E.A.)
[31] Records of UP Historical Museum.   [32] *Ibid.*
[33] Dodge, *Papers*, vol. 158 (original manuscript). "$82,000 a mile" is C.E.A.'s figure, based on 53½ miles.

will find that nearly all your losses occurred west of Granger [October 1868]. Up to that point the work was managed reasonably well and cost fair prices . . . If Evans (and the others) had carried out their orders, you would have been millions worse off than you are . . . *I defy any man to contradict it, that all our losses, all our thieving, all our wrongs, come directly or indirectly from Durant and Seymour's orders, and it is no use trying to charge it off to any one else.* They had full, unlimited power, used it to its full extent, fed the directors with prospects of big dividends, the press with great ability, and took full care personally of themselves. Now they are trying to shift the responsibility to the poor devils who were under them . . . .[34]

Oakes, now at Omaha after visiting his and Blair's road at Sioux City, wrote Oliver on June 21: ". . . Davis says his contract was for timber and ties to go to Humboldt Wells and he is going to make you take enough to do it. They have no copies of Durant's contracts out here. You had better examine them and see what you have got to do." [35]

Hodges wrote one of his intimate letters to Dodge on June 27, giving him conditions as they were in the Boston office, ". . . Mr. Oakes Ames has returned. He is the stanchest friend to your interests and to Mr. Snyder of any of the stockholders, and whenever he or his brother desires it, the board goes with them and against Mr. Duff who seems to be opposed to all the old hands on the road." [36]

Bushnell Lists Debts to Contractors: Bushnell, still at Echo, and as optimistic as ever, sent in a long report on debts to contractors in a letter to "Oliver Ames, President, and J.M.S. Williams" on July 3:

I am hard at work with Reed and Kennedy who have their accounts in very good shape for adjustment and we find the snugg little sum of $2,783,192.42 due which they make no question of. Besides this there is the J.W. Davis claim for a large sum for ties and timber on hand not received we having paid them over $66,105.26 more than our Books call for.

Mr. Kennedy, Cashier for contractors by direction of Mr. Duff and myself, is authorized to draw on J.M.S. Williams Treas UPRR Co for the balance [now] due of $1,457,134.34 and interest at the rate of 7% on time that will average from 3 to 4 and 6 months from this date—And it will be absolutely necessary for me to make some arrangement for at

---

[34] Dodge, *Autobiography*, p. 980. (Italics by C.E.A.)
[35] Records of UP Historical Museum.   [36] Dodge, *Autobiography*, p. 984.

least 200,000 of this amount in cash . . . before they will allow me to leave this vicinity . . . . And you will please excuse me for saying that no man in Boston will consent to sell our UP stock at 50 after Duff and I get back and report what we shall be able to report of this Road and its present and prospective business when properly handled.[37]

Bushnell followed this up two days later with another letter to Treasurer Williams:

We have made provision for the settlement of nearly everything outstanding by drawing on you at sight for $50,000 at sight and on 30 days for $100,000, which I endorsed and borrowed the money from my friend Warren Hussey (gentile banker of Salt Lake City), where I spent last even in conference with B. Young and his Elders, etc. . . . The gross amount [of drafts] will not vary much from $1,500,000 . . . .

The men were all about here waiting for their money, having pledged their vouchers for money to live on, contractors having pledged theirs to considerable extent to raise money to pay off men they had discharged. I think of the $2,750,000 we owe out here or did when we came out, *$750,000 is proffitt to the contractors,* but I do not think there has been but a very small proportion of dishonesty practiced on us of what I had expected to unearth.[38]

B. Young Taken Care of: Brigham Young was given a note for $346,000, but in the end his account was compromised by arbitration, and he accepted in settlement a large supply of surplus materials, stored at Echo, which he used in the construction of his Utah Central.[39]

Davis "& Associates" collected $50,000 of their claims after litigation running into 1871.[40]

Other Debts: 1. In addition to the $2,750,000 of debts to contractors which Bushnell and Duff had succeeded in temporarily funding at Echo, as shown above, the company was heavily obligated to the Seven Trustees of the Ames–Davis contracts and to the CM. The latter's claims aggregated four millions, but were offset by the UP's counterclaims, based upon asserted overpayments under the two construction contracts. These accounts remained unsettled for many years.[41]

2. Dodge himself was compelled to appeal for relief. He wrote Wil-

[37] Records of UP Historical Museum.   [38] *Ibid.* (Italics by C.E.A.)   [39] *Ibid.*
[40] *Ibid.*   [41] *Ibid.*

liams from Council Bluffs on July 7: "Can I draw for $15,000 on engineering account? In cutting off all my forces except those on bridge . . . has taken considerable, also the settling up and discharge of Oregon Branch has taken more than I can carry. Banks are carrying for me all they want to." [42]

3. Colonel Hammond, on relieving Snyder as General Superintendent on July 22, found unpaid operating payrolls for March, April, May, and June totaling $770,090 to which the July rolls would add $320,000. [43]

4. The track and structures only recently built had already commenced to show need of repairs. Dodge advised Hammond in July that all the masonry foundations of the bridges between Laramie and Echo were worthless. Cottonwood ties to be replaced by the end of 1870 numbered 323,000. [44]

5. Thomas H. Bates, a Division Engineer of the UP, brought suit in September for $20,368 for ties furnished during the preceding winter and for $18,924 additional amounts disbursed by him on location. [45]

6. General B.F. Butler wrote from Lowell on October 11 for the balance of his fees for services and advice at the New York meeting of 2 October 1867, and for a retainer fee in behalf of the UP before the Federal Courts. [46]

7. Charges for the construction of the Missouri River bridge were coming to substantial amounts. [47] Due to financial stringencies, all work was suspended on July 26 and not resumed until 10 April 1870. Dodge was soon relieved of his active duties there.

Under the weight of these burdens, the Directors were compelled to borrow large sums on short term notes, the total running up to $12,754,952. [48] Included was the demand note for $2,000,000 given the CM by the UP on August 8, which seemed to have been looked upon as a contingent liability rather than a firm obligation.

In the middle of July, the UP first mortgage bonds were down to 88 and the stock to 20. [49] It was impossible to pledge the land grant bonds at over 50 per cent.

Ham Refuses to Work on Contractors' Accounts: B.F. Ham wrote Treasurer Williams an important letter on July 19 about his accounting problems:

[42] *Ibid.*   [43] *Ibid.*   [44] *Ibid.*   [45] *Ibid.*   [46] *Ibid.*
[47] *Ibid.*   [48] U.S. Pacific Railway Commission, pp. 5042–5043.
[49] Dodge, *Autobiography,* pp. 996, 998.

Mr. Crane showed me his papers. The difficulty with making up the statement is at the west end. Kennedy shows us his balance sheet but Crane cannot tell which items belong to the Ames Contract and which to the Davis Contract. A settlement made here might prove just like the one with the CM did on Hoxie contract viz—that the Cashier had spent more money than was charged to him on that contract. The settlement of the contractors books is a job I don't want. *I straightened up the Hoxie books and tried hard to control the books on the Ames contract. I did not succeed, and now I don't care to have anything to do with them.* I do not see however how any settlement can be made here until the balance sheet is forwarded from Echo showing division of Expenditure there together with statement of indebtedness.[50]

Land Sales Commence: On July 28 the office of the UP Land Department was opened for business in Omaha, attractive pamphlets were distributed, and sales of land began. Under the Acts of 1862 and 1864, the UP eventually, after "completion," received from the Government, by patents, a free grant of 11,401,175 acres of open land.[51] The Land Department now offered its property in tracts of 40 acres and upwards at prices varying between $2 and $10 per acre, with a deduction of 10 per cent for cash payments. By November 1871, 480,000 acres had been sold for $2,031,000, or $4.23 each.[52] UP land grant bonds were accepted at par in payment for land. The purchaser was given a clear title, free of all incumbrances. Most of the first sales were in the fertile farming and grazing lands of the Platte Valley. A neat one-story frame house, with from two to four rooms, could at that time be built there at a cost of from $200 to $600. Purchasers of 160 acres or more were given free railroad tickets to explore for sites. Detailed instructions were also issued in the pamphlets on how to obtain tracts in the even-numbered Government sections within UP limits, under the Pre-Emption Act of 4 September 1841, or the Homestead Act of 20 May 1862 (amended 15 July 1870). On 10 May 1869, the Government profited by doubling the price of its land from $1.25 to $2.50 an acre. But because of rapid sales at low prices, the major share of price appreciation in subsequent years was realized by the purchasers or their successors, and *not* by the railroads.[53]

For example, in September 1869 Dodge bought a parcel of 320

---

[50] Records of UP Historical Museum. (Italics by C.E.A.)

[51] *Ibid.;* U.S. Pacific Railway Commission, p. 936.

[52] *Guide to the Union Pacific Railroad Lands, 12,000,000 Acres,* 4th ed., 1871. See also map on inside front and back covers of this book.

[53] Records of UP Historical Museum.

acres in Colfax County, Nebraska (which took in Columbus), for $8 an acre and sold it a few years after at $11 an acre. In later years, the same piece went for $213 an acre, including buildings and other improvements.[54]

Kinsley Iron Works: On July 5 and 15, Oliver made entries about the Kinsley Iron and Machine Company: "Went over to Canton with Mr. Oakes Ames. looked through the works. Things are looking well and the value of the works are doubled since we took them. At annual meeting July 15 announced 106,000 profit & made dividend of 50 per cent." Close to North Easton, this plant, of which Oliver was then President and Director, and Oakes a Director, was managed by Frank Morton Ames, Oakes's third son.

Effort to Borrow from CM Stockholders: On August 6, Oliver noted in his diary, "Passed resolution to give a Bonus of 30 shares of Stock in UPRR to such stockholders as should pay 1000$ for a Land Grant Bond and 20 shares to such as shall pay 1000$ for 1st Mtg.bond."

This proposition was made by the Seven Trustees in an ambiguous circular dated 11 August 1869.[55] Its purpose was to borrow back, for a while, part of the generous allotments of profits made to the CM stockholders in 1868.[56] In view of the depressed prices of UP securities, the Trustees had to make very attractive terms. They offered to *buy* from any stockholder (for every 200 shares of stock held) who was willing to *lend* them $2,000 (with interest at 12 per cent per annum) a package consisting of $1,000 6 per cent first mortgage bond, $1,000 7 per cent land grant bond, and a bonus of 50 shares of UP stock, as Oliver had said in a different way. These securities, to be issued by the UP to such stockholder, were to be pledged until 26 February 1870 in payment of very pressing bills for railroad construction.[57] At the then *market* value the package was worth say $2,900, that is, $850 for the first mortgage, $550 for the land grant, and $1,500 for the 50 shares, probably around 30.[58]

In case anyone failed to take his package, it would be distributed in equal proportions to those who accepted.

By August 20, a total of $550,000 had been loaned by 19 stockholders against $275,000 first mortgages, $275,000 land grants, and 13,750 shares. But on that day, McComb stopped further distribu-

---

[54] *Ibid.*   [55] *Wilson Rep.*, p. 358.   [56] See table, p. 259.
[57] Records of UP Historical Museum.   [58] See Appendices A, C.

tions under the circular by getting a court injunction.[59] Bushnell had loaned 33 per cent of the total, and Rowland G. Hazard (Sr.) 27 per cent, but neither the Ameses nor Durant had come in.[60]

When Hazard's "loan" totaling $150,000 and interest was tendered him on the due date, 26 February 1870, he refused to accept payment or to return the securities, claiming that by the terms of the circular and contract the deal was not in fact a loan, but a *purchase!* In due course, the Trustees, of whom Durant was one, brought suit in the Massachusetts Supreme Court against Hazard to recover the securities. Hazard proposed his claim be arbitrated but was turned down.[61]

Because of the action by Hazard and a number of others, this disappointing effort of the Trustees became known as the "Evasion Loan." [62]

The next loan, more successful, is discussed in Chapter 10, pages 395–398.

Hodges Worried: F.S. Hodges, upset by the gyrations of the mortgage bonds between 103 and 65 in the past seven months, wrote Dodge from Roxbury, Massachusetts, on August 30:

The 1st mortgages were today offered for 85 with no bids above 84½ . . . . I don't know what can break the market down so . . . if Government should take the road they would have to assume the bonds . . . . *It is my opinion that no one here will ever get the true figures of the cost of the road. No two reports from the New York books ever agree.*[63]

Oliver Settles with B. Young in Person: On September 6, Oliver started on a three-week trip West, going as far as Promontory. This was the period when the "Five Eminent Citizens" were examining the road, but he did not mention them. He called on President Brigham Young and "Was rec'd very much distinction. Was not so well impressed as I expected. Salt Lake is quite a nice place for the country . . . Road over the Mts [Laramie to Cheyenne] very good." [64] However, he arranged for payment of $940,138 to Young, thereby reducing a claim of $1,139,081 to $198,943—the latter amount was left to future arbitration, as stated previously.[65]

[59] Oliver Ames's diary, 20 Aug. 1869.   [60] *Wilson Rep.*, p. 633.
[61] Records of UP Historical Museum.   [62] *Ibid.*
[63] Dodge, *Autobiography*, p. 1011 (italics by C.E.A.); see also Appendix A.
[64] Oliver Ames's diary, Sept. 16 and 20.
[65] Records of UP Historical Museum; see also pp. 356, 279.

Black Friday Gold Panic: September 24 was "Black Friday" on the New York Stock Exchange and in its adjacent Gold Room. Jay Gould and Jim Fisk had teamed together to knock down more railroad security prices and then buy them up. Their method this time was a fantastic corner on gold itself. During September they succeeded in advancing its price from 133 to 144 by Thursday, the 23rd. In the buying panic of Wall Street dealers who had sold short, the next day (Friday) gold soared to 162½ by noontime. President Grant, at last aroused to action, suddenly ordered Secretary Boutwell to throw in millions of gold for sale "at the market." At this news, the price skidded back to 130. The Gold Board closed for four days in hysteria. Gould, tipped off on the Administration's last minute decision, secretly sold heavily near the top, deliberately leaving Fisk still buying. Fisk was painfully scorched as was, indeed, a large part of Wall Street.[66]

During the period of this bold speculation, most security prices dropped sharply with the rise in gold. The stock of the Chicago and North Western, for instance, slumped on the Exchange from 86 to 63. The UP first mortgages, even though payable in gold, declined from 88 only two weeks previously to 82, and the currency land grants to 54. By October 2, the markets were quieting down, and there were large bids for the mortgages at 84, with the company offering at 87. The land grants were back to 60 for cash, and to 50 as collateral for loans.[67]

Hodges wrote Dodge on Black Friday, "Oakes Ames don't flinch any, though it has mostly fallen on him the last summer." [68]

Oliver Optimistic: Oliver, just back from his trip West, and apparently unmoved by Black Friday's panic, scribbled in his diary on September 30, "Prepared Report for yr. to be forwarded to Secretary of Interior accompanied by report of Chief Eng'r. Report shows no great earnings to be taxed for. Expressed confidence in Road's future business." And, even more cheerfully, on October 15, "Things seem to be going along very well and Returns from Road look favorable. I shall, I think, bring out our things right."

Dodge to Leave: Oliver wrote Colonel Hammond on November 12, "We are desirous of having you take the full charge of Road and its repairs. Gen'l Dodge as Chf. Engr says in a recent letter that he will

---

[66] Grodinsky, *Jay Gould,* pp. 77–79; Swanberg, *Jim Fisk,* pp. 142–155; *Commercial & Financial Register,* 1870, p. 15.

[67] Records of UP Historical Museum.   [68] Dodge, *Autobiography,* p. 1015.

close up all connexion with the Road turn over all things to you and devote his time to the Bridge . . . ." But work on the bridge had been temporarily suspended on July 26.[69]

Suez Canal Competition: Only six months after the Golden Spike, on November 20, the Suez Canal was opened to vessels drawing less than 24.4 feet. This came as no surprise to anyone, as work had been under way for 10 years. Yet, now at one stroke, any possible advantage the Pacific Railway route might have over the all-ocean Europe-China route was cut off. Instead, the westward expansion of commerce would rise, like a phoenix, to fulfill the fondest dreams of railroaders. The Union Pacific and other transcontinental steel links were destined, over the decades, to become more of a treasure to the nation's economic health than ever had been imagined, even by Asa Whitney.[70]

On December 6, the Forty-First Congress, Second Session, convened, and Oakes returned to Washington. Three days later, Treasurer Williams followed him up with an urgent letter, "Think we are in need of such money that you had better part with all you can get any one to take and pay for . . . . If you can help us please do so." [71]

Hodges wrote Dodge another newsy letter from Boston on December 20:

> I deeply regret to hear you have been unwell again. It was hoped by your friends that the out-door life would entirely prevent troubles of this kind . . . . Earnings are to be about $600,000 for December . . . . Your credit balance here is $7,731 . . . . There is no reason why they should not pay you that $15,000; but Mr. [Oliver] Ames' letter to Col. Hammond to pay you has such conditions that he could not tell anything about it . . . . If I could only get Mr. Ames alone to speak about it, I think I could arrange it.[72]

High Cost of Loans: On December 24, just in time to dampen Oliver's Christmas yet another year, Dillon wrote him that the UP had negotiated a 60-day $600,000-gold loan from Dabney, Morgan and Company (predecessor of J.P. Morgan & Co.), *but,* as an indication of bankers' opinions of the UP's credit at that time, *at a rate of 17½ per cent.* It was computed by B.F. Ham as 7 per cent for interest, 9 per cent commission at 1½ per cent for 60 days, and 1½ per cent

[69] See p. 357.   [70] See p. 7.   [71] Records of UP Historical Museum.
[72] Dodge, *Autobiography,* p. 1031.

commission to Mr. Clarke (the negotiator) at ¼ per cent for 60 days, exclusive of a payment for individual endorsement. "This I consider outrageous, if you give the bonds themselves as collateral, . . ." wrote Dillon, "I think our parties should take the loan themselves for about 14 or 15% or less, if they can make it." [73]

Earnings and Interest on Debt: A statement of the *operating* earnings for the last three years follows: [74]

Cal. Yr.	Total Earns.	Total Operating Expenses (incl. taxes)	Net	Miles (end of yr.)
1867	$3,465,000	$1,404,000 [a]	$2,061,000	536
1868	5,063,000	4,169,000 [a]	894,000	982
1869	8,192,000 [b]	6,161,000 [a]	2,031,000	1,039

[a] "As per general ledger, operating department; Annual Reports for 1867, 1868 and 1869 not at hand."
[b] Divided as follows: Passengers, $4,077,000; Freight, $3,395,000; Mail, $268,000; Express, $236,000; and Miscellaneous, $216,000—Total earnings, $8,192,000.

But the interest payable on the total funded debt, which is not included above, was alone costing the UP more than $4,000,000 a year by the end of 1869. A year later, after the land grant and income bonds were all issued, the annual rate would reach $5,338,615. Included in these figures is a 25 per cent gold premium on the coupons of the first mortgage bonds. The 1869 balance sheet appears in a report of the U.S. Pacific Railway Commission, pp. 5032–33.

C. Freight Rates, Passenger Fares, Wages, and Services

Through freight and passenger service between Omaha and Sacramento commenced on May 15, five days after the Golden Spike.

Freight Rates: Oliver wrote Dodge on June 1:

. . . We should not let Passengers lay over 20 hours at Promontory to curse the Road . . . .
Your idea about freight is quite too low. It should not be carried at less than 5 cts—3 cts will not pay the cost . . . . I have been hoping to

[73] Records of UP Historical Museum.
[74] U.S. Pacific Railway Commission, pp. 5266–5272; see also p. 261.

see earnings . . . to justify our expectations of returns from its trafic sufficient to pay up interest & make Dividends on Stock . . . . If we could
do anything with our Stock we might put enough of it on the market to
finish up, but at present no sale could be made.[75]

In Boston, he made a diary notation on June 5: "Huntington &
Crocker here today to talk about fixing prices for passengers & freight
from Omaha to San Francisco. Could agree on the rates but not on
the Division. They want to charge more for their end per mile than
we have. Unable to agree. Want to fix price of Road again."

He wired General Superintendent Snyder on June 15, "Fare fixed
from Omaha to Promontory $76. Central charge from Promontory to
San Francisco $57. Get out tickets and advertise." [76]

Dodge still could not agree at all on the freight rates proposed at
Boston and wrote Government Director Brooks from Council Bluffs
on June 19: "On freights our rates are now prohibitive, ranging from
8½ to 11 cents per ton per mile. I would reduce immediately to 3
and 5 cents and would make special rates in New York, Chicago and
San Francisco." [77]

Wages: On July 19, Secretary Rollins answered a Commissioner's
question about wages on the Pacific Railway by saying that common
laborers were paid $3 to $3½ a day; that they were employed 10 hours
a day. "They generally 'earn' $2 a day," he wrote. "During construc-
tion, wages ranged from 2 to 5 & 7 dollars a day, & hours from 10 to
14 & 16. Instances occurred where these wages & hours were far
exceeded." [78]

Passenger Fares: Colonel Hammond, the new General Superintendent, wrote Oliver on August 5 that after another revision, the UP
passenger fares were as listed below: [79]

		First Class	Emigrant	Emigrant from Chic. or St. Louis
New York–Chicago		$ 20.00	$13.00	
Chicago–Omaha		19.00	10.00	$10.00
Omaha–Promontory		63.33	26.81	28.52
Promontory–San Fran.		47.67	20.19	21.48
N.Y.–San Francisco		$150.00	$70.00	$60.00

[75] Dodge, *Papers,* vol. 158 (original manuscript).
[76] Records of UP Historical Museum.
[77] Dodge, *Autobiography,* p. 981.   [78] Records of UP Historical Museum.
[79] *Ibid.*

Traveling conditions were very crude for most of the passengers, who at first were largely curious sightseers. There were no dining cars yet, and the stops for meals at station "eating-houses" were very brief, usually only 20 or 30 minutes.

Passenger and Freight Services: George F. Mayer of Hammond's office wrote Hodges on September 6 about train schedules:

1. We run one express passenger and two freight trains daily each way.

2. Our passenger trains run from Omaha to Promontory in 54 hours, and from Promontory to Omaha in 60 hours [an average of 19 miles an hour]. Freight trains run through going west in about 4 days; coming east in 4 days and 6 hours [an average of 11 miles an hour].[80]

3. Passenger trains average about 2 sleepers, 2 first class, and 1 smoking car, besides baggage and mail; and carry about 110 or more through passengers.

4. Freight trains average about 22 cars leaving Omaha, but a portion of these are way freight, perhaps 20% on an average, and by putting on a heavy 40-ton engine the whole train is taken over the hills as a general thing without doubling up.

5. No second class or emigrant passengers are allowed on express trains. They are carried on freight trains, 2nd class or caboose cars being furnished for that purpose.[81]

In October the "running time from Omaha to Sacramento was on Passenger trains 100 hours; on Freight trains 7½ or 8 days." [82]

The "U.P. Timetable No. 22" of December 5 again listed three trains a day each way between Omaha and Ogden (the CP by now had taken over Promontory). One train was the "Hotel Express"; one, the "Daily Express"; and the third was "Mixed" (passenger and freight). It also stated, "All First Class Passenger Trains are Accompanied by Pullman's Palace Drawing Room and Sleeping Cars." These averaged about 40 feet in length.

Timetable of June 1870: By 20 June 1870, conditions of travel had improved greatly. Sightseers were being encouraged by numerous enthusiastic guidebooks to try out the Pacific Railway. The UP "Time Table No. 24" of this date included some interesting information and advertisements printed on the back. There were only two trains a day each way, the "Daily Express" and the "Mixed." The latest word in luxury, the "Hotel Express" ran weekly in place of the

[80] *Ibid.*   [81] *Ibid.*   [82] *Ibid.*

"Daily Express" on the same hours. It left Omaha Thursdays at 1:20
P.M., arriving at Ogden Saturdays at 4:45 P.M. Returning, it left
Ogden Mondays at 8:00 A.M. and arrived at Omaha Wednesdays at
2:10 P.M. It was advertised as "Made up of Splendid Drawing Room,
Sleeping and *Dining Room* Cars, and Elegant Smoking Cars—All the
luxuries of a first class hotel on wheels." Hauling five or six cars,
handled with hand brakes and link and pin couplers, it had a
scheduled speed of about 19.5 miles per hour for the 53-hour run
between Omaha and Ogden.[83]

Some further significant details of this June 1870 timetable for
passengers follow: [84]

| | | Time of Day | Elapsed Time [a] | | | Through Fare Rate | |
			Hours	Days	Miles	1st Class	2nd Class
	Via Eastern Roads						
Lv.	New York	9.30 am	0	0	0		
Arr.	Omaha	11.30 pm [b]	62	2.6	1,393		
	Via U.P.						
	"Daily Express" (No.3)						
Lv.	Omaha	1.20 pm [b]	0	0	0		
Lv.	Cheyenne	12.30 pm [b]	23	1.0	516	$ 38.75	$ 31.00
Arr.	Ogden	4.45 pm [c]	53	2.2	1,032	77.40	62.00
	Via Central Pacific						
Lv.	Ogden	6.00 pm [d]	0	0	0		
Arr.	Sacramento	11.25 am	42	1.7	744		
	Via Western Pacific						
Lv.	Sacramento	11.45 am	0	0	0		
Arr.	San Francisco	6.00 pm	6	0.3	138		
	SUMMARY [a]						
	Omaha to Sacramento		95	4.0	1,776	$100.00	$ 80.00
	Omaha to San Francisco		102	4.2	1,914	100.00	80.00
	New York to San Francisco		178	7.4	3,307	$136.00	$110.00 [e]

[a] The overall time, including stops. On this basis, the speed averaged about 19 miles
an hour.
[b] Omaha time.
[c] Laramie time.
[d] Sacramento and San Francisco time.
[e] $65.00 for third class, or "emigrant."

Connections at Ogden for Salt Lake City, via Brigham Young's
37-mile Utah Central, could be made for a $2 fare, it was advertised.
A one-way trip took 2 hours.

Also mentioned were two "fast" freight trains daily each way,

[83] *Ibid.; History of the Union Pacific Railroad*, dated 10 May 1919 (50th Anniversary), p. 38.
[84] Records of UP Historical Museum.

advertised to "make the transit between oceans in 17 days." (This meant an average speed of 8.1 miles per hour.)

D. The Five Eminent Citizens' Report

It will be recalled that in August, President Grant had appointed a board of "Five Eminent Citizens," in accordance with the Joint Resolution of Congress of April 10, to ascertain the sums of money necessary to complete the two roads under the Government specifications.[85] His choices for the job were Samuel M. Felton (Chairman), former Representative Hiram Walbridge, General Cyrus B. Comstock, General E.F. Winslow, and J.F. Boyd. Dodge noted, "These gentlemen were all able men. Felton, Winslow, and Boyd were noted railroad men. General Comstock of the regular Army [and an aid-decamp to President Grant] and General Winslow of Iowa had been connected somewhat with railroads since the Civil War. Mr. Walbridge was a distinguished citizen and well known throughout our country." [86] During most of September, Dodge was on the UP with the Commissioners to help with their examination. By the 25th, their inspection was done, and the Chief Engineer returned to Council Bluffs with them.[87] On October 30, their long and thorough report was completed.[88]

On the UP, they itemized current deficiencies totalling only $1,586,100 on the 1,032 miles between Omaha and Ogden,[89] compared with $6,489,550 on 890 miles named by Browning's Special Commission of three back on 23 November 1868.[90] In addition, between Ogden and Promontory $206,000 was needed. On the CP, the expenditures due were set at only $576,650. In retrospect, the demands on both roads were very modest, as within the next four years the two lines actually spent several times these sums.[91]

The list of requirements dealt largely with temporary work on bridges and culverts, ballasting, widening embankments, filling of trestles, and changes to reduce grades. Dale Creek bridge was approved. Their report was unexpectedly favorable:

The location of the accepted line is highly creditable to the engineers of the company. There are deviations from this accepted line at Promon-

---

[85] See p. 306.   [86] Dodge, *Autobiography*, p. 1023.   [87] *Ibid.*, p. 1014.
[88] Senate Executive Document No. 90, 41st Cong., 2nd Sess. (serial no. 1406).
[89] Dodge, *Autobiography*, p. 1024, fn. 4.   [90] See p. 253.
[91] Records of UP Historical Museum; Reports of Government Commissioners, pp. 1869–1874.

tory Mountain and at Uintah, which should be corrected; and at Omaha
the bridge line should be built to avoid the present heavy grade . . . .
After examining the lists of rolling stock, material and supplies . . . and
making a liberal allowance for immediate future wants, we find a surplus
here of about $1,800,000 in value.

    . . . Both companies are day by day bringing [their roads] nearer to
the standard required by law. This great line, the value of which to the
country is inestimable, and in which every citizen should feel a pride,
has been built in about half the time allowed by Congress, and is now
a good and reliable means of communication between Omaha and Sacramento, well equipped and fully prepared to carry passengers and
freight with safety and dispatch, comparing, in this respect, favorably
with the majority of the first-class roads in the United States.[92]

Dodge, obviously greatly pleased, added in his autobiography:

This was such a favorable report to the company, and coming from
the character of the men that it did, it virtually stopped the critiscisms
that were in the country and in Congress as to how the roads had been
built. The simple facts were that, the pressure for speed from all over
the country, from Congress and the Government, forced the company to
leave a good deal of the permanent work such as piers for bridges, stations, shops, etc., until Fall, after their track was laid. This work they
performed as rapidly as possible and both companies spent a great deal
more money, in bringing the roads up to what they considered a first-
class railroad and what the operations of the road required, than any
of the commissioners found were required.[93]

E. McComb's Injunction

Henry S. McComb was a very stubborn man, particularly when it
came to his money. Also, he was either avaricious or, like Durant,
rather stupid about people, or both.[94] Now that he had been ejected
from the UP board, along with the Doctor, his enmity broke the last
bond of cooperation. On August 18, there was a meeting of the UP
Directors, at which J.R. Duff Jr. resigned and Dodge was put in, as
had been pre-agreed. Also, the Honorable James Brooks became a
regular Director, instead of a Government Director, in place of Ezra
Baker, who had resigned. The next day Oliver noted, "McCombs
here. wants copy of Ames Contract & its transfers. Will give it
to him." [95]

[92] Dodge, *Autobiography*, p. 1024.   [93] *Ibid.*, pp. 1024–1025.   [94] See p. 210.
[95] Oliver Ames's diary; see also p. 240.

On August 20, Oliver wrote in his diary, "McCombs had injunction served on Trustees to stop the distribution of farther sale of Bonds & Stock under the circular of Aug 6 issued by Trustees. Submitted the case to Bartlett who will attend the hearing tomorrow morning." [96] The next day, "Went up to court this morning on injunction case. McCombs & Durant on Case. was discharged without a hearing. McCombs says he is willing to come in and do his part if we will only show him what there is to be done." But obviously he was not going to subscribe to any new capital.

Rollins, in Boston, wrote Oliver on November 16:

Mr Oakes Ames has sent you a telegram in regard to the dangers of having balances etc in New York at present time, and requests me to write you . . . . He thinks no transfer should be made in New York and that all bonds should be delivered here or in Wash. in case you make a settlement with the Central. No doubt if any property is found in N.Y., a very desperate effort will be made to obtain possession of it, in some way through the New York courts.[97]

On November 25, Oliver, as Chairman of the Trustees, wrote H.C. Crane, as Assistant Treasurer of the Trustees, "As you are restrained by the New York Courts from removing the Books of the Contractors beyond their jurisdiction will you please deliver to Mr. B.F. Ham copies of all the Books of the trustees in your possession." [98]

F. The UP Sells Its Ogden–Promontory Track to the Central

Pursuant to the agreement of April 9, the Joint Resolution of Congress of April 10, and the joining of the roads on May 10,[99] negotiations were soon commenced for the transfer to the Central of the line between Ogden and Promontory which had been built by the UP. They were complex and protracted. In fact, many years passed before all details were settled.

As has been mentioned, Dodge wrote Oliver on May 26 that the UP no longer wanted the road, "with its 116-foot grades, 10° curves, and high trestles." [100] Dodge wanted to get rid of it.

---

[96] He meant the circular of Aug. 11; see also p. 359.
[97] Records of UP Historical Museum.
[98] Durant, *Papers*, 1–3–27–26.   [99] See pp. 317–318.
[100] See p. 349; Dodge, *Annual Report*, 1 Dec. 1869, p. 29.

Oliver wrote Dodge June 1, ". . . [You say] that Crocker Genl Supt of the Central had an interview with you and desires to settle matters. We are very desirous of doing so . . . just as soon as they are willing to fix a Basis of equal justice so that we shall have the cost of construction of our Road and fair interest . . . ." [101]

Oliver, in Boston, next wrote Vice-President Huntington on June 29:

> Our Chief Engineer . . . has submitted to you the cost of construction, & an estimate of the earth & rock removed between Ogden & Promontory, & also estimate of cost of incidental expenses, together with cost of super-structure. We wish at as early a day as practicable, to turn over this road to you in accordance with the Joint Resolution of Congress . . . and receive the pay therefor. We wish to arrange at the terminous of our Road, the required Station Houses for our business . . . .[102]

Dodge stated in a letter to Treasurer Williams on July 19, "The Central do not intend to . . . pay a fair price for it if they can help it, but do intend to make a row to fight for the bonds to Ogden, go to Congress, lie, howl, and finally steal the road . . . ." [103]

From Boston on July 21, Oliver wrote Duff:

> . . . Huntington seems anxious to get the Road, But will not be willing to pay what he ought . . . . Lambard saw Huntington who said he ought not to pay over 1,500,000 . . . . This is less than the Bonds we receive from Govt will amount to. We better get our Bonds & *then* we will get 2,500,000 from him which will be nearer the true value & actual cost . . . . We have sent Rollins & Painter is at Wash. with Wade working to get our bonds.[104]

The First Offer: In the course of these discussions the UP finally made a definite proposition. On August 3, Duff (Chairman of the Committee), Oakes Ames, and Dillon wrote Huntington as follows:

> For the purpose of making a speedy adjustment of all unsettled matters . . . we propose to sell you our road from a point *six miles west of Ogden* to Promontory, at cost, which is about $87,000 dollars a mile [$4,132,500 for 47½ miles].
>
> We further propose if you are disposed to sell that portion of the road from Corinne *east,* to the point named above, to *pay* you therefor $110,000

101 Dodge, *Papers*, vol. 158 (original manuscript).
102 Records of UP Historical Museum.
103 Dodge, *Autobiography*, p. 999.   104 Records of UP Historical Museum.

per mile [$1,870,000 for 17 miles], notwithstanding this portion cost much less [per mile] than the road between Corinne and Promontory . . . .[105]

Huntington did not accept. The first proposal evidently was too high, and the second obviously barred a connection to Salt Lake City and was 17 miles further away from Ogden.

The Second Offer: The UP next made an offer to sell the 47½ miles for the total cost estimated by Reed and Dodge of $4,387,254.80 (about $92,000 a mile), including $381,542.50 deficiencies. But the CP argued that the UP had been extravagant in building, and that the cost of grading, bridging, and track-laying, without equipment, was reasonably only $50,000 to $60,000 a mile ($2,375,000 to $2,850,-000). This also was rejected.[106]

Sold: It was not until November 17 that a general agreement on the price was concluded. After some further bickering, the UP finally sold to the CP about 48½ miles of its road, from Promontory to a point 5 miles west of Ogden, for a consideration of about *$2,853,000,* or less than *$59,000 a mile.* Payment was not completed until August 1870. Allowing for a market discount of about 9.4 per cent on the CP bonds delivered, and for a cash payment 9 months later, the author's summation of the transactions is as follows: [107]

		Approx. Mkt. Value
$1,338,000	U.S. Subsidy bonds at par, turned over by CP by December 31	$1,338,000
1,502,000	CP 1st Mtg. Bonds at about 90.587 delivered by December 31, but "to be kept out of the market for a year."	1,360,620
$2,840,000		$2,698,620
60,000	CP 1st Mtg. Bonds at about 90.587, delivered in 1870	54,350
$3,000,000	Total Bonds	$2,752,970
$ 100,000	Cash paid in August 1870, "to settle the dispute."	$ 100,000
	Eventual Approximate Value of Transaction	$2,852,970
		($58,824 a mile)

Oliver finally noted in his diary on December 29, "Meeting of Exec Com. authorized signing of the papers to attach to agreement

[105] *Ibid.* (Italics by C.E.A.)   [106] *Ibid.*
[107] U.S. Pacific Railway Commission, pp. 3808, 4748, 5048; *Wilson Rep.,* p. 637; Records of UP Historical Museum; Balance Sheet of UP on 31 Dec. 1869.

made with Central P Rd transferring to them the Road west of Ogden." [108]

The agreement being made, the transfer point was moved from Promontory to Ogden on or about December 1, and the CP commenced operating from there, apparently by sufferance, and without written lease until 1875. Then Gould found that the CP had been using the 5-mile stretch just west of Ogden, a part of the UP main line, without lease payment. This small mileage was not a part of the 48½ miles sold. But the lease claims of the UP remained unsettled until as late as 1884.[109]

The actual junction of the roads was fixed by further agreement on 25 June 1870 (pursuant to an Act of Congress on May 6) at 5 miles west of the Utah Central crossing at Ogden. The U.S. bonds on the 5 miles, which had been issued to the CP by Browning, were turned over to the UP in 1870.[110]

Reflections: The main considerations in this confused Promontory deal follow:

1. The price was freely negotiated; Congress apparently resisted taking part in most of it.

2. The cash loss to the UP on construction alone over the 48½ miles was $1,124,036, if Dodge's final actual-cost figure of June 17 of $82,000 a mile [111] and the table above are accepted. If Reed's estimate of $87,000 a mile were to be considered, the loss would be $242,500 greater.[112]

(Dodge was asked years later by the U.S. Pacific Railway Commission why such a great concession was made by the UP. He said he could offer no explanation, but added, "I know there was a great contest over it; and we preferred to sell rather than they should build a road alongside of us." An important consideration, no doubt, was the UP's desperate financial situation in 1869.) [113]

3. The UP abandoned the grading it had done west of Promontory, near Independence Springs (204 miles from Ogden) and Humboldt Wells (222 miles from Ogden) at a cost of over $200,000.[114]

---

[108] Presumably he meant "5 miles west of Ogden," yet that important 5 miles caused much further wrangling. The overall distance from Ogden to Promontory was 53½ miles.

[109] Records of UP Historical Museum.   [110] *Ibid.*   [111] See p. 354.

[112] See p. 333.

[113] Records of UP Historical Museum; U.S. Pacific Railway Commission, pp. 3799–3801 (testimony of Dodge).

[114] Records of UP Historical Museum.

4. The work done by the Central east of Promontory during 1869 and 1870 cost $751,963. This line was abandoned, the company taking the road built by the UP over the same route.[115]

5. The Central gained its point of an entry to Ogden and the Salt Lake valley traffic, as Huntington had always threatened he would do. The "Big Four" had no notion of resting content with their eastern terminal marooned in the desert.

6. President Johnson's and Secretary Browning's favoritism in the distribution of the U.S. bonds was at last mollified, but the Central had gained the use of precious working capital at a most critical period, at the expense of the UP.

7. Congress disgracefully had allowed over 200 miles of overlapping grading to be built before acting definitively.[116]

G. *Dodge's Last Annual Report*

The Chief Engineer's long delayed third and farewell report covered the surveys of 1868 (including those to Oregon) and the operations of 1869 up to 1 December 1869, the date of the report. A few excerpts from his concluding remarks are quoted: [117]

Reduction of Grades and Curves.

All grades ascending both eastward and westward can be reduced to 60 feet per mile, except those over the three mountain ranges, should the commerce of the road demand it; and in many cases . . . where sharp curves now occur, the curvature can be much ameliorated.

Missouri River Bridge and Transfer.

Very little work in the sinking of piers has been done on the bridge, although a large amount of material has been bought and manufactured, and sufficient has been done to determine . . . the practicability of the plan adopted . . . . The Missouri River is now the only obstacle to travel between the Atlantic and Pacific . . . . In my opinion the transfer can be cheapened and simplified so as to avoid the great annoyance and tax upon travel. We should receive all passengers and freight on the east bank of the Missouri River, placing the transfer in the hands

---

[115] U.S. Pacific Railway Commission, p. 4748.   [116] See p. 318.
[117] See p. 265 for the part covering 1868.

of one company and under one management. If they do not desire to cross their cars, then let the trains on each side run to the river bank, and the passengers step from the cars to the boat . . . . It is unnecessary . . . to force four competing roads to each put in boats . . . . I have known passengers to be kept two hours in omnibuses [horse-drawn] making a transfer that could be made in fifteen minutes, and baggage to get so wet as to seriously damage it . . . . Under our management it could be made to yield a fair profit, and the cost reduced at least one-half . . . . The completion of the bridge at an early day is a necessity. We can push the work at almost any speed directed.

Surveys.

Some 15,000 miles of instrumental lines have been run, and over 25,000 miles of reconnaissances made, from the Missouri to the Californian state line, covering a width of 200 miles, north and south.

Progress of the Work.

Each day taught us lessons by which we profited for the next . . . . Our improvement in the art of railway construction was marked by the progress of the work; 40 miles of track having been laid in 1865; 260 in 1866; 240 in 1867, including ascent to an elevation of 8,235 feet above the ocean; and during 1868, and to May 10, 1869, 555 miles, all exclusive of side and temporary tracks, of which over 180 miles were built in addition.[118]

The first grading was done in the autumn of 1864, and the first rail laid in July, 1865. When you look back to the beginning at the Missouri River, with no railway communication from the east, and 500 miles of the country in advance without timber, fuel, or any material whatever from which to build or maintain a road, except the sand for the bare road-bed itself, with everything to be transported, and that by teams, or at best by steamboats, for hundreds and thousands of miles; everything to be created, with labor scarce and high, you can all look back upon the work with satisfaction, and ask, under such circumstances, could we have done more or better.

The Achievement.

The country is evidently satisfied that you accomplished wonders, and have achieved a work that will be a monument to your energy, your

[118] However, to be exact, this adds up to 1,095 miles of track, 9 miles too much. Presumably the 555-mile figure should have been 546. The author's calculation of 1,086 miles to Promontory is made up of 40 miles in 1865, 265 in 1866, 231 in 1867, 446 in 1868, and 102 in 1869 (plus 2 miles to the "initial point" north of Omaha). See pp. 120, 162, and tables on pp. 235, 295, 336.

ability, and to your devotion to the enterprise through all its gloomy as well as its bright periods; for it is notorious that, notwithstanding the aid of the government, there was so little faith in the enterprise that its dark days—when your private fortunes and your all was staked on the success of the project—far exceeded those of sunshine, faith, and confidence.

This lack of confidence in the project, even in the West, in those locations where the benefits were manifest, was excessive . . . . Laborers even demanded their pay before they would perform their day's work . . . . Probably no enterprise in the world has been so maligned . . . but now . . . it is almost without exception pronounced the best new road in the United States.

Its location . . . has received the praise of some of the ablest engineers . . . . That it yet needs work to finally complete it, no one denies, but whatever is necessary is being done.

A Forecast.

Its future is fraught with great good. It will develop a waste, will bind together the two extremities of the nation as one, will stimulate intercourse and bring harmony, prosperity and wealth to the two coasts . . . . The local trade will increase gradually until the mining, grazing and agricultural regions through which it passes will build up and create a business that will be a lasting support to the company.

Acknowledgments.

In closing the surveys of the road and reporting its final completion, I take pleasure in acknowledging the services of those who have been directly connected with my department—the engineers in charge of divisions, the chiefs of parties and their assistants; many of them commenced with the enterprise, while others of their comrades fell in the line of duty, but never deserted their posts. They have been mentioned so often in the various reports that it is not necessary for me to name them.

The chiefs of the running department, Messrs. Snyder and Hoxie, and their subordinates, always rendered promptly and efficiently any aid asked by my department. I am also under obligations to the superintendent and chiefs of construction, the commanders of the department and their staffs. In fact, all officers with whom I have come in contact or asked favors of, from the highest to the lowest, have responded promptly, and their aid has been of no little advantage to us in pushing forward the enterprise. Without it the company would have been subjected to serious expenditures for escorts, arms, ammunition, and guards of all kinds . . . . During the entire construction a relentless, determined war has been waged all along the line by different tribes of the Plain Indians with scarcely any interruption, and peace was not brought about until after we had long passed the hostile country and got beyond their reach.

Very respectfully, your obedient servant,

G. M. Dodge
Chief Engineer [119]

Oliver Ames, Esq.,
President Union Pacific Railroad, Boston, Mass.

The General lived to see his "Forecast" come true.

H. Summary of 1869

This was a stormy, complex year of closing the gap in the first transcontinental railroad at a point acceptable to both companies, yet keeping out of bankruptcy. The very size of the Union Pacific had magnified the number and intensity of the problems, especially those of financing fearful expenses while earned subsidy bonds were unfairly withheld, also preventing the issues of company First Mortgages. Not until the unfriendly Johnson administration ended on March 4, and Grant came in, did the UP get any comfort from the White House. Congress remained suspicious of both roads, and especially of Durant.

As 1869 opened, the Directors first learned of the awful plight caused by the Doctor's unbridled determination to rush construction through the Wasatch Mountains in winter. His objective—profit—was understandable; but his bad planning, mismanagement, and wild extravagance resulted instead in a crushing cost just for construction of at least $80,000 a mile. The unexpected fiasco staggered even the four members of the Executive Committee who in July, 1868, had unwisely voted him full authority on construction and changes in the line. In the general demoralization which ensued, the line was plundered by some dishonest sub-contractors and employees. His "crazy gamble" with parallel construction as far west as Humboldt Wells, instead of winning subsidies and construction profits, cost the UP precious time.

Oliver felt obliged to plead with Oakes to cut down his debts and make no new speculative investments.

[119] Dodge, *Reports of the Chief Engineer*, 1868–1869, pp. 19–23.

The confused Browning, Johnson's Secretary of the Interior, brazenly favored the Central Pacific, and wrongfully insisted that the Union Pacific must meet the Central Pacific as far east as Echo Summit, even though the UP had already graded many miles beyond the key town of Ogden, and had brought the completed track into that town on March 7. To cap it all, on the very last day of his term, Johnson broke his promise to Oakes that no subsidies would be issued to the CP in advance of the completed track. This enabled Huntington to irretrievably capture $2,400,000 U.S. subsidy bonds for grading work merely claimed to have been done on 180 miles between Ogden and Ives Pass. When finally completed, the U.S. Bonds on this stretch, at $32,000 a mile, would amount to $5,760,000, all to the Central Pacific. Dodge submitted a long affidavit claiming that the Central's demand for these bonds was based on a fraudulent map filed with Browning. Oliver earnestly protested to Congress, but to no avail.

Grant's first order on taking office on March 4 was to annul Johnson's directives against the UP, but to suspend further issue of subsidy bonds to both roads. Next he demanded that Durant be put out of office.

Not until March 11 did the majority of the Directors rescind all of Durant's authority on the line. From then on, a committee consisting of Duff, Dillon, and Grant's Government Director Price was given the tremendous task of cleaning up the mess at Echo.

As a result of the outrageous Fisk raid on the UP at a critical moment in March, a Tammany Hall receiver for the CM broke open the safe, and the market value of UP securities tumbled by several millions. Furthermore, Fisk caused the regular annual meeting of stockholders for election of Directors to be postponed. Thereby Durant's final ouster was delayed until after the Golden Spike ceremonies.

Even while Congress, alarmed at long last, was debating action to force the roads to cease the senseless grading past each other over the same route, Dodge, Hooper, and Hazard (without Oliver's knowledge) signed an agreement on April 9 with Huntington to meet at Promontory. As a result, the UP had to sell to the CP all the track it had built, or was to build, between Ogden and Promontory. The gladiator scene suddenly vanished. Congress gladly adopted this agreement the next day, and Grant appointed a competent commission of "Five Eminent Citizens" to inspect the entire length of both roads for deficiencies. Further, to thwart Fisk's dealings with crooked

New York judges, Congress authorized the UP to move its headquarters to Boston, which was done on May 2.

On April 29 the UP started building eastward from Promontory to meet its own tracklayers. On April 30 the CP arrived at Promontory, after making a new record of laying 10 miles of track in a day. Durant arranged to be "kidnapped" on the way West by Davis's tie-cutters. After delays from washouts and inadequate bridging in Weber Canyon, the Golden Spike was finally driven at Promontory with simple but historical ceremony on May 10. Oakes, Oliver, Huntington and a majority of the Directors of both roads were unable to attend. "Now that the road is finished," queried depressed Oliver that day in Boston, "how shall we put it in the best running order, and our finances in satisfactory shape?"

On May 25 the UP stockholders held their delayed meeting in the safe city of Boston. There Durant was at last removed as Director and Vice President, and four of his friends, including McComb, were put off the Board. The Ames group, too late, came into firm working control for the first time. But Durant still had heavy UP and CM stockholdings, and still could use corrupt courts.

Internal strife had been the UP's greatest weakness from the beginning.

In the meantime the financial condition of the UP was slumping from bad to worse. Heavy drafts were pouring in from the West, with no money to meet them. As early as January, 1869, the stockholders had met to see if they could raise enough money amongst themselves to avoid bankruptcy of the road. By April 10 most of them had honorably agreed to use part of their $12,838,000 profit allotments received in 1868 to buy First Mortgage and Land Grant Bonds, with a good bonus of common. The Ameses responded generously, and the total amount subscribed was $7,657,000 at market value.

Oliver Ames and Dodge, both exhausted by extreme exertions, exchanged sharp recriminations concerning past events. On July 3 Bushnell reported from Reed's office at Echo that unpaid amounts due contractors were down to $2,783,000. But unsettled obligations, especially those due Brigham Young, forced the Directors to borrow as much as $12,755,000 on short-term notes.

Paying traffic on the UP began to pick up after through service between Omaha and Sacramento commenced on May 15. Late in July work was suspended on the important Missouri River bridge at Omaha for lack of funds. But the UP Land Office opened for business and commenced sales to settlers.

McComb brought an injunction in August with his important suit against Oakes Ames and the Credit Mobilier, claiming title to 375 shares of CM.

The reckless gold panic created by Fisk and Gould culminated on September 24, thereafter called "Black Friday." The prices of UP bonds, and all securities traded on the Exchange, were hard hit, just at a time which hurt the UP most. The First Mortgage Bonds had a volatile year. They fell from a high in February of 103 to 65 during the Fisk raid in March, recovered in May to 93, dropped again during Black Friday to 82, and closed the year at about 85. The 7% Land Grant Bonds, first issued in April, ranged between 60 and 50.

The Five Eminent Citizens appointed by Grant in April turned in an unexpectedly favorable report in October. Deficiencies on the UP by then had been reduced to $1,586,100, and on the CP to $576,650. Both roads were declared "well equipped and fully prepared to carry passengers and freight with safety and dispatch."

On November 17 the two roads, after many months of dispute, came to an agreement on the price the UP was to receive from the CP for its 48½ miles between Promontory and a point 5 miles west of Ogden. The amount settled on, $2,853,000 ($59,000 a mile), created a loss to the UP estimated at about $1,124,036. The UP was in no financial position to barter: it was in desperate need of the money. Anyway the Central probably would have extended its own road into Ogden, rather than be marooned in the desert. The junction and transfer point was moved from Promontory to Ogden in December.

But hardly was the missing link in the Pacific Railway welded at Promontory than, on November 20, the Suez Canal was opened. Exciting visions of "China Trade" vanished. However, unexpectedly large traffic from the opening up and growth of the Great West was to far more than make up the loss, as the years rolled on. Dodge's faith in the future, as expressed in his last annual report, was to be confirmed.

In December the UP had to pay a 17½% interest rate on a large, short-term loan from a prominent New York bank, so low had its credit fallen.

Net operating earnings for 1869 of $2,031,000 fell far short of covering the annual interest cost on the bonded debt outstanding at the end of the year of over $4,000,000.

Professor Fogel made a cogent contribution to the history of the Union Pacific with a painstaking estimate of the "social return or unpaid benefits" brought about by the opening up of land in the four states through which the railroad passed. Using the theory of rent, he computed that the value of the UP lands between Omaha and Ogden, 40 miles on each side of the track, increased from under $6,000,000 in 1860 to over $158,000,000 in 1880. Furthermore, he calculated that the "increase in national income in 1880 due to the productivity of labor and capital on the lands made available by the UP but not reflected in the company's receipts," was nearly $16,000,000. He concluded, "Clearly, then, from a social point of view the Union Pacific was a most profitable adventure. There can be little doubt that the government was economically justified in intervening to build a road that would not have been built by unaided private enterprise." [120]

[120] Fogel, pp. 97–103.

10

Insolvency

Dodge Resigns—Oakes Insolvent—UP Finances Most Desperate—Cabinet Members "Raid" the UP—Report to Stockholders by Oliver Ames—The Pennsylvania Takes Control—Missouri River Bridge Problems—New York Central Takes Control from the Pennsy—Deficient Net Income

A. Dodge Resigns

The pioneering Union Pacific was finished and no longer needed a locating Chief Engineer. Great new railroads still were to be built, and fine opportunities beckoned to civil engineers like General Dodge, who had proved his ability and mettle in war and rail. So he laid out his plans.

On 8 November 1869, he wrote General Sherman, ". . . I believe that I ought to, in justice to myself and to others, quietly retire. My work as an engineer is completed, and any work of that kind I have no taste for. The road is becoming settled a thousand miles away, a mere plaything for Wall Street, to be put up or down as a few may dictate . . . ." [1] Sherman replied by letter that Dodge was probably right in his conclusion. At about the same time, Dodge wrote President Ames of his intention to resign as soon as possible. He still had to finish his farewell report for 1868 and 1869, he had work to do on the Missouri River bridge, and his involved railroad accounts must be closed.

On 8 January 1870, ill at home in Council Bluffs, Dodge virtually turned over the repairs of the road to the "running department" in a letter to Colonel C.G. Hammond, the new General Superintendent of the UP.[2] Next he got a few last words off his mind. On January 17,

---

[1] Dodge, *Autobiography*, p. 1027.   [2] *Ibid.*, p. 1032.

he mailed a "private" letter to Sidney Dillon, a Director, Member of the Executive Committee, one of the Seven Trustees of the UP, and President of the Credit Mobilier, as follows:

I have been on the point of writing you for some time, just to say to you that on the road now, or under present influence, you appear to have very few friends. It seems to be the endeavor to pull down anyone who prefers to work efficiently and honestly; so far as I observe, they take pleasure in building up the rascalities and corruptions of Durant, rather than say a word commendatory of those who brought the Company to a full knowledge of their condition. I believe I am about the last friend you have in the administration. Wilson, Price and myself, as well as Snyder and Hoxie, are not afraid to say what we think; all this is private but you should know it.[3]

He submitted his resignation as Chief Engineer to Oliver on January 25 in these words:

. . . I saw Mr. Hammond and explained my desires as to the future. That hereafter I did not wish to take charge of or be responsible for the engineering on the road, and as he wished to get in his estimate for the next year, I prefer that it should be done under his supervision, or by such person as the company may select. That I would close up all my office matters, etc., myself but if it meets with your approval, would relinquish all charge of the engineering on the line of the Railroad. I am responsible yet for a large amount of property, Government and railroad, which I am getting in shape as fast as possible.

I am still unable to do much but gaining slowly. If this meets with your approval, please say so . . . .[4]

Then because, as he said, "there were all kinds of rumors afloat out west in relation to changes and account charges and reports of what the Directors were saying in Boston," he dispatched a second, and "private," letter to Oliver dated January 26:

It has been intimated to me out here by some parties who have been in Boston that a charge is made against me of expending some money in repairs, unauthorized and that I raised the money out here to pay for them, etc. Now if any such charge has been made it is due to me that I should know it, for I have not expended a cent on repairs or construction that I am aware of that was not ordered . . . . I have raised large amounts of money on line for running department, sometimes for the current expenses of my Department but it was always when the company was short of funds, and with the full approval of the Company . . . . I know that Mr. Durant will do me all the harm he can and will influence others all he can as he has good reason to hate me, and I care nothing for his ill-will or good-will but the rest of the Company I have the desire to retain the confidence of and want to meet any charge that pertains against me.[5]

In reply, Oliver delivered a gracious testimonial on the 29th:

Yours of the 25th inst., tendering your resignation as Chief Engineer of the Union Pacific Railroad Company is received.

In accepting your resignation, permit us to express to you our thanks for the eminent services you have rendered this company and the country, in so admirably locating this great national highway.

When we consider the great difficulties and dangers that beset you on all sides while locating the road, through an uninhabited country, and the rapidity with which the work was accomplished, we are gratified and surprised that you have finished the work in so perfect and acceptable a manner. We now have one of the best railroads in the country, notwithstanding it was located and built with a rapidity without precedent in the history of railroad enterprises.

I enclose herewith vote of thanks, adopted by the Executive Committee, in consideration of services in behalf of this company, and hope you will find elsewhere the same hearty appreciation of your valuable services as we now most cheerfully accord to you.[6]

Dodge finished his "Review of the Building of the Union Pacific," written many years later, with this sentence, "I retained my position as a Director in the company, taking an active interest in it up to the time it went into the receivers' hands. My services during that period will appear later in the Dodge Records now being compiled."[7] Actually, he was a Director from August 1869 to March 1873, from March 1875 to November 1878, and from January 1880 to July 1897 —probably the longest service of any Director of the Union Pacific.

The life story of this remarkable man, only thirty-nine years of age at the time that he left the UP, is summed up in Chapter 4, pages 129–139.

---

[5] *Ibid.*, p. 1033.　　[6] *Ibid.*, p. 1112.　　[7] *Ibid.*, p. 1113.

B. Oakes Insolvent

Changes in Directors: Oakes Ames's contract with the UP having been successfully completed, he made himself available as a Director of the company for the first time, and on 9 March 1870 was so elected at the annual meeting of stockholders held in Boston. Oliver continued as President, and the Ames group still remained in firm control of company affairs. Bushnell was again carried on as the only Director from the Durant group. Dodge was re-elected, and James Brooks (once a Government Director) was put back on the Board, replacing Bates. Dexter was not taken on, to make room for Oakes. There were no changes among the five Government Directors. Besides Oliver, the Executive Committee now consisted of John Duff (Vice-President), Dillon, Glidden, Atkins, Bushnell, and James F. Wilson (Government Director).[8] J.M.S. Williams continued as Treasurer and E.H. Rollins as Assistant Treasurer and Secretary.

Oakes's Many Activities: Oakes was going on sixty-seven, and his burdens were increasing at a period when they should have been lightening. The Forty-First Congress, Second Session, did not adjourn for the summer and fall until July 15; elections for the Forty-Second Congress were coming up in November; the financial condition of the UP was ever critical; the McComb suit was cooking; and he always had the Shovel Works to think about, on top of his wide-flung investments, many debts (but more assets), outside business connections, and family.

Evelina Has a Stroke: No sooner had Oakes and Evelina returned home from Washington on Sunday morning, July 17, than she had a stroke. She was sixty-one. Her diaries of those years no longer can be found, and Oliver's diary is the only known source of information about this sad blow. He wrote that day, "Oakes' wife has had a Paralytic Shock which has crippled her very much with great difficulty —Mr. Oakes Ames is quite recovered from his Diabetis. Chaffin preached, not able to finish his sermon."

Oliver to Resign: In September Oliver told the Executive Committee that he was intending to resign soon as President.[9] On October 3

---

[8] See table, p. 240 (adapted from Union Pacific, *Official Register*). See p. 345 for the previous election of 25 May 1869, in which Durant was removed from office.

[9] Oliver Ames's diary, Sept. 8.

he went west for a last inspection trip. Returning on November 5, he noted, "I have the greatest confidence that we shall be able to make a better show than we have ever done since the road opened." He did not get back in time for the November elections, when Oakes was chosen for the House of Representatives for the last time.

Oakes Joins Durant's Pool: On October 1, Oakes joined with Durant, Bushnell, and Dillon in a secret pool to buy and support the UP stock on the New York Stock Exchange where it had just been listed and was at 24. The transactions were to be as directed by Durant, reputed to be clever in such things. In all, 12,000 UP shares and $100,000 income bonds were put up by them as collateral.[10] This may have cost them some big money, as by December 9 the stock was at 9.[11] *But already Durant had begun secretly to sell his own stock in a big way.*[12]

Oliver Had Asked Oakes to Retrench: Nearly two years earlier, Oliver had written a long letter to Oakes pleading with him to cut down his speculations and debts.[13] That visional letter is quoted in full, now being of no small import:

N. Easton
Hon Oakes Ames   *Jan 10th 1869*
Dear Bro
    The date at the Head of this page reminds me of your entrance upon the 66th year of your life and it also admonishes me that we have but a few more years to pass through the toil and turmoil of the World Below before we shall be called to the higher and Better life. With the new year I have come to the conclusion to withdraw as soon as possible from my connexion with Pacific Railroad and outside business and devote myself to putting my property in such shape that I may feel that it is not all placed at hazard of an unfortunate speculation or a misplaced confidence. I am now 61 years of age and may not calculate with much confidence upon more than 10 years more perhaps not five of Life. I feel that I should now draw in my outside matters and look for safe and reliable investments where my time will not be occupied as in this Pacific Railroad management in fighting to protect its interests against the Thousand Thieves that are on every side robbing it
    I understand that this year by our mutual agreement was to be one of retrenchment and reform that no new speculations were to be

---

[10] Durant, *Papers,* 3–3–12–18.   [11] See Appendix A.
[12] See p. 399.   [13] See pp. 302–303.

entered but all our efforts were to be turned to reducing our indebtedness & I am going to do it. I started last year with a Ballance due me from O A & Sons of 350,000$ the same amt 350,000 was due by you to the concern. I see in the new a/c that you have doubled your indebtedness which is now 700,000$ to the Firm while mine remains about the same as last year. I expect to add to my credit about 150,000$ from profits of Shovel works and Kinsley I. & M Co & Plow Co . . . .[14]

I think your true Policy is in view of your large indebtedness to sell off your Stocks, and reduce your outside indebtedness. Your Cedar Rapids of which you have a 1,000,000, would sell I suppose for more than par and would put you out of debt sufficiently to carry along the rest of it easy. I would not at your stage of life be harrassed by debt as you must be all for the difference between what you could now get for the Stock and what you think it is worth I think I should get my neck out of this yoke of bondage before another year is over. If we save Pacific RR and our interests there we want to raise 500,000$ to do it and have got to put our necks to this burden.

You better come over to NY next Wednesday and we can see if any arrangement can be made to raise our share of the money.

I hope we shall be able this year to keep our promise to go into no new thing

Your Brother
Oliver Ames [15]

Probably Oakes did not answer by letter, as they were to meet soon. What he thought about it can be only a guess. Perhaps he decided that the Cedar Rapids stock could be sold higher later on, when it would be helped by the growing traffic to and from the UP. In addition to faithfully giving still more aid to the struggling UP, he did take on many "new things," and continually borrowed more from the banks to carry them. As a private banker himself, that was the way. Or perhaps he was, at his age, unconsciously beginning to lose his touch for successful investments. Maybe he thought that Oliver was too conservative, or was unduly depressed by the weight of his problems in the UP. Most likely of all, Oakes had more irons in the fire than he could handle.

Oakes Goes Insolvent: Be that as it may, Oliver first revealed his new worries soon after he returned from the West by writing in his diary of 16 November 1870: "Am feeling uneasy about Oakes matters

---

[14] The portion omitted here appears on p. 308.
[15] Original letter, in the possession of the Ames family.

do not see how he is going to get along with his payments without involving O Ames & Sons in great loss. He seems crazy almost to involve himself in every new scheme."

Then follow many diary entries, which speak for themselves:

Nov. 17—Mr. Oakes has great difficulty in saving money to meet his notes. Endorsed 100,000$ notes of Peter Butler on Ames Plow Co . . . at request of Oakes Ames for some of his matters.

Nov. 20, Sun.—Had a talk with Mr. Oakes Ames on his affairs and he promises to retrench and sell off his property and get out of his entanglements.

Nov. 24—Spent the day mostly in looking over my securities and Co's and getting a statement of Brothers Oakes liabilities and assets. He thinks he has 2,500,000 surplus after paying all up. I don't know what to think of it.

Nov. 28—Alley says he is inquired of daily about Mr. Oakes Ames Position and responsibility, and has to give replies favorable and does not know what to say. Thinks he ought to retract.

Nov. 30—Have had headache and poor day and discouraged about the prospect of Mr. Oakes Ames getting his.

Dec. 3—Saw Eager this morning and had a long talk on condition of Kinsley I & M Co. He wants Mr. Oakes Ames if possible to pay up the Dec. notes and we can later take care of the rest.

Dec. 4, Sun.—Spent a considerable portion of day in Office looking up the records of Property of Mr. Oakes Ames. He shows a very large amt. of Securities to offset his Liabilities.

Dec. 5—Called this morning on Mr. Bartlett and showed him the papers exhibiting Mr. Oakes Ames property and Liabilities. Looks well but must in his opinion get some one to sell off and reduce. Says that I can not secure any one and recommends not to pay my debts of OA shops. Showed exhibit to Atkins.

On this day the Forty-First Congress, Third Session convened, and presumably Oakes went to Washington to remain until 20 April 1871, except for some trips back and forth.

Dec. 6—Am greatly distressed by condition of Mr. Oakes Ames matters. Spent large part of day looking over his Exhibit with Alley & Atkins and they think he can be carried along and work out if he will consent to sell off. Oakes has gone to NY tonight to see if he can sell off anything there.

Dec. 9—Quite a panic today in Pacific Securities on a/c of movement in Congress looking to some change in law to affect lands of the Co.

Incomes went down to 51 and Land Grants to 64 but rallied a little towards night. Mr. Oakes at home from NY did really nothing in NY but get his mortgage.

The *Financial Review,* 1875, page 53 said, "Union Pacific stock fell off to 9 in consequence of stoppage of Oakes Ames and other temporary embarrassments." Earlier in the year, in March, the stock had sold at 45½; the first sale on the Stock Exchange on 24 September 1870 was at 24; and by May 1871, it was up to 37⅞.[16] Durant's pool of 1 October 1870 must have found the going rough.[17] To go on with Oliver's diary notes:

Dec. 11, Sun.—Mr. Chaffin preached. Cannot take much interest in anything outside of Mr. Oakes Ames involvement.

Dec. 20—Letter from Swain showing state of Treadwell's affairs to be awful in the extreme. Mr. Oakes Ames must lose a million dollars by the operation.

Treadwell and Company Fails: Treadwell and Company, 118 Milk Street, Boston, were proprietors of the small Antrim Shovel Works built in North Easton in 1865.[18] Assets were figured at $780,000 but liabilities at $1,700,000. The secured creditors, of whom Oakes was one, might recover about 30 per cent of their investment.[19] The creditors' committee estimated the value of Oakes's investment in Treadwell at about $751,000.[20] During the year 1870, Treadwell and Company's net debt to Oakes in cash and loans ranged from $363,370 on July 27 to $180,099 on December 27. Oakes was obviously trying to save them from bankruptcy, and even as late as October and November was making new loans and cash payments to them ranging between $5,000 and $50,000 every few days, which they were paying off in large amounts whenever they could.[21] But in the end, Oakes's own insolvency probably was touched off by their failure as the year closed.

Oliver's diary goes on:

Dec. 24—Called Brooks and Ball this morning and arranged to put Treadwell & Co. into insolvency. Had a meeting of the Ames Plow Co. & voted to authorize me to sign the papers putting them in.

---

[16] See Appendix A.   [17] See p. 385.   [18] Winthrop Ames, pp. 238–239, 240.
[19] Oliver Ames's diary, 31 Dec. 1871.   [20] See p. 392.
[21] Oakes Ames's cash and ledger books, May 1868 through Dec. 1870, ledger pp. 392–393.

Still another Christmas was ruined for the Ameses—and many other persons.

Dec. 28—Ames Plow Co. went to protest today and Mr. Oakes Ames has come to the conclusion that he will be unable to go on and must ask an extension. It is a terrible blow to me.[22]

Dec. 29—Called on Mr. Bartlett this morning with Oakes & Glidden and talked of our case. Called in Coolidge & Bates and they recommend us to ask for an extension which they think will be granted freely.

Dec. 30—Called on Mr. Choate for advice who says go on just as though nothing had occurred, paying as usual. Had interview with Col. French and he recommends that we take sufficient time to sell off enough to pay up—2 years, says 6, 12, 18 and 24 months, and as much earlier as possible . . . . Expect to get out of the Road in March.

Jan. 1, 1871—Worked on statement to present to our Creditors showing condition of Oakes Ames & O Ames & Sons—Mr Oakes Ames statement does not show as well as I expected.

Jan. 3—Statement of Ames Plow Co. showing after deducting loss by Treadwell a Surplus of 202,000. Committee of leading Creditors consisting of Upton, Coolidge, Bates, Gunner Walker Alley & Atkins after looking over Statements they decided to recommend an Extension of our Creditors of to 12, 18 & 24 mos.

Creditors' Committee Extends Credit: "Report of the Investigating Committee.

"In response to a call for a meeting of the creditors of Oakes Ames, Oliver Ames & Sons, the Ames Plow Company, and the Kinsley Iron and Machine Company, about one hundred gentlemen assembled in the office of Oliver Ames & Sons, 38 Sears Building, January 9, 1871. The Hon. John B. Alley was chosen president, and Seth Turner, secretary. Mr. Alley presented the following report." [23]

At the solicitation of the Messrs. Ames and their friends, together with requests from some parties largely interested, the undersigned were induced to act as a committee to investigate their affairs, and to give the result to this meeting. This course was deemed advisable cheafly for the reason that much time would be saved, and promptness was an essential element in obtaining a satisfactory adjustment. The liabilities are so large, the property involved so immense, and of every description, that

[22] The Ames Plow Co. had 4,000 shares, of which 41.5 per cent was owned by Oakes and Frank M. Ames, 41.5 per cent by Oliver and his son and daughter, 14.8 per cent outside the family, and 2.2 per cent by Oliver Ames & Sons. (Oliver Ames's diary, 12 Dec. 1871.)

[23] Boston *Transcript*, 9 Jan. 1871.

the best interests of all required that there should be no unnecessary delay in agreeing on the course to be pursued.

The Committee find upon examination, the liabilities and assets to be as follows:

Mr. Oakes Ames' indebtedness and liabilities amount to
the sum of $ 7,386,179
Of this amount $4,000,000 is secured by collateral, esti-
mated to be worth at its market value about $5,000,000
Leaving, of unsecured debts, about $3,000,000
His assets amount to $10,781,986
Leaving a balance, after paying all his debts, of $ 3,395,807

This estimate is based upon what we regard as a fair valuation of what may be realized out of the property, if reasonable time is given to dispose of it. It is estimated that Oliver Ames & Sons are endorsers upon the obligations of Oakes Ames, to the extent of about $3,000,000.

Oliver Ames & Sons owe in notes and accounts $ 685,363
They have assets to the amount of $ 3,033,709
Exclusive of about $1,000,000 due them from Mr. Oakes
Ames leaving a balance of assets of $ 2,348,346

This we regard as a moderate estimate of their property, and have no doubt this amount can be fully realized.

The liabilities of the Ames Plow Company amount in notes
and accounts to $ 418,001
   Their assets amount to $ 1,020,682
   Leaving a balance of $ 602,681

The Kinsley Iron & Machine Co's. liabilities are $ 8,536
   Their assets are $ 400,790
   Leaving a balance of $ 392,254

The whole amount of the liabilities above is $ 8,498,075
   The assets of all are $15,237,165
   Which leaves a balance of $ 6,739,089

This does not include the private property of the members of the firm of Oliver Ames & Sons, except that of Oakes Ames. That would swell this balance to considerably above $8,000,000. We feel that in this estimate everything is valued no higher than it would bring under proper and judicious management. Their assets comprise every variety and description of property, most of it exceedingly valuable, and if the creditors will grant them the necessary time to dispose of their property without too much sacrifice and their business continued, which is very large and immensely profitable, we have no hesitation in saying unqualifiedly that we believe every obligation will be met by the payment of both principal and interest. The high character of the parties, their undoubted ability, large experience and unquestioned integrity, give assurance to the creditors that however liberal they may be in granting time to them to turn their property, not a moment longer will be taken than is actually necessary to protect the interests of all; and while the committee do not feel that so long a time as they propose will be absolutely essential, yet considering the parties with whom they are dealing, they feel that it is best, with so large a portion of the property unavailable at present, to recommend that the creditors grant an extension, and are allowed to manage their affairs themselves, in their own way, that every dollar of this indebtedness will be liquidated before the expiration of the time proposed.

(Signed)	Elisha Atkins	John B. Alley
	F. Haven	John T. Coolidge
	Jas. H. Beal	Geo. B. Upton
	T. W. Walker	B. E. Bates
	Seth Turner	

"On motion of Mr. Andrew T. Hall of Tremont National Bank, the report of the committee was adopted by unanimous vote. The leading creditors then signed an agreement to extend their credit in accordance with the recommendation of the committee and the meeting was dissolved.

"*(Note)* The report omits to state that the Ames Plow Company are liable by indorsement on Oakes Ames liabilities for $409,000; and the Kinsley Iron and Machine Company are similarly liable to $353,-000. These amounts, being included in the indebtedness of Oakes Ames, do not appear in the assets or debts of either company." [24]

Oakes's Holdings: To give a general idea of the kind and number of investments held by Oakes on 1 January 1871, the main items are listed, in order of size, in the table on page 392.

While most of the loans and securities are speculative and heavy in new railroads, the proportion of common stocks to total investments is conservative at $37\frac{1}{2}$ per cent. Clearly, Oakes was not "bankrupt," but due to the very inactive markets for all except his UP securities, he was unable to raise enough cash to meet the immediate demands of some of his banks and other creditors. He was therefore "insolvent," and would be given time to pay off, in the best interests of all.

[24] *Ibid.* For comments, see Boston *Journal,* 10 Jan. 1871, and Boston *Commonwealth,* 14 Jan. 1871.

LOANS

	Value
Treadwell & Co.[25]	$ 751,000
Sioux City Construction Co. and undivided bal.	674,500
Butler, Sise & Co., etc.	270,000
Milladon Plantation, La.	250,000
Plattsburg & Montreal Rr.	250,000
N. Orleans & Chatt. Rr., W. Div.	248,000
Harrisburg R.R. Ass'n.	200,000
Central Branch, U.P. Rr.	100,000
Booth Mortgage	100,000
Northampton St. Property	100,000
22 others under $100,000	506,096
	$3,449,596

BONDS

	No.	Price	Value
U.P. Rr. 1st Mtge.	689	78	$ 537,420
U.P. Land Grants	673	60	403,800
Incomes	1,070	40	428,000
			1,369,220
N. Orl. Mob. & Chatt. Rr.	650	90	585,000
N. Orl. Mob. 2nd Mtg.	800	40	320,000
Davenport & St. Paul Rr.	807	75	605,250
Cedar Rapids & M.R. Rr.	205	85	174,250
11 others under $100,000			242,500
			$3,296,220

STOCKS

	Shares	Price	Value
Cedar Rapids & Mo. R. Rr. com.	11,845	80	$ 947,600
Cedar Rapids & Mo. R. Rr. pfd.	2,069	100	206,900
Iowa R.R. Land Co.	13,920	50	696,000
Union Pacific Rr.	28,000	12½	350,000
Credit Mobilier of America	1,995	25	48,775
Chicago, Iowa & Nebraska Rr.	2,712	120	325,440
U.S. & Brazil Mail Steamship Co.	3,987	75	298,025
Pacific Guano Co.	1,725	100	172,500
New Orleans, Mobile & Chattanooga Rr.	8,000	20	160,000
Ames Plow Co.	1,560	100	156,000
Kinsley Iron & Machine Co.	870	180	156,600
Iowa Falls & Sioux City Rr.	1,146	100	114,600
Sioux City & Pacific Rr.	2,000	50	100,000
19 others under $100,000			304,630
			$4,037,070

Total Loans, Bonds, and Stocks held by Oakes Ames
at values appraised by the creditors $10,782,886

More quotations from Oliver's diary:

Jan. 14—Oakes returned from NY but gets nothing to pay his debts. I fear he has no realizing sense of his position and we shall all be Bankrupt in 6 mos.

[25] See p. 388.

Jan. 21—Income Bonds went up today to 59½ flat and Stock to 24.

Jan. 26—Application made today to put us into bankruptcy.[26]

Horatio Ames Dies: Just at this unfortunate moment, Horatio Ames, brother of Oakes and Oliver, died on January 28, aged sixty-six. The cause was a gangrenous sore on his foot combined with diabetes. A huge man, six foot six inches and 300 pounds, he was an iron master and gunfounder. A family problem, he caused Oakes and his father much worry about money troubles.[27] He had become well known in Washington for his huge, seven-inch, rifled, welded-wrought-iron cannons which he had finally persuaded Lincoln to buy for the Navy. But before a shot could be fired against the Confederates, the War was over. Horatio was again destitute.[28] Oliver dutifully made the eight-hour trip by train to Falls Village near Salisbury, Connecticut, to find Horatio had just passed on.[29]

Miscellaneous: The Forty-Second Congress opened on 4 March 1871, and Oakes answered the roll call. On April 20 the First Session expired, and Oakes went home, presumably for the rest of the year, as the Second Session would not convene until December 4.

By May, the UP stock had rallied to the year's high of 37⅞, compared with only 9 on December 9 last. Not until 1875 would it be much higher.

"Had a sharp pain," wrote Oliver on July 13, "which I think may proceed from my diabetes."

The annual meeting of the Kinsley Iron and Machine Company was held on July 20. Oliver said, "They show a very handsome profit for last year. Voted to make a dividend of 37% to be paid to stockholders in notes of Oakes Ames." Frank Ames was doing a good job managing the company in Canton.[30]

On September 18, Oliver noted: "Let Mr. Oakes Ames have today 40,000$ and took 54 Income Bonds as collateral, which I have put in safe. I furnished 20,000$ and OA & Sons 20,000$ of above loan."

The Massachusetts elections of November 7 resulted in a complete Republican triumph. At the age of thirty-six Frederick Lothrop Ames, Oliver's only son, was elected a member of the Commonwealth's Legislature (a Senator, Oliver wrote the next day).

[26] The application was denied.   [27] Winthrop Ames, pp. 106–107.
[28] Bruce, pp. 279–281.   [29] Oliver Ames's diary.
[30] Winthrop Ames, pp. 123, 238.

Oliver paid $23,800 to Oakes for 200 of his 546 shares of the National Bank of Easton, and on November 18 loaned $25,000 to Oakes for 2½ months at 9 per cent with $40,000 UP income bonds as collateral. On December 13, Oliver bought for himself $50,000 land grant bonds at 79½.

Oakes's Account Books: Only two of Oakes's personal account books now can be found. Massive, and bound in heavy leather crumbling with age, they were originally kept at the offices of Oliver Ames and Sons in North Easton or Boston. The *"Cash—Oakes Ames"* book runs from the end of May 1868 to the end of 1871, with the exception of an unexplained gap during June, July, August, and September 1870. The *"Ledger—Oakes Ames,"* with a separate index, covers the period from the end of May 1868 only to the end of 1870. They do not reveal more than routine purchases and sales of the UP stock.

The countless details of how he carried on his business as a private banker are interesting. He had active accounts with many banks in Boston, Easton, and New York, largely open concurrently. Certainly the most important was the National Bank of Commerce, incorporated in 1869 in New York, and now the Morgan Guaranty Trust Company of New York. Others, in order, were the Merchants National Bank, the Columbian National Bank, the National Bank of Easton, the First National Bank, Massachusetts, the National Webster Bank, and the Exchange National Bank. As to his investment bankers and stockbrokers, he mostly used, in order of activity, the partnership firms of Page, Richardson & Co.; Morton, Bliss & Co.; Kidder, Peabody & Co.; Blake Brothers & Co.; and Walker & Brother. As a part of his business he made loans to, and received loans and deposits from, a great many individuals and industrial companies. Of greatest importance, of course, were his investments in the UP and speculations in a handful of embryo railroads. Apparently he handled the details of all this business alone, except for his accountant. How he could have kept his positions in his head, as he was said to do, is astounding.

One thing remains evident. These account books do not contain records of Oakes's important transactions in the securities of the Union Pacific and Credit Mobilier. The promoters took care to see that certain records of their actual profits from construction remained undisclosed, despite the Congressional investigations. So it seems highly probable that Oakes and Oliver also kept some very private books. If not destroyed, unfortunately they are not available.

C. UP Finances Most Desperate

The Plight of the UP: After the Golden Spike, it will be recalled, the UP was painfully lugging a floating debt of nearly $13,000,000 in short term notes.[31] Also, more rolling equipment had to be bought, as well as substantial renewals made of rails and cottonwood ties. The UP resorted to selling more 7 per cent land grant and 10 per cent income bonds, which brought these issues up to a maximum of $10,400,000 and $9,355,000.[32] At the same time, the Seven Trustees again sought to borrow back several millions of the $12,800,000 allotments of profit.[33] But to accomplish this in a weak market,[34] it developed that these two bond issues had to be sold at a fearful discount of 36 per cent, or $7,154,000, and even then a huge amount of 120,000 UP shares had to be issued.[35] This alone is proof enough of the desperate predicament of the company. Furthermore, interest on the funded debt (even excluding the controversial interest on the U.S. Subsidy bonds) was thereby increased to the point where it would not be fully covered by earnings during 1871 and 1872.[36]

Bond Trades of 1869 and 1870 Recover $5,000,000: The first of these complex bond transactions, all made during the second half of 1869 and first half of 1870, was the so-called "Evasion Loan" of 11 August 1869.[37]

Not having raised enough money with which to pay the bills then, a second offer was made in a circular, dated Boston, 22 September 1869. It invited another loan by willing stockholders to the Seven Trustees for account of the CM, whereby the Trustees would again *buy* the securities. This time there was no question but that it was a loan, no interest was allowed, and only income bonds and stock were used as bait. The tersely worded proposition is quoted in full below:

To the stockholders of the Union Pacific Railroad Company:
The trustees having completed the work of construction and equipment of the Union Pacific Railroad, and having received a payment for the same in 10 per cent, income-bonds, payable September 1, 1871, or within five years, at the option of the company, also stock of the Union

---

[31] See p. 357.
[32] *Wilson Rep.*, p. 639 (testimony of E.H. Rollins, Asst. Treasurer of the Union Pacific).
[33] See p. 259.   [34] See Appendix C.
[35] *Wilson Rep.*, pp. 639, 749–750; see also Appendices C, E. This brought the stock up to the final amount of 367,623 shares.
[36] See pp. 428–429.   [37] See pp. 359–360.

Pacific Railroad Company, and being desirous of closing up the trust, and paying up all outstanding liabilities, propose to each party interested in the trust the following terms:

For two of said income-bonds of $1,000 each, and forty shares of the stock of the company, the trustees will take $1,600, cash, and as agents for the Union Pacific Railroad Company, and by way of compromise and adjustment, will also give the party taking said bonds, one other of said bonds of $1,000, upon the surrender to us, as such agents, of a certificate of agreement of July 3, 1868, by which the Union Pacific Railroad Company promise to deliver, when practicable, one of its first-mortgage bonds. Payment for the said bonds will be received as follows: [in nine semi-monthly installments, of 10% or 15% each, between 1 October 1869 and 15 February 1870, inclusive].

Any shareholder notifying the subscriber on or before the 1st day of October will be entitled to his *pro rata* portion of these securities.

Any stockholder failing to take his portion of the securities in thirty days from the date of this circular will forfeit his right thereto, and said securities will be divided *pro-rata* to those stockholders who are willing to take them.

By order of the trustees.

John A. Rice
Assistant Treasurer Trustees [38]

Dividing that package in half for simplicity, its market value was probably about *$800* for the $1,000-income bond, and $600 for 20 free shares apparently worth 30—a total of, say, *$1,400,* plus some value for exchanging a first mortgage certificate into an income bond. From 1 October 1869 through 15 February 1870, when cash payments were due the Trustees, the income bonds were selling over-the-counter between a probable low of 70 and an actual high of 90, but averaging near 80.[39]

Oliver wrote in his diary of 15 February 1870:

Durant here selling out his Income Bonds and Stock. I hope he will sell all out. Hazard here & wants to be allowed what he claims in payment for losses he suffered by not having 1st Mtg. Bonds credited him for Income Bonds.

And again, the next day, he gives some evidence of prices:

Durant & Hazard here selling off their Income Bonds at 80, 85 & 90 + and equal amt of Stock. Hazard put in a protest which was refused and

[38] *Wilson Rep.,* pp. 359, 637–638.   [39] See Appendix C.

he was denied his Bonds unless he signed a paper approving the action of Trustees in making the divisions.

And on February 25, further information: "Bought 30 Income Bonds which cost me 22,737.50 (about 75¾)."

But H.C. Crane said that "$5,811,000 bonds were sold by the company to the trustees at 60 . . . and were sold by the trustees at 80." [40] This implied a profit of $1,162,200 to the CM at the expense of the UP. Also, B.F. Ham testified under questioning that "without any authority whatever" he had entered the transactions in the books at $600 for the bond, which necessarily left $200 for 20 shares of stock at *10*.[41] Both his prices and Crane's were wrong. As the Wilson Committee claimed, the bonds really were bought at 80, and the shares were just a stock dividend, in modern words.[42]

In the end, as a result of the circular of 22 September 1869, the Trustees succeeded in borrowing $4,672,000 in cash from those stockholders who chose to go along, each in his own amount, for which the UP issued to them $5,840,000 income bonds and 116,800 shares of stock. The Trustees also received certificates for $2,444,000 first mortgages to be exchanged into a like amount of incomes.[43]

Oliver scribbled an interesting memo about the repayment of his loans in the back of his 1870 diary under the heading of "Circular of September 22, 1869":

I get for 561,600$ Income Bonds	702,000
" " " 351,000 Ctf. for Income Bonds	351,000
& Bonus of 14,040 of Stock	1,404,000
	2,457,000

Above all taken Jan. 10, 1870.

On 22 September 1870, Oliver made this important entry, "Williams [44] plan to sell our Income Bonds for 800$ and give 20 shares of stock to sweeten it." That day $52,000 first mortgage bonds sold at 80.[45] The land grants were at about 69, the incomes near 71, and the stock, say, 25, all on the New York Stock Exchange.[46]

So, after the elapse of a year to the day, the Trustees terminated the whole loan by *paying back* to each stockholder the same amount he had lent, leaving him with the same blocks of bonds and stocks that he had had originally. No profit or loss had been forced on anyone.

[40] *Wilson Rep.*, p. 631.   [41] *Ibid.*, pp. 645–647.   [42] *Ibid.*, p. xvi.
[43] *Ibid.*, pp. 627–628, 359.   [44] J. M. S. Williams, Treasurer of the Union Pacific.
[45] Oliver Ames's diary.   [46] See Appendices A, C.

There since has been some difference of opinion as to whether the promoters really made the profit of $1,168,000—the difference between 80 and 60 on $5,840,000 incomes. From the evidence stated, the answer is—no profit.

The purchasers and amounts of income bonds finally *sold* by the Trustees after 22 September 1870 are detailed in an incomplete list in the Wilson Report, pages 634–35.[47] Of a total of about $3,628,000 bonds showing, 16 per cent were bought by Oliver and 14 per cent by Oakes. Duff bought 5 per cent; Bushnell, Dillon, and McCormick, 4 per cent each; and McComb, Hazard, Lambard, and Hooper, 3 per cent each. These 10 alone took 59 per cent of the total. Durant declined to help, as expected.

So concludes an attempt to clarify an important, but confusing and little-understood episode in the financing of the Union Pacific; namely, that a large number, but not all, of the promoters faithfully risked, for a critical 12 months, some $5,000,000 of their $13,000,000 allotment of profits on construction.[48]

Later, some exaggerated criticisms of these deals appeared in the New York *Daily Bulletin,* which did not understand their nature. On 14 January 1871, President Oliver wrote a long explanatory letter to the New York *Evening Post.* A few sentences are here quoted:

It was months before the stockholders could be induced to take six millions, not ten [of the income bonds], upon those favorable terms; and it was not until the earnings . . . had made certain in their minds . . . that interest on all bonds could be paid . . . that they came forward and took their proportion. Those who thus deferred to the last moment . . . did in many instances soon throw their bonds and stock upon the market, and realized a handsome profit thereon. . . . But this class were few in numbers, and comprised none, I think, of the present management. The pecuniary necessities of the company absolutely required the distribution in this form, as almost their only resource, and surely no injustice was done, for every stockholder was offered his *pro rata* share, and urged to take it.[49]

Fisk Again: To turn to other events of 1870, Oliver, much bored, wrote on March 22, "Had writ served on Co. by Fisk and attached desk of Williams and summoned us to appear before the Supreme

---

[47] Presumably incomplete because of a printing error.

[48] See pp. 258–261; *Wilson Rep.,* p. 442 (testimony of Clark, without the amounts given).

[49] *Boston, Past and Present,* pp. 212–213 (gives Oliver Ames's public rejoinder in full).

Court the 1st Tues of Apr." [50] At about this time the UP and CM changed their official attorneys to Messrs. Emott, Hammond and Pomeroy, and dismissed the services of Messrs. Tracy and Olmstead, notifying Durant that they would no longer pay any bills of his counsel.[51]

Oliver Helps Bushnell: On April 23, Oliver offered to help Bushnell: "Had conference with Bushnell & was unable to settle his matter. Gave him up 1,000 of the 2,000 share of Stock I was holding as security. I feel like doing what I can for him." Apparently Oliver was lending him sorely needed money.

Final UP Payment to Contractors: Oliver made this note on May 5: "Meeting of Ex Committee voted to pay 3,000,000$ extra to meet demands upon them." That would be the last issue of stock by the UP to the CM on account of construction and would bring the stock up to its final amount of 367,623 shares.[52]

Durant Sells Out: Durant and his relations (W.F. and T.F. Durant, and H.C. Crane, Trustee, and so forth) were at their high water mark of holdings of UP stock on 26 February 1870, according to the company lists of stockholders. As the Doctor had previously warned, he tried to clear out on the first good opportunity after the construction profits ended. But he did not have much luck, as 61 per cent of it was dumped below 27 during the five-month period between September 1870 and March 1871. The following table gives some details, particularly about his position around 1 October 1870.[53]

Date	UP Shares Held by Durant Family	Per Cent of Shares Outstanding	Price Range During Period When Sold [54]
26 Feb. '70	37,282 [55]	11.0	
Shares *Sold*	5,230 [56]		45—24 [57]
1 Oct. '70	32,052 [58]	8.8	
Shares *Sold*	22,666 [59]		27— 9 [60]
25 Feb. '71	9,386 [61]	2.6	
Shares *Sold*	9,182		39—20
24 Feb. '72	204 [62]	0.05	

At least once he caught some good prices. Through John Pondir's firm, on 6 March 1870, he worked off 2,000 shares at $42\frac{5}{8}$, as well as

[50] See p. 326.   [51] Durant, *Papers*, 1-3-26-72 (Oliver Ames to Durant, 2 Feb. 1870).
[52] *Wilson Rep.*, p. 750. It was dated July 29 on the books. See also Appendix E.
[53] See p. 385 concerning Durant's pool to "support" the stock.   [54] See Appendix A.
[55] *Wilson Rep.*, p. 605.   [56] See p. 385.
[57] Quoted from *Commercial & Financial Chronicle*.   [58] Durant, *Papers*, 3-3-12-6.
[59] See p. 385.   [60] First listed on the New York Stock Exchange 24 Sept. 1870.
[61] *Wilson Rep.*, p. 608.   [62] *Ibid.*, p. 602.

$96,000 income bonds at 82¾.[63] On 22 March, J.M.S. Williams wrote Oakes, who was in Washington, that "there had been quite a lively movement in the stock," which was at 45½, a new high. The first mortgages were at 84½, land grants at 73¾, and incomes at 85.[64]

The Hazards Sell Out: R.G., Rowland, Isaac P., and other members of the Hazard family had owned 23,852 shares on 26 February 1870. Two years later they had only 685 shares. They also had sold mostly in the low period below 27.[65] Further details are not available.

Oakes Sells Heavily, Oliver Hangs On: The actions of the Ameses were quite different from those of Durant and the Hazards.

As to Oakes,[66] sometime after February 1870, he *bought* 5,079 shares, raising his investment by 1 October 1870 to a maximum of 29,067 shares, or 7.9 per cent of all the stock outstanding.[67] Then, when he suddenly found he must relieve his creditors to the best of his ability, he sold nearly all out as follows: Within the next five months, while the price was below 27, he sold 8,960 shares;[68] during the following 12 months, when the price was between 39 and 20, he parted with another 14,090 shares. This left Oakes and his own family with only 6,017 shares, or 1.6 per cent of the total. By these moves alone, guessing an average price of 26 on the 23,050 shares liquidated, he raised some $600,000 cash for the benefit of his creditors.

However, Oliver and his son Fred never got overextended. They permanently held on to practically all of their large amount, which in February 1872 stood at 9 per cent of the 367,623 shares outstanding.

The Ameses as a Family: As a result of Oakes's sales, the investment of the Ameses as a whole was reduced from a maximum of 58,671 shares, or 17.4 per cent of all the UP stock, to 39,055 shares, or 10.6 per cent. The transactions are reviewed in the table on page 401.

Who Were the Buyers?:   To sum up, just during the short but sharp period when the stock was between 27 and 9, Durant sold 22,666 shares; the Hazards 5,730; and Oakes 8,960. These three moves alone

[63] Durant, *Papers*, 1–3–41–8.

[64] Records of UP Historical Museum; see also Appendices A, C.

[65] *Wilson Rep.*, pp. 605, 607, 601; Durant, *Papers*, 3–3–12–16.

[66] Including one-half of the shares held by Oliver Ames & Sons, plus small amounts held in trust and by his two sons, Oakes Angier and Oliver (later Governor), and his daughter-in-law, Catherine H. Ames.

[67] See p. 385 concerning Durant's pool.

[68] See p. 415; "Report to the Stockholders, 8 Mar. 1871," by Oliver Ames, pp. 8–9; see also pp. 404–405.

caused a total of 37,356 shares to change hands at bargain prices. The question naturally arises, who were the buyers? Vice-President John Duff and his son, it seems, bought an even 26,000 shares, but then sold them all during the next 12 months, presumably making a good turn.

UP Shares Held by All the Ameses

Date	Oakes & Family [a]	Oliver & F.L. Ames [a]	Total	Per Cent of Shares Outstanding	Price Range During Period When Sold [69]
26 Feb. '70	23,988	34,683	58,671 [70]	17.4	
Shares *Bought*	5,079	1,185	6,264		45—24 [71]
1 Oct. '70	29,067	35,868	64,935 [72]	17.7	
Shares *Sold*	8,960	None	8,960		27— 9 [73]
25 Feb. '71	20,107	35,868	55,975 [74]	15.2	
Shares *Sold*	14,090	2,830	16,920		39—20
24 Feb. '72	6,017	33,038	39,055 [75]	10.6	

[a] Including one-half of the 5,140 shares held by O. Ames & Sons through February 1871, then 2,140 shares in February 1872.

The answer is that a whole new group had suddenly taken advantage of the UP's most acute weakness to pick up stock. Morton, Bliss and Company, one of Oakes's brokers,[76] had accumulated 17,700 shares for a client or themselves; and James S. Suydam, a newcomer, had picked up 13,216. Leaving out the short term gamble of the Duffs, these two moves trace well enough the bulk of the offsetting purchases of 37,356 shares. But still more new buyers were to come in. A year later, on the February 1872 list, appear 42,800 shares in the name of George B. Grinnell and Company; 14,900 for Edward Brandon; and 8,400 for George M. Pullman of Pullman's Palace Car Company. Altogether, nine new names holding at least 6,000 each made up a total of 124,227 shares.[77] That was a big 35 per cent of all the common stock outstanding. What had happened?

D. Cabinet Members "Raid" the UP [78]

Current Interest on Subsidy Bonds Demanded: In the last months of 1870 some most extraordinary events occurred which had a devas-

---

[69] See Appendix A.   [70] *Wilson Rep.,* p. 605.
[71] Quoted from *Commercial & Financial Chronicle.*   [72] Durant, *Papers,* 3-3-12-6.
[73] First listed on the New York Stock Exchange 24 Sept. 1870.
[74] *Wilson Rep.,* p. 607.   [75] *Ibid.,* p. 601.   [76] See p. 395.
[77] *Wilson Rep.,* pp. 601–604.
[78] The term "raid" was used by Horace Clark repeatedly in his testimony before the Wilson Committee (*Wilson Rep.,* pp. 433, 449–450). He used it as "a market expression . . . whereby the market value of the securities is depressed. . . . This might be done by the assertion by the Government of an alleged right . . . which would probably lead the road into bankruptcy."

tating effect on the struggling UP. Indeed, by contributing to the break in the stock at the very moment of Oakes's insolvency, and sales by Durant and Hazard, *the events caused the builders of the road to lose control.*

In September 1870, President Grant had appointed Amos T. Akerman of Georgia as Attorney General in place of the resigning Ebenezer R. Hoar of Massachusetts. Akerman held office for only a year. His first move was to state that all of the subsidized railroads must repay to the Treasury the entire interest on the Subsidy bonds currently, as it fell due semi-annually, rather than let it continue to accrue until the bonds matured 30 years later. To the UP, this meant an overwhelming cash payment of $1,634,191 every year. The Secretary of the Treasury, George S. Boutwell of Massachusetts, Grant's first selection for this office in March 1869, and Acting Secretary of the Interior W.T. Ott (Jacob D. Cox had just resigned, perhaps because he could not agree) were inspired by Akerman to take action.

Pursuant to the Act of 25 June 1868, Cox had requested the presidents of all railroads with Subsidy bonds to file an annual report as of June 30, so as to conform with the Government's fiscal year.[79] Oliver had done so, at considerable effort and company expense. Thereupon Oliver received a demand from Ott (as did the other railroads) that his report be amended to show the amount of unrepaid interest on the Subsidy bonds. Dated 29 September 1870, Ott's letter was worded:

It has been observed that . . . you do not include the interest on the bonds issued by the United States to the company in aid of the construction of the road, which has been paid by the United States and not repaid by the company. By the Treasury Statement for the month of June last, I find the amount . . . not repaid to be $1,602,157.98. The company, as the law stands, are required to pay this interest; and, unpaid, it is a debt of the company's and should be properly included in their statement of indebtedness.

Your attention is called to the foregoing, to the end that the report in this respect may be properly corrected.[80]

Acts of 1862 and 1864: To be sure, the Act of 1862 had been clumsily and hurriedly drawn, due to pressures of the Civil War. Section 5 thereof (which referred to these bonds) specified only that ". . . to secure the repayment of the United States . . . of the amount

---

[79] Secretary of the Interior, *Correspondence*, vol. 3, pp. 155–156.   [80] *Ibid.*

of said bonds so issued and delivered to said company, together with all interest thereon which shall have been paid by the United States, the issue of said bonds and delivery to the company shall ipso facto constitute a first mortgage on the whole line of railroad . . . ." The Act of 1864, Section 10, in effect merely changed the first mortgage to a second mortgage.[81] Neither act provided that the interest must be repaid currently. However, by 1 July 1872, the UP voluntarily had refunded $1,289,577, or 35 per cent, of the $3,713,371 coupons then paid by the Treasury, leaving $2,423,794 owed.[82]

The *Commercial & Financial Chronicle* of 24 December 1870 (pp. 814–15) ran the following important article, probably at Akerman's request:

THE PACIFIC RAILROAD COMPANIES
AND THE INTEREST ON THE SUBSIDY BONDS

The Attorney General has rendered an opinion in which, after quoting at large the provisions of law bearing on the question, he says:

". . . Upon application to the company to reimburse this interest the company refuses, contending that the Government has no valid claim upon the company for reimbursement of interest until the principal of the bonds shall be due, except as to one half of the compensation for services rendered by the company for the Government, and as to the 5% of the net earnings of the road after its completion. If the company is right, the amount which the company will thus owe the Government at the expiration of thirty years will be nearly treble the principal of the bonds, and more if interest on the paid coupons is charged against the company; and while this heavy debt shall be accumulating against the company, the Government will all the time be paying to the company one half of the value of the services rendered to it by the company. Without a wonderful increase in value there is no probability that the road and all the pertinent property will be worth at the end of 30 years the thus increased debt then due the Government, after the first mortgage creditors shall have been satisfied. Meanwhile the company may be paying dividends to its stockholders out of the earnings which natural justice would apply to the relief of that creditor through whose benefactions the road has been mainly built. A construction which leads to such results ought not to be adopted unless clearly required by the language of the law . . . .

"My conclusion, then, is that the Government may lawfully claim from

[81] See pp. 16, 31.   [82] Secretary of the Treasury, *Report,* 1872, pp. 41–42.

the company the amount of the interest in question, as such interest is paid by the Government.

"The Government may retain the entire amount of compensation for services . . . applying the same to the interest paid by the United States, unless such interest shall have been repaid by the company, and in that event, one half of the compensation for such services may be reserved and applied to the principal of the bonds."

Boutwell Retains All UP Earnings from Government: At the same time, late in 1870, the Secretary of the Treasury, relying on the Attorney General's opinion, went further and issued an order withholding all, instead of one-half as before, of the earnings of the subsidized roads realized on transportation for Government account. This included such items as "mail, troops, munitions of war, supplies, and public stores." The entire amount would be held by him against repayment of the U.S. Subsidy bonds, principal and interest, until both were fully repaid. The UP's full earnings on Government traffic averaged about $743,000 a year for the next three years.[83] But Section 6 of the Act of 1862, which Akerman apparently was thinking of, clearly had been amended by Section 5 of the Act of 1864 so as to cut the withholding in half.[84]

Thus Boutwell added still more fuel to Akerman's ravaging fire, which it took the U.S. Supreme Court to douse. Up to now the law had not been interpreted that way. In any event, it just was too early to impose new burdens on new railroads whose potential earning power not yet had been developed.[85] But eventually, as the companies well knew, they would have to pay back the subsidy loans with all accumulated interest, or go broke.

To add insult to injury, someone in the Treasury Department, without any apparent reason, arbitrarily refused to allow the Subsidy bonds to be used as a basis for the currency-issue of the national banks and treated them as the debts of the Pacific Railways, rather than of the Government. Clark later said, "Discredit was thrown upon the bonds, and down they went, perhaps 10 per cent . . . I do not know who did it."[86]

Congress Makes Remedy: After many long debates, both Houses of Congress nullified the actions of Grant's three Cabinet members by

[83] U.S. Court of Claims, U.P. *v.* U.S., 1879, vol. 13, p. 463.
[84] The Acts are quoted in White, pp. 104, 111.   [85] See pp. 33–41.
[86] *Wilson Rep.*, p. 432 (testimony of Clark); for Oliver Ames's report to the stockholders 8 Mar. 1871, see p. 415.

passing the Act of 3 March 1871.[87] The Treasury was ordered to pay the railroads one-half of the Government transportation account as originally. A powerful lobby, including Bushnell and General Dodge, assisted in the passage of this bill.[88] Clark stated that he never would have owned a bond or share of the UP but for the Act of March 3.[89]

UP Badly Hurt: By the last week of December, when Ackerman's *Chronicle* article appeared, great damage had been done to the credit of the UP at the worst possible moment. As Oliver bitterly stated in his "Report to the Stockholders" dated 8 March 1871, "No corporation could withstand such attacks."[90] Not only had the stock crashed to the low of 9, the first mortgages fell from 83 to 73, the land grants from 72 to 53, and the incomes from 73 to 33.[91] Even the payment of the January 1 coupons of the first mortgage bonds had been put in serious jeopardy.[92] Oakes's investment in the Sioux City and Pacific, a subsidized road, had also been hurt.[93]

The Courts Favor the Railroads: Two years later, Congress vacillated, and although legislating against the railroads, authorized them to bring suit in the U.S. Court of Claims. The UP did so, and the Court of Claims upheld the railroads. In an appeal by the Government, the U.S. Supreme Court affirmed the Court of Claims. At least one part of the wrangle which continued on until 1897 was settled by the following judgment of the Supreme Court in October 1875:

> The words "to pay said bonds at maturity"[94] . . . imply obviously an obligation to pay both principal and interest, when the time fixed for the payment of the principal has passed; but they do not imply an obligation to pay the interest as it accrues, and the principal when it is due . . . . It is necessary to superadd other words in order to extend the condition so as to include the payment of semi-annual interest as it falls due. Neither on principle or authority is such a plain departure from the express letter of the statute warranted.[95]

Bushnell Raises Desperately Needed Money: Back in November 1870, the UP Executive Committee had passed a resolution author-

---

[87] Records of UP Historical Museum; see also p. 410 (Oliver Ames's diary, Mar 4); 16 Statutes at Large 525.

[88] *Wilson Rep.*, p. 530 (testimony of Bushnell).   [89] *Ibid.*, p. 410.   [90] See p. 415.

[91] See Appendices A, C.   [92] See pp. 407, 410.   [93] See p. 85.

[94] *Act of 1862*, Section 6; White, p. 104.

[95] Trottman, pp. 129–130 (quotes 91 U.S. 72); White, p. 75.

izing the issue of $2,500,000 10 per cent bonds to finance the building of the Missouri River bridge. The Trustees under this mortgage were Oliver, Atkins, and Duff. Only $1,225,000 of them were issued, and they were delivered to Bushnell, who thought he had some buyers. There was great difficulty in placing them on the market, partly because Government legislation was lacking which would allow the company to make a mortgage, and partly because all the UP bonds were then heavily depressed by the Cabinet raid.[96]

Authority was finally given by the Bridge Act of Congress of 24 February 1871 to issue $2,500,000 8 per cent gold bonds due in 25 years, with a sinking fund to retire them. Of these new bonds, $1,225,000 were delivered to Bushnell in exchange for the 10 per cent issue. The remainder were turned over to the new Bridge Bond Trustees, who were J. Edgar Thompson; J. Pierpont Morgan of Drexell, Morgan and Company; and Elisha Atkins. These bonds were sold at 80. Bushnell received his bonds at the same price, but subsequently was charged $60,000 discount, the reason for which does not appear. Thus the UP raised $2,060,000 cash at a critical moment. The original cost of the bridge as then figured was $2,254,259.[97]

The new bonds were sold in London by J. Pierpont Morgan, the negotiations for the sale being handled by Andrew Carnegie.[98]

Bushnell Tells How He Did It: Some interesting details of this deal come out of the Wilson Committee's seemingly endless questioning of Cornelius Bushnell on 3 February 1873.[99] These Congressmen were attempting to prove that he had improperly expended, or used for his own benefit, $126,000 that had been charged on the UP books as "special legal expenses," namely, $24,500 to Dodge for services in procuring passage of the Act of 3 March 1871, $19,000 paid to Thomas A. Scott on private account, and $82,500 retained by Bushnell on his own account.

The question was put, "Do you recollect being at a meeting of the Union Pacific Directors held in Boston on the 8th and 9th of March, 1871, when an item of $126,000 was under investigation?" Answering affirmatively, salesman Bushnell added, "I will make here a statement with a great deal of pleasure. I will have to go back a little, and state the reasons why the committee came to the conclusion they did." He

---

[96] See pp. 402–405. [97] Records of UP Historical Museum; see also p. 421.
[98] *Ibid.;* Andrew Carnegie, *Autobiography.* [99] *Wilson Rep.,* pp. 528–541.

then recounted in his colorful but sometimes unprecise or incomplete
way:

In December 1870, after the action of the Secretary of the Treasury
Boutwell, our securities went down almost out of sight, and we had not
the money on hand to pay the interest on our First Mortgage bonds,
due on the first of January. We had expended the money, some $700,000,
in commencing the building of the Omaha bridge. We had no collaterals
on hand to raise the money, except a 10% Bridge bond . . . and it was
impossible to raise any money on them . . . . I had an immense amount
of UP stock which I had loaned out, and I could not afford to have it
utterly lost . . . . The majority of the Directors were very anxious to pay
the First Mortgage coupons and some were willing to indorse notes of
the Company . . . for 3 or 4 months, provided we would put up these
Bridge bonds at 50 cents on the dollar. I took these indorsements on the
notes of the Company Treasurer, and the Bridge bonds, went to New
York, and raised the money to pay the interest. I indorsed the notes
myself also, and became involved to the amount of $600,000 or $700,000.
. . . We paid our interest. Of course I went to work at once to see how
we could provide the means to pay these notes at maturity, by disposing
of our Bridge bonds and our Land Grant bonds, and thus get the Company out of debt. I went to Philadelphia and had two or three interviews
with Colonel Scott and J. Edgar Thompson, who said to me that if I
would make some arrangements whereby the Company would be got
out of debt, they would take hold, and advance me a large amount of
money to carry the securities; but on no other condition than that the
Company should be relieved of its floating debt, and provision made for
the building of this bridge across the Missouri.[100]

I came home and sat down, and figured up the prices of the securities.
The Land Grants were at 54 and 55, and the best we could realize on the
Bridge bonds was 50, which left us in debt more than a million dollars
to complete the bridge after we should sell the bonds at that rate. It was
a very extreme case, and required a very extreme and extraordinary
effort.[101]

I went on to Boston and made a proposition to the Company to buy
the $2,136,000, or thereabouts, of the Land Grants . . . I proposed to buy
them for myself and those who were associated with me, at 70 and accrued interest; and I proposed to buy the $2,500,000 10% Bridge bonds
at 80 and interest. Of course that was far above the market price, but it
was absolutely necessary to buy them at that high price in order to pay
the floating debt. They accepted my proposition . . . .

[100] *Ibid.*, pp. 356–357.
[101] *Ibid.*, pp. 356–357. Spence testified that the Union Pacific sold all the Income,
Land Grant, and Bridge bonds it owned (totaling between $4,000,000 and $5,000,000),
and 30,000 shares of UP stock.

I started instantly for Philadelphia, and made an arrangement for money with Colonel Scott, and drew for five or six hundred thousand dollars on New York. As soon as I received the money I started for Washington. I came here mainly, almost entirely, to secure legislation of Congress, whereby the Union Pacific should be authorized to place a mortgage on the bridge, which would make the bonds a better security so that I could dispose of them . . . I arrived here and undertook, myself, to present the case, as I always do.

I met the Iowa Representatives here, and they said to me frankly that there was a good deal of jealousy between Council Bluffs and Omaha about that bridge, and that they would not move a hair's breadth until General Dodge should confer with them . . . I saw that there was nothing for me to do but to telegraph Dodge, at Council Bluffs, to come on, which I did, stating that I would pay him for all his expenses and trouble. He came here, and met me. I told him what I wanted. He at once said that he had borrowed every dollar he could get on his Union Pacific stock, along in the summer, in New York, to carry on his business—I think some pork-packing business—and that that damned Boutwell ring had ruined him; that his brokers had sold him out, and he was ruined. I said, "I cannot help that, but do you go to work and help me to carry this bill through, and I will pay you for your expenses and time, and make up all you have lost."

He went to work (everybody knows how the General can work when he sets out), and in less than fifteen days we had the bill through Congress just exactly as we wanted it [102] . . . I got up and had printed and distributed the opinions of the best lawyers and the reports of the committee, and all that sort of thing, and gave them to everybody where they could be of service.

Now as to the $126,000. We went home to Boston and had our annual election, but it became evident to me that I could not carry out this purchase, and take up these securities, without help from the Company. I said so to Colonel Scott. I could not pay him back the money which he had advanced me without some help, for I had given from half a million to a million dollars more for the securities than they were worth in the market. He said, "We will fix that up when we get to Boston," but that he must have a little of his money returned to him.

We had a committee appointed [in the UP].[103] I went before that committee and stated the case—that I had promised General Dodge to make him good . . . . He figured up what he wanted for his services, and what would cover his losses, and I agreed to pay it. This was the $24,500. I asked Colonel Scott how much he wanted on account, and he said $19,000

[102] The *Act of 3 Mar. 1871*, concerning the interest question; 16 Statutes at Large 525.
[103] *Wilson Rep.*, pp. 189–190 (testimony of Rollins). The date was 9 Mar. 1871, and the members were Scott, Dodge, Duff, and J. F. Wilson.

or $20,000. I gave him $19,000. The balance of $82,500 I handed over at once to the Treasurer of the Company, in payment for bonds which I got that day from him to take to New York.[104]

That explained in two pages of testimony the whole $126,000 turned over to Bushnell, but the Wilson Committee then used up ten more pages of questions and answers, largely repetitious, without learning much else; except to hear Bushnell wistfully remark, "I think I ought to have had more."

A week later, Thomas A. Scott verified Bushnell's testimony. He described what had taken place in these words:

He [Bushnell] was carrying a large amount of the Land Grants and Income bonds of the Company, that were taken by himself and associates in order to place the Company in reasonable financial condition by providing for its interest due in January, and to provide money to lift and pay off the floating debt of the Company. I had made this a condition before agreeing to accept the Presidency, that all its old complications with the Credit Mobilier, unadjusted floating debt, and other questions of that character, should either be actually paid off or placed in such condition as to relieve the Company from embarrassment from that source. To accomplish this purpose, Mr. Bushnell and his associates agreed, as I afterward understood, to purchase from the Company, very much above their current market values, four or five millions of the bonds referred to, no doubt with the prospect on their part that the improved financial condition of the Company, and the revived credit of the new organization, would ultimately relieve them from loss.

But this they found to be a slow process and the load a heavy one. I do not know who the associates of Mr. Bushnell were, but I think they were bankers of New York and Boston. Mr. Bushnell finally and fully, I believe, carried out all his obligations to the Company, and its credit by these various movements was preserved intact, and all its obligations met at maturity.[105]

Scott also swore he knew of no UP money used directly or indirectly with members of Congress to secure the passage of the Act of 3 March 1871, to secure the preceding Omaha Bridge bill approved 24 February 1871, or to secure the election of any member of Congress.[106]

In fact, this official attempt at smearing merely established for history that Bushnell's action, as a heavy stockholder and party in in-

---

[104] *Ibid.*, pp. 528–541 (testimony of Bushnell).
[105] *Ibid.*, p. 650.   [106] *Ibid.*, pp. 649, 651.

terest, had enabled the UP to meet its excessive floating debt of over $2,000,000 in a time of most acute crisis.

But the control of the road had shifted.

Oliver Helps Save Default on First Mortgages: On 29 December 1870, at the eleventh hour, Oliver made this significant entry: "Signed 5 notes of UPRR as Prest and endorsed them by O. Ames & Sons & Oliver Ames for 100,000$ each to raise money for interest." He was referring to the first mortgage coupons payable January 1.

Again, on 4 March 1871: "Congress passed the resolution instructing Treasurer to pay UPRR one-half of earnings as heretofore." [107] By May the stock had peaked at 38, up from 9 in five months.[108]

CM Offers to Settle with UP: It will be recalled that the CM held a $2,000,000 demand note of the UP as an adjustment in payment for construction under the Hoxie contract.[109] On 18 January 1871, 33 of the CM stockholders, representing 48 per cent of the shares, signed an offer to settle the matter once and for all, if the UP would issue to them "$700,000 income bonds and the balance in UP stock, both at their par value." [110] The UP refused, probably influenced by the new group, even though at market prices then of about 59 and 24, respectively,[111] the cost to the UP would have been only $728,000. Conspicuous by failing to sign were CM stockholders Durant, the Hazard family, McComb, Gray, Bardwell, McCormick, Holladay, Opdyke, and Lambard. Their reasons are not available. By that time, the stockholders of the CM were entirely different from those of the UP.

E. Report to Stockholders by Oliver Ames

Oliver Resigns as President: On 8 September 1870, Oliver tersely noted in his diary, "Ex Comm. in session. I propose to resign my position as President." Already the die had been cast. Some months later, following the annual meeting of the UP stockholders on 8 March 1871, he withdrew his name for re-election as President and Member of the Executive Committee. However, he agreed to continue as a Director.

---

[107] See pp. 404–405.   [108] See Appendix A.   [109] See p. 357.
[110] Durant, *Papers*, 1–2–33–14.
[111] Oliver Ames's diary, Jan. 21; see also Appendices A, C.

On 8 March 1871, Oliver gave his first and last report to the stock-holders. It covered the year 1870. In view of the welter of new troubles Oliver was having, most of it must have been prepared by T. E. Sickels, Chief Engineer and Superintendent. But the last section, "Credit Shaken by the Government," looks like the hand of the President.

The Report

EARNINGS.

During the past year, notwithstanding the great depression of business in California, the net earnings have been sufficient to meet the interest upon our entire bonded debt; [112] and it is confidently expected that the ensuing year will show much better results.

SNOW PROTECTION.

We have very much improved our road during the past year, by smoothing and perfecting the road-bed, strengthening our snow-sheds where they showed signs of weakness last winter, increasing the amount of our snow-fences; and so effectually has our road been protected during the past winter from obstruction by snow, that we have in no instance missed our connection at either end of our line; while the roads east, through Iowa, have been detained over twenty-four hours. The great danger anticipated from the snows of the Platte Valley and Laramie Plains, has proved groundless; and the Union Pacific Railroad can be run with more certainty of being unobstructed by snows than the rail-roads of New England and New York.

REPAIR SHOPS MOVED TO EVANSTON.

Our repair-shops at Bryan and Wahsatch have been a source of great anxiety to us on account of the temporary nature of their construction, their great liability to fire, and the difficulty of removing our locomotives, should a fire occur. We decided last fall to remove from these shops, and put up new stone shops at Evanston, of sufficient capacity to accommodate the machinery and store the engines now sheltered at both of these shops. We commenced the construction of our shops at Evanston, but not early enough to complete them before the winter set in with such severity as to force us to postpone their completion till spring. They will be

---

[112] Presumably based on Sickels' statement: "The expenses of transportation, in view of the experience already attained in operating the road, can be stated with an approximation of accuracy, and will not be found to exceed 50 percent of receipts; leaving a balance of $5,000,000 as the net profits of the year's business." This proved far too optimistic.

ready for occupation early in May. They are finely located on Bear River, with an abundance of pure water, and in the immediate vicinity of one of the most extensive coal-fields on this continent.

MISSOURI RIVER BRIDGE.

The want of a bridge over the Missouri River, at Omaha, to connect the eastern railroads with the Union Pacific, has been one of the most annoying incidents connected with the trip to California. The uncertain and turbulent character of the river, with its shifting banks, has made its passage uncertain, and frequently extremely tedious. During the past year, we have been actively at work upon the bridge, and hope to have as permanent and durable a structure as can be made, ready for use the ensuing summer.

Mr. T. E. Sickels, the chief engineer of the Company, submits a report in detail, upon the construction and present condition of the Missouri-river bridge, from which I extract the following facts:—

The bridge is of 11 spans, of 250 feet each, 50 feet above high water, resting upon one stone abutment now completed; and 11 iron piers, all in place, and the larger part of them already sunk from 60 to 72 feet in the sand, and resting in the bed-rock.

All piers will be completed by the time the superstructure is ready to be placed in position.

The pneumatic system, used in sinking the piers, is specially applicable to the construction of foundations for bridges across rivers similar to the Missouri. Lignite, bones, &c., have been found to a depth of 50 feet below low water, showing a scouring of at least that depth; and the bed-rock, when reached, shows invariably a smooth surface, worn by attrition of sand upon it. The shortest time in which any column was sunk was seven days; and the greatest depth any column has reached in twenty-four hours was $18\frac{1}{2}$ feet.

The west approach to the bridge is 7,000 feet long. The material for it is very rapidly moved, and it will be completed by April 1.

The east approach is $1\frac{1}{2}$ miles long, rising from the tableland in Council Bluffs to the bridge grade at 35 feet per mile. This approach requires 468,000 cubic yards of earth; and there has been put in by steam-shovels and three trains of cars during the past winter 82,700 cubic yards.

With energetic prosecution of the work, Mr. Sickels is of opinion the bridge can be completed this year.

The bridge is being constructed for highway-travel on the same level with the track of the railway. The revenue arising from this travel and the transportation by cars, taking as a basis the present transfer of cars, freight, and passengers, between the roads terminating in Council Bluffs, Iowa, and the Union Pacific, and the foot-travel between Council Bluffs and Omaha, Mr. Sickels finds to be for the year 1870, at the rates charged, $176,430. In view of the rapid growth of Council Bluffs and Omaha, which now have a population of 29,000, the large immigration induced by the cheap lands along the line of the road, the development of the Utah silver-mines, and of the agricultural and mineral lands generally, adjacent to the road, with the assured great increase in the trade in Texas cattle, the estimate for 1871 may be set down to be $275,000.

An Act has been obtained from Congress, authorizing a mortgage of the bridge.[113] We propose, now, to issue $2,500,000 of 20 years, 8 per cent mortgage bonds, to provide means for the completion of the bridge. The tolls on the bridge will be fixed at a rate sufficient to pay the interest on the bonds, and set apart enough to a sinking fund to redeem them at maturity. It is proposed to make the bridge a carriage-way for the accommodation of travel between the cities of Omaha and Council Bluffs, and from which it is expected to derive an income largely in excess of the additional cost, and without interference with its use for railroad purposes.

MINING DEVELOPMENTS.

The increased facilities opened by the railroad for reaching the mining districts have greatly stimulated the development of the mines. Colorado and Utah are now opening some of the richest mines yet discovered in our country. The mines in the vicinity of Salt Lake are exciting great attention. It is estimated that from ten to fifteen thousand settlers and miners will be drawn there the ensuing season. The amount of ores to be sent over our road to smelting works east and in England is estimated to be from 500 to 1,000 tons daily; while the machinery and supplies necessary to develop successfully and profitably the mines will give a very large westward business to our road. Our prospects of business from Salt Lake City and its vicinity are very encouraging; and I shall be greatly disappointed if it shall not be more than double what it was last year. Our coal-mines have proved fully equal to our most sanguine expectations, both in regard to the superior quality of the coal as a steam generator and the extent of the deposit. It is believed that there is no better coal in this country for locomotive service, and none where it can be more cheaply mined. Iron ore, of very superior quality, and in vast quantities, has been discovered in the vicinity of Cheyenne and Laramie. We have promise of an iron district here that will be able to compete successfully with the most favored localities of our country. Extensive iron works must spring up on the line of our road, and we shall be furnished with cheap iron for all its uses. Coal and iron, the most necessary and essential materials for the construction and operation of a rail-

[113] *Act of 24 Feb. 1871;* see also p. 406.

road, are found on the line of our road in unlimited quantities, and of the finest quality. They are the sure guaranties that our road can be maintained and operated at the lowest rates.

SALE OF LAND GRANTS.

The sale of our lands and the settlement of the country on the line of our road have been very satisfactory; and a large increase of our business must be derived from this source. Our land agent, Mr. Davis, anticipates a very large influx of settlers the coming season, whose purchases must greatly reduce our indebtedness on Land Grant Bonds. One of the most promising sources for the increase of the business of our road is stock-raising on the Platte Valley and Laramie Plains. Parties who have been in this business for the past two years have realized very satisfactory profits; and the rapid increase of the flocks and herds indicates that we may soon expect to transport hundreds of car-loads of beef and cattle daily to Chicago and eastern markets. These immense plains, covered with the most nutritious grasses, which have been in past ages the pasture of countless herds of buffalo that have been driven off by advancing civilization, are now open for the flocks and herds of the enterprising settler. The pasturage is unlimited, and the extent of the business is only limited by the capacity of eastern markets for consumption.

Cattle that were purchased last summer for $13 each, and have cost but $1 since for their care, are now being sold for $24 each. It does not cost over from $5 to $8 to raise a steer up to three years old, that will weigh from eight to ten hundred pounds. These plains cannot be settled up for many years; and they offer to capital one of the most flattering openings for safe and profitable investments.

CHINA TRADE.

Since the opening of our road, we have been seeking to secure the transportation of the teas and silks of China and Japan. Arrangements have been recently made that will, we think, secure a large portion of this business overland; and we expect during the coming season a very large increase of our receipts from this source.

MONTANA TRAFFIC.

A business that has run for a long period in one channel is changed from its course with great difficulty. We shall find from year to year new business and new sources of income. The Montana business from the east, previous to last year, went almost entirely up the Missouri River by steamboats. Last year, a portion of it went over our road. This year, I think it will almost entirely go over our road, leaving it at Evanston, Ogden, and Corinne, for Montana, on wagons.

CREDIT SHAKEN BY THE GOVERNMENT.

The great mutations which have taken place in our securities the few months past perhaps demand some explanation.

After we had saved the Government millions upon millions on the cost of its transportation over the plains and to the Pacific; after we had done away with the necessity of keeping a cordon of soldiers for eighteen hundred miles, to secure the safety of emigration and of trans-continental trade; after we had opened the vast interior to settlement seven years earlier than required of us by our charter,—the action of some of the departments of the Government became so hostile to us as to shake the credit of the corporation. The Treasury Department first refused to receive United States Pacific Railroad Bonds as a basis for banking, and thus lessened their mercantile value; next selected and set apart these bonds in its monthly publications of the public debt, as if not a portion of the debt of the United States, but of our road exclusively; thus apparently indicating its irresponsibility, and thereby again lessening their value; then published monthly, not only the indebtedness, with the interest, but the deficit of interest, as if due by us, and left unpaid; and then, worst of all, and hardest of all, withheld from us all our earnings in the transportation of letters, newspapers, packages, and of the army and navy, all of which hitherto we had been paid one-half of, as under Act of Congress. The Treasury Department was fortified in the last act of injustice by an opinion of the Attorney General. These repeated blows against this the great work of the age, so unexpectedly directed, shook our credit for a time; for it was soon seen and felt that no corporation could withstand such attacks, and hence those wide and wild variations in the market-value of our securities.[114] The Judiciary Committee of the United States Senate (every member except one) offset their legal opinion, that the interest was not due, against the opinion of the Attorney General, that it was all due; and every other committee in both Houses of Congress before whom the question was brought agreed with the Judiciary Committee of the Senate. Both Houses of Congress finally reversed the action of the Treasury Department and of the Attorney General (the House of Representatives without a division); and the result is the restoration of the credit of the company, with a great advance in all its securities.

Oliver Ames,
President Union Pacific Railroad Company

This was followed by a statement of operations of the Transportation Department for 1870 by T. E. Sickels to Oliver Ames, President, dated 1 March 1871. It is not quoted here.

[114] See pp. 404–405.

The UP balance sheet as of 31 December 1870, reconstructed by the accountants for the U.S. Pacific Railway Commission in 1887, appears in the report of the U.S. Pacific Railway Commission, pp. 5046–47.

F. The Pennsylvania Takes Control

It has become obvious that it was the Pennsylvania Railroad which had accumulated enough stock and bought enough bonds during the Cabinet "raid" and the two months following to warrant their taking a working control of the Union Pacific. The Pennsy was a powerful road, with gross earnings of over $30,000,000, headed by J. Edgar Thompson, an important financier from Philadelphia. Within three years of the Golden Spike, the control of the UP had shifted, never to return to the original promoters.

COMPOSITION OF UP BOARD BY GROUPS [a]

8 MARCH 1871 TO 6 MARCH 1872		
Ames Group	*Government*	*Pennsylvania RR Group*
DIRECTORS AND MEMBERS EXECUTIVE COMMITTEE (7)		
C. S. Bushnell	Jas. F. Wilson	A. Carnegie
S. Dillon		G. M. Pullman
J. Duff (V.P.)		T. A. Scott (Pres.)
DIRECTORS (13)		
Oakes Ames	J. C. S. Harrison	J. E. Thompson
Oliver Ames	H. Price	
E. Atkins	D. S. Ruddock	
J. Brooks	B. F. Wade	
F. G. Dexter		
G. M. Dodge		
L. P. Morton		
R. E. Robbins		
TOT. DIRS.: 11	5	4

[a] Adapted from Union Pacific, *Official Register; Wilson Rep.*, p. 597. (For period 11 Mar. 1868 to 8 Mar. 1871 see p. 240.)

The Pennsy asked for, and got, the Presidency and three other Directorships. Thomas A. Scott of Philadelphia, a Vice-President, became the President. The other three Directors were J. Edgar Thompson, President of the Penn, and an original Director of the UP in 1863; Andrew Carnegie, then only thirty-six; and George M.

Pullman of the Pullman Palace Car Company. Scott, Carnegie, and Pullman also were put on the Executive Committee, thereby equalling the Ames group on that committee. But Scott, Thompson, and Carnegie were to last only for a year, for reasons to be explained later.[115]

In the Ames group, Gordon Dexter was re-elected after a year's absence and two new names were added—Levi P. Morton of Morton, Bliss and Company and Royal E. Robbins. To make room for the seven names above, the following old-timers were left out: Lambard, Alley, McCormick, Glidden, R.G. Hazard, Fred Nickerson, and Chapman.

No changes were made in the five Government Directors. The make-up of the UP Board for the next twelve months is shown in the accompanying table.

J.M.S. Williams was relieved as Treasurer by E.H. Rollins (also Secretary) on 8 April 1871. Sussex D. Davis was appointed Assistant Secretary (a new office) by President Scott on 9 March 1871, but served only during Scott's term of a year.

IF & SC Ties up with UP: In the summer of 1871, the Iowa Falls and Sioux City Railroad reached its goal, Sioux City, and so closed the last gap in the line between Chicago and the UP at Fremont via Dubuque, Fort Dodge, and the Sioux City and Pacific Railroad. Oakes was a Director, and largely interested with Blair in the construction company.[116]

G. Missouri River Bridge Problems

"Old Muddy":   The bridge over the mighty Missouri River, second only to the Mississippi in length, was by far the most difficult engineering problem of the UP. Over a 50-year period the average discharge of water past Omaha was estimated at 35,000 cubic feet per second, which is very large, but in the peak flood of 1881, for instance, it ran ten times that amount. In the flood of April 1867, water covered some of the UP tracks at Omaha.[117] The river now and then completely changes its channel in a flat flood plain as wide as 4 miles between the high, washed-back bluffs of Omaha and Council Bluffs. During extreme floods, most of this plain might be covered by a rise

[115] See p. 423.   [116] See pp. 86–87.   [117] See p. 233.

of 10 feet above normal high. At low summer water, however, the channel is well defined, and runs close to the Omaha bluffs, where it might be only 750 feet in width and perhaps 20 to 25 feet in depth. Although soundings vary greatly, its bed probably consists of some 10 to 45 feet of the usual alluvial soil, sand, and gravel washed down from a drainage area above Omaha of 323,000 square miles, or over 10 per cent of the area of the nation, excluding Alaska. "Old Muddy," it is nicknamed. Smooth bedrock, on which the piers of the bridge should rest if possible, was found to vary from about 30 to 70 feet below low water mark.

The Ferry: Starting in the summer of 1867, after Oakes's Cedar Rapids and Missouri River Railroad had arrived at Council Bluffs,[118] a special freight-car ferry, the *H.C. Nutt,* hustled to and fro between the two levees, transferring cars and passengers from one railroad to the other. But every winter, the river was sheeted with thick ice. Then holes were cut through it and tall piles driven into the alluvial sand to support a temporary wooden trestle bridge.[119] Come spring, the tracks and trestle were removed before the flooding waters rushed over the ice, carrying away the piles. Then the *H.C. Nutt* resumed its shuttle service. The following December, new piles were driven through the ice. The cost was less than $14,000 a year, and the Cedar Rapids road took a share.

Dodge Knew the River: As far back as 1853, Grenville Dodge, then only twenty-two, had first become familiar with the general aspects of the crossing. That year Henry Farnam and Durant, contractors for the Mississippi and Missouri River Railroad, had instructed their engineer, Peter A. Dey, "to investigate the question of the proper point . . . to strike the Missouri to obtain a good connection with any road that might be built across the continent . . . . I was assigned to the duty," said Dodge, "and surveys were extended to and up the Platte Valley, to ascertain whether any road . . . would thus overcome the Rocky Mountains . . . . I extended the examination westward to the eastern base of the mountains and beyond (to the Great Salt Lake) . . . . The practicability of the route demonstrated to me that through this region the road must eventually be built." [120] Long before joining the UP, therefore, Dodge had staked out what he thought would be the best crossing from Council Bluffs: a straight line directly west

---

[118] See p. 85.   [119] A sketch of the first winter bridge appears in Illus., Group 1.
[120] Dodge, *Report of the Chief Engineer,* 1868–1869, pp. 20–21; see also p. 21.

from the projected M & M depot at present Commercial and Nebraska Streets, over the river, and up to the table where Omaha's Marcy Street now stands. This line became known as the "M & M," or South Omaha crossing. It was there that the bridge was finally built.

Bridge Delayed by Lack of Funds: But there were other problems for the UP besides those of mere physiography. Omaha, the UP's only point for delivery by boat of the vast quantities of material of all kinds used during construction, was being left far behind by the rapidly advancing end-o-track. The Cedar Rapids and Missouri River had reached Council Bluffs, and the Rock Island and the Burlington were expected to arrive in 1869. Still the bridge was not built, even though the Golden Spike had been driven. It was evident that the real reason for the costly delay was lack of funds. The ferry would have to do for some years more.

After Dodge joined the UP in 1866, he made very extensive soundings, surveys, and studies of all possible crossings. His search went on until a contract for the bridge was let, even though he was mostly preoccupied on the line of road. He consulted with J.L. Williams and T.E. Sickels of the UP and with the most noted bridge experts of the country. In his autobiography, he left some 40 long pages of their correspondence, covering the most minute details.[121] No exploratory work could have been done more conscientiously.

The Best Crossings: The choice was finally reduced to one of two good crossings. Both involved a high bridge. As Dodge said in December 1866:

(1) It does away with all expenditure in confining the channel, which I consider an experiment . . . . (2) It relieves the company from the hostility of the boating interest, gives no excuse for the long list of lawsuits that all drawbridges have had to meet, obviates unfriendly legislation, and gives a boatable channel under the bridge at all seasons, no matter what freaks the yearly freshets may play with the river. (3) It is almost impossible to place obstacles in the current of the channel which will turn it . . . . (4) A high bridge once built, all expense has been incurred . . . and (5) The cost of a high bridge over a low one . . . is not [excessive considering] the objections to a low bridge.[122]

In a purely engineering point of view, without regard to the advantage

---

[121] Dodge, *Autobiography*, pp. 1064–1104.   [122] *Ibid.*, p. 1065.

of crossing directly at Omaha, or the use of our own depot grounds, I am decidedly of the opinion that the best point . . . is at Child's Mill [about 5 miles below the ferry]. It is shortest, gives best grades, and leaves out entirely the 66 feet grade at Omaha . . . . It can be put up . . . in shortest time, with least cost, gives us a high bluff to abut against on west side, with plenty of distance to rise to grade on east side, and shortens through distance 7.1 miles.

If desirable to avail ourselves of the crossing at Omaha, for the use of our shops and grounds, the best point . . . is the M. & M. crossing . . . . It will cost more than at Child's Mill . . . because of increased length on west side to reach table south of city, while it has the advantage at east side of reaching high water table 600 feet from bank of river.[123]

Government Director Jesse Williams estimated the cost of the Child's Mill bridge at $1,632,000 and the M & M at $2,426,000 in a report to Oliver on 25 November 1867. Seymour and Durant were for the low drawbridge at "Telegraph pole" leading directly to the UP shops, estimated at $1,775,000.

In February 1868 the UP bridge committee, headed by McComb, recommended that the Board decide on the Child's Mill crossing. But when this became known, a great disturbance was created at Omaha and Council Bluffs, where "the citizens" thought it was too roundabout a way to get into Omaha, and they might lose the eastern terminus.

The M & M Crossing Chosen: On March 25 the UP Board met, and, now supported by Dodge, finally changed over in favor of the M & M crossing. But not without extracting promises of a donation from Omaha of 10 acres of depot grounds and right of way for connection from the bridge to the constructed line at about 20th Street, and from Douglas County $250,000 7 per cent 20-year bonds towards the cost of constructing the bridge.[124] Council Bluffs also was touched for a depot building and $200,000 in bonds which, however, were never delivered.

At this time, Government Director Jesse Williams, who had supported Dodge's views all the way along, relieved his mind by writing Dodge a letter on March 28 about a proposed separate company for the bridge:

Although the U.P. will keep a majority of the stock . . . the Vice President will control chiefly, and he will make a flimsy job of it; always

123 *Ibid.*, pp. 1064–1067 (Dodge to Durant, 3 Dec. 1866).
124 Records of UP Historical Museum.

endeavoring to control the plans which will drive from it every competent engineer. If he could have his own way no engineer not entirely subservient and who would make estimates to order would stay in his employ. This would not do for the bridge, nor will it answer for his penny-wise and pound-foolish economy to be introduced on the bridge . . . Col. Seymour's report [recommending a low bridge at Telegraph pole], which I enclose, is a curiosity.[125]

Contract with Boomer Fails: During Dodge's absence in the summer of 1868, bridge matters were held up by the company until they could see where the funds could be raised to build it. Finally, on 4 September 1868, they made a $1,089,500 contract with L.B. Boomer and Company of Chicago. "This contract," said Dodge, "was a blind for the purpose of inducing men to come in and furnish money for building the bridge, but it was a failure."[126] Boomer did only $310,637 worth of work before his contract expired on 15 September 1870.

Oliver noted in his diary of March 10, "Meeting of Bd of Dirs. had a discussion on subject of fixing initial pt. on East side of Mo. R. 12 votes no, 3 yeas. The desire was to make Council Bluffs & not Omaha the place of transfer . . . Put Gen'l. Dodge in charge of Bridge Committee."

Work Resumed by UP: On 10 April 1870, work on the bridge was resumed, this time by the UP itself with Chief Engineer Sickels in charge, Dodge having resigned. Oliver offered Chapman $10,000 a year "to go out and look after building bridge."[127]

The total cost of the bridge, according to the UP expense books, was $2,254,259 including Boomer's $310,637.[128] But the U.S. Pacific Railway Commission, in 1887, after adding the discount of $440,000 on bonds sold to finance it, as well as interest of $172,205 on the bonds paid or accrued before the bridge was completed, found the real cost to be $2,869,898.[129]

The Bridge Is Opened: On or about 1 April 1872, the bridge was opened for traffic. The distance from the initial point in Council Bluffs to the point 5 miles west of Ogden was now 1,042.5 miles. This extra 3.9 miles was not subsidized, thanks to Durant. The bridge has been rebuilt twice, each time stronger to take the heavier weights of

[125] Dodge, *Autobiography*, p. 1082. [126] *Ibid.*, p. 1097; see also p. 275.
[127] Oliver Ames's diary, June 11.
[128] Records of UP Historical Museum. [129] See p. 406.

more modern locomotives and cars. The present double-tracked trestle was erected in 1916.

Eastern Terminus Changed: On 17 February 1872 the UP Government Directors, of whom James F. Wilson was the member of the Executive Committee, addressed a letter to the Honorable C. Delano, Secretary of the Interior, objecting to the failure of the company to establish its eastern terminus at Council Bluffs. After citing pertinent parts of the Act of 1 July 1862, Section 14, requiring a single line of railroad from the western boundary of Iowa; Lincoln's executive order of 7 March 1864; and the amending Act of 2 July 1864, Section 9 (authorizing ferries and bridges across the Missouri), the Government Directors ended their contention with these words:

On inquiry we find that the Union Pacific Railroad Company, on or about 6 January 1872, by John Duff, its vice-president, entered into an agreement in writing with the city of Omaha, in which it is declared that "the eastern terminus of the Union Pacific Railroad Company shall be and remain at said city of Omaha." This provision of said agreement, together with all others tending to change the eastern terminus of said road from the east to the west side of the Missouri River, or tending to shift the responsibility of maintaining said bridge from said company to its connecting lines, we find to be in direct and palpable violation of its charter and detrimental to the interests of the public.

This was a conscientious step for them to take, for it had been a great advantage to the company to operate only from Omaha ever since Durant had circumvented Lincoln by "losing" his first order and breaking ground near the ferry landing at Davenport and Seventh Streets, Omaha.[130] Dodge had consistently maintained that "by law, by economy of operation [not construction], and by ample terminals, Council Bluffs should have been the actual terminus." [131] After the bridge was in operation, Iowan parties brought suit under the Act of 24 February 1871, which provided that nothing should be so construed as to change the eastern terminus from the place where it was fixed under existing laws; and under the Act of 3 March 1873, which required a U.S. Circuit Court to determine all cases of mandamus to compel the company to operate its road as required by law. The U.S. Supreme Court finally affirmed in October 1875 the deci-

---

[130] See p. 26.   [131] Dodge, *How We Built the Union Pacific*, p. 66.

sion of the Circuit Court in favor of the Iowans and required the bridge and all parts of the UP and branches to be "operated as one continuous line." The decision, of course, rendered invalid the agreements with Omaha and Douglas County, so far as they required the company to make up and terminate its trains in Omaha.[132]

So, in spite of the Doctor's calculations and policies, the UP terminus is still in Council Bluffs, 3 miles east of the bridge, at the Union Depot known as the Union Pacific Transfer, near Ninth Avenue and Twenty-first Street. There rises a 56-foot replica of the Golden Spike, its sharp tip pointing skyward and its bronze plaque inscribed with these words: "Eastern Terminus of the Union Pacific Railroad, Fixed By Abraham Lincoln, President of the United States."

H. New York Central Takes Control from the Pennsy

Pennsylvania System Defaults: In the meantime, in the winter of 1870–1871, when the UP was so hard pressed, it negotiated a large loan from the Pennsylvania Railroad, the condition being that the latter should have representation and control. According to Carnegie, and apparently through a misunderstanding, Scott, without the knowledge of Carnegie and Pullman, sold the collateral which the UP had pledged for the loan.[133] They were charged with having sold out the collateral for their personal profit. Carnegie relates in his autobiography that "at the first opportunity we were ignominiously but deservedly expelled from the Union Pacific Board." [134]

Horace Clark Steps in: Horace Francis Clark was born on 29 November 1815 at Southbury, Connecticut, the son of a Presbyterian minister. A graduate of Williams College at the age of eighteen, he was admitted to the New York Bar Association four years later. Marrying a daughter of "Commodore" Cornelius Vanderbilt, he made his home in New York City. In 1856 he was elected to the Thirty-Fifth U.S. Congress as a "Hardshell" Democrat, and was re-elected to the Thirty-Sixth Congress as an independent. On leaving Washington,

---

[132] Records of UP Historical Museum.
[133] *Wilson Rep.,* pp. 356–357 (testimony of B.W. Spence).
[134] Records of UP Historical Museum.

he resumed his law practice but abandoned it when railroads began to occupy most of his attention.[135]

He became a Director of Vanderbilt's New York Central and Hudson River Railroad, and then President of the Lake Shore and Michigan Southern. These two roads made a "water-level" connecting line of 982 miles between New York and Chicago, via Buffalo and Toledo. He was also a Director of the Toledo, Wabash and Western Railroad (the Wabash), then running between Toledo and St. Louis. Associated with him as Directors on all three roads were Augustus Schell and James H. Banker of New York.[136] Clark was also a member of the Executive Committee of the Union Trust Company of New York and Chairman of the Executive Committee of the Western Union Telegraph Company.

When called, in February 1873, to testify before the Wilson and Poland Committees, Clark answered all questions frankly, willingly, and intelligently, and in such pertinent detail that 78 closely printed pages were used on him in the report. "I have no secrets," he stated repeatedly. He showed remarkable familiarity with the history, administration, and finances of both the UP and CM, considering that he had had no office whatever with the road prior to March 1872. Invited to subscribe to the CM in 1866, he had turned it down: "I deemed the venture too hazardous . . . without, perhaps, judging correctly as to the future . . . I thought the road, if built, could not be so managed that it could pay its running expenses . . . . After the Act of March 1871 I became interested in it by reason of the very large interest I then had and now have in its eastern connections." [137]

Questioned by J.M. Wilson, Chairman, as to how much UP stock he had purchased, Clark replied that after 1 January 1872, together with Schell and Banker, he bought perhaps 40,000 shares at 30 to 35 in the open market; and then, after March 6, exercised a "60-day call," or option, purchased through Morton, Bliss and Company on about 25,000 shares additional at around 30. The sellers of the call he thought included Morton, Duff, Oakes Ames, Oliver Ames and Sons, Samuel Hooper and Company, and Dexter. He did not remember who else. He would not have exercised it, he said, if the coming election of Directors had turned out otherwise than it did. One condition was that he would become President. His inducements, he claimed, were that (never taking any compensation in the way of

---

[135] *Dictionary of American Biography*, vol. 4; *Harper's Weekly*, 12 July 1873; New York *Times*, 21 June 1873.
[136] Poor, *Manual*, 1871–1872.   [137] *Poland Rep.*, p. 431.

salary) he wanted the advantage which would result from a share in the traffic of the UP, and the advantage that might result from an increase in the value of the stock and a change in administration. The Vanderbilt roads might get none of the UP traffic, he went on, if its control were to be in the hands of a competing line such as the Pennsylvania.[138]

COMPOSITION OF THE UP BOARD BY GROUPS [a]

6 MARCH 1872 TO 5 MARCH 1873		
Ames Group	*Government*	*N. Y. Central Group* [b]
DIRECTORS AND MEMBERS EXECUTIVE COMMITTEE (7)		
Oakes Ames	Jas. F. Wilson	H. F. Clark (Pres.)
S. Dillon		G. M. Pullman
J. Duff (V.P.)		A. Schell
DIRECTORS (13)		
Oliver Ames	J. C. S. Harrison	J. H. Banker
E. Atkins	J. H. Millard	
J. Brooks	H. Price	
C. S. Bushnell	D. S. Ruddock	
F. G. Dexter		
G. M. Dodge		
L. P. Morton		
R. E. Robbins		
TOT. DIRS.: 11	5	4

[a] Adapted from Union Pacific, *Official Register; Wilson Rep.,* p. 597. (For period 8 Mar. 1871 to 6 Mar. 1872 see p. 416.)
[b] Clark, Schell, and Banker replaced Scott, Thompson, and Carnegie.

Thus it happened that the new Board changed radically for the second time in a year. Still a third change would happen soon. The UP was fast becoming one of the active, leading, and speculative stocks on the Exchange. Ten times the issue had turned over there during 1872.[139] From a low of 20¼ in October, the stock rose steadily to 30 by the end of the year, and then peaked out again at 42 in April. During these six months, the land grants moved up from 71 to 84¾, and the incomes from 71 to 87.[140] But the panic of 1873 was yet to come.

Oakes on Executive Committee: Oakes was placed on the Executive Committee for the first time, taking Bushnell's place. Very probably

[138] *Wilson Rep.,* pp. 665–666, 454.
[139] *Ibid.,* p. 410 (testimony of Clark).   [140] See Appendices A, C.

this was at the request of Clark. When asked to express his ideas of Oakes Ames's general character as a businessman in connection with the affairs of the company, Clark answered:

I know Oakes Ames very well. I first met him in 1872. I have had business relations with him since that time. He has always attended the meetings of the Board, and has always exhibited a very deep interest in the affairs of the Company . . . . He is without that accuracy, and without, perhaps, that peculiar culture which some men have acquired. I think very well of Mr. Ames . . . . I should not regard him as a full man in his explanations. He is not a man of many words. I believe him to be a thoroughly honest man.[141]

I. Deficient Net Income

The net earnings as reported publicly by the Union Pacific in the years 1870–1872 show only earnings from the expenses of railroad operations. They omit figures on net income (or deficit) after paying interest on the company's own bonds. There is no mention of the amounts paid or payable on account of the Government loan. Therefore, earnings for the calendar years 1870, 1871, and 1872 are shown in sections A and B in the following table only in brief outline. The calculations made later by the U.S. Pacific Railway Commission vary slightly from those of the UP.

However, complete details of both railroad operations and debt are given in section C in the following table, by adapting certain valuable data reported by the U.S. Court of Claims for the fiscal years ending November 5. This brief summary is important to a comprehension of the railroad's principal problem. The picture is rather staggering.

	1870	1871	1872
		(in $1,000s)	
A. PER UNION PACIFIC REPORTS [a]			
Earnings	7,625	7,522	8,893
Expenses	4,677	3,601	4,801
Net Earnings from Railroad Operations	2,948	3,921	4,092
B. PER U.S. PACIFIC RAILWAY COMMISSION [b]			
Earnings	7,567	7,522	8,893
Expenses	4,790	3,601	4,801
Net Earnings from Railroad Operations	2,777	3,921	4,092

[141] *Poland Rep.,* p. 437 (testimony of H.F. Clark).

C. PER U.S. COURT OF CLAIMS [c]

NET EARNINGS FROM RAILROAD OPERATIONS AND NET INCOME OR (LOSS) AFTER
(A) INTEREST ON COMPANY DEBTS, AND (B) PAYMENTS ON ACCOUNT OF
U.S. SUBSIDY BONDS

Line [d]	1870	1871	1872
		(Yr. ending Nov. 5)	
OPERATING EARNINGS		*($1,000s)*	
1. Commercial passenger	3,643	2,992	2,950
5. Commercial freight	2,668	2,906	3,870
7. Company freight [e]	482	362	404
4. Express	285	308	324
8. Telegraph	9	2	——
9. Ferry	65	——	——
10. Omaha bridge	——	——	218
11. Car-service [e]	58	48	16
13. Rent of building at termini or on line of road [e]	18	17	17
14. Surplus in fuel and material accounts	——	121	9
12. Miscellaneous [e]	116	94	113
Total Company Account	7,344	6,850	7,921
2. U.S. passenger	272	198	298
3. U.S. mail	271	285	284
6. U.S. freight	236	228	157
Total Government account	779	711	739
Total Operating Earnings	8,125	7,563	8,659
OPERATING EXPENSES			
1. Conducting transportation expenses [e]	830	671	747
2. Motive-power expenses [e]	1,779	1,229	1,681
3. Maintenance of cars expenses [e]	609	302	368
4. Maintenance of way expenses [e]	1,403	966	1,552
5. General expenses (including taxes)	445	398	354
6. Ferry expenses	55	——	——
7. Deficiency in fuel and material account	76	——	——
8. Legal expenses	85	49	58
9. U.S. revenue stamps	7	1	2
10. Salary account	16	54	29
11. Government Directors	4	3	6
12. Government Commissions	2	——	——
13. Expense account [e]	26	24	12
14. Telegraph earnings refunded	——	——	3
15. Omaha Bridge, expenses of operating	——	——	90
16. Car-service (use of cars of other companies)	——	——	——
18. Expenses of Land and Town Lots Dept.	41	61	88
19. Taxes on land and town lots	36	85	89
26. Construction of Omaha Bridge (in excess of sales of mortgage bonds)	——	——	——
27. Expenditures for station buildings, shops, fixtures, etc.	897	67	498
Total Operating Expenses	6,311	3,910	5,577
Net Operating Earnings	1,814	3,653	3,082
INTEREST, ETC., ON COMPANY DEBTS			
17. Discount and interest on floating debt	409	188	142
20. Interest on 1st Mortgage bonds	2,015	1,715	1,657
21. Interest on Land Grant bonds	554	602	641

Line [d]	1870	1871	1872
	(Yr. ending Nov. 5)		
	($1,000s)		
22. Interest on Income bonds	674	882	936
23. Interest on Sinking Fund bonds	——	——	——
24. Interest on Omaha Bridge bonds	——	——	98
25. Premium on gold to pay coupons	——	118	149
28. Requirements of Sinking Fund for Omaha Bridge bonds	——	——	38
29. Premium on Omaha Bridge bonds redeemed	——	——	——
Total Interest, etc., on Company Debts	3,652	3,505	3,661
Net Income or (Deficit)	(1,838)	148	(579)
Net Income or (Deficit) After Actual Payments on Account of U.S. Subsidy bonds			
30. Half of Earnings on Government Transportation a/c [f]	325	528	335
5% of "Net Earnings" (Operating), estimated [g]	91	183	154
Total Reserves Currently Payable to the Treasury	416	711	489
Final (Deficit), Estimated	(2,254)	(563)	(1,068)

[a] U.P. *Report to Stockholders*, 1875, pp. 18–19. Dillon was President then.

[b] U.S. Pacific Railway Commission, 1887, pp. 5266–5272; see also p. 261.

[c] Rearrangement of findings of U.S. Court of Claims, U.P. *v.* U.S., 1879, vol. 13, pp. 461–470.

[d] Line numbers are those in tables of U.S. Court of Claims.

[e] This line was in dispute, and adjustment was made.

[f] In other words, "An assumed payment of a portion of the interest on the Government subsidy bonds by the application to it of half the Government transportation account." U.S. Court of Claims, U.P. *v.* U.S., 1879, Vol. 13, p. 465.

[g] Full payment of interest on the 6% U.S. Subsidy bonds would have been $1,634,000 a year.

Annual Average for 1870–1872: Over the three years, 1870–1872, which commenced on 6 November 1869, the official date of completion, the findings of the U.S. Court of Claims and the U.S. Supreme Court in 1875 indicated the following facts: On an average annual basis, operating earnings were $8,116,000 and operating expenses were $5,266,000—leaving net operating revenues of $2,850,000. But after deducting interest, and so forth, on company debts of $3,606,000, there was an average *deficit* of $756,000.

Furthermore, after currently paying $539,000 to the Treasury for the two reserves specified in the Acts of 1862 and 1864, as partly estimated in the table, the final average deficit was increased to $1,295,000.

Annual Average for 1873–1875: But during the next three years, 1873–1875, according to the same sources, results proved to be sharply worse in spite of a 40 per cent increase in gross operating earnings and smaller payments to reserves. The final annual deficit averaged $2,805,000—more than double the deficit of the first three years of the road's operation.

Annual Average for 1870–1875: Going back over the full *six* years covered by the Court of Claims report, that is, from 6 November 1869 to 5 November 1875, gross operating earnings were $9,721,000 a year, on the average. But net operating earnings were only $2,202,-000 a year. Interest on company debt was a high $3,762,000, leaving a deficit in net income of $1,506,000. After allowance for the Subsidy reserves of $490,000 *the final yearly deficit was $2,050,000.*

An Adjustment Decreed: In December 1877, the U.S. Court of Claims finally adjusted the contentious Subsidy accounts up to that date in the following words:

Upon the foregoing facts the conclusion of the law was, that the defendants [the Government] were entitled to recover, under their counterclaim, as five per cent. of the claimant's [the UP's] net earnings, from November 6, 1869, to November 5, 1874, inclusive, the sum of $1,402,602.28; which sum is made up in the manner set forth in the opinion of the Chief Justice, concurred in by Richardson, J.; and that the claimant was entitled to recover $593,627.10, as one-half of the compensation due from the defendants to it for services rendered; and that for the difference between those sums, to wit, $808,975.18, judgement should be rendered in favor of the Government.[142]

Worst of All: Most serious of all, however, even then nothing would be left to provide for the balance of the unrepaid interest on the Subsidy bonds; to wit, $1,634,000 less $490,000, or $1,144,000 a year. *If repaid, the final deficit for these six years would be $3,194,000 a year.* For this to be covered, after interest on company debt, nearly impossible *net* operating earnings of $5,396,000 a year would be required just for the company to break even. Nothing would be earned on the stock, and, of course, no dividends would be paid. (But they were, by Jay Gould!)

Already it was apparent that unless some tremendous improvement in net income after company interest was to occur, insolvency of the Union Pacific would be inevitable sometime in the 1890's, when the $27,000,000 of Subsidy bonds would begin to come due, plus all the unrepaid interest. Compounded semi-annually at 6 per cent, interest on $27,000,000 accumulates in 30 years to two and a half times the principal, making $67,500,000. Then most of this, less the amount of reserve already set aside, would have to be paid in one

---

[142] U.S. Court of Claims, U.P. *v.* U.S., 1879, vol. 13, p. 470.

lump sum; and, of course, the principal also would have to be repaid or refinanced.

But in the judgment of the U.S. Supreme Court, that had been the intention in 1864 of the war Congress, which had insisted that the Pacific railways be built at once, regardless of cost.[143]

[143] See p. 30.

11

Political Passions Displace Reason

McComb's Blackmail—The Wilson Inquisition—The Poland Inquisition—Defense of Oakes Ames Before Congress—The Vote of Censure

A. McComb's Blackmail

McComb's Background: Colonel Henry S. McComb of Wilmington, Delaware, was a leather merchant and manufacturer, in which trade he made a considerable fortune during the Civil War. But according to Alley (also in that business), although of "fine appearance, he had a bad name." [1] A close associate of Durant's from the earliest days of the UP, he was his representative in major purchases of equipment, shop machinery, and materials. As one of the Doctor's partners in the Hoxie contract pool, he became an original CM stockholder with 1,000 of the 16,000 shares outstanding (25 per cent paid) in October 1864.[2] He was a Director of the UP from October 1863, and a member of the Executive Committee from October 1867, until ejected from all offices in the UP along with Durant, shortly after the Golden Spike.[3] Until then, he was also one of the Seven Trustees of the Oakes Ames contract, but never an officer of the CM. On 20 August 1869, he got out an injunction to stop the Trustees from borrowing from the stockholders under the so-called "Evasion Loan." [4]

Fant's Subscription Bounces: McComb's seemingly endless troubles with the CM began on 3 March 1866, when he tried to persuade a banker friend in Richmond by the name of H.G. Fant to subscribe to

---

[1] *Poland Rep.,* p. 93; Records of UP Historical Museum.
[2] See pp. 43, 47–48, 112.   [3] See p. 346.   [4] See pp. 359–360.

431

250 shares. Perhaps to facilitate matters, he elected to draw a draft on Fant and send it to the CM, whose Treasurer made an entry on the books this way: "Dr. To capital stock $25,000. For 250 shares, subscription of H.S. McComb, for account H.F. Fant, Virginia, and draft made on him this day for the amount." But three months later, June 29, a closing entry was worded: "Dr. To cash $25,000. For draft of H.S. McComb, for account subscription of H.G. Fant, March 3, 1866, for 250 shares stock returned dishonored and subscription cancelled." [5] Obviously, Fant had finally decided he would not take the stock. Nor did McComb want it, as he already had 500 of the 25,000 shares fully paid.[6]

McComb Claims It After All: However, a year and a half later in January 1868, after the Oakes Ames contract had been ratified by all UP stockholders; after the CM stockbook had been closed for good at 37,500 shares; and after the first division of profits had been declared —at last the stock commenced to go up.[7] So McComb then demanded that his 1866 "subscription" be made good. The other CM stockholders, even his friend Durant, just laughed at him for making such a preposterous claim. Obviously, he was turned down. By this time he had built up his holdings to 750 shares, the seventh largest position.[8]

Durant's Unpaid 650 Shares: In the meantime, a scandalous, or at best puzzling, situation had arisen about some unpaid stock, as has been told in detail.[9] To sum it up, when Durant had been voted out as President of the CM and Dillon had succeeded him, it was discovered that a block of 650 shares was standing on the books in Durant's name, without a penny having been paid for it. Apparently, the Doctor, while in command, had never intended to take them down, whether for his own account or for undeclared friends, until the market should begin to move. Yet every dollar of construction capital had been needed badly. So, to stake his claim, he had the block transferred to himself. The CM Directors now ordered him to transfer it to Dillon in trust, which he did. They then re-transferred it, *against payment* by the individual in full at par and interest—370

---

[5] *Poland Rep.*, pp. 53, 57. (Answers of defendants filed 10 Feb. 1870, McComb *v.* the CM, Supreme Court, January term, 1868, No. 19, Equity.)
[6] See p. 127.   [7] See pp. 214–215.   [8] See p. 194.   [9] See p. 198.

shares to Durant for his parties and 280 shares to Oakes for his parties. A committee of nine large CM stockholders (Oakes, Oliver, Dillon, Duff, Alley, and Bardwell; also Durant, Bushnell, and McComb himself) had met and discussed the situation with care. They all, *including McComb,* signed a brief agreement worded as follows:

We, the undersigned, . . . understanding that $65,000 of the capital stock of this company, held in trust by the president, has been promised certain parties by T.C. Durant and Oakes Ames, do hereby consent to and advise the transfer of said stock to such parties as they, the said Durant and Ames, have agreed upon and designated, say, to Durant parties $37,000, and Ames parties $28,000.[10]

Although McComb had been throwing in claims for his friends, too, the committee decided that he should have none, in view of his dubious statements to President Dillon.[11] McComb was furious, not because pal Durant had gotten 370, but just because Oakes had been favored over himself. He immediately began writing Oakes to give him some, and an exchange of letters resulted, which got Oakes and everyone else into dire trouble.

The Suit Commences: On 11 November 1868, McComb opened up in the Supreme Court of Pennsylvania at Philadelphia the much publicized lawsuit against the CM.[12] He claimed for himself 250 of the shares allotted to Oakes and all the large profit dividends paid on them; and, for good measure, charged that Oakes had been given the 250 shares merely for the "deliberate purpose of corrupting members of Congress." [13]

At first, he referred vaguely to certain personal letters which Oakes had written him early in 1868. In them Oakes had named some prominent Congressmen, all friends of his, who had already been promised some of the CM stock which he was now holding "in trust" (no actual trust deed). In one letter, Oakes naively had said he would distribute some of these shares geographically "where they will do

---

[10] *Poland Rep.,* p. 18 (Oakes).
[11] *Ibid.,* p. 58. (Defendant's answer to 33rd question, filed 10 Feb. 1870, McComb *v.* the CM.)
[12] See p. 256.   [13] *Poland Rep.,* p. 15 (Oakes).

the most good to us." Oakes had also named other Congressmen to whom he might be obliged to fulfill commitments already made.[14]

The Blackmail: Oakes's unguarded letters, thus drawn out by McComb, probably would not have strengthened McComb's case in court, but they did give him leverage for a personal settlement with Oakes. Sure enough, Judge J.S. Black, McComb's lawyer in Wilmington, thereupon came to Oakes or Alley three times and urged that the suit be compromised: that the letters were very damaging to many a high official in the Government as well as to Oakes. *If he would pay $100,000, the letters would not be exposed.*[15] Nor would they reach the public eye if he would acknowledge that he held the stock "in trust" for McComb.[16] But Oakes repeatedly and steadfastly refused to pay a penny of blackmail.

In a prepared statement, Oakes testified, "I told him to publish the letters if he chose. I knew I had done or said nothing that meant anything wrong to a fair mind. The remark he puts in my mouth, viz, that all members of Congress are bribed, etc, is entirely untrue. I said nothing of the kind to him." [17] Alley said that Oakes had told him, "Don't allow the judge or McComb to blackmail your company by any such threats, as I have never done anything wrong, and I know I have nothing to fear from any transactions of mine in regard to this or any other company." [18]

Oakes kept no copies of his longhand letters to McComb, and apparently could not recall exactly what he had written. But his friends had enough confidence in him to be convinced that the suit would come to nothing and that McComb really was just blackmailing.[19]

Nor did Oakes retain McComb's letters. He said, "I do not generally keep letters unless they are business letters of importance . . . . My papers are at Easton. I think it very likely I burned these letters . . . . I did not suppose anything in these letters would ever be considered as referring to bribery or anything of that sort, and I did not regard them as important." [20]

The Evidence Goes Public: But it seemed that McComb was bound to have his pound of flesh, if no money. He finally put the letters in

---

[14] *Ibid.*, pp. 4–7 (McComb); see also pp. 203, 210–213.
[15] Davis, p. 177; Crawford, p. 100.   [16] *Poland Rep.*, p. 22 (Oakes).
[17] *Ibid.*, pp. 22–23.   [18] *Ibid.*, p. 92.   [19] *Ibid.*, pp. 91–94 (Alley).
[20] *Ibid.*, p. 33 (Oakes).

evidence before the Master in Chancery. These records were kept out of sight for a while, but "by the most singular chance" were revealed to a Democratic newspaper correspondent in the midst of the Presidential campaign. Some allege they were stolen.[21] Whether McComb had first given an interview to the reporter apparently was not established. Certainly parts of the article as printed look as though they were the words of McComb.

In the meantime, his agitations were largely the cause of another costly suit. The State of Pennsylvania took action against the CM for about a million dollars of taxes on the "fabulous" profits which would be due the State under the terms of the charter, if McComb's story was correct.[22] It also involved the $2,000,000 note the UP allegedly owed the CM under the Hoxie contract.

In the end, McComb's claims were not settled until 12 January 1881, when he was paid a trifling consideration.[23]

The Sun *Scoops the Suit:* President Grant and Horace Greeley, campaigning for the coming election, were at extremities of political bitterness over Reconstruction policies when, like a bolt from the blue, the New York *Sun,* on September 4, published a blistering, sensational, and grossly inaccurate synopsis of the evidence taken in the Philadelphia Chancery. This Democratic paper had sensed the exact moment to strike viciously at the CM, and perhaps swing victory away from the well-entrenched Republicans.

Wrote Rowland Hazard in 1881:

It is difficult to know how the printed testimony which follows can be made to sustain the charges. There must have been an extremely unstable condition of public morals at Washington when such scantily supported accusations could have produced such terror in the accused, and such a wild excitement in the country. Suddenly the name "Credit Mobilier" was in every one's mouth .... No one knew what it meant, but nothing was too atrocious or too monstrous to be believed. According to the *Sun,* Ames had distributed, as bribes, thirty thousand shares of the stock, worth nine millions of dollars! [24]

[21] Hazard, p. 34; see also p. 486 (Butler).
[22] Records of UP Historical Museum; *Wilson Rep.,* pp. 267–270.
[23] U.S. Pacific Railway Commission, pp. 871–872.
[24] Hazard, p. 34.

Following is the beginning of the *Sun*'s article:

THE SUN

New York, Wednesday, September 4, 1872
39th Year—Price 2 cents

THE KING OF FRAUDS

How the Credit Mobilier Bought
its Way Through Congress.

COLOSSAL BRIBERY

Congressmen who Have Robbed the
People, and who now Support
the National Robber.

HOW SOME MEN GET FORTUNES.

Princely Gifts to the Chairmen of
Committees in Congress.

From 2,000 to 3,000 shares Each to
Henry Wilson, Schuyler Colfax,
George S. Boutwell, John A. Bingham,
James A. Garfield, the Pattersons,
Eliot, Brooks, Dawes and
James G. Blaine.

Correspondence of the Sun.

Philadelphia, Sept. 3—The revelations contained in the sworn testimony accompanying this need no explanatory introduction. It is the most damaging exhibition of official and private villainy and corruption ever laid bare to the gaze of the world. The Vice-President of the United States, the Speaker of the House of Representatives, the chosen candidate of a great party for the second highest office in the gift of the people, the chairman of almost every important committee in the House of Representatives—all of them are proven, by irrefutable evidence, to have been bribed . . . .

The history of the suit which is the means of giving this exposure to the public is somewhat curious. It seems that Henry S. McComb, who has filed a bill of

equity in the Supreme Court of Pennsylvania against the Credit Mobilier, was one of the original incorporators of the Union Pacific Railroad Company, as well as one of the favored few who get into the inside ring. He was an active manipulator of both the railroad company and the Credit Mobilier, and, as will be seen by his testimony, he made piles of money out of both. But some of his good friends, it seems, were not willing that he should have all that rightfully belonged to him. He had subscribed for 250 shares–$250,000 worth–of the stock of the Credit Mobilier for one H.G. Fant, then of Richmond, Va. He gave his draft on Fant to the treasurer of the company in payment of this stock; but Fant failed to honor the draft, and thus threw the load on McComb, who agreed to take Fant's stock. But there was some difficulty . . . about an imperfect power of attorney from Fant, and when that was corrected the President was out West and there was no certificates signed. Before the President returned he had been deposed by another faction headed by Ames, and the stock had become so valuable that they determined to cheat McComb out of his stock. He demanded it time and again, but the Ames faction would not let him have it. He then threatened to bring suit . . . .

McComb had adroitly drawn two letters and several verbal statements from Oakes Ames, explaining how he had distributed the stock among the prominent members of Congress, and he determined to use this information to bring Ames and his faction, who are still controlling the company, to terms. Accordingly, in 1869, he filed his bill in equity in the Supreme Court of Pennsylvania. After a great deal of manoeuvring the counsel for McComb applied for an examiner to take testimony in the case. A Wilson Norris of Philadelphia was appointed, and the testimony of McComb has thus far been taken.

By the most singular chance this testimony has been placed in my hands, and I hasten to lay it before THE SUN'S millions of readers.

Then follows the testimony, in six complete columns of fine print on the front page, and six more on page 2.

Further excited editorials and articles appeared in the *Sun* of September 5, 6, and 7, and in Greeley's own New York *Tribune* of September 7. The 1868 and early 1869 rumors of corruption in the Pacific railways had been largely forgotten with the elation over the Golden Spike. But at these fantastic charges they were revived a hundredfold. Congress, the press, and the country became impassioned. Reason had few listeners—truth could wait.

Grant Elected: In spite of McComb's charges, General Grant, still the war hero, won his second term on November 5, with Senator Henry Wilson of Massachusetts as Vice-President. The electoral vote was 272 to 66; the popular vote much closer, at 3.6 millions to 2.8 millions. The Democrats voted only half-heartedly for Horace Greeley, a former political foe, so he carried but six states, all Southern. He was a genius, and honest; but eccentric, vain, and impractical. A few weeks after the campaign, which had been relentlessly personal, Greeley was dead from over-exertion.

During November, the UP stock went down to a low of $30\frac{5}{8}$, compared with a high for the year in April of 42.

Oakes's Circular: After all the fuss in the papers, Oakes issued an explanatory circular to his constituents, although he was not a candidate for re-election. He openly styled the charges as "infamous," made only for McComb's purpose of obtaining money from the company wrongfully. He said in part:

The sworn statements of myself and others, made and filed in the same suit, lying side by side in the same record, could have been published with the charges, had it suited the political purposes of the *New York Sun* . . . . The list of names given by McComb, as indorsed on my letter and published, was written by himself, as he stated under oath at the hearing in Pennsylvania. He had no authority from me for making any such statement . . . .

I may have done wrong in my efforts to aid this great national enterprise; if so, I am unconscious of it. I have always regarded it as among the most creditable and patriotic acts of my life.[25]

[25] The circular is quoted in full in *Boston, Past and Present*, pp. 429–430; Ames Family, *Oakes Ames*, pp. 33–34; see also p. 94.

If Oakes had not had the resoluteness and honesty to refuse black-mail payments, history would not have had a multitude of enlightening facts about the enterprise. But what price virtue!

B. The Wilson Inquisition

1. CONGRESS GETS BUSY

The Third Session of the Forty-Second Congress convened on 2 December 1872. As might be expected, the Congressmen immediately went to work on Union Pacific affairs. Representative James G. Blaine of Augusta, Maine (Republican), at once left the Speaker's chair to propose the appointment of the Poland Committee.[26] On 6 January 1873, Representative J.M. Wilson of Indiana presented a resolution for another investigation.[27] Worded in a confused and verbose way, it was intended to "inquire and ascertain if the Government had been defrauded, and if so to devise a remedy." [28] This Select Committee, appointed by Samuel S. Cox, Speaker pro tempore, consisted of five member lawyers: Jeremiah Morrow Wilson (1828–1901) of Connersville, Indiana (Republican), Chairman; Samuel Shellabarger of Springfield, Ohio (Republican); George F. Hoar of Worcester, Massachusetts (Republican); Henry W. Slocum of Brooklyn, New York (Democrat); and Thomas Swann of Baltimore, Maryland (Democrat), once President of the Baltimore and Ohio. Such was the Wilson Committee.

Wrote Rowland Hazard in 1881: "Both the Wilson and Poland Committees attempted to sit with closed doors, but the outcry against this was so furious that they were obliged to open them." So each day, the press regaled its readers with all the sensational details. There were quotations of choice questions and answers, and sides were taken according to political leanings. Secrecy was tabooed. For instance, even Aaron F. Perry, one of the counsel appointed by the President to carry on the Government suit against all the Pacific Railway companies, was not only present but also participated in the Wilson questioning.[29]

On January 10, the Committee commenced its hearings. Before finishing on February 19, some 37 persons had been interviewed. It took 831 pages of small type to set it all down.

[26] *Cong. Globe,* 2 Dec. 1872, p. 11. See p. 459.
[27] Davis, pp. 178–179 (text of resolution).
[28] Hazard, p. 35.   [29] *Wilson Rep.,* p. 96.

2. SOME WILSON TESTIMONY

Below are a few quotations from sworn statements giving some interesting comments that are not found elsewhere in this book.

By Bushnell

I have thought a great many times that . . . the great cost of constructing the road was about balanced by the earnings for the years saved by the speedy construction.[30]

The Government Directors are the most squeamish men that ever lived about taking any responsibility. We had always to take the responsibility, except when we started to build the road. Mr. Jesse Williams took some responsibility in showing us how the road ought to have been built, and it cost us five or ten millions of dollars by reason of his taking that responsibility.[31]

Dr. Durant is a very reticent man, and all those reports of the engineers (about the ease or difficulty of crossing the Rockies) went to his department, and nobody ever saw them. I was as intimate with him as anybody, and I never saw them.[32]

By Alley

The interest account was a very important item among the causes of the haste in building. The principal reason, said Alley, was this:

In 1866 very much to the astonishment of the U.P., the Central Pacific, with the Kansas Pacific and some other roads, came here for additional legislation. The country being exceedingly anxious that the road be built in the shortest possible time . . . Congress was induced (as we thought, very unjustly and against its plighted faith to us) to . . . allow the two companies to build until they met . . . . This, of course, occasioned at once a strong feeling of rivalry to get at those points which it was very important to both should be got at, and it occasioned a dispute . . . which resulted in grading alongside of each other . . . which was a great loss to both companies. Mr. Huntington, in the conversations I had with him, said that it was a case of life and death to the Central Pacific, and that at any cost . . . they must get to those points on account of the connections which they would give them, and in order to prevent our road from coming in and cutting them out of those connections and destroying their road.

Question: Was there any reason except the saving of the interest and

---

[30] *Ibid.,* p. 49. [31] *Ibid.,* p. 535. [32] *Ibid.,* pp. 550–551.

the desire to command the point of junction? *Alley:* There was . . . also
the desire to comply with the general wish of the country, and of Congress, and everybody, to get the road through as fast as possible.[33]

By Durant

As to the reasons why the Seven Trustees were given irrevocable
proxies for six-tenths of the UP stock, Durant said:

> One was that the stock was increasing all the time, and it was difficult
> to keep track of it. Another was that the CM was the guarantor of the
> contract. Their stockholders owned a large majority of the stock of the
> UP, and it was for the purpose of keeping track of the thing that this
> plan was resorted to . . . . The Trustees wanted to protect outside stock-
> holders who had no interest in the CM. Their assent was required to
> the contract.[34]

To the question whether, before Oakes Ames took his 667-mile
contract, "anybody was given an opportunity to take that contract
and take their pay out of this money thus provided to be paid in on
stock," Durant replied,

> The Company could not advertise for contracts payable in cash, be-
> cause they had no cash, and the stockholders would not pay up; they
> would not make new subscriptions.[35]
>
> *Question:* How did the Company hope to pay for the making of the
> road, when they had no stock either promised or paid in? *Answer:* Be-
> cause the contract with Oakes Ames guarantees in itself to the Company
> the funds to complete the road. It proposed to take their bonds, and it
> agreed to pay the discount beyond a certain amount on them. It then
> provided that in case the bonds, the Government and first-mortgage,
> were not sufficient to complete the road, they will subscribe, or procure
> to be subscribed, at par, stock sufficient to furnish the funds to complete
> the road . . . . The Seven Trustees themselves subscribed the [balance of]
> stock to make the road.[36]

By Clark

Congressman George F. Hoar had a preconceived and determined
notion that the principal wrong was that the promoters had not paid
$100 a share in "real money" for the UP stock. He now tested out
Clark's opinion on the subject:

---

[33] *Ibid.,* p. 563; see also p. 141.   [34] *Ibid.,* pp. 72–73.
[35] *Ibid.,* p. 87.   [36] *Ibid.,* p. 87.

Hoar: Suppose the existing stockholders of this company, the men who own the stock today, were to pay in, as something due on their stock, the amount of $30,000,000 of the capital, $100 a share, so that the existing capital would remain just as it is now, and the company would have the $30,000,000 in the treasury—what, in your judgement, would be the effect on the strength of the company, and what would be the likelihood of the stockholders receiving a remunerative profit on their investment? [37]

Clark: The state of the case which you put is the case of the road with $30,000,000 in its treasury. I should think that the road would be unquestionably prosperous.

Hoar: What do you think would be the likelihood of its being able to make remunerative returns hereafter to the persons who so paid in that $30,000,000?

Clark: You are dealing in unknown quantities, and the future of railroads is all uncertainty.

Hoar: Do you not think that with the resources which the question I have put supposes, there would be such a vast development of business between the Atlantic and Pacific as would make the returns on such an investment highly remunerative?

Clark: I think it would make remunerative returns. I do not understand exactly what you mean by highly remunerative. A railroad to make returns that are remunerative must be able to maintain itself in a good condition and pay 8 per cent. to its stockholders . . . I should want more than that for a highly remunerative road. I should not look for that in a great many years from the Union Pacific Railroad.

Hoar: Not with those resources?

Clark: No, sir; I think there is no traffic that requires any very large expenditure, except for the maintenance of the track. It is a tolerably well completed road. Your thirty million dollars I do not think would add much to the earnings. It would give solvency and strength. But I think that if it had thirty million in its treasury now, the bulk of it should be at once appropriated to the payment of its debt. That is what I should advise.

Hoar: It would remove the embarrassments occasioned by its present indebtedness and probable insolvency?

Clark: I think there is no man connected with railroads that does not know that there is danger in debts.

Hoar: The object of my question, I will explain to you, is to ascertain, if I can, what would have been likely to be its history, supposing that the capital stock had been actually and in good faith paid in in cash, instead of its having been subscribed under contracts by which in reality, as some witnesses say, the company got, instead of 100 per cent. in cash, 30 per cent. in road-building for every share of its capital stock.

[37] *Ibid.,* p. 400.

The object of my question is to learn of the present president of the road what, in his judgement, would have been likely to have been its condition and the value of the property to the men who built it if that had not been done.

Clark: It is entirely conjectural. I am hopeful as to the future growth and settlement of the country. I think that, in respect of this road, it is as well established as many other roads, and there will be a large increase of its traffic . . . . If the company had that money and did not owe a debt, I think it might divide a good deal of it among the stockholders . . . .

Hoar: You think, as I understand you, that if this 36 millions of capital had been paid in cash it would have been of no use . . . ?

Clark: Permit me to say that your question assumes that the money could have been paid in; I do not believe it . . . . You could not have got the money. But, assuming that you did get it, admitting that those Boston gentlemen paid up that 36 millions . . . . the road would have to be built by days' work. You could have got no contractor to take a contract when he had to freight his material at such vast expense, and where he had to have a standing army to protect his laborers from Indians. I do not think that any prudent, responsible contractor would have been found to take the contract at any price . . . . And let me say that I think it was the wildest contract that I ever knew to be made by a civilized man . . .[38]

In answer to a question by Shellabarger about a possible amendment or repeal of the Act of 1862, Section 18, Clark replied:

This is a public franchise, created by eminent domain, and subject to the control of the sovereign power, as are all franchises . . . . The moral question is still left open, whether the Government could make such amendment . . . as would violate the private rights of third parties who have reposed on the faith of Government acts. Your question involves another point . . . . What is the right of the Government in this property? . . . The Government made no gift to the Union Pacific Railroad Company except of lands and right of way . . . but lent its credit, and took a lien in the nature of a second mortgage on the road for the amount of $27,000,000. The Government paid no money; it merely lent its credit. It gave every alternate section on account of the valuable consideration which inured to it of rendering the sections retained of some value. The relation of the Government to this company in respect of its property is nothing more nor less than that of a creditor with a lien. I have never been able to see how the Government is injured, provided the road is maintained and the Government debt is paid . . . .

[38] *Ibid.*, p. 405.

The Government reserved the right (and it was, I think, a most unfortunate circumstance for this company that that was part of the arrangement) to appoint 25 per cent of the governing body. The transactions in the past have been approved by those Government Directors, and it seems to me that the Government is estopped . . . from the claim that it can make amendments . . . as to affect the rights of such [innocent third] parties.

In relation to the subject of recovering these moneys . . . assuming that the Credit Mobilier scheme was a violation of . . . equity jurisprudence, and that the profits . . . can be brought into the . . . Union Pacific, to whom would that money belong? Not to the Government . . . which is only a creditor. The Government is not a stockholder . . . and did not choose to build this road with its own capital . . . It is true it is interested in the maintenance of the road and in its having sufficient strength . . . to do the Government service; and that perhaps would be a very proper subject of inquiry . . . . But the money divided among the stockholders of the Credit Mobilier cannot . . . be grasped by the Government except as an act of spoliation . . . .

I think that the relation of trustee and *cestui que trust* does not exist between the Government and the Company . . . . The Government cannot complain of any act which does not infringe on its right of eminent domain, or obstruct or interfere with the purpose for which the act was passed. The Government made the bargain. It may have been wise or unwise. I think the object of the Government was to get a road built, and the Government got it. I do not think it could have got it in any other way. The Government, instead of advancing its own capital, instead of building the road itself, saw fit to make a contribution of its credit to a limited extent, and to call upon citizens to furnish the balance in one shape or other. They did it—our predecessors did it, and we succeeded to their rights. We now say to the Government, "Perform the contract and we will."

. . . Legislation has run through Congress which puts the Government in the position of saying to the Union Pacific Railroad Company, "You shall do this work, and we will not pay the money for it. We insist that you keep the road in order . . . open against the winter storms, and if additional locomotives are rendered necessary by the increase of the mails, we demand that you supply them, but we will withhold the compensation." [39]

By Oakes Ames

People thought I was crazy to make such contracts and go into such contracts and go into such an enterprise. Governor Washburn of Massa-

[39] *Ibid.*, p. 433.

chusetts came to me before I took that contract and offered to loan me $50,000, which they had at the Greenfield Savings Bank. I asked him what security they wanted. He said, "What security can you give?" I mentioned my brother and other names. I also gave him $50,000 in stock as collateral. Immediately after I took that contract he called on me to pay back the loan at a time when it was inconvenient to pay it back. He said that the contract was a reckless thing, and that he would not consent that I should have the money; that the directors said they would not trust a man who would take such a contract. That is the way the thing was looked upon.[40]

I thought it was a good contract to take, and supposed I was going to make 20 per cent on it.[41]

By Oliver Ames

I took my interest in it [the final increase in the CM stock to $3,750,-000] which was large, (I was next to the largest stockholder in the railroad company at that time), with very great reluctance and fear, and at that time Mr. Oakes Ames said he thought there were parties here in Washington who would take some of that stock; that he had talked with them about it; and the stock was promised to them then. It was agreed [by the Directors] that he should have it. That is my recollection of the first mention of it. If I am right . . . about the time when this increase of stock was made, the transfer of the stock of these books to Mr. Oakes Ames was made quite long after it was sold to him.[42] . . . My recollection is that it was promised to him earlier than December, 1867.[43] . . . It was not worth more than par [then] . . . I know I did not feel that I was giving up anything in resigning my interest in those shares.[44]

I never believed in bribing members of Congress. I did not believe it was a thing that could be done.[45]

By Dillon

As a railroad contractor, which has been my business all my life . . . I say here that I would not take that contract today, nor any other contract, unless I could make 20 per cent on it . . . . And when they talk $16,000,000, or 19 per cent profit on a contract like that, with all the risk they run—the risk of every one of us being bankrupt if we could not sell our bonds or got through in the right shape—I say it is an outrage.[46]

---

[40] *Ibid.*, p. 29.
[41] *Ibid.*, p. 30. He meant that he supposed the promoters as a whole should make 20% on the cost of the contract. See p. 456.
[42] *Ibid.*, p. 279.   [43] *Ibid.*, p. 282.   [44] *Ibid.*, p. 283.   [45] *Ibid.*, p. 300.
[46] *Ibid.*, pp. 502–511; see also p. 148.

3. THE WILSON FINDINGS

The surprisingly harsh findings of the Wilson Committee appear in the first 26 pages of Report No. 78, House of Representatives, Forty-Second Congress, Third Session, 20 February 1873. Parts of the principal points are quoted in order below:

A. All that the Government stipulated to do in aid of this enterprise has been done [including the right of way through the public land, space for depots, the eventual grant of 12,000,000 acres of land in alternate sections, and the loan of $27,000,000 U.S. bonds due in 30 years].[47]

B. The United States was not a mere creditor . . . the railroad was not a mere contractor . . . . The law created a body politic and corporate, bound, as a *trustee,* so to manage this great public franchise and endowments that not only the security for the great debt due the United States should not be impaired, but so that there should be ample resources to perform its great public duties in time of commercial disaster and in time of war.[48]

C. The moneys borrowed by the corporation, under a power given them, only to meet the necessities of the construction and endowment of the road, have been distributed in dividends among the corporators. The stock was issued, not to men who paid for it at par in money, but who paid for it at not more than 30 cents on the dollar in road making. Some of the Government Directors have neglected their duties, others have been interested in the transactions by which the provisions of the organic law have been evaded. At least one of the commissioners [Wendell] appointed by the President has been directly bribed to betray his trust by the gift of $25,000.[49] The chief engineer was largely interested in the contracts for its construction.[50] There has been an attempt to prevent the exercise of the reserved power in Congress by inducing influential members of Congress to become interested in the profits of the transaction.[51]

D. The Hoxie Contract and its assignment were a device by which the persons who were the active controllers of the Union Pacific caused it to make a contract with themselves for the construction of a portion of its road, by which they got possession of all the resources which it would be entitled to by the completion of said portion; and by which they evaded . . . the requirement that the stock should be fully paid in money . . . . The interests of the Union Pacific Railroad Company were utterly disregarded.[52]

E. Having procured the assignment to themselves of this contract, they

---

[47] *Ibid.,* pp. i–ii.   [48] *Ibid.,* p. iii.   [49] *Ibid.,* p. iv; but see pp. 288–289.
[50] *Ibid.,* p. iv; but see p. 136.   [51] *Ibid.,* p. iv.   [52] *Ibid.,* pp. iv–v.

were liable individually as partners for all debts . . . . They therefore procured corporate powers as a shield . . . by securing the control of a corporation afterwards known as the Credit Mobilier of America . . . which took upon itself the control of the Union Pacific Railroad Company . . . . By this means the persons who under the guise of a corporation that was to take the contract to build the road held complete control of the corporation for which the road was to be built. These things accomplished, they took charge of construction under the Hoxie Contract, and the portion of the road lying between Omaha and the 100th meridian [246 miles] was constructed under it.[53]

F. [The next 667 miles were built under the Oakes Ames contract. Durant had declared that the CM would never have another contract and was using injunctions. This contract was the compromise reached between Ames and Durant].[54]

At the time this contract was made there was an understanding that it was for the benefit of those who were also shareholders of the Credit Mobilier. Mr. Ames was only the medium through whom these shareholders should receive the benefits . . . . On the 15th day of October, 1867, it was assigned by a tripartite agreement to seven trustees . . . all stockholders in the Union Pacific and in the Credit Mobilier. Oliver Ames was in the anomalous position of president of the railroad company making the contract, and one of the parties to whom it was assigned, and all of them were Directors of the railroad . . . . In order to secure any of the proceeds of this contract, the stockholders of the Credit Mobilier who owned stock in the Union Pacific Railroad Company were compelled to give an irrevocable proxy to these seven trustees to vote in all cases six-tenths of their railroad stock . . . . For two years the trustees exercised the entire control thus acquired . . . . These trustees . . . were manifestly not especially looking after, or proposing in the future to very carefully guard the interests of the Union Pacific Railroad Company. If any one doubts that its interests were to be disregarded and the interests of the contractors vigilantly cared for, that doubt must be readily dispelled by reading the agreement entered into the day after the Oakes Ames Contract was assigned to them.[55]

G. The Davis Contract was made with J.W. Davis, a man of but little, if any, pecuniary ability [and not expected to perform the contract], for the construction of the remainder of the road to its western terminus, a distance of 125 miles. It was upon the same terms as the Ames Contract, and was assigned to the same board of trustees.[56]

H. Your committee present the following summary of the cost of the entire road to the railroad company and to the contractors, and the profit, as appears by the books, with all securities at *par* value:[57]

---

[53] *Ibid.*, pp. vi–vii.   [54] See pp. 184–192.   [55] *Ibid.*, pp. ix–xi; see also p. 189.
[56] *Ibid.*, p. xiii; see also pp. 254–256.   [57] *Ibid.*, p. xiv.

	Cost to Railroad	Cost to Contractors	Profit
Hoxie Contract	$12,974,416	$ 7,806,183	$ 5,168,233 *
Ames Contract	57,140,103	27,285,142	29,854,961
Davis Contract	23,431,768	15,629,634	7,802,134
	$93,546,287	$50,720,959	$42,825,328

* To this should be added amount paid CM on acount of 58 miles   1,104,000 [a]

TOTAL PROFIT ON CONSTRUCTION $43,929,328

[a] However, the item of $1,104,000 represents double counting. Fogel, p. 66.

I. Estimating all the securities at their *cash* value and the stock at 30 (which is the value the parties have placed on it), Mr. Ham gave the following exhibit as to the profits on the above contracts: [58]

Hoxie Contract

$ 1,125,000	1st Mtg. Bonds @ 85	$ 965,250
$ 5,147,233	Stock @ 30	1,544,170
		$ 2,509,420

Ames and Davis Contracts combined

$ 3,777,000	1st Mtg. Bonds @ 90	$3,399,300
$ 4,400,000	Certificates for 1st Mtg. Bonds, afterwards converted into Income bonds at	4,425,000
$ 5,841,000	Income bonds @ 60	3,486,600
$24,000,000	Stock @ 30	7,200,000
$ 2,346,195	Cash	2,346,195
		$20,857,095

TOTAL CASH PROFIT ON ENTIRE CONSTRUCTION $23,366,515 [a]

[a] This was misunderstanding Ham's testimony. Ham said the profit was not over $9,000,000. See p. 457.

It appears then, speaking in round numbers, that the cost of the road was $50,000,000, which cost was wholly re-imbursed from the proceeds of the Government bonds and first-mortgage bonds; and that from the stock, the income-bonds, and land-grant bonds, the builders received in cash value at least $23,000,000 as profit, being a percentage of about 48 per cent. on the entire cost.[59]

The committee have examined . . . the parties who have been participating in these transactions as to the amount of profits. Their testimony . . . has been widely variant.[60]

Your committee have earnestly endeavored to get the exact cost of the road to the Company and to the contractors; and if they have failed, it is because those who should know, and have had the opportunity to inform the committee, have failed to give the information. The books

[58] *Wilson Rep.*, pp. xiv–xv.

[59] *Ibid.*, p. xvii. (No further comment on the details of profits appeared in the report.)

[60] *Ibid.*, p. xvii.

have been kept in such a way, and the transactions have been of such a character, as that their true nature has been very much disguised.[61]

J. The committee deem it proper here to direct attention . . . to the following transactions in disbursement of portions of the assets of this road, which seem . . . to have been wrongful, and to demand the immediate and grave consideration of the present Directors of the Union Pacific . . . of securing the recovery of the property . . . from those who are responsible for . . . these illegal disbursements:

a) $126,000 paid to Bushnell on 9 March 1871 as "special legal expenses." [62]

b) $50,000 paid to Governor Dix as a purchase by the railroad of its own stock at par.[63]

c) $25,000 paid to a Government commissioner [Wendell] to secure the acceptance of a portion of the road as completed.[64]

d) $435,754 allowed to Durant as "suspense account." [65]

K. If these gentlemen assumed great risks from which others shrank, and thereby great benefits inured to the public, they should have all due credit. But we think they differed from other capitalists, not in taking a risk, but in having discovered that the road could be built at vast profit without risk, the resources furnished by the Government being more than ample for the purpose . . . . This claim that no unreasonable profit has been made is not supported by the testimony. *The risk, as has been shown, was wholly that of the Government.*[66]

L. There are many persons connected with the Credit Mobilier who held their stock openly . . . and who seem to have had no share in its management, and no knowledge of the wrongful use of its stock or of the funds of the railroad. . . . As Mr. J.M.S. Williams said, "They thought they were only dealing with their own property; they did not think they had anything to do with the Government." [67]

M. Instead of securing a . . . powerful . . . company . . . able to maintain its impartiality . . . in dealing with all connecting lines, [the Union Pacific Railroad Company] is now weak and poor, kept from bankruptcy only by the voluntary aid of a few capitalists who are interested to maintain it, and liable to fall into the control of . . . adroit managers, and to become an appendage to some one of the railroads of the East. In 1871 it fell under the control of . . . the Pennsylvania Railroad Company; and its present control and the manner in which it was procured are sufficiently shown by the testimony of Hon. Horace F. Clark, the present president.[68]

N. The right of the Government to regulate fares when the road pays

---

[61] *Ibid.*, p. xiv.   [62] Ibid., p. xvii; see also p. 408.   [63] See p. 192.

[64] See p. 288.   [65] See pp. 27–28; *Wilson Rep.* p. xviii.

[66] *Wilson Rep.*, p. xx. (Italics by C.E.A.)

[67] *Ibid.*, pp. xx–xxi.   [68] *Ibid.*, p. xxi.

10 per cent on its cost is rendered nugatory . . . by recording a fictitious and not an actual statement of the cost of the road.[69]

O. Your committee . . . have labored under great disadvantages. The books containing the records of these transactions are voluminous and complicated. The estimates of engineers made before the letting of the various contracts cannot be found. The presence, as a witness, of General Dodge, the chief engineer, under whose supervision the principal part of the work was done, could not be procured . . . although telegrams were sent to him, inviting his attendance, and a deputy sergeant-at-arms was sent for him, who has diligently sought him for weeks, but has been unable to find him . . . . Your committee . . . believe that he has been purposely avoiding the service of the summons.[70]

Mr. John J. Cisco, who was treasurer of the Union Pacific, was unable to attend by reason of illness.

Governor Dix, who was president, could not be present by reason of his executive duties as governor of the State of New York.

Having these difficulties to encounter, your committee do not present the foregoing figures in relation to the money value of profits . . . as being exact.

Many of the incidents to the transactions have not been investigated as thoroughly as was desired, for want of time.

The committee have given much consideration to the question of remedy. To discuss it fully would extend this report, already too long.[71]

P. We think the facts we have stated would furnish ground for judgement of forfeiture of all the franchises of the corporation . . . . But . . . it would be unjust to forfeit the rights of the present stockholders, a large majority of whom have bought their stock in good faith in the market, for the wrong-doing of their predecessors.[72]

Q. Any distribution of the proceeds of these funds [lands and bonds] as profits to stockholders is illegal, as violative of the declared purposes of the trust.[73]

R. We have then, the case of a corporation which is a trustee, in the management of persons who have divided the trust funds among themselves, who have promised to pay for its capital stock in cash, which promises they have not kept, and on which they are still liable . . . . A suit can be maintained by any *cestui que trust* to compel the collection of these assets . . . . It will be no answer to this statement to say that the ultimate security of the United States has not been impaired. This is far from being true in fact.[74]

S. If we are wrong in this opinion, there is no remedy except by resorting to the extreme power of repealing the act. Those questions are judicial. We propose a simple method of raising and determining them

---

[69] *Ibid.*, p. xxii.　　[70] *Ibid.*, p. xxii; see also p. 136.　　[71] *Ibid.*, p. xxiii.
[72] *Ibid.*, p. xxiii.　　[73] *Ibid.*, p. xxv.　　[74] *Ibid.*, p. xxv.

in one suit, and of securing so far as we can the administration of the fund according to law in the future.[75]

T. The committee, then, find that there are persons connected with the Credit Mobilier holding such bonds as are contemplated by the order of the House. They are not holders of the same in good faith and for value, but did procure the same illegally. We do not recommend that the United States refuse to pay these bonds or their interest without a judicial ascertainment of the facts. We think that so many persons hold the first-mortgage bonds in good faith that the said mortgage ought not to be set aside.[76]

We respectfully report the accompanying bill, and recommend its passage.

> J.M. Wilson.
> Saml. Shellabarger.
> Geo. F. Hoar.
> H.W. Slocum.

Thomas Swann filed a Minority Report asking for recommendations in reference to certain members of Congress who had transactions with Oakes Ames, as detailed in the Poland Report.[77]

The Bill Recommended: *An Act* to amend an act entitled "An act to aid in the construction of a railroad and telegraph line from the Missouri River to the Pacific Ocean," and so forth.

Be it enacted by the Senate and House of Representatives of the United States of America in Congress assembled. [Sec. 1]. That the Attorney-General shall cause a suit in equity to be instituted . . . [by] the United States against the Union Pacific Railroad Company, and against all persons who may . . . have subscribed for or received capital stock in said road, which stock has not been paid for in full in money, or who may have received as dividends or otherwise, portions of the capital stock of said road . . . or other property, unlawfully, . . . or who may have received as profits or proceeds of contracts for construction . . . moneys or other property, which ought in equity to belong to said railroad, or who may . . . have unlawfully received from the United States bonds, moneys, or lands, which ought in equity to be accounted for and paid to said railroad company or to the United States, and to compel payment for said stock, and the collection and payment of such moneys, and the restoration of such property or its value either to the railroad or to the United States, whichever shall in equity be held entitled thereto.

Sec. 2. That said suit may be brought in the circuit court in any cir-

---

[75] *Ibid.*   [76] *Ibid.*   [77] *Ibid.*, p. xxvi.

cuit, and all said parties may be defendants in one suit. Decrees may be . . . enforced against any one or more parties defendant without awaiting the final determination of the cause against other parties . . . .

Sec. 5. That no dividend shall hereafter be made by said company but from the actual net earnings thereof, and no new stock shall be issued, or mortgages or pledges made on the property or future earnings without leave of Congress, except for the purpose of funding and securing debts now existing, or the renewals thereof.

Sec. 6. That no director or officer of said road shall hereafter be interested . . . in any contract therewith, except for his lawful compensation as such officer.

Sec. 7. That any director or officer who shall pay, or declare, or aid in paying or declaring any dividend, or creating any mortgage or pledge prohibited by this act, or who shall offend against Section 6 thereof, shall be punished by imprisonment not exceeding two years, and by fine not exceeding $5,000.[78]

Subsequent Action: The bill which accompanied the Report was never passed by the Forty-Second Congress. It was laid on the table, lost in the stampede to adjourn on March 4. But later the Forty-Third Congress included Section 1 of the proposed Act, almost word for word as set forth above, in the "Legislative, Executive and Judicial Appropriation Bill." [79]

4. SOME COMMENTS ON THE WILSON REPORT

From: Crawford, The Credit Mobilier of America, *1880*

When we come to the *report* as written by the Committee, we must dissent from the conclusions reached by them. They could not, at least they did not, understand the relations existing between the Credit Mobilier and the seven trustees, and the Union Pacific road . . . . They did not discern that the Credit Mobilier had lost its entire capital in the construction . . . They failed to understand the relations of the government to the Pacific roads, and imagined that the government had loaned them a large amount of money for construction, when in fact the government had never loaned them a cent . . . . They could not understand the relations of cost and profits, and in their attempt to show some great fraud, made out the profits of construction to amount to more than $43,000,000, with a cash value of some $23,000,000, when the cash value of the profit actually made was but a trifle over $8,000,000. The minds of the committee were so evidently biased that they could see nothing in its true light, could understand nothing as it actually was, but thought

---

[78] *Ibid.,* p. xxvi (quotes the Act in full).   [79] 17 Statutes at Large 508; see also p. 531.

(probably because so many of their constituents did, and they were very anxious to be returned to Congress) that there was fraud on every hand, and that no men could carry through so gigantic a scheme and remain honest.[80]

From: *Davis,* The Union Pacific Railway, *1894*

Such another example of special legislation, or edict, cannot be found in the statute books of the United States—to such an extremity did the members of Congress conceive the nation to have been driven in its efforts to control its corporate creature. The whole trouble was in the puerile and improvident legislation of 1862 and 1864.[81]

From: *White,* History of the Union Pacific Railway, *1895*

[The Wilson Committee] investigated thoroughly, but, like the Poland Committee, with preconceived notions always in mind. Both committees took testimony so voluminous that neither the members of Congress nor the newspaper men nor the ordinary student of current affairs could hope to digest it. That the committees themselves did not digest it is shown by various statements incorporated into their reports which the testimony does not bear out at all. The country demanded condemnatory reports from the committees, and it got them. The widespread jobbery of the war period had to be denounced, and the Credit Mobilier case presented the occasion for such a denunciation. It was an evidence of a change of attitude by the public, of an aroused public conscience. If the spirit of reform had not taken this mode of expression it would have found some other.[82]

From: *Trottman,* History of the Union Pacific, *1923*

Instead of calling attention to the broader features of the railroad problem, and to the fact that the Union Pacific–Credit Mobilier arrangement was merely an example of uncontrolled railroad finance, the Wilson Report makes a personal attack upon a group of men who had followed the usual method of financing a new railroad enterprise. The effect of watered capitalization and of speculative railroad management upon the public is not even alluded to.[83]

From: *Fogel,* The Union Pacific Railroad, *1960*

It was ironic, indeed, that Congress in shunning a government enterprise as an invitation to profligacy should have instead spawned the Credit Mobilier scandal. *To the investigators of 1873* this twist of fate

---

[80] Crawford, pp. 117–118. [81] Davis, pp. 192–193; see also pp. 34–35.
[82] White, p. 79. [83] Trottman, p. 78.

was entirely attributable to the dishonesty of the men to whom the work had been entrusted. The Union Pacific was in a state of near prostration because it had been built by a group of men who wantonly disobeyed the "express directions" of Congress, who maliciously abrogated the various safeguards that Congress had put into these enactments.[84]

The size of the stock issue *per se* had no bearing on the financial stability of the firm. The solvency of the Union Pacific turned on the company's ability to meet the interest payments on its bonded debt. Hence the size of the stock issue entered into the question of solvency only to the degree that it induced an increase in the amount of debt . . . . And here the record seems to indicate that the greatest portion (perhaps 85 percent) of the proceeds of the various bond sales were used to meet necessary construction costs and operating expenses.[85]

The second irony of the Acts of 1862 and 1864, then, is this: Even if the promoters . . . had scrupulously limited themselves to the profit justified by the risk they had borne, the attempt to build the road under . . . these enactments would still have resulted in a bonded debt which exceeded the cost of construction and in interest charges which amounted to between 113 and 124 percent of the net income of the road in 1872.[86] With respect to the post-construction financial stability of the firm, the great deficiency was not in the character of the promoters but in the character of the enactments.[87]

If the promoters, in a great burst of generosity, limited themselves to but *one-half* of the "justifiable" profit (of $11,100,000) the interest charge would still have ranged between 95 and 106 percent of the net earnings of the road.[88]

Regardless of whether one chooses to think of them as "daring innovators" or as "unmitigated cheats," the promoters cannot be held responsible for either the long or the short run financial instability of the Union Pacific. The responsibility must be placed at another door—the door of Congress . . . . While the Act of 1862 reduced the amount of private equity capital needed to finance the Union Pacific, it did not, in any way, free the prospective purchaser of stock from the risk of losing his investment. Quite the contrary, the particular form of government aid projected in the Act increased the risk to equity capital by saddling the road with a large bonded debt.

The Act of 1864 did little, if anything, to induce investors to purchase the stock . . . . The clause permitting the railroad to use its own first mortgage bonds doubled the debt that equity had to carry, thus greatly increasing the risk to prospective stock purchasers . . . . It is true that the clause also increased the potential return to equity by increasing its "leverage" . . . . At the same time this clause invited the entry of specu-

---

[84] Fogel, pp. 53–54. (Italics by C.E.A.)   [85] *Ibid.*, p. 55.
[86] See p. 454.   [87] Fogel, p. 55.   [88] *Ibid.*, p. 88.

lative promoters of the type associated with the Credit Mobilier. By allowing the road to issue its own first-mortgage bonds, Congress created a situation in which clever manipulators, willing to hazard very great risk, could foresee the possibility of reaping a fortune great enough to tempt them into taking up the enterprise. Indeed, under the Acts of 1862 and 1864 this was the only basis upon which private business could be induced to build the road. The outcome that the Wilson committee so much deplored was not the result of an unfortunate but avoidable accident that allowed the project to fall into the hands of "heartless speculators." The final outcome—the enervation of the Union Pacific— was built into the Acts . . . by a Congress that failed to understand the implications of the risk that the investing public attached to the construction of a Pacific railroad.[89]

The building of the Union Pacific is more than an episode in history; it is a great American myth. The story of how this proud enterprise was ruined by rapacious promoters is as integral a part of the myth as the romantic versions of the explorations that preceded the road, the battles with the Indians, the armies of men pounding an Anvil Chorus across the plains, the race to the finish, and the driving of the golden spike . . . . Once formed, myths are sturdy things; they can withstand the findings of a dozen documented studies. The myth of the Union Pacific is probably invincible.[90]

5. WHAT WERE THE PROMOTERS' PROFITS?

According to Fogel

Professor Fogel's broad approach is that the Union Pacific's piercing problems arose fundamentally because it was not only a "premature enterprise," but also a "mixed enterprise" which involved both Governmental and private control and capital.[91] As to the profits made, he says:

There are as many estimates of the profit of the promoters as there are studies of the subject . . . . The bookkeeping systems . . . were "disgraceful"; the financial records contained in the report and hearings of the Wilson committee are fragmentary; the market value of the securities in which the promoters were paid is uncertain. Indeed, these factors make a precise determination of the profit . . . impossible.[92]

Nevertheless, Fogel estimated an upper limit of about $16,500,-000 [93] and a lower limit of about $13,000,000.[94] Taking a mean of $14,750,000 and a cost of $59,166,272, the ratio of profit would have

---

[89] *Ibid.*, pp. 89–90, fn. 105.   [90] *Ibid.*, p. 110.   [91] See p. 37.
[92] Fogel, pp. 68–69.   [93] *Ibid.*, p. 70.   [94] *Ibid.*, p. 71.

been 25 per cent. However, he believed that a conservative estimate of a "reasonable or justifiable" profit would have been $11,100,000, or 18.7 per cent.[95]

On the other hand, the Wilson Report found that the profit, also based on the estimated cash value of the securities when received, was $23,366,320.[96] This conclusion was either an error made in the rush of events or was a biased exaggeration.

Whatever the reason, Wilson, in reporting the actual cost of the railroad from Omaha to Promontory at $50,720,959,[97] failed to allow for certain necessary expenditures by the contractors of $8,445,313, although they were presented by Ham in writing.[98] The breakdown of the contractors' expenditures was:

Discount and interest		Legal expenses	$ 235,009
(on short term loans)	$2,581,180	Govt. commissioners	136,037
Equipment	1,460,676	Bridging	124,048
Engineering	890,866	Right of way	96,787
Station buildings	730,388	Roadway and track	95,399
Preliminary expenses	487,230	CR & MR Rr.	75,000
Expense	421,968	Telegraph	53,736
Shops and tools	398,429	Govt. Directors	52,593
Snowsheds	293,570	U.S. Revenue stamps	50,650
Fencing	249,428	Express outfit	12,319
			$8,445,313

Adding these legitimate expenditures, the total cost (at cash values) would raise Wilson's figure of $50,720,959 exactly to Fogel's figure of $59,166,272.[99]

By the same correction, Wilson's profit would drop from $23,366,515 to $14,921,202 which is not too far from the mean of Fogel's upper and lower limits, or $14,750,000.

Furthermore, deducting the CM paid-in capital of $3,750,000, which became a total loss to most of the stockholders and was a legitimate expense of construction, the Wilson profit is reduced to $11,171,202. This is very close to Fogel's idea of what a "reasonable or justifiable" profit would have been.

According to Alley

The dividends upon that contract [Oakes Ames's] were the only profits amounting to anything ever made by the Credit Mobilier or anybody

---

[95] *Ibid.*, pp. 84–85, and fn. 96.   [96] See p. 447; *Wilson Rep.*, p. xv.

[97] *Wilson Rep.*, pp. xiv, xvii.

[98] *Ibid.*, pp. 636–637. The "interest on bonds paid during construction of $4,000,000," and losses of $10,740,748 on the four classes of long-term bonds are not a part of "actual cost," and are deducted from Ham's total "actual cost" of $73,907,019.

[99] Fogel, p. 71.

else in building the road, and these profits were between $8,000,000 and $9,000,000, estimating it on this basis: The road was finished . . . in May, 1869. I took the average market-value of the stock and bonds which they received in payment of this contract between that date and January 1, 1870.[100]

The Credit Mobilier has never yet received back its capital. And if you deduct that amount . . . and the interest on the same, you will find that the profits on the stock of the Credit Mobilier . . . will be very much less than the par value of the stock . . . . That explains my declaration that the profits really counted out only between eight and nine million dollars.[101]

According to Oakes Ames

My present judgement is that we made some $8,000,000 or $9,000,000 on the Oakes Ames contract . . . . Part of it came out of Credit Mobilier stock, which is not now worth 25 cents on the dollar. Its capital has been worked up on these contracts . . . .[102] I supposed I should make about 20 per cent on the contract.[103]

A vast amount of error has been disseminated and prejudice aroused in the minds of many by . . . extravagant statements of the profits accruing from the different contracts . . . . The actual cost, in money, of building the road was about $70,000,000, and all statements of a less cost are based upon mere estimates of engineers who never saw the work . . . . The actual profit on this expenditure, estimating the securities . . . at market value when received, was less than $10,000,000, as can be . . . established in any court . . . . A profit of from 20% to 30% is not unreasonable; [considering] the risk, no man could reasonably object to a profit of 50%.[104]

According to Bushnell

I sold my profits as favorably, I think, as anybody, and at the rate at which I sold them the whole profits of the company, all told, under this contract [Oakes Ames's] would have been less than $11,000,000.[105]

We made our whole money in an incredibly short time in building the road from Cheyenne 150 miles west, but not a dollar can be shown that we made west of that 150 miles, and I do not believe we made one dollar east of Cheyenne.[106]

[100] *Wilson Rep.*, p. 5.   [101] *Ibid.*, p. 558.
[102] *Ibid.*, p. 30. By "worked up" he meant "used up."
[103] *Ibid.*, p. 28. He meant that he supposed the promoters as a whole should make about 20 per cent on its cost. See p. 444, fn. 41.
[104] *Cong. Globe*, 25 Feb. 1873, pp. 1723–1727, "Defense of Oakes Ames."
[105] *Wilson Rep.*, p. 547.   [106] *Ibid.*, p. 546.

According to Durant

The Committee failed to ask Durant what the profit was, and he made no statement about it.

According to Ham

The trustees under the Ames and Davis contracts were compelled . . . to sell the securities . . . at so large a discount . . . that the actual amount divided . . . at its cash value I should consider worth not more than $9,000,000.[107]

According to Hazard

The greater part of the profit received by the contractors for building the road was in the stock of the Railroad Company. The trustees of the stockholders of the Credit Mobilier took it at par in payment of their contract. If it turned out to be of no value, their profit was largely gone . . . [Each stockholder] received by purchase at $4.50 a share and by dividend, 615% in stock of the Union Pacific . . . . At the time it was received . . . it was *worth, to hold*, about 50. On this basis, the total profit received by the stockholders of the Credit Mobilier was about $15,000,000 . . . . A fairer criterion would be to take the (market) value of the stock as estimated at the time . . . . I inquired of the best informed directors, and came to the conclusion that 10 was a high *value* to place on it. On this basis, the total profit would be about $6,000,000.[108]

According to Clark

Construction companies with which I have been connected . . . furnish all the capital and take all the securities for better or worse. The amount of a fair profit depends upon the extent of the risk. A man who furnishes $2,000,000 to build a road connecting with great trunk lines would not think he made too much profit if he made 100 per cent, and that is a case where success is almost certain . . . . Railroad enterprise is about as hazardous a business as can be.[109]

To sum up the promoters' profits, a cash value of about $11,000,-000, or 18.6 per cent of their established costs of $59,166,272, seems to be a reasonable enough estimate, all testimony and opinions considered.

[107] *Ibid.*, p. 645.   [108] Hazard, pp. 27–29. (Italics by C.E.A.)
[109] *Wilson Rep.*, p. 435.

6. CONCLUSIONS ON THE WILSON PROCEEDINGS

In a few ways, the hearings of the Wilson Committee were constructive. Interesting information was divulged which otherwise might never have been publicized. Some of the secret workings of a railroad construction company were revealed at last. The verbal testimony was transcribed excellently by the stenographer. One thousand copies were nicely printed for skimming by Congressmen, and, more practically as it happened, for the future perusal of historians and students of politics and economics. The five committeemen labored long and hard to the best of their ability, handicapped by a time limit far too short.

But in other ways, the hearings seem inept and injudicious. The reputation of the Forty-Second Congress as a whole, and several members thereof, was compromised forever. At home, the five lawyers may well have been able prosecuting attorneys, but the investigation was no trial before judge and jury. It was an inquisition by the sovereign Government, and a harsh one at that.

The legal ability of the Committee can be questioned. They had little understanding of the financing and operations of railroads and far less of construction companies such as the CM. Their notions were preconceived, haughty, and stubborn. Their bias was exposed by suspicion of wrongdoing on the part of nearly every person interviewed and by their evident desire to appease the prejudiced and uninformed opinions of their constituents and the press. Hours were wasted on minute examinations of trivial, alleged misappropriations of money, none of which were proven. Many of their questions were sadly lacking in penetration and merely brought forth equally inadequate answers. Often the questions were redundant, producing only irritation and the same replies over and over again.

Considering the evidence taken, how could these lawyers have disregarded Ham's written testimony about $8,445,000 of legitimate construction costs and inflated the promoters' profits by that much? [110] How could they have passed over the repeated testimony concerning the inevitable loss of $3,750,000 of the promoters' capital? The hearings were far too long in view of the time limit. Some persons were permitted to talk too much. The findings were too confused to be understood even by the committeemen themselves, far less by Congress, the press, and the public. As a result, the Wilson proceedings were dwarfed by the Poland proceedings, with all the latter's color

[110] See p. 438.

allusion to Mr. C.C. Washburn, and this I will explain in connection with my proposal in the letter of the 22d of February,[113] for they belong to the same subject:

It had become tolerably well known to all the world that the road was likely to be a success, and those of us who had risked the chance had won a prize. There appeared to be a disposition then to complain of the grants that had been offered without opposition. There was first a complaint made by Mr. Washburn of the value of the land-grants. In view of this I desired that we should put it out of the power of any one to take from us what we had, in my view, paid the Government for. It was to get these land-grants as private property. I wanted them sold and the bonds divided. Mr. Alley thought we could not afford to do this; and the event proved he was right. It was also complained that we were excessive in our charges for freight and transportation, not that we exceeded our legal right, but it was proposed to trammel that right. Being a mere private right I had always found it difficult to induce any one to take the trouble to look at the case. I did not want any assistance or privilege, but that our legal vested rights should not be taken from us. I thought we had fairly bought or earned them, and I knew if any one would examine he would see this. For this reason I wanted more shares to be issued; for I have found that there is no difficulty in inducing men to look after their own property. But no one seemed to think this was necessary, and it never was done.

Before any publication of these transactions a threat of exposure was communicated to me . . . . The price of secrecy offered was the compromising with McComb. Though perfectly aware of what I had done and my motives, so confident was I in my innocence of all evil design, that I refused to pay one dollar . . . . Mr. McComb says, in his evidence, he offered to surrender these letters and deny he had any such if I would settle his claim, or something to that effect. He repeatedly made such offers, and I always refused to have anything to do with him after the charges he had made in the suit.[114]

Other excerpts from Oakes's written testimony can be found below.[115] Excerpts from his verbal testimony also appear.[116]

I do not think I ever saw the Credit Mobilier books . . . . I was never a Director.

In answer to a question as to whether, in any negotations with members of Congress there was any purpose . . . of exercising any influence over them, or to corrupt them in any way, Oakes said:

[113] See p. 212.   [114] *Poland Rep.*, p. 22.
[115] See pp. 56–57, 94–95, 106, 199–200, 210, 215.   [116] See pp. 199, 200, 209, 211, 212.

I never dreamed of it; I did not know that they required it, because they were all friends of the road and my friends. If you want to bribe a man you want to bribe one who is opposed to you, and not bribe one who is your friend.[117]

Answering the question how long it was before the time that the stock was awarded to him that he had conversations with Congressmen, Oakes said: "Probably a few months before, *or at the session of Congress before—the summer before.*" [118]

It was frequently alleged in our New York consultations that there would be an investigation into the affairs of the Pacific Railroad, and I always said I would like to have an investigation. I knew that I had never done anything that I feared to have investigated. It was alleged that things had been done before I had any connection with the road, in connection with obtaining the original charter, which would not bear investigation.[119]

Asked what was his motive in endeavoring to induce members of Congress to become shareholders in the CM and UP, Oakes said:

My object was to have associated with us men of influence and character who would investigate and see for themselves in regard to the rights and privileges of the Union Pacific Railroad Company . . . . There was a prejudice against the railroad. It was charged that we were a set of scoundrels and swindlers, who had committed all kinds of crimes against the public.[120]
Question: So you think the 93 shares is 50 per cent additional stock on the 250?
Oakes: Yes, sir. I should have had 125 shares instead of 93. I only got 93.[121]
Question: You received the stock [343 shares] as trustee; for whom were you acting as trustee?
Oakes: I was not acting as trustee for anybody. I put it in that way to distinguish it from the stock . . . which I held before for myself . . . . I was not authorized by anybody to act as trustee . . . . I acted as the agent of these parties [of Congressmen] . . . . It was a private transaction between myself and them.[122]
Question: Whence did the money come from that constituted the profits of making the road?
Oakes: I suppose it came from the sale of bonds. The profits were

---

[117] *Poland Rep.*, p. 32.   [118] *Ibid.*, p. 32. (Italics by C.E.A.)   [119] *Ibid.*, p. 33.
[120] *Ibid.*, p. 36.   [121] *Ibid.*, p. 41.   [122] *Ibid.*, pp. 42–43.

what they got for building the road more than the actual cash cost of the road. I supposed they were entitled to a profit.[123]

Question: What is your explanation of the sensitiveness which has been shown here by members of Congress and others on the subject of having any connection with it?

Oakes: It was in consequence of the slander and abuse heaped upon the Credit Mobilier. They became frightened; they thought it might affect their re-election, and they wanted to slip out of it the easiest way they could; I knew of nothing else. I cannot see anything wrong in the transaction, and I do not think any of these gentlemen did.

Question: If there is nothing wrong in it, why not come out boldly and make an explicit acknowledgment to the country of their connection with it? Why this general effort to conceal?

Oakes: That I cannot explain. Here are Mr. Boyer, Mr. Wilson, and Mr. Bingham, who have come forward . . . and did not appear to feel ashamed of it . . . .

Question: Why could you not naturally . . . say you had given Mr. Patterson so much, or Mr Bingham so much, without referring to them by their States?

Oakes: I might have done that just as readily as to have written what I did, but it would have taken me longer to write it. Mr. McComb was talking about the location of it. He thought I was placing too much in one locality. He did not call for names . . . I was endeavoring to get people everywhere to invest in it.[124]

Question [January 22]: Have you made a memorandum of it all [the transactions with Congressmen]?

Oakes:..Yes, I took a copy of the memorandum I made and brought it with me. When I went home you asked me to look over my books. I did, and found I had received $534 from Mr. Colfax, and I found I had charged him with $1,200 in June . . . .

Question: What was the character of the book in which the memorandum was made?

Oakes: It was a small pocket-memorandum, and some of it on slips of paper.[125]

Now follows the remainder of Oakes's testimony concerning the actual details of the transactions with each of the Congressmen to whom he sold stock. Up to about this time, January 22, he had apparently been avoiding direct answers to certain questions, so as to protect some wavering friends. But when a few of them, like Colfax,

[123] *Ibid.,* p. 45.   [124] *Ibid.,* p. 272.   [125] *Ibid.,* p. 281.

seemed to expect that he would perjure himself for their benefit, Oakes was sadly obliged to fetch extracts from his memorandum book kept in North Easton.[126] His detailed *written* record of five years previous became incontrovertible evidence.

The story is concluded in the same person-by-person alphabetical order as was begun in Chapter 4.

Representative Allison (now out of office)

Allison returned his 10 shares of CM and 10 of UP to Oakes, without gain or loss, apparently in March 1872. This was after Allison's political opponents had criticized his holding 10 shares of Sioux City and Pacific stock. Purely for that reason, Allison stated, "It was a prudent thing to have no interest in these matters." [127] But the Mc-Comb suit must have caused a rift between them, and they had little or no correspondence. There was much uncertainty or indifference about the accounting on the part of both Allison and Oakes, particularly about the final title to the stocks.

Representative Bingham

Bingham testified frankly and fully. He said:

In December 1870 I requested Mr. Ames to close these contracts [for 20 shares CM], as I wished to use my money . . . . I never supposed Mr. Ames contracted with me for corrupt purposes. I know that I had no corrupt purpose in contracting with him . . . . I had done nothing that in my judgement required either apology or explanation. I accept Mr. Ames's statement made to the committee . . . and I accept his statement [of his accounting to me] . . . The aggregate amount I received on the Credit Mobilier account was less than $6,000. After the settlement in 1870 I had no interest at all in the Credit Mobilier; I never held or received a certificate of stock, and, by the terms of the contract, was not entitled to any. We closed the whole matter.[128]

Representative Colfax (now Vice-President)

On January 24, Colfax said to Oakes at the hearings: "When I testified the 7th of January, and had closed all my statement . . . why

---

[126] *Ibid.*   [127] *Ibid.*, pp. 307–308 (Allison), 290–293 (Oakes); see also pp. 203–204.
[128] *Ibid.*, pp. 191–192, 195, 196; see also p. 204.

did you not cross-examine me then in regard to my statement that I had received no dividend?" *Oakes*: "I did not want to contradict you. I was in hopes the thing would never be brought up again." [129] Again, on February 11, Oakes testified, "I intended to make it as favorable as I could to Mr. Colfax, but when I heard it was said they intended to break me down I could not do otherwise than state everything." [130]

The committee used 42 pages interviewing the Vice-President of the United States about the 20 shares of CM. It is possible to recount only a few details here. Colfax had vehemently denied any connection with the CM during his campaign of 1872 and, worst of all, continued to do so even after he was confronted with Oakes's memorandum book. Instead of coming out with the truth, that he was merely an innocent investor, he clung to the claim that he had withdrawn from his 1867 contract with Oakes. "I told Mr. Ames [in 1868] that no profits, present or prospective, could induce me to buy into a lawsuit . . . and that I must recede entirely from the transaction . . . . He [Oakes] assented to this, and nothing was said as to the money I had paid him." [131] This was the check for $534.72 which Oakes had received from Colfax on 5 March 1868.[132] Also, Oakes had paid him $1,200 via the Sergeant-at-Arms, for the cash dividend just received.[133]

Colfax went on: "Now, when I said to you that I was sorry for your misfortunes [the insolvency], and that I would not require you to return the $500 that I had paid you, why did you not state to me that you had paid me $1,200 against that, and that there was nothing to return?" Oakes replied, "I do not understand your version of the matter at all. When you spoke to me about that matter, you knew you had the $1,200, and so did I; there is proof of that on the [memorandum] book, and what is the use of trying to get around it? There is no getting around it or over it. The record shows for itself that I gave you the check." [134] The Committee accepted Oakes's evidence as true.

This one incident proves well enough that Colfax was perjuring himself. In fact, Colfax's testimony was so full of inaccuracies, fabrications, and contradictions that it finally became evident to all that he was trying to lie his way out of having had any interest in the Credit Mobilier. So, instead of saving his political career, he ruined it. It is interesting to note that not once is the name of Colfax mentioned in the findings of the Committee.[135]

[129] *Ibid.*, p. 322.   [130] *Ibid.*, p. 470.   [131] *Ibid.*, p. 82 (Colfax).
[132] *Ibid.*, p. 451 (Oakes's memorandum).   [133] *Ibid.*, p. 453 (Oakes).
[134] *Ibid.*, p. 325; see also p. 204.   [135] *Ibid.*, pp. i–xix; see also p. 204.

Representative Dawes

Shortly after buying 10 shares of CM and paying Oakes for them at par and interest, Dawes learned that Duff Green had commenced a suit in Pennsylvania against the CM. "I told him [Oakes] I did not want any such stock. He replied, 'Well, you need not take it. I will pay you back your money and 10 per cent interest if you prefer.' . . . He settled with me in that way." [136] Dawes returned the stock and the dividends thereon, and had no further participation in the matter.

Representative Garfield

General Garfield testified in 1873: "I had heard that the company was involved in some kind of controversy with the Pacific Railroad, and that Mr. Ames's right to sell the stock was denied. When next I saw Mr. Ames I told him I had concluded not to take the stock. There the matter ended, so far as I was concerned, and I had no further knowledge of the company's operations until the subject began to be discussed in the newspapers last fall . . . . I never owned, received, or agreed to receive any stock of the Credit Mobilier or of the Union Pacific Railroad, nor any dividend or profits arising from either of them." [137]

However, Oakes's memorandum book showed otherwise. The Committee found that he had agreed with Oakes to take 10 shares of CM, but did not pay cash for them.[138] There was no communication between Ames and Garfield on the subject until the investigation began.[139] The General considered the $329 as a "loan" by Oakes to him, which he "repaid." [140]

Garfield, unlike Colfax, was smart enough to make no further denials before the Committee.[141] As a result, he managed to get re-elected to Congress and eventually become President of the United States.

He told the Committee, "Mr. Ames never said any word to me that indicated the least desire to influence my legislation in any way." [142]

Representative Kelley

The case about these 10 shares of CM is identical to General Garfield's, except that in addition to the $329 cash paid by Oakes in June 1868, the latter paid Kelley $750 in money in September, which

---

[136] *Ibid.*, pp. 113 (Dawes), v, 20, 450 (Oakes); see also pp. 204–205.   [137] *Ibid.*, p. 129.
[138] See p. 205.   [139] *Poland Rep.*, p. vii.   [140] *Ibid.*, p. 129 (Garfield).
[141] See p. 205.   [142] *Poland Rep.*, p. 130.

was considered as a "loan" by Kelley.[143] Said the latter, "Neither my self-respect will permit me to believe that I was sought to be bought by that operation which I believed was purely personal . . . or that Mr. Ames was stupid enough to invest his money with any such view in one who, for more than a quarter of a century, had been an enthusiast in the work for the promotion of which he was supposed to be purchased." [144]

Representative Logan (now Senator)

As with Garfield and Kelley, in June 1868 Oakes paid Logan the credit balance of $329 due from 10 shares of CM. In the following month Logan became apprehensive because of a letter he had received, and he returned the money with, he thought, $2 interest. "I had no hesitation in making the agreement with Mr. Ames at the time, so far as any suggestion of corruption or wrong in the matter was concerned. I did not think of such a thing, and I had no suspicion that Mr. Ames did . . . . He and I were good friends." [145]

Senator Patterson

In 1868, Oakes delivered Patterson a certificate for 30 shares of CM stock bought prior to August 1867 and standing in the name of Oakes Ames, Trustee.[146] But Patterson claimed in a sworn statement of 16 January 1873: "I never received, directly or indirectly, nor did any one ever hold for me in trust, one penny's worth of stock of the Credit Mobilier." [147] Patterson delivered the certificate to Morton, Bliss and Company, and later received through Oakes dividends thereon of some $5,000 in cash, 300 UP shares, and $2,400 in UP income bonds.[148] (Of course, the $3,000 he paid for the CM stock was to become a loss.) Furthermore, on 6 May 1871 he signed a receipt to Oakes for some of the cash and unsold UP securities, including a specification that "30 shares of stock in the Credit Mobilier were still due on the transaction." [149]

The motive for Patterson's sadly false statements and technical equivocations seemed to be that his rival for the Senate seat in 1872 had charged that "the Credit Mobilier was a fraudulent concern, and that those engaged in it perpetrated a fraud on the country." [150] At

---

[143] *Ibid.*, p. vii; see also pp. 205–206.   [144] *Ibid.*, p. 200.
[145] *Ibid.*, pp. 346–348 (Logan); see also p. 206.
[146] *Ibid.*, pp. 266–267, 444 (Oakes); see also p. 206.
[147] *Ibid.*, p. 185.   [148] *Ibid.*, pp. 352, 457–458 (Oakes).   [149] *Ibid.*, p. 337.
[150] *Ibid.*, p. 263 (Oakes).

the same time he said that his "investment in Union Pacific stock and bonds was both honest and honorable, and I regret it was not larger."

As in Colfax's case, Oakes at first obliged the Senator in his pleadings for protection before the Committee. Asked, "Why did you consent to help Mr. Patterson . . . in his skulkings?" Oakes answered, "Because I am kind hearted, and want to help everybody . . . . I did not think there was anything wrong in his holding the stock." [151] But in the end, the memorandum book was accepted as proof that Patterson had indeed bought the 30 CM shares and received all of the dividends accruing from them.

The Select Senate Committee to Act on Senators, who made their own investigation, found that Patterson's testimony before them and the Poland Committee was "a contradictory relation of the transaction between him and Mr. Ames; a suppression of material facts, and a denial of other facts which must have been known to him." [152]

Representative Scofield

In July 1868 Oakes said, "Scofield got frightened in some way, as he states, in relation to his personal liability, and I settled the matter with him." [153] He bought back the 10 shares of CM stock at cost, as he had agreed he would do if Scofield was not entirely satisfied.[154] The balance was adjusted in money, except that Oakes believed Scofield made 10 shares of UP stock out of the settlement, while Scofield was not so sure.[155] The Poland Committee considered it was unimportant to settle this difference. They finally determined that "since the settlement, Mr. Scofield has had no interest in the Credit Mobilier stock, and derived no benefit therefrom." [156]

Senator Henry Wilson (now Vice-President elect)

As related before, Oakes bought back the 20 shares of CM stock and returned all the money he had received from Senator Wilson and his wife, with 10 per cent interest added.[157]

The Senator made some significant remarks before the Committee on 16 January 1873:

> . . . In this transaction with Mr. Ames, I have done nothing which I did not feel that, as a member of Congress and a man, I had a perfect right to do; nothing to be palliated or excused; nothing I am called

---

151 *Ibid.*, pp. 272–273.
152 Crawford, pp. 147–148 (Resolution in full); see also p. 489.
153 See p. 206; *Poland Rep.*, p. 299 (Oakes).   154 *Poland Rep.*, p. 21 (Oakes).
155 *Ibid.*, pp. 300, 353, 455–456 (Oakes).   156 *Ibid.*, p. vi.   157 See p. 207.

upon to apologize for . . . . I was actuated by no improper motives . . . . Conscious of my innocence, I feel outraged at the charges which have been made against me, and I believe no greater wrong was ever perpetrated than has been perpetrated on many honorable gentlemen, who could not be influenced by the Pacific Railroad, or all the railroads of the country.[158]

To which Niblack of the Committee made an equally pertinent comment:

Let me ask whether this odium which has been created in the public mind has not, to some extent, arisen from mistakes which some gentlemen have made in endeavoring to conceal their connection with it.[159]

Oakes then questioned Wilson: "Did you not ask me, when I suggested this stock to you, if we expected to want any legislation in Congress upon the subject, and did I not answer that we did not want any?"

Wilson answered: "You told me that you wanted nothing; that all the legislation your road required had been passed years before. If there had been any question on that point, I should never have consented that my wife's money should have been so invested."[160]

Representative James F. Wilson (now out of office)

Oliver bought at cost the 10 shares of CM (ex-dividend) which Wilson, at the insistence of McComb, had solicited and bought from Oakes before he became a Government Director.[161] Wilson testified on 18 January 1873:

I did not have any idea in the whole transaction that Mr. Ames, Mr. McComb, or anybody else was trying to influence my action as member of Congress. They knew, everybody knew, that I was a friend of this enterprise. Under the same state of facts I would do over again everything I did in connection with it . . . . If Mr. Ames was around bribing anybody, I do not suppose it would have entered his mind to bribe a person who, from the start, was as true a friend to the Pacific Railroad legislation as a person could be.[162]

3. THE POLAND FINDINGS

"We are not trying a case between anybody. This is a proceeding in rem., if I may so express it. *It is more in the nature of an inquisition*

---

[158] *Poland Rep.*, p. 189.   [159] *Ibid.*, pp. 189–190.   [160] *Ibid.*, p. 190.
[161] See p. 208; *Poland Rep.*, p. 457.   [162] *Poland Rep.*, pp. 218–219.

than a trial." So declared Chairman Poland on February 11.[163] His Committee's report, or findings, appear in the first 19 pages of Report No. 77 of the House of Representatives. After setting forth the general historical background of the CM, the UP, and the Oakes Ames contract, they arrived at some astonishing conclusions, the more important of which are quoted in part below:

> In relation to the purpose and motives of Mr. Ames in contracting to let members of Congress have Credit Mobilier stock at par, which he and all other owners of it considered worth at least double that sum, the committee, upon the evidence taken by them and submitted to the House, cannot entertain doubt. When he said he did not suppose the Union Pacific Company would ask or need further legislation, he stated what he believed to be true. But he feared the interests of the road might suffer by adverse legislation, and what he desired to accomplish was to enlist strength and friends in Congress who would resist any encroachment upon . . . the rights . . . already secured, and to that end wished to create in them an interest identical with his own. This purpose is clearly avowed in his letters to McComb . . . . He gives the philosophy of his action, to wit, "That he has found there is no difficulty in getting men to look after their own property." The committee are also satisfied that Mr. Ames entertained a fear that, when the true relations between the Credit Mobilier and the Union Pacific became generally known, and the means by which the great profits expected to be made were fully understood, there was danger that congressional investigation and action would be invoked . . . . The committee believe that Mr. Ames, in his distributions of stock, had specially in mind the hostile efforts of Mr. Washburn of Wisconsin and Mr. Washburne of Illinois, and desired to gain strength to secure their defeat . . . .[164]
>
> The committee do not find that Mr. Ames . . . entered into any detail of the relations between [the CM and UP], or gave them [the buyers] any specific information as to the amount of dividends they would be likely to receive . . . . They all knew from him, or otherwise, that the Credit Mobilier was a contracting company to build the Union Pacific road, but it does not appear that any of them knew that the profits and dividends were to be in stock and bonds of that company . . . . Mr. Ames made no suggestion that he desired to secure their favorable influence in Congress in favor of the railroad company, and whenever the question was raised as to whether the ownership of this stock would in any way . . . embarrass them in their action . . . he assured them that it would not.[165]
>
> The committee, therefore, do not find . . . that they [the buyers] were aware of the object of Mr. Ames, or that they had any other purpose in

163 *Ibid.,* p. 449. (Italics by C.E.A.)　　164 *Ibid.,* pp. iii–iv; see also p. 213.
165 *Ibid.,* p. viii.

taking this stock than to make a profitable investment . . . [nor do] they find any corrupt purpose . . . founded upon the fact of [the buyers'] non-payment alone.

Those gentlemen who surrendered their stock to Mr. Ames before there was any public excitement . . . do not profess to have done so upon any idea of impropriety in holding it, but for reasons affecting the . . . security of the investment.

The committee have not been able to find that any of these members of Congress have been affected in their official action in consequence of their interest in Credit Mobilier stock.[166]

It has been suggested that the fact that none of the stock was transferred to those with whom Mr. Ames contracted, was a circumstance from which a sense of impropriety, if not corruption, was to be inferred. The Committee believe this is capable of explanation without such inference . . . . A transfer from Mr. Ames to new holders would cut off the right to dividends from the trustees, unless they also became parties to the agreement. [This was] the true reason why no transfers were made.[167]

There was a satisfactory reason for delay on Mr. Ames's part to close settlements . . . for dividends. In the fall of 1868 Mr. McComb commenced his suit . . . which is still pending . . . . Mr. Ames was not . . . anxious to have the stock go out of his hands until that suit was terminated . . . .[168]

No one of the above named members of the House appears to have had any knowledge of the dealings of Mr. Ames with other members.[169]

The committee do not find that . . . the gentlemen, in contracting with Mr. Ames, had any corrupt motive or purpose . . . or were aware that Mr. Ames had any, nor did they suppose he was guilty of any impropriety or even indelicacy in becoming a purchaser . . . . Had it appeared that they were aware of the enormous dividends upon this stock, and how they were to be earned, we could not thus acquit them.

Congress never intended that the owners of the road should execute a mortgage on the road prior to that of the Government, to raise money to put into their own pockets, but only to build the road . . . . They resorted to the device of contracting with themselves . . . and [fixing] a price high enough to require the issue of bonds to the full extent, and then divide the bonds . . . under the name of profits on the contract . . . . The sudden rise of value of Credit Mobilier stock was the result of the adoption of this scheme. Any undue and unreasonable profits [170] thus made by themselves were as much a fraud upon the Government as if they had sold their bonds and divided the money without going through the form of denominating them profits on building the road. Now, had these facts been known to these gentlemen, and had they understood they

---

[166] *Ibid.*, p. viii.   [167] *Ibid.*, p. viii; see also p. 202.   [168] *Ibid.*, pp. viii–ix.
[169] *Ibid.*, p. ix.   [170] There were none. See pp. 454–457.

were to share in the proceeds of the scheme, they would have deserved the severest censure.[171]

The only criticism the committee feel compelled to make on the action of these members in taking this stock is that they were not sufficiently careful in ascertaining what they were getting.[172]

Members of Congress are not subject to be impeached, but may be expelled, and the principal purpose of expulsion is not as punishment, but to remove a member whose character and conduct show that he is an unfit man to participate in the deliberations and decisions of the body, and whose presence in it tends to bring the body into contempt and disgrace. In both cases it is a power of purgation and purification to be exercised for the public safety, and in the case of expulsion, for the protection and character of the House.[173]

The Committee quoted in full the 6th section of the Act of February 26, 1853, 10 Stat. United States, 171, the sense of which will appear from this abstract of its one and only sentence:

If any person . . . shall . . . offer or give any money . . . bribe . . . or reward . . . to any member of the Senate or House . . . after his election . . . with intent to influence his vote on any . . . matter . . . brought before him in his official capacity . . . and shall thereof be convicted, such person . . . *and the member . . . who shall in anywise accept . . . the same* . . . shall be liable to indictment as for a high crime and misdemeanor *in any of the courts* of the United States having jurisdiction; . . . and shall, *upon conviction thereof,* be fined not exceeding three times the amount so offered . . . and imprisoned in the penitentiary not exceeding three years; and *the person so convicted of so accepting . . . the same . . . shall forfeit his office* . . . and shall forever be disqualified to hold any office . . . under the United States.[174]

Then the Committee judged that "the facts reported in regard to Mr. Ames and Mr. Brooks would have justified their conviction under [this] statute." [175]

Finally, they produced for action two severe resolutions in these words:

The committee submit to the House and recommend the adoption of the following resolutions:

1. Whereas Mr. Oakes Ames . . . has been guilty of selling to members of Congress shares of stock in the Credit Mobilier of America, for prices

---

[171] *Poland Rep.,* p. ix.   [172] *Ibid.,* p. x. (Italics by C.E.A.)
[173] *Ibid.,* p. xiv; for comment, see pp. 484–486 (speech of B.F. Butler).
[174] *Ibid.,* p. xviii. (Italics by C.E.A.)   [175] *Ibid.,* p. xix.

much below the true value of such stock, with intent thereby to influence the votes and decisions of such members in matters to be brought before Congress for action: Therefore,

Resolved, That Mr. Oakes Ames be, and he is hereby, expelled from his seat as a member of this House.

2. Whereas Mr. James Brooks . . . did procure the Credit Mobilier Company to issue and deliver to Charles H. Neilson, for the use and benefit of said Brooks, fifty shares of the stock of said company, at a price much below its real value, well knowing that the same was so issued and delivered with intent to influence the votes and decisions of said Brooks, as a member of the House, in matters to be brought before Congress for action, and also to influence the action of said Brooks as a Government director in the Union Pacific Railroad Company: Therefore,

Resolved, That Mr. James Brooks be, and he is hereby, expelled from his seat as a member of this House.[176]

These resolutions did not pass, as will be related further on.[177]

4. SOME COMMENTS ON THE POLAND REPORT

From: Hazard, The Credit Mobilier of America, *1881*

The idea had gone abroad that the people had been swindled and Congress had been bribed. The letters of Ames to McComb and McComb's interpretation of them made out a *prima facie* case. The untrue and evasive denials [of ownership of Credit Mobilier stock], and the attempt to investigate with closed doors, only deepened the popular impression of wickedness. The political managers [Democrat and Republican] were in despair. It was necessary to do something to purge Congress, and make it stand once more pure in the eyes of the people.

Under these circumstances, it is not strange that the reports of the Wilson and Poland committees should lean in favor of Congress, and throw blame on the Credit Mobilier and Oakes Ames. An extra-judicial committee could hardly be expected to make a calm, judicial report. But the future historian, as he reads those reports and learns the decisions reached by Congress upon the state of facts presented, may well moralize over the frailty of human justice, when confronted with popular prejudice and selfish fear.

The Poland Committee found Oakes Ames guilty of bribery, and they recommended his expulsion. It was useless to point out that no Act was before Congress at the time of the alleged bribery, or before, or after it, for which Ames was seeking votes. Ames was guilty in the abstract. No person whom he had bribed or sought to bribe was produced, nor was

[176] *Ibid.,* p. xix.   [177] See pp. 483, 488.

any object he had attempted to accomplish suggested. The offence was alleged to have been committed in a previous Congress, but the committee recommended his present expulsion . . . .

Public men must be very careful not to put themselves in a position where their interests will dictate their public acts. But whether the holding of Credit Mobilier stock, or of National Bank stock, or being the owner of stock in a company affected by the tariff, is a disability for a member of Congress, must be determined each man for himself. It is evident, however, that Ames was not guilty of bribery.[178]

From: *Crawford,* The Credit Mobilier of America, *1880*

The only evidence of bribery before the committee was that of Mr. McComb, which was so sifted as to prove every material statement made by him to be without the shadow of a foundation; but it must have been upon this that the committee based their findings, or else on their own imaginations, for there was nothing else . . . .

The evidence [in the report] was so bulky, the Congressmen had not the time to investigate it or study it, and therefore could not discover the fearful errors into which the committee had fallen.[179]

From: *Davis,* The Union Pacific Railway, *1894*

The result of the investigation is degrading. The evidence taken by Poland . . . did not convict Ames of bribing, or Brooks of being bribed. The report had found that Ames had been guilty of bribery, but that no one had been bribed. Members, it seemed, had been bribed without knowing it, and Ames had bribed them without telling them what he expected them to do in return for their bribes. It was a most miserable effort to appease public clamor by offering up to it the two most convenient victims . . . one a Republican, the other a Democrat.[180]

From: *Oberholtzer,* A History of the United States Since the Civil War, *1922*

Oakes Ames was a direct, outspoken man, unfortunate in the choice of his words . . . He had had a long struggle to secure the cooperation of capitalists, and it was of material assistance if he could say that a number of men whose names were favorably known in politics were in it . . . The moral view of such transactions were plainly tolerant, when men like Colfax, Garfield, Henry Wilson, James F. Wilson, and Allison would stop to listen to such proposals.

That Ames had any corrupt purpose in selling to friends, or that their action was influenced on this account, was not proven. Nor is so much demonstrable in the light of later examinations . . . However indiscreet he

---

[178] Hazard, pp. 35–36.   [179] Crawford, pp. 183, 185.   [180] Davis, p. 202.

may have been, no man could be brought to sincere belief in a wilful intention of wrong-doing on the part of this public spirited and useful man.[181]

From: *Riegel,* The Story of the Western Railroads, *1926*

In reality these men were the victims of an awakened public conscience. The practices in which they had indulged had been countenanced by preceding generations, and had carried with them no taint of wrong-doing. Oakes Ames, in particular, deserves sympathy. All through the investigations he was perfectly frank in his testimony and seemingly had no desire to conceal any of his actions. Up to the time of his death, shortly after the House vote of censure, he was unable to understand wherein he had erred.[182]

From: *Dodge,* How We Built the Union Pacific Railway

There was no man connected with the Union Pacific who devoted his time and money with the single purpose of benefit to the country and government more than Oakes Ames, and there never was a more unjust, uncalled for, and ungrateful Act of Congress than that which censured him.[183]

From: *Boston* Post *(a Democratic paper), 20 February 1873*

It is a finding that will be riddled with the shafts of contemptuous ridicule from one end of the country to the other.

From: *Oakes Ames, Two Letters*

On 18 January 1873, Oakes wrote:

Dear Wife:

I sent you a telegram today that all will come out right. Don't feel uneasy on my account, as there will be no stain on my reputation, whatever others may do. Am sorry that you feel so badly. Remember the scriptures say that "whom the Lord loveth he chasteneth." You must see by that passage that I am in high favor in the right quarter. The committee are in session this evening, and I must close. Good night! Borrow no trouble on my account. My health is good.—Yours, Oakes.

The unknown newspaper which published this letter—"which has never before seen print, attesting his honesty, calmness under severe trials, and confident faith in the justice of his countrymen,"—then added, "No man with a guilty soul would write such a letter." [184]

---

[181] Oberholtzer, pp. 600–607.   [182] Riegel, p. 79.   [183] Dodge, p. 39.
[184] Scrapbook clipping (no date) of F. M. Ames, p. 62.

On 22 February 1873, Oakes wrote his daughter-in-law, Mrs. Oakes Angier Ames of North Easton, from the House of Representatives:

Dear Katie:

I have your letter giving your sympathy and affectionate regard for me in this unjust report of the Poland Committee for which I thank you. I shall beat them I think as there has been no wrong or improper act on my part, and cannot believe that the house will so decide, but we shall see how many cowards there are on the Republican side of the house & how many of the Democrats will vote against me to blacken the Republican Party. I think they will insist that all these men that are said to have rec'd. stock from me will be put in the bill and be expelled with me. But I have not much fear of being expelled.

Thanking you again for your kind and affectionate letter

I remain Yours Truly

Oakes Ames [185]

In the House of the Forty-Second Congress were about 134 Republicans, 104 Democrats, and 5 others; while in the Senate were 52, 17, and 5 respectively.

5. CONCLUSIONS ON THE POLAND PROCEEDINGS

Both the Poland and Wilson investigations were, of course, ordered by Congress in response to public clamor following a widespread impression that the Union Pacific and the people of the United States were victims of a gigantic fraud. In fairness to the five Poland lawyers, they carried out their orders in a manner which, compared with the Wilson inquisition, was more considerate of the feelings of the persons interviewed. Furthermore, they wasted less time. They had a sincere desire, no doubt, to develop the facts to the fullest extent possible under the impassioned and hectic conditions existing. Yet these Poland Congressmen, quite humanly, were swayed by fear of their own defeat at the polls. So in the nature of things their conduct could hardly be judicious.

However, on many key points their findings seem wrong:

A. The Committee on the Judiciary of the House, to which the Poland testimony was referred, soon made it evident that the House really had no jurisdiction in the case at all, the alleged offenses having

[185] Original manuscript in possession of a member of the Ames family.

occurred before the existence of the Forty-Second Congress.[186] Yet this same Committee, after finding Ames and Brooks guilty, proceeded not only to recommend the severest possible punishment, but to act on the floor of the House as prosecuting attorneys to have the punishment inflicted.

B. No actual, specific act of bribery by Oakes was alleged and proved. Nor was any motive for bribery charged by those on the receiving end.

C. The Congressmen who contracted with Oakes were unlawfully exonerated, for obviously it takes two persons to complete a bribe.

D. Actually, it developed that all of Oakes's contracts with Congressmen *were negotiated during sessions of Congress prior to the first declaration of dividends on December 12,* which first caused the stock to rise above par.[187] Some contracts even may have been made during a Special Session of the Fortieth Congress which convened on November 21 and met every day until December 2, when the regular Second Session opened. This fact unfortunately was overlooked by Oakes, his lawyer, and all others except Alley. The Poland Committee "did not find any negotiations prior to December 2." [188] They found that Oakes "contracted with a considerable number during December, for prices much below the true value of the stock." [189] Yet the Tripartite agreement was not even completed until December 20, when Durant and McComb signed.[190]

E. Even if the stock sold at $200 a share or higher,[191] $100 of its true value must be deducted, as the stock became depleted when the road was finished. Theoretically, it would become worthless after the last dividend was paid.[192]

F. There was no actual "market" for the stock at any time, and, once above par, "prices" were highly controversial.

G. All charges of bribery and corruption were made by McComb alone, and his affidavits and testimony were not only generally untrue but malicious, involving attempted blackmail.[193] Yet the Committee obviously allowed themselves to be swayed by his testimony.

H. The amount of money involved in each sale to Congressmen, averaging $1,500, was insignificant in relation to the total $3,750,000 par value of the stock issued, both in shaping favorable legislation and influencing a "market" price.[194]

[186] *Cong. Globe,* p. 1651.
[187] See pp. 203–208, 444; Crawford, p. 179; Ames Family, *Oakes Ames,* p. 25.
[188] *Poland Rep.,* p. iii.   [189] *Ibid.,* p. xix.   [190] See p. 192.
[191] *Poland Rep.,* p. xviii.   [192] See pp. 214–215.   [193] See pp. 431–438.
[194] See pp. 203, 479.

I. Poland's idea of "continuing corrupt intention" by Ames and Brooks is impossible to understand.[195]

J. Presumption of guilt, rather than of innocence, was the keynote throughout both inquisitions. This and the hurry to close before the terms of Ames and Brooks expired best explain the errors made.

K. Finally, the outstanding fact was that Oakes Ames was convicted not so much on what he did, as on what it was *supposed* he was *thinking* of doing.

D. Defense of Oakes Ames Before Congress[196]

On 25 February 1873, two days before Congress took a vote, Oakes's long personal defense, prepared by his lawyer, Richard McMurtrie, was read by the Clerk, the Honorable E. McPherson, "in splendid style." [197] In the words of Hazard, "it is a remarkable paper, and ought to have produced some effect." Perhaps it did help to reduce the punishment first recommended. Due to lack of space, only the more important parts of it can be quoted:

Before the House proceeds to the consideration of the resolution reported on Tuesday last by the special committee charged with the investigation of alleged transactions with certain members of this body, in the disposition of shares of capital stock of the Credit Mobilier, I desire to submit the following statement:

The charges on which said resolution is based relate to events so intimately connected with a portion of the history of the construction of the Union Pacific railroad that I shall ask the indulgence of the House while I proceed to trace such history in greater detail than would otherwise be necessary.

Oakes then briefly outlined the Acts of 1862 and 1864,[198] which were "a scheme appealing to the patriotism and loyalty of the capitalists of the United States, as the instrument whereby future separation of the Pacific from the Atlantic States would be rendered forever impossible." He went on:

The alleged corrupt transactions imputed to me are all charged to have been initiated in December, 1867. Glance for a moment at the situa-

[195] *Poland Rep.*, p. xviii; see also pp. 480, 484.
[196] *Cong. Globe*, 25 Feb. 1873, pp. 1723–1727; Crawford, pp. 186–213 (in full); Ames Family, *Oakes Ames*, pp. 109–125 (in full).
[197] Diary of Governor Oliver Ames, who was present.
[198] See pp. 29–30, 95, 140–141, which quote parts of this speech.

tion of the Union Pacific Company and my connection with it at that time. After a long and ineffectual struggle, the final construction of the road had been assured by my intervention in its affairs. No one doubted that it would be rapidly pushed to completion . . . . The company had no reason to apprehend unfriendly or hostile legislation . . . . The whole country was loud in demonstrations of approval of the energy and activity which we had infused into the enterprise . . . . Government officials of every grade whose duties brought them in contact . . . were clamorous for increased speed of construction . . . . Praises everywhere filled the press. As a matter of history, no legislation, at all affecting the pecuniary interests of the company, were asked for three years and a half after the date of the alleged sales by me of Credit Mobilier stock, and then only in settlement of a purely judicial question, suddenly and without warning sprung upon it, in a critical period of its fortunes, and in relation to which no controversy had ever been made . . . .[199]

If the charge [against me] is true, it is predicated upon three facts, all of which should be shown to the satisfaction of this body, in order to justify the extreme measures recommended by the committee.

1st. The shares must have been sold at prices so manifestly and palpably below the true value as to conclusively presume the expectation of some other pecuniary advantage in addition to the price paid.

2nd. The shares must have been of such a nature as that their ownership would create in the holder a corrupt purpose to shape legislation in the interest of the seller.

3rd. Some distinct and specific matter or thing to be brought before Congress, and on which the votes and decisions of members are sought to be influenced, should be alleged and proved.

It is by no means clear, from the testimony, that the stock was sold at a price less than its true value. It was not on the market; it had no market value . . . . It had no current price, and the amount for which it could be sold depended upon the temperament of the buyer, and his inclination to assume extraordinary risks . . . or solid investments. It is in proof [here] by witnesses largely interested in railroad construction . . . and of great financial ability . . . that when this stock was offered to them at par, it was instantly declined, by reason of the enormous risks involved. . . . Apart from some proof that a small amount of this stock changed hands between persons addicted to speculation, at about 150, nothing is shown in reference to its value, except that it . . . had no ascertained price. To overturn the presumption of innocence, and substitute the conclusive imputation of guilt, from the simple fact of such a transaction occurring between men who had long maintained the most friendly personal relations . . . is to overturn all the safeguards afforded . . . by the

[199] See pp. 401–410.

common law, and in lieu thereof establish an inquisitorial code, under which no man's reputation is safe . . . .

When the Oakes Ames contract was completed, and the consideration thereof divided in cash . . . the interest of a holder of Credit Mobilier stock in the Union Pacific Railroad Company, and everything pertaining to it, was at an end (and the stock had no further real value) . . . .

To say that the Washburne bill, which professed to deal exclusively with the operation of the road, in the hands of the company, after it had been built and turned over by the contractors, was a measure feared, and to protect the railroad company, against which the stock in question was sold to members of Congress, seems to me to invoke the last extreme of credulity . . . .

For the first time in the history of any tribunal, this body has before it an alleged offender without an offense. Any person accused in the courts of the country, under like circumstances, might well, when called upon to plead to the indictment, insist that it failed to charge a crime. I am charged by the committee with the purpose of corrupting certain members of Congress, while it, at the same time, declares said members to have been unconscious of my purpose, and fails to indicate the subject of the corruption. In other words, the purpose to corrupt is inferred, where the effect of corrupting could not by possibility be produced, and where no subject for corruption existed. No lawyer who values his reputation will assert that an indictment for bribery could stand for an instant in a common-law court, without specifically alleging who was the briber, who was bribed, and what precise measure, matter or thing was the subject of bribery. There can be no attempt to bribe without the hope and purpose of corruptly influencing some person or persons in respect to some particular act. Until, therefore, it is alleged and shown not only who tendered a bribe, but who accepted or refused it, and what was the specific subject-matter of the bribery, any conviction which may follow the alleged defense must rest upon the shifting and unstable foundation of individual caprice, and not upon the solid rock of justice administered under the restraints of law . . . .

The position, however, that the fault—if such exists—is a continuing offense, is so extraordinary that I cannot forbear a reference to it. Since the Credit Mobilier stock sold by me passed into the hands of the several members of Congress . . . I have been, in the judgement of the committee, a perpetual and chronic offender against the dignity and honor of the House . . . and must so continue to the end of the world. So long as a single share of this stock shall not be restored, but shall remain in the hands of the several receivers . . . my offense goes on . . . . And yet, notwithstanding the world is now apprised of my alleged corrupt intentions . . . the parties who alone have the power, but fail to release me from the necessity of continuing my offenses by return of the stock, are themselves without blame . . . . The committee declare that want of knowledge alone of the corrupt intention of the seller excused the buyer, while holding and owning the proceeds of the sale.

I beg to be correctly understood. I allege nothing against those members of Congress who purchased stock. I am simply following the reasoning of the committee to its logical results . . . under the Act of 26 February 1853, every penalty denounced upon him who shall "give any valuable thing to any member of Congress with intent to influence his vote" is alike launched with impartial severity against any member "who shall accept the same," not knowingly, wilfully or feloniously, but in *anywise* accept the same . . . .

Aside, then, from the letters addressed to Mr. McComb, it is impossible to infer the motives attributed to me by the committee . . . . A candid consideration of their object and purpose, must, I think, carry to any unbiased mind the conviction that my motives were very far from those ascribed to me. Dr. Durant, Mr. McComb, and myself were each anxious to secure as large a portion as possible of the shares of Credit Mobilier stock, and professedly for the same purpose; namely, for disposition to those persons with whom, from past favors or personal friendship, we were willing to share opportunities of profitable investment. I had no desire or expectation to further enrich myself . . . . These obligations had been incurred not only to members of Congress, but to many private citizens; they had been contracted early in the year 1867, when the stock could not be sold above par, and it was to meet these contracts that I made special efforts to obtain the stock. No distinction was made between members of Congress and unofficial friends . . . . I sold to both alike stock at its par value, in accordance with my agreement. When, therefore, Mr. McComb objected to my receiving so large an amount, and entered upon a struggle to prevent it, I naturally addressed to him such arguments as, in my opinion, would make the deepest impression upon his mind . . . I urged upon him that I had so disposed of the stock as to enhance the general strength and influence of the company, for whose welfare his solicitude was not less than my own . . . I now concede that [my letters] contained expressions liable to be construed against the purity of my motives . . . . Written hastily in the press of business . . . in that personal confidence ordinarily existing between parties jointly concerned in financial enterprises . . . I never for an instant imagined that from them could be exacted proof of the purpose of corrupting members of Congress . . . which I solemnly declare I never entertained. The insignificant amounts sold to each member . . . the proven fact that I never urged its purchase, and the entire lack of secrecy—ordinarily the badge of evil purposes—ought, in my judgement, to stand as a conclusive refutation of the offences charged . . . I submit that a long and busy life spent in the prosecution of business pursuits, honorable to myself and useful to mankind, and a reputation hitherto without stain, should of its weight overcome charges solely upheld by the unconsidered and unguarded utterances of confidential business communications.

So far as I am pecuniarily concerned, it would have been better that I had never heard of the Union Pacific. At its completion the company found itself in debt about six millions of dollars, the burden of which fell upon individuals, myself among others. The assumption of the large portion of this liability allotted to me, followed by others necessary to keep the road in operation until there should be developed in the inhospitable region through which it runs a business affording revenues sufficient to meet running expenses and interest, finally culminated in events familiar to the public, whereby losses were incurred greatly in excess of all profit derived by me from the construction of the road.

The Secretary of the Treasury in a communication to the House, bearing date May 20, 1872 . . . estimates the amount of principal and interest which will be due from the Union Pacific Railroad Company, at the maturity of the government bonds, at the present rate of payment, at $58,157,000, assuming that the saving to the government of all the different classes of transportation in the future will be the same as in the past (a supposition entirely on the side of the United States, for it will in fact increase in almost geometrical progression), and the result is a total saving, at the date of the maturity of the bonds of $64,344,000, a sum in excess of the principal and interest due at that time to the amount of $6,187,000 . . . . To attempt to grasp the national benefits which lie outside the domain of figures, but are embodied in the increased prosperity, wealth, population, and power of the nation, overtasks the most vivid imagination.

There is but one power that can destroy its ability to perform all its obligations to the government; there is but one agency that can render it incapable of paying all its indebtedness, to the last dollar, namely the Congress of the United States. It alone can so cripple, weaken, or destroy the company as to make the loan of the government to it a *total loss.*

Oakes finally concludes his defense as follows: [200]

These, then, are my offences: that I have risked reputation, fortune, everything, in an enterprise of incalculable benefit to the government, from which the capital of the world shrank; that I have sought to strengthen the work, thus rashly undertaken, by invoking the charitable judgement of the public upon its obstacles and embarrassments; that I have had friends, some of them in official life, with whom I have been willing to share advantageous opportunities of investment, that I have

[200] *Cong. Globe,* p. 1727; Ames Family, *Oakes Ames,* pp. 124–125; Crawford, pp. 212–213.

kept to the truth through good and evil report, denying nothing, concealing nothing, reserving nothing. Who will say that I alone am to be offered up a sacrifice to appease a public clamor or expiate the sins of others? Not until such an offering is made will I believe it possible. But if this body shall so order that it can best be purified by the choice of a single victim, I shall accept its mandate, appealing with unfaltering confidence to the *impartial verdict of history* for that vindication which it is proposed to deny me here.[201]

E. The Vote of Censure

A heated, hectic debate on the Poland resolution began on 25 February 1873 and consumed the larger part of three days. The House had referred the testimony to its Committee on the Judiciary, with instructions to enquire whether impeachment was warranted of any Congressman or Senator not a member of the Forty-Second Congress, and whether further investigation should be ordered.[202]

The Honorable Benjamin Franklin Butler (1818–1893), Republican of Lowell, Massachusetts, who had been a Major-General in the war, a lawyer and a Representative since 1866, and in 1882 was to become Governor of Massachusetts on the Democratic and Greenback ticket, made the report on behalf of the Judiciary Committee.[203] They found that as the alleged offenses were committed more than five years ago, within the jurisdiction of the Supreme Court of the District of Columbia; and as the House of Representatives has no legal nor constitutional right to use its power of expulsion of its members as punishment for crimes done by a member before his election thereto, that the punishment of all offenses against the laws should be *after trial by jury and judgment of a court* of competent jurisdiction. Further, that the District Attorney (the prosecuting officer of the United States for the District of Columbia) shall present testimony to the grand jury, and take such action as law and justice shall deem appropriate. All but one member of the Judiciary Committee endorsed the report.[204]

As the debate proceeded, it became clear that the view of the Judiciary Committee had substantial support, and that the required two-thirds of the House (162 needed) could not be induced to vote for expulsion.

[201] Italics by C.E.A.   [202] *Cong. Globe,* p. 1651.
[203] Ames, Blanche A., *Adelbert Ames, 1835–1933,* pp. 559–561.
[204] House of Representatives, *Report No. 81,* 24 Feb., 14 pp.

Butler's Defense of Oakes Ames: Butler also made an eloquent speech on February 26, lasting for an hour and a half, in defense of Oakes Ames and, rather incidentally, Brooks. Some of his views concerning Oakes are quoted below:

I have spoken in many forums; in those where the lives of men hung wavering in the scale of justice; but never have I spoken where I felt that a precedent was being discussed which must settle for all time the rule of right of the representatives of the people in the House of Representatives of the Congress of the United States . . . so that if we err, when bad men shall get power, when party passion shall take the place of reason, a justification may be found for action that may result in detriment to the Republic. . . . There is no precedent in this country or in England for the procedure that we now witness this day of punishing a man for an offence committed more than three years before his election, of which he stands unconvicted by the verdict of any jury or the judgement of any court . . . . It is the immutable principle of the law of our fathers, that no man shall be held to answer for a crime on any pretense whatever by anybody on earth, except upon the presentment of a grand jury . . . . The safety is in the fact that a man is to be tried by his peers, his neighbors in the vicinage, for any act done by him. He is not to be brought five hundred miles from home to be tried by those who know him not. If you will try Oakes Ames in North Easton, or in the county of Plymouth, you will find that it will take much more than crying over the allegations when you make them to such a jury to convict him. They will tell you that they know Mr. Ames to be what my colleague (Mr. Banks) told us he knew he was, an honest man, a truthful man . . . . You, the law-makers, stand between the wrong and the right always, and you must give every man his full rights under the law, however wrong in act you deem him to have been.

Let me glance at the assertion that we must purify the House. Well, sir, how long since has this necessity of purification been upon us? We have sat here with these two men, as corrupt as they may be, and their corruption is alleged to be here only as a conspiracy these long years. We have four days more only to sit with them. They are no worse now than five years ago, upon the finding of the committee . . . . If we are contaminated already, turning these men out will not stop the operation of the virus. (Laughter and applause) . . . We have full right and power to protect ourselves here in the House from every danger, yea, inconvenience; *but we have no right to use this power of protection for punishment. That is the point* . . . .

Who is there who does not believe substantially every word Oakes Ames says in his testimony? Your committee have certified to its truth. Who, then, does not believe he is an honest man? Surely not those who allowed him to be the trustee of their property; and he kept debit and credit about it in his simple blacksmith way, but kept it with an accuracy which shows more of truthful honesty than the account books of the most resplendent counting room in the land. We have here an honest man, a patriotic man, a truthful man, and we are to expel him lest we should be contaminated with honesty, truth, and patriotism. (Applause) . . .[205]

If he had chosen then to lie, to quibble, he would have been safe, as the committee admit . . . .

He agreed with his associates that he would give, by purchase, to certain gentlemen then in Congress and out of it . . . an interest in this stock. Said he, in the truthful simple language of the old blacksmith, "I find I know enough of Congress to know that it is very difficult to get men to attend to something that they do not know anything about. Now, I will give a man a chance to buy some of this stock, and then he will be watchful to see that no wrong is done to the road, and a wrong done to the road is a wrong to the Government." That is the extent of his offending . . . If anything is made certain so far as the report of the committee is concerned, nobody is or has been bribed by Oakes Ames . . . .

After the dividend of December 13, 1867, the stock . . . was worth a great deal. As Mr. Ames said, a great many men would like more of it than he had promised, . . . and he was troubled to get enough to comply with their wishes. But they were shy about it before this dividend . . . And to get them to take the bribe he had to guarantee them 10% interest . . . Now, whoever heard of guaranteeing interest on a bribe?

The stock went up; a lawsuit came on, and men began to think, with the ideas prevalent, that it might not be well to be the holders of it; and they began to get rid of it as well as they could, and some to say that they had had nothing to do with it.

But Ames . . . sold none of his stock to get rid of it . . . . When McComb threatened him with the exposure of what he had done, feeling innocent, he defied him. When McComb sued he defended himself. He felt like an innocent man, he acted like one. His conduct guarantees his rectitude.

Now let me say that if every man . . . had stood precisely as Ames does, had stated as he did the exact truth when the oath of God was upon them requiring it, this storm would have blown over and made hardly a ripple upon the surface of public opinion. (Several members: That is so.) The trouble has arisen because men in the late canvass got shaky and incautiously denied their connection with it. (Laughter) . . .

The press, that damnable engine of libel and slander, has pursued him (Oakes) remorselessly, till his name has become a by-word and a reproach. Editors of newspapers send their missives here to tell us what is our duty to do under these circumstances; as if all purity as well as all knowledge

[205] See pp. 471–472, findings of Poland Committee.

resided in the editors of newspapers, and none was to be found in the Representatives of the people. Why, sir, how did this Credit Mobilier affair first get out? A newspaper reporter stole the documents from a lawyer's office and sold them to a newspaper for money, which published them to make money.[206] That was receiving stolen goods knowing them to be stolen, to begin with! (Laughter). That is what the newspapers call their business enterprise . . . . I thank heaven for one thing, if nothing more: I am a man that God made, not the newspapers. (Applause and laughter) . . .

If you send him from this House in the attempt to disgrace him, you will fail . . . . A man with that character cannot be disgraced; there is not a man of you today, even after you drive him out, who would not go and take his hand, and be glad to take it—it is the hand of an honest man.

If every gentleman in the House will vote on the facts as they are, and as every man in the House knows them to be in his inmost soul, he would vote for Oakes Ames's acquittal in a moment . . . and vote without fear or favor.

Butler then went on briefly to defend Brooks also, and ended as follows:

The last place on earth in which to settle a judicial question is in a deliberative, popular assembly; and therefore our fathers wisely, as I think, insisted that nothing like punishment should be dealt out by a deliberative assembly, and that punishment should be done only by a court.

We are not fit to try a case here; we cannot give it patient investigation and accurate analysis of the testimony; we cannot apply the rules of evidence . . . . We never should attempt to administer justice at all. We can protect ourselves from that which is around us which is noisome, unhealthy, corrupt, or improper, but to go back and punish men, that we never can do—never, never.[207]

Farnsworth's Speech: Another effective defense of Oakes Ames was made in the House on February 25 by Brig. General Richard F. Farnsworth of St. Charles, Illinois, a Republican Congressman for 14 years. A few parts are quoted below: [208]

Since the committee have made their report there has scarcely been time for any member of the House . . . to become master of the testimony

[206] See pp. 434–437.
[207] *Cong. Globe, Appendix*, pp. 176–182; Oakes and Blanche A. Ames, *Credit Mobilier —Speech of Hon. Benjamin F. Butler*, privately printed, 1944.
[208] *Cong. Globe, Appendix*, pp. 127–131.

in all its bearings . . . . In all fairness, I give to the committee what I believe it deserves, credit for intentional fairness, for great patience and industry in the performance of the very delicate and disagreeable duty devolved upon them.

It [the committee] was under the apprehension that there might be in the future, in some indefinable shape which could not be anticipated, some legislation proposed or done . . . which should be hostile to the rights of the Pacific railroad . . . This intention or design of Mr. Ames to influence the members who purchased the Credit Mobilier stock was never in any instance communicated to them . . . . The committee also say that "they have not been able to find that any of these members of Congress have been affected in their official action in consequence of their interest in Credit Mobilier stock" . . . Nor is it charged that Mr. Ames urged any one to take it.

Then what in brief is the statement of the committee against Oakes Ames? It is, first, that he bribed his friends; second, that they did not know they were bribed; third, that they were not affected by the bribe; and fourth, that neither Ames nor the persons bribed knew what those persons were to do, or abstain from doing, in consideration for the bribes.

And yet this committee concludes this report by charging that Mr. Ames is guilty of bribery because he made these sales of stock. Now I cannot so understand the law of the land. One man cannot commit bribery any more than one person can commit a conspiracy, or any more than one person can commit matrimony. (Laughter) . . . A man does not bribe his friends . . . Bribes are offered to those who are disinclined, in order to prevail upon them to do what the briber desires them to do . . .

The committee do not find that holding the Credit Mobilier stock was not legal . . . [or that it] would disqualify a man from voting . . . on matters affecting the Union Pacific . . . Yet they propose to expel him from Congress . . . because he sold some of it . . . They propose to expel Mr. Brooks . . . because he did not sell it . . . because he bought some of it . . . Now this is the dilemma in which this committee has placed itself . . .

I do not think it was the correct thing to contrive that sort of machinery by which this company became builders of that road . . . Go back and punish the men . . . who contrived the iniquity, if it was one.

I think the purchasing of or speculation in this stock by members of Congress was very imprudent, but I do not cast a stone at them. I know that there is clamor; and I verily believe that if these two resolutions are adopted, and these two men are singled out to be made the scapegoats and pack-horses for all the sins of Congress, that it will be in obedience to the clamor, and to a vitiated and iniquitous demand on the part of the public press for a victim.

What new thing has Mr. Oakes Ames done that you did not know before? The only new thing is that he sold stock, but everybody . . . knew of the existence of the Credit Mobilier. Is its stock any more wicked now than it was four years ago? We all knew he held it then, and it was allowed to pass over. And now, when he is within seven days of bidding goodbye to this Hall, it is proposed to expel him? . . . For one, I will not follow his retreating footsteps from this Capital to plant a dagger in his back.

The Final Vote: Finally, on February 27, the debate was brought to an end by Congressman Aaron A. Sargent of California (Republican), who moved the following "modified" compromise in place of the Poland resolution: [209]

Resolved, That the Special Committee be discharged from the further consideration of the subject.

Resolved, That the House absolutely condemns the conduct of Oakes Ames, a member of this House from Massachusetts, in seeking to procure Congressional attention to the affairs of a corporation in which he was interested, and whose interest directly depended upon the legislation of Congress, by inducing members of Congress to invest in the stocks of said corporation.

Resolved, That this House absolutely condemns the conduct of James Brooks, a member of this House from New York, for the use of his position as government director of the Union Pacific Railroad, and a member of this House, to procure the assignment to himself or family, of stock in the Credit Mobilier of America, a corporation having a contract with the Union Pacific Railroad, and whose interest depended directly upon the legislation of Congress.

The resolution on Ames was passed by a roll call vote of 182 to 36 (22 not voting); and on Brooks by 174 to 32 (34 not voting).[210]

During the proceedings, Oakes occupied his seat (2 East) on the floor of the House, directly in front of the Speaker, in plain view of all. A bouquet of rare flowers, the gift of some Massachusetts ladies, was on his desk. He sat there silent, immovable, a deathly pallor on his countenance, calmly awaiting the decision. The moment it had been announced and the sentence recorded, there "ensued upon the floor a scene without parallel. Men who had just joined in the vote of condemnation against Mr. Ames, gathered around him to ask his pardon for having done so. They said to him, 'we know that you are

[209] *Cong. Globe,* 27 Feb. 1872, pp. 1830–1831.

[210] Among those not voting were Ames, Bingham, Dawes, Garfield, Kelley, and Scofield; *Cong. Globe,* pp. 1832–1839.

innocent; but we had to do it in order to satisfy our constituents.' The scene is a fact, and the names of those who thus spoke can be given." [211]

Mr. Brooks, ending 20 years of service, occupied his own seat (85 East), looking more like a corpse than a human being.

In the meantime, the Select Committee of the Senate reported that same day a resolution: "That James W. Patterson be, and hereby is, expelled from his seat as a member of the Senate." But other Senators demanded more time for its consideration, and it was left over for the next session. Patterson's term expired on March 4, and the resolution was not again heard of.[212]

But if the House did not have the right to punish Oakes Ames by expulsion, as was agreed, how could they have the right to punish him by censure?

Political passions had displaced reason, indeed.

The "Salary Grab Act": Only four days after the censure, and on the very last day of the Forty-Second Congress, the House passed by 103 yeas, 84 nays, 53 not voting, the so-called "Salary Grab Act," raising, among others', their own salaries and those of Senators from $5,000 to $7,500 a year, *retroactive for two years so as to include the Forty-Second Congress.* J.A. Garfield, who reported the appropriation bill, of which this was a part, in answer to a question from the floor, stated, "The raise involved an annual increase of about $750,000, but to the present Congress about $1,250,000." [213] Ames and Brooks did not vote. Both had gone home.

But such vociferous opposition arose from outside that the "Salary Grab Act" was soon revoked.

[211] Crawford, p. 216. The scene is confirmed in writing by the Hon. Ginery Twitchell, who was seated next to Oakes at the time; see Ames Family, *Oakes Ames,* p. 99. See also Hazard, pp. 40–41.

[212] See pp. 467–468.

[213] *Cong. Globe,* 3 Mar. 1873, p. 2099.

12

Death of Oakes Ames

Oakes Back Home: On March 5, Oakes was re-elected both a Director and a member of the Executive Committee of the UP. Oliver was re-elected a Director, and the next year to the Executive Committee in Oakes's place, offices which he held to his death.[1]

Disillusioned by the censure of Congress and saddened by the perjury of some of its leading members, but relieved to be free of Washington, Oakes returned at once to North Easton. "I have got home among my friends," he remarked to an acquaintance. "They know me, and I mean to stay." His neighbors, townsmen, and constituents throughout the Second District, whom he had represented for ten years, arranged a gay reception of about 400 persons for March 13 in the new Ames High School, with the Easton Brass Band, an elegant supper, and some appropriate speeches. When Oakes rose, he spoke very briefly but with a good share of his old fire:[2]

My Friends and Neighbors—I should be less than human not to be grateful and happy at this great gathering of my constituents, to show their confidence and faith in my honor, truth and integrity. I am not in the habit of speech making, as you all know.

I have, as you are aware, been the principal subject of abuse for the past six months. The press of the country has been full of what is called the Credit Mobilier scandal.

The whole offense, if offense it can be called, is in selling sixteen thousand dollars of stock to eleven members of Congress, at the same price I paid for it, and at the same price I sold the stock to others; and if the parties purchasing the stock had simply told the truth, and said they had a right to purchase it, that would have been the end of it. But from the fact of their denial, the public suspected there must be something criminal in the transaction; and to find out what the crime was,

[1] Union Pacific, *Official Register;* see also p. 425.
[2] Boston *Journal,* Mar. 14; Ames Family, *Oakes Ames,* pp. 46–47.

Congress appointed a committee to inquire if Oakes Ames had bribed any member of Congress.

The result was the appointment of the notorious Poland committee. That committee was engaged nearly three months, and the result of all its labors was to badly damage the characters of some men high in office for truth and veracity. But the object of the committee, to see if Oakes Ames bribed any member, was admitted "not proven." But that committee made the wonderful discovery that I was guilty in selling stock for less than it was worth, but the parties taking the stock and keeping it were very innocent; and that I had the extraordinary ability to give men a bribe without their knowing it; and to do they did not know what.

That's the sum and substance of the Credit Mobilier, which has kept the country in a state of excitement for the past six months. (Applause and cheers).

An attending reporter from the Boston *Herald,* always against Ames, noted in small print:

Oakes Ames had a pleasant reception where it did him "most good" at home. Oakes continues to think that his method of making friends in Congress "for a scheme liable to encounter adverse opinion" is not open to the least objection. The "absolute censure" of two-thirds of his former congressional associates has not availed to change his opinion.

Some of Oakes's friends begged him to take up the cudgels and fight for vindication. But he reportedly answered, "No, that would only hurt others still living. History can be the judge." After all, it is not necessary to feel too sorry for Oakes at this time. A pious man, steadfastly sure of having done no wrong, his fortitude in adversity must have been great. "The world's work has always been done by men who have suffered pains or taken pains." [3]

Over sixty-nine years of age, quite a full life for that period, Oakes had encountered a formidable chain of unforeseeable ill fortune during the four years since the thrill of the Golden Spike. Saving the credit of the completed railroad suddenly became far more difficult than he had expected. Assuming too big a share of the burden, he became insolvent. Then followed the loss of control to the Pennsylvania.

So it is difficult to believe, as so often has been surmised, that the censure was the cause of Oakes's death. Far more probably, it was the

[3] Charles H. Brent, *Good Treasure*, Day 22, The Forward Movement, Cincinnati, Ohio.

cumulative effect of the overwork, strain, and disappointments of his last four years.

Death: Be that as it may, the first sign of illness in a lifetime appeared on April 28. Oakes's son Oliver noted it this way in his diary: "Father had a bad time in Boston today—a terrible pain in his stomach." Two days later: "Father looked completely worn out this morning, having had a night of terrible pain. But he went to Boston, & came out at 2:40. He could hardly walk to house from depot." For several days, although very weak, he seemed to be recovering. But on May 5 an apoplectic stroke with paralysis set in, complicated by pneumonia. He was unable to speak. The affliction had become hopeless. On Thursday, 8 May 1873, with the immediate family at his bedside, Oakes quietly passed away.

James Brooks had died only a week earlier at an age of sixty-three.

The Transcript *Eulogy:* Out of a score or more newspapers over the country reporting his death, only one will be quoted. That is the Boston *Evening Transcript,* then reputed to be the most intelligent journal serving one of the nation's centers of culture. A long editorial under date of 9 May 1873, repeated in the Boston *Weekly Transcript* of May 13, is quoted in part:

Hon. Oakes Ames breathed his last in North Easton at half-past nine o'clock P.M. yesterday . . . . From his youth up to his last hour Mr. Ames was no ordinary person. There was nothing negative about him, and one so positive in every fibre of his nature could not live as he lived, achieve what he achieved without making his mark with deep-cut lines on his day and generation.

He won the right to have his diligent, active, public-spirited past; his support with head, heart and means of many projects for the good of others and the public good; his career of indomitable energy and far-seeing sagacity, and his honesty and comprehensiveness in business matters,—he won the right to have these borne in mind for his commendation. Those who esteemed and loved him the most will concede that in the vigor of his impulses, the unconquerable persistency of his will, and the resoluteness of his whole bearing, he was not likely to be always so politic, persuasive or tender as to escape criticism; while at the same time it is safe to assert that even of such as only knew him in public, few would venture to question his personal integrity or doubt the fairness of his personal motives, as they clearly existed in his own consciousness . . . .

We must go to North Easton to see where and how the subject of this obituary, through years of unwearied and clear-sighted industry, threw his individual energies into a manufacturing concern he did his full part to build up, enlarge, perfect and lift to the high position of being the first of its class in the world. The growth and success of an establishment calling into existence and comprising nearly the whole of a prosperous village; giving livelihood to thousands and contributing no small portion to the industrial wealth of the State, it is not necessary to describe. Just now, however, it is of pertinent interest as one of the monuments to the memory of the deceased; inscribed, as it were, all over, not only with the proofs of his ability as a financier, but also of his sound judgment and the understanding of his heart. Men talk of the merchant prince: Oakes Ames was a mechanic prince; proud of his calling; pursuing it in an enlightened and even philanthropic manner, so that others should partake of the gains and benefits of the "Shop" as well as its owners. We have not the space to picture the scene of the skillful assiduity in which he took so large a part; but to visit it, see its mansions, churches, schools, and ever-increasing activities, is to have visibly manifested not a little of the organizing, persevering, fair-dealing and liberal characteristics of its financial manager.

These characteristics soon and naturally made him influential and gave him wide repute as a man of note; simple in manners, sturdy and outspoken in bearing, upright and downright, loyal to the core, and ambitious for the well-being of the community as well, in certain directions, for his own advancement. He was chosen the representative of his district in Congress in 1862, and rechosen up to his resignation as a candidate last autumn. In possession of a large and growing fortune, he entered upon various enterprises, chiefly the building of railroads, outside and apart from his operations as a manufacturer. At a critical hour he took hold, with his usual boldness, of the Union Pacific. He believed in its practicability when others more than doubted. His daring courage never faltered; his steady faith never wavered. He enlisted cooperation, assumed the perils of a leading operator, and to him, more than to any one man besides, the country is indebted for the greatest and most marvelous internal improvement of the age.

Without assuming that he was insensible to possible and probable pecuniary gains for himself, those who knew him best will never doubt that there was a large element of genuine patriotism in the views which induced him to determine and to carry out the determination to open that gigantic highway from the river, through the wilderness and over the mountains to the ocean. His heart, as well as his head and his pocket, was in the execution of that project; and he risked everything heroically for its accomplishment . . . .

Thus to trace, in meagre outline, the career of Oakes Ames, is to give him his rightful place as one of the industrial and financial master spirits of the times, and also to suggest what were the qualities of temperament, the intellectual and moral traits that made up his power, and gave him his triumphs. He was no common man; though proud to be a man of the people. Eager for success, there was no pretension or petty egotism in his ambition. Fearless, frank, and even rough and rugged in his carriage, he was of a kindly disposition. Simple in all his tastes and habits, . . . plain almost to homeliness in his whole address, there was about him hardly a touch of narrow exclusiveness; no desire to be, by the purchase of factitious consideration, other than he was in the thorough manliness of his nature. He was every inch of him an American and a New Englander, a true democrat and a believer in the worth and dignity of work. By habit and constitutional proclivity he was a utilitarian; and hence the type of his eminence. Such was Oakes Ames in his more public relations; of all he was in other relations, to win and keep the esteem, confidence and affection of neighbors, friends and kindred, those who were nearest and dearest to him know only too well as they mourn the loss of his counsels, his kindness and the firm grasp of his guiding hand.

"A man is not completely born until he be dead."—*B. Franklin.*

The Funeral: The whole village of North Easton went into mourning Friday, and the Shovel Works were closed for two days.

The funeral was held on Sunday, May 11.[4] Despite a drenching, dismal, easterly storm, fully 3,000 friends of Oakes came to pay their last respects. There were special trains from Boston, Fall River, Taunton, and Canton. Others near enough drove in by carriage. Among many notable persons were Vice-President Henry Wilson, Senator Boutwell, Governor Washburne, the Lieutenant Governor and high officials of the State Senate and House, the mayors of Boston and several neighboring towns, and the officers of the New Orleans, Mobile and Texas Railroad. Unfortunately, only Rollins represented the UP, all the Directors being absent on a trip West.

The family, and the pallbearers who were faithful employees of the family, rode in carriages to the burial service and were followed on foot by "some four or five hundred well-dressed, intelligent-appearing, and orderly operatives of the Shovel Works . . . . The procession moved in the heavy rain to the family burial place at the cemetery some mile and a half distant on the Taunton road." [5] Shortly after the present Unity Church was dedicated in 1875, Oakes's remains and

---

[4] Boston *Post,* 12 May 1873; Boston *Commonwealth,* 17 May 1873; Ames Family, *Oakes Ames,* p. 49.
[5] Boston, *Old Colony Press,* 14 May 1873.

his father's were moved to the present Village Cemetery of North Easton, adjoining the church.[6] There, close to the top of a lovely, wooded knoll, in the Ames family lot, a moderately tall shaft or obelisk of granite, placed next to the sarcophagus of Oliver Sr., honors Oakes's memory.

Tributes by Oakes's Railroads: At the annual meeting of the stock-holders of the Cedar Rapids and Missouri River Railroad held at Cedar Rapids on 21 May 1873, the following resolution was unanimously adopted:

Resolved—That in the death of Hon. Oakes Ames, this company has lost one of its warmest and most attached friends. Associated with the enterprise from its commencement, as a Director and its chief stockholder, his devotion to its interests, his energy, sound judgement, and liberality were equally conspicuous. Neither depressed by adverse circumstances nor unduly elated by prosperity, his councils were wise, judicious, and far sighted. We speak of him as we have known him through long years of intimate official and personal relations, feeling that in view of the peculiar circumstances surrounding his death, we should greatly fail in our duty to a generous and high minded associate if we omitted to spread upon our records this memento of our appreciation of his worth.[7]

A meeting of the Directors of the Union Pacific was held in Boston on 25 June 1873, at which the following resolution was unanimously adopted:

Resolved, That intelligence of the death of *Hon. Oakes Ames,* a member of this Board since 1870, has been received by us with profound sorrow, and we desire to express and put on record our high estimate of his strong, manly character, and our deep sense of his especial usefulness to this corporation. We esteemed him for his far-sighted enterprise, resolution, patience, cheerfulness, and sterling integrity. His interest in the Union Pacific Railroad commenced long ago, and his good offices to the company can hardly be overestimated.

He had faith when all was doubt, courage when courage was needed, resources when others had none. In the darkest period of war and financial distrust, his indomitable spirit urged forward the building of this road, and sustained its credit. In its behalf he carried great burdens of care and debt.

[6] Chaffin, pp. 500–501; Gov. Oliver Ames's diary, 27 Nov. 1876.
[7] Gov. Oliver Ames, *Papers.*

Now that all those cares have ended, the popular voice entitles him *"Builder of the Union Pacific Railroad."*

We sincerely mourn the loss of a friend so true, an associate so trust-worthy, and a citizen so valuable to his State and the Nation.[8]

A Letter: Only one of the many letters received by the family at this time will be quoted. Dated 16 May 1873, from Washington, it was addressed to Oakes Angier Ames by the Honorable Nathaniel G. Ordway of New Hamshire, Sergeant-at-Arms of the House of Representatives, Forty-Second Congress. It is quoted in part as follows:

. . . I had almost forgotten witnessing your father's will . . . During the ten years which I have been an officer of the House of Reps., and that your father held a seat in Congress, my relations with him were most pleasant—in fact a portion of the time of a very intimate character, and I can assure you that no man knew his course and action as a member of Congress better than myself.

I have some very strong articles of matters which have occurred during these ten years which, if known to the public, would prove beyond question or cavil his integrity and devotion to the interests of his constituency which he so well represented.

I remember on one occasion that a Southern member of Congress who was a member of the Committee on Pacific R.R. and who happened to have some measure before the Committee on Roads & Canals of which your father was a member, requested me to confer with your father in regard to his measure and ascertain his views, if possible, in regard to the measure before the Committee on Roads & Canals remarking at the same time that I could say to Mr. Ames that he was on the Pacific R.R. Committee and could reciprocate any favor that he could extend to him. Mr. Ames' reply was perfectly characteristic: "Tell him I can give no assurances what my action will be in his case until I have heard the evidence. I have large interests in the Pacific R.R. and should be glad to have the Pacific R.R. Committee sustain me in carrying through the great enterprise in which I am engaged but I am the representative of a large constituency and I cannot give my vote in favor of a measure which does not commend itself to my judgment even though the Pacific Rail Road suffers in consequence of my action." This is only one of many similar facts that have come under my observation during your father's service in Congress.

Of course these manifestations of his true character are not new to you but in view of the terrible ordeal through which he had passed dur-ing the past winter—suffering as he did under wanton and wicked mis-

---

[8] *Ibid.* (original resolution); Ames Family, *Oakes Ames*, p. 50; records of UP Historical Museum.

representation by the newspapers and others, and more especially from men who had thought to sacrifice him to shield themselves, I have taken the liberty in this letter to let you know that your father had many true friends and those who knew him best never doubted his inherent and native honesty and integrity and who knew that it was his indomitable will that gave the Pacific Road—the great highway of nations—to the Country . . . .[9]

Oakes's Principal Positions of Responsibility

Oliver Ames & Sons	Partner
Ames Plow Co.	Director
Cedar Rapids & Missouri River RR	Director
Central Branch Union Pacific RR	Director
Chicago, Iowa and Nebraska RR	Director
Easton Branch RR	Director
Emigrant Aid Society (Boston)	Director
Fremont, Elkhorn & Missouri Valley RR	Director
E. W. Gilmore & Co.	Partner
Iowa Falls and Sioux City RR	Director
Iowa Land Company	Director
Kinsley Iron and Machine Co.	Director
Lackawanna Steel Co.	Partner
Massachusetts Executive Council to the Governor	Member
Massachusetts, U.S. Representative from	Congressman
Mississippi and Iowa Central RR	Director
New Orleans, Mobile & Texas RR	Director
North Easton Savings Bank	Trustee
Old Colony & Newport RR	Director
Sioux City & Pacific RR	Director
Union Pacific RR	Director, Contractor, Executive Committee

[9] Gov. Oliver Ames, *Papers.*

13

Interlude

Oakes Ames's Estate 8 May 1873—Clark Dies and Jay Gould Takes Over—The Panic of 1873—The Rule of Gould Over the UP—Adams Elected President—Gould Returns But Dies—The Inevitable Bankruptcy of the UP—Governor Oliver Ames Settles Oakes's Estate

A. Oakes Ames's Estate 8 May 1873

When Oakes's last will dated 21 December 1868 was opened, it was found that his two elder sons, Oakes Angier and Oliver, were named executors of his estate.[1] This Oliver was really the third of that name in the Ames family of North Easton, but he always signed officially as "Oliver Ames 2d." For purposes of simplicity, throughout this book he is referred to as "Governor Oliver," there being no other Oliver Ames who was a governor. For the next eight years he assumed the brunt of the vast load of untangling Oakes's complicated and widely dispersed estate, which he did successfully, considering the obstacles which arose.[2]

On 27 May 1873, Governor Oliver wrote in his diary, "Called on W. Hutchins for legal advice. He says banks & others cannot sell collateral unless they have written consent to do so—except at 60 day notice. Says Executors cannot renew notes or give new ones nor give extra collateral. UP stock down to 26, and all calling for more margins. Bad day for us. Incomes down to 55, Land Grants 70. Oakes with me & Aaron also."

It was not until just before the panic of 1873 exploded in September that he was able to piece together a comprehensive list of the assets and liabilities as of the date of death. Governor Oliver once

---

[1] Files of Register of Probate, Taunton, Mass.   [2] See pp. 516–526.

publicly admitted that he "always had a fondness for figures," [3] but even so his list probably is not complete and accurate. As some of the details are pertinent to this story, however, an adaptation of his findings is presented in condensed form in the following table.

VALUE AS OF 8 MAY 1873, DATE OF DEATH [4]

ASSETS

STOCKS	Shares	Price	Value
Iowa R.R. Land Co.	14,289	50	$ 714,450
Cedar Rapids & Mo. Riv. Rr.	12,163	50	608,150
Union Pacific Rr.	13,600	31	421,600
Iowa Falls & Sioux City Rr.	4,663	85	396,355
Kinsley Iron & Machine Co.	870	250	217,500
U.S. & Brazil Mail Steamship Co.	3,987	50	199,350
Pacific Guano Co.	1,700	75	127,500
Cedar Rapids & Mo. R. Rr., Preferred	1,041	85	88,485
Bradley Fertilizer Co.	750	100	75,000
Chicago, Iowa & Nebraska Rr.	689	100	68,900
Credit Mobilier of America	2,741	25	68,525
Sioux City & Pacific Rr.	2,862	20	57,240
Blair Town Lot Co.	2,015	25	50,375
Metropolitan Steamship Co.	535	75	40,175
National Bank of Easton	300	130	39,000
Sioux City Town Lot Co.	846	25	21,150
New Orleans, Mobile & Texas Rr.	17,452	0	0
Central Branch Union Pacific Rr.	666	0	0
Fremont, Elkhorn & Mo. Val. Rr.	495	0	0
Fifteen others under $20,000			103,115
Total Stocks			$3,296,820

BONDS	Par Value ($1,000)	Price	Value
Union Pacific Rr. Incomes	1,194	71	$ 847,740
New Orleans, Mobile & Texas Rr.:			
N.O., M. & Chattanooga Rr. 1st Mtge.	454	40	181,600
Ditto, Certificates for 1st Mtge.	400	15	60,000
Ditto, 2nd Mtge. (8%)	1,006	15	150,900
Ditto, Guaranteed	146	50	73,000
N.O., M. & Texas Rr. Certificates for 1st Mtge.	217	15	32,550
Ditto, Incomes	766	0	0
Total			$ 498,505
Delaware & Hudson Canal	215	96	206,400
Union Pacific Rr., Land Grants	234	74	173,160
Louisiana State (8%)	205	50	102,500
Sioux City & Pacific Rr.	146	68	99,280
Fremont, Elkhorn & Mo. Val. Rr.	49½	100	49,500
Cedar Rapids & Mo. Riv. Rr.	43½	86	37,410
Boston, Hartford & Erie Rr.	82	38	31,160
Washington & Ohio Rr.	41	70	28,700
Atchison & Pike's Peak Rr. (Central Br. UP)	27	80	21,600
Five others under $20,000			27,470
Total Bonds			$2,113,970

[3] Ames Family, *In Memory of Oliver Ames*, p. 34.
[4] Adapted from Gov. Oliver Ames, *Papers*.

ACCOUNTS RECEIVABLE	*Value*
Good Accounts	
Texas & New Orleans Rr. (Gentry Rd.)	$ 240,000
Milladon Sugar Plantation, La.	200,000
W. L. Bradley	169,936
Notes Receivable	160,499
New Orleans, Mobile & Texas Rr.	132,000
Northampton Street Property	100,000
Booth Mortgage	100,000
Douglass Mining Co.	100,000
Fifteen others under $25,000	172,599
Total	$1,375,034
Doubtful Accounts	
Copper Mines	$ 600,000
Peter Butler	195,158
Butler, Sise & Co.	106,100
Nine others under $40,000	185,378
Total	$1,086,636
Total Accounts Receivable	$2,461,670
Total Assets	$7,872,460

LIABILITIES	*Value*
Oliver Ames & Sons [5]	$1,879,886
$111M U.P. 1st Mtges. due them (@ 85)	94,350
$100M U.P. Land Grants due them (@ 74)	74,000
Total	$2,048,236
Notes Payable on Time	1,631,514
Sterling Exchange	1,066,910
Notes Payable on Demand	270,425
Kinsley Iron & Machine Co.	235,493
A. A. Reed Guaranty	200,800
Union Trust Co.	150,000
Sundry Accounts	112,524
$104M Cedar Rapids Rr. bonds due Oliver Ames Jr.	89,440
Loans	56,300
Total Liabilities	$5,861,642

SUMMARY

ASSETS		*% of Assets*
Railroad and Other Stocks	$3,296,820	42
Railroad and Other Bonds	2,113,970	27
Good Accounts Receivable	1,375,034	17
Doubtful Accounts Receivable	1,086,636	14
Total Assets	$7,872,460	100
Liabilities	$5,861,642	75
SURPLUS	$2,010,818	25
Less: Doubtful Accounts Receivable	1,086,636	14
SURPLUS [6]	$ 924,182	11

[5] Presumably net liability, after deducting the value of his interest in the firm's assets.

[6] Oakes Ames's real and personal properties are not included.

The summary figures in the table show considerable shrinkage from January 1871, when Oakes was declared insolvent. At that time, his assets were estimated by the creditors' committee at a fair value of $10,781,986 and liabilities at $7,386,179—leaving a surplus of $3,-395,807.[7]

Governor Oliver Ames: Governor Oliver, now aged forty-two, had been taken into Oliver Ames and Sons as a partner ten years previously when his grandfather died.[8] During that period, while Oakes and Oliver were building the UP, he was an important factor in the success of the Shovel Works. But being executor now took most of his time. When that job was nearly ended, he entered politics as a Republican Senator in the Massachusetts Legislature during 1880 and 1881, followed by four terms as Lieutenant Governor during the calendar years 1883–1886. Then came three terms as Governor of the Commonwealth during 1887–1889. During this administration, he succeeded in getting the aging State House restored and enlarged.

He always took a keen interest in the affairs of the Union Pacific. Gould had him on the Board from March 1874 to March 1877. Particularly, he was a loyal supporter of the role his father played therein, and remained firmly convinced that the actions of Congress against Oakes and the UP were most unjust.[9]

Very prominent in business affairs, he was a Director of some three dozen companies. He served with over 18 railroads (including the Cedar Rapids, the New Orleans, Mobile and Texas, and the Central Branch UP, as well as the UP). Also, he was on the Board of nine industrial companies, five banks, and two insurance companies.[10] In addition he was President of the Merchants Club and the Art Club of Boston.

In June 1888 heart trouble developed from overwork on official duties and personal affairs. Although able to finish out his term as Governor, after a long illness he succumbed on 22 October 1895. He was survived by his wife, Anna Coffin Ray, and six children, to whom he left a large fortune.

B. *Clark Dies and Jay Gould Takes Over*

Jay Gould (1836–1892), when asked by the United States Pacific Railway Commission in 1887 whether he recalled the circumstances

---

[7] See pp. 384–392.   [8] See p. 66.   [9] See pp. 536–537.
[10] Ames Family, *In Memory of Oliver Ames (Gov.)*, pp. 15–16; Chaffin, pp. 646–647, 658–659; Winthrop Ames, p. 210.

of his earliest financial or business connection with the Union Pacific, testified as follows:

Yes, sir. In the spring of 1873 I met Mr. Clark and Mr. Schell at Chicago. Mr. Clark was president of the road,[11] and he and Mr. Schell [12] had been out over it and were on their return trip . . . They spoke so highly of the property that it induced me to send an order down to New York to buy that stock. I was on a trip over the Chicago & Northwestern, and I sent an order down, I think, to begin at 35 and buy the stock— buy it on a scale down. Well, it seems that Mr. Clark was then ill. He returned, and when I was off up in the woods he grew worse, and his brokers discovered that he would have to die, and they took the opportunity to sell his stock, and my orders caught it. After I got home the stock kept going down,[13] and I got alarmed about it and began to inquire into the condition of the property,[14] and finally I met Mr. Alley and asked him what was the trouble with the Union Pacific. "Why," he said, "there was trouble enough. They have an immense floating debt, being carried at enormous rates—several millions of dollars—and they have got ten millions of income bonds coming due very soon," and he said he did not see how the company could avoid a receivership. Of course that alarmed me. The stock had got down to about 14,[15] and I inquired to see what directors there were that would help to stand by the property.

I soon discovered that Oliver Ames and Sidney Dillon were the two that could be relied upon. They had a large interest in the stock . . . I think my interest by the end of 1873 was about 100,000 shares. I sent for them and had an interview . . . about the financial condition of the company. I found that the directors had been charging a commission for indorsing, and that the notes were carried at a very high rate of interest. I protested against that and said that I would stand in and take my share of the notes and we were to put it right down to legal interest. We did so. Shortly after I made a further proposition that we should fund this floating debt, and I think I took a million of the bonds above the market price. We funded the debt.[16]

---

[11] Clark had been associated with Gould in 1872 in efforts to acquire the Chicago & Northwestern, and later the Erie. Grodinsky, pp. 105–106, 108.

[12] Augustus Schell, Treasurer of the Chicago & Northwestern.

[13] In May the price dropped from 32¾ to 25¼ on the Exchange, and in June to a low of 22. In July it recovered to 29⅜ (see Appendix A). Thus Clark's sales did not affect the market substantially.

[14] This was probably before he placed the order. Gould always investigated *before* buying.

[15] In November during the panic; see Appendix A.

[16] U.S. Pacific Railway Commission, pp. 446–447 (testimony of Gould).

President Horace F. Clark died on 20 June 1873, six weeks after Oakes. The stock was then at 26. Thus it happened that the working control of the Union Pacific changed hands for the third time in three fast years. Gould admitted that he was "not a very good hand at dates," and the timing in this testimony, 14 years after the event, is not exactly correct. At least, he said, "I knew nothing about the Union Pacific until 1873." [17]

This time the master would not be another great Eastern railroad, but one man, who would run it as a powerful and absolute dictator for the next 11 years. In retrospect, this may have been another disaster for the UP, for over the long run Clark would have been more scrupulous and probably a better, wiser leader, with much less interest in the market. Certainly, Congress would have had more confidence in him, which would have been a great advantage. Yet Gould, in his ruthless manner, expanded both property and gross earnings to an amazing degree, both through new construction and consolidation with other roads.

C. The Panic of 1873

Late in 1873, a year so fateful to the UP, the nation was afflicted with a financial panic which, up to that time, was the most severe ever experienced. The entire credit system of the country collapsed, followed by a depression lasting several years. Its primary cause was the rapid overbuilding and overcapitalizing of the railroads. The mileage of roads operated at the end of 1872 had *doubled* to 66,171 miles since the end of the war.[18]

Jay Cooke and Company of Philadelphia, as sole financial agent of the Federal Government, had made a superb record in negotiating the sale to the public of over two billion dollars of U.S. long term bonds to finance the Civil War. Now, as pioneers in the investment banking field,[19] they undertook to raise $100,000,000 for the construction of the Northern Pacific from Duluth to Tacoma. A syndicate of bankers was formed to arrange a stock bonus of 50 per cent on subscriptions to the 7.3 per cent bonds at 88, with a profit of 12 per cent in cash plus 20 per cent in stock to themselves on all bonds sold. But

---

[17] *Ibid.*, pp. 448–449.

[18] Bureau of the Census, *Historical Statistics of the United States, Colonial Times to 1957*, Series Q15, p. 427.

[19] See p. 34.

the capitalists of America and Europe were already loaded with vast quantities of railroad bonds which the public could or would not buy. Congress was unwilling to vote any aid. The currency was inflated, gold had risen to 119, the average yield on American railroad bonds was up to 7¾ per cent, and interest rates on short-term commercial paper were over 12 per cent and rising. As far as Cooke was concerned, the Northern Pacific owed him $1,500,000. After every effort to meet a hopeless situation, he ordered his firm to announce suspension of payments on the morning of Thursday, September 18, and the panic was sparked.[20]

After three days of bedlam in "the Street," marked by "uproar and ceaseless squabbles on the floor, surging crowds in the gallery and outside on Broad Street, and wild rumors as stocks continued to jump and tumble," the Stock Exchange and the Gold Exchange, for the first time, closed their doors. The Stock Exchange did not reopen for six trading days. President Grant soon arrived, and the Treasury, in a psychological step designed to relieve the shortage of cash, offered to buy unlimited amounts of certain issues of Government bonds at par in gold. But by Tuesday, September 23, an ominous list of 66 firms and banks already had suspended payments. Most notable among the New York banks were Union Trust Company,[21] National Trust Company, and Bank of the Commonwealth; and, among the New York private bankers and brokers, Jay Cooke and Company, Fisk & Hatch, and Henry Clews and Company.[22]

The price of the UP stock was at 21 on September 18, and three days later, when the Union Trust failed, it declined to 15, according to Governor Oliver. On the 25th he noted, "Round in New York to borrow money on stock, but could not succeed." [23] The lowest price of 14¾ was not reached until November 7. About the same time, the first mortgage bonds hit a low at 65⅞, the land grants 57½, and the incomes 35.[24] There is no reliable evidence that any important amount of UP stock was sold for account of Oakes's estate during the panic, nor to Gould during 1873. While Gould saved his commitment in the UP, his personal secretary wrote later that it left him a "comparatively poor man . . . . I doubt if any man parted with more cash and securities than did Mr. Gould by reason of the catastrophe." [25]

---

[20] Much later, after all claims were paid, including principal and interest, Jay Cooke & Co. reopened and continued successfully.

[21] The late Horace F. Clark had been president.

[22] New York *Weekly Tribune*, 24 Sept. 1873.   [23] Gov. Oliver Ames's diary.

[24] See Appendices A, C.   [25] Grodinsky, p. 121.

D. *The Rule of Gould Over the UP*

The complex manipulations of Union Pacific affairs by Jay Gould are beyond the scope of this book. But a summary, as brief as possible, is advisable to tie together its main threads.

Gould, only thirty-eight, was first elected Chairman of the Board of the UP and to the Executive Committee on 11 March 1874. The shares voted at the annual meeting were 304,000, of which Gould's proxies totalled 167,000.[26] Governor Oliver also for the first time went on the Board, and Oliver Jr. on the Executive Committee, each replacing Oakes. Gould never became President or held another office. Sidney Dillon was his choice for top executive throughout his rule. Wrote Charles F. Adams, while President years later, "Mr. Dillon was Gould's representative—he never consulted anyone except Mr. Gould, and Mr. Gould . . . gave orders without consulting Mr. Dillon at all. These orders were implicitly obeyed."[27] On this basis, Dillon cannot be criticized.

Almost immediately troubles began. A rate war among the transcontinental roads was reducing the profit on freight. It was intensified by the fact that the Pacific Mail Steamship Company (in which Gould was accumulating stock for control) was diverting nearly all of the China trade via the Isthmus of Panama.[28] The UP stock, having hit a low of 14¾ during the panic, recovered to 39 in March 1874 on Gould's election.[29] It was during 1873 and 1874 that Gould bought most of his stock, probably at prices ranging between 15 and 30, averaging not over 25.[30]

New UP Sinking Fund Bonds: In 1875 the $9,355,000 10 per cent income bonds were maturing, and in February, Gould succeeded in refunding them, at the same time paying off the remainder of the floating debt, with a new issue of $14,500,000 8 per cent sinking fund bonds due in 1893. These were a second mortgage on the grants of land, and a third mortgage on the railroad. The UP thus benefited substantially from his superior credit.

Dividends Commenced: On 3 March 1875, Gould wrote Secretary-Treasurer Rollins, "Tell our friends to hold on to their U.P. stock.

---

[26] Gov. Oliver Ames's diary.   [27] Records of UP Historical Museum.
[28] *Ibid.* The canal was not opened until 1914.   [29] See Appendix A.
[30] Records of UP Historical Museum.

There is not much floating stock left in this market, and it is being absorbed to be held for dividends *not far off.* As soon as the market is cleared the price will advance to above 50. Within two years, if I live, I mean to plant this stock to par." [31] A second letter on March 11 said, "I shall not sell a share of my stock at any price, as I can see par for it within the next 18 months." These were pretty good tips, for from 40 in March it doubled to 80 in June, the sharpest rise to date.

Gould customarily kept track of persons buying and selling stock by calling for the stock list. On 7 June 1875, President Dillon wrote Edward King, the new President of the Union Trust Company, transfer agents for the UP:

Please give Mr. Gould any information he may desire from the Transfer Books . . . furnishing him list of stockholders when desired. This order is to be good until revoked.

Gould was carrying out his carefully laid plans for making an appropriate fortune out of the UP. On 1 July 1875, he vindicated the rise by initiating dividends, even though legally unauthorized. Starting at $1\frac{1}{2}$ per cent, they were continued quarterly at 2 per cent (an annual rate of $8 per share) from 1 October 1875 to 1 April 1878, inclusive. The dividend due July 1878 was passed because of the Thurman Act of May 7. Payments were then reduced to $1\frac{1}{2}$ per cent from October 1878 to January 1881, and finally raised to $1\frac{3}{4}$ per cent from April 1881 to April 1884 inclusive. Thus, including the two increases in the amount of stock issued,[32] total cash dividends paid by the old Union Pacific Railroad Company and the new *Railway* Company aggregated, in $8\frac{3}{4}$ years, the tidy sum of $28,650,770.[33] But in accomplishing this bold move, Gould slighted prudent management, which might have set up adequate reserves for maintenance and emergencies; particularly, he subordinated the accumulating interest on the Government Subsidy debt.

On 16 July 1875, he wrote Rollins, "I think . . . Union Pacific a grand purchase (at about 72) for *permanent investment.* I should like to see some of the floating stock thus absorbed." This was despite his July estimate for 1875 operations that, with gross earnings at $12,000,-000 and operating net at $7,200,000, the road would show a deficit of some $87,000 after allowing $2,941,000 for 8 per cent dividends.[34] It

[31] *Ibid.*
[32] Increased from 367,623 shares to 507,623 in 1880, and to 608,685 in 1881.
[33] U.S. Pacific Railway Commission, p. 4810 (testimony, reports of accountants).
[34] Records of UP Historical Museum.

was also after rigid restriction of expenditures—always one of his main but unwise policies.

A bearish editorial in *The Railway World* of Philadelphia on 17 July 1875 reflected some cynical thoughts of the time:

There still seems to prevail a blind, unreasoning confidence in a rising tide, which is one of the most curious riddles ever given for solution in Wall Street.

The truth is that one man holds almost undisputed sway over the movements of the Stock Exchange. Under his potent spell, Union Pacific, from an apparently desperate condition and attenuated figures upon the stock list, rises to prosperity and dividends . . . . Such are the wonders worked in the stock market by Jay Gould, and this is the solution of the riddle. Wall Street is not governed by ordinary currents. It is no question of values; it is not even a matter of prospective advantages; the only point worth knowing is, what the arch-speculator is going to do. The whole street is moved by his nod, or the wave of his hand; if he sneezes, the stock exchange sneezes, and the curbstone operators sneeze . . . No such example of one-man power has ever been known in Wall Street . . . . Under these extraordinary circumstances, to write of the New York stock market is simply to describe the movements of Jay Gould . . . .

"Margin requirements" on New York Stock Exchange margin accounts were then only 10 per cent (compared with modern rates of 50 per cent to 70 per cent), but interest charges then were usually 7 per cent. Commission rates on stocks were only $\frac{1}{8}$ of one per cent on the par value ($12.50 per 100 shares).[35]

After backing to 61 in October, the next month the stock climbed to a new high of $82\frac{3}{4}$, not to be exceeded for four years.[36]

One of Gould's first moves in the UP had been to repudiate the Wardell contract of 1868, and in this he was supported eventually by the U.S. Supreme Court.[37] He had been wrong but vehement that the CM and Ames-Davis contracts were fraudulent, but doubted that action at law would succeed "because of laches," or expiration of legal time limits.[38]

In June 1876, Gould held 160,000 shares, on which, excluding some of his own stock registered in names of various nominees, dividends were being paid to him. By the beginning of 1878, he reached an all-time maximum of some 200,000 shares.

[35] *Financial Review*, 1875, p. 18. [36] See Appendix A. [37] See pp. 247–248.
[38] Records of UP Historical Museum.

The Thurman Act: The contentious and potent Thurman Act of 19 June 1878 [39] amended the Act of 1862, Section 6, so as to require the UP (and Central Pacific) to segregate 25 per cent—rather than 5 per cent—of their conjecturable yearly "net earnings" and deposit them in a Subsidy bond sinking fund held by the U.S. Treasury. Furthermore, the monies were to be invested in Government bonds, which, because of their high premium prices, yielded the roads only about 2 per cent. No dividends could be paid while such annual payments were in default. However, under various pretexts, Gould had not seen fit to set anything aside for three years.[40]

In fact, by the end of 1878, studies of annual reports revealed that actually he was doing little to improve the physical condition and net income of the UP. His reputation among traders, too, sank to a new low. The market worth of his huge block of UP had been relatively stable for three years between 58 and 73 only because he did not, in fact could not, sell it. His attitude towards the Thurman Act and his paper losses in other large ventures had reduced the collateral value of his bank loans, it was reported, down to one-half of the market price.[41]

On 9 January 1879, the Supreme Court delivered its verdict on the suit involving the recommendations of the Wilson Committee appearing in Section IV of the Act of 3 March 1873. The Court rejected the claim of the United States to recover the profits made on construction and strongly upheld the UP and the CM (U.S. *vs.* UP *et al.,* 98 U.S. 569).

Gould Sells Heavily: But almost overnight his problems were solved. Yet on February 17, despite previous repeated "permanent investment" declarations, Gould accepted a bid of $65 to $70 a share for 70,000 shares, made by a powerful syndicate headed by Russell Sage and James R. Keene.[42] The syndicate members were correctly bullish on the market, while Gould stayed bearish. By the autumn of 1879 he had liquidated all but 27,000 of his 200,000 shares of UP at an average price of about 70. The apparent profit of around $40 a share was near $7,000,000, plus some $20 a share, or $3,500,000, received in dividends.[43]

[39] 20 Statutes at Large 169.

[40] Grodinsky, p. 420. In 1875 and 1876, the Government had foolishly rejected two propositions by Gould to make annual payments that would be sufficient, with compound interest, to meet the entire subsidy debt and interest at maturity (Records of UP Historical Museum).

[41] Grodinsky, pp. 159–162.   [42] Records of UP Historical Museum.

[43] U.S. Pacific Railway Commission, p. 474 (testimony of Gould).

Kansas Pacific Consolidation: Retaining his directorship in the UP in spite of sales, with the new-found funds he acquired firm control of both the nearly defunct Kansas Pacific Railway Company and the annoying little Central Branch Union Pacific (no relative of the UP).[44] Dillon, the UP President, was also made President of the Kansas Pacific. Although not a part of this story, Gould bought from the St. Louis interests for $3,000,000 the entire stock of the big and expanding Missouri Pacific Railroad and kept it permanently. The Missouri Pacific and the Central Branch UP had been threatening to build from the Missouri to Denver, which would have reduced the traffic of the Kansas Pacific. That, in turn, would have hurt his plans to merge the Kansas Pacific into the UP system.

So Gould, thoroughly prepared, now made a classic but ruthless play. *He informed his fellow Directors in the Union Pacific that, unless they merged with the Kansas Pacific, he was going to extend his road through Colorado all the way to Ogden and there connect with the Central Pacific, and compete for transcontinental traffic.*[45] The Union Pacific was hopelessly trapped. For a long time the Directors had wanted and expected a merger.[46] But they had never imagined such a price—"take it or leave it." Gould may have been partly bluffing, but he stood his ground.

Finally, on 24 January 1880, driven by fears of calamity, the old Directors gloomily yielded to consolidation with the Kansas Pacific and its bankrupt subsidiary, the Denver Pacific Railway and Telegraph Company—at Gould's original terms.[47] The end result was that the stock of the new company, Union Pacific *Railway* Company, was increased by $14,000,000 par, from 367,623 to 507,623 shares, the latter figure being the sum of the shares of all three companies. The new stock was then issued, *share for share,* in exchange for the old stock of each company.[48] The bonds of all three roads were left untouched, thereby greatly increasing the UP's debt. The Kansas bonds alone totalled over $30,000,000. Simply by the conversion, Gould's holding of UP dividend-paying stock was increased by over 99,000 shares, then selling at about 93. His total profit on the deal at the time

[44] See p. 522.

[45] U.S. Pacific Railway Commission, pp. 505–509 (testimony of Gould), 657 and 660–662 (testimony of F.L. Ames).

[46] Among the Directors were F.L. Ames (the second largest stockholder), Atkins, Dexter, Dillon and Dodge.

[47] *Articles of Union and Consolidation of the Union Pacific Railroad . . . into the Union Pacific Railway Co.,* Boston, 24 Jan. 1880.

[48] The Kansas Pacific had 100,000 shares out, and the Denver Pacific 40,000 shares. Neither had paid any dividends.

apparently was around $4,424,000 on an outlay of $576,000.[49] In addition, he would make $2,000,000 profit on the eventual sale of the 99,000 shares, and $2,500,000 in dividends on the same shares to be received eventually.[50]

Before the end of 1880, the UP stock rose to 103, and later, on 2 July 1881, to an all-time high of 131¾. Perhaps such optimism in a general bull market was in anticipation of the larger flow of traffic and the higher, less competitive rates which would ensue—a correct forecast, for a time.

Such is the surprising climax of the Congressional Act of 1866, Section 1, about which Oakes had complained so bitterly.[51]

Gould's Most Constructive Period: Commencing with this consolidation of the Union Pacific, Gould reversed himself and became the spearhead of a new bull market. It was generated by the resumption of specie payments for the first time since the Civil War. By the end of 1879, the old paper dollar was selling at par with gold.

The transformation of Gould from a trader into a business leader of national proportions was one of the most startling events in American business history. His accomplishments in the three years of 1879, 1880 and 1881 were unprecedented in the business and financial life of the country, and in a sense have never been repeated since . . . . He succeeded indeed in lifting himself up by his financial boot straps.[52]

Oregon Short Line: Gould's next move was the long delayed building of the Oregon Short Line to complete a UP road to tidewater in the northwest and compete with the Central Pacific, which had begun to divert its UP traffic to the Southern Pacific route. The idea of such a route had started with General Dodge in 1868, and a good line was surveyed that year largely along the old Oregon trail.[53] The company was incorporated by Act of Congress in 1881 as a subsidiary of the UP.[54] UP stockholders received rights to buy for $1,000 cash a $1,000 bond and 5 shares (par value $500) of the Oregon Short Line.[55] One-half of the stock was kept by the UP for purposes of control, in return for a guarantee of interest on the bonds. Such backing made the subscription a success, and the road was built by

---

[49] Records of UP Historical Museum. Of this $4,424,000 profit, $1,000,000 was through sale of St. Joseph & Western RR. bonds.

[50] Records of UP Historical Museum.   [51] See pp. 140–141, 315.

[52] Grodinsky, p. 165.   [53] See p. 265.   [54] 22 Statutes at Large 185.

[55] U.S. Pacific Railway Commission, pp. 92–93 (testimony of Adams).

the construction department of the UP during 1881–1882 at a cost of $25,000 a mile.[56] Starting at Granger, Wyoming, the road ran in a northwesterly direction to Huntington, Oregon, on the Idaho state boundary, a distance of about 550 miles. It was one of the largest construction jobs of the early eighties. Here it waited until December 1884 for the Oregon *Railway* and Navigation Company, which was building eastward from Portland, with steamship connections from Tacoma and San Francisco. Three years later, the Oregon Navigation leased its track and equipment to the "Short Line." For some years, with the Northern Pacific completed more suddenly than expected, the guaranteed interest was a drag on the UP, but eventually the whole road to Portland was turned over to the UP and became profitable.

Utah and Northern: The Utah and Northern Railroad had been started as a narrow-gauge line shortly after the Golden Spike by Brigham Young, but it was no more than a spur northward from Ogden for the Mormon settlers. Late in 1880, Colonel Joseph Richardson decided to rebuild it to Butte, Montana, where the growing copper industry was then centered. But on reaching Pocatello, Idaho, he ran out of funds. Gould, having planned to build the Short Line through that point, bought the bonds from Richardson at 40 per cent, received the stock as a bonus, and turned them over to the UP at cost. In eight months during 1881, the UP built the remaining 250 miles from Pocatello to Butte.[57]

Other Branch Lines: By June 1884, Gould had built a number of other feeder lines, the most important of which were in the farming plains of eastern Kansas and Nebraska, in the mountainous mining area of Colorado around Leadville, and in the wastes of central Utah to Frisco of that state.

Just during the three years (1881–1883) of feverish speculation throughout the nation, the UP spent nearly $25,000,000 in branch line construction.[58] The UP bond issues then were all selling at premiums of 4 per cent to 31 per cent, and the stock ranged between 80 and 131¾. To aid financing, in 1881 the UP issued 101,062 shares of treasury stock at par, which for the first time were sold at a premium, bringing the outstanding issue to 608,685 shares.

[56] *Ibid.*, pp. 92–93 (testimony of Adams).

[57] *Ibid.*, pp. 572 (testimony of Gould), 2154 and 2173 (testimony of John Sharp); Records of UP Historical Museum.

[58] U.S. Pacific Railway Commission, p. 3970 (testimony of accountants).

Gould's Zenith: By the end of 1881, Gould had reached the peak of his career. His empire consisted of these systems:

Western Railroads	Miles of Road Operated
Union Pacific	4,269
Wabash	3,348
Texas & Pacific	1,392
Missouri, Kansas & Texas	1,286
Denver & Rio Grande	1,065
Missouri & Pacific	904
International Great Northern	776
St. Louis, Iron Mountain & Southern	723
Utah Central	280
	14,043

In addition, he controlled for a short time three eastern systems: the Delaware, Lackawanna and Western; the Central of New Jersey; and the New York and New England, which added 1,811 miles. The total was 15,854 miles,[59] or over 15 per cent of the 103,108 miles of road then operating over the nation.[60] (This would be the largest proportion controlled by any man until the empire of E.H. Harriman in 1906.)

His Profits in UP Stock: It has been estimated that during Gould's regime in the Union Pacific from 1873 through 1884, plus one more year to complete liquidation, market operations in the stock alone netted him capital gains of $9,000,000 through sales of 272,000 shares of stock,[61] and $4,424,000 by the Kansas Pacific consolidation.[62] In addition, he gathered in some $6,000,000 of dividends on the stock. *Thus his total personal gain was at least $19,500,000.*[63] Even if the calculation be only approximate, certainly this figure is far greater than the highest reasonable estimate of the entire profit of all the promoters in constructing the UP from Omaha to Ogden.[64]

The UP Crumbles: But business and market cycles revolve relentlessly. Wild speculation in time generates its own cure. From the excessive heights of 1881, a long bear market got under way. The heyday of the Union Pacific was over. Gould's virtual monopoly in the West began to totter. By the opening of 1884, he was in deep trouble with the UP. The stock was down to 75.[65] The net floating debt was over $5,000,000 and in six months it would be $7,000,000, even according to Gould's annual reports. Net operating earnings, which had

[59] Grodinsky, p. 354.
[60] Bureau of the Census, *Historical Statistics,* Series Q15–22, p. 427.
[61] See pp. 508–509.   [62] See p. 510.   [63] Records of UP Historical Museum.
[64] See pp.454–457.   [65] See Appendix B.

peaked at $12,097,000 in 1882,[66] were so poor that in his report for 1883 he resorted to "approximate figures (that were) deceptive . . . and misleading . . . making comparisons with the preceding year utterly useless," [67] complained Adams publicly, evidently in excuse for his recent recommendations to buy the stock for investment. In those years reports were not supervised by a public authority.[68]

Gould Sells Out: But already Gould had decided to get out. Starting probably in 1882 and continuing through the first quarter of 1884, during which the stock may have been between 120 and 70, he gradually sold a large part of his holdings. One authority estimates that, by 1885, he got an average of 70 to 75 for *all* of his stock.[69] Gould had sold as best he could in small parcels to the investing public, who, according to the company under Adams, and as Gould well knew, were small investors, women, and trustees—already owners of the great bulk of the outstanding stock at high costs, attracted by the quarterly dividends.[70] At this time, over one-third of the stock was held in New England.[71]

The straw that broke the camel's back was Gould's own disregard of the Thurman Act. In April 1884, a vindictive House passed an amendment to again increase the sinking fund contributions, this time from 25 per cent to 55 per cent, and the stock dropped to 63. Then a U.S. Senator brought in a report which would exact penalties from the company for paying unauthorized dividends, as well as severe penalties against all Directors who had voted for them. The stock kept plummeting until, in June, it hit a low of 28.[72] This Governmental "raid" really worked.

E. Adams Elected President

Deeply shocked, Gould rose boldly to a desperate situation. He called upon Charles Francis Adams Jr. to personally appeal to Congress and save the company from immediate bankruptcy. Adams was a grandson of President John Quincy Adams and a Director of the UP since March 1883. He had a good reputation in Washington through his many incisive, critical writings on management of railroads.

He succeeded in making an arrangement with Senator Hoar (of

---

[66] U.S. Pacific Railway Commission, p. 5266 (testimony of accountants). The company's annual report showed $14,188,000.

[67] *Railway Review*, 6 Sept. 1884, p. 464; Johnson and Supple, p. 252.　　[68] See p. 40.

[69] Records of UP Historical Museum.

[70] Union Pacific, *Annual Report*, 1884, p. 111 (by President Adams).

[71] Johnson and Supple, p. 241.　　[72] See Appendix B.

Wilson Report notoriety) whereby Gould and his group were to be eliminated, the UP was to pay back dues for 1883 on the Thurman Act, and the dividend due in July 1884 was to be passed. The UP consented on June 18, and Gould turned over proxies for his remaining stock to Adams. He had been saved—financially. On the same day, Adams was elected President, displacing Dillon.

A Gould-led general bull market immediately carried the UP back to 58. By 24 March 1885, when he resigned from the Board, it was at about 45. (In the meantime he had lost the Wabash and the Texas Pacific, but held the Missouri Pacific.) Congress abandoned threats of increases in the Thurman requirements. Dividends were ended for good. But the UP was left in lamentable financial and physical condition, thanks to Gould's lust for personal gain.

The new President placed executive authority in the General Manager at Omaha, and did all he could to strengthen the company, for a while. But he was unable to overcome the ingrained Congressional antagonism, which had spread to many communities on the line and to numberless investors who had been hurt. Furthermore, the rate wars continued unabated. In 1887, the United States Pacific Railway Commission made its prodigious investigation into the whole affairs of the UP and the other subsidized roads. The stock rose to 71 late in 1889, but by the close of 1890 the floating debt again had risen, this time to over $7,000,000, the highest since the days of construction. Most discouraging of all was Adam's inability, try as he might, to reduce the excessive capitalization as the years sped ominously towards the time of bond maturities.

F. *Gould Returns but Dies*

Why Jay Gould chose to come back to the UP will remain a mystery. Perhaps it was because bankruptcy was impending, with all its openings for deals. Or perhaps it was because Adams was hurting his pet Missouri Pacific, and he wanted to fix that.[73] In any event, early in 1890 Gould found he had 15 or 20 million dollars available for operations, and in November he again purchased control. Upon learning this, Adams at once resigned, on 26 November 1890, and Gould (with Sage) stepped in as Director and member of the Executive Committee.[74] The price was then around 45. Sidney Dillon, ever since 1873 Gould's man, was once more installed as President. But in

---

[73] Records of UP Historical Museum.   [74] Johnson and Supple, pp. 260–261.

April 1892, Dillon resigned because of ill health, and on June 9 he died at the age of eighty.

Gould had never fully recovered from his upsetting experiences of 1884. After a long illness he passed away on 2 December 1892, aged 56. His estate was reported as worth $100,000,000.[75] He never disclosed his plans for the future. The way was open to E.H. Harriman.

All in all, Jay Gould's influence on the economic life of the nation during his business career was unsurpassed. A lone wolf, he accumulated more enemies than friends. The former noisily made him the scapegoat for their failures, the latter did not air their successes in following him. So his "press" was poor.

A shrewd, courageous, and tireless speculator, Gould furnished big equity capital for big, growing railroads, and thereby created massive new wealth, particularly in the West. For example, during the years 1879–1882 he built 1,250 miles of new road just for the Union Pacific System. The most violent rate wars in history were initiated and led by him. The permanent lower rates which followed benefited both producers and consumers by reducing costs of transportation. Traffic naturally expanded.

On the other hand, he was a ruthless wrecker of other people's property. At his convenience he broke contracts, pools, and territorial agreements made in good faith. Often he sold a security while close and trusting associates were buying it, or vice versa.[76] As in the case of the Kansas Pacific consolidation, he adapted to his own purposes the low state of business ethics prevailing. Uninterested in mechanics and labor, he envisaged no improvements for his roads. In fact, his inadequate maintenance resulted in bad service to shippers and passengers. The $29,000,000 in dividends he ordered paid by the UP were of vast profit to himself, but were most unsound, and contrary to the intent of the lawmakers. Disregard for the Thurman Act only intensified the wrath of Congress. He left the UP vastly more over-capitalized than ever. In sum, Gould, like Durant and Fisk, apparently had no permanent policy but to add to his own power and fortune.

G. *The Inevitable Bankruptcy of the UP*

In October 1893, during still another nationwide panic, three large stockholders of the Union Pacific, namely, the executors of the estate of Frederick Lothrop Ames (who had died only the month before),

[75] New York *Times*, 4 June 1967 (Russell Edwards).   [76] See p. 361.

Edwin F. Atkins (son of Elisha), and P.B. Wyckoff, entered a petition for receivership. It was promptly granted. The Government, with three of the five receivers, was placed in control. Four years of wrangling followed. The stock continued downward from 20 until in January 1896 it reached the historic low of 3½. In July 1897, when at 7, an agreement was finally reached on an *assessment* of $15 a share, payable in cash, by subscription at par to part of a new issue of preferred stock. Upon payment of the assessment, the common sold at 22, and went on up, with E.H. Harriman the big buyer.

The bankruptcy was due mostly to the unbearable weight of the Government's bond aid in the original construction to Ogden. When the receivership at last was wound up on 31 October 1897, and practically all of the $27,236,512 Subsidy 6 per cent thirty-year bonds had come due, the interest thereon had accumulated to $47,736,065—nearly twice the amount of the principal.

Both principal and interest were paid off that day—a total of $74,-972,577. Of this, $16,524,353 was interest already paid by the UP over the years; $18,194,618 was realized from the liquidation value of the UP sinking fund assets held by the Government; and the balance, $40,253,606, was raised in cash by the banking firm of Kuhn, Loeb and Company and their associates.[77]

So the nation's taxpayers did not lose a penny, principal or interest, on their subsidy to the Union Pacific—that is, except for the time, energy, and money Congress lost in debating over it. Perhaps that can be forgotten, if not forgiven. At least, the Subsidy was a good thing for the lawyers and an exceedingly vital thing for the pioneering promoters.

The keynote of this story remains: The original railroad closed the missing transcontinental link on time, and thereby the nation was benefited.

H. Governor Oliver Ames Settles Oakes's Estate

Oakes Ames's estate at the time of his death apparently showed a net value of $924,000.[78] No sooner had the appraisal been completed, however, than the panic of 1873 broke out. Governor Oliver sold as little as possible of the securities during that demoralized market.[79] In fact, the Ames family were bullish on the UP stock. On 25 February 1874, the Governor noted in his diary, "In N.Y. Met Uncle Oliver at 5th Avenue Hotel. He says Union Pacific is all right & gave me orders to Smith to buy 2000 UP at 35 or less. Smith bought them at 34⅞." Uncle Oliver must have been talking with Rollins, or even Gould.[80] But no doubt the estate had suffered severely, as a year after the panic, on 4 October 1874, the Governor wrote, "G.K. Davis gave me a new statement showing indebtedness at $3,988,701, assets $3,625,315, and net *debt* $363,386." On that date the UP was at about 35 again. The estate was declared insolvent, and put under the protection of the Probate Court.

Governor Oliver was elected a Director at the annual meeting of the UP on 11 March 1874, filling the vacancy caused by his father's death, and voting 13,860 shares held by the estate.[81] Oliver Jr. replaced Oakes on the Executive Committee. It will be recalled that this also was the date of Gould's first appearance on the Board and Executive Committee.

Oliver Ames & Sons: A review of the shovel operations of Oliver Ames & Sons partnership, or corporation, since the Civil War helps to explain one of Governor Oliver's larger difficulties with the estate. Unfortunately, the net profit of each year (a secret of the partners), and the portion of it that was distributed by dividends, are not available. Ordinarily most of it was paid out. But annual reports were made regularly of the number of dozens of shovels, scoops, and so forth, sold, the value of the sales, together with the undivided profit and loss account left at the year-end, as below: [82]

OLIVER AMES & SONS

Calendar Year	Sales (Dozens of shovels)	Sales Value	Sales Value (per dozens of shovels)	Undivided Profit on Books at end of year
1865	86,640	$1,255,165	$14.50	$342,903
1866	90,536	1,230,162	13.60	257,499
1867	91,182 [83]	1,297,003	14.20	341,968
1868	107,630	1,464,927	13.60	427,810
1869	114,026	1,534,988	13.45	444,669
1870 [84]	110,426	1,306,158	11.90	424,032
1871	120,124	1,469,985	12.25	475,490
1872	122,200	1,568,458	12.80	552,246
1873	101,973	1,346,621	13.20	373,988
1874	102,268	1,273,768	12.45	not available
1875	98,512	1,173,436	11.90	not available
1876	89,019	964,062	10.80	181,013
1877 [85]	100,052	972,464	9.72	not available
1878	103,009	934,104	9.60	not available
1879	115,110	985,555	8.50	not available

[80] See p. 506.   [81] Gov. Oliver Ames's diary.
[82] Gov. Oliver Ames, *Papers* and diaries.
[83] This was 53 per cent of all the shovels made in the U.S. that year.
[84] The year of Oakes Ames's insolvency.
[85] On 1 Jan. 1877 the partnership was incorporated.

At the end of 1870, the time of Oakes's insolvency, the assets of the firm were $3,033,706 at market value. They consisted of stocks $672,-776; bonds $340,290; accounts receivable $631,016; inventory $310,-470; shops and machinery $554,400; and real property $524,754. The two largest single entries, included above, were "book accounts all good," $404,374 (under accounts receivable), and 31,058 shares of UP stock at 13, $403,754 (under stocks).

Oakes and Oliver Jr. each had a one-third interest in the business while living, and their sons the remainder. How Oakes got deeper into debt to the Shovel Works, while Oliver Jr. increased his surplus, is shown by the following year-end book figures of Oliver Ames & Sons:

Dec. 31	Oakes's Deficit	Oliver's Surplus
1868	$ 350,000 [86]	$350,000
1869	700,000	350,000
1870	1,000,000 [87]	not available
1871	1,241,000	not available
1872	1,563,000	not available
1873	2,221,000	623,000

It is clear that the Shovel Works were in trouble due to Oakes's brave but unwise attempts to save both the UP and Treadwell and Company by drawing down his account at the firm. General Dodge quoted Oakes as saying to him, "We must save the credit of the road. I will fail." [88] Immediately after his death, the remaining four partners drew up an agreement among themselves to require Oakes Angier and Oliver "2d," as executors of his estate, to pay off the debts as fast as possible, and restrict themselves, as below:

"It appears," they said, "that Oakes Ames did in his lifetime draw from the copartnership large sums of money, beyond the amount of capital contributed by him, and that his estate is indebted therefor to said copartnership to an extent which his executors . . . are now unable to discharge and pay . . . . From time to time he used the copartnership as endorser of paper to be employed in his own private business, which paper is now outstanding and in part overdue . . . and the executors are now unable to take up said paper." Therefore they agreed to extend the life of the firm for three years from 8 May 1873 (as provided in the original agreement forming Oliver Ames & Sons on 1 December 1863), and to allow the firm name to be used as endorser upon paper to take up and renew Oakes's unpaid notes and

[86] See p. 386, Oliver Ames's letter to Oakes Ames, 10 Jan. 1869. [87] See p. 390.
[88] Dodge, *How We Built the Union Pacific*, pp. 40, 128.

obligations—*provided* that they be reduced as rapidly as possible, and that the executors, personally and as executors, indemnify and save harmless the copartnership from all loss or damage arising from the use of the firm name. The profits were to be divided one-third to Oliver Jr., one-sixth to Fred, and one-half to Angier and Oliver 2d, personally and as executors. But the last two were not to draw more than (blank) thousand dollars each in any one year, until the indebtedness of the estate to the firm had been paid.[89]

Four months after this agreement, the panic of 1873 commenced.

Oliver Jr. began to think about incorporating so as to limit personal liabilities. Governor Oliver noted in his diary of 20 July 1874, "Uncle O spoke about making a corporation to buy real estate and business, saying that he was liable to be taken away suddenly, and the same trouble of settling up would occur again." On October 15, nephew Oliver entered, "Talk with Choate about Corporation. Said cap. stk. could be made small by Corp. giving notes for working capital." And five days later, "Had talk with Uncle O about corporation. He now talks of higher price for property, for fear estate will not pay in full." Nine days later, "Had talks with Uncle O & Choate about price of property—agreed to $600,000 and to $500,000 as capital of corporation." On December 7, "In B. Uncle O on way in said he would let us have Sinking Funds to borrow on, and we let him have Cedar Rapids stock as collateral, so we could borrow at 7% the money we want." Two days later, "In New York. Called on Edward King at Union Trust Co who promised me 45,000 on Sinking Funds. Called on Mutual Life who gave me loan of 220,000." The next day, Sunday, "Received from Uncle O 100,000 Sinking Fund bonds & let him have 1800 shares Cedar Rapids & 200 I.F. & SC RR as collateral—I to use Sinking Funds to raise money at Union Trust Co."

Unfortunately, the Governor's diary for 1875 and the diaries of Oliver Jr. since 1871 are not available. Apparently, lengthy arguments continued between firm and estate about equitable appraisals of assets.

On 26 July 1876, the Governor noted, "In B. Took notice from Uncle O. that he was going to sell Estate collaterals & requesting we meet him." Three days later, "In B. Met Uncle O. with Oakes & Fred and agreed on prices for assets of old firm. Fixed UP at price of today [59]. Uncle O. to take it. Had very pleasant meeting."

The Corporation commenced business on 1 January 1877. The

---

[89] Gov. Oliver Ames, *Papers.*

first balance sheet follows: Assets $935,407; Liabilities (including $400,000 for capital stock) $754,384; and Profit & Loss $181,023.[90] On February 8, Governor Oliver received his certificate for 1,000 shares of the capital stock. He also noted that day, "Oliver S. Chapman fell dead in J.V. Kettles store this morning."

Oliver Jr. died on 9 March 1877. Oakes Angier succeeded him as President. Fred now had a half interest in the shovel business.

By 1880, Oliver was getting interested in Massachusetts politics and was already a State Senator, serving on the Railroad Committee. On November 22 of that year, he made his last diary reference to the affairs of the estate and Shovel Works: "In B. Paper for settlement signed by Fred & myself & taken to Oakes for signature. I gave Davis check 439,830.83 to pay amount of compromise debt. UP advanced to 101½, & KP consols (Kansas & Pacific bonds) to 101¾."

On December 11, he added, "Gould told me that UP is a sale (at about 110), & a good purchase at 90. Debt too large." But after hitting 131¾ in 1881 it did not reach 90 until 1883, and then plummeted to 28 the next year.[91]

Gould Goes for the CM: The $2,000,000 demand note (with accrued interest), which the UP had given the CM on 4 August 1869 for alleged nonpayment of construction under Durant's Hoxie contract, was still dishonored.[92] In July 1875, with UP dividends being paid and the stock above 70, the Executive Committee of the CM, threatened by a suit from Durant,[93] decided to sue the UP for payment. Gould at once wrote Oliver Jr.:

Yours of July 16 read. I am sorry to notice what you say [as to bringing] a suit against the Union Pacific Rd. as it necessitates similar action on the part of the Union Pacific against the stockholders of the Credit Mobilier, and is stirring up a dirty cesspool just at a time when we want to stand well at Washington . . . . The action will be a serious blunder.[94]

Notwithstanding the threat, the CM brought suit on 19 July 1875, and a long war opened. Gould promptly counterattacked. Careful to find only evidence that Gould wanted, his lawyers informed him that the Hoxie contract was indeed "fraudulent." Gould then threatened

---

[90] *Ibid.*   [91] See Appendix B.

[92] See pp. 357, 410; *Wilson Rep.*, pp. 304–306 (testimony of Atkins, who held it in trust).

[93] Durant, *Papers*, 3–3–8–13, July 21.   [94] Records of UP Historical Museum.

that his own suit would be withdrawn only if all the CM stock was surrendered promptly to the UP, without recompense to the holders. Bluffed out, an agreement to do this was signed by Oliver Jr., Dillon, Bushnell, Duff, and numerous others a few months later. But Durant, McComb, Opdyke, Hazard, Governor Oliver, and one or two others refused. Gould commenced separate suits against some of them, but not against the Governor. The latter, however, was penalized for his opposition, and for bringing an injunction against Gould, by being dropped from the UP Board in March 1877.[95]

At the same time, Gould extended his offensive by challenging even the validity of the contracts of the Seven Trustees and their distributions of profits in 1868. Governor Oliver succeeded in blocking this temporarily.[96] Nothing came of it after the rulings of the U.S. Supreme Court much later. But for years relations between the UP and CM were intricate and tense, with suit after countersuit. By this time the stockholders of the two companies were far from being the same individuals.

By June 1878 Gould had acquired for the UP a majority of the CM stock, without paying a penny, and only in consideration of a release of liability to the CM holders. Thereupon Gold made himself President of the CM, which office he held until its dissolution in 1890. Governor Oliver, who had disagreed all the way with his uncle's conciliation of Gould, as executor of the estate refused to give up any stock, as stated above.[97] On 15 February 1879, he was appointed by a court as receiver of the CM in Pittsburgh, following one of Hazard's suits. The Governor wrote in his diary of 5 March 1879, "UP elections. Had talk with Gould. He called me his adversary. Told him I should go for him soon." On 29 April he noted, "In N.Y. Had writ served on me by Union Pacific on acct of Cr Mr."

At last, in September 1883, a Massachusetts court ruled that even if there had been any fraud in the Hoxie contract, that deal was valid because the UP Directors had ratified its assignment to the CM in 1865.[98] Gould's equity suit against the CM was dismissed, but the CM suit was still pending. Now Gould had no alternative but to negotiate for the purchase of the Governor's CM. In May 1884, the price was fixed at $20 a share for 13,532 CM shares, plus $75,000 for

---

[95] U.S. Pacific Railway Commission, pp. 814–815 (testimony of Gov. Oliver Ames); Gov. Oliver Ames's diary, 6 Mar. 1877.

[96] Records of UP Historical Museum.

[97] Oliver Ames's diary, 17 Jan. 1879 and 15 Feb. 1879; U.S. Circuit Court, Eastern District of Pennsylvania.

[98] See pp. 97–98.

legal and other expenses—a total of $345,640. A portion of the stock having been controlled by Bushnell, some $11,000 additional was paid to him for securing its surrender.[99] Governor Oliver stated that he received $316,735 in notes of the UP, accompanied by some UP 5 per cent bonds as collateral on the notes.[100] In Oakes's estate there had been, on his death, 2,741 CM shares.[101] No information is available to make up the obvious differences in the number of shares, unless Hazard's holdings are included. But the Governor, almost alone, had prevented Gould from securing the relinquishment and cancellation of the two-million-dollar note.

Deals in Central Branch Union Pacific RR Co.: The "Central Branch Union Pacific," as it became known, was a creation of the Acts of 1862 and 1864. It was designed to be a branch line extending westward from the Missouri at St. Joseph and Atchison to meet another branch line from Kansas City, the Union Pacific Eastern Division, which in turn would meet the Union Pacific at the 100th meridian.[102] But it did not work out that way at all. When its Government Subsidy of $16,000 a mile and grants of land ran out at its 100th milepost at Waterville in northeastern Kansas, the CBUP (as it will be called here) stopped too. But when the Kansas Pacific (originally the U.P.E.D.) was allowed to run all the way to Denver by the Act of July 1866, the CBUP was left with no western connection. Heavily overbonded, it defaulted interest and went into receivership. The 10,000 shares of stock (par $100) had no value nor market. Yet the road (with its six engines and 131 cars in 1870) continued to serve a rich agricultural land. R.M. Pomeroy of Boston was President, while Oakes Ames (until 1873) and Effingham H. Nichols, A.S. Barnes, and C.S. Parsons of New York were among the dozen Directors. By 1879 they had built an additional 188 miles as feeder lines radiating around Waterville. These roads were consolidated to form the Atchison, Colorado and Pacific Railroad Company, which was leased to the CBUP.

When Oakes Ames died, he left 666 shares of CBUP, appraised at $1 a share, and $27,000 bonds. On 8 May 1877, Governor Oliver, working thoroughly on the estate as always, wrote in his diary, "At 8 o'clock started out over Central Branch UP. Decided to build road to Concordia (50 miles west of Waterville) if aid is to be had." He

---

[99] U.S. Pacific Railway Commission, p. 5168 (accountants' testimony).
[100] Gov. Oliver Ames's diary, 4 Apr., 16 and 17 May, 1884.
[101] See p. 499.   [102] See pp. 12, 85, 509.

and Pomeroy shrewdly conceived the idea that, by starting to build westward at a moderate outlay, they could at least threaten to extend all the way to Denver, and become a competitor of Gould's Kansas Pacific or Missouri Pacific, or of the Chicago, Burlington and Quincy, each of which wanted more of the UP's traffic. Six months later, Oliver was on the road again and noted, on November 26, "In Atchison. Attended meeting of CBUP & was elected Director." On 20 February 1878, he made an entry in his diary, "In B. Sold at auction for estate 666 shares Central Br. UP at $1 per share." The court's permission had been granted.[103]

Between February 1878 and November 1879, Oliver purchased altogether for his personal account 2,896 shares at prices ranging from 1 to 125.[104] At the same time he was helping to finance a new extension to Kirwin, 130 miles west of Waterville. With authority on 1,688 shares from Pomeroy, 1,000 from Nichols, 500 from Barnes, and 164 from Parsons, he offered five-eighths of the whole issue, or the control, to Gould.

The story is best told by his 1879 diary:

January 1, 1879: I have 1111 shs. CBUP which cost me $23,980 (21½ a share).

May 1: In N.Y. Pomeroy saw Gould who says he is inclined to work in harmony with us in our Kansas Rr, if he can have ⅓ interest.

September 13: In B. called with Pomeroy to see Higginson & also to see [Charles E.] Perkins. Proposed to him consolidation of Burl [Burlington & Missouri River Rr., controlled by Chicago, Burlington & Quincy] & CB. He said he was favorable to it.

October 16: In N.Y. Called on Dillon & saw Gould who asked for information about our CBUP. Told them it was better for them to buy us out than it was to fight us.

October 22: In N.Y. Called on Jay Gould & saw him about CBUP, offering it to him for $300 per share for 5700 shares. He said he would refer matters to directors & intimated he would purchase if we would take securities in part payment. Mr. Barnes & Nichols & Pomeroy all agreed to put matter in my hands. I was nominated to the Senate by acclamation at Taunton today.

October 31: In N.Y. Dillon wrote Judge Emmott to stop suit. Bought 100 CBUP for $1600.

November 6: In N.Y. Met Gould, Dillon & Sage & talked till 5½ o'clock—they bulldozing me—but I held firm. They having small opinion of agricultural roads. Agreed to meet them in morning. Pomeroy says I cannot trade with them. I feel that I will.

[103] Gov. Oliver Ames, *Papers.*   [104] Records of UP Historical Museum.

November 7: In N.Y. At 11 o'clock met Gould and in about 30 minutes made a trade with him selling 6,250 shares of CBUP at $250 per share payable ½ in new UP 6% bonds & ½ in Kansas Pac. consolidated bonds, 6%. Gould wrote agreement which we both signed. Gould & Sage were delighted with their trade & so was I, and all our party. Gould told me he would allow me [a price of] 200 for 1,000 shares more. Left for home on the boat. Sales amounted to $1,562,500. Gould & Dillon say they want me to be a director in the Union Pacific R.R.

November 11: In N.Y. Made agreement with Gould to take 1000 CBUP at 175 in addition.

November 14: In N.Y. Dillon asked me to buy stock in Union Pacific so I bought 200 for 18300 at Wood & Davis—they to carry at 6%.

November 19: In N.Y. Gould gave me a written agreement to take the balance of stock at 150 within 30 days.

November 20: The Cr Mr case argued in Boston today.

November 21: In B. A great panic in stocks—off from 1 to 20%. I bought 200 UP at 82.

November 24: In B. RR [CBUP] opened to Kirwin today.

December 4: In B. UP Directors quarterly meeting & no quorum. So I was not elected Director.

December 9: In N.Y. Finished trade for 6,250 shs: Gave Pomeroy 422,000, Nichols 250,000, Barnes 125,000, Parsons 41,000, Self 724,000. [Total $1,562,000 in the railroad bonds at par.]

December 26: In B. Talked from Boston office with Lena at my house through telephone first time.

18 February 1880: In N.Y. Leased CBUP to Missouri Pacific for interest on bonds & leases.

Gould also bought 1,366 more shares from Oliver after the 6,250-share trade, bringing his total cost on 7,616 shares up to $1,826,500. He turned them all over to the Kansas Pacific at cost, taking in payment Kansas Pacific and Union Pacific 6 per cent bonds in equal amount at par.[105] The deal had cost him nothing personally.

Governor Oliver was one of the few persons who successfully opposed Jay Gould on his own grounds.[106]

The Estate Is Closed: Oliver was advised by Shattuck, his lawyer, that he could "go on and settle the estate without fear, as no new case could affect them." During February and March 1878, for example, the executors sold at auction for only $44,000 a dozen or so stocks and bonds which at Oakes's death had been worth about $972,000. Most of this loss was in only a portion of the securities of the New

[105] *Ibid.*   [106] *Ibid.*

Orleans, Mobile and Texas Railroad, and the associated State of Louisiana bonds which had been judged invalid. These were sold by the executors for $16,000 while the estate cost had been $594,000.[107] In fact, it is probable that altogether Oakes lost some two million dollars by helping to build railroads in the South soon after the war.

Governor Oliver bought portions of the two most valuable stocks by taking 443 shares of the Cedar Rapids and 443 shares of Iowa Railroad Land Company, both at 65 while they both had been appraised at 50 on 8 May 1873.[108] (One share of Land Company had been given for each share of the railroad.)

Taken as a whole, the Iowan railroads had been Oakes's first and most profitable ventures. But it would be impracticable, if not impossible, to accurately trace all of Oakes's more important profits and losses, even if confined to the administration of the estate, and without any consideration of the meager records of such transactions during his life as are now available.

Oakes's Bequests: The estate was finally closed on 24 June 1881, after an incessant, difficult pull of 8 years. All debts were paid, either in full or as compromised by agreement with creditors at the time the estate was insolvent. All legacies were paid, and properties were distributed in accordance with Oakes's will dated 21 December 1868,[109] as here paraphrased:

1st. To Evelina O. Ames, his wife: $100,000 and all the furniture, horses and carriages, and the use of the house for lifetime.

2nd. To Susan E. French, his daughter: $2,000 per year for lifetime (capitalized at $25,000).

3rd. To each grandson (there were 6): $25,000.

4th. To each granddaughter (there were 10): $20,000.

5th. To Frank M. Ames, his son: All his interest in the Kinsley Iron & Machine Co. and his interest in the houses, lands, and buildings bought or received from the estate of Lyman Kinsley in Canton.

6th. To Oakes Angier Ames and Oliver Ames, his sons: All his real estate in Easton, Canton, Braintree, and West Bridgewater; with all machinery, tools, and fixtures connected in any way with the shovel business.

7th. $50,000 in seven per cent Railroad Bonds, the income from which shall be used for the support of schools in, and for the benefit of the children in what is now School District No. 7 in North Easton.

[107] Oliver Ames's *Papers* and diaries.
[108] Oliver Ames's diary, 11 June 1877; see also p. 499.
[109] Register of Probate, Taunton, Files.

8th. "What property there may be remaining after paying out the above sums shall be equally divided between my three sons Oakes Angier Ames, Oliver Ames, and Frank Morton Ames."

The legacies paid in cash totalled $475,000 and the properties distributed were appraised at $818,000, a total of $1,293,000.[110] The value at the time of Oakes's death, excluding doubtful accounts receivable and real property, had been $924,182.[111]

[110] Gov. Oliver Ames, *Papers.*   [111] See pp. 500, 516.

14

Death of Oliver Ames Jr.

The Unity Church: Perhaps the most reposed moments of Oliver's later life were spent planning and building the beautiful and substantial Unity Church of North Easton. Started early in 1874, it was finished and dedicated on 26 August 1875. It was to become his finest personal memorial. He bought a large plot of land gently rising from the north side of his residence, and at its summit placed the church and connecting chapel. On Main Street is the parsonage, and back of the church is the cemetery. He gave all, with a fund for their permanent maintenance, to the Unitarian Society of North Easton, a parish formed twenty years earlier with the help of Oliver Sr.[1]

A perfect gem, Unity Church is Gothic in design and cruciform in shape. The walls are of a warm pinkish syenite stone, the very tall spire of bluish syenite, both cut from nearby quarries. The handsome interior woodwork is of black walnut. In the left transept, under Oliver's bust, is a memorial tablet in reddish brown marble, designed by H.H. Richardson. The architect was Oakes's and Oliver's 30-year-old nephew, John Ames Mitchell, who later became the founder of the original *Life* magazine.

But Oliver's health already had begun to decline. "On 2 March 1877 he was attacked with pneumonia, and after an illness of less than a week, on Friday, March 9, he breathed his last, and passed on to the reward of the faithful and good." [2] His age was sixty-nine, within a few days of the life span of Oakes. The funeral services were held on Monday, a cold, damp day with leaden sky. All work was suspended, and the schools were closed. A special train brought two or three hundred friends from Boston and elsewhere. Among those present were Directors and officers of the Union Pacific, with many prominent

---

[1] Ames Family, *A Memorial of Oliver Ames,* p. 10; Chaffin, p. 411; Mary Ames Frothingham, *History of Unity Church;* see also pp. 65–66.

[2] Ames Family, *A Memorial of Oliver Ames,* p. 11; Easton *Journal,* 17 Mar. 1877.

men from Taunton, Fall River, New Bedford, and other places both in and out of the State. Oliver's remains rest at the large granite sarcophagus high in the family plot close to the church he built, in the rolling, wooded Village Cemetery which he gave and provided for—the father's monument between the brothers'.

Oliver's wife, Sarah Lothrop Ames, survived him only by months. Their two children were Helen Angier Ames (1836–1882), unmarried; and the Honorable Frederick Lothrop Ames (1835–1893), a Fellow of Harvard College during his last five years, and a Director of the Union Pacific for 16 years, from 1877 until his decease in the year of its receivership.

Tribute by the UP: A tribute by those who knew Oliver Ames best speaks for itself:

At a meeting of the Board of Directors of the Union Pacific Railroad Company, held in the city of New York, March 15, 1877, the following Resolutions were unanimously adopted:—

Resolved, that, whereas death has deprived us of the presence and counsel of Mr. Oliver Ames, one of our oldest and most esteemed Directors, it is fit and proper that his associates in the direction of the Union Pacific Railroad Company should express the official and personal regard which they had for the deceased, and their unaffected grief at his sudden death in the full tide of his usefulness.

Mr. Ames came into this Board at a period when high character, financial ability, and extended reputation were indispensable to the Company's success. His experience in great enterprises was then a matter within the public knowledge. From 1866 to 1877 he remained a Director, and was President from 1866 to 1871. Throughout this long service, his name has been like a tower of refuge and strength. His faith in the capacity and future of our road, early formed, was unfaltering. In periods of financial peril, his means and credit were most generously placed at the disposal of our treasury. His daily presence and timely word of counsel have contributed very largely to the good reputation which the Company has attained. With his official intercourse with members of this Board have been united acts of personal friendship which will cause us to hold him ever in affectionate remembrance.

And to his ability, culture, wealth, station, and dignified but unostentatious manners, were added the kind heart and the open hand of a Christian gentleman.

Resolved, that the Secretary be requested to transmit a copy of these Resolutions to the family of the deceased.[3]

3 Ames Family, *A Memorial of Oliver Ames,* pp. 81–83.

Ames Free Library: By will, he left $50,000 in trust to build of syenite stone and to maintain the handsome Ames Free Library on Main Street, next to the Oakes Ames Memorial Hall. It was opened on 10 March 1883 with further aid from his heirs, particularly his wife, who contributed $25,000.[4] The architect was H.H. Richardson. In the reading room of black walnut is a massive, finely carved fireplace of red sandstone, with a bronze medallion of Oliver over the center by the well-known sculptor, Augustus Saint-Gaudens. A tablet in his memory reads, "A man of unassailable integrity and wise generosity. He lives in these gifts to the town: The Ames Free Library, Unity Church, Unity Church Parsonage, The Village Cemetery, The Oliver Ames Fund for Easton Highways and the Oliver Ames School Fund." Hanging on the wall by the stairway is an excellent portrait of him by Lazaro. The Librarian, who at the time of this writing is Miss Irene M. Poirier, lives in the apartment on the second floor. David Ames, son of John Stanley Ames, is currently President of the five Trustees.

Other Bequests: In addition, $100,000 was bequeathed in trust to the Town of Easton, half for maintenance of roads, and half for the support of schools.

He also left $35,000 to the Plymouth Society. It was used to create the figure of Faith surmounting the 81-foot monument "To Our Fore-Fathers," erected in 1889 on the summit of the hill rising from Plymouth Rock. In all, there are more than 11,000 donors to this nationwide tribute.

Oliver's Principal Positions of Responsibility

Oliver Ames & Sons	Partner
Ames Plow Co.	President, Director
Atlantic and Pacific RR	Director
Bristol County National Bank	Director
Chicago & North-Western System	Director
Colorado Central RR	Director
Denver Pacific RR	Director
Easton Branch RR (Old Colony)	Director
Emigrant Aid Society (Boston)	Director
First National Bank, Mass.	Founder, Director
E.W. Gilmore & Co. (North Easton)	Partner

---

[4] Chaffin, pp. 378–379. The annex is the relatively recent gift of Mrs. William Hadwen Ames (Fanny E. Holt), daughter-in-law of Governor Oliver Ames.

Kansas Pacific RR	Director
Kinsley Iron and Machine Co.	President, Director
Massachusetts Senate	State Senator
Massachusetts Total Abstinence Society	Vice-President
National Bank of Easton	President, Director
North Easton Savings Bank	Trustee
Old Colony and Newport RR	Director
Sioux City & Pacific RR	President, Director
Taunton Insane Asylum	Trustee
Union Pacific RR	President, Director, Executive Committee

15

Reason Returns

Supreme Court Upholds the Union Pacific—Oakes Ames's Sons Undertake His Defense—The UP Builds a Monument to Oakes and Oliver Jr.—The Oakes Ames Memorial Hall and Its Dedication—Massachusetts Pays Her Tribute to Oakes Ames

A. Supreme Court Upholds the Union Pacific

The bill recommended by the Wilson Committee was not passed exactly as first drafted, but Section 1 thereof[1] was included without change as Section IV of the Legislative, Executive, and Judicial Appropriation Bill for the fiscal year ending 30 June 1874, known as the Act of March 3, 1873.[2] As a result, the Attorney General, in the name of the United States, did bring suit in equity in the inconveniently remote U.S. Circuit Court for the District of Connecticut against 170 defendants, including the Union Pacific and such Credit Mobilier stockholders as had received "illegal" distributions of profits. It was supposed that the amounts recovered would be restored to the U.S. or the UP, as demanded by the Forty-Second Congress.

But the Connecticut Circuit Court (Justice Hunt) held that the United States could not sue for any recoveries, even if fraudulently taken, so long as there was no impairment to the security of the Subsidy by the U.S. and so long as the railroad continued to perform its public duties as required by the Charter. The UP interposed a demurrer[3] to the complaint of the United States, claiming that since it was a potential beneficiary, it improperly had been made both a

---

[1] See pp. 450–451; *Wilson Rep.*, p. xxvi (quotes the Act in full).
[2] 17 Statutes at Large 508.
[3] Demurrer: A pleading that allows the truth of the facts stated by the opposite party, but denies that they are sufficient to constitute a good cause of action or defense in law.

plaintiff and a codefendant in the same action. The Circuit Court ruled that no case had been made by the Government.

The United States appealed, and the litigation went the way of all Pacific Railway cases—to the U.S. Supreme Court. Six long years would go by to cure the errors of the Wilson Committee. Finally, on 9 January 1879, Mr. Justice Miller, concurring with the Circuit Court, read the Supreme Court's 25-page opinion.[4] Some of the more poignant findings are quoted below.

There is, therefore, no ground for relief on account of money due by defendant to plaintiff . . . .

The Government made its contract and bargained for its security. It had a first lien on the road by the original act of incorporation, which would have made its loan safe in any event. But in its anxiety to secure the construction of the road—an end more important to the Government than to any one else, and still more important to the people whom it represented—it postponed this lien to another mortgage, that the means might be raised to complete it. The Government has the second lien, however, and it has the right to appropriate one-half of the price it pays for the use of the road—a very large sum—annually, and five per cent of the net earnings of the road, which may become much larger, to the extinction of this debt . . . .

It is difficult to see any right which the Government has as a creditor to interfere between the corporation and those with whom it deals. It has been careful to look out for itself in making the contract, and it has the right which that contract gives. What more can it ask?

It is true that there is an allegation of insolvency. But in what that insolvency consists is not clearly shown. It has a floating debt. What railroad company has not? It is said it does not pay the interest on its debt to the United States. We have shown that it owes the United States no money that is due. There is no allegation that it does not pay the interest on all its own funded debt. The allegation as it is would be wholly insufficient to place the corporation in bankruptcy even if that was not forbidden by the Act under which this bill is drawn. The facts stated are utterly insufficient to support a creditor's bill by the United States. That requires a judgment at law, an execution issued, and a return of *nulla bona*. Here there is no judgment, no money due, and no sufficient allegation of insolvency.

[4] U.S. *v.* U.P. *et al.*, 98 U.S. 569 (suit to collect 5 per cent on net earnings of company); Supreme Court No. 3, October term, 1878, appeal from the Circuit Court of the U.S. for the District of Connecticut. Justices Swayne and Harlan dissented, except as to the constitutionality of Section IV of the Act of 3 Mar. 1873. Hazard, pp. 39–40, quotes the opinion. See p. 509.

We are unable, therefore, to see any relief which the United States would be entitled to in a Court of Equity under this bill, on account of its contract relations with the defendant.

The bill has established no right in the Government, under this clause, or under any clause of the Act, to recover in its own right any property or money from this corporation . . . .

This brings us to the consideration of the last ground of relief which we propose to notice, and which, with the alleged right to have a decree in favor of the Company against the individuals and corporations who have defrauded it, is most earnestly insisted on here.

The Proposition is that the United States, as the grantor of the franchises of the Company, the author of its charter, and the donor of lands and of rights and privileges of immense value, and as *parens patria*, is a Trustee, invested with power to enforce the proper use of the property and franchises granted for the benefit of the public.

The *legislative* power of Congress over this subject has already been considered, and need not be further alluded to. The trust *here* relied on is one which is supposed to grow out of the relations of the corporation to the Government, and which are cognizable in the ordinary courts of equity without any aid from legislation.

It must be confessed that with every desire to find some clear and well-defined statement of the foundation for relief under this head of jurisdiction, and after a very careful examination of the authority cited, the nature of this claim of right remains exceedingly vague . . . .

If the United States is a Trustee, there must be *cestuis que trust*. There cannot be the one without the other, and the Trustee cannot be a Trustee for himself alone. If the legal right and the use is in the same party, and there are no ulterior trusts, it ceases to be a trust.

Who are the *cestuis que trust* for whose benefit this suit is brought? If it be the defrauded stockholders, we have already shown that they are capable of asserting their own rights; that if this suit should be successful, no means are provided by the statute for securing those rights in it, and there is nothing in the statute which indicates any such purpose.

If the trust concerned relates to the rights of the public in the use of the road, no wrong is alleged capable of redress in this suit, or which requires such a suit for redress . . . .

The liberal manner in which the Government has aided this Company in money and lands is much urged upon us as reasons why the rights of the United States should be liberally construed. This matter is fully considered in the opinion of the court already cited, in the case of The U.S. vs. Union Pacific Railroad Company, 91 U.S.R., 72, in which it is shown that it was a wise liberality, for which the Government has received all the advantages for which it bargained, and more than it expected. In the feeble infancy of this child of its creation, when its life and its usefulness were very uncertain, the Government, fully alive to its importance, did all that it could to strengthen, to support, to sustain it. Since it has grown to a vigorous manhood, it may not have displayed the gratitude which so much care called for. If this be so, it is but another instance of the absence of human affections which is said to characterize all corporations. It must, however, be admitted that it has fulfilled the purpose and realized the hopes in which it was founded; that the Government has found it a useful agent, enabling it to save vast sums in transportation of troops, mails, and supplies, and in the use of the telegraph.

A court of justice is not called upon to enquire into the balance of benefits and favors on each side of this controversy, but into the rights of the parties as established by law, as founded in their contracts, as recognized by the established principles of equity, and to decide accordingly. Governed by this rule, and by the intention of the Legislature in passing the law under which this suit is brought, we concur with the Circuit Court in holding that no case for relief is made by the bill, and the decree of that court dismissing it is accordingly affirmed.[5]

On this ruling Hazard makes the following comments:

The Court intimates that if any one has a claim, it is the defrauded stockholders: "If any such there be," the decision says in one place. But there were no defrauded stockholders. They prosecuted no claim.

With regard to the Government, the decision is clear that no claim exists, and it appears that Congress, under the stimulus of fear of a popular clamor, passed an unjust, tyrannical, and cruel edict, for which the Court finds no legal or equitable basis . . . .

The vindication of history to which he [Oakes Ames] appealed is tardily making itself heard. The arguments before the Courts, the decisions of the Courts, the contributions to the literature of the subject by such men as Henry T. Blake, Edward Atkinson, and Henry V. Poor, and now this book of J.B. Crawford, which is more of a history than has before appeared, all are tending to bring about the vindication which Ames confidently looked forward to. When the whole history is fully understood, it will be seen that however certain members of Congress may have smirched their consciences with lies, the builders of the Pacific Railroad, the holders of stock in the Credit Mobilier, who advanced their money when no one else would, and who, by their energy and perseverance, carried the road through to completion, are entitled to the thanks of the nation and to the honor of posterity.[6]

---

[5] U.S. *v.* U.P.R.R., *et al.*, 98 U.S. 569.   [6] Hazard, pp. 40–41.

President Sidney Dillon closed his Annual Report to Stockholders for 1878, pp. 14–15, as follows:

The numerous decisions of the Supreme Court have settled most questions which were in controversy between the Government and the Company, thus enabling them to work together in harmony, and to the better interests of both.

After several years of uncertainty and legal contest with the Government as to the construction of portions of the Charter . . . the U.S. Supreme Court has made several decisions, setting forth fully the relations of both, and settling finally these questions.

The decisions in most cases have been in favor of the Company, and it is to be congratulated that it may now stand upon these decisions, and know for all time what its obligations are, and the amount of the fixed charges against it.

The claims of the Government and its construction of our Charter has been the only cloud upon the securities of the Company. These decisions determine all claims and clear away every doubt.

To sum up this vital phase in the history of the Union Pacific, it developed that in spite of the Wilson Committee, supported as it was by the Forty-Second Congress, not a dollar of the profits on construction received by the CM stockholders was ever returned to either the Union Pacific or to the United States. The Executive Committee of the UP refused to sue the CM for recovery of the profits, in spite of Chairman Gould's vigorous efforts to do so for his own gain. The obvious reason was that the majority of the UP stockholders, who were also CM stockholders, themselves had received such profits.[7] Nor was the United States legally entitled to them, in the opinion of the Supreme Court.

So the UP stock, which was selling at 58 in January 1879 just before the court verdict was released, being freed from claims of the U.S., soared in a general bull market to an all time record high of 131¾ in 1881.[8]

B. Oakes Ames's Sons Undertake His Defense

In the heat of General James A. Garfield's campaign for the Presidency in 1880 against his Democratic opponent, Garfield's biography

[7] U.S. Pacific Railway Commission, p. 713.

[8] See Appendices A, B. Yet during this period the stock outstanding was increased from 367,623 shares to 608,685 shares. (See pp. 510, 511.)

was published. In that book, and with Garfield's prior knowledge, an attempt was made to vindicate his testimony against Oakes in the Credit Mobilier investigation of 1873. It was Ames, not Garfield, the claim went, who was the "perjured scoundrel" about the $329 dividend.[9] This indiscreet attack, made on Oakes only for momentary political advantage, naturally inspired Oakes's sons to take up the cudgels. They sent an 11-page printed statement about their father to the editors of the Boston *Sunday Herald,* who published it in full on Sunday, 8 August 1880. A great many other newspapers in Boston and elsewhere either printed it fully or made their own shorter comments on it. No new facts about the CM case were set forth by the Ameses; their object was merely to make a general defense of Oakes Ames. It was high time they did so, with the Supreme Court's favorable decision on the Wilson Committee bill already out for a year and a half.

The statement is not quoted in full here, as the story of Oakes's part in the building of the UP has already been covered in this book. The first and last paragraphs, however, read as follows:

OAKES AMES AND THE CREDIT MOBILIER

To The American People, Irrespective Of Party:

We, the undersigned, sons of Oakes Ames, desire to be heard, in justice to the memory of our father, who can no longer speak for himself. The revival of interest in the political scandal known as the "Credit Mobilier," growing out of an alleged complicity therein by the Republican candidate for the Presidency, makes the present a fitting time for a true statement of that extraordinary affair. When even General Garfield, in what purports to be an extract from his forthcoming biography, has totally failed to comprehend the facts, how can the public at large be expected to understand them? Such a statement is due alike to a public benefactor whose last days were clouded with obloquy, to the great enterprise with which he was identified, to the good name of both political parties, some of whose trusted leaders have been assailed, and to the honor of the nation, which has been compromised by the opprobrium cast upon its representatives. It is in the interest, not of any individual or of any party, but of truth and equity and common sense, that we appeal to the people and the press of the United States for a reconsideration . . . .

In appealing for justice to our father's memory, we do not take the attitude of apologists. A righteous indignation against fraud must not

[9] See p. 466; Brooklyn *Daily Eagle,* 9 Aug. 1880.

assail a great and good man whose life was honorably associated with the most useful industrial achievement of his age. History will surely record the Credit Mobilier Construction Company and the Oakes Ames contract as legitimate and necessary means, without which the Union Pacific Railroad could not have been built. But we gladly accept the present occasion to vindicate the memory of our father, because the generation which knows the facts and can testify to his upright and blameless life will soon pass away. Today there live thousands of men in New England, thousands more in the Middle States and the great West, who have had business relations with him, who know what we say is true, and who will testify of their own knowledge—"Oakes Ames was an honest man."

Oakes A. Ames
Oliver Ames
Frank M. Ames [10]

General Garfield won the election and was inaugurated in March 1881. Only four months later, he was shot by a mentally unbalanced assassin, and he died in September.

C. The UP Builds a Monument to Oakes and Oliver Jr.

The first person to publicly suggest a monument to Oakes was the Honorable John B. Alley, who exclaimed before the Poland Committee: "If the American people could know all the facts, instead of bestowing upon Oakes Ames one word of censure, they would far sooner erect a monument to his name in grateful recognition of his eminent services." [11] For this reflection, Alley "was made the butt of great ridicule, and the very proposition was treated with derision." [12]

At a meeting of the stockholders of the Union Pacific held in Boston on 10 March 1875, the following resolution was unanimously passed:

Resolved, That in honor of the memory of Oakes Ames, and in recognition of his services in the construction of the Union Pacific Railroad, to which he devoted his means and his best energies with a courage, fidelity, and integrity unsurpassed in the history of railroad construction, the Directors are requested to take measures, in coöperation with such

---

[10] Ames Family, *Oakes Ames,* pp. 127–138. The paper, prepared by H.B. Blackwell, was signed by the brothers on 4 Aug. (Oliver Ames's diary of that date).
[11] *Poland Rep.,* p. 85.   [12] Boston *Commonwealth,* 11 Mar. 1875.

friends as may desire to contribute, for the erection, at some point on the line of the road, of a suitable and permanent monument.[13]

After waiting five years for the Supreme Court decision, the Union Pacific commenced construction of the monument in September 1880 and completed it in October 1882 at a cost of $64,773, which was charged to UP income account in 1884. The contractors were Norcross Brothers of Worcester, Massachusetts, one of the largest building companies in America. In direct supervision was their general foreman, Captain A.L. Sutherland. He had some 85 workers, of whom the stonemasons, quarrymen, granite cutters, and blacksmiths were from Massachusetts, while the ordinary laborers were local. They were quartered in a large frame building erected for them in Sherman, with a recreation room, dining room, and kitchen. Excellent board was provided at $4 a week. But they were forbidden liquor and gambling. The stone was hewn from a typical grotesque outcropping half a mile to the west, with the help of a derrick 103 feet high, and was skidded over the sagebrush by ox teams.

Sherman, Wyoming, was then a lively little community with several hundred residents, a station house, a water tank, two railroad section houses, a schoolhouse, a post office, two hotels, two saloons, and a general store. All trains were inspected there before descending the heavy grades east and west.[14]

The monument is of simple, pleasing, pyramidal form in two steps, 60 feet square and 65 feet high. It is composed of random-sized blocks of crystalline granite, having a general salmon-pink color in sunlight. On close inspection, the rock is seen to be mottled with pink feldspar, glassy quartz, black mica, and hornblende. Near the top, facing north towards the railroad, are carved into the stone in large letters these words: "In Memory of Oakes Ames and Oliver Ames." On the east side is an 8-foot square granite plaque of the head and shoulders of Oakes, in half-relief, while to the west is a matching one of Oliver Jr. Good likenesses, these are the work of one of the most talented American sculptors, Augustus Saint-Gaudens.[15] Each plaque is inscribed only with a small monogram "OA" and the day and year of birth and death. Sad to say, the noses on the plaques of both brothers are now broken off, perhaps by the rifle fire of passing

[13] Ames Family, *Oakes Ames,* pp. 50–51; Records of UP Historical Museum.

[14] Charles S. Fitz, an old-time conductor on the UP, in *The Union Pacific Magazine,* May 1924; Records of UP Historical Museum. (Another article with photographs of the monument appears in the Mar. 1923 issue of the same magazine.)

[15] See p. 529.

hunters in need of a target, or more charitably, by frost, gale winds, and flying sand. In a sheltered crevice between blocks, there resided, at least in 1965, a shrewd, fat badger.

The architect of the monument was Henry Hobson Richardson, then no doubt America's leading figure in his profession and only forty-two years old. He designed Trinity Church (his greatest work) and the First Baptist Church, both of Boston; Sever and Austin Halls of Harvard, from which he was graduated; and many commercial and public buildings and libraries. Living in Brookline, Massachusetts, he became a warm friend of the Ames family. In North Easton, he designed for them the Oakes Ames Memorial Hall, the Ames Free Library, and the railroad station, and for F.L. Ames, two residential buildings.[16] In Boston, he made preliminary sketches for the winter home of Governor Oliver, at the corner of Commonwealth and Massachusetts Avenues,[17] but he died in 1886 before their completion.

His style was inspired by the Romanesque architecture of southern France, particularly Auvergne. He studied after training at the Beaux-Arts in Paris. The design of the Ames Monument is "entirely original . . . and uniquely fitting for a family and a railroad that were impressively successful in an era of rugged self-assertion. Against the background of the Rockies, the pyramid is like an abstract mountain itself, a dramatic statement in granite about the persistence and vigor of a pair of industrial movers." [18]

It was decided by the Directors of the UP that the Ames Monument should be placed at the highest elevation on the line. This was at the original Sherman station, 8,275 feet above sea level. Today, a wilder or more grandly lonely spot could not be found, nor one more dramatic in the history of the building of the railroad.[19] From the height of a gradually rolling, southward spur of the broad tableland of the Sherman Pass over the Black Hills is a breathtaking sight of the great Front Range of the Colorado Rockies to the south. Their shining white crests, dark blue in the haze of summer, are surmounted by Long's Peak, 14,255 feet high and 65 miles away. Westward lies the great forested Medicine Bow Range, only 30 miles to the southwest but terminating at conspicuous Elk Mountain, 70 miles to the northwest, where the railroad swings around it.[20] The wide Laramie Plains are hidden in the fertile valley between the Medicine Bow and Black

---

[16] Photograph of the gate-lodge is used as the frontispiece in Chaffin.
[17] Ames Family, *In Memory of Oliver Ames*, photograph, p. 48.
[18] H.R. Dietrich, Jr., in *Annals of Wyoming*, Apr. 1966.
[19] See pp. 116–118, 224–228.   [20] See p. 228.

Hill mountains. To the southeast, the open plains stretch towards the South Platte River, over 100 miles away. Northward are the nearby heights of the Black Hills, with their strangely tumbled mounds of dark pinkish rock. Underfoot, all is greenish grass, gray sagebrush, and sandy salmon-pink soil. Above, on a fine day, is the brilliantly blue sky typical of high altitudes, with great fleecy white clouds racing by on a chilly west wind. Their hurrying shadows, as far as the eye can reach, lend the only motion to the landscape.

But now the monument has no railroad or town.[21] In 1900–1901, the new Directors relocated the line southward over the dozen miles between Buford and Hermosa. Thereby the maximum grade was reduced from 98 to 43 feet a mile, without increasing the mileage. The saving in maintenance from abandoning the Dale Creek bridge was offset by the cost of a tunnel near Hermosa. The highest elevation on the UP was reduced by 262 feet, but the panoramic view was lost, and the town of Sherman disappeared completely. Not a trace is left. A new station house, also named Sherman, was erected at a point 3½ miles southeast of the monument.

In 1916, the Directors voted to move the pyramid, "so long lonely and near forgotten," [22] to some point adjacent to the new line, at an estimated cost of $16,000. But World War I came, and perhaps no other site as fine as the first could be found. Whatever the reason, the project was never carried out. Perhaps it is just as well, for with passenger traffic vanishing to a fraction of its old volume and with the fine transcontinental Lincoln Highway and Monument nearby, more people are able to enjoy it at leisure, with the fun of a little adventurous motoring. Yet it is sorrowful to ponder that even to this day there is no hard surfaced road between highway and pyramid, nor even adequate signs erected on each side of the main thoroughfare to point the way for passing motorists. Now they can get only a distant glimpse of the monument at one or two spots. Nor, of course, is it visible to inquisitive railroad passengers, except by a remote peep from the eastbound train only. New westbound tracks are still further away.

Today, the Ames Monument can be found only by driving on the Lincoln Highway some 17 miles eastward from Laramie, or 33 miles westward from Cheyenne. If from the latter, the nearest landmark beyond Buford is the historical marker for the "Tree in Solid Rock" on the roadside. This is the tree "which the foreman of each passing

---

[21] See map, Illus., Group 4.   [22] Sabin, p. 8.

train never failed to drench with a bucket of water." [23] About 2 miles further westward is a turnoff to the pyramid. The little side-trip is well worthwhile. The 100-year-old raised grading can be detected running east and west a few hundred feet north of the monument, and there is a nearly vanished cemetery noted on the map just north of the site of old Sherman.[24] A mile and a half north of the highway is the fantastic Vedauwoo Glen; and there is the impressive Lincoln statue at "The Summit," 10 miles from Laramie, offering a fine view eastward of the crest of the Black Hills.

At the monument is a relatively new, but half-broken, Wyoming State Marker swinging between two posts, which originally read as follows:

AMES MONUMENT

Erected by Union Pacific Railroad as a memorial to Oakes and Oliver Ames, brothers from Boston, who arranged financial support, making possible the original construction of the Union Pacific.

At the personal request of President Lincoln, they pledged their financial resources and the shovel manufacturing firm owned by the family, to continue the building of the Railroad when the project faced failure due to its pioneering nature through hostile country.

Built where the town of Sherman once stood, which was the highest elevation on the U.P., the monument is 65 feet high. Commenced in 1880, completed October 1882. Because of line improvements in 1900, the Railroad now runs four miles south.[25]

D. *The Oakes Ames Memorial Hall and Its Dedication*

In the meanwhile, Governor Oliver had already decided to build a lasting memorial to his father in the hometown of North Easton. On 15 March 1879, just before his Central Branch Union Pacific deal with Gould,[26] he noted in his diary, "In Boston. Richardson [27] in and said he would send me several sketches for town hall." And two days later, "In Boston. Richardson went out to library,[28] & I took him to site of proposed hall. He said it was superb." On 26 September, he

[23] Tablet erected by the Historical Landmark Commission of Wyoming.

[24] U.S. Geological Survey, Sherman Mountains Quadrangle, 1948 (1958 ed.), scale 1 inch to the mile.

[25] Wyoming State Archives and Historical Department, Cheyenne: letter to the author dated 1 Dec. 1965; see also p. 89.

[26] See pp. 522–523.

[27] Henry Hobson Richardson; see also p. 539.   [28] See p. 529.

wrote, "In Boston. Oakes [Angier] said he would put $16,000 into Memorial Hall—and no more. All above that at my expense." Three days later, "In Boston. Signed contract with Norcross [29] to build Memorial Hall at N. Easton—price $29910 extras $1666 if put on."

The massive, castle-like Oakes Ames Memorial Hall was finished in November 1881. It is placed conspicuously on the turn of Main Street at Lincoln Street, next to the Ames Free Library.[30] The first story, 96 feet long, and the tall, highly decorated octagonal tower nearest the road are of local pinkish-gray syenite stone from a nearby quarry, cut in random sizes. The generous trimmings, particularly the arcade of five prominent arches in front, are red sandstone. The second story is faced with harmonizing red brick. The steeply pitched roof of red tile remotely suggests a pyramid. Indeed, it was erected at the same time as the Ames Monument in Wyoming, was designed by the same architect, and was executed by the same builder. At the front door is a stone tablet inscribed: "THIS BUILDING WAS ERECTED IN MEMORY OF OAKES AMES BY HIS CHILDREN." Inside, on the first floor, are two small halls; on the second is the large, high main hall.

The dedication exercises, held on 17 November 1881, were attended by a large number of prominent people, including four or five hundred arriving by special train from Boston. The first and shortest speech was by Governor Oliver himself, who said:

The building in which we are assembled is erected in honor of our father, the late Oakes Ames, to stand as a monument to his public services and to his private worth. This, the Oakes Ames Memorial Hall, we dedicate today to the use and for the benefit of the people of Easton. To you [addressing Mr. Lewis H. Smith, Chairman of the Board of Trustees of the Oakes Ames Memorial Hall Association],[31] the Trustees appointed to receive and care for the building, we now present the keys, trusting that the building will prove a source of pleasure and convenience to the good people of the town.[32]

Following Mr. Smith's acceptance in behalf of the town, a number of letters of tribute to Oakes were read aloud. Speeches were then

[29] See p. 541.

[30] Other early photographs appear in Ames Family, *Oakes Ames,* p. 55, and Ames Family, *In Memory of Oliver Ames,* p. 40.

[31] This corporation has entire control of all the property and its management. The town can have "the full and free use of the premises, without payment of rent for all the ordinary purposes of a Town Hall," according to the Deed of Trust. But the town never chose to use it as a town hall.

[32] Ames Family, *Oakes Ames,* p. 59.

made by Governor John D. Long; Ex-U.S. Senator George S. Boutwell; [33] Rev. Edward Everett Hale; and Judge Thomas Russell, who adapted Milton's 1652 ode, *To the Lord General Cromwell,* to Oakes:

> *Thou chief of men,*
> *Whom through a cloud not of war only, but detractions rude,*
> *Guided by faith and matchless fortitude,*
> *To high success thy glorious way hast ploughed.*
> *Peace hath her victories*
> *No less renowned than war.*

Among the great number of letters answering the invitation to attend the dedication, some 80 are quoted in *Oakes Ames, a Memorial Volume,* pages 80–107. All were finely expressed praises of Oakes's character, and some were of special interest. It is possible to quote here only a few of them, each in small part at that.

Tributes

From the Honorable James G. Blaine, U.S. Congressman from Maine 1863–77, Speaker of House 1869–75, and Secretary of State under Garfield and Harrison:

I knew your father well, having been a member of the House of Representatives the entire period of his service in that body. He was distinguished among his associates, both in and out of Congress, for solidity and uprightness of character, for sterling sense, for sound judgment, for extraordinary energy, and for manly courage. He was a model of simplicity and sobriety in his habits of life, and large wealth without pride of purse, and always had the quickest and kindliest sympathy with young men in their early and difficult struggles . . . He enjoyed the profoundest confidence of those who knew him best.

From the Honorable Henry L. Dawes, U.S. Senator from Massachusetts, Member of the House of Representatives 1857–73, and Member of the Senate Committee on Indian Affairs:

Mr. Ames was indeed a great man, and accomplished in his lifetime a great work. He built his own monument, which will outlast the marble and the brass fashioned to keep others in mind. While others were fighting battles for the unity of the nation, he bound it into one with iron bonds which no force can break asunder. We rightly crown with laurels

[33] See p. 544.

the hero who led our armies to victory, and I rejoice that the nation is not forgetting him who, with no less courage or hazard, by the arts of peace achieved a victory more grand and far-reaching in its consequences than was ever won over men on the field of battle.

From the Honorable John Sherman, U.S. Senator from Ohio, Chairman of the Senate Finance Committee, Secretary of the Treasury under President Hayes, author of the Sherman Antitrust Law, Secretary of State under President McKinley, and brother of General William Tecumseh Sherman:

It would have given me great pleasure to have accepted your invitation, and in this way shown my respect for the important and valuable services rendered by Oakes Ames to his country and State. I knew him well at the time he was bearing the heavy load of the construction of the Union Pacific Railroad, when but few of his detractors would have had the courage to take his place.

From the Honorable George S. Boutwell, Governor of Massachusetts 1851–52, U.S. Congressman 1863–69, Secretary of the Treasury under Grant 1869–73, and U.S. Senator 1873–77:

For a period of about twenty years I enjoyed . . . the friendship of Mr. Oakes Ames . . . . He was born to an inheritance of active business. He accepted its duties and administered its trusts with a manly fidelity and comprehensive intelligence which advanced yet higher the already honorable name of his family . . . . In the use of vast wealth he was liberal and wise in private and public charities and contributions, and generous to excess in the aids he extended to business associates and acquaintances. *He was tolerant of hostility, forgetful of injuries, and persistent in his friendships.*[34] Of men of wealth and capacity for action he was among the first.[35]

From the Honorable Nathaniel G. Ordway, Governor of Dakota Territory:

The stupendous public and private enterprises with which the name of Oakes Ames will stand indissolubly connected are monuments to his energy, fidelity, and greatness, which misrepresentation can never obscure . . . . He was one of the ablest and best men I have ever known in public life.[36]

[34] Italics by C.E.A. See p. 404.
[35] This was not a letter, but a part of his speech at the dedication of the hall.
[36] Quoted in part from an original letter in Gov. Oliver Ames, *Papers.*

From the Honorable John B. Alley:

It was my privilege to be associated most intimately for many years with Oakes Ames in the councils of the nation—in business pursuits of vast importance . . . involving the nation's well being, as well as his own, in social discourse and private friendship—and I can most truly say that I have never met a man whose life was more in obedience to what he believed the principles of justice and right demanded, than was that of my late honored friend . . . .

—To those who knew him personally he needed no vindication—for they knew him to be incapable of doing any great public or private wrong.[37]

From the Honorable Benjamin F. Butler:

Nothing would give me greater personal satisfaction than by my presence to testify my regard for Oakes Ames as a man, my great appreciation of his character as a statesman, and my admiration of his brave and enterprising spirit, which gave to this country the Union Pacific Railroad. Without him, I am confident that that great link which binds the East and the West . . . would not have been made within this generation, if at all. Other interests might have prevented it in the future . . .

Supposed political necessities and fears of newspaper attacks caused certain men, who, if they had half of Mr. Ames's courage and one-quarter of his honesty, would have scorned to do such a deed, to attempt to protect themselves by interposing him as a shield between them and acts which were only wrong because the denial of them was a confession of that implication, and which, if [they], as in the case of some of them, had been courageously avowed, would never have made a ripple even upon the turbid stream of political strife . . .

My relations to him as his colleague made me entirely familiar with the whole subject . . . Oakes Ames was one of the best, most unselfish, most upright, and most brave and true of all the public men I have ever known.

From the Honorable Richard F. Farnsworth, U.S. Congressman from Illinois:

I knew Mr. Oakes Ames well, having served many years in Congress with him, and have great respect for his memory; for in these elements of character which constitute genuine human greatness—energy, courage, sterling integrity, and truth—he was certainly the peer of any man.

[37] *Ibid.*

From the Honorable Ginery Twitchell, U.S. Congressman from Brookline, Massachusetts 1867–73; President, Atchison, Topeka & Santa Fe Rwy., 1870–74:

I once bargained with Oakes Ames for a parcel of real estate in Brookline, which I was to have for $4,500, in case he sold it at all. It was sold by his agent, in his absence, for $6,000. He was not legally bound to me; but, with his usual magnanimity, directed his agent to pay me even the whole purchase-money, or to institute proceedings to recover the estate for me, if I desired to secure it.

I recall another instance of his integrity. A quantity of iron, which he had imported for use in his business, and insured, having apparently been injured by wet and rust, the insurance company had the damage appraised, and paid him $2,500 as the result. But on coming to use the iron, he discovered that there really had been no damage, and he voluntarily refunded the money.

Oakes Ames needed only to be known in order to be appreciated. That justice may be publicly done his memory is my most sincere wish.

From William S. Eaton, Esq., of Boston:

I had bought a note signed by Thomas Douglass, I think for about $5,000. Shortly after, I met Mr. Oakes Ames on State Street, and asked him about Douglass' standing and credit. He answered cautiously . . . but thought Douglass was good, and was a regular buyer from his firm. I asked him what he would buy the note for, describing the one I held. He named a rate, and I accepted it. He said, "Well, I cannot take it now, as I am just going away for several days, but will come to your office and get it when I return."

Before he returned Douglass failed. A week after, Oakes Ames came in and asked for the note. I said, "Douglass has failed, and I have no claim on you for the amount." He replied, "He hadn't failed when I agreed to take the note. Take off the interest, and I will give you a check." And he did so.

I have told this story to many of our merchants, and do not find one who knew him who is at all surprised . . . .

From the Honorable Josiah B. Grinnell, Clergyman, U.S. Congressman from Iowa 1863–67, Founder of Grinnell, Iowa, and Grinnell College:

I knew Oakes Ames well for nearly twenty years . . . He was possessed of a comprehensive mind for affairs, and his heart expanded with the widest and warmest sympathies . . . . He was of strictly temperate habits; so schooled in economy that, while in Congress, he chose a comparatively inexpensive mode of life, in order to save money to devote to charity.

In Iowa, no name wears more honor than his, for he periled his fortune to build the first railroad across our State . . . As a legislator, no man's opinions were more eagerly sought or highly prized than his, particularly in currency and revenue matters. Mr. Conkling would say, "This you understand, Ames; others do not." Mr. Thaddeus Stevens, chairman of the Ways and Means Committee, on all doubtful matters counted on Oakes Ames to save a measure or kill it, though he never made a motion or a speech . . . .

He once pencilled a memorandum promise that at some future day he would begin the founding of a professorship in Iowa College with a gift of $6,000; but he died without money. Then there came a notice from his executors that "there is no money, but the wishes of father will be sacredly respected when we are able, without reference to legal considerations." They were respected, when Hon. Oliver Ames sent the college $6,000, with interest.

From Wendell Phillips, Esq., of Boston, eminent orator and anti slavery leader:

I am very sorry I cannot be present and pay my tribute of respect to one of the most honest, patriotic, devoted, and far-sighted men that Massachusetts has lent to the national councils in our day. While he stood head and shoulders above all her Representatives in furthering the material interests of the nation, he was equally distinguished above most of them by his clear view of what honor and justice demanded of us and by his manly, outspoken and self-sacrificing efforts to make that the law of the land. I held him always in special honor, and felt it a privilege to call him my friend, admiring his sturdy and straightforward honesty of life and purpose as a type of what a true man in a republic should be.

From Aaron S. Reid, Esq., of New York:

After I had been utterly ruined through the effects of the war on my Southern customers, I met Oakes Ames on the street. He inquired what I was doing. I told him I was doing nothing, but thought I could get business if I had the capital. He said in reply that he had no idle money at the time, but that if his notes for $10,000 would be of any benefit to me they were at my command . . . . The financial condition I was then in made the offer one of great generosity—one I shall always remember, as friends in adversity are always scarce. But that was his opportunity.

From B.B. Johnson, Esq., U.S. Marshall's Office, District of Massachusetts:

I was in Washington . . . during the terrible influx of the wounded into the hospitals there . . . I had occasion to need funds often that the Massachusetts State Agent did not furnish, to relieve the wounded. Your father visited two of the hospitals with me . . . several times, and said, "When you need money call on me. Don't let any poor fellow suffer, if you can help it." He slipped $25 into my hands then, and other sums frequently afterward, not waiting to be asked, but himself seeking to know the wants. His unostentatious, genuine generosity; his words and conduct, always impressed me.

Letters also came from all six governors of Massachusetts serving during the period 1866 to 1880: Alexander H. Bullock, William H. Claflin, William B. Washburn, William Gaston, Alexander H. Rice, and Thomas Talbot.

E. Massachusetts Pays Her Tribute to Oakes Ames

Early in 1883, a movement got under way to urge Congress to cancel its censure of Oakes Ames. The Honorable Marshall P. Wilder wrote the Ames brothers:

I rejoice to learn that there is to be an application to Congress to wipe out from its records that most unwise, unjust, and cruel censure of your honored father, and I beg the privilege of adding my name and influence (if I have any) to blot out this most improvident act of our national assembly, which otherwise must forever be a disgrace to American history.[38]

On 8 March 1883, the Honorable Effingham H. Nichols,[39] in New York, wrote an eloquent letter, which was printed in an eight-page leaflet and widely distributed: [40]

Hon. Oliver Ames, Lieutenant Governor of Mass.
My Dear Sir:
I see that a resolution has been introduced in the Legislature of Massachusetts, requesting their Representatives in Congress to initiate

[38] Ames Family, *Oakes Ames,* pp. 104–105.
[39] Nichols was a lawyer and a Director of the Central Branch Union Pacific.
[40] Ames Family, *Oakes Ames,* pp. 105–107.

measures, with a view to expunge from the minutes of the House of Representatives the vote of censure passed in March, 1873, on your honored father the late Hon. Oakes Ames . . . . [Then follows a review of the findings.]

Fortunately the action of the Wilson Committee was comparatively harmless, except as to the cost and expenses to which innocent parties were subjected, and the financial embarrassments which grew out of the delay incident thereto. The calm and considerate action of the Courts stood in strange contrast with that of a committee of politicians, swayed and governed by public clamor, popular prejudice, and personal considerations.

Not so with the action of the Poland Committee. The wrong which they initiated was then and there consummated, and a vote of censure passed upon one of the most honest, sincere, frank and far seeing of public men . . . . [Then follows an opinion of Oakes's character and accomplishments.]

When I consider these facts, and recall your honored father and that kindness of heart and simplicity of manner which so endeared him to his friends and associates, I have grave doubts about the propriety of the resolution introduced in your Legislature, to which I have referred. I would rather read in the public enactments of the Legislature of the old Commonwealth of Massachusetts, the State where he was born and lived and died, resolutions expressing their faith and confidence in their late fellow citizen, Oakes Ames, and commending his example to the on-coming generations as that of a great public benefactor; and leave to the House of Representatives of the United States to volunteer such action, as respects its records, as time and a recurring sense of justice shall dictate . . . .

Your father has left an honorable name—a name which will live in history when the granite monument to his memory and that of his brother, on the summit of the Rocky Mountains, shall have crumbled to dust, and the names of his calumniators shall have been forgotten.

With sincere respect,
I am very truly yours,
Effingham H. Nichols

Evidently his suggestion carried weight on Beacon Hill. It was unlikely that Congress had the authority to expunge from the records an act legislated by a previous Congress. The Commonwealth finally concurred that it would merely ask Congress to recognize, if it would, in its own way, the tribute being made by Massachusetts.

On 26 April 1883, General Nathaniel P. Banks, a member of the Poland Committee of 1873, wrote a long letter from Waltham, Massachusetts, to the Honorable David Randall, Senator, and to the Honorable John S. Williams, Representative of the Legislature of Massachusetts, which he closed as follows:

The citizens of Massachusetts can honorably unite in the proposal now made that the Legislature "express its gratitude for his work, and its faith in his integrity of purpose and character, and ask for a like recognition thereof on the part of the national Congress."

As one of the committee appointed by the House of Representatives, in Congress, to consider the part borne by Mr. Ames in these transactions, and concurring in its final judgment, I should most cheerfully support such declaration, and doubt not that it will be approved by the people of Massachusetts and the United States.[41]

On April 23 the State Senate, and on May 7 the State House of Representatives, unanimously adopted the Resolution, a reproduction of which appears on the next page.

[41] *Ibid.,* pp. 140–143.

Commonwealth of Massachusetts.

IN THE YEAR ONE THOUSAND EIGHT HUNDRED AND EIGHTY-THREE.

RESOLUTION

Relating to the Resolutions of the Forty-Second Congress censuring the Hon. Oakes Ames.

RESOLVED, *In view of the great services of Oakes Ames, representative from the Massachusetts Second Congressional District for ten years ending March 4, 1873, in achieving the construction of the Union Pacific Railroad, the most vital contribution to the integrity and growth of the national Union since the war;*

In view of his unflinching truthfulness and honesty, which refused to suppress, in his own or any other interest, any fact, and so made him the victim of an intense and misdirected public excitement and subjected him to a vote of censure by the Forty-Second Congress at the close of its session;

And in view of the later deliberate public sentiment, which, upon a review of all the facts, holds him in an esteem irreconcilable with his condemnation, and which throughout the whole country recognizes the value and patriotism of his achievement and his innocence of corrupt motive or conduct;

Therefore, the legislature of Massachusetts hereby expresses its gratitude for his work and its faith in his integrity of purpose and character, and asks for like recognition thereof on the part of the national congress.

Senate, April 23, 1883.

Adopted. Sent down for concurrence.

S. N. GIFFORD, Clerk.

House of Representatives, May 7, 1883.

Adopted in concurrence.

EDWARD A. McLAUGHLIN, Clerk.

The above resolution was adopted unanimously by both the Senate and the House of Representatives.

Tribute to Oakes Ames Expressed in a Resolution
by the Massachusetts Legislature
(Ames Family, *Oakes Ames, a Memorial Volume.*)

Appendices

APPENDIX A

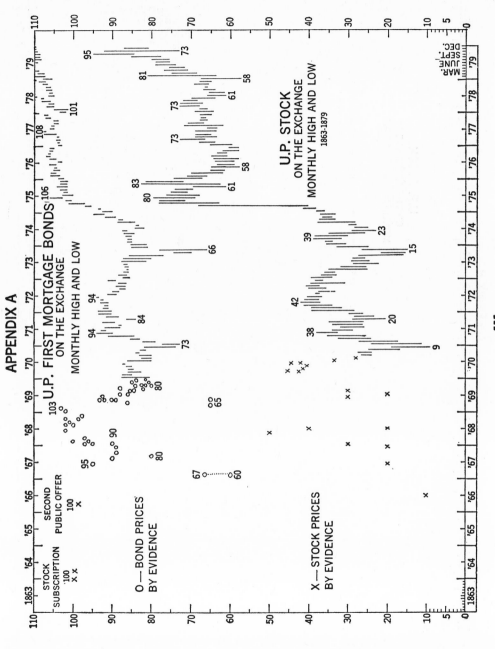

U.P. FIRST MORTGAGE BONDS
ON THE EXCHANGE
MONTHLY HIGH AND LOW

U.P. STOCK
ON THE EXCHANGE
MONTHLY HIGH AND LOW
1863-1879

STOCK SUBSCRIPTION

SECOND PUBLIC OFFER

O — BOND PRICES BY EVIDENCE

X — STOCK PRICES BY EVIDENCE

555

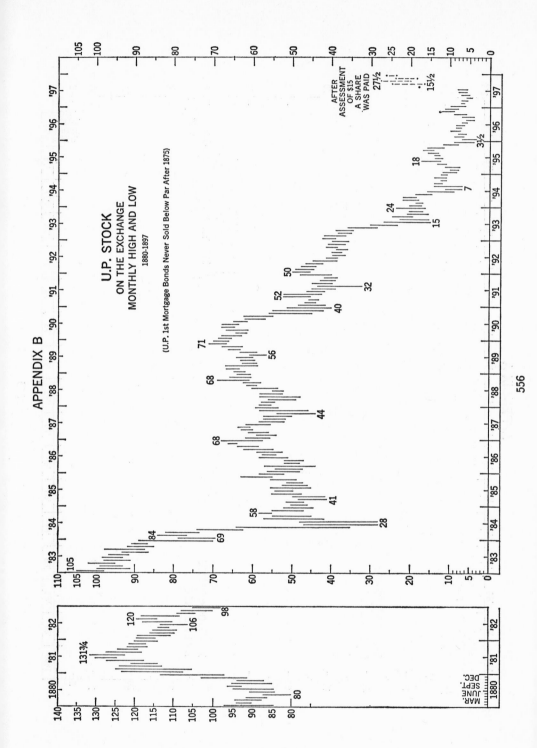

APPENDIX B

U.P. STOCK
ON THE EXCHANGE
MONTHLY HIGH AND LOW
1880-1897

(U.P. 1st Mortgage Bonds Never Sold Below Par After 1875)

AFTER
ASSESSMENT
OF $15
A SHARE
WAS PAID

556

APPENDIX C

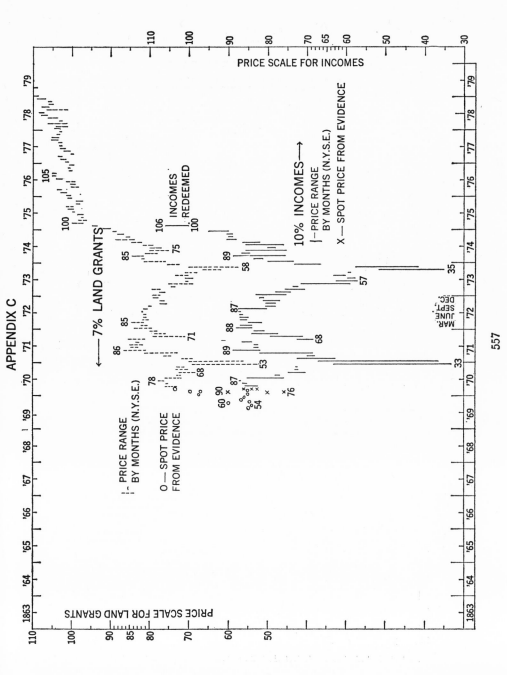

PRICE SCALE FOR INCOMES

PRICE SCALE FOR LAND GRANTS

←— 7% LAND GRANTS

|— PRICE RANGE
BY MONTHS (N.Y.S.E.)

O — SPOT PRICE
FROM EVIDENCE

INCOMES
REDEEMED

10% INCOMES —→

|— PRICE RANGE
BY MONTHS (N.Y.S.E.)

X — SPOT PRICE FROM EVIDENCE

557

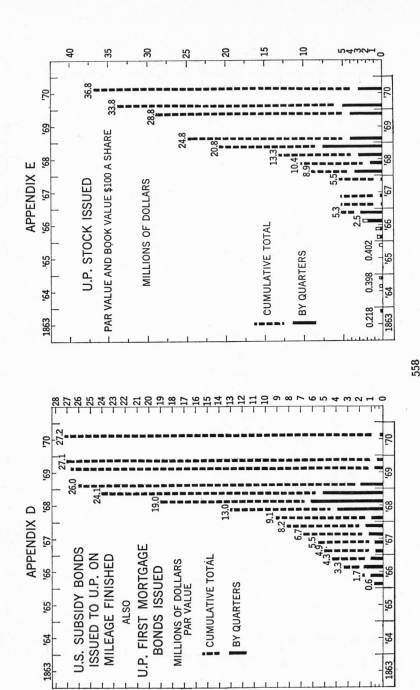

558

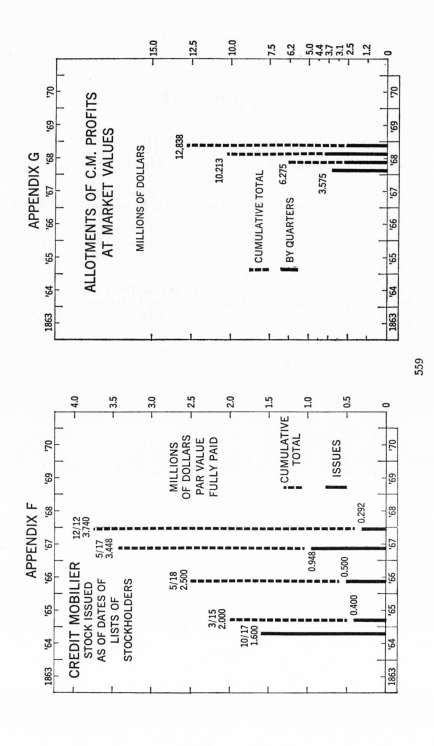

APPENDIX F

CREDIT MOBILIER
STOCK ISSUED
AS OF DATES OF
LISTS OF
STOCKHOLDERS

MILLIONS
OF DOLLARS
PAR VALUE
FULLY PAID

CUMULATIVE
TOTAL

ISSUES

12/12
3.740

5/17
3.448

5/18
2.500

3/15
2.000

10/17
1.600

0.292

0.948

0.500

0.400

APPENDIX G

ALLOTMENTS OF C.M. PROFITS
AT MARKET VALUES

MILLIONS OF DOLLARS

12,838

10,213

6,275

3,575

CUMULATIVE TOTAL

BY QUARTERS

559

Appendix H

Union Pacific Principal Directors [1]
Terms of Office, Other Offices Held, 1863–1893 [2]

Adams, Charles F., Jr., 3/83 to 11/90; U.P. Pres. and Exec. Com.

Alley, John B., 10/67 to 5/69 and 11/69 to 3/71; Seven Trustees; C.M. Dir. and Exec. Com.

Ames, Frederick L., 3/77 to 9/93; [3] U.P. Exec. Com. throughout.

Ames, Oakes, 3/70 to 5/73; U.P. Exec. Com.; 1st Mtg. Bonds Trustee.

Ames, Oliver, Jr., 10/66 to 3/77; U.P. Pres. and Exec. Com.; Seven Trustees; Mo. Bridge Mtg. Trustee.

Atkins, Edwin F., 1/89 to 10/93; [4] U.P. Exec. Com.

Atkins, Elisha, 5/69 to 12/88; U. P. Vice-Pres. and Exec. Com.

Baker, Ezrah H., Jr., 3/77 to 6/88; U.P. Vice-Pres. and Exec. Com.

Bates, Benjamin E., 10/67 to 5/69 and 3/74 to 1/78; U.P. Exec. Com.; Seven Trustees.

Bushnell, Cornelius S., 10/62 to 3/74; U.P. Exec. Com. and Finance Com.; Seven Trustees; Mo. Bridge Com.; C.M. Dir. and Exec. Com.; Railway Bureau Mgr. and Exec. Com.

Cisco, John J., 10/64 to 5/69; U.P. Treas.

Clark, Horace F., 3/72 to 6/73; U.P. Pres. and Exec. Com.

Clark, S. H. H. 3/76 to 3/85 and 4/91 to 10/93; [4] U.P. Pres., Vice-Pres., Gen. Mgr., and Exec. Com.

Dexter, F. Gordon, 10/67 to 3/71 and 9/71 to 10/93; [4] U.P. Exec. Com.

Dillon, Sidney, 10/66 to 6/92; U.P. Pres. and Exec. Com.; [5] Seven Trustees; C.M. Pres., Dir., and Exec. Com.; Railway Bureau Mgr.

Dix, John A., 10/63 to 10/67; U.P. Pres. and Exec. Com.

Dodge, Grenville M., 8/69 to 3/73, 3/75 to 11/78, and 1/80 to 10/93; [4] U.P. Chief Engineer.

Duff, John R., Sr., 10/66 to 12/74; U.P. Vice-Pres. and Exec. Com.; Seven Trustees; Land Grant Mtg. Trustee; Railway Bureau Mgr. and Exec. Com.

Durant, Thomas C., 10/63 to 5/69; U.P. Vice-Pres. and Exec. Com. Chm.; Gen. Mgr.; Finance Com. Chm.; Gen. Agent; Seven Trustees; C.M. Pres., Dir., and Exec. Com.: Railway Bureau Chm. and Exec. Com.

Glidden, William T., 10/67 to 3/68 and 5/69 to 3/71; U.P. Exec. Com.

Gould, Jay, 3/74 to 3/85 and 11/90 to 12/92; U.P. Board Chm. and Exec. Com.; C.M. Pres.

Hazard, Rowland G., 5/69 to 3/71; C.M. Dir. and Exec. Com.

Lambard, Charles A., 10/63 to 10/67 and 3/68 to 3/71; U.P. Exec. Com.; Railway Bureau Mgr.

McComb, Henry S., 10/63 to 5/69; U.P. Exec. Com.; Seven Trustees; Mo. Bridge Com. Chm.

Opdyke, George, 10/63 to 10/66; U.P. Exec. Com.

Pullman, George M., 3/71 to 3/73; U.P. Exec. Com.

Sage, Russell, 11/78 to 3/85 and 11/90 to 10/93; [4] U.P. Exec. Com.

Scott, Thomas A., 3/71 to 3/72; U.P. Pres. and Exec. Com.

Sharp, John, 12/74 to 4/92; Subcontractor; rep. of Brigham Young.

[1] Excluding Government Directors.   [2] Receivership of U.P. began in Oct. 1893.
[3] F.L. Ames died in Sept. 1893.   [4] Also served as Director after Oct. 1893.
[5] Served on U.P. Exec. Com. without break from 1869 to 1892.

560

Major References

General

Ames, Evelina Gilmore, *Diaries.*

Ames, Frank Morton, *Scrapbook.*

Ames, Oakes, *Cash and Ledger Books,* 1867–1872.

Ames, Oakes, *Letters.*

Ames, Oliver, & Sons, *Papers.*

Ames, Oliver, Jr., *Diaries,* 1864, 1867–1871.

Ames, Governor Oliver, *Diaries,* 1873, 1874, 1876–1880, 1883–1886.

Ames, Governor Oliver, *Papers.*

Ames, Governor Oliver, *Scrapbook.*

Ames, Oakes and Blanche A., *Credit Mobilier—Speech of Hon. Benjamin F. Butler in the U.S. House of Representatives, February 27, 1873.* Privately printed, 1944, 38 pp.

Ames, Oakes A., Oliver (Governor), and Frank M., *Oakes Ames and the Credit Mobilier.* North Easton: 9 August 1880; also includes *Defense of Oakes Ames, Read in the House of Representatives Feb. 25, 1873,* 47 pp.

Ames, Winthrop, *The Ames Family of Easton, Massachusetts.* Privately printed, 1938, 248 pp., illustrated.

Ames Family, *A Memorial of Oliver Ames (Jr.).* Privately printed, 1877, 99 pp., illustrated.

Ames Family, *In Memory of Oliver Ames (Governor).* Privately printed at Boston, Mass., 1898, 122 pp., illustrated.

Ames Family, *Oakes Ames, a Memorial Volume.* Cambridge, Mass.: Riverside Press, 1883, 143 pp., illustrated.

Ames Family, *Papers.*

Bancroft, Hubert Howe, *Chronicles of the Builders of the Commonwealth, Historical Character Study.* San Francisco: The History Company, 1891. Vol. v, chap. 10, "Lives of Oakes and Oliver Ames," 119 pp.

Bancroft, Hubert Howe, *History of California.* San Francisco: The History Company, 1890, vol. vii, 1860–1890.

Bancroft, Hubert Howe, *Oakes Ames,* inscribed "Corrected and put in typewriter by Col. S. J. Menard 1891 and presented to Oliver Ames," 79 typed pp.

Blair, John I., "The Journal of John I. Blair; Surveying the First Railroad Across Iowa," Anthony L. Cassen (ed.), *Annals of Iowa,* Summer 1960, 41 pp.

Boston, Past and Present. Cambridge: Riverside Press, 1874, 543 pp., illustrated.

Biographies of Oliver Ames, Sr., Oliver Ames, Jr., and Oakes Ames.

Bruce, Robert V., *Lincoln and the Tools of War.* Indianapolis: The Bobbs-Merrill Company, Inc., 1956, 368 pp., illustrated.

Chaffin, William L., *History of the Town of Easton, Massachusetts.* Cambridge: John Wilson and Son, University Press, 1886, 838 pp., illustrated.

Crawford, J. B., *The Credit Mobilier of America.* Boston: C. W. Calkins & Co., 1880, 229 pp., no index.

Davis, John P., *The Union Pacific Railway.* Chicago: S. C. Griggs and Company, 1894, 247 pp., maps, no index.

Dictionary of American Biography. New York: Charles Scribner's Sons, 1928, 20 vols.

Dodge, Grenville M., *Autobiography.* Iowa State Department of History and Archives, Des Moines.

Unpublished typescript, 1865–1871, 1277 pp.; no index of names, only of paragraph topics.

Dodge, Grenville M., *Biographical Sketch of James Bridger, Mountaineer.* Kansas City: R. M. Rigby Printing Co., 1904, 18 pp.

Dodge, Grenville M., *How We Built the Union Pacific Railway, and Other Railway Papers and Addresses.* 171 pp., illustrated, no index.

Dodge, Grenville M., *Papers.* Iowa State Department of History and Archives, Des Moines, and Council Bluffs Free Public Library.

Correspondence concerning the Union Pacific Railroad, reports, diaries, personal recollections, letters.

Dodge, Grenville M., *Romantic Realities. The Story of the Building of the Pacific Roads.* Paper read before the Society of the Army of the Tennessee at Toledo, Ohio, 15 September 1888, 24 pp.

Driggs, Howard R., *The Old West Speaks.* Englewood Cliffs, N.J.: Prentice-Hall, Inc., 1956, 220 pp.; water-color paintings by William H. Jackson.

Driggs, Howard R., *The Pony Express Goes Through.* New York: Frederick A. Stokes Company, 1935, 208 pp.; water-color paintings by William H. Jackson.

Durant, Thomas C., *Papers.* Iowa City: Leonard Collection, Library of the State University of Iowa.

Thirty steel filing drawers. Each document is identified by four hyphenated numbers.

Encyclopedia of American Biography, 1898.

Ferguson, A. N., *Diary of October 12 and 13, 1866, on U.P. Surveying Trip*. Records of U.P. Historical Museum.

Fogel, Robert W., *The Union Pacific Railroad—A Case in Premature Enterprise*. Baltimore: The Johns Hopkins Press, 1960, 129 pp.

Frothingham, Mary Ames, *History of Unity Church, North Easton, 1875-1935*. Privately printed, 20 pp., illustrated.

Galloway, John D., *The First Transcontinental Railroad*. New York: Simmons-Boardman Publishing Corporation, 1950, 319 pp., illustrated.

Grodinsky, Julius, *Jay Gould, His Business Career, 1867-1892*. Philadelphia: University of Pennsylvania Press, 1957, 627 pp.

Hayes, William E., *Iron Road to Empire—The History of the Rock Island Lines*. New York: Simmons-Boardman Publishing Corporation, 1953, 306 pp., illustrated.

Hazard, Rowland, *The Credit Mobilier of America, A Paper Read Before the Rhode Island Historical Society, February 22, 1881*. Providence: Sidney S. Rider, 1881, 42 pp.

Jameson, Jesse H. (ed.), *SUP News*, April-May 1959, August 1959. Official publication of National Society, Sons of Utah Pioneers.

Johnson, Arthur M., and Supple, Barry E., *Boston Capitalists and Western Railroads*. Cambridge: Harvard University Press, 1967, 416 pp., tables, maps.

Leonard, Levi O., and Johnson, Jack T., *A Railroad to the Sea*. Iowa City: Midland House, 1939, 277 pp., illustrated.

Lincoln, Abraham, *Papers*. Library of Congress, Manuscript Division, Washington, D.C.

National Cyclopedia of American Biography. New York: James T. White & Co.

New England Historical and Genealogical Register. Boston.

Nichols, Effingham H., *The Late Hon. Oakes Ames. A Letter Addressed to Hon. Oliver Ames, Lieut. Gov. of Mass*. New York, 8 March 1883, 8 pp.

Oberholtzer, Ellis Paxson, *A History of the United States Since the Civil War*, vol. ii, 1868–1872. New York: The Macmillan Company, 1922, 649 pp.

Parry, Henry C., "Letters from the Frontier—1867," *Annals of Wyoming*, October 1958, 17 pp.

Parry, Henry C., "Observations on the Prairies: 1867," Edward O. Parry (ed.), *Montana, the magazine of western history*, October 1959, 13 pp.

Perkins, J. R., *Trails, Rails and War, The Life of General G. M. Dodge*. Indianapolis: The Bobbs-Merrill Company, 1929, 371 pp., illustrated.

Poor, H. V., *Manual of the Railroads of the United States*, 1871–1872.

Quiett, Glenn Chesney, *They Built the West, An Epic of Rails and Cities*. New York: Appleton-Century-Crofts, 1934, 569 pp., illustrated.

Reed, Samuel B., *Compilation of Letters to His Wife and Family, 1864–1869*. Records of U.P. Historical Museum.

Riegel, Robert Edgar, *The Story of the Western Railroads*. New York: The Macmillan Company, 1926, 345 pp.

Sabin, Edwin L., *Building the Pacific Railway*. Balboa Island, California: Paisano Press, Inc., 1919, 317 pp., illustrated.

Sandburg, Carl, *Abraham Lincoln, The Praire Years and The War Years*. New York: Dell Publishing Co., Inc., 1959, 3 vols.

Seymour, Silas, *Incidents of a Trip Through the Great Platte Valley*. New York: D. Van Nostrand Company, 1867.

Stennett, W. H., *Yesterday and Today—A History of the Chicago and Northwestern Railway System*. 3rd ed. Chicago, 1910, 201 pp., illustrated.

Stone, Elizabeth Arnold, *Uinta County—Its Place in History*. Laramie: Laramie Printing Company, 1924, 276 pp.

Swanberg, W. A., *Jim Fisk: The Career of an Improbable Rascal*. New York: Charles Scribner's Sons, 1959, 310 pp., illustrated.

Trottman, Nelson, *History of the Union Pacific, A Financial and Economic Survey*. New York: The Ronald Press Company, 1923, 412 pp., illustrated.

Waterman, Merwin H., *Investment Banking Functions*. Ann Arbor: School of Business Administration, University of Michigan, 1958, 190 pp.

White, Henry Kirke, *History of the Union Pacific Railway*. Chicago: University of Chicago Press, 1895, 129 pp., charts.

Wick, B. L., "John I. Blair and His Associates in Railway Building in Iowa," *Annuals of Iowa,* October 1914.

Newspapers, 1865–1883

Boston:
   Commonwealth; Courier; Daily Advertiser; Daily Globe; Daily Traveller; Evening Times; Evening Transcript; Herald; Journal; Old Colony Press; Post; Traveller.

Brockton (Mass.) *Weekly Gazette.*

Brooklyn *Daily Eagle.*

Cedar Rapids (Iowa) *Daily Republican.*

Chicago *Daily Review.*

Council Bluffs (Iowa) *Nonpareil.*

Easton (Mass.) *Journal.*

Haverhill (Mass.) *Gazette.*

Massachusetts *Ploughman.*

New York:

Herald; The Nation; Post; Shoe and Leather Reporter; Sun; Times; Tribune; Weekly Tribune.
Omaha:
Herald; Republican.
Philadelphia *Railway World.*
Providence *Journal.*
Sacramento *Union.*
Springfield (Mass.) *Republican.*
Taunton (Mass.) *Daily Gazette.*
Worcester *The Daily Spy.*

Periodicals

American Railroad Journal. New York, 1863–1873.
American Railway Engineering Association, "Construction of the Pacific Railroad," *Bulletin,* vol. xxiii, July 1921.
Annals of Iowa. Des Moines: Iowa State Department of History and Archives. Quarterly.
Annals of Wyoming. Cheyenne: Wyoming State Archives and Historical Department. Biannual.
Chicago *Railway Review.*
Commercial & Financial Chronicle (or *Chronicle*), New York. Weekly.
The same company also published the *Commercial & Financial Register* and the *Financial Review,* both annuals.
Frank Leslie's Illustrated Newspaper.
Harper's Weekly.
Montana, the magazine of western history. Helena: The Historical Society of Montana. Quarterly.
North American Review.
The Palimpsest. Iowa City: The State Historical Society of Iowa. Monthly.
Vermont Life Magazine. State of Vermont.
SUP News. Salt Lake City: National Society, Sons of Utah Pioneers. Monthly.

Union Pacific Railroad

A Brief History. 15th printing, January, 1959, 32 pp., illustrated.
Along the Union Pacific, The Overland Trail and the Union Pacific Railroad, 15 February 1958, 48 pp., illustrated.
Articles of Union and Consolidation of the Union Pacific Railroad Co., the Kansas Pacific Railway Co., and the Denver Pacific Railway Co.

into the Union Pacific Railway Co., Dated January 24, 1880; and the By-laws of the Union Pacific Railway Co. Boston: Printed for the company.

Dodge, Grenville M., *Reports of the Chief Engineer to the President, with Accompanying Reports of Chiefs of Parties,* 1866–1869 inclusive.

Dodge, Grenville M., *Report to the Board of Directors on a Branch Line to Puget Sound,* 1 December 1867.

Durant, Thomas C., *Report to the Board of Directors in Relation to the Surveys Made up to the Close of the Year.* New York, 10 April 1865, 8 pp.

With appended Reports by J. A. Evans, 24 pp.; F. M. Case, 11 pp.; S. B. Reed, 15 pp., maps; and S. Seymour, 9 pp., map.

Durant, Thomas C., *Report to the Board of Directors in Relation to the Operations of the Engineer Department, and the Construction of the Road, up to the close of the year.* New York, 10 April 1866, 19 pp.

With appended correspondence; Report by J. A. Evans, 23 pp., maps; Report by S. B. Reed, 18 pp., maps; and 64 pp. of correspondence concerning the change of location west of Omaha, including letters by S. Seymour, J. A. Dix, the Secretary of the Interior, and Colonel J. H. Simpson, U.S. Engineer Corps.

Guide to the Union Pacific Railroad Lands, 12,000,000 Acres. 4th ed. Omaha, 1871, 48 pp., maps.

History of the Union Pacific Railroad. Issued by the Railroad on the Occasion of the Celebration, on May 10, 1919, of the 50th Anniversary of the Driving of the Golden Spike. 42 pp.

Map of U.P. from Cheyenne to Ogden, Showing Changes of Line, 1 November 1900, Drawing No. 8824.

Official Register of Directors and Officers, 1863–1889, Revised and Extended to July 1, 1897.

Records of the Union Pacific Historical Museum. Omaha.

Report of the Consulting Engineer on the Location and Construction of a Bridge Across the Missouri River, 31 December 1866, 27 pp., map.

Reports to Stockholders, Annual.

Reports Union Pacific R.R. 1861–1866. About 400 pp., maps, lithographs by surveyors.

A bound collection of numerous reports by Durant, Government Directors, engineers, surveyors, geologists; standards of construction, etc.

Russell, A. J., *The Great West Illustrated in a Series of Photographic Views,* vol. i. Union Pacific Railroad Co., 1869.

The Union Pacific Bulletin. Passenger Traffic Department, monthly, illustrated.

The Union Pacific Magazine, 1922–1933. Illustrated.

The Union Pacific Railroad Company, Chartered by the United States. Progress of Their Road. 540 Miles Completed December 1867. 32 pp., map.

United States Government

The titles listed are publications of the Government Printing Office, Washington, D.C., unless otherwise specified.

Acts and Joint Resolutions of Congress and Decisions of the Supreme Court of the United States, Relative to the Union Pacific, Central Pacific and Western Pacific Railroads, 1897, 255 pp.

Biographical Directory of the American Congress, 1774–1961. 1863 pp.

Bureau of the Census, *Historical Statistics of the United States, Colonial Times to 1957.* 1960, 789 pp.

Congressional Record (Congressional Globe before 1874).

Court of Claims decisions relating to the Union Pacific.

Department of Commerce, *Statistical Abstract of the United States.* Annual.

Department of the Interior, Bureau of Indian Affairs, *Indians of the Central Plains,* and *Indians of Montana Wyoming.* 1966, each 20 pp., illustrated.

Executive Documents of the Senate.

Geological Survey Bulletin 612, *Guidebook of the Western United States; Part B, The Overland Route.* 1915, 244 pp., maps, illustrations.

Geological Survey Bulletin 1212, *Boundaries of the United States and the Several States.* 1966, 291 pp., maps, illustrations.

Government Commissioners of the Union Pacific Railroad, *Reports to the Secretary of the Interior,* 1869–1874.

Government Directors of the Union Pacific Railroad, *Reports to the Secretary of the Interior,* 1864–1884.

House Reports.

Pacific Railroad Congressional Proceedings in the 37th, 38th and 41st Congresses. West Chester, Pa.: F. S. Hickman, 1875, 332 pp.

Pacific Railway Commission, *Senate Executive Document No. 51, 50th Congress, 1st Session.* 1887, 5561 pp.

Poland Report, *Credit Mobilier Investigation, House Report No. 77, 42nd Congress, 3rd Session.* 1873, 523 pp.

Report of Board Convened to Determine a Standard for Construction of the Pacific Railroad Made to Hon. James Harlan, Secretary of the Interior, with Accompanying Documents. 24 February 1866, 50 pp.

Reports of Explorations and Surveys to Ascertain the Most Practicable and Economic Route for a Railroad from the Mississippi River to the

Pacific Ocean. By various engineers of the U.S. Army under direction of the Secretary of War. 1853–1856, 13 vols. Senate Executive Document No. 78, 33rd Congress, 2nd Session, Serial Numbers 758–768.

Secretary of the Interior, *Annual Reports,* 1863–1869.

Secretary of the Interior, Record Group 48, Lands and Railroad Division, *Correspondence with Oliver and Oakes Ames Concerning the Union Pacific Railroad,* 1866–1870.

Secretary of the Treasury, Reports, 1865–1897.

Secretary of War, Reports, 1863–1869.

Senate Reports.

Statutes at Large.

Supreme Court decisions relating to the Union Pacific.

Wilson Report, *Affairs of the Union Pacific Railroad Company, House Report No. 78, 42nd Congress, 3rd Session.* 1873, 812 pp.

Index

Missouri River bridge, 408, 418-423; *see also* Missouri River bridge
Oregon, first surveys to, 230, 265, 510-511
papers and documents, 139, 383
and Reed, *see* Reed, Samuel B.
salary, 130, 140, 233
vs. Seymour, 224, 227, 274, 276, 280
and Sherman Pass, *see* Sherman Pass
and UP, agreement for junction with CP, 316-320; Chief Engineer, 130, 134, 138, 139-140, 185, 224-225, 381; and construction costs, 273; Director, 240, 346, 383, 560; eastern terminus, *see* "Initial point" questions; forecasts future, 375-376, 379; on freight rates, 242-243, 364; Grant's emissary to, 316; lays out towns, 161, 223, 276, 291, 334; loans to, 351, 357, 362, 382-383; not responsible to contractors, 224; relations with Army, 139, 264-265, 282-284; reports to, 158, 265-268, 373-376; stockholder, 408; surveys and engineering, *see* Surveys; threatens to resign as Chief Engineer, 284; vision of a Pacific railway, 9, 130-132, 418
and J. M. S. Williams, 347
and Wilson Comm., 136, 449
Dodge, Julia Phillips, 129
Dodge, Lettie, 134, 139
Dodge, Nathan, 131
Dodge, Ruth B., 130, 133, 134, 136, 139
Dodge, Solomon, 129
Dodge, Sylvanus, 129, 131
Douglas County, Nebr., 103-104, 420, 423
Douglass Mining Co., 500
Douglass, Thomas, 546
Drew, Daniel, 24, 175, 324
Drexell, Morgan & Co., 406
Dubuque & Sioux City R.R. (Illinois Central), 86-87
Duff, John Robertson, Jr., 151, 240, 346, 401
Duff, John Robertson, Sr., 149-151
and Alley, 150
and Oakes Ames, 150, 348, 355
and Bushnell, 172, 326
career, 149-151
and CP, 370
character, 149-151, 172, 303, 355
Comm. on Location and Construction, 170
and CM, 109-110, 432-433; stockholder, 112, 127, 149, 168, 194
and Dillon, 149, 353
and Durant, 109-110, 281, 321-322, 329, 433; "kidnapped" with, 321-323, 335-336; votes power to, 281, 329
vs. Fisk, 326
at Golden Spike ceremony, 338
vs. Gould, 149, 521
on Oakes Ames contract, 149-150
Railway Bureau Mgr. and Executive Comm., 114, 149

and Seven Trustees, 149-150, 188, 189, 560
as speculator, 149, 150, 401
trustee, land grant mtg., 149; Missouri River Bridge mtg., 406
and UP, Director, 149, 151, 178, 240, 416, 425, 560; and eastern terminus, 422-423 (*see also* "Initial point" questions); Executive Comm., 149; *vs.* Government Directors, 150; loans to, 149, 151; and "outside" contractors, 150; on stock value, 150; stockholder, 195, 401; and unpaid bills at Echo, 306, 349, 353, 356; Vice-President, 149, 416, 425
Wilson Rep. testimony, 150, 166-167
Durant, Charles W., 21
Durant group *vs.* Ames (or New England) group, *see* Ames group
Durant, Heloise, 20
Durant, Heloise Timbrel, 20
Durant, Lathrop & Co., 20
Durant, Thomas Clark, *vs.* Alley, 23, 76, 180, 186-187, 281-282
and Oakes Ames, 105
vs. Oliver Ames Jr., *see* Ames, Oliver, Jr.
and authority to change grades, 274-285, 287-290, 315, 329, 333, 345
and Judge Barnard, 152, 164, 324, 325, 326
and Bellevue crossing of UP, 99-102
and J. I. Blair, 81, 107
and Blickensderfer, *see* Blickensderfer, Jacob, Jr.
and Boomer (Gessner) contract, 151-152, 163-164, 190
and Boyer, *see* Boyer, Benjamin M.
and Brooks, *see* Brooks, James
and Bushnell, *see* Bushnell, Cornelius S.
career, 20-25
and Casement brothers, 124, 287
character, 20-29, 49, 92, 100-103, 152, 170, 182, 243, 263-264, 272, 275, 278-284, 287, 315, 322-323, 329-333, 346, 352-353, 354-355, 439, 515
and Cheyenne, Wyo., 276-277
and Chicago, Rock Island & Pacific R.R., 21, 22, 197
and construction, costs increased by, 260, 266, 280, 287, 288, 331, 333; deficiencies, *see* Construction; delays in, 45, 60, 102-103, 121, 280; and equipment, *see* Construction; for quick profit, 23, 181, 233, 266-267, 280; speed and extravagance, 23, 260, 266, 284, 287-288, 289-290, 297, 312, 329-333, 353, 354-355
and Council Bluffs, 104
and CM, 45-49, 97, 121, 127, 128, 152, 166-167, 410; Director, 98; Executive Comm., 98, 169; his group of stockholders, 48-49, 112, 127, 168, 194, 244-245; New York agency of, 47-48; no contracts under Ames group, 152, 167; payment to, 49; President, 22, 113, 169; relations with

Durant, Thomas Clark *(cont.)*
engineers and department heads, 161;
removed from office, 25, 169-170; stock,
sale of, 167; stockholder, 48, 112, 127,
166-167, 168, 194, 244-245, 520-521; unpaid subscriptions to stock, 197-198, 432-
433
and "Davis" contract, 254-260, 279-280, 332-
333, 356-357
death, 25
vs. Dey, 43-44, 98-99
and Dix, 19-20, 61, 99, 192
vs. Dodge, 100, 139, 225, 266-267, 275, 278,
282-284, 332-333; *see also* Dodge *vs.*
Durant
and Duff, 109-110, 150, 321-323
early life, 20-21
Echo Summit problems, *see* Echo Summit
problems
and Evans, *see* Evans, James A.
extravagance of, 23, 58, 182, 260, 266, 287,
289-290, 297, 333
and Fisk, 186-187, 282, 301, 323-327
at Golden Spike ceremony, 338, 340-341
"Grand Excursion" picnic, 119
vs. Grant, 217, 282-285
"Great Pacific Railway Excursion," 153-154
and Harlan, 101-102
vs. R. G. Hazard, 49, 111
his "General Orders," 263-264, 275-278
and Hoxie contract, 41-45, 49, 97, 98, 151-
152, 163-164, 358, 445, 520-521
vs. Indians, 217, 263-264
interest in Kansas Pacific Rwy., 28, **100**
investment philosophy, 20-23
"kidnapped" by Davis's tie-cutters, 321-
323, 335-336
land muddles, 103-104
and Laramie, Wyo., 276-277
lawsuits, 24, 25, 27, 49, 104
letters, to Oakes Ames, 108, 109; to Oliver
Ames Jr., 325, 341-342
and Lincoln's order for initial point, 26-
27, 99, 104, 422
and Lincoln's railroad car, 159-160
lobbying in Washington, 27-29
and McComb, 327, 432
and Mississippi & Missouri R.R., *see* Mississippi & Missouri R.R.
and Missouri River bridge, 27, 420, 422,
423
muddles around Omaha and Bellevue, 98-
103
and Oakes Ames contract, *see* Oakes Ames
contract
Omaha land speculations, 99, 103-104
"ox-bow" route, 98-103
papers and documents, 325
and personalities of the promoters, 180-
182
Poland Rep. testimony, 24, 190, 333

Railway Bureau Chrm. and Executive
Comm., 113
and Reed, *see* Reed, Samuel B.
Rock Creek line lengthened, 266-267
Seven Trustees, 188-192, 560
and Seymour, *see* Seymour, Silas
and Sherman Pass, *see* Sherman Pass
as speculator, 20-24
and G. F. Train, *see* Train, George Francis
trips, to Europe, 238; to the West, 163,
272, 287, 289
and UP, agent, 151-152, 274; and Comm.
on Location and Construction, 277-278;
Director, 19, 98, 178, 240, 416, 425, 560;
early control of, 18-20, 22-23, 29, 97-98,
113; Executive Comm., 22, 178, 255, 281,
345; Finance Comm. Chrm., 22-23;
ground broken, 25-26; income bonds
sold, 396; and "initial point," 26, 27, 104,
423; injunctions, 25, 152, 164, 169, 170,
182, 188, 277, 282; loans to, 398; and
New York office, 76; organization of, 18,
19, 175; and original capital, 45, 127-
128; partnership pool, 43, 45, 48, 175;
pool to support stock, 385, 388, 399, 555;
and presidency, 155; removal from office,
25, 261, 345, 378; reports, 99, 115, 116, 120;
stock sold, 182, 385, 396, 399, 555; stock
subscriptions, 18, 104, 186-187; stockholder, 18-19, 195, 399-400; and sub-
contracts, 280, 322-323, 332; surveys for,
115; "suspense-account," 27-28, 455;
Vice-President, 19, 22, 178, 240
versatility, 28
vision of a Pacific railway, 21, 22, 180
and Wardell coal contract, *see* Wardell
coal contract
vs. J. L. Williams, *see* Williams, Jesse L.
and J. M. S. Williams, *see* Williams,
J. M. S.
Wilson Rep. testimony, 18-19, 24, 45,
48, 151, 164, 169, 191, 248, 440, 457
yachts, 22
Durant, T. F., 399
Durant, William Clark, 21
Durant, William Crapo, 20
Durant, William Franklin, 104, 399
Durant, William West, 20
Dutch Flat (in Sierras), 140

Early, Major Gen. Jubal, 30
"Eastern base" of Rockies, 15, 157, 168, 184,
225, 227, 239
Eastern terminus, *see* "Initial point" ques-
tions
Easton Branch R.R., 69, 497, 529
Easton, Mass., 67, 75, 529, 542
Eaton, William S., 546
Echo (Echo City), Utah, 286, 294, 322, 330,
336, 345, 355, 357

578

Echo Canyon problems, 6, 114, 147, 230, 266, 268, 286
Echo Summit problems, 230, 266, 269-271, 279, 284, 286, 287-288, 290, 295
Eddy, J. M., 220
Eicholtz, Col. Leonard H., 335, 338
Eliot, Thomas D., 203, 208, 212, 436
Elkhorn, Nebr., 233
Elkhorn River, Nebr., 82, 83, 98, 119, 131, 233
Elk Mountain, Wyo., 228, 539
Elm Creek, Nebr., 263
Emancipation, Proclamation of, 70
Emigrant Aid Society (Boston), 69, 497, 529
Emigrants, 114, 415
Emory, Utah, 295, 336
Emott, Hammond & Pomeroy, 399
Engine No. 1, "Gen. Sherman," 119
Engineering, see Surveys
Engines, 45, 119, 235-236, 290, 342-343, 411
Ericsson, Capt. John, 175
Erie Canal, 20, 146
Erie Rwy., 324
Evans, James A., 115, 140, 156, 158, 181, 222, 227, 228, 265-266, 276, 294, 338, 353, 355
Evans, John, 316
Evans Pass, Wyo., see Sherman Pass
Evans, West, 340
Evanston, Wyo., 230, 294, 295, 411-412, 414
Evarts, William M., 290
"Evasion loan," 360, 395, 431
Ewing, Thomas, 257, 290, 302
Excavators, 118, 286, 290, 412

Fairview Cemetery, Council Bluffs, 139
Fant, H. G., 431-432, 436
Farnam & Durant, 21, 418
Farnam, Henry, 21, 24, 43, 130
Farnsworth, Richard F., 486-488, 545
Federalists, 64
Felton, Samuel M., 367
Fencing, 411, 455
Ferguson, Arthur N., 145-146, 218-219, 264
Ferries, 25, 85, 418, 422
Fessenden, William P., 246
Fetterman, Lieut. Col. William J., 144
Fifth Avenue Hotel (New York), 166, 188
Finances, 126-129, 154-155, 173, 175-176, 348, 384-394, 395-401, 426-430; difficulties, 9-10
Financial Review, 388
First National Bank (Mass.), 394, 529
Fisk, James, Jr., 24, 57, 187, 258-260, 282, 286, 301, 315, 323-328, 361, 379, 398-399, 515
Fisk & Hatch, 504
Floating debt of UP, 45, 105, 154-155, 165, 167, 172, 251, 256, 302, 322, 326, 357, 362, 395-401, 407-409, 482, 502, 505, 512, 532
Floods, 160, 232-233, 417-418

Fogel, Robert William, 36-37, 166, 379-380, 452-455
Forbes, W. D., 112, 127
Fort Bridger, Wyo., 2, 5, 6, 8, 215, 322
Fort D. A. Russell, Wyo., 215, 234, 263
Fort Dodge, Iowa, 87
Fort (Camp) Douglas, Utah, 215-216, 230
Fort Kearney, Nebr., 5, 6, 124, 145, 215
Fort Laramie, Wyo., 5-6, 8, 115, 215, 282
Fort Leavenworth, Kans., 5, 135, 142
Fort McPherson, Nebr., 215
Fort Phil Kearney, Wyo., 144, 220-221
Fort Sanders, Wyo., 215, 222, 223, 264, 272, 275, 283, 284
Fort Sedgwick, Colo., 215, 219
Fort Smith, Ark., 9
Fort Steele (Fred Steele), Wyo., 228, 264, 291, 295
49th parallel, 3, 8
42nd parallel, 3, 8, 78, 81, 83
Fowler, Joseph S., 203, 208, 212, 246
Franeker University, Netherlands, 62
Franklin Academy (North Andover, Mass.), 74
Freeman, Leigh, 293
Free-Soil party, 69, 111, 179
Freight rates, 16, 213, 242-244, 262, 316, 349, 351, 363-364, 461
Freight trains, 363-365, 379
Fremont, Elkhorn & Missouri Valley R.R., 86, 87, 303, 499
Fremont, Gen. John C., 2, 135
Fremont, Nebr., 82, 84, 86, 87, 99, 124, 126, 417
French, Charles H., 168
French, Col. Jonas H., 389
French, Susan E. Ames, 525
The Frontier Index, 293
Frost, G. W., 140, 349
Frothingham, Mary Ames, 527n.
Fuel, 118, 374
    See also UP, coal
Funded debt, see Bonded debt of UP

Gadsden Purchase, 4, 9
Galena & Chicago Union R.R., 79, 81
Garfield, James A., 203, 205, 212, 436, 466, 467, 474, 489, 536, 537
Gaston, Gov. William, 548
Gentry R.R., see Texas & New Orleans R.R.
Gessner contract, see Durant, Thomas Clark
Gettysburg, 19, 26
Gibbons, Gen. J. C., 216
Gilbert, Horatio, 108, 127, 168, 194, 195
Gilbert, Horatio, Jr., 168, 194, 195
Gilmer, Wyo., see Bear River City, Wyo.
Gilmore, E. W. (& Co.), 168, 194, 497, 529
Gilmore, Evelina Orville, 67
    See also Ames, Evelina Gilmore
Gilmore, Joshua and Hannah Lothrop, 67

Glidden, William T., 58, 86, 87, 112, 127, 168, 178, 188, 194, 195, 240, 304, 305, 346, 384, 417, 560
Glidden & Williams, 14, 58, 110, 169, 306, 326
Godfrey, C. O., 247-248
Gold prices, *see* United States
Golden Spike, the, 340-342
Golden Spike ceremony, 87, 147, 301, 315, 335-344, 378
Golden Spike monument (Council Bluffs), 423
Golden Spike monument (Promontory), 343
Gould, Jay, *vs.* Adams, 513-514
  and Gov. Oliver Ames, 520-524
  and Oliver Ames Jr., 516-517, 521
  "Black Friday" on the Exchange, 361, 379; *see also* Fisk, James, Jr.
  and Central Branch Union Pacific R.R., 522-524
  vs. Central Pacific, 510
  character, 503, 506-507, 512-513, 514-515
  and Horace F. Clark, 502
  and Congress, 508, 513, 515
  constructive period, 510-512
  and CM, President, 521; stockholder, 520-521, 535; *vs.*, 507, 520-521
  death, 515
  and Denver Pacific Rwy., 509-510
  and Dillon, *see* Dillon, Sidney
  vs. Duff, 149, 521
  vs. Durant, 520-521
  vs. Fisk, 361, 379
  vs. R. G. Hazard, 111
  vs. Hoxie contract, 42-43, 520-522
  investment philosophy, 502, 505-507, 508-510, 512-515
  and Kansas Pacific R.R., 316, 509-510, 512, 515
  vs. Oakes Ames contract, 507
  and Oregon Short Line, 510-511; *see also* Oregon Short Line
  and panic of 1873, 504
  and rate wars, 505, 515
  reputation, 507, 512-513
  vs. Seven Trustees and profit allotments, 520-521
  vs. Thurman Acts, 508, 513, 515
  and UP, Board Chrm., 505; Director, 505, 514, 560; dividends on, 451, 505-508, 510, 512, 514, 515, 520; on Executive Comm., 505, 514; and maintenance of property, 506, 508, 515; rule over, 503, 505-513; sinking fund bonds, 505; stockholder, 502, 504-513; stock profits, 509-510, 512-513; and stock speculation, 506, 507
  and Wardell coal contract, *see* Wardell coal contract
Government Commissioners of UP, 14, 126, 153, 160, 251-254, 330-331, 455
Government Directors of UP, 14, 25, 32, 44,

56, 98, 150, 248-249, 285, 422, 439, 443, 445, 455
Government standards for Pacific railways, 160, 297
Grades, *see* Track grades
Grading, 17, 31-32, 45, 104, 118, 257, 287-288, 289, 311, 353-354, 373
  cost, *see* Cost
  progress of, 45, 98-99, 104, 118
Graft on the road, 288-290, 300-301, 314, 331, 332, 334, 350-355
Grand Island, Nebr., 233
Granger, Wyo., 230, 295, 355, 511
Granite Canyon, Wyo., 235, 271, 295
Grant, Ulysses S., 3, 25, 90, 132, 134, 135, 136, 137, 144, 216, 217, 239, 250, 256, 282-284, 293, 301, 312, 314, 316, 341, 342, 345, 361, 376, 377, 435, 437, 504
Grass Creek, Utah, 247
Gray, G. Griswold, 112, 127, 168, 169, 194, 195, 410
Gray, H. W., 43, 112, 127
Great Britain, 3, 10
Great Divide Basin, 222, 229, 230
Great Northern Rwy., 8
Great Salt Lake, Utah, 2, 6, 9, 14, 114, 146, 229, 230, 267
Greeley, Horace, 435, 437
Green, Duff, 46, 282
Green River, Wyo., 124, 229, 295
Green River (the), Wyo., Utah, 2, 114, 115, 146, 228, 229
Grey, Zane, *The U.P. Trail*, 292
Grimes, James W., 127, 128, 168, 194, 195, 203, 212, 246
Grinnell, George B., & Co., 401
Grinnell College, Iowa, 81, 546
Grinnell, Josiah B., 546

Hale, Edward Everett, 543
Hall, Andrew T., 391
Hallet, Samuel, 28
Ham, Benjamin F., 54n., 55n., 136, 169, 177, 239, 252, 269, 362, 369, 397, 447, 455, 457
Hammond, Col. C. G., 346, 357, 361, 364, 381-382
Ham's Fork (the Green River), Wyo., 230
Hannibal & St. Joseph R.R., 119, 150, 153
Harbaugh, Springer, 19, 98, 160, 169, 171, 178, 183, 188, 233
Harkness, Dr. W. H., 338
Harlan, James, 11, 31, 101, 102, 144, 160
Harriman, Edward H., 102-103, 512, 515, 516
Harris, D. L., 240
Harrison, J. C. S., 240, 416, 425
Hart, Alfred A., 339
Harvard College, 62-63, 66, 528
Hastings & Dakota R.R., 88
Hastings, Minn., 88
Haven, F., 391

Hazard, Isaac Peace, 111, 112, 127, 168, 194, 195, 400
Hazard, Mary Peace, 111
Hazard, Rowland, 5, 27, 28, 45, 48, 112, 168, 194, 195, 197, 435, 438, 457, 474-475, 478, 534
Hazard, Rowland Gibson, 49, 80, 111-112, 127, 168, 169, 171, 191, 194, 195, 240, 317, 346, 360, 396, 398, 400, 402, 417, 521, 560
Hazard family, 111, 194, 195, 400, 402, 410
"Hell on wheels" towns, 126, 161, 232, 234, 291, 293, 334
Henderson, John B., 246
Henefer, Utah, 6
Henry Clews & Co., 504
Henry, John E., 24, 43, 98, 100, 106, 110, 178
Hermosa, Wyo., 540
Herndon House, Omaha, 26, 154
Hewes, David, 342
Hill, Ralph N., Jr., 72n.
Hilliard, Wyo., 293
Hills, L. L., 159, 219-220, 222, 223
Hillsdale, Wyo., 235
Hoar, Ebenezer R., 402
Hoar, George F., 438, 440, 450, 513-514
Hodges, F. S., 222, 230, 231, 355, 360, 361, 362, 365
Holladay, Benjamin, 112, 127, 168, 194, 195, 410
Holman, W. S., 33n.
Hooper, Samuel, 107, 128, 203, 317, 398
Hooper, Samuel, & Co., 112, 127, 168, 194, 195, 424
Hopkins, Mark, 13, 91
Hot Springs (Bonneville), Utah, 336, 349
Hotchkiss, Henry, 168, 194, 195
House, Jacob E., 140, 161, 273
Howard, John M., 309, 313, 318
Hoxie contract, see Durant, Thomas Clark
Hoxie, Herbert M., 24, 41-43, 45, 97, 140, 153-154, 233, 338, 375, 382
   See also CM; Durant, Thomas Clark; Gould, Jay
Hudnutt, J. O., 265
Humboldt River, Nev., 116, 159, 231
Humboldt Wells, Nev., 260, 266, 267, 268, 287, 311, 312, 318, 350, 372, 376
Humphreys, Capt. A. A., 130
Huntington, Collis P., 13, 29, 91, 141, 260, 308-309, 312, 313, 317, 370, 371, 373, 378, 439
Huntington, Oreg., 511
Hurd, M. F., 338
Hussey, Warren, 356
Hutchins, W., 499

Illinois Central R.R., 78, 130, 147
Independence Springs, Nev., 372
Indian problem, 115-116, 142-144, 216-217
   See also Dodge, Grenville M.

Indian tribes near UP, 141-142
Indians, 144
   and Oliver Ames Jr., 222
   and Browning, see Browning, Orville H.
   Dodge vs., see Dodge, Grenville M.
   Durant vs., 217, 263-264
   and Andrew Johnson, 142
   raids on emigrants, 5, 9, 115-116, 131, 142, 217, 219, 220, 232, 236-237
   and right-of-way lands, 15
   vs. UP, 58, 95, 115-116, 125, 126, 135, 143-145, 159, 215-223, 229, 236-237, 263-265, 375-376, 442
   vs. U.S. Army, 5, 9, 141-144, 217-218, 220-221, 236-237, 442; see also U.S. Army
"Initial point" questions, 12, 26, 27, 85, 99, 101, 104, 132-133, 421-423
   See also Durant, Thomas Clark
Injunctions and UP financing, see Durant, Thomas Clark; McComb, Henry S.
Interest, on bonded or funded debt, 262, 289, 298, 363, 379, 395, 427-430
   on floating debt, 105, 154, 172-173, 239, 252, 301-302, 344, 362-363, 369, 502
   unrepaid, on U.S. subsidy bonds, 16, 402-404, 405, 415, 429-430, 506-507, 508, 516
International Great Northern R.R., 512
Interstate Commerce Commission, 40
Iowa, 26, 77-78, 88
Iowa Board of Railroad Commissioners, 43
"Iowa Branch" of UP, 12, 26-27
Iowa Central Air Line R.R. Co., 80
Iowa City, Iowa, 21, 79
Iowa Falls, Iowa, 87
Iowa Falls & Sioux City R.R. Co., 86-87, 88, 247, 392, 417, 499, 519
Iowa Land Co., 79, 497, 525
Iowa Rail Road Contracting Co., 80
Iowa Railroad Land Co., 79, 392, 499, 525
Iowa State Dept. of History and Archives, Des Moines, 139
Iowa State Univ. of Science & Technology, Ames, 84
Irish labor, 285, 293, 328, 350
   See also Labor on the UP
Iron, see Rails
Iron men, 285
Iron ore, 31, 159, 413-414
Ives Pass, Nev., 311, 377

Jay Cooke & Co., 503-504
Jefferson, President Thomas, 1
Jenks, Barton H., 168, 194, 198
Johnson, President Andrew, 70, 90, 99, 102, 134, 142, 144, 153, 232, 239, 245-246, 288, 309, 311, 312, 373, 377
Johnson, Arthur M., 37-38
Johnson, B. B., 548
Johnston, James B., 194, 195
Joliet, Ill., 78, 147
Jones, David, 127, 168, 194, 195

War of 1812, 3, 64
Wardell coal contract, 247-248, 507
Wardell, Thomas, 247-248
Warren, Gen. G. K., 252, 253, 308, 330, 347
Wasatch Mountains, 6, 9, 222, 230, 328, 337
Washburn, Cadwalader C., 211, 213, 242, 461-462, 470, 480
    See also Ames, Oakes; Poland Committee and Report
Washburn, Gov. William B., 443-444, 494, 548
Washburne, Elihu W., 29n., 470
Washington, D.C., 70-71, 341
Washington & Ohio R.R., 499
Water, 58, 95, 116, 292, 412
Waterman, Mervin H., 34
Waterville, Kans., 522
Weber, Utah, 288
Weber Canyon (River), Utah, 9, 114, 230, 288, 290-291, 314, 336, 338
Webster, J. D., 240
Wells, Fargo & Co.'s stages, 242
Wells, Judge, 169
    See also Durant, Thomas Clark
Wendell, Cornelius, 288-289, 445, 448
West Bridgewater, Mass., 62, 63, 68, 525
"Western base," of Rockies, 15, 184n.
of Sierra Nevadas, 15
Western R.R., 148
Western Stage Co., 83
Western Union Telegraph Co., 6, 424
Westport, Mo., see Kansas City, Mo.
Whig party, 75
Whiskey traffic, 272
White, Henry Kirke, 452
White, W. M., 218
Whiting, Judge, 82
Whitney, Asa, 7, 362
Wilder, Marshall P., 548
Williams & Guion, 127, 168
Williams, Horace, 80
Williams, Jesse L., 24, 98, 156, 171, 178, 240, 248, 249-253 passim, 279, 283, 419, 420, 439
Williams, J. M. S., and Oakes Ames, 107, 400
    and Oakes Ames's Iowan railroads, 79, 86

and Oliver Ames Jr., 321
career, 58
character, 58-60, 113
vs. Congress, 58-60
and CM, 58-60, 113; Director, 58, 169; Executive Comm., 58, 169; stockholder, 112, 127, 194
and Dodge, 321, 329, 347, 370
vs. Durant, 23, 24, 110-111, 113, 168, 169, 329
vs. Fisk, 398-399
and UP, contracts proposed, 168-169, 171; Railway Bureau, 58; stockholder, 195; stockholders' loans repaid, 397; Treasurer, 58, 321, 346, 355, 370, 417
Wilson Rep. testimony, 23, 54, 58-60, 448
Williams, John S., 549-550
Williamson, Gen. J. A., 294, 338
Williamson, Lieut. Col. R. S., 308, 330, 347
Willow Island, Nebr., 161
Wilson Committee and Report, 55-56, 256, 288-289, 397, 398, 406, 409, 438-459, 531, 535, 536, 549
Wilson, Henry, 203, 207, 212, 436, 437, 468-469, 474, 493
Wilson, James Falconer, 203, 208, 240, 382, 384, 408n., 416, 422, 425, 463, 469, 474
Wilson, Jeremiah M., 424, 438, 450
Wilton Springs, Utah, 286
Wind River Range, Wyo., 131
Winslow, Gen. E. F., 367
Winthrop, Gov. John, 62
Wisner, Nebr., 87
Wister, Owen, 228
Witherell, Sarah Ames, 66
Wood & Davis, 524
Wyckoff, Cora Dillon, 148
Wyckoff, Peter B., 148, 516
Wyoming Basin, see Great Divide Basin
Wyoming Coal & Mining Co., 248
Wyoming Territory organized, 4, 277

Young, Brigham, 19, 26, 98, 116, 146, 178, 230, 267, 279, 332, 356, 360
Young, Joseph A., 279

Z-tracks at Echo Summit, 290

PIONEERING
THE
UNION PACIFIC

*A Reappraisal of
the Builders of
the Railroad*

CHARLES EDGAR

AMES

Unlike other books about the nation's first transcontinental railroad, *Pioneering the Union Pacific* is largely a detailed narrative of the ordeals and achievements of the daring men who made its original construction possible. Many previous histories of the road suffer from incomplete and sometimes inaccurate recording of its complicated financing through a seemingly mysterious company, unfortunately labelled the Credit Mobilier of America. In reality it was merely one of the construction companies so commonly used in that era to assist in the extremely risky financing of new railroads. Fresh light is cast on its intricate operations by quoting from many hitherto unpublished manuscripts, diaries, and other records.

Intimate revelations of the characters and personalities of Oakes Ames, Oliver Ames, Grenville Dodge, Thomas Durant — and many others—develop new insight into the dramatic history of the greatest feat of construction in the United States up to that time. The Ames brothers were major stockholders and promoters of the Union Pacific and leaders of the New England group of capitalists who joined them in 1865. After a devastating quarrel between the Ames and Durant groups which threatened an end of construction before it even reached the Rocky Mountains, Oakes Ames, a Congressman in Washington, underwrote an ingenious plan known as the Oakes Ames Contract. Its purpose was the financing of the last two-thirds of the road in a way which could be accepted by Durant, the original promoter. Oliver Ames was President during most of the period of construction. General Dodge, renowned for his Civil War record, was the able Chief Engineer and surveyor, and at one critical time was also a Representative in Congress.

The author has objectively endeavored to portray the past in its own true setting by quoting as far as practicable the words of men then living. The book covers the creation of the Union Pacific by inadequate acts of Congress, recounts the drastic Congressional investigations as a result of which Oakes Ames was censured, covers briefly the expansive but over-costly regime of Jay Gould, and ends with the inevitable bankruptcy of the company in 1893.

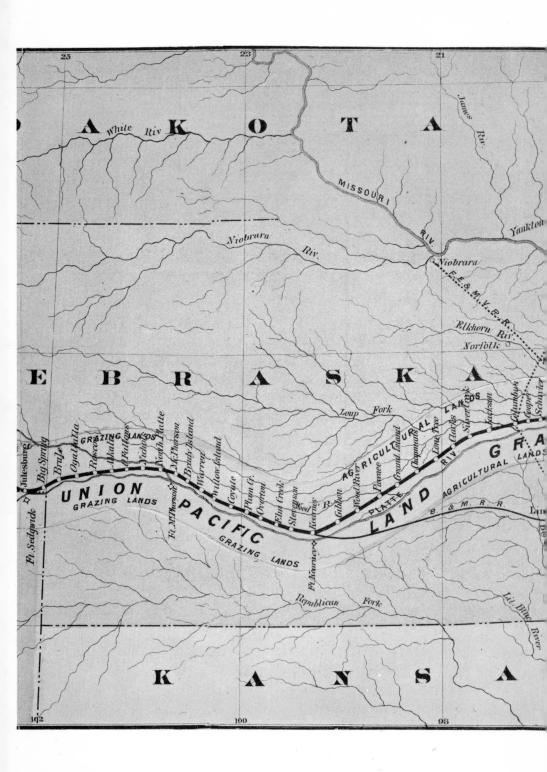